IN CONGRESS WE TRUST?

This book reveals how Congress quietly shaped American elections across more than a century of constitutional development. Far from a passive observer, Congress used its authority to influence key controversies, from the expansion of slavery in new territories to the reconstruction of the post–Civil War electorate. Congress exercised power under the Elections Clause, the Guarantee Clause, and later the Fourteenth and Fifteenth Amendments to combat voter suppression, reimagine representation, and determine who could (and could not) participate in American democracy. Even as Jim Crow laws disenfranchised millions, Congress continued to review and sometimes overturn the elections of its own members, refusing to cede complete control to the states. In doing so, Congress routinely subordinated federalism concerns to the demands of politics. *In Congress We Trust?* provides a new perspective on who truly governs our system of elections by showing that federal authority has been broad, lasting, and decisive.

Franita Tolson, Dean of University of Southern California (USC) Gould School of Law, is one of the nation's leading experts on election law and constitutional history. She has testified before Congress on voting rights, advised lawmakers and institutions on election reform, and served as a consultant on redistricting and voting rights litigation nationwide. A frequent media commentator for outlets such as CNN, MSNBC, and *The New York Times*, Tolson is also a coauthor of the leading election law casebook, *The Law of Democracy* (Foundation Press, 2022).

CAMBRIDGE STUDIES ON CIVIL RIGHTS AND CIVIL LIBERTIES

This series is a platform for original scholarship on U.S. civil rights and civil liberties. It produces books on the normative, historical, judicial, political, and sociological contexts for understanding contemporary legislative, jurisprudential, and presidential dilemmas. The aim is to provide experts, teachers, policymakers, students, social activists, and educated citizens with in-depth analyses of theories, existing and past conditions, and constructive ideas for legal advancements.

General Editor: Alexander Tsesis, Loyola University, Chicago

In Congress We Trust?

ENFORCING VOTING RIGHTS FROM THE FOUNDING TO THE JIM CROW ERA

FRANITA TOLSON

University of Southern California

Gould School of Law

CAMBRIDGE
UNIVERSITY PRESS

CAMBRIDGE
UNIVERSITY PRESS

Shaftesbury Road, Cambridge CB2 8EA, United Kingdom

One Liberty Plaza, 20th Floor, New York, NY 10006, USA

477 Williamstown Road, Port Melbourne, VIC 3207, Australia

314–321, 3rd Floor, Plot 3, Splendor Forum, Jasola District Centre, New Delhi – 110025, India

Cambridge University Press is part of Cambridge University Press & Assessment, a department of the University of Cambridge.

We share the University's mission to contribute to society through the pursuit of education, learning and research at the highest international levels of excellence.

www.cambridge.org
Information on this title: www.cambridge.org/9781009781619
DOI: 10.1017/9781009781657

When citing this work, please include a reference to the DOI 10.1017/9781009781657

First published 2026

Cover Credit: Douglas Rissing / iStock / Getty Images Plus

A catalogue record for this publication is available from the British Library

Library of Congress Cataloging-in-Publication Data
NAMES: Tolson, Franita author
TITLE: In congress we trust? : enforcing voting rights from the founding to the Jim crow era / Franita Tolson.
DESCRIPTION: 1. | New York : Cambridge University Press, 2026. | Includes bibliographical references and index.
IDENTIFIERS: LCCN 2026000700 | ISBN 9781009781640 hardback | ISBN 9781009781657 ebook
SUBJECTS: LCSH: Constitutional law – United States – History | Suffrage – United States – History | Discrimination – United States – History | Reconstruction (U.S. history, 1865–1877) | African Americans – Suffrage – History
CLASSIFICATION: LCC KF4550 .T65 2026
LC record available at https://lccn.loc.gov/2026000700

ISBN 978-1-009-78164-0 Hardback
ISBN 978-1-009-78161-9 Paperback

Contents

Acknowledgments

This book is dedicated to my nephew, BB, who supported me throughout the entirety of this project but didn't live to see it published. BB was an angel here on earth, and one of those people with whom one is blessed to be able to spend even a bit of time. Being his aunt was one of the greatest honors of my life. Even though he is no longer here with me, he is still my biggest cheerleader in spirit.

This book has been a labor of love, hate, frustration, pride, and sadness ... of every emotion one could possibly imagine. The range of emotions is not surprising given the topic, and that made the writing journey difficult at times. Despite it all, I am grateful to God for not only helping me see this project through but also helping me to remove the ceiling on my aspirations. Articles? Sure. Essays? No problem. But a book seemed well outside of my purview ... until it didn't. This book is proof that God's plans for us are so much bigger than the dreams we have for ourselves.

My family has been a critical support throughout the writing process and the process of self-growth that I had to undertake to finish this project. My children – Brianna, Alexander, and Isabella – were so patient with me through the long hours that I toiled on this book. My kids are my everything, and their constant positivity and unwavering belief that I could do this is what pushed this project over the finish line.

I am deeply grateful to my mom, Wyona (who consistently called to ask if the book was finished and enlisted her prayer warriors to support my efforts – thank you); my sister, Marcie (who graciously reminded me that if I took much longer on the project, history would probably repeat itself again); my sister, Lynette (who had no patience with any of my doubts about this project); and my niece, Tamoya (who was much nicer in her messaging but pretty much echoed that same sentiment).

I have so many people in my family who also provided vital infrastructure as I labored on this book in a decade that has canvassed some of life's highest highs and lowest lows – my nephew, Darien (my spirit and fellow political animal); my nephew, Derek Jr. (whose peaceful demeanor was necessary at vital times); my brother-in-law, Derek (my second dad who I have to constantly remind that he loves me a lot); and my brother-in-law, Bernard (whose worried texts about the poor state of our democracy reaffirmed the need for this project).

I lost my father, Frank Smith, a few years ago, and I know that he would be so proud right now. So much of my success is thanks to the lessons that he taught my sisters and I, including the value of hard work and the benefit of ignoring stupid people. I miss him every day, but I am also grateful that the universe saw fit to expand my family amid loss with two nieces by marriage (Jaeidah and Kierra) and my cute new grand-niece, Alivia Rose. I'm grateful beyond words for this crew.

Like with family, I could not have completed this project without a LOT of support in the legal academy. There are far too many people to list here, but I do have to give a few special shout outs. Lisa Bernstein shepherded my career since its infancy and convinced me that law teaching was a viable path. She has helped so many people reach their potential, and I am lucky to count myself among that group. My gratitude to her knows no bounds.

I have to give a special thanks to Guy Charles, who has read almost everything I have ever written and supported my career since the early days. To be able to learn from someone as brilliant as Guy is not an opportunity that I have taken lightly or have let gone to waste; I have long recognized it for the privilege that it is. Guy likes to toil in the background, but I can't let this moment pass without noting publicly that I wouldn't be the scholar I am or have the career that I have had without him. Needless to say, this book wouldn't exist either.

Guy also introduced me to Rebecca Brown and who knows what my story would be had that not happened. I will never forget that Rebecca took a chance on me, and she is the reason that I am at USC. Simply put, she changed my life. Not only did she chair the committee that hired me, she is also the person who summed up my scholarly existence as "helping people to vote" – so simple a concept, yet vital for providing me with direction about what it is that I am here to do. Rebecca also made the "conlaw" part of my scholarly profile stronger. Things shift when you have clarity of purpose, which Rebecca gave me, and I owe her more than I can ever repay.

I have also had many research assistants over the years whose assistance with this project was immeasurable, including Christopher Cabral, Justin Chasalow, Jacqueline Concilla, Landon Dial, Alivia DuQuet, Thomas Fogal Burlan, Matletha Fuller, Nathan George, Chinelo Ikem, Shayna Jackson, Priya Jupudi, Steve Kolbert, Emily Kong, Jason Byrd, Morgan Brock-Smith, Janine Raduechel, Simone Rudolf-Dib, Mina Saffarian, Kirsten Sencil, Katherine Sims, Charlene Smith, Stephanie Quinones, and Victoria Woodward.

I owe a special thanks to Marshall Amaya, my smart and hardworking research assistant for the last two years, who has put in countless hours cite checking and proofreading the final manuscript. It has been a treat to watch your intellectual growth from a young undergraduate to a class of 2026 law graduate. You are going to be a terrific professor in your own right someday.

I owe a debt to the librarians at Florida State University (FSU) College of Law (where I first started this project) and USC Gould School of Law (where I finished it). Their patience with my many emails knows no bounds, from locating difficult sources to fielding dozens of book requests. I am also indebted to Jennifer Allison, my indefatigable editor who patiently worked through the manuscript and provided feedback that resulted in a much better written product.

I am also grateful for the support of two of the best deans to ever do it – Andrew Guzman (USC) and Don Weidner (FSU). Now that I am a dean, I appreciate the importance of having an administration who is supportive of scholarship. I have been lucky in this respect, twice. Having a great team in place has been vital for me as I continue to write and publish during my deanship. For that, I owe thanks to my Vice Deans – Donald Scotten, Jordan Barry, Lybby Carroll, and Stephen Rich – for standing in the gap so I can wear multiple hats.

There are so many people I have to thank for this book that I am almost certain to miss someone important. My apologies for that.

Finally, to my grand-dog Liberty, thank you for keeping me company during the long nights working on this book. Also, stay off my couch.

Introduction

The Lost Story of Federal Voting Rights Enforcement

Questions about the scope of Congress's authority over voting rights and election administration have long shaped American constitutional debate. Today, that tension is more acute than ever, and the uncertainty over where federal power ends and state sovereignty begins has made even modest legislation vulnerable to judicial invalidation. In recent years, the U.S. Supreme Court has been especially aggressive in policing the boundaries of congressional authority, sharply limiting Congress's ability to remedy systemic inequities and instead asserting that control of the franchise rests primarily with the states. Yet the Court's approach overlooks a deeper historical truth. From the founding era to the present, Congress has at times asserted its power robustly and creatively, even in periods of judicial obstruction, and its role in shaping the nation's electoral landscape has always been pivotal – even when contested, uneven, or ineffective.

Take, for example, the election of Charles Miller Shelley, a brigadier general in the Confederate Army and, later, a congressman representing Alabama's Fourth Congressional District. While Shelley has been lost to history, he was no different than many other Democrats in the late 1870s. He first served as a soldier in the "Lost Cause," and then, following the Confederacy's defeat, embraced a brutal formula for regaining and holding political office in the post–Reconstruction South: violence, intimidation, and the wholesale suppression of Black votes. Shelley's voter suppression efforts paid significant dividends for his political ambitions. The congressional district that he would go on to represent was a Democratic gerrymander that had packed many of the state's Republican and African American voters in the district.[1] Yet Shelley had good reason to believe that his quest to win the seat in the majority Republican district would be successful. In his first congressional run in 1876, Democrat Shelley was able to emerge victorious because voters split between

1 "Smith v. Shelley," in James H. Ellsworth (ed.), *Digest of Election Cases: Cases of Contested Elections in the House of Representatives, Forty-Seventh Congress* (Washington, D.C.: Government Printing Office, 1883), p. 19 ("The census returns of 1880 now show that there are now in the counties composing the district 135, 881 persons of the negro race and 32, 855 white persons" and there is "a majority of 18,000 Negro Republican voters over white Democratic voters in the district.").

the two Republican candidates. His next re-election campaign in 1878 was easier than his 1876 effort because of the Democrats' overwhelmingly successful voter suppression tactics in that short two-year period: Shelley received 55 percent of the vote even though, in terms of whole numbers, he received almost 9,000 fewer votes than he had in his plurality win two years earlier.[2] The trend held and Shelley was re-elected in 1880 and again in 1882.

Thanks to adverse court decisions during this period, Black voters in the fourth district faced an uphill battle in challenging their disenfranchisement, difficulties that should have guaranteed Shelley's victory for the foreseeable future. In *United States v. Reese*, decided in March of 1876, the Supreme Court invalidated Section 4 of the Enforcement Act of 1870, which provided criminal penalties for "all persons who shall, by force, bribery, threats, intimidation, or other unlawful means, ... hinder, delay, prevent, or obstruct ... any citizen from doing any act required to be done to qualify him to vote or from voting at any election[.]"[3] Congress enacted the 1870 Act pursuant to its power under both the Fifteenth Amendment, which prohibits race-based voting discrimination, and the Elections Clause of Article I, Section 4, which empowers Congress to enact legislation that governs the time, place, and manner of federal elections.

In invalidating Section 4, the Court ignored that the statute was predicated on dual sources of authority. Focusing solely on Congress's power to enforce the Fifteenth Amendment, the Court held that the statute exceeded the scope of this authority by criminalizing the actions of state officials for any denial of the ballot rather than just race-based denials.[4] According to the Court, "states, as a general rule, regulate[] in their own way all the details of all elections."[5] Because the Fifteenth Amendment did not alter this basic structure, Section 4 represented "a radical change in the practice and...should be explicit in its terms."[6]

For most students of this period, the judicial invalidation of Section 4 of the Enforcement Act was the end of the story for the unfortunate voters in the fourth district, and a triumph for Southern Redeemers laying the groundwork for a White ruling class to govern after the withdrawal of federal troops from the South.[7] But the

2 Ibid.

3 *United States v. Reese*, 92 U.S. 214, 217 (1876) (quoting Act of May 31, 1870, 16 Stat. 140 (1870)). The Court also invalidated Section 3 of the statute, which penalized election officials who wrongfully prevented individuals from performing actions necessary to qualify as voters. Ibid., 218.

4 Ibid., 219 (arguing that Section 4 of the Act interfered with the state's authority to choose the qualification of electors).

5 Ibid.

6 Ibid.

7 See, e.g., Ellen D. Katz, "Reinforcing Representation: Congressional Power to Enforce the Fourteenth and Fifteenth Amendments in the Rehnquist and Waite Courts' (2003) 101 *Michigan Law Review* 2341–2408, 2348, 2350–2352 (noting that "*Reese* and *Cruikshank* thwarted federal power to protect the southern black population and facilitated the end of Reconstruction"); ibid., n. 54 (detailing the scholarly consensus on *Reese* and *Cruikshank*). *But see* Michael Perman, *Struggle for Mastery:*

real story was complicated – more accurately described as a historical labyrinth – and, for this reason, has been easy to overlook.

Intervention actually came not from the courts, but from Congress itself. The House of Representatives, acting pursuant to its authority to judge the elections of its members under Article I, Section 5,[8] set aside Shelley's 1882 re-election in the Fourth Congressional District because of the extensive disenfranchisement of Black voters. During the election, Democratic County supervisors never opened the polls in Black precincts but manned polling places in majority White locations so that votes could be cast for Shelley.[9] The failure to open polling locations was often followed by stern warnings from election administrators about the illegality of voting in the absence of inspectors.[10] Other supervisors refused to count the election day returns from majority-African American precincts, deeming the votes legally insufficient.[11] In areas where African Americans voted despite the active interference of election officials, ballots were turned over to the sheriff of the County, yet no returns were ever delivered to the election supervisors.[12] Those ballots that were delivered were "held to be irregular, informal, and insufficient" under state law and therefore not counted.[13]

Alabama law provided that election administrator and inspector "malconduct, fraud, or corruption" in the counting of votes was sufficient to challenge an election, but this provision was not effective in preventing the disenfranchisement of Black voters.[14] Instead, it was the House Committee on Elections, when assessing the legality of Shelley's election, who determined that the failure to count legally-cast ballots from qualified voters rendered the election invalid. The Committee concluded, "[T]here must have existed a well-planned and previously arranged conspiracy on the part of Democratic election managers … but such a scheme, if formed, cannot be allowed to be successful, as the committee have no difficulty on the proof in finding that an election was held according to law and what the vote actually was."[15]

Because of these voting irregularities, the Committee determined that the votes of African American electors had been illegally discarded. Once these votes were

Disenfranchisement in the South 1888–1908 (Chapel Hill: UNC Press, 2003) (discussing how Black people continued to vote and build coalitions with other racial groups for decades after the presumed end of Reconstruction).

8 "Each House shall be the Judge of the Elections, Returns and Qualifications of its own Members, and a Majority of each shall constitute a Quorum to do Business; but a smaller Number may adjourn from day to day, and may be authorized to compel the Attendance of absent Members, in such Manner, and under such Penalties as each House may provide." United States Constitution Art. I, s. 5.

9 "Smith v. Shelley," in Ellsworth, *Digest of Election Cases*, p. 37.

10 Ibid., p. 32.

11 Ibid., p. 22.

12 Ibid. (discussing Martin's Precinct, Dallas County and noting that the "ballots were counted, the returns made out, placed in a box, and returned to the sheriff of the county and delivered to him, but when opened by the county supervisors no returns found and none counted").

13 Ibid., p. 36.

14 Ala. Code chap.4, Art. I, § 302(1) (1876).

15 "Smith v. Shelley," in Ellsworth, *Digest of Election Cases*, p. 36.

counted, Congress determined that the actual winner of the election was the contestant, Republican James Q. Smith, rather than Shelley, who had been declared the winner by the state.

The contested election case of *Smith v. Shelley* is a paradigmatic example of how Article I, Section 5, in expressly delegating to Congress the power to judge the elections of its members, became a powerful tool to address race discrimination in voting through means other than judicial enforcement of the Fourteenth and Fifteenth Amendments. The Amendments had significantly broadened the scope of federal power over elections, but unfavorable court decisions and decreased federal military oversight after the 1876 presidential election had neutered their effectiveness.[16] But up to, and even after, the supposed end of Reconstruction, an emboldened Congress used its other constitutional powers over elections – some of which had long lain dormant – to shape state political systems, even as White Southerners aggressively pushed for a return to the racial hierarchy that predated the Civil War.[17] The mid-to-late nineteenth century contains a rich and overlooked history that reveals a repository of federal authority over elections that was triggered (or ignored) less for reasons of federalism, and more so due to pragmatic, principled, or partisan considerations.

In Congress We Trust? Enforcing Voting Rights from the Founding to the Jim Crow Era seeks to disrupt the federalism narrative that has assumed an outsized role in debates over the future of our democracy, offering a new perspective on federal power over elections. Courts and commentators have assumed that the states are supreme in election regulation, but as *Smith v. Shelley* illustrates, Congress's institutional role vis-à-vis the courts and the states in regulating voting and elections has been much more extensive and involved than the legal scholarship has acknowledged to date.

Congressional power is multi-faceted, deriving from the Constitution's individual rights provisions like the Fourteenth and Fifteenth Amendments, which empower that body to enforce the Amendments' terms against the states through "appropriate" legislation.[18] As most scholars recognize, the right to vote protected by these

[16] See generally *Slaughter-House Cases*, 83 U.S. 36 (1872); *Civil Rights Cases*, 109 U.S. 3 (1883).

[17] See, e.g., Chandler Davidson, "The Voting Rights Act: A Brief History," in Bernard Grofman and Chandler Davidson (eds.), *Controversies in Minority Voting: The Voting Rights Act in Perspective* (Washington, D.C.: Brookings Inst., 1992), p. 8 ("In its Reconstruction Act of 1867, passed over [President Andrew] Johnson's veto, Congress required as a condition for readmission to the Union that the rebel states call conventions, to which blacks could be elected as delegates, in order to devise new constitutions guaranteeing voting rights to black men. By the time registration was completed that year, more than 700,000 southern blacks were on the rolls, comprising a majority of registered voters in several former Confederate states.").

[18] Section 1 of the Fourteenth Amendment provides that:

> All persons born or naturalized in the United States, and subject to the jurisdiction thereof, are citizens of the United States and of the State wherein they reside. No State shall make or enforce any law which shall abridge the privileges or immunities of citizens of the United States; nor shall any State deprive any person of life, liberty, or property, without due process of law; nor deny to any person within its jurisdiction the equal protection of the laws.

Amendments is undoubtedly important for understanding the scope of federal power over elections.[19] But our understanding of the scope of this right, particularly when conceptualized as an exercise of political power, is unduly narrow.

During the antebellum era, political rights consisted of a state-defined right to vote, mostly exercised by White men,[20] and a natural right to alter or abolish government, nominally retained by everyone.[21] These rights fall under the umbrella of what I term the "Constitution of Political Rights."[22] With the ratification of the Fourteenth and Fifteenth Amendments, Reconstruction radically changed the

United States Constitution Amend. 14, s. 1. The Supreme Court has interpreted the Equal Protection Clause of the Fourteenth Amendment to protect a fundamental right to vote in state elections, *Harper v. Virginia State Board of Elections*, 383 U.S. 663 (1966), and the Voter Qualifications Clause of Article I, Section 2, requiring federal voters to "have the qualifications requisite for the electors of the most numerous branch of the state legislature," to create a right to vote in federal elections. *Wesberry v. Sanders*, 376 U.S. 1, 17 (1964). Similarly, the Fifteenth Amendment reads:

> The right of citizens of the United States to vote shall not be denied or abridged by the United States or by any State on account of race, color, or previous condition of servitude.

United States Constitution Amend. 15, s. 1. The enforcement provisions in the Fourteenth and Fifteenth Amendments are identical: "The Congress shall have the power to enforce, by appropriate legislation, the provisions of this article." United States Constitution Amend. 14, s. 5, United States Constitution Amend. 15, s. 2.

19 Franita Tolson, "The Constitutional Structure of Voting Rights Enforcement" (2014) 89 *Washington Law Review* 379–439; Travis Crum, "The Superfluous Fifteenth Amendment?" (2020) 114 *Northwestern Law Review* 1549–1630; Henry L. Chambers, Jr., "Colorblindness, Race Neutrality and Voting Rights" (2002) 51 *Emory Law Journal* 1397–1468; Katz, "Reinforcing Representation"; Michael T. Morley, "Remedial Equilibration and the Right to Vote under Section 2 of the Fourteenth Amendment" (2015) 2015 *University of Chicago Legal Forum* 279–329.

20 Alexander Keyssar, *The Right to Vote: The Contested History of Democracy in the United States* (New York: Basic Books, 2000).

21 In paragraph 2, the Declaration of Independence decreed that "whenever any Form of Government becomes destructive of these ends, it is the Right of the People to alter or to abolish it, and to institute new Government, laying its foundation on such principles and organizing its powers in such form, as to them shall seem most likely to effect their Safety and Happiness." United States Declaration of Independence, para. 2 (1776). The right to abolish the government was enshrined, with similar language, in some state constitutions that were ratified the same year. For example, the relevant clause in the Pennsylvania state constitution reads as follows: "[T]he community hath an indubitable, unalienable and indefeasible right to reform, alter, or abolish government in such manner as shall be by that community judged most conducive to the public weal." Constitution of the State of Pennsylvania art. V (1776). The word "majority" was used to qualify "community" in a similar clause in the Constitution of Virginia: "[A] majority of the community hath an indubitable, inalienable, and indefeasible right to reform, alter, or abolish it, in such manner as shall be judged most conducive to the public weal." Constitution of the State of Virginia s. 3 (1776). This right was also contemplated by the Founders as they debated the U.S. Constitution, as evidenced by James Madison's invocation of the "transcendent and precious right of the people to 'abolish or alter their governments' as justification for a new Constitution." James Madison, "The Federalist 40," in John C. Hamilton (ed.), *The Federalist: A Commentary on the Constitution of the United States* (Philadelphia: J.B. Lippincott & Co., 1864), p. 315.

22 Other political rights include the right to serve on a jury and run for political office. See Akhil R. Amar, "The Bill of Rights as a Constitution" (1992) 100 *Yale Law Journal* 1131–1210, 1164. These rights are beyond the scope of this book. See also Travis Crum, "The Unabridged Fifteenth Amendment" (2024) 133 *Yale Law Journal* 1039–1161.

nature of these rights, who can exercise them and, importantly, which government (state or federal) was charged with their protection.

Federal authority to regulate voting and elections also derives from structural provisions of the Constitution that are less widely studied. These provisions serve as express delegations of power to Congress, rather than the courts, the executive branch, or the states. I refer to these provisions collectively as the "Constitution of Political Structure":

- The Guarantee Clause of Article IV, Section 4, through which Congress "guarantee[s] to every State in this Union a Republican Form of Government";[23]
- The Elections Clause of Article I, Section 4, which allows Congress to "make or alter" state regulations governing the "Times, Places, and Manner" of federal elections;[24]
- Article I, Section 5, which empowers each house of Congress to "be the Judge of the Elections, Returns, and Qualifications of its own members";[25] and
- Section 2 of the Fourteenth Amendment, which requires Congress to penalize states that abridge or deny the right to vote by reducing their representation in the House of Representatives.[26]

While the individual rights provisions of the Fourteenth and Fifteenth Amendments receive an outsize amount of scholarly attention and commentary, this book focuses primarily on how these provisions interact with the Constitution of Political Structure, and in doing so, enrich a narrative that has been incomplete. As this book argues, one of the overlooked legacies of the Reconstruction project is that congressional power to regulate state and federal elections was significantly broader

[23] United States Constitution Art. IV, s. 4. This provision states:

> The United States shall guarantee to every State in this Union a Republican Form of Government, and shall protect each of them against Invasion; and on Application of the Legislature, or of the Executive (when the Legislature cannot be convened) against domestic Violence.

[24] United States Constitution Art. I, s. 4. The text reads:

> The Times, Places and Manner of holding Elections for Senators and Representatives, shall be prescribed in each State by the Legislature thereof; but the Congress may at any time by Law make or alter such Regulations, except as to the Places of chusing Senators.

[25] United States Constitution Art. I, s. 5.

[26] United States Constitution Amend. 14, s. 2. This section provides that:

> Representatives shall be apportioned among the several States according to their respective numbers, counting the whole number of persons in each State, excluding Indians not taxed. But when the right to vote at any election for the choice of electors for President and Vice President of the United States, Representatives in Congress, the Executive and Judicial officers of a State, or the members of the Legislature thereof, is denied to any of the male inhabitants of such State, being twenty-one years of age, and citizens of the United States, or in any way abridged, except for participation in rebellion, or other crime, the basis of representation therein shall be reduced in the proportion which the number of such male citizens shall bear to the whole number of male citizens twenty-one years of age in such State.

when Congress acted pursuant to its authority under the Constitution of Political Structure, or alternatively, enacted legislation pursuant to more than one source of constitutional authority under the Constitutions of Political Structure and Political Rights. This legislative framework stands apart from the legal fiction that currently exists – that Congress regulates elections, both state and federal, in a singular, clause-bound fashion, the perimeter of which is determined by our federalist system. Yet, it is this latter interpretation, which gained prominence after Congress completely retreated from its multi-clausal approach in enforcing Reconstruction at the turn of the twentieth century, that currently holds sway in the Supreme Court's jurisprudence.

I.1 CAN CONGRESS DO THAT? CRAFTING ELECTION POLICY AMID JUDICIAL UNCERTAINTY

In the 1950s and 1960s, the greatest barrier to meaningful civil rights legislation was not the Supreme Court; instead, it was the Senate filibuster. Sitting in juxtaposition to this fact is that one of the greatest advocates for civil rights during this period was the Senate majority leader, and later President, who had stolen the 1948 Democratic Senate primary election – his first theft was a 1930 college election[27] – by stuffing the ballot box in a majority-minority precinct in a remote Texas County.[28] Thanks to precinct thirteen in Jim Wells County, Lyndon Baines Johnson defeated former Texas governor Coke Stevenson by eighty-seven votes. This precinct was controlled by the head of the Democratic Machine in South Texas, George Berham Parr (the so-called "Duke of Duval"[29]) who used fraudulent votes to help Johnson eke out the win in repayment for Johnson's assistance in helping Parr to obtain a presidential pardon for his income tax conviction two years earlier.[30] This fraud would not have been possible but for Parr's control of the Latino vote in the County until 1975, depriving these voters of any meaningful control over selecting their candidate of choice.[31]

Odd start for a man who stewarded some of the earliest civil rights legislation through the Senate in the 1950s, and as President in the 1960s, delivered the most

27 Robert A. Caro, *The Years of Lyndon Johnson: The Path to Power* (New York: Penguin Books, 1981), p. 25 ("To obtain the power that he wanted, Lyndon Johnson, who was alleged to have won his seat in the United States Senate in a stolen election in 1948, stole his first election at college, in 1930…He was, in fact, so deeply and widely mistrusted at college that the nickname he bore during all his years there was 'Bull' (for 'Bullshit') Johnson.").

28 Robert A. Caro, *The Years of Lyndon Johnson: The Means of Ascent* (New York: Vintage Books, 1990), p. 187.

29 Ibid., p. 186.

30 Ibid., p. 191 (noting that "Coke Stevenson was going into the campaign with his great popularity. But before the campaign began, Johnson had a 25,000-vote head start.").

31 David Montejano, *Anglos and Mexicans in the Making of Texas, 1836–1986* (Austin: University of Texas Press, 1987).

expansive federal legislation to protect minorities in a century.[32] On June 11, 1964, a bipartisan majority of the Senate voted, for the first time, to end a filibuster of a federal civil rights bill, invoking cloture after 75 days and clearing the way for the passage of the Civil Rights Act of 1964.[33] Earlier civil rights bills, enacted in 1957 and 1960, had only seen the light of day because Johnson, as Senate majority leader, had negotiated compromises with the southern bloc to ensure passage (although these compromises had substantially weakened the impact of these bills).[34] Seeking to avoid similar difficulties with the proposed Voting Rights Act, President Johnson conferred with the relevant stakeholders behind closed doors, gaining agreement on key terms among civil rights leaders, civic leaders, authorities from southern states, and key Republican congressmen prior to introducing the measure on Capitol Hill.[35]

The passage of the Voting Rights Act of 1965 represented a watershed moment for federal voting rights policy, comprehensively changing our political system rather than adhering to the incremental change that had defined federal intervention up to that point.[36] It was clear that the question of whether Congress had the power to enact this legislation was as much a question about political will and maneuvering as it was about constitutional constraints. Yet, in the more than half century since the passage of the Voting Rights Act, Congress has consistently tied its own hands when enacting

[32] Caro, *The Means of Ascent*. In 1948, Johnson ran for the Senate as a traditional states' rights, segregationist southern politician. According to his biographer, Robert Caro:

> On civil rights, [Johnson] attacked President Truman's attempts to create a FEPC [Fair Employment Practices Committee] ('because if a man can tell you whom you must hire, he can tell you whom you cannot employ'), and to end the poll tax (because "it is the province of the state to run its own elections'). He was against the proposed laws against lynching "because the federal government has no more business enacting a law against one form of murder than against another.'

Ibid., 196.

[33] John H. Averill, "Civil Rights Bill: Swift Senate Passage Expected Filibuster Silenced, 71 to 29," *Los Angeles Times*, June 11, 1964; "Senate Approves 1, Defeats 3 Rights Bill Amendments: Byrd Starts All-Night Filibuster," *Atlanta Daily World*, June 10, 1964.

[34] "Advance Agreement on Voting Rights Sought: President Johnson, Aids Consult with Negro Leaders, GOP on New Legislation," *Los Angeles Times*, March 9, 1965.

[35] Ibid.

[36] Section 5 of the Voting Rights Act ("VRA") requires covered states to, prior to implementing changes to their voting laws, seek confirmation from the federal government that the proposed changes do not establish a "qualification, prerequisite, standard, practice, or procedure" for voting that has "the purpose and … the effect of denying or abridging the right to vote on account of race or color." Voting Rights Act of 1965, Pub. L. No. 89–110, codified as amended at 52 U.S.C. § 10301 (2012), s. 5. Section 5 prohibits those changes that have a "retrogressive" effect on minority communities – i.e., minorities are worse off under the new law than its predecessor. *Beer v. United States*, 425 U.S. 130, 141–142 (1976). Under the VRA, nine states – mostly in the deep South, along with a few jurisdictions scattered throughout several other states – were covered by Section 5 until the Supreme Court's decision in *Shelby County v. Holder*, 570 U.S. 529 (2013), which invalidated the Act's coverage formula. United States Department of Justice, "Jurisdictions Previously Covered by Section 5," www.justice.gov/crt/jurisdictions-previously-covered-section-5 [https://perma.cc/BBE3-Z28J] (last updated November 29, 2021).

new legislation, feeding into the judicially crafted fantasy that Congress's power over elections must be rarely used, narrowly construed, and specifically targeted.

Congress's acquiescence in these artificially constructed boundaries was on full display when the 116th Congress introduced its very first bill in the House of Representatives, H.R. 1, aptly titled the "For the People Act of 2019."[37] Proposed pursuant to the Elections Clause, H.R. 1 was Congress's most ambitious attempt to restructure our system of federal elections in a generation. Among other things, the bill addresses campaign spending, expands voter registration, proposes independent redistricting commissions, prohibits felon disenfranchisement, and bolsters election security.[38] By upending the manner in which federal elections are traditionally regulated, which is primarily through state law, H.R. 1 would have been one of the most novel and expansive exercises of federal power over elections in decades.[39] Had it ever become law, however, H.R. 1 would have been on a collision course with one of the most conservative Supreme Courts in history. Congress has regulated federal elections at various points in our history, but federal legislation has become relatively rare as the Court has increasingly rejected the expansive exercise of federal authority in this domain.

During its short lifespan, the bill saw its fair share of opposition. For example, the Heritage Foundation, a conservative think tank and lobbying organization,[40] argued that H.R. 1 is unconstitutional because the proposed law would interfere with the states' constitutional authority to determine voter qualifications and administer elections.[41] Its report on the bill alleged that H.R. 1 would "[s]eize the authority of states to regulate voter registration and the voting process by forcing states to implement early voting, automatic voter registration, same-day registration, online voter registration, and no-fault absentee balloting."[42]

Congress's reliance on the Elections Clause as the sole justification for the 2019 version of the Act invited this critique. Although the subject of the Clause is the

37 For the People Act of 2019, H.R. 1, 116th Cong. (2019).

38 In March 2019, the House passed H.R. 1 by a vote of 234 to 193, but then Majority Leader Mitch McConnell did not bring the bill to the Senate floor. Ella Nilsen, "House Democrats Just Passed a Slate of Significant Reforms to Get Money Out of Politics," *Vox*, March 8, 2019, www.vox.com/2019/3/8/18253609/hr-1-pelosi-house-democrats-anti-corruption-mcconnell [https://perma.cc/CJV8-NKMG] (describing H.R. 1 as "dead on arrival in the Senate"). The bill was reintroduced in the 117th Congress as H.R. 1, the "For the People Act of 2021." For the People Act of 2021, H.R. 1, 117th Cong. (2021).

39 The VRA and in particular, its preclearance regime, imposed federal oversight for certain state political systems. Voting Rights Act of 1965, Pub. L. No. 89–110, codified as amended at 52 U.S.C. § 10301 (2012). The Elections Clause gives Congress comprehensive power to regulate federal elections and does not require any continuing evidence of racial discrimination for federal oversight to remain valid. See Franita Tolson, "Reinventing Sovereignty?: Federalism as a Constraint on the Voting Rights Act" (2012) 65 *Vanderbilt Law Review* 1195–1259, 1228–1233.

40 Heritage Foundation, "About Heritage," www.heritage.org/about-heritage/mission [https://perma.cc/6B4L-PHCJ].

41 Heritage Foundation, "The Facts about H.R. 1 – The For the People Act of 2019," February 1, 2019, www.heritage.org/sites/default/files/2019-02/FS_182_0.pdf [https://perma.cc/E85Q-HH2M].

42 Ibid., 1.

"times, places, and manner" of federal elections,[43] H.R. 1 arguably went further, with provisions that also had implications for voter qualifications such as its requirement that individuals with felony convictions be enfranchised for federal elections.[44]

In the 2021 version of H.R. 1, Congress heeded this message. Relying on the Elections Clause, the Guarantee Clause, and the Fourteenth, Fifteenth, Nineteenth, Twenty-Fourth, and Twenty-Sixth Amendments, the 117th Congress reintroduced H.R. 1, now titled the "For the People Act of 2021," as the first bill in both the House and the Senate (as S.R. 1) in the new Congress. Congress attempted to short circuit the federalism-based arguments that threatened to derail the first H.R. 1 by invoking additional constitutional provisions that empower it to regulate both voter qualification standards and the time, places, and manner of federal elections. Notably, these are not provisions that fell out of the sky in the two years between versions of the bill; rather, their inclusion reflected Congress's belated realization that it had substantially underestimated the scope of its own authority.[45] Although these bills never became law,[46] H.R. 1/S.R. 1 could provide a practical blueprint for how

43 "The Times, Places and Manner of holding Elections for Senators and Representatives, shall be prescribed in each State by the Legislature thereof; but the Congress may at any time by Law make or alter such Regulations, except as to the Places of chusing Senators." United States Constitution Art. 1, s. 4.

44 Franita Tolson, "The Elections Clause and the Underenforcement of Federal Law" (2019) 129 *Yale Law Journal Forum* 171–184.

45 See Statement of Franita Tolson, *The Elections Clause: Constitutional Interpretation and Congressional Exercise*, H. Comm. on House Admin., 117th Cong. (July 12, 2021) (written testimony), available at https://docs.house.gov/meetings/HA/HA00/20210712/112883/HHRG-117-HA00-Wstate-TolsonF-20210712.pdf; Statement of Franita Tolson, *Evidence of Current and Ongoing Voting Discrimination*, Subcomm. on the Const., C.R. & C.L. of the H. Comm. on the Judiciary, 117th Cong. (July 27, 2021) (written testimony), available at https://docs.house.gov/meetings/JU/JU10/20210727/113962/HHRG-117-JU10-Wstate-TolsonF-20210727.pdf; Statement of Franita Tolson, *Restoring the Voting Rights Act: Combating Discriminatory Abuses*, Subcomm. on the Const. of the S. Comm. on the Judiciary, 117th Cong. (September 22, 2021) (written testimony), available at www.judiciary.senate.gov/imo/media/doc/Tolson%20Testimony1.pdf.

46 In September 2021, a key Democratic Senator who opposed H.R. 1/S.R. 1 in its current form, Senator Joe Manchin from West Virginia, worked with a group of Democratic Senators to propose a narrower version of national legislation – The Freedom to Vote Act. Wendy R. Weiser, Daniel I. Weiner, and Emil M. Pablo, "Breaking Down the Freedom to Vote Act," Brennan Center for Justice, September 23, 2021, www.brennancenter.org/our-work/research-reports/breaking-down-freedom-vote-act [https://perma.cc/M9NC-ZSBN]. In January 2022, Senate Democrats combined into an omnibus election bill the Freedom to Vote Act with another proposed piece of voting legislation: The John Lewis Voting Rights Act. Brian Naylor, "The Senate is Set to Debate Voting Rights: Here's What the Bills Would Do," *National Public Radio*, January 18, 2022, www.npr.org/2022/01/18/1073021462/senate-voting-rights-freedom-to-vote-john-lewis-voting-rights-advancement-act [https://perma.cc/NK4B-2LFY[. That bill, otherwise known as the Voting Rights Advancement Act, or H.R. 4, was passed by the House on December 6, 2019, and would respond to the Supreme Court's decision in *Shelby County v. Holder*, which struck down the coverage formula for the Voting Rights Act of 1965. Caitlyn Oprysko, "House Passes Voting Rights Package Aimed at Restoring Protections," *Politico*, December 16, 2019, www.politico.com/news/2019/12/06/house-passes-voting-rights-package-077112 [https://perma.cc/NG8S-YWPV]. On January 18, 2022, the day after Martin Luther King Jr.'s Birthday (observed), Senate Democrats brought the combined Freedom to Vote / John R. Lewis Voting Rights Advancement Act to the floor for debate. Carl Hulse, "Senate Opens Voting Rights Debate, With Legislative Defeat Looming," *New York Times*, January 18,

Congress should utilize the full scope of congressional power moving forward, particularly in light of recent proposals to shift significant authority over elections back to the states.[47]

In Congress We Trust? provides historical and theoretical grounding for these debates, offering an important and timely clarification about the scope of federal power over elections. In recent years, a more diverse and representative Congress began to rediscover the breadth of its constitutional powers, drawing on long-overlooked provisions and underused authority in an effort to safeguard the nation's electoral system. For a time, this marked a quiet but meaningful departure from the institutional reluctance that had long characterized legislative oversight of elections. Yet the aftermath of the 2024 election has complicated this trajectory. Faced with renewed political pressures while demonstrating inexplicable deference to its sister branches, Congress has grown more cautious once again, hesitant to assert its constitutional prerogatives with the same vigor, or alternatively, acting in ways that are contrary to is constitutional role.[48] Updating our understanding of this shifting dynamic is not only timely but essential, as it reflects the evolving institutional position of Congress in defending the foundations of American democracy.

This book offers a blueprint for policymakers, serving as a reminder that congressional authority over election regulation surpasses that of the states in more instances than is commonly known. As illustrated by Alabama's hotly disputed congressional election at issue in *Smith v. Shelley*, Congress has pursued election reform not only through the widely known Reconstruction Amendments, but also through the comparatively obscure structural provisions that are the focus of this book.

The book will also appeal to courts and commentators struggling to understand how the United States can implement a system of elections that is as accessible and inclusive as the Constitution theoretically permits. A progressive election system is possible because Congress is a co-equal branch of government with the Supreme Court.

2022, www.nytimes.com/2022/01/18/us/politics/senate-voting-rights-debate.html [https://perma.cc/2MD4-6TRW]. After Senate Republicans filibustered the bill, Joe Manchin and another Senate Democrat (now Independent), Kristen Sinema, joined with the 50 Republicans to reject a voting-related carve-out to the filibuster that would have allowed the bill to proceed. Li Zhou, "Democrats' Failure on Filibuster Reform Will Haunt Them," *Vox*, January 19, 2022, www.vox.com/2022/1/19/22881837/senate-filibuster-vote-voting-rights-joe-manchin-kyrsten-sinema [https://perma.cc/V5B9-E6KP]. At the time that this book went to press, the failure to reform the filibuster allowed these fifty-two Senators to prevent a final vote on the bill, effectively eliminating its chances of passage.

47 The Leadership Conference, "Project 2025: What's at Stake for Voting Rights," August 2024, https://civilrights.org/wp-content/uploads/2024/08/Project-2025-Voting-Rights.pdf.

48 See Franita Tolson, "Whose Congress Is This, Anyway? Some Thoughts on the Constitutionality of the SAVE Act," *Democracy Project*, February 4, 2026, https://democracyproject.org/posts/whose-congress-is-this-anyway-some-thoughts-on-the-constitutionality-of-the-save-act (arguing that the proposed SAVE Act, which would disenfranchise thousands through its requirement of documentary proof of citizenship to vote in federal elections, is unconstitutional because Congress does not have "the authority to impose federal rules that violate the principles of republicanism that Congress [under the Guarantee Clause] is constitutionally obligated to protect").

Not only is Congress tasked with protecting the right to vote from undue encroachment by the states, but Congress has also historically played a role in interpreting the scope of its own authority independent of the courts.[49] In ignoring that Congress regulates at the intersection of structure *and* rights rather than just structure *or* rights, the case law and the scholarly literature have promoted a state-centered vision of our electoral system that more adequately reflects Madison's original Constitution of 1789 rather than the Constitution that emerged, redefined for a new era, after the ratification of the Twelfth, Thirteenth, Fourteenth and Fifteenth Amendments.

Congress's deference to, and tacit endorsement of, the Madisonian conception is not surprising given the Supreme Court's pronouncement over two centuries ago, in *Marbury v. Madison*, that, "It is emphatically the province and duty of the judicial department to say what the law is."[50] Some scholars have rejected *Marbury*'s core tenet, shifting attention to the nonjudicial actors whose behavior also bear on constitutional meaning.[51] Mark Tushnet, for example, has argued that judicial supremacy is not (and indeed cannot) be absolute, despite the Supreme Court's assertions to the contrary, because implementation of the Court's dictates by nonjudicial actors has just as much import for constitutional meaning as the judicial opinion itself.[52]

49 Compare Gregory Ablasky, "Beyond the Indian Commerce Clause" (2015) 124 *Yale Law Journal* 1012–90 (detailing how constitutional understandings of federal authority over Indian affairs developed over time outside of the courts); Vicki C. Jackson, "Pro-Constitutional Representation: Comparing the Role Obligations of Judges and Elected Representatives in Constitutional Democracy" (2016) 57 *William & Mary Law Review* 1717–1788 (describing the normative role of elected officials in Congress as "advanc[ing] the purposes of constitutional democracy within their own constitutional system" in ways that include, but are not limited to, constitutional and statutory interpretation).

50 *Marbury v. Madison*, 5 U.S. 137, 177 (1803).

51 See, e.g., Joshua A. Chafetz, *Congress's Constitution: Legislative Authority and Separation of Powers* (New Haven: Yale University Press, 2017) (detailing the power that Congress has, beyond its lawmaking authority, that allow it to assert its authority vis a vis the other branches); Jerry Mashaw, "Rethinking Judicial Review of Administrative Action: A Nineteenth Century Perspective" (2011) 32 *Cardozo Law Review* 2241–2254 (discussing how it would be beneficial, for the purposes of the separation of powers, for Congress, rather than the courts themselves, to establish the parameters of judicial review of executive agency actions); Bertrall L. Ross II, "Against Constitutional Mainstreaming" (2011) 78 *University of Chicago Law Review* 1203–62 (arguing against the constitutional validity of the Supreme Court's practice of "constitutional mainstreaming," in which the Court interprets statutes "as a superlegislature … in accordance with the constitutional values it prizes," rather than interpreting them in accordance with congressional intent as indicated in subsequent legislative enactments); Anne J. O'Connell, "Agency Rulemaking and Political Transitions" (2011) *Northwestern University Law Review* 471–534 (arguing that courts should take political transitions in consideration when reviewing agency rules); Louis Fisher, "The Curious Belief in Judicial Supremacy" (1991) 25 *Suffolk University Law Review* 85–116, 87 (arguing that a model of constitutional interpretation "in which all three branches … insist[] on independent construction" is superior to the emergent "unrealistic expectation that the Supreme Court can resolve every constitutional dispute that comes its way").

52 Mark Tushnet, *Taking the Constitution Away from the Courts* (Princeton: Princeton University Press, 1999), pp. 154, 169, 227 (distinguishing between the "thick" constitution, which are the "detailed provisions describing how the government is to be organized" and the "thin" constitution that elevates broad principles such as equality and liberty and arguing that disagreement about the meaning of the "thin" constitution is best conducted by the people, not the courts).

In Congress We Trust? joins this debate and centers Congress as a consequential, nonjudicial actor in the interpretation of constitutional provisions that regulate voting and elections. Seeking to clarify the historical record, this book describes the constitutional and political evolution of congressional power, from an unduly narrow and sparsely used version of federal authority to regulate elections in the early decades of the Founding to one in which federal power was exercised liberally and in the aggregate, deriving from multiple constitutional provisions, during the Reconstruction period. The book concludes by detailing Congress's retreat – sparked by politics, not law – from exercising this broad authority in the late nineteenth and early twentieth centuries, a retreat that has spearheaded a federalism narrative in which the states, rather than Congress, are generally sovereign over the regulation of all elections.

Before the Civil War, Congress already possessed broad authority to regulate voting and elections through the Constitution of Political Structure. This authority was – importantly – unconstrained by federalism and substantially increased with the ratification of the Reconstruction Amendments, enhancing Congress's institutional role relative to the courts and the states. By expanding the Constitution of Political Structure and altering the Constitution of Political Rights, these Amendments shifted significant authority to protect voting rights from the states to Congress, merging the natural right to alter or abolish government with the right to vote. No longer just a privilege granted by states or constrained by courts, voting became a right that Congress had a constitutional duty to protect – broadly, affirmatively, and with significantly less deference to judicially defined parameters that narrowly confined Congress's enforcement authority to "appropriate legislation."

Focusing on the evolution of congressional power through the Constitutions of Political Structure and Political Rights reveals a larger story about the creation and death of the political norms that govern our system of elections. Through this lens, the book explores the role of politics and partisanship in shaping the boundaries of federal power over elections. The Supreme Court currently views principles of federalism as the main constraint on federal power over elections, but *In Congress We Trust?* marshals significant historical evidence that Congress's decision whether to adhere to federalism norms, particularly when enforcing the Constitution of Political Structure, was significantly shaped and influenced by partisan considerations. In other words, Congress had broad authority to regulate elections pre–Civil War, but political norms dictated that it act with caution and restraint. Operating under the label of federalism, Congress followed these norms until it became politically inconvenient to do so. The dispute over the 1842 Apportionment Act[53] and the events surrounding the Kansas–Nebraska Act[54] are two notable examples discussed

53 An Act for the Apportionment of Representation Among the Several States According to the Sixth Census (Apportionment Act of 1842), ch. 47, 5 Stat. 491 (1842).

54 An Act to Organize the Territories of Nebraska and Kansas, ch. 59, 10 Stat. 277 (1854).

in these pages that illustrate the ease with which these federalism norms were disregarded in the face of partisan politics.

The norms surrounding the Constitution of Political Rights similarly reveal a complicated story about federal power over elections and the need to limit the natural right to alter or abolish government to prevent societal upheaval. Premised on the idea that the people exercise collective sovereignty, the right of the people to alter or abolish government flourished during the country's first few decades. As scholars such as Akhil Amar and Christian Fritz have argued, this authority operated independently of official mechanisms of constitutional amendment provided by state constitutions and through the Article V amendment process.[55] The right was long revered as a justification for breaking from unruly monarchs and, perversely, as a defense for a narrowly defined electorate since people retained this political right even if they could not vote.

Larry Kramer, for example, has pointed to alter or abolish (or as he terms it, "constitutional mob action") as a form of popular constitutionalism that negates the need for the robust judicial review that we have today.[56] Historically, the people engaged in constitutional amendment and interpretation in their day-to-day practices. These practices manifested through implementation of state and federal constitutional provisions and in the creation of new precedents (which extended to the outright rejection of unconstitutional laws).[57] On this view, the people, as the governed, were tasked with the ultimate responsibility of determining the legality of official action.[58]

[55] See Akhil R. Amar, "The Consent of the Governed: Constitutional Amendment Outside Article V" (1994) 94 *Columbia Law Review* 457–508, 458; Christian G. Fritz, "Recovering the Lost Worlds of America's Written Constitutions" (2005) 68 *Alabama Law Review* 261–293, 268. See also Christian G. Fritz, *American Sovereigns: The People and America's Constitutional Tradition before the Civil War* (Cambridge: Cambridge University Press, 2009).

[56] Larry Kramer, *The People Themselves: Popular Constitutionalism and Judicial Review* (New York: Oxford University Press, 2004), pp. 24–28 (noting that the people resisted unconstitutional laws through voting, petitioning the government, speaking out in public meetings, boycotts, and finally, constitutional "mob" action that Kramer referred to as "a direct expression of popular sovereignty").

[57] Ibid., Chapter 1 (discussing the founding era understanding of fundamental law as based in part on the British notion of a customary constitution that can improve without changing, modified by usage and prevailing standards). The American constitutional tradition has long been one in which the people, as sovereigns, have resisted laws that they believed to be unjust or unconstitutional. See, e.g., Allison LaCroix, *The Interbellum Constitution: Union, Commerce, and Slavery in the Age of Federalisms* (New Haven: Yale University Press, 2024), pp. 384–409 (discussing the case of Joshua Glover and Wisconsin residents' opposition to the Fugitive Slave Act). Other examples include the people's resistance to the Stamp Act, which provided a basis for the Anti-Federalists to advocate for the protection of the rights to assemble and petition that would ultimately be enshrined in the First Amendment; popular resistance to Prohibition and the Eighteenth Amendment, ultimately leading to its formal repeal in 1933; the boycotts, protests, and noncompliance central to the Civil Rights Movement, which resulted in the passage of a number of federal statutes and constitutional provisions in the 1960s; and opposition to the Vietnam War, which triggered large scale noncompliance and public protests in the 1960s and 1970s and eventually led to the informal demise of the draft.

[58] Kramer, *The People Themselves*, p. 24 ("The community itself had both a right and a responsibility to act when the ordinary legal process failed, and unconstitutional laws could be resisted by community members who continued to profess loyalty to the government and to follow its other laws.").

Contrary to these longstanding political norms, however, invocations of the right to alter or abolish government were rarely respected when politics made adhering to the norm impossible. Domestic uprisings such as the Whiskey Rebellion,[59] Shays' Rebellion,[60] the Dorr Rebellion,[61] and finally, the rise of the Confederacy, would challenge the reverence previously enjoyed by the right to alter or abolish government. This breakdown of norms proved that institutional actors like Congress had to help American Democracy because its excesses, particularly in the case of the Confederacy, were real and not imagined. As some scholars have noted,[62] Reconstruction was indeed the second founding, necessitating the creation of a new legal and political framework to: (a) mitigate the right to alter or abolish

[59] In response to a federal excise tax on whiskey enacted by Congress in 1791, after several years of muted protests, Anti-Federalist farmers in western Pennsylvania who were opposed to the tax converged on Pittsburgh and engaged in a violent "insurrection," which the federal government quelled by sending in a multi-state militia. Saul Cornell, *Other Founders: Anti-Federalism and the Dissenting Tradition in America, 1788–1828* (Chapel Hill: University of North Carolina Press, 1999), p. 195.

[60] Shays' Rebellion took place in Massachusetts during the winter of 1786–87, when an insurgent militia, angered by high taxes and debt-collection enforcement, attacked Massachusetts government institutions. Richard D. Brown, "Shays' Rebellion and the Ratification of the Federal Constitution in Massachusetts," in Richard Beeman, Stephen Botein, and Edward C. Carter II (eds.), *Beyond Confederation: Origins of the Constitution and American National Identity* (Chapel Hill: University of North Carolina Press, 1987), p. 115. The government responded by not only violently suppressing the rebellion and suspending laws that guaranteed civil rights, but also by barring some members of the "Shaysite army" from voting in the state's 1787 gubernatorial election. Ibid., pp. 116–19. Many citizens who did not consider themselves Shaysites viewed this action by the government, which was spearheaded by Governor James Bowdoin, as a clear misuse of government power, and it cost Bowdoin his reelection to the governorship. Ibid., pp. 119–121.

[61] The Dorr Rebellion took root in 1842, when the state of Rhode Island effectively had two governments. Robert W. Coakley, *The Role of Federal Military Forces in Domestic Disorders, 1789–1878* (Washington, D.C.: Center of Military History, U.S. Army, 1988), pp. 119–120. One was the "Charter" government, organized under the state's original charter, under which the only people who were permitted to vote were "freeholders" who held property and their oldest sons. Ibid., p. 120. The other government was established by reformists referred to as "suffragists," who found the voting rights regime under the Charter to be inequitable. Ibid. The latter group became known as "Dorrites" after Thomas Wilson Dorr was elected its governor. Ibid., p. 122. The Dorrites found enough support that the Charter government's governor made multiple requests to the federal government for military assistance. Ibid., pp. 120–123. Although the Dorrites were able to assemble some armed forces, they were no match for the Charter government's militia. Ibid., pp. 123–125. Dorr was eventually convicted of treason, sentenced to life in prison, and pardoned after a year. Ibid., pp. 125. However, the rebellion he led did eventually yield his desired result: by November 1842 the state of Rhode Island had a new constitution "providing for practically universal manhood suffrage." Ibid.

[62] Eric Foner, *The Second Founding: How the Civil War and Reconstruction Remade the Constitution* (New York: W.W. Norton & Company, 2019); Kermit Roosevelt III, "Reconstruction as Revolution: The Fourteenth Amendment and the Destruction of Founding America" (2023) 25 *University of Pennsylvania Journal of Constitutional Law* 1073–1096. See also Kermit Roosevelt III and Kellen McCoy, "Second Founding, Second Redemption" (2024) 26 *University of Pennsylvania Journal of Constitutional Law* 1369–1423 (describing *Students for Fair Admissions v. President and Fellows of Harvard College*, 143 S. Ct. 2141 (2023), the decision striking down affirmative action in higher education, as one in which the Supreme Court, ironically embraced the reference to Reconstruction as a "Second Founding").

government; (b) recognize African Americans as full participants in the political community; and (c) expand Congress's power over elections and the right to vote. However, the scholarship has not fully assessed how this chapter in our history demonstrated the breadth of federal power over elections, through constitutional provisions (both new and old), in response to an ever-changing political situation. This gap in the literature has likewise affected Congress's willingness to exercise the full scope of its authority, with that body needlessly ceding constitutional ground to the Court based on a false federalism narrative.

I.2 CONGRESS, THE COURTS, AND THE DANGERS OF A CLAUSE-BOUND INTERPRETIVISM

In the nineteenth century, New Orleans was known – not for its amazing cuisine, vibrant musical culture, and amazing nightlife – but rather, for its public health crisis, a reputation earned in part from how butchers in the city mishandled meat with poor waste disposal, lack of refrigeration, and unhealthy conditions. The stench that came from animal carcasses tossed in the street unfortunately defined the city more than Mardi Gras, its second line brass bands, and its elaborate parades.[63] By centralizing all slaughtering in a single location, New Orleans tried to address the rise of cholera and yellow fever among its inhabitants, but it unwittingly gave rise to the first case to test the boundaries of the recently ratified Fourteenth Amendment.[64] A group of butchers filed suit, claiming that the 1869 New Orleans law that created a slaughterhouse monopoly violated their economic rights in violation of the Privileges or Immunities Clause of the Fourteenth Amendment.[65]

In ruling against the butchers, the Supreme Court held that the Privileges or Immunities Clause did not protect economic rights, but only a narrowly defined category of federal rights (such as the right to interstate travel, the right to access the federal courts, and the right to sail the high seas).[66] As the dissenters in the case argued, this interpretation of the Clause – to protect rights already guaranteed elsewhere in the Constitution – rendered the Privileges or Immunities Clause "a vain and idle enactment, which accomplished nothing, and most unnecessarily excited Congress and the people on its passage."[67]

[63] See Jonathan Lurie and Ronald M. Labbe, *The Slaughterhouse Cases: Regulation, Reconstruction, and the Fourteenth Amendment* (Lawrence: University Press of Kansas, 2005), pp. 25–26 ("In New Orleans, animals were routinely herded through the streets. Slaughtering sometimes took place out in the open within sight of the public. Carts loaded with slaughterhouse waste were driving, leaking and reeking, through the streets to 'nuisance wharves,' where the waste was supposed to be dumped into the river. But much of it was simply discarded into the streets and gutters or left to rot and fester in butchers' backyards.").

[64] Ibid., p. 47 ("An Act to Protect the Health of the City of New Orleans, and to Locate the Stock Landings and Slaughter Houses").

[65] Ibid., p. 71.

[66] *Slaughter-House Cases*, 83 U.S. 36, 79 (1872).

[67] Ibid., 96 (Field, J., dissenting).

The *Slaughter-House Cases* have been widely reviled by commentators, particularly those who point to the case as the explanation for why the Due Process Clause of the Fourteenth Amendment has, in the last century, uncomfortably become a source of implied fundamental rights that were arguably meant to be protected by the Privileges or Immunities Clause.[68] At the heart of *Slaughter-House* lies a deeper problem, however: the danger of interpreting a constitutional provision in isolation, disconnected from adjacent clauses that shape and inform its meaning. That kind of clause-bound formalism not only narrows the universe of protected rights,[69] it also narrows the scope of institutional power to enforce them. While *Slaughter-House* is often invoked as a cautionary tale about the judicial contraction of individual rights, Congress, too, has sometimes succumbed to a similarly restrictive interpretive approach. By treating its own enforcement powers under the Reconstruction Amendments as more limited than the Constitution arguably requires, Congress has often reinforced the very constraints that decisions like *Slaughter-House* put in motion.

The irony is striking. When Congress adopts the Supreme Court's clause-bound methodology – narrowly grounding its legislative authority in a single constitutional provision as it did with H.R. 1 – that body often finds its efforts deemed

[68] See John H. Ely, *Democracy and Distrust* (Cambridge: Harvard University Press, 1980), p. 18 (arguing that "'substantive due process' is a contradiction in terms – sort of like 'green pastel redness.' One might assume that this doesn't matter, that it is revisionism for the sheer hell of it, since I've advertised that the Fourteenth Amendment does contain provisions – notably the Privileges or Immunities Clause … that contain the sort of invitation to substantive oversight that the Due Process Clause turns out to lack."). See also Akhil R. Amar, "Forward: The Document and the Doctrine" (2000) 114 *Harvard Law Review* 26–134, 123 ("Does a documentarian gain anything by changing the label on the lid of the black box of unenumerated rights from 'substantive due process' to 'privileges or immunities of citizens?' Perhaps a little. Because the very phrase 'substantive due process' teeters on self-contradiction, it provides neither a sound starting point nor a directional push to proper legal analysis. …But given that the origins of substantive due process doctrine are not particularly admirable – Dred Scott and Lochner haunt this swamp – perhaps we can do better."). But see Jamal Green, "Constitutional Rhetoric" (2016) 50 *Virginia Law Review* 519–543, 532 ("While there may be a strong case against substantive due process on historical or prudential grounds, the textual case against it is remarkably weak.").

[69] My references to "clause-bound formalism" or "clause-bound methodology" should be distinguished from John Hart Ely's invocation, and criticism of, a "clause-bound interpretivism" that is limited to the written constitution and ignorant of any norms that cannot be traced to the document. See Ely, *Democracy and Distrust*, pp. 11–42 (cautioning against a "clause-bound interpretivism"). My use of this term is slightly different – where courts interpret a constitutional provision in isolation from any other provisions of the written constitution that may bear on its meaning as well as any norms relevant to the text. While this book does not focus exclusively (or primarily) on the courts, per se, my view of congressional power would lend itself to an interpretive approach that expands on Akhil Amar's theory of intratextualism. See Akhil Amar, "Intratexualism" (1999) 112 *Harvard Law Review* 747–827. While Amar focuses on like words or phrases within the document, I would expand this approach to advocate for assessing the meaning of related constitutional provisions as a collective rather than treating each provision independent and assigning meaning within an interpretive vacuum. See Tolson, "Constitutional Structure of Voting Rights Enforcement," 379–439 (applying intratextualism to advocate for a judicial interpretation of the Elections Clause and the Fourteenth and Fifteenth Amendments that is coherent and internally consistent).

constitutionally suspect by the very Court it emulates. For decades, the Court has misconstrued the overlapping (and sometimes conflicting) authority over elections that Congress shares with the states.[70] Retracing the path set by the *Slaughter-House Cases*, the Court has embraced an increasingly rigid view of federal power – one that prioritizes structural federalism over substantive rights.

Foreshadowing the key points against H.R. 1 in the Heritage Report, the Court's decision in *Shelby County v. Holder* has the dubious honor of undermining a federal statute that has long protected the right to vote while simultaneously circumscribing Congress's enforcement authority under the Fourteenth and Fifteenth Amendments on federalism grounds.[71] In *Shelby County*, the Court invalidated the coverage formula of Section 4(b) of the Voting Rights Act, which required those jurisdictions with a history of race-based discrimination in voting to preclear all changes to their election laws with the federal government. Because the formula used forty-year-old data to single out certain jurisdictions for federal preclearance, but not others that might have acted illegally, the Court held that this provision violated the "equal sovereignty" of the states.[72] Since the coverage formula did not account for the decrease in racial discrimination in voting in covered jurisdictions over the last three decades, the Court insinuated that the formula impermissibly gave minority groups a political advantage over the majority at the expense of state sovereignty.[73] In framing the challenge to the Voting Rights Act as a false choice between safeguarding federalism and protecting minority voting rights, the Court's attempt to strike a balance between these principles has led to a jurisprudence that is inconsistent, insufficiently protective of voting rights, and overvalues state sovereignty over elections.[74]

The Court has taken a similar approach with legislative redistricting. The false dichotomy between expansive voting rights and state sovereignty has breathed new life into racial gerrymandering claims,[75] where the Court has struggled to balance the sometimes conflicting obligations that state legislatures have under state and federal law to ensure that minorities can elect their candidate of choice. But the Court has

70 Compare *Shelby County v. Holder*, 570 U.S. 529 (2013) with *South Carolina v. Katzenbach*, 383 U.S. 301 (1966).

71 *Shelby County v. Holder*, 570 U.S. 529 (2013). See also Guy-Uriel Charles and Luis Fuentes-Rohwer, "The Voting Rights Act in Winter: The Death of a Superstatute" (2015) 100 *Iowa Law Review* 1389–1439, 1391, 1421–1422. The Supreme Court's recent decision in *Louisiana v. Callais* joins *Shelby County* in effectively gutting the VRA - in this case, Section 2 of the Act. 608 U.S. __ (2026).

72 *Shelby County*, 570 U.S. at 539–545, 555–556.

73 Ibid., 534–535, 543–545, 556–557. This issue of segregating political losses from losses attributable to racial discrimination has long been a concern for the Court. See, e.g., *Whitcomb v. Chavis*, 403 U.S. 124 (1971).

74 See Tolson, "Reinventing Sovereignty?,"1200.

75 See, e.g., *Cooper v. Harris*, 581 U.S. 285 (2017) (holding that North Carolina's gerrymander was based on race and, therefore, unconstitutional). But see *Alexander v. NAACP*, 602 U.S. 1 (2024) (suggesting that plaintiffs have to produce at least some direct evidence to win on racial gerrymandering claims and a purely circumstantial case would not be enough, especially if the state has a partisan defense).

also sanctioned partisan justifications that can legitimize these same regressive and problematic plans.[76] It was once true that an excessively gerrymandered redistricting plan raised federal constitutional concerns, even if the Supreme Court doubted its ability to police them,[77] but now the Court has signaled that states enjoy unfettered authority to pursue partisan ends. The Court makes its unjustifiable deference to the states clear in a recent 2024 case, *Alexander v. NAACP*, where it asserted a presumption that the legislature acted in good faith while gerrymandering districts to harm a particular class of voters.[78] Other cases in which the Court showed undue solicitude to the states, such as those involving voter identification laws and various restrictive voting regulations,[79] illustrate that the storied position of state sovereignty as the focal point of our federalist system holds steady, even when unwarranted.[80]

The federalism narrative has persisted despite the substantial authority that Congress has under the Constitution of Political Structure to regulate federal, and to a lesser extent, state elections. Oddly enough, each of the structural provisions that are the focus of this book has made an appearance at least once in the last ten U.S. Supreme Court terms, but in most cases, for reasons other than clarifying the scope of congressional authority over voting and elections.

For example, Congress has never enforced Section 2 of the Fourteenth Amendment, but the Court has relied on its terms in analyzing the scope of Section 1 of that provision, resolving disputes over felon disenfranchisement and redistricting by reference to Section 2's text and legislative history.[81] In 2016, the Court decided *Evenwel v. Abbott*, holding that the one person, one vote rule enshrined in Section 1 of the Fourteenth Amendment did not require states to draw districts containing an equal number of voters.[82] Relying on the legislative history of Section 2, the Court argued that the framers of that Amendment rejected a standard for drawing districts based on total population. Is *Evenwel* relevant to the state's authority over

76 See *Rucho v. Common Cause*, 588 U.S. 684 (2019) (holding that partisan gerrymandering claims present a political question and are not justiciable in federal courts). See also *Louisiana v. Callais*, 608 U.S. __ (2026).

77 See *Vieth v. Jubilierer*, 541 U.S. 267 (2004).

78 See *Alexander v. NAACP*, 602 U.S. 1, 6 (2024) ("Legislators are almost always aware of the political ramifications of the maps they adopt, and claims that a map is unconstitutional because it was drawn to achieve a partisan end are not justiciable in federal court. Thus, as far as the Federal Constitution is concerned, a legislature may pursue partisan ends when it engages in redistricting.").

79 See, e.g., *Crawford v. Marion County Election Bd.*, 553 U.S. 181 (2008) (declaring that Indiana's voter ID law was valid because it furthered the state's interest in preventing election fraud).

80 See Tolson, "Reinventing Sovereignty?" 1196–1198, 1200.

81 *Richardson v. Ramirez*, 418 U.S. 24, 54–56 (1974), decided over four decades ago, concluded that Section 2's express exemption of disenfranchisement grounded on prior conviction of a felony meant that states do not violate the Equal Protection Clause by excluding these individuals from the franchise. *Richardson* was the blueprint for the Court's later deployment of Section 2 to torpedo the argument the redistricting had to be based on total voters.

82 *Evenwel v. Abbott*, 578 U.S. 54, 1130–1133 (2016). But see *Reynolds v. Sims*, 377 U.S. 533, 594 (1964) (Harlan, J., dissenting) (refuting that Section 1 protects a right to vote and pointing to Section 2 as the only remedy for voting rights violations).

redistricting and the Court's interpretation of Section 1? Yes. But is the decision central to understanding congressional power to enforce Section 2? Not so much.[83]

Article I, Section 5 – like Section 2 of the Fourteenth Amendment – has also made an appearance in the case law in the last decade, albeit for reasons other than its delegation to Congress of authority to determine who should sit within its chambers. In its 2014 decision *NLRB v. Noel Canning*, the Supreme Court invoked this clause's prohibition on either congressional chamber being able to adjourn for more than three days without the consent of the other to discern the meaning of "recess" for purposes of the Appointments Clause of Article II, Section 2.[84]

Outside of *Noel Canning*, the Court has not substantially weighed in on the scope of Article I, Section 5 in at least five decades. In the last case to do so, *Powell v. McCormick* (decided in 1969),[85] the Court held that, although Congress has authority to judge the "elections, returns, and qualifications" of its members under this provision, it could not do so in a way that adds to the qualifications for office listed in Article I, Section 2.[86] Thus, Congress could expel Adam Clayton Powell pursuant to its authority under Article I, Section 5, but it must first seat him because Congress was not constitutionally authorized to exclude any person, duly elected, who meets the age, citizenship, and residency requirements in Article I, Section 2.[87] By considering Congress's power under Article I, Section 5 in conjunction with the qualification requirements in Article I, Section 2, *Powell* synthesized related constitutional provisions to ensure internally consistent and coherent constitutional meaning. Yet no recent cases discussing the scope of federal authority over elections

83 The lack of guidance from the courts has led some commentators to fill in the blanks about what Section 2 might require. For example, some have argued that Section 2 requires that the U.S. Census Bureau include a citizenship question on the American Community Survey to enforce the penalty of reduced representation. See, e.g., David B. Rivkin Jr. and Gilson B. Gray III, "How to Put Citizenship Back in the Census," *Wall Street Journal*, July 4, 2019, www.wsj.com/articles/how-to-put-citizenship-back-in-the-census-11562264430 (arguing that Section 2 of the Fourteenth Amendment requires the addition of a citizenship question on the census). For scholarship on Section 2's relevance to the census, see, e.g., Delaram Takyar, "'The Cornerstone of the Stability of Our Government': The Forgotten Penalty Clause and Electoral Reform in the Aftermath of the 2020 Election" (2021) 39 *Yale Law & Policy Review Inter Alia* 1–12; Michael Hurta, "Counting the Right to Vote in the Next Census: Reviving Section Two of the Fourteenth Amendment" (2015) 94 *Texas Law Review* 147–173. See also *Department of Commerce v. New York*, 139 S. Ct. 2551 (2019) (finding that, under the Enumeration Clause, Congress, and by extension the Secretary of Commerce, can inquire about citizenship for purposes of the census, but this decision is reviewable under the Administrative Procedure Act).

84 *NLRB v. Noel Canning*, 573 U.S. 513, 526–536 (2014).

85 395 U.S. 486, 550 (1969).

86 "No Person shall be a Representative who shall not have attained to the Age of twenty five Years, and been seven Years a Citizen of the United States, and who shall not, when elected, be an Inhabitant of that State in which he shall be chosen." United States Constitution Art. I, s. 2.

87 *Powell v. McCormack*, 395 U.S. 486, 559 (1969) ("[W]e hold that, since Adam Clayton Powell, Jr., was duly elected by the voters of the 18th Congressional District of New York and was not ineligible to serve under any provision of the Constitution, the House was without power to exclude him from its membership.").

have considered how Article I, Section 5 interacts with other provisions that delegate authority to Congress, and not the courts, over voting and elections.

This oversight stems from the Supreme Court's desire to keep the constitutional structure, which expressly delegates to Congress authority over various areas of the political system, separate and distinct from the right to vote under the Fourteenth and Fifteenth Amendments, which empower Congress subject to parameters set by the Court. The Court maintains these silos even when issues regarding the Constitutions of Political Structure and Political Rights are present in the same case, oftentimes leading to calamitous results.

For example, both of these constitutions made an appearance in *Rucho v. Common Cause*, which held that partisan gerrymandering claims were nonjusticiable despite evidence that these gerrymanders rendered meaningless the votes of those in the opposition party.[88] In *Rucho*, the plaintiffs challenged congressional redistricting plans in North Carolina and Maryland as unconstitutional partisan gerrymanders in violation of the First and Fourteenth Amendments as well as Article I, Section 2 and the Elections Clause. In rejecting these claims, the Court asserted that any argument "that partisan gerrymanders violate the core right of voters to choose their representatives is an objection more likely grounded in the Guarantee Clause," which "does not provide the basis for a justiciable claim."[89]

Notably, the reapportionment cases, starting with *Baker v. Carr* in 1962,[90] were premised on the idea that judicial intervention was warranted *precisely* because the failure to redistrict violated the voters' right to choose their representatives under the Fourteenth Amendment. *Baker* rejected the argument that the political nature of malapportionment, which, in the Court's view, made it a justiciable "political case" rather than a nonjusticiable "political question," meant that such claims could not be judicially resolved.[91] In making a distinction between "political questions" and "political cases," *Baker* sought to evade the line of precedents finding Guarantee Clause claims to be nonjusticiable.[92] But in doing so, the Court inadvertently rendered the Clause's broader purpose and meaning inconsequential as it relates to issues other than justiciability, choosing instead to confine core questions of voting and representation to the Equal Protection Clause.[93] By treating partisan gerrymandering as a structural harm beyond the

88 *Rucho v. Common Cause*, 588 U.S. 684 (2019).

89 Ibid., 716–717.

90 369 U.S. 186 (1962).

91 Ibid., 217 ("The doctrine of which we treat is one of 'political questions,' not one of 'political cases.' The courts cannot reject as 'no law suit' a bona fide controversy as to whether some action denominated 'political' exceeds constitutional authority.").

92 Ibid., 289–290.

93 Ibid., 218 ("We shall discover that Guaranty Clause claims involve those elements which define a 'political question,' and for that reason and no other, they are nonjusticiable. In particular, we shall discover that the nonjusticiability of such claims has nothing to do with their touching upon matters of state governmental organization.").

purview of federal courts,[94] *Rucho* exploits *Baker*'s distinction between political questions and political cases, and obscures that the Guarantee Clause's conception of republicanism marries rights-based questions about the disbursement of political power with structural questions about how political power should be aggregated and organized.

Rucho also rejected the argument that the Elections Clause, by providing Congress with the power to enact legislation that overrides state election laws, presented a manageable standard to resolve partisan gerrymandering claims. The Elections Clause allows Congress to serve as an express check on partisan gerrymandering in the absence of meaningful judicial standards to govern such claims, even though, according to the *Rucho* Court, the Clause did not delegate exclusive authority to the political branches over redistricting.[95] It is unclear why the Court left open the possibility of an Elections Clause challenge to partisan gerrymandering should manageable standards ever develop, even though the Elections Clause claim involved the same underlying (presumably nonjusticiable) Guarantee Clause argument that North Carolina deprived voters of the right to choose their representatives. The Court had rejected this claim as derivative of the Guarantee Clause because they viewed it as a challenge to the republican nature of state governments rather than an overreach by state governments in setting the times, places and manner of federal elections, or alternatively, as an abridgment or denial of the right to vote. But the Guarantee Clause implications of partisan redistricting would still be present even if manageable standards under the Elections Clause exist.

With the Elections Clause, the Court has struggled to articulate a coherent approach when cases, like *Rucho*, involve issues touching on both the structure of our system of elections and the individual right to vote. For example, in *Arizona v. Inter Tribal Council of Arizona*, decided in 2013,[96] the Court confronted whether the National Voter Registration Act (NVRA), enacted pursuant to the Elections Clause, permitted states to require documentary proof of citizenship as a prerequisite to registering to vote in federal elections, even though the Act itself imposed no such requirement.[97] Recognizing that the Elections Clause gives Congress broad authority over federal elections, the Court nonetheless struggled with the conflict between voter registration (a permissible "manner" regulation) and proof of citizenship (a voter qualification that falls within the state's domain). The Court's reticence to confront the issue head on – by finding that states can challenge application of the NVRA through the administrative process if the statute frustrates their ability to enforce their voter qualifications – likely stemmed from five decades of priming in

94 *Rucho v. Common Cause*, 588 U.S. 684, 707 (2019) ("Federal judges have no license to reallocate political power between the two major political parties, with no plausible grant of authority in the Constitution, and no legal standards to limit and direct their decisions.").

95 Ibid., 705–706.

96 570 U.S. 1 (2013).

97 Ibid., 19–20.

which many of these core democratic disputes have been treated as matters of structure or individual rights, but not both.

Thinking about the Constitution in neat and convenient silos means that there has been no consideration of the full spectrum of congressional authority over elections as a matter of both constitutional rights and constitutional structure. Piecemeal efforts consider structural provisions in a vacuum, as a means of illuminating the scope of individual rights, the nature of the constitutional structure, or alternatively, to flesh out the judiciary's constitutional obligations. This approach follows a long history of Supreme Court intra-clausal interpretivism that has little to do with clarifying how Congress has deployed these provisions or ensuring consistent and coherent meaning.[98] Even the Elections Clause, certainly better theorized than the rest, has nonetheless been marginalized due to the failure to consider its meaning and scope in the broader context of congressional power over elections.[99]

Unsurprisingly, the *Shelby County* Court's blind adherence to federalism principles, together with its faulty logic that the preclearance regime was unconstitutional because the exigency that justified its existence – virulent racism – no longer exists,[100] has created confusion about the *actual* scope of congressional power to regulate elections as a practical matter. *Shelby County* rested on a very narrow interpretation of Congress's authority under the Fourteenth and Fifteenth Amendments, essentially adhering to a vision of the constitutional structure that predates the Reconstruction Amendments.

From this perspective, the sin of *Shelby County* is not only the neutering of a significant provision of one of the most successful civil rights statutes in history, but also that it leaves a legacy of constitutional interpretation that fails to engage the full spectrum of congressional authority in this area. The Court focused on the substantial federalism costs of the VRA, ignoring that the Act arguably could have been sustained based on sources of authority beyond the Fourteenth and Fifteenth Amendments.[101] Interpreting federal authority over elections in the aggregate, based on all of the provisions from which such power derives, would properly account for the allocation of authority between Congress and the states over elections that emerged after the Reconstruction Amendments. This approach would create a theoretical framework that is centered in 1870 rather than 1789, and account for both constitutional rights and constitutional structure in election regulation.

98 See, e.g., *Evenwel v. Abbott*, 578 U.S. 54 (2016) (relying on the text of Section 2 of the Fourteenth Amendment to interpret the scope of Section 1 of the Fourteenth Amendment); *Richardson v. Ramirez*, 418 U.S. 24 (1974)(same); *Minor v. Happersett*, 88 U.S. 162 (1874) (same).

99 See, e.g., *Rucho v. Common Cause*, 588 U.S. 684 (2019) (rejecting the First and Fourteenth Amendment challenges, in part, because Congress could address partisan gerrymandering under the Elections Clause but doing so without any discussion of how Congress has actually deployed this authority).

100 *Shelby County v. Holder*, 570 U.S. 529, 547 (2013) (citing increases in African American voter participation to illustrate that preclearance requirements for selected states is no longer justified).

101 Tolson, "Reinventing Sovereignty?," 1241.

I.3 IN CONGRESS WE TRUST? A ROADMAP

The longest filibuster in history would not be the only hurdle that the Civil Rights Act of 1964 would have to overcome before it took its place as one of the most transformational pieces of legislation in American history. Within two hours of becoming law, Moreton Rolleston, owner of the segregated Heart of Atlanta Motel, filed a lawsuit challenging the 1964 Act as a violation of the Takings Clause of the Fifth Amendment and as exceeding the scope of Congress's power under the Commerce Clause. Rolleston was fully committed to segregation, forbidding African American patrons at his hotel and including a rider in the deed to his private home that people of African descent could never purchase or stay at the property.[102] Rolleston – like General Charles Miller Shelley – will eventually be lost to history or, preferably, recalled as a side character in the story of how Congressman John Lewis conducted a sit-in at the counter of the restaurant in Heart of Atlanta Motel.

Rolleston will also likely be remembered in one of history's greatest ironies because his property was purchased by African American media mogul Tyler Perry in 2005. Rolleston sued Perry to regain control of the property (even though he hadn't been the owner since losing the property in unrelated litigation in the 1990s[103]) before eventually being jailed for contempt and barred from filing any additional lawsuits.[104]

But more importantly for our purposes, his lawsuit challenging the 1964 Civil Rights Act presented an opportunity for the Supreme Court, for the first time in almost a century, to endorse a view of federal authority where congressional power was assessed in the aggregate, as Congress sought to create a new blueprint for civil rights and enforce the commitment to democracy and racial equality promised by long dead constitutional provisions.

Congress passed the Civil Rights Act of 1964 pursuant to its authority under the Commerce Clause and Section 5 of the Fourteenth Amendment.[105] In some ways, Congress's reliance on the Commerce Clause was additive, a safeguard in response to an unfavorable Supreme Court decision in the late nineteenth century that invalidated an earlier Civil Rights Act (of 1875) and circumscribed Congress's ability to reach private discrimination.[106] But at least three members of the Court argued that the Commerce Clause, as a source of congressional authority for the Act, was not

[102] Amy R. Dobson, "The Full Circle Moment behind the Record-Breaking Sale of Tyler Perry's Former Mansion, Now Owned By Steve Harvey," *Forbes*, June 24, 2010.

[103] *Rolleston v. Cherry*, 487 S.E.2d 354 (Ga. App. 1997).

[104] Dobson, "Full Circle Moment."

[105] *Heart of Atlanta Motel v. United States*, 379 U.S. 241, 249 (1964).

[106] See, e.g., *Civil Rights Cases*, 109 U.S. 3, 11 (1883). The *Heart of Atlanta Motel* Court declined to revisit the *Civil Rights Cases*, finding that the 1964 Act was constitutional under the Commerce Clause. *Heart of Atlanta Motel*, 379 U.S. at 250–51.

the only provision that Congress could have invoked to justify its terms.[107] As Justice Black noted in his concurrence,

> In the view of the Commerce Clause it is not possible to deny that the aim of protecting interstate commerce from undue burdens is a legitimate end. In view of the Thirteenth, Fourteenth and Fifteenth Amendments, it is not possible to deny that the aim of protecting Negroes from discrimination is also a legitimate end [under the Necessary and Proper Clause].[108]

While any one of these clauses would have arguably been sufficient justification for the Act,[109] especially if coupled with the Necessary and Proper Clause,[110] federal authority is at its most expansive when Congress legislates pursuant to more than one provision.[111]

This book builds on that insight. It examines Congress's authority over voting and elections as similarly aggregate – rooted not in any single clause, but in the interaction among multiple, often overlooked constitutional provisions – to offer two major contributions. First, it shows the historical connection between the Constitution of Political Structure and the Constitution of Political Rights in the regulation of state and federal elections. By focusing on congressional oversight in this area from the founding to the early Jim Crow era, this book presents a stark contrast to narratives that often center on either (a) how Congress and the courts have shaped the modern electorate since the 1960s[112] or, (b) how both of these institutions have, at various points throughout the history of the United States, abdicated their responsibilities to protect the right the vote.[113] The story of voting rights in America is not just about the non-linear march toward universal suffrage;[114] it is also a story about the enlargement and concentration of federal power over the course of two centuries.

[107] *Heart of Atlanta Motel*, 379 U.S. at 260 (Black, J., concurring) (arguing that the Act is valid under the Commerce Clause and the Necessary and Proper Clause); Ibid., 279 (Douglas, J., concurring) (joining Court's Commerce Clause opinion but preferring that the Court's holding be based on Section 5 of the Fourteenth Amendment); Ibid., 292–293 (Goldberg, J., concurring) (noting that the Act is constitutional under the Commerce Clause and Section 5 of the Fourteenth Amendment).

[108] Ibid., 276–277 (Black, J., concurring).

[109] Ibid., 279 (Douglas, J., concurring). See also *Katzenbach v. Morgan*, 384 U.S. 641 (1966) (holding that Congress, under Section 5 of the Fourteenth Amendment, could enact legislation that expanded rights beyond those recognized by the courts).

[110] See, e.g., the Civil Rights Act of 1866, ch. 31, 14 Stat. 27; the Ku Klux Klan Act of 1871, ch. 22, 17 Stat. 13 (both enacted pursuant to the Thirteenth Amendment and the Necessary and Proper Clause).

[111] *Heart of Atlanta Motel*, 379 U.S. at 280 (Douglas, J., concurring) ("In determining the reach of an exertion of legislative power, it is customary to read various granted powers together.").

[112] See, e.g., Ari Berman, *Give Us the Ballot* (New York: Farrar, Straus and Giroux, 2016); Richard L. Hasen, *The Supreme Court and Election Law: Judging Equality from Baker v. Carr to Bush v. Gore* (New York: New York University Press, 2006).

[113] See, e.g., Michael Waldman, *The Fight to Vote* (New York: Simon & Schuster, 2022); Carol Anderson, *One Person, No Vote* (New York: Bloomsbury Publishing, 2019).

[114] See, e.g. Keyssar, *The Right to Vote*; Anderson, *One Person, No Vote*.

A central argument of this book (and its second major contribution to the literature) is that Congress's understanding of its constitutional power has not been static. Rather, this authority has evolved dramatically over time, moving from a narrow, clause-bound approach to one that has reflected a more expansive, multi-clausal view of federal authority during key periods in American history. In the early years of the republic, Congress tended to regulate federal elections by anchoring its actions in single, isolated provisions of the Constitution. However, political controversies over slavery and the exigencies of war necessitated that Congress change its election regulation practice and aggressively draw on numerous constitutional provisions, both new and old, to force systemic change.

The history will show that, prior to the Civil War, the desuetude of certain clauses, notably the Elections Clause and the Guarantee Clause, was not driven exclusively by respect for federalism; rather, it reflected institutional pathologies, partisan concerns, and constitutional text that treated state regulation as a discretionary default unless circumstances dictated greater congressional intervention. Despite the current Court's singular focus on federalism, Congress, like any institutional actor, legislates (or fails to legislate) for a multitude of reasons that cannot be neatly packaged in the language of constitutionalism.[115]

Part I (Chapters 1 and 2) focuses on the Constitution of Political Structure and argues that the Guarantee Clause, the Elections Clause, and Article I, Section 5 defined the basic parameters of the federal–state relationship over elections during the founding and antebellum periods. Notably, Congress's deference to the states when acting pursuant to these provisions was not driven solely by abstract concerns about federalism. In many cases, Congress determined its level of involvement based on (a) whether federal intervention would exacerbate disputes over the extension of slavery in the territories and (b) whether state election procedures adequately ensured the continued existence and legitimacy of federal elections consistent with republican ideals. This was an era defined by a respect for versions of federalism and republicanism that centered on the state as the primary organizational force for state and federal elections until politics (and war) made this deference untenable.

The founding generation coalesced around the Guarantee Clause as the touchstone for an ideal government structure in the American system because of an almost universal sentiment, after the ratification of the Twelfth Amendment, that republicanism required that the preferences of the majority hold sway. While the meaning of republicanism was contested, the Clause arguably allowed Congress to intervene in state political systems, both at the point of admission to the Union and on a continuing basis, whenever there was a threat to republican ideals.

Chapter 1 highlights the changing definitions of republicanism in light of the adoption of the Twelfth Amendment, debates over slavery, and the admission of

115 See LaWanda Cox and John H. Cox, "Negro Suffrage and Republican Politics: The Problem of Motivation in Reconstruction Historiography" (1967) 33 *The Journal of Southern History* 303–330.

new states. The Twelfth Amendment elevated the voters to a central position in republican theory by creating an expectation that the president be the choice of a majority of those who wield political power on behalf of the state. This version of majoritarianism, filtered through the medium of political parties, also became a limit on the types of political systems that states could adopt in accordance with the Guarantee Clause. However, Congress's power under the Clause was stunted because of a slaveocracy that consistently made federalism arguments to protect that institution, even when such arguments were contrary to newly redefined republican ideals.

Chapter 2 discusses how Congress pushed back against this abuse by powerful slave interests after the controversy over the Kansas–Nebraska Act,[116] fully embracing its constitutional obligations in the name of election integrity. Indeed, Congress's willingness to assert itself vis-à-vis the states was notable given its commitment, for much of the early nineteenth century, to defer to political systems in which election winners were chosen from a process legitimized by clear rules and a definitive outcome. These goals generally trumped any desire to use electoral disputes as a vehicle for asserting the supremacy of federal law or to promote views of republican government that stood in tension with the form preferred by states seeking admission to the Union. Deference to state law brought coherence and administrative ease to a system in which multiple states had de facto control over federal elections.[117] Even when state procedures were not ideal, Congress deferred to state authority to promote broader values of ease and predictability.

As this chapter shows, federalism did not necessarily mandate this deference. On occasion, Congress had to intervene in state political systems and reassert the primacy of federal law, negating any inference that the states were truly sovereign over elections. This chapter's discussion of early federal election legislation, such as the

[116] An Act to Organize the Territories of Nebraska and Kansas, ch. 59, 10 Stat. 277 (1854).

[117] That Congress would be conservative and reserved in regulating federal elections is consistent with at least some views of federal power under the Clause at the country's founding. See Tolson, "Reinventing Sovereignty?," 1224–1225 (discussing proposals in Massachusetts and New Hampshire that would limit Congress's power under Elections Clause to only those situations in which states failed to call for congressional elections or where state legislation endangered rights otherwise protected by Constitution). During their constitutional conventions, some states included language in their proposed amendments reflecting their desire that the federal government defer to state election laws. New York provides an example of this: "Congress shall not make or alter any Regulation in any State respecting the times places and manner of holding Elections for Senators or Representatives, unless the Legislature of such State shall neglect or refuse to make Laws or Regulations for the purpose, or from any circumstance be incapable of making the same; and then only until the Legislature of such State shall make provision in the premises…." "Ratification of the Constitution by the State of New York (July 26, 1788)," in *Documentary History of the Constitution of the United States of America, 1786–1870*, 3 vols. (Washington, D.C.: Department of State, 1894), vol. 1, p. 197. Rhode Island's proposed constitution, submitted two years after New York's, includes identical language. "Ratification of the Constitution by the State of Rhode Island and the Providence Plantations (May 29, 1790)," in *Documentary History of the Constitution of the United States of America, 1786–1870*, 3 vols. (Washington, D.C.: Department of State, 1894), vol. 1, p. 315.

Apportionment Act of 1842 and the decision to seat representatives elected in violation of this federal law, shows that Congress made purely partisan decisions to weigh in on issues long considered to be the domain of the state, further undermining the inference that Congress was constrained by federalism during this period.

Importantly, this book builds on the idea that one cannot understand Congress's place in our system of elections without appreciating that decisions to exercise the federal government's power over elections were predominantly rooted in politics rather than federalism. The book illustrates this principle by showing the dependent relationship between the scope of federal power over elections and the robustness of the underlying right to vote. During Reconstruction, this relationship would, for a time, find a home in the Constitution of Political Rights, subject to congressional regulation, but its beginnings were very different. Prior to the Civil War, the norm was that the political community entitled to exercise the right to vote was defined almost exclusively by state law. During the founding and antebellum eras, there was little room for federal intervention in states with a limited suffrage, but as the political community grew, so too did federal power.

Using the lens of political community, Part II (Chapters 3 and 4) focuses on the Constitution of Political Rights, and argues that the U.S. Constitution's mandate that Congress guarantee to every state a republican government, judge the elections of its members, and legislate with respect to the times, places and manner of federal elections was an implicit limit on the power that states had to create, shape, and protect their political communities. These communities include the enclave of voters ("We the Voters") and the broader community of nonvoters ("We the People"). Political community, as a theoretical concept, has played an important role in how the atom of sovereignty was divided among the federal government, the states, and the people. Community is defined by denoting the scope of rights that any person is entitled to as a matter of law and that the government is bound to respect.

For much of our history, the states, with little input from the federal government, have determined the boundaries of their political communities and the rights of those within. The question of who should have access to the ballot has been bloody and contested precisely because the Constitution, as ratified in 1789, gave states the authority to heavily police these communities, and states constantly reconceptualized those boundaries to limit influx. Scores have died challenging the boundaries of the political nomos.[118] These communities have been defined based on citizenship, geography, religion, race, gender, age, profession, length of residency, and financial means, to name the most common characteristics.[119] Whether by barring

118 See Chapter 6.

119 Chilton Williamson, *American Suffrage: From Property to Democracy, 1760–1860* (Princeton: Princeton University Press, 1960), p. 15 (discussing voting restrictions as applied to "free Negroes in the Carolinas, Georgia, and Virginia" and "legal discriminations against Catholics in some colonies even where there were no Catholics or very few.").

active military from voting,[120] or limiting the ability of college students to participate in local elections,[121] political communities have been artificial constructs, enforced by law, that exist to divvy up and protect scarce resources among the "haves" while excluding the "have nots."

As Chapter 3 discusses, the political community of "We the People" represented all of those individuals in the American polity who could claim the protection of the federal government (including women, children, and property-less White men) but who were not necessarily voters.[122] The Founders believed that government could limit the electorate and still be republican in form because "We the People" retained their natural right to alter or abolish government even if they could not vote, and states preserved this right when amending their constitutions during the Confederation period from 1776 to 1789.[123] The right's presence in state constitutions allowed the founding generation to claim that no one was truly without political power to influence government (which might have otherwise prompted federal intervention to enforce the republican guarantee), effectively leaving in place the privileged classes who would choose representatives and voters from among their ranks.

In contrast, the community of "We the Voters" had suffrage rights, but their access to the ballot was closely policed by the state. The right to vote was treated

120 *Carrington v. Rash*, 380 U.S. 89 (1965).

121 See Joseph A. Bollhofer, "Disenfranchisement of the College Student Vote: When a Resident is Not a Resident" (1983) 11 *Fordham Urban Law Journal* 489–524, 521; Michael Wines, "The Student Vote Is Surging. So Are Efforts to Suppress It," *New York Times*, October 24, 2019, www.nytimes.com/2019/10/24/us/voting-college-suppression.html [https://perma.cc/BH4G-C5RP].

122 During the Constitutional Convention, Alexander Hamilton advocated for apportionment based on total population, reasoning that "[t]here can be no truer principle than this – that every individual of the community at large has an equal right to the protection of the government." "Comments of Alexander Hamilton (June 29, 1787)," in Max Farrand (ed.), *Records of the Federal Convention of 1787*, 2 vols. (New Haven: Yale University Press, 1911), vol. 1, p. 473.

123 In paragraph 2, the Declaration of Independence decreed that "whenever any Form of Government becomes destructive of these ends, it is the Right of the People to alter or to abolish it, and to institute new Government, laying its foundation on such principles and organizing its powers in such form, as to them shall seem most likely to effect their Safety and Happiness." United States Declaration of Independence, para. 2 (1776). Among the rights established by the Declaration of Independence is the right to "alter or abolish" any form of government that fails to secure people's "unalienable rights," including those to "Life, Liberty and the pursuit of Happiness." United States Declaration of Independence, para. 2 (1776).

The right to abolish the government was enshrined, with similar language, in some state constitutions that were ratified the same year. For example, the relevant clause in the Pennsylvania state constitution reads as follows: "[T]he community hath an indubitable, unalienable and indefeasible right to reform, alter, or abolish government in such manner as shall be by that community judged most conducive to the public weal." Constitution of the State of Pennsylvania art. V (1776). The word "majority" was used to qualify "community" in a similar clause in the constitution of Virginia: "[A] majority of the community hath an indubitable, inalienable, and indefeasible right to reform, alter, or abolish it, in such manner as shall be judged most conducive to the public weal." Constitution of the State of Virginia s. 3 (1776). This right was also contemplated by the Founders as they debated the U.S. Constitution, as evidenced by James Madison's invocation of the "transcendent and precious right of the people to 'abolish or alter their governments' as justification for a new constitution. Madison, "The Federalist 40" p. 315.

as a property right, denial or abridgment of which was subject to recovery in tort. At the founding, the electorate consisted of a small subset of Americans who could meet varying requirements concerning property ownership, age, gender, race, and citizenship. Post–Twelfth Amendment, states could no longer exclude those entitled to be in the community of "We the Voters" without running afoul of republican principles. In other words, once an individual was deemed part of the political community entitled to vote in both state and federal elections,[124] states could not abridge or deny their right to vote without violating the Guarantee Clause's requirement of republican government.[125]

Despite broad text authorizing federal enforcement of the republican guarantee, the founding and antebellum eras were defined by deference to state level determinations regarding who possessed political rights and the circumstances under which the right to alter or abolish had been properly exercised. The Dorr Rebellion, detailed in Chapter 4, presented the paradigmatic example of an unresponsive state government that had impermissibly narrowed the community of "We the Voters" to maintain power. Yet the federal government refused to intercede on behalf of Dorr and his supporters even after they went through formal legal processes to displace the incumbent legislature. The Dorr Rebellion was but one illustration of how political calculation, rather than legal or moral principle, dictated the terms upon which political communities were policed prior to the Civil War.

The right to vote and the right to alter or abolish government, both of which would ultimately become the foundation of the Constitution of Political Rights, were defined by state law for the period leading up to the Civil War, and congressional attempts to protect the right to vote directly were virtually nonexistent. Instead, Congress used its authority under the Elections Clause to "make or alter" state regulations and its authority to judge the elections of its members under Article I, Section 5, to police federal elections. When acting pursuant to these provisions – key aspects of the Constitution of Political Structure – Congress interpreted its authority as broadly as circumstances warranted, which indirectly impacted, and in some cases, limited, the states' authority to determine the membership of "We the Voters."

124 Article I, Section 2 provides, in part, that:

> The House of Representatives shall be composed of Members chosen every second Year by the People of the several States, and the Electors in each State shall have the Qualifications requisite for Electors of the most numerous Branch of the State Legislature.

United States Constitution Art. I, s. 2.

125 See William M. Wiecek, *The Guarantee Clause of the U.S. Constitution* (Ithaca: Cornell University Press, 1972), pp. 18–19 ("'Democracy', referring to a distinctive form of government, meant the direct, complete, and continuing control of the legislative and executive branches of government by the people as a whole … all but extreme conservatives by 1787 conceded that a 'democratic element' was essential, or at least unavoidable, in the composition of state governments."). James Madison defined a pure democracy as "a Society, consisting of a small number of citizens, who assemble and administer the Government in person." Madison, "The Federalist 10," p. 109.

By the late 1850s, disputes over slavery and economic issues forced Congress to abandon the conservative posture that defined the first half of the nineteenth century. For example, controversy over the Kansas–Nebraska Act, which involved leading Missouri residents fraudulently voting in territorial elections to get Kansas admitted as a slave state, forced Congress to utilize the Constitution of Political Structure to police voting rights (in this case fraudulent voting). And this was not the only area that saw fundamental change because of slavery politics.

In the onslaught of secession, President Abraham Lincoln and Congress were forced to rethink not only the continued viability of the right to alter or abolish government, but also to conceptualize a new version of the political community of "We the Voters" – one premised on loyalty to the Union rather than racial and economic restrictions. As Chapter 4 shows, the narrowing of the natural right to alter or abolish government, as a right belonging to numerical minorities rather than the institutional state, paralleled discussions about who should be tasked with exercising the political power of the state. The traditional planter class could no longer be trusted with a right of revolution meant to be used sparingly, which necessitated broader access to nonviolent forms of political power. Thus starts a longstanding disagreement in every corner of the Union – from the Executive to Congress to the Supreme Court – about which individuals have demonstrated sufficient virtue to be enfranchised, and even more importantly, who decides? Ultimately, Black people, previously thought unworthy to be a part of "We the People" or as holders of any political rights, challenged existing paradigms and forced Congress's hand.

Picking up on this inquiry, Part III (Chapters 5 and 6) discusses Reconstruction, focusing on Congress's post–Civil War power over voting and elections, which was often at odds with the Supreme Court's interpretation of that authority. Reconstruction was defined, in large part, by the marriage between the Constitutions of Political Structure and Political Rights. This synergy was necessary because the exigencies of war required the creation of new political norms regarding the right to vote, republicanism, and federalism. This expansion of federal power ultimately set Congress on a collision course with the Court as Congress liberally interpreted its constitutional obligation to ensure republican government.

Changing norms, together with the need for new political communities following the demise of the southern planter class, necessitated federal intervention in state political systems. Toward this end, Congress used its power under the Elections Clause, the Guarantee Clause, Article I, Section 5, and the Reconstruction Amendments, the latter of which expanded Congress's power to define the community of "We the Voters."[126] After confederates relied on the alter or abolish power to secede from the Union, Congress required southern states, as a condition of reentry,

[126] See Rebecca Zietlow, "Vision and Revision: Exploring the History, Evolution, and Future of the Fourteenth Amendment: Juriscentricism and the Original Meaning of Section Five" (2004) 13 *Temple Political & Civil Rights Law Review* 485–513, 488, 505–506 (discussing how "the Reconstruction Era

to expand voting rights. Voting rights, exercised by a broader swath of the population, supplanted the natural right to alter or abolish government as the mechanism through which the people could express their sovereign authority. Chapter 5 shows that this shift from the alter or abolish right to suffrage as the preferred vehicle for government accountability paralleled the expanded federal presence in the election realm during this period. It was this understanding of the right to vote, derived almost entirely from state constitutions (which were adopted by some of the most racially diverse conventions in history) and infused with moral authority usurped from the natural right to alter or abolish government, that lay at the heart of the new political community that Congress created in enacting Section 2 of the Fourteenth Amendment.

Through Section 2 of the Fourteenth Amendment, congressional Republicans formally recognized the political existence of African Americans. This group had previously been denied such recognition: first, with the Supreme Court's 1856 *Dred Scott* decision[127] and, then post–Thirteenth Amendment, with the adoption of the Black codes in southern states that relegated this group to quasi-slave status.[128] The hope was that Section 2 would penalize states by reducing their representation in Congress for disenfranchising African American men who were now entitled to membership in the political community of "We the Voters." The expansion of federal power and the evolution of the right to vote became manifest in this new political community that emerged from the ashes of the Civil War; namely, an electorate that was no longer predominantly White and privileged.

Chapter 6 illustrates that Congress sought to protect African Americans, not only through Section 2, but also through the Fifteenth Amendment, the adoption of which was an explicit rejection of the clause-bound approach to regulating elections and voting that had existed, however sparingly, prior to the Civil War. Congress's authority to impose the penalty of reduced representation for any abridgment of the right to vote was intended to be an important supplement to Congress's power to enact broad legislation to combat racial discrimination in voting. The debates surrounding these provisions also demonstrated Congress's intent to read its authority

Congress embraced the role of protecting 'rights of belonging,' that is, rights that promote an inclusive vision of who belongs to the national community" such as the right to vote).

[127] *Dred Scott v. Sandford*, 60 U.S. (19 How.) 393 (1856).

[128] See Walter L. Fleming, "Race and Labor Problems: 'Black Codes,'" in Walter L. Fleming (ed.), *Documentary History of Reconstruction: Political, Military, Social Religious, Educational & Industrial, 1865 to the Present Time*, 2 vols. (Cleveland: The A.H. Clark Company, 1906), vol. 1, pp. 243–312 (includes excerpts of so-called "Black Laws" or "Black Codes," which were antebellum laws enacted in southern states that applied to formerly enslaved Black people). The formerly enslaved were also kidnapped and sent to countries such as Cuba and Brazil in the wake of emancipation. "Comments of Senator Sumner," 39th Congress, 1st Session, January 9, 1866, 36 *Congressional Globe* (Washington, D.C.: Globe Office, 1866), pt. 1, p. 146 (introducing a resolution to address the issue of enslaved persons who, post-Thirteenth Amendment, were "kidnapped and transported to Cuba and Brazil to be held as slaves…").

under the Reconstruction Amendments in tandem with the provisions of the original Constitution that emerged from Reconstruction redefined: the Guarantee Clause, the Elections Clause, and Article I, Section 5. These provisions gave Congress a role in defining the political community entitled to exercise this newly redefined right to vote, a right that was now federally protected and disconnected from its property-like status. Voting now served as the vehicle through which "We the People" could more easily join the community of "We the Voters" and express their political power.

Each provision contributed to the creation of this new collective. The Guarantee Clause legitimized much of the Reconstruction program, especially as Congress brought the southern states under federal control to facilitate the creation of their new postwar governments. The Enforcement Acts, adopted pursuant to the Elections Clause and the Fourteenth and Fifteenth Amendments, punished those who sought to disenfranchise African Americans seeking to exercise their new rights. Article I, Section 5 likewise functioned as an ex-post check on broad disenfranchisement, with Congress refusing to seat beneficiaries of such wrongdoing, like Shelley, in its chambers.

The story of these constitutional provisions, with their limitless potential to alter the political landscape, also sheds light on Congress's post-Reconstruction failures in a way that the scholarship has not fully appreciated. Importantly, Part IV (Chapters 7–9) argues that Congress, in crafting the Reconstruction Amendments, wanted to preserve its authority to exclude those it deemed undesirable from the political community of "We the Voters," which significantly undermined later efforts to protect Black voters. The preservation of some elements of the pre–Civil War constitutional framework – that is, the absence of an affirmative right to vote – when combined with the judicial invalidation of many key aspects of the Reconstruction project provided Congress with the exit for which the institution was searching as Reconstruction became less viable politically.

The Panic of 1873 and widespread economic and social unrest made the Reconstruction project untenable for many Republicans.[129] The desire to minimize the federal presence in the South not only created a tension with the republican ideals and equality norms that Congress sought to impart on the states, but the lack of enforcement of these new political norms at a critical juncture undermined their ability to constrain political actors (even those who were once allies) moving forward. Chapter 7 shows that Congress's hypocrisy and complicity in the treatment of Chinese people, women, and the initial beneficiaries of federal

[129] The years immediately after the Civil War saw an explosive expansion into the west, which included the building of several railroad lines. However, by late 1873, the inability to secure investments, both in the United States and Europe, to meet the funding needs of this railroad expansion, together with the ongoing economic depression in the South following the Civil War, essentially meant that "the depression was everywhere," which caused nearly two weeks of "panic [that was] so wild on the New York Stock Exchange that the governors of the clearing house closed it down and refused to allow sales to go on record." Frederic L. Paxton, *History of the American Frontier, 1763–1893* (Boston: Houghlin Mifflin Company, 1924), pp. 513–521.

intervention – African Americans – diminished Congress's standing as a counterpoint to the exclusionary tactics used by states.

This loss of moral authority undermined later efforts in the nineteenth century to protect African American voting rights from an onslaught of state disenfranchisement efforts. Violent uprisings across the South, from the Colfax Massacre of the 1870s to the Wilmington Insurrection of the 1890s, further complicated Congress's already precarious standing on these issues, especially given its ongoing war with a Supreme Court intent on limiting congressional power. As Chapter 8 details, the Federal Elections Bill of 1890, which would have instituted federal supervision of congressional elections, as well as several proposed bills seeking to implement the penalty of Section 2 of the Fourteenth Amendment, discussed in Chapter 9, were casualties of Congress's failure to capitalize on the full scope of its authority at a time in which such efforts were politically palatable. Instead of using the Constitutions of Political Structure and Political Rights to ensure that African Americans would be permanent fixtures in the political community of "We the Voters," politics guaranteed that they would remain transient and temporary visitors.

With the failure of these efforts, Congress sporadically used its power under Article I, Section 5 to police racial discrimination in voting, even though much of the disenfranchisement written in law was ostensibly race-neutral. As illustrated in Chapter 9, Congress fought back against these restrictive regimes, which were adopted across the South over the course of the 1890s and set the tone for the exclusion of Black voters from American politics for almost a century. Congress's efforts during this period bring this book back to a reoccurring theme: that political limitations were more of a barrier to the broad implementation of federal power over elections than constitutional constraints like federalism.

Indeed, the controversy over federal enforcement efforts reveals that there were political risks attendant to legislating toward the outer limits of constitutional power, risks that tended to manifest at the ballot box. Republicans enacted five Enforcement Acts in the early 1870s, which contributed to the 1874 defeat that cost them control of Congress for the first time since the Civil War. Similarly, Republicans' support for the Federal Elections Bill cost them in the 1890 elections, with fissures in the Republican caucus ultimately leading to the bill's defeat in 1891, followed by huge Republican losses in the 1892 elections.[130] The 1890 bill, although proposed pursuant to the Elections Clause, was the first time since Reconstruction that the Republicans attempted to merge their authority under both the rights-bearing and structural provisions of the Constitution; in other words, the proposal was a time, place, and manner statute designed to strengthen the 1870s Enforcement Acts – all of which were enacted pursuant to the Fourteenth and Fifteenth Amendments as

[130] Richard M. Valley, "Partisan Entrepreneurship and Policy Windows: George Frisbie Hoar and the 1890 Federal Elections Bill," in Stephen Skowronek and Matthew Glassman (eds.), *Formative Acts: American Politics in the Making* (Philadelphia: University of Pennsylvania Press, 2007), p. 127.

well as the Elections Clause – to protect voters in both the North and the South. The failure of this bill meant that the effort to further de-silo these sources of authority had also failed.

Instead, the piecemeal, case-by-case enforcement efforts that Congress undertook pursuant to Article I, Section 5 became an incomplete alternative to the broad legislation that was needed, signaling the limits of federal power when Congress does not tap into the full spectrum of its authority to address systemic voting discrimination. As was true in the antebellum era, contested elections brought before each house illustrate the difficulty of disentangling politics from any federalism concerns underlying Congress's motivations for deploying (or neglecting) its constitutional duties. In the end, politics won, and Congress abandoned its efforts to protect voting rights in federal elections by the early twentieth century.

After the clarification of the historical record offered by the book,[131] the Epilogue explores the implications of this history for modern disputes between the Supreme Court and Congress. Given that the history offered in these pages stops around 1910, and as such is necessarily incomplete, the Epilogue seeks to draw a somewhat limited comparison between the Voting Rights Act of 1965 – in particular, the preclearance regime of Sections 4(b) and 5 – and past congressional voting rights efforts during Reconstruction and its aftermath. Notably, the Voting Rights Act was built on the framework created by moderate Reconstruction-era Republicans, but the Act also reflects lessons learned from a nineteenth century Supreme Court hostile to broad federal power.

The Roberts Court has ignored both this framework and these lessons. The Court insists on interpretating congressional power over elections in a manner that

[131] The historical narrative in this book is not, and does not seek to be, comprehensive. Readers will notice that there is virtually no discussion of Congress's power under Article II, Section 1, Clause 3 to count the electoral college votes – or of the contested elections that arose under this provisions in 1800, 1824, 1876, and 1888 – beyond the limited focus on how the Twelfth Amendment, and its changes to the presidential election process, altered our understanding of what majoritarianism requires under the Guarantee Clause. Also excluded is any discussion of the Electoral Count Act of 1887. There is also very little focus on Congress's power under Section 3 of the Fourteenth Amendment to disqualify those who commit insurrection from running for certain state and federal offices, limited only to those instances in which this provision was relevant to Congress's power to judge the elections of its members under Article I, Section 5 as well as various Reconstruction-era legislation.

While this project seeks to understand the political valence of constitutional arguments made throughout this period – a topic that Article II and Section 3 undoubtedly have some bearing on – I am primarily interested in overlooked or under-theorized structural provisions that directly affected the composition of the political community of "We the Voters." Article II concerns the procedure for allocating and counting electoral college votes, a provision that has fundamentally changed the trajectory of U.S. history at various points (most notably, in 1876) but involves political decisions that only tangentially touch on the actual and theoretical composition of the electorate. Congress has never rejected a state's electoral college votes on the grounds that the underlying vote was fraudulently obtained, which makes this provision of limited relevance to the current project. In the same vein, by excluding ex-confederates from office, Section 3 is arguably less about who can vote rather than who can run for office. As such, this provision is also beyond the scope of this project.

misconstrues the original constitutional structure, minimizes the nation's march toward a more inclusive suffrage, and discounts the changes to this structure by the Civil War Amendments. The Court's perception that states retain sovereignty over elections that must be protected from federal overreach is a relic of a history that has been grossly misunderstood and misinterpreted.

As this book shows, Reconstruction fundamentally altered our system of federalism, resulting in more active federal oversight in which Congress was willing to aggregate its powers to protect voting rights. To be sure, the Reconstruction Amendments did not completely displace the states' authority to define voter qualifications. Nonetheless, the Amendments fundamentally changed the terms of federal engagement, making it impossible to return to the world envisioned by the Founders, even during the period after Reconstruction in which the aggressive policing of state and federal elections declined.

For this reason, it is important for Congress to understand the scope of its authority, particularly in the face of conflicting and sometimes incoherent judicial precedents. The Epilogue shows how Reconstruction-era voting rights legislation was a model for both the preclearance regime of the Voting Rights Act and recent bills seeking to regulate state and federal elections such as the aforementioned H.R. 1 as well as H.R. 4, which would have reauthorized the coverage formula of the Voting Rights Act. These comparisons not only illustrate that these bills are significantly more modest than their historical counterparts but also refute the federalism narrative that has hampered federal authority in this area over the past three decades.

PART I

Federalism and Republicanism as Political Norms

The Structural Constitution, State Political Systems, and the Regulation of Federal Elections

The congressional elections of 1789 were the country's first test of its commitment to nonpartisan elections, designed to elicit the selection of individuals who, according to *The Federalist* 52, "have an immediate dependence and intimate sympathy with the people."[1] One of these elections involved a face-off between two future presidents – James Monroe and James Madison – as they each sought to represent Virginia's Fifth Congressional District. While historians dispute whether the overwhelmingly Anti-Federalist district was gerrymandered at the behest of Patrick Henry to disadvantage Madison – after all, his home County was placed in a district with five other counties that voted against the Constitution he had championed – Madison emerged as the winner in a close race.[2]

In 1789, Madison would not have described his accusations that the district was gerrymandered to disadvantage him as being situated in "partisan" intent. Instead, he likely would have characterized the gerrymandering as opposition from those who were against the newly enacted Constitution.[3] By the summer of 1792, however, he would have surely described the political situation in the new government as partisan.

1 Alexander Hamilton, "The Federalist 52," in John C. Hamilton (ed.), *The Federalist: A Commentary on the Constitution of the United States* (Philadelphia: J.B. Lippincott & Co., 1864), pp. 404–405.

2 Elmer C. Griffith, *The Rise and Development of the Gerrymander* (Chicago: Scott, Foresman and Company, 1907), pp. 31–37. See also Thomas R. Hunter, "The First Gerrymander? Patrick Henry, James Madison, James Monroe, and Virginia's 1788 Congressional Districting," (2011) 9 *Early American Studies* 781–820, 782.

3 Noble E. Cunningham, *The Jeffersonian Republicans: The Formation of Party Organization, 1789–1801* (Chapel Hill: University of North Carolina Press, 1957), p. 7 ("In Congress men disagreed, but no one suggested that the divisions in that body sprang from party associations; and the voting record

Specifically, he would have blamed fissures in the governing Federalist Party coalition for the creation of nascent, ill-defined political organizations that would influence elections and constitutional politics over the course of the next decade.[4]

Political parties emerged because few, if any, delegates achieved the bulk of their preferred outcomes during the Constitutional Convention. As historian Jeff Broadwater has observed, "Madison went to the Philadelphia Convention in May 1787 committed to a congressional veto over state laws and a broad delegation of powers to the new government, but he got neither."[5] Instead, the Constitution expanded federal power in other ways. It specifically provides for congressional oversight of federal elections, rather than delegating complete control of these elections to the states. While there may be no congressional veto over state laws, there is a congressional veto over state election laws that govern federal elections.

This provision, the Elections Clause, gives Congress the power to "make or alter" state regulations that govern the elections of representatives and senators. Alexander Hamilton referred to this power in *The Federalist* 59 as an affirmation of the "plain proposition" that "EVERY GOVERNMENT OUGHT TO CONTAIN IN ITSELF THE MEANS OF ITS OWN PRESERVATION"[6] (The emphasis is his, not mine). Although states retain significant authority over voter qualification standards, the "distinctive characters of the republican form" that Madison described in *The Federalist* 39 required a government built around majority rule rather than "a favored class" of society.[7] For all that Madison thought that he lost after leaving Philadelphia in September 1787 – he was hoping for a national government that was far more powerful than its state-level counterparts – he gained a uniquely blended structure that is both federalist and nationalist, empowered to oversee state and federal elections to an extent that Madison had not originally anticipated.

The country's first half century was initially defined by versions of federalism and republicanism that centered the states as the primary organizational force in our federal political system. Yet the rise of partisanship in the 1790s, as well as the emergence of the first (1792–1824) and second (1828–54) party systems tested the boundaries of the new government,[8] forcing Congress to probe the limits of its authority within the

of the members of the First Congress reveals no significant evidence of members voting together with any degree of consistency suggestive of party groupings.").

4 Ibid., p. 23 ("James Madison, one of the leading Federalists of 1787, was in 1792 a leader of the growing opposition to the policies of the new government, and he was soon to be joined by not a few leading men who had been advocates of the Constitution ...").

5 Jeff Broadwater, *James Madison: A Son of Virginia and a Founder of the Nation* (Chapel Hill: University of North Carolina Press, 2012), p. 97.

6 Alexander Hamilton, "The Federalist 59," in John C. Hamilton (ed.), *The Federalist: A Commentary on the Constitution of the United States* (Philadelphia: J.B. Lippincott & Co., 1864), p. 448.

7 James Madison, "The Federalist 39," in Hamilton (ed.), *The Federalist*, p. 302.

8 This chapter discusses, in detail, the workings and conflicts of the parties in these systems, especially as they relate to federalism, the admission of new states, and voting rights. However, a brief overview of the major players may be helpful. The two parties of the first party system were (1) the Federalists,

Constitution of Political Structure. Madison would become one of the chief opponents of broad federal authority. Politics would color and, eventually, alter his former pro-nationalist world view. By the election of 1800, the first party system was well on its way to becoming part of the fabric of the American system of government. This came after a decade in which policy disagreements, population growth, and grassroots activism led to the creation of two relatively defined political organizations, Federalists and Democratic Republicans, both seeking to win elections to stem the worst impulses that each camp tended to ascribe to the other.[9] Federalism and republicanism were no longer pure structural principles to organize the state/federal relationship. The politics of the day meant that these terms would also become gloss for partisan positions.

The infusion of intense partisanship into the American political system meant that many of the provisions of the Constitution of 1789 had an entirely different import and meaning by 1800. For example, Article II, Section 1 provides that, "Each state shall appoint, in such manner as the Legislature thereof may direct, a number of electors, equal to the whole number of Senators and Representatives to which the State may be entitled in the Congress."[10] The electors then, "meet in their respective states and vote by ballot for two persons," to be President and Vice President.[11] *The Federalist* 64 predicted that the Electoral College, along with the selection of senators by state legislatures, would result in the appointment of "men the best qualified for the purpose, and in the manner most conducive to the public good."[12] These men would accomplish this by avoiding "the activity of party zeal, taking advantage of the supineness, the ignorance, and the hopes and fears of the unwary and interested [that] often places men in offices by the votes of a small proportion of the electors."[13]

What the Framers could not have predicted was that political parties would facilitate and breed partisanship that increased the salience of state elections. The importance of state elections for the composition of the national government shifted the focus from electing men best equipped for the job to electing men who had the best political organizations behind them. Case in point: the intense partisan wrangling that occurred in elections for the New York General Assembly in May 1800,

whose membership included Alexander Hamilton and (2) the Democratic-Republicans, with which James Madison and Thomas Jefferson were affiliated. "The First and Second Party Systems, 1787–1854," in Michael Shally-Jensen (ed.), *Political Campaigns, Candidates, and Debates [1787–2017]: Defining Documents in American History* (Ipswich: Salem Press/Grey House, 2018), vol. 1, pp. 1–2, Gale eBooks, https://go.gale.com (accessed February 12, 2023). During this period, "Democratic-Republicans" were also referred to as "Jeffersonian-Republicans," or, simply, "Republicans." The second party system was comprised of three parties (1) the Democratic Party of Andrew Jackson, (2) the short-lived National Republican Party of John Quincy Adams, and (3) the Whig Party of Henry Clay (comprised of National Republicans, anti-Jackson Democrats, and other groups). Ibid.

9 Broadwater, *James Madison*, pp. 85–86.

10 United States Constitution Art. II, s. 1.

11 Ibid.

12 John Jay, "The Federalist 64," in Hamilton (ed.), *The Federalist*, p. 483.

13 Ibid., p. 484.

months before the November presidential election. Future Vice President Aaron Burr recruited candidates for the General Assembly, tying them to George Clinton, a popular six-term governor of the state, and campaigned relentlessly, resulting in a sweeping Republican victory for all thirteen of New York's General Assembly seats.[14] The Republican dominance in the spring elections ensured that Thomas Jefferson would receive all of New York's electoral votes for president that fall. Partisanship infected the Constitution's federalist structure, creating a cooperation and cohesiveness across branches thanks to the party label.[15]

The chaos of the 1800 election, in which Congress resolved the stalemate over whether Aaron Burr or Thomas Jefferson would be president,[16] ultimately led to the enactment of the Twelfth Amendment.[17] This Amendment not only changed the process for selecting the president, but it also altered our understanding of what constitutes a Republican form of government in this new partisan environment. In 1787, it was unclear whether majoritarianism, which Madison and others advocated as central to the Guarantee Clause's requirement that each state have a Republican government, had to reflect the will of a majority of the people in the state. The Twelfth Amendment clarified that republicanism only had to reflect the will of a majority of the voters, and it did so by sanctioning a system in which the legitimacy of the presidency was tied to a decisive Electoral College win.[18]

With the Twelfth Amendment, "We the Voters" became more important than "We the People" in the theory of republicanism that, through the Guarantee Clause, underlies our system of government. This new structure also indirectly affected the scope of federal power over elections by forcing the founding generation to revisit its original conceptions of how political power should be deployed and by whom. In other words, could territories that disenfranchised significant portions of their

14 John R. Sharp, *American Politics in the Early Republic: The New Nation in Crisis* (New Haven, CT: Yale University Press, 1993), pp. 233–234.

15 Compare, however, to Daryl J. Levinson and Richard H. Pildes, "Separation of Powers, Not Parties," (2006) 119 *Harvard Law Review* 2312–2386.

16 On February 17, 1801, after casting thirty-six separate ballots to determine the winner of the 1800 presidential election, the House of Representatives finally elected Thomas Jefferson to the presidency over Aaron Burr. "Aaron Burr," in Mark A. Hatfield, *Vice Presidents of the United States, 1789–1993* (Washington, D.C.: United States Government Printing Office, 1997), pp. 35–36. Burr responded with "indignation" at rumors of his role in inflaming the tensions during this series of votes, including the intimation that "he was soliciting Federalist support in an attempt to wrest the presidency away from Jefferson." Ibid., p. 35.

17 Enacted the fall of 1803 and intended to prevent a repeat of the chaos that had taken place during the previous presidential election, "the Twelfth Amendment … changed the method of election by requiring electors to designate one vote for a presidential candidate and the other for a vice-presidential candidate." Ibid., p. 36. This rule was "[i]ntended to prevent an unscrupulous vice-presidential candidate (or his supporters) from subverting the electoral process[.]" Ibid.

18 Professor Edward Foley contends that the Twelfth Amendment anticipated that the president would emerge as the winner of a compound majority of majorities in the states key to his electoral college victory. Edward Foley, *Presidential Elections and Majority Rule: The Rise, Demise, and Potential Restoration of the Jeffersonian Electoral College* (New York: Oxford University Press, 2020).

electorates be denied entry into the Union? Additionally, once new states were admitted, does the Guarantee Clause require Congress to continue to police their political systems? Put another way, can Congress impose uniform election requirements on the states to facilitate republican principles? Can Congress refuse to seat representatives elected in violation of a federal law that no longer enjoys majority support? Or, more controversially, can they refuse to seat representatives to make a statement about the legitimacy of the government at the state level?

The answer to these questions was not immediately apparent and instead became settled over time due to two factors (1) the ebbs and flows of partisan polarization and (2) the disintegration of political norms in which Congress had left to the states the job of figuring out these answers. In the early decades of the republic, including the so-called Era of Good Feelings that followed the War of 1812,[19] Congress was reluctant to use its constitutional powers to their full conceptual limits and deferred to the states over both voter qualification standards and regulations governing the time, place, and manner of federal elections. However, as political communities became increasingly defined by partisan affiliation, and slavery politics became increasingly polarizing, Congress was willing to deploy its authority for partisan ends in influencing the boundaries of these communities. Even the application of "clear" constitutional text, such as Congress's authority to "judge" the elections of its members, became heavily influenced by partisan considerations.

The decades leading up to the Civil War revealed that partisanship had long dictated the use (or nonuse) of many of the constitutional provisions that we now think of as being constrained by structural principles like federalism. After the Twelfth Amendment was enacted, the centrality of the voting population to the accomplishment of partisan end goals – that is, winning elections and enacting policy under a mandate of popular sovereignty – was acknowledged. This opened the door for Congress to be more aggressive about shaping the contours of the community of voters that the Twelfth Amendment viewed as the relevant coalition for legitimizing the election of the president. For example, the Whigs enacted the 1842 Apportionment Act[20] under the guise of ensuring that congressional elections adhered to republican principles and better reflected the preferences of the people. The Act required districted elections, which benefited the Whigs over

19 In the presidential election of 1816, Republican James Monroe defeated the Federalist candidate, Rufus King. This event essentially signaled the end of the Federalist Party and ushered in what became known as the "Era of Good Feelings," during which the previous period of especially fierce partisanship appeared, at least on the surface, to abate somewhat. Robert C. Byrd, "The Era of Good Feelings: 1817–1824," in Robert C. Byrd (ed.), *The Senate, 1789–1989: Addresses on the History of the United States Senate*, 4 vols. (Washington, D.C.: United States Government Printing Office, 1988), vol. 1, pp. 69–86. Although the period known as the "Era of Good Feelings" is said to have persisted through 1824, politicians in the national government still found several things to fight about, including negotiations with Spain over the acquisition of Florida and admission of "slave" states versus "free" states. Ibid.

20 An Act for the Apportionment of Representation among the Several States According to the Sixth Census (Apportionment Act of 1842), ch. 47, 5 Stat. 491 (1842).

their Democratic counterparts and was the first truly partisan election legislation. Debates over the Act's constitutionality signaled that many of the "federalism" concerns that had long stymied the use of federal power over elections were discarded in politically polarizing times.

Congress also resolved a number of election cases under Article I, Section 5 that defy this federalism narrative. During this period, Congress sometimes set aside elections in their entirety or seated the "losing" candidate.[21] These findings sometimes required a new election or that excluded votes be added to the vote count, even if the state had declared a winner in the previous contest. In the notable case of *Spaulding v. Mead*, for example, Congress counted votes that were invalid under state law due to error by state officials, finding that body's authority to "judge" returns under Article I, Section 5 included "everything required by way of ascertaining and proclaiming the result from the moment the election is closed."[22] As a result, Congress seated Spaulding instead of Mead, who had been certified the winner of the election by the governor of Georgia.

By the mid-nineteenth century, increasing election fraud and the manipulation of electoral rules for partisan gain led Congress to more frequently assert its authority over federal elections. Put another way, Congress was forced by circumstances to loosen, and ultimately discard, its self-imposed federalism constraints. Notably, Congress used its power under the Elections Clause and Article I, Section 5 to invalidate congressional elections in Kansas after violence over slavery and electoral fraud called into question the legitimacy of those elections.[23] As slavery politics became more contentious, Congress contemplated whether new slave states should be admitted and aggressively exercised its constitutional authority to refuse to seat pro-slavery members elected in fraudulent elections. While not uniformly successful, these efforts to navigate slavery politics through Congress's power over elections illustrate how the Constitution of Political Structure had largely been constrained by political norms, rather than constitutional limitations like federalism.

21 See, e.g., "John P. Van Ness: Hearing before H. Comm. on Elections, 7th Cong. (1801)," reprinted in Chester H. Rowell, *A Historical and Legal Digest of all the Contested Election Cases in the House of Representatives of the United States from the First to the Fifty-Sixth Congress, 1789–1901* (Washington, D.C.: Government Printing Office, 1901), p. 49 (vacating a seat where representative accepted a military commission).

22 See, e.g., "Spaulding v. Mead: Hearing before H. Comm. on Elections, 9th Cong. (1805)," reprinted in Rowell, *Contested Election Cases*, p. 4 (noting that "this was the first case in which it was proposed to change the result of an election by counting votes which could not be counted under State law").

23 In 1856, the House of Representatives conducted several hearings over of multiple claims that the election for the Kansas House seat between John W. Whitfield and Andrew H. Reeder had been conducted illegally. See Asher C. Hinds, *Hinds' Precedents of the House of Representatives of the United States*, 5 vols. (Washington, D.C.: United States Government Printing Office, 1907), vol. 1, sections 825–827, pp. 1071–1078).

1

Federal Power under the Guarantee Clause amid Changing Notions of Republicanism

With his boyish face, square glasses, closely shaven head, and buttoned-up shirt, Michael Baca looked the part of an inquisitive graduate student attending Northern Arizona University.[1] By all appearances, Baca did not look like a member of the Electoral College seeking to challenge his legal obligation to vote for Hillary Clinton, the winner of Colorado's popular vote in the 2016 presidential election.[2] Yet Baca, who wanted to throw the election into the House of Representatives to avoid a Donald Trump presidency, was a named plaintiff in one of the most important faithless elector cases to ever reach the Supreme Court. Four years after Colorado replaced Baca as an elector after he cast his vote for John Kasich,[3] the Supreme Court decided *Chiafalo v. Washington*[4] and its companion case, *Colorado Department of State v. Baca*.[5] These cases presented the issue of whether presidential electors are obligated to vote in accordance with the winner of the state's popular vote, as required by state law, or if they have independent discretion to cast their ballot for the candidate of their choice.[6]

A Bernie Sanders supporter who styled himself as a "Hamilton" elector, Baca argued that presidential electors can exercise independent judgment in casting their ballot and state law cannot bind them to vote for a particular candidate.[7] *The Federalist No.* 68 spoke of such independence among electors, with Alexander Hamilton writing that the president should be selected by "men most capable of

1 Erin Powell, "Colorado Elector Wants Electoral College to Dump Trump," KUSA: 9NEWS, November 16, 2016, www.9news.com/article/entertainment/television/programs/next-with-kyle-clark/colorado-elector-wants-electoral-college-to-dump-trump/352671785.

2 In Colorado, Clinton beat Trump with 48.2% of the vote to 43.4%. "2016 Presidential Election Results," *New York Times*, August 9, 2017, www.nytimes.com/elections/2016/results/president.

3 Jacob D. Shelley, "'Faithless Elector' Challenge Goes to Supreme Court," Congressional Research Service, May 12, 2020, https://crsreports.congress.gov/product/pdf/LSB/LSB10462.

4 591 U.S. 578 (2020).

5 Ibid.

6 Petition for Writ of Certiorari at i, *Colorado Department of State v. Baca*, 591 U.S. 578 (2020).

7 Respondents' Brief in Support of Certiorari at 20, *Colorado Department of State v. Baea*, 591 U.S. 578 (2020).

analyzing the qualities adapted to the station."[8] This view of electors was also consistent with the founding generation's general conception of voters as those who cast their ballots independently, free of third-party coercion.[9] But *The Federalist No. 68* also spoke of electors as representatives of the people:

> It was desirable that the sense of the people should operate in the choice of the person [the elector] to whom so important a trust was to be confided. This end will be answered by committing the right of making it, not to any preestablished body, but to men chosen by the people for the special purpose, and at the particular conjuncture.[10]

In *Chiafalo*, the Supreme Court struck the balance by recognizing the role of both political parties and electors as conduits of majority preferences, such that states can punish and remove electors who cast ballots for anyone other than the winner of the state's popular vote in the presidential election.[11] While Baca channeled Hamilton as his inspiration, the Court instead endorsed a post–Twelfth Amendment Jeffersonian vision of the Electoral College. From this perspective, the Amendment "brought the Electoral College's voting procedures into line with the Nation's new party system" and codified the expectation that the elector would "'vote the regular party ticket and thereby carry out the desires of the people' who had sent him to the Electoral College."[12] Or, as the *Chiafalo* majority succinctly put it, "No independent electors need apply."[13]

The *Chiafalo* decision also implicitly recognized that the controversy over faithless electors placed two defining characteristics of republican government on a collision course. One strand dealt with founding-era notions of elector independence, in which virtuous individuals exercised their own objective judgment about what was best for the masses. According to the second strand, electors served as intermediaries, or an aspect of representative government intended to mirror majoritarian sentiment within the republic. The fact that two of the most important facets of American-style republicanism can be in disharmony illustrates how republicanism's definition has evolved over time and, more importantly, has been dictated by political norms. During this country's first decades, political elites reimagined republicanism, turning away from state-level preferences regarding the structure of their political systems, to carve out a larger role for partisan politics.

8 Alexander Hamilton, "The Federalist 68," in John C. Hamilton (ed.), *The Federalist: A Commentary on the Constitution of the United States* (Philadelphia: J.B. Lippincott & Co., 1864), p. 508.

9 See *Baca v. Colorado Department of State*, 935 F.3d 887 (10th Cir. 2019).

10 Hamilton, "The Federalist 68," in Hamilton (ed.), *The Federalist*, p. 508.

11 *Chiafalo v. Washington*, 591 U.S. 578 (2020).

12 Ibid., 594 (citing *Ray v. Blair*, 343 U.S. 214, 224 n.11 (1952)). The Court also noted that the Twelfth Amendment "both acknowledge[ed] and facilitate[ed] the Electoral College's emergence as a mechanism not for deliberation but for party-line voting." Ibid.

13 Ibid.

1.1 THE GUARANTEE CLAUSE, REPUBLICAN GOVERNMENT, AND THE CREATION OF STATE POLITICAL SYSTEMS

Republicanism, despite being a constitutional "requirement" for the composition of state political systems, was ill-defined during the founding period.[14] Theorists have

[14] Republicanism remains ill-defined. See Alexander Hamilton, "The Federalist 9," and James Madison, "The Federalist 10," in Hamilton (ed.), *The Federalist*, pp. 97–112.

The Founders were greatly influenced by French philosopher Montesquieu (1689–1755). In his foundational work *The Spirit of the Laws*, he compared three types of governments: republic, monarchy, and despotism. Throughout the work, he offers various descriptions of "republics" and "republican governments," including, but not limited to, the following:

A "republican" government "executes the laws after more mature deliberation" than monarchies.
A "republican government is that in which the body, or only a part of the people, is possessed of the supreme power[.]"
"[V]irtue is necessary in a republic."
Speaking about the republics of ancient Greece: "In every republic, the legislator had in view the happiness of the citizens at home, and their power abroad[.]"
"[E]very republic ought to have a particular regard to manners."

Baron de Montesquieu, *The Spirit of the Laws*, Thomas Nugent (trans.), 2 vols. (New York: D. Appleton and Company, 1900), vol. 1, pp. xxi, 9, 31; vol. 2, pp. 495, 557.

Similarly, the definition of "republicanism" in the *Stanford Encyclopedia of Philosophy* provides two conceptions of this theory:

> In the first sense, republicanism refers to a loose tradition or family of writers in the history of western political thought, including especially: Machiavelli and his fifteenth-century Italian predecessors; the English Republicans Milton, Harrington, Sidney, and others; Montesquieu and Blackstone; the eighteenth-century English commonwealthmen; and many Americans of the founding era such as Jefferson, Madison, and Adams. The writers in this tradition emphasize many common ideas and concerns, such as the importance of civic virtue and political participation, the dangers of corruption, the benefits of a mixed constitution and the rule of law, **etc.**; and it is characteristic of their rhetorical style to draw heavily on classical examples – from Cicero and the Latin historians especially – in presenting their arguments. …
>
> [T]here exists considerable historiographical controversy – with respect to who the tradition's members are, and their relative significance; with respect to how we should interpret its underlying philosophical commitments; and with respect to its role (especially vis-à-vis liberalism) in the historical development of modern political thought. This brings us to the second sense of the term "republicanism." In contemporary political theory and philosophy, it most often refers to a specific (and still contested) interpretation of the classical republican tradition, associated especially with the work of Quentin Skinner; together with a research program dedicated to developing insights from this tradition into an attractive contemporary political doctrine, associated especially with the work of Philip Pettit. According to Republicans in this second sense (sometimes called "civic Republicans" or "neo-Republicans"), the paramount republican value is political liberty, understood as non-domination or independence from arbitrary power.

"Republicanism," in *Stanford Encyclopedia of Philosophy* (2006, updated 2022), https://plato.stanford.edu/entries/republicanism/ (emphases added).

With respect to the definitions offered by the *Stanford Encyclopedia of Philosophy*, this book is primarily concerned with republicanism in the first sense, although both schools seem to assume that independence from arbitrary power is an important cornerstone of republicanism. After all, it was concerns about a lack of independence (in the civic republican sense) that led many in the founding generation – followers of classical republicanism – to conclude that a narrow electorate was consistent with republican theory.

never reached consensus on which forms of government aligned with republicanism, even as this concept has been held out as the ideal since antiquity.[15] Plato once defined a republic as a "well-ordered" community ruled by "guardians ... who in their whole life show the greatest eagerness to do what is for the good of their country, and the greatest repugnance to do what is against their interests."[16] Aristotle and Cicero similarly viewed a republic as any government that worked for the good of the whole.[17]

Later writers adopted a definition of republicanism that could encompass an aristocracy or an oligarchy, provided that the ruling class acted on behalf of the majority. Montesquieu, for example, described a republic as "that in which the body, or only a part of the people, is possessed of the supreme power," while at the same time using the term "republic" to describe a monarchy, an aristocracy, and a democracy.[18] He considered republicanism consistent with any of those forms of government so long as there were laws enforced by rulers who, acting with virtue and honor, checked abuses of power.[19] Some of these forms of government (a monarchy being the most obvious example) were difficult, although not impossible, to reconcile with the focus on a robust civic life and the emphasis on the common good underlying republican ideals.[20]

15 In fact, an 1866 speech by Senator Charles Sumner on the history of the Guarantee Clause from the founding to the post–Civil War period drew on many of the classical philosophers discussed in this section. Charles Sumner, "Equal Rights of All: the Great Guarantee and Present Necessity, for the Sake of Security, and to Maintain a Republican Government," February 5–6, 1866, 39th Congress, 1st Session, *Congressional Globe* (Washington, D.C.: Congressional Globe Office, 1866), pp. 673–687. In 1972, William Wiecek, a professor of law and history at Syracuse University, wrote what is considered to this day to be the definitive history of the Guarantee Clause. William Wiecek, *The Guarantee Clause of the U.S. Constitution* (Ithaca: Cornell University Press, 1972).

16 Plato, *The Republic: Book III*, Benjamin Jowett (trans.) (London: Sirius Publishing, 2020), p. 104.

17 According to Aristotle, when the power of the state is "in the hands of one person, or a few, or many; and when either of these apply their power for the common good, such States are well governed." *Aristotle's Politics: A Treatise on Government*, William Ellis (trans.) (London: George Routledge and Sons, 1895), book III, chap. VII, p. 93. Cicero characterized this principle as follows: "[I]n no other state, save where the power of the people predominates, has liberty any home." *The Republic of Cicero*, G. W. Featherstonhaugh (trans.) (New York: G. & C. Carvill, 1829), chap. XXXI, p. 60.

18 Baron de Montesquieu, *The Spirit of Laws*, Book Two, p. 10.

19 Baron de Montesquieu, *The Spirit of Laws*, Book Three, p. 14 ("I have already observed that it is the nature of a republican government that either the collective body of the people, or particular families, should be possessed of supreme power; of a monarchy, that the prince should have this power, but in the execution of it should be directly by established laws..."). See also ibid., p. 15 (noting that the governing aristocracy can restrain themselves "by a very eminent virtue, which puts the nobility in some measure on a level with the people and may be the means of forming a great republic"); Ibid., p. 16 (arguing that it is honor that constrains the monarch and honor "can be found only in countries in which the constitution is fixed, and where they are governed by settled laws.")

20 As Gordon Wood has argued, republicanism is not necessarily inconsistent with monarchism, but having emerged from a monarchy, the Framers were not interested in any government that involved ruling by a king. According to Wood, "For most educated elites in the eighteenth century, monarchism and republicanism often blended and blurred to the point where the two at times seemed virtually indistinguishable," and that "few persons talked openly of deposing kings and instituting

Like the political theorists from whom they drew inspiration, Madison and the other founding fathers did not feel pressed to develop a clear definition of republicanism. Other than drawing knowledge from the great republics of classical antiquity, this generation treated the concept as unnecessary of explanation and ingrained in the psyche of the young country.[21] In *The Federalist* 39, Madison described a republic as a "government which derives its powers directly or indirectly from the great body of the people, and is administered by officers holding their offices during pleasure, for a limited time, or during good behavior."[22] The idea of government by the people rather than by the nobility was a recurring theme in classic republican thought.

Self-governance also avoided a system in which the people would be pawns in the power struggles among the privileged few, which could lead to an increased risk of revolution among the masses. By partaking in the selection of their rulers, who would presumably be virtuous individuals committed to translating popular preferences into policy, the people would happily submit to their authority in return. As Machiavelli observed,

> He who obtains sovereignty by the assistance of the nobles maintains himself with more difficulty than he who comes to it [sovereignty] by the aid of the people, because the former finds himself with many around him who consider themselves his equals, and because of this he can neither rule nor manage them to his liking. But he who reaches sovereignty by popular favour finds himself alone, and has none around him, or few, who are not prepared to obey him.[23]

The idea that sovereignty lies with the people, who then delegate decision-making to a smaller representative body, was one of the primary advantages of a republic over a democracy. A republic, according to *The Federalist* 10, could better mitigate the mischiefs of faction because "the greater number of citizens, and greater sphere

elected republican governments." Gordon S. Wood, *The Creation of the American Republic, 1776–1787* (Chapel Hill: University of North Carolina Press, 1998), p. 7. He explained how both concepts could reasonably coexist: "People, even good aristocrats, could be loyal monarchists and still ardently promote republican values," which included "its morality, its freedom, its sense of friendship and civic duty, and its vision of society." Ibid., p. 8. Wood argued that this belief emerged in response to the development of Enlightenment thinking: "Republicanism as a form of life was too pervasive and too much involved with being liberal and enlightened to be seen as subversive or as antimonarchical." Ibid.

21 Wiecek explained this as follows: "The word 'republican' may well not have had any single and universal denotation to the men who inserted it into the guarantee clause. It may, in fact, have had no meaning at all. John Adams complained late in life that 'the word *republic* as it is used, may signify anything, everything, or nothing.'" Wiecek, *Guarantee Clause*, p. 13. According to Wood, "the principles of republicanism permeated much of what the colonists read and found attractive. In fact, 'the true principles of republicanism are at present so well understood,' so much taken for granted, so much a part of the Americans' assumptions about politics, that few felt any need formally to explain their origin." Wood, *American Republic*, p. 48.

22 James Madison, "The Federalist 39," in Hamilton (ed.), *The Federalist*, p. 302.

23 Niccolo Machiavelli, *The Prince* (Bulgaria: Pretorian Books, 2019), Chapter IX (originally published 1532)

of country, over which [a republic] may be extended" makes it more difficult for "unworthy candidates to practice with success the vicious arts by which elections are too often carried."[24]

By creating a virtuous intermediary to translate the preferences of the majority, Madison believed that the dispersiveness of the underlying population and the patriotism of the chosen representatives would prevent a cabal from obtaining power and enacting policies contrary to majority preferences.[25] In thinking that republicanism required some form of majority rule, translated through a medium that was sufficiently representative, Madison was not alone. There was almost universal agreement that, in addition to obligating the federal government to come to the aid of states facing rebellion,[26] the Guarantee Clause required that states enfranchise some portion of their population to legitimize these intermediaries who made policy.[27] In short, republicanism required accountability.

This approach, no matter how rhetorically appealing, had its detractors. Republicanism suffered from its historical connection to monarchy, despite its intended purpose being to counter the then-prevailing view of kings as all-powerful rulers accountable only to God and not the people. This connection led many opponents of the Constitution to question the new government that the founding generation sought to create.[28] Writing under the pseudonym "Columbian Patriot," one such opponent referred to a Republic as a "many-headed monster" that was

24 James Madison, "The Federalist 10," in Hamilton (ed.), *The Federalist*, p. 109.

25 See ibid., pp. 109–110.

26 See ibid. See also Jonathan Toren, "Protecting Republican Government from Itself: The Guarantee Clause of Article IV, Section 4" (2007) 2 *New York University Journal of Law and Liberty*, 371–410, 405 (arguing that the purpose of the Clause is "(1) protect[ing] the existing states from upheaval; (2) preventing the states from changing their government to one not republican; and (3) protecting the union as a whole from disintegration.").

27 Countless scholarly works have been written on what constitutes a republican form of government, and most scholars agree that republicanism requires that states extend political rights to their citizens. See, e.g., John Hart Ely, *Democracy and Distrust: A Theory of Judicial Review* (Delanco: Legal Classics Library, 1980), pp. 122–123 (noting that the Guarantee Clause could be the source of the Court's voting rights jurisprudence); Akhil Reed Amar, "The Central Meaning of Republican Government: Popular Sovereignty, Majority Rule, and the Denominator Problem" (1994) 65 *University of Colorado Law Review* 749–786, 749 (arguing that republican government requires that "the structure of day-to-day government – the Constitution – be derived from 'the People' and be legally alterable by a 'majority' of them").

28 Even where a king was a hereditary ruler, republican theorists argued that the king was accountable to law (not just God) and that his power derived from the trust of the people. John Milton, writing in 1650, expanded on this point as follows: "It being thus manifest that the power of Kings and Magistrates is nothing else, but what is only derivative, transferr'd and committed to them in trust from the People, to the Common good of them all, in whom the power yet remaines fundamentally, and cannot be tak'n from them, without a violation of their natural birthright, and seeing that from hence Aristotle and the best of Political writers have defin'd a King, him who governs to the good and profit of his People, and not for his own ends…" John Milton, *The Tenure of Kings and Magistrates* (London: Matthew Simmons, 1650), p. 11. Milton believed that a "Monarchy unaccountable, is the worst sort of Tyranny; and least of all to be endur'd by free born men." Ibid., p. 13. As he made clear,

"founded on principles of monarchy – a democratick [sic] branch with the *features* of aristocracy – and the extravagance of nobility pervading the minds of many of the candidates for office."[29]

A famous Anti-Federalist commentator using the pseudonym "Brutus" wrote a series of essays opposing ratification, similarly warning that America could not be a republic because its size and diversity of population would inevitably lead to the selection of leaders who lack virtue. "They will use the power when they have acquired it to the purposes of gratifying their own interest and ambition," he wrote, "and it is scarcely possible, in a very large republic, to call them to account for their misconduct, or prevent their abuse of power."[30]

Another Anti-Federalist, writing under the name "Federal Farmer," likewise cautioned that the proposed constitution was "calculated ultimately to make the states one consolidated government,"[31] which would make it easy for the aristocratic few to usurp the power of the people.[32] According to these critics, not only was creating a republic in these conditions impossible, but the fact that the Constitution failed to include a bill of rights to safeguard the people made the descent into despotic government a virtual certainty.[33]

While Columbian Patriot, Brutus, and other Anti-Federalists insisted that the republic proposed by the new constitution was contrary to "the fundamental

> It follows lastly, that since the King or Magistrate holds his autoritie of the people, both originally and naturally for their good in the first place, and not his own, then may the people as oft as they shall judge it for the best, either choose him or reject him, retaine him or depose him though no Tyrant, merely by the liberty and right of free born Men, to be govern'd as seems to them best.

Ibid., pp. 14–15.

29 A Columbian Patriot, "Observations on the Constitution (Feb. 1788)," in Bernard Bailyn (ed.), *Debate on the Constitution: Federalist and Antifederalist Speeches, Articles, and Letters During the Struggle over Ratification*, 2 vols. (New York: Library of America and Viking Press, 1993), vol. 2, pp. 288–289. "Columbian Patriot" was the pseudonym used by Mercy Otis Warren, a female political writer and propagandist, who opposed the Constitution on the grounds that it did not have a Bill of Rights. But see James Madison, "The Federalist 39," in Hamilton (ed.), *The Federalist*, p. 302 ("It is essential for such a government that it be derived from the great body of the society, and not from an inconsiderable proportion, or a favored class of it; otherwise a handful of tyrannical nobles, exercising their oppressions by a delegation of their powers, might aspire to the rank of republicans, and claim for their government the honorable title of republic.").

30 Anonymous, "Essays of Brutus 1," in Herbert J. Storing (ed.), *The Complete Antifederalist*, 7 vols. (Chicago: University of Chicago Press, 1981), vol. 2, pp. 363–372.

31 The Federal Farmer, "Letter I, October 8, 1787," letter, available at: https://leefamilyarchive.org/papers/essays/fedfarmer/01.html.

32 The Federal Farmer, "Letter 4, October 12, 1787," available at https://leefamilyarchive.org/papers/essays/fedfarmer/04.html (criticizing the Article 5 amendment process based on this rationale). He notes, "[W]hen power is once transferred from the many to the few, all changes become extremely difficult; the government, in this case being beneficial to the few, they will be exceedingly artful and adroit in preventing any measures which may lead to a change; and nothing will produce it, but great exertions and severe struggles on the part of the common people." Ibid.

33 Ibid.; Anonymous, "Essays of Brutus 2," in Storing (ed.), *The Complete Antifederalist*, vol. 2, pp. 363–372.

principle of a free government,"[34] those who would later govern the new nation under the party label of "Federalists" refuted the argument that the new government would institute a monarchy or oligarchy. Edmund Randolph expressed his belief, during the Constitutional Convention, that "a republican government must be the basis of our national union; and no state in it ought to have it in their power to change its government into a monarchy."[35]

James Wilson similarly argued, during the ratification debates in Pennsylvania, that there are "but three forms of government: monarchy, aristocracy and a republic or democracy, but as the only form that left power in the hands of the people, only the last was suitable for the new nation."[36] Wilson's comments exemplified that republicanism was commonly lumped with democracy, given that both forms of government placed ultimate authority in the people.[37] The founding generation was less focused on distinguishing republican government from its democratic counterpart – even though they recognized the dangers of the latter – because they believed a monarchy or aristocracy posed a greater threat to the new nation.[38]

Even Thomas Paine, who would become controversial and provoke the ire of the Federalists because of his writings in later years, argued that "monarchy and succession have laid (not this or that kingdom only) but the world in blood and ashes. 'Tis a form of government which the word of God bears testimony against, and blood will attend it."[39] Paine further observed that, "[t]he nearer any government approaches to a Republic, the less business there is for a king."[40] *The Federalist* 43

34 A Columbian Patriot, "Observations on the Constitution (Feb. 1788)," in Bailyn (ed.), *Debate on the Constitution*, vol. 2, pp. 289.

35 "Speech of Edmund Randolph on June 11, 1787," in Max Farrand (ed.), *Records of the Federal Convention of* 1787, 3 vols. (New Haven: Yale University Press, 1911), vol. 1, p. 206.

36 "Speech of James Wilson on November 26, 1787," in Jonathan Elliott (ed.), *Debates in the Several State Conventions on the Adoption of the Federal Constitution*, 2nd ed, 4 vols. (Washington, D.C.: Jonathan Elliott, 1836) vol. 2, p. 433.

37 That combination persists today, since some countries have styled themselves as "democratic republics." Of course, one such country was East Germany, and another is North Korea, which shows the subjective meaning that can be attached to words and labels.

38 Wilson offers a helpful tripartite framework for monarchy/aristocracy/republic-democracy:

> There are three simple species of government-monarchy, where the supreme power is in a single person; aristocracy, where the supreme power is in a select assembly, the members of which either fill up, by election, the vacancies in their own body, or succeed to their places in it by inheritance, property, or in respect of some personal right or qualification; a republic or democracy, where the people at large retain the supreme power, and act either collectively or by representation.

Ibid. See also Amar, "Central Meaning," 758 ("In debates over the Constitution, republican government was regularly contradistinguished from monarchy and aristocracy, but rarely from democracy.").

39 Thomas Paine, "Common Sense (1776)," reprinted in William M. Van der Weyde (ed.), *The Life and Works of Thomas Paine*, 10 vols. (New Rochelle: Thomas Paine National Historical Association, 1925), vol. 2, pp. 97–110, 114–120, 120–122, *available at* http://press-pubs.uchicago.edu/founders/documents/v1ch4s4.html.

40 Ibid.

presented the Guarantee Clause as a bulwark against these "aristocratic or monarchical innovations," with Madison noting that, "Whenever the States may choose to substitute other republican forms, they have a right to do so and to claim the federal guaranty for the latter. The only restriction imposed on them is that they shall not exchange republican for anti-republican Constitutions; a restriction which, it is presumed, will hardly be considered as a grievance."[41]

From these discussions, one can distill that republicanism promoted a type of majority rule that required elected officials to: (1) act virtuously, (2) for the good of the whole, and (3) periodically stand for election to be held to account for any misdeeds by some portion of the population.[42] Periodic elections would ensure that elected officials act in the interest of the whole and defy the notion of a hereditary ruler or ruling class. Participation by those most invested in society, who exhibit sufficient independence,[43] promoted majority rule by treating "We the People" as a homogenous entity with politically discernible preferences best communicated by this virtuous few.[44]

Identifying the portion of the population qualified to select virtuous rulers, and by implication, legitimize their policies as good for the whole, increasingly became the touchstone for authentic republican government. Republican theory required that electors be free of arbitrary constraints imposed by others; as Blackstone recognized, "The true reason of requiring any qualification, with regard to property, in voters, is to exclude such persons as are in so mean a situation that they are esteemed to have

41 James Madison, "The Federalist 43," in Hamilton (ed.), *The Federalist*, pp. 341–342.

42 As Roger Sherman argued during the ratification debates, a republican government is one that has three branches of government, including legislative and executive branches determined "by periodical elections, agreeably to an established constitution; and that what especially denominates it a republic is its dependence on the public or people at large, without any hereditary powers," a view that appeared to be common during this period. "Letter from Roger Sherman to John Adams, July 20, 1789," in Charles Francis Adams (ed.), *The Works of John Adams, Second President of the United States*, 10 vols. (Boston: Little and Brown, 1851), vol. 6, p. 437. See also James Madison, "The Federalist 39," in Hamilton (ed.), *The Federalist*, p. 302 (defining a republican government as "a government which derives all of its powers directly or indirectly from the great body of the people; and is administered by persons holding their offices during pleasure, for a limited period, or during good behavior"); see also Wiecek, *Guarantee Clause*, p. 17 ("The negative senses of 'republican' that is nonmonarchical and nonaristocratic commanded the assent of most Americans in 1787. Beyond this it is unsafe to generalize about the precise meaning of the term."); Wood, *American Republic*, p. 53 ("The sacrifice of individual interests to the greater good of the whole formed the essence of republicanism and comprehended for Americans the idealistic goal of their Revolution").

43 William Blackstone, *Commentaries on the Laws of England: Book the First of the Rights of Persons* (Oxford: Clarendon Press, 1765), p. 165 (noting that a lack of political independence would "would give a great, an artful, or a wealthy man, a larger share in elections than is consistent with general liberty.").

44 Wood, *American Republic*, p. 57 ("What made the Whig conception of politics and the republican emphasis on the collective welfare of the people comprehensible was the assumption that the people, especially when set against their rulers, were a homogeneous body whose 'interests when candidly considered are one.'").

no will of their own. If these persons had votes, they would be tempted to dispose of them under some undue influence or other."[45]

The requirement of "nominal" participation by the people, even if only a privileged few, likely precluded the establishment of a monarchy, dictatorship, aristocracy, or permanent military rule, even if through a valid majority vote.[46] In late eighteenth century republican theory, "there were no hereditary distinctions, no 'empty ornament and unmeaning grandeur,' where only sense, merit, and integrity commanded respect" so that the silent majority excluded from the community of voters had an equal opportunity to become a part of it (at least in theory).[47] Thomas Jefferson corroborated this sentiment, writing to Alexander von Humboldt, a prominent Prussian philosopher and scientist, that, "The first principle of republicanism is that the lex majoris partis [majority rule] is the fundamental law of every society of individuals of equal rights."[48]

The requirement of majority rule was an explicit limit on the ability of the states to substantially disenfranchise their populations. *The Federalist* 52 explicitly connected the right to vote to notions of republican government:

> The definition of the right of suffrage is very justly regarded as a fundamental article of republican government. It was incumbent on the Convention therefore to define and establish this right, in the Constitution. To have left it open for the occasional regulation of Congress, would have been improper for the reason just mentioned. To have submitted it to the legislative discretion of the States, would have been improper for the same reason .... To have reduced the different qualifications in the different States, to one uniform rule, would probably have been as dissatisfactory to some of the States, as it would have been difficult to the Convention. The

45 1 *Blackstone Commentaries*, p. 165.

46 See Wiecek, *Guarantee Clause*, pp. 22–23 (describing one of the strands of republican thought at the founding as based on the idea that "government is founded on the consent of the governed and therefore should reflect the will of the people" which in turn fed into the "agency" concept of government where "the people are the principals, their elected representatives the agents chosen to carry out the popular will.").

47 Wood, *American Republic*, pp. 46–47.

48 "Thomas Jefferson to Alexander von Humboldt, 13 June 1817," *Founders Online*, National Archives, https://founders.archives.gov/documents/Jefferson/03-11-02-0361. [Original source: J. Jefferson Looney (ed.), *The Papers of Thomas Jefferson*, vol. 11, *19 January–31 August 1817* (Princeton: Princeton University Press, 2014), pp. 434–435.]. See also "Speech of Charles Pickney of May 14, 1788, Debates in the Convention of South Carolina," in Jonathan Elliott (ed.), *The Debates, Resolutions, and Other Proceedings in Convention, On the Adoption of the Federal Constitution*, 1st ed, 4 vols. (Washington, D.C.: Jonathan Elliott, 1830), vol. 3, p. 389 ("A Republic is where the people at large, either collectively or by representation, form the Legislature."). See also John Taylor, *Construction Construed and Constitutions Vindicated* (Richmond: Shepard & Pollard, 1820), p. 312 ("The end of this guarantee is 'a republican form of government.' The meaning of this expression is not so unsettled here as in other countries, because we agree in one descriptive character as essential to the existence of a republican form of government. This is representation. We do not admit a Government to be even in its origin republican, unless it is instituted by representation; nor do we allow it to be so, unless its legislation is also founded upon representation.").

> provision made by the Convention [Article I, Section 2] appears, therefore, to be the best that lay within their option. It must be satisfactory to every State; because it is conformable to the standard already established, or which may be established by the State itself. It will be safe to the United States; because, being fixed by the State Constitutions, it is not alterable by the State Governments ....[49]

Importantly, this passage suggests that there is no uniform right of suffrage at the federal level and the right varies by state; nevertheless, the right to vote in state and federal elections must exist in some form because it is the hallmark of a republican form of government.[50]

Supporters believed that tying the success of the new government to the health and vitality of the franchise in the states was key to ratification.[51] The link between state and federal electors in Article I, Section 2, which tied the qualifications for voting in federal elections to those established for the most numerous branch of each state's legislature, ensured that the qualifications of either group would be the same. In *The Federalist* 45, Madison observed that "[e]ven the House of Representatives, though drawn immediately from the people, will be chosen very much under the influence of that class of men, whose influence over the people obtains for themselves an election into the State Legislature."[52]

The relatively low property qualifications then in existence meant that a sizable number of White men would be able to vote post-ratification. A supporter of the Constitution calling himself "A Landholder" wrote a spirited defense in the *Connecticut Courant*, noting that, among the advantages of the new government, "Every freeman is an elector. The same qualifications which enable you to vote for state representatives, give you a federal voice. It is a right you cannot lose, unless you first annihilate the state legislature, and declare yourselves incapable of electing, which is a degree of infatuation improbable as a second deluge to drown the world."[53]

Perhaps most significantly, states were compelled, through the constitutional text, to define their political communities in accordance with the principles of republican theory. That meant more than simply holding elections – it required that the electorate be composed of individuals with enough independence to cast their votes free from coercion or domination by powerful interests. The Guarantee Clause

49 Alexander Hamilton (or James Madison), "The Federalist 52," in Hamilton (ed.), *The Federalist*, pp. 403–404.

50 See ibid.

51 See ibid.; see also James Madison, *Debates in the Federal Convention of 1787 Which Framed the Constitution of the United States of America*, Gaillard Hunt and James Brown Scott (eds.) (Amherst: Prometheus Books, 2007), p. 351 (debate over whether qualifications of federal electors should be included in the Constitution).

52 James Madison, "The Federalist 45," in Hamilton (ed.), *The Federalist*, p. 361.

53 "A Landholder" (Oliver Ellsworth), "Reply to Elbridge Gerry of November 26, 1787," *Connecticut Courant*, reprinted in Bailyn (ed.), *Debate on the Constitution*, vol. 1, pp. 236–237 (arguing that "State representation and government is the very basis of the congressional power proposed").

functioned as a safeguard in this regard: it set a constitutional floor beneath which no state could fall in structuring its system of representation. This requirement was reinforced by the link between state and federal electors in Article I, Section 2. Together, these provisions gave the federal government a critical backstop. If a state failed to designate voters at all – or constructed its electorate in a way that undermined basic republican principles – the federal government could step in to ensure that *someone* retained the right to vote, especially given that these restrictions could also affect the federal electorate.

Delegates to the constitutional convention worried instead about a different problem. They expressed concerns about disqualifying voters who would otherwise be eligible to vote under state law, with some opining that this development could lead the people to ultimately reject the proposed constitution.[54] According to James Wilson, "[i]t was difficult to form any uniform rule of qualifications for all the States" because "it would be very hard [and] disagreeable for the same persons at the same time, to vote for representatives in the State Legislature and to be excluded from a vote for those in the Nat[ional] Legislature."[55] Other delegates proposed freehold requirements for federal electors, but critics argued that imposing a property restriction could derail ratification because property qualifications, deemed by some to be too "British," were not a prerequisite to voting in all states.[56]

[54] See ibid., p. 354. Benjamin Franklin argued that he did not think "the elected had any right in any case to narrow the privileges of electors" because the elected often used subterfuge to circumscribe the right to vote. As James Madison described in his notes:

> He [Franklin] quoted as arbitrary the British Statute setting forth the danger of tumultuous meetings, and under that pretext narrowing the right of suffrage to persons having freeholds of a certain value; observing that this Statute was soon followed by another under the succeeding Parliam[en]t subjecting the people who had no votes to peculiar labors & hardships. He was persuaded also that such a restriction as was proposed would give great uneasiness in the populous States. The sons of a substantial farmer, not being themselves freeholders, would not be pleased at being disenfranchised, and there are a great many persons of that description.

Ibid.

[55] Ibid., p. 351.

[56] See Madison, *Debates in the Federal Convention*, p. 352 (comments of Oliver Ellsworth). Oliver Ellsworth stated:

> How shall the freehold be defined? Ought not every man who pays a tax, to vote for the representative who is to levy & dispose of his money? Shall the wealthy merchants & manufacturers, who will bear a full share of the public burdens be not allowed a voice in the imposition of them – taxation and representation ought to go together.

Ibid. See also Constitution or System of Government, Agreed to and Resolved Upon by the Representatives in Full Convention of the Delaware State art. 4 (1776) (incorporating by reference 7 Geo. II, § 2 (1733)) (requiring that electors "be a freeholder" or "be otherwise worth Forty Pounds of lawful money"); Constitution of the State of New York art. VII (1777) (requiring electors to either be a freeholder or "have rented a tenement therein of the yearly value of forty shillings"); Fundamental Orders of Connecticut (1639), 1 (providing that "choice shall be made by all that are admitted freemen").

The fear, rightly so, was that the people would rebel against creating a system that mimicked the one that they had repudiated.[57] Oliver Ellsworth argued, "[t]he people will not readily subscribe to the Nat[ional] Constitution if it should subject them to be disenfranchised. The States are the best Judges of the circumstances [and] temper of their own people."[58] "What will the people there say, if they should be disenfranchised?" asked George Mason. He concluded that, "A power to alter the qualifications would be a dangerous power in the hands of the [Federal] Legislature."[59] Ultimately, the delegates decided to let states determine voter qualifications for federal elections to avoid outlining criteria that, in disenfranchising otherwise qualified voters, would create unnecessary tension with the concept of majority rule.[60]

Opponents of the new constitution nonetheless fought any proposal that could be construed as disenfranchising those already within the community of voters, contending that this was fundamentally inconsistent with republican ideals. For example, critics treated the absence of annual elections to be a subversion of the people's right to vote, equivalent to a freehold requirement or outright denial of the franchise.[61] A letter appeared in the *Independent Gazetteer* in November 1787, arguing that, under the proposed Constitution, "[a]nnual Elections are abolished,

57 Madison, *Debates in the Federal Convention*, p. 353 (comments of George Mason). George Mason stated

> We all feel too strongly the remains of antient prejudices, and view things too much through a British medium. A Freehold is the qualification in England, and hence it is imagined to be the only proper one. The true idea in his opinion was that every man having evidence of attachment to & permanent common interest with the Society ought to share in all its rights & privileges.

Ibid. See also A Declaration of Rights Made by the Representatives of the Good People of Virginia (1776), Sec. VI (requiring only that men have "sufficient evidence of permanent common interest … with the community"); Madison, *Debates in the Federal Convention*, pp. 353–354 (comments of James Madison) (arguing that "[a] very small proportion of the Representatives [in England] are chosen by freeholders. The greatest part are chosen by the Cities and boroughs, in many of which the qualification of suffrage is as low as it is in any one of the U.S.," but noting that "it was in the boroughs and Cities … that bribery most prevailed"). But see ibid., p. 355 (comments of Nathaniel Ghorum) (disputing that the "[c]ities & large towns are … the seat of Crown influence & corruption" and arguing that the "[t]he elections in Philadelphia, New York & Boston where the Merchants, & Mechanics vote are at least as good as those made by freeholders only").

58 Madison, *Debates in the Federal Convention*, p. 351 (comments of Oliver Ellsworth) (arguing that "[t]he right of suffrage was a tender point, and strongly guarded by most of the State Constitutions").

59 Ibid. (comments of George Mason).

60 Ibid., p. 354 (comments of John Rutledge) (arguing that "restraining the right of suffrage to the freeholders a very unadvised [idea]" because it "would create division among the people and make enemies of all those who should be excluded"); see also ibid. at 351 (comments of George Mason) (noting that "[e]ight or nine States have extended the right of suffrage beyond the freeholders").

61 *See* "Cato," "Can an American Be a Tyrant? On the Great Powers of the Presidency, the Vagueness of the Constitution, and the Dangers of Congress" (1787), in Bailyn (ed.), *Debate on the Constitution*, vol. 1, pp. 401 ("The most general objections to the first article [which comprises the election of the house of representatives and the senate], are that biennial elections for representatives are a departure from the safe democratic principles of annual ones.").

and the people are not to re-assume their rights until the expiration of *two*, *four* and *six* years."[62]

While supporters of the Constitution conceded that "the doctrine of frequent elections has been sanctified by antiquity," they maintained that longer terms of office were necessary to govern effectively at the federal level because "[i]t is not by riding post to and from Congress, that a man can acquire a just knowledge of the true interests of the union."[63] Noah Webster similarly rejected the argument that biennial elections undermined the right to vote, arguing that the proposed timing of federal elections did not disturb the underlying rights of the people because the "only barrier against tyranny ... is the *election of Legislators* by the yeomanry of the State. Preserve *that*, and every privilege is safe."[64]

After the ratification of the Constitution, republicanism – and its focus on majority rule – would be further refined through constitutional amendment and the entry of new states into the Union. These events illustrated that the federal government was not only invested in the composition of state electorates, but also in ensuring that the very structure of state government comported with republican ideals. However, the rise of political parties and the contentiousness of the presidential election of 1800 altered the terms upon which the states and the federal government would engage these concepts, particularly the principle of majority rule.

1.2 MAJORITY RULE BUT WHICH MAJORITY? THE TWELFTH AMENDMENT AND THE EVOLUTION OF REPUBLICAN GOVERNMENT

Timothy Pickering had a resume that any modern politician would envy. A hero of the Revolutionary War, he served as Postmaster General, Secretary of War, and

62 See "Reply to Wilson's Speech of November 6, 1787, an Officer of the Late Continental Army (William Findley?)," *Independent Gazetteer*, reprinted in Bailyn (ed.), *Debate on the Constitution*, vol. 1, p. 100.

63 "Fisher Ames on Biennial Elections and on the Volcano of Democracy, January 15, 1788," reprinted in Bailyn (ed.), *Debate on the Constitution*, vol. 1, pp. 891–95 (arguing that "Biennial elections [are] ... an essential security to liberty" because it allows time for "reflection and information" so as to discourage people from "nourish[ing] factions in their bosom"); see also James Madison, "The Federalist 53," in Hamilton (ed.), *The Federalist*, pp. 411–412 ("No man can be a competent legislator who does not add ... a certain degree of knowledge of the subjects on which he is to legislate ... part [of which] can only be attained ... by actual experience in the station which requires the use of it."); Alexander Hamilton (or James Madison), "The Federalist 52," in Hamilton (ed.), *The Federalist*, pp. 405–407 (drawing on the history of British elections, where election frequency went from every seven years to every three; Irish elections, which "were regulated entirely by the discretion of the crown"; and elections in the colonies, which "varied for one to seven years," in order to show that "biennial elections under the federal system, cannot possibly be dangerous to the requisite dependence of the house of representatives on their constituents").

64 "America" (Noah Webster), "Reply to the Pennsylvania Minority of December 31, 1787," reprinted in Bailyn (ed.), *Debate on the Constitution*, vol. 1, pp. 554–555. (arguing that "the right of election is above [Congress's] control: it must remain in the people, and be exercised once in two, four or six years").

Secretary of State under President Washington. He continued the last post for the Adams Administration. He later served as both a Senator and a Representative from Massachusetts. As an ardent Federalist and New Englander, however, one title is notably absent from his resume: secessionist.

The election of 1800 was not only the first in which political parties were decisive to the outcome. It was also the first election that necessitated a transfer of power from one party to another.[65] To be frank, Pickering did not take the loss well. He detested Jefferson. Much of his opposition centered on the two things: (1) the declining influence of his party, and (2) his concern that the policies of the Jefferson Administration would destabilize the Northeast as the center of influence in the country.[66]

In 1803, Pickering conspired with several prominent Federalists, including sitting Vice President Aaron Burr, to secede from the Union and create a northern Confederacy.[67] Pickering's efforts would fare no better than those of his southern counterparts more than fifty years later. As historian Kevin Gannon has documented, the Federalists failed to secure political wins in state elections throughout the Northeast in 1804, which would have drummed up popular support for any secessionist efforts.[68] Burr failed to win the governorship in New York (a win that would have, perhaps, prevented him from being the villain in the world's best musical),[69] and the secession movement died.

Pickering endorsed secession because he felt kinship with the revolutionaries who had invoked the right to secede a little more than two decades prior. But by the early nineteenth century, alter or abolish was on the decline as a vehicle to express dissatisfaction with the government. The unsuccessful secessionist conspiracy in which Pickering and Burr were involved helped show that politics, rather than extralegal mob violence, was the preferred method to resolve conflict. The decline in legitimate invocations of the alter or abolish right, as Chapter 4 will show, had much to do with who was invoking the right rather than the moral force and legality of the invocation.

Either way, political elites hoped that majority support, filtered through political parties, would drive debate and resolution of every major political issue. This proved mostly true until southern secession in 1860. In the interim, conversations

65 John Ferling, *Adams vs. Jefferson: The Tumultuous Election of 1800* (Cary: Oxford University Press, 2004). Thomas Jefferson, a Democratic Republican (also referred to as "Jeffersonians" or "Republicans," although not the same Republican Party founded in the 1850s), ascended to the presidency in 1801 by defeating President John Adams, a Federalist. Adams' presidency, controversial as it was, is remember less for what he accomplished and more for the fact that he left office peacefully after he lost the election.

66 Kevin M. Gannon, "Escaping 'Mr. Jefferson's Plan of Destruction': New England Federalists and the Idea of a Northern Confederacy, 1803–04" (2001) 21 *Journal of the Early Republic* 413–443, 414.

67 Ibid.

68 Ibid.

69 Diep Tran, "Everything You Need to Know About 'Hamilton' on Broadway," *New York Theatre Guide*, January 10, 2023, www.newyorktheatreguide.com/theatre-news/news/everything-you-need-to-know-about-hamilton-on-broadway [https://perma.cc/PVQ9-YT6V].

around the prospect of secession took place in the framework of popular politics (i.e., southern secession was publicly tied to the outcome of the 1860 presidential election) rather than as the type of covert backroom conspiracy that marked Pickering's efforts. Pickering failed because he did not publicly unite northern Federalists in a fashion similar to southern Democrats who coalesced around the slavery issue a generation later. He did not appreciate just how much the rise of political parties and increasing polarization had changed the relationship between the government and the governed.

For the founding generation, the structure of republican government – and the electorate who would safeguard its principles – should be determined by the states. But political elites challenged this intention within a few short years by proposing the Twelfth Amendment. The Twelfth Amendment, ratified in 1804, requires that electors vote for the president and vice president on separate ballots. The Amendment also provides that if no candidate garners a majority of the electoral votes, the top three vote getters (instead of the top five as under the original Constitution) go to House of Representatives, where the candidate who receives a majority of the votes (with each state delegation having one vote) becomes president.[70]

Based on its text, the Twelfth Amendment looks like a technical fix to the problems that plagued the disputed election of 1800. Rather than being a mere technicality, however, the Amendment was more far-reaching, bringing suffrage further within the purview of the federal government and establishing that republican principles should dictate the structure of presidential elections. Its text, structure, and history reflected the view that, in selecting a president, republicanism does not require the outcome to reflect the majority of the state population, just the will of a majority of the voters.

To the latter point, *The Federalist Papers* foreshadowed this shift from "We the People" to "We the Voters" by explicitly linking the concept of virtue that was central to effective governance to the size of the republic. Hamilton, quoting Montesquieu, noted that a federative republic "may support itself without any internal corruptions…As this government is composed of small republics, it enjoys the internal happiness of each; and with respect to its external situation, by means of the association, of all the advantages of large monarchies."[71] The internal happiness of each state, or "small republic," likewise turned on a need to "break and control

[70] United States Constitution Amend. XII (June 15, 1804).

[71] Alexander Hamilton, "The Federalist 9," in Hamilton (ed.), *The Federalist*, pp. 100–101. But see "Letter of Timothy Pickering to Richard Peters, December 24, 1803," in Henry Adams (ed.), *Documents Relating to New England Federalism, 1800–1815* (Boston: Little, Brown, and Co., 1877), p. 338 ("I will rather anticipate a new confederacy, exempt from the corrupt and corrupting influence and oppressional of the aristocratic Democrats of the South. There will be – and our children at furthest will see it – a separation"); "Letter of Timothy Pickering to George Cabot, January 29, 1804," in Henry Adams (ed.), *Documents Relating to New England Federalism, 1800–1815* (Boston: Little, Brown, and Co., 1877), pp. 340–341 (doubting the practicability of a long-continued union" and pointing to New England as the 'last refuge' of federalism.").

the violence of faction" even from within. Madison warned in *The Federalist* 10 that faction was a threat that, if magnified across jurisdictions, could undermine a "well constructed Union."[72] Thus, the shift from prioritizing the preferences of unpredictable numerical majorities to those of smaller electoral majorities more likely to act with virtue was probably inevitable.

By tying the legitimacy of the presidency to the selection of electors who reflect majority will, the Twelfth Amendment endorsed a view of republican government that was voter-centered, rather than population-centered. In altering the 1787 design, the Amendment's drafters, both in what they changed about the original Electoral College and in what they left the same, clarified that "majoritarianism" centered on political influence rather than population. The text preserved the ability of state legislatures to choose how to select electors and was consistent with the original design. And the Amendment's use of passive voice regarding the tallying of Electoral College votes ("and the votes shall be counted") represented a power that has evolved over time, one that allows Congress to affirmatively weigh in on the state process for selecting electors.[73] But the Jeffersonian conception of majoritarianism, unlike the Madisonian vision, anticipated that the president would garner the support of those who held the political power in the state, either through the popularly elected state legislature that chooses electors, or through electors selected by voters directly.[74]

The requirement that electors vote for president and vice president on separate ballots might have seemed like a commonsense response to the 1800 Electoral College tie between Thomas Jefferson and Aaron Burr that almost plunged the country into chaos. However, this aspect of the Twelfth Amendment was deeply tied to respect for the principle of majority rule. By tinkering with the 1787 system, the Framers wanted the president to emerge from an electoral process in which he (or she) was the preference of a compound majority of majorities in states central to his (or her) Electoral College victory, rather than a mere plurality winner. The latter would undermine republicanism's commitment to majority rule, as was the case when Aaron Burr emerged as a presidential contender in the election of 1800 despite not being the popular preference.[75] His selection was contrary to republican ideals in which the preferences of the voters were supposed to hold sway.

72 James Madison, "The Federalist 10," in Hamilton (ed.), *The Federalist*, p. 104.

73 Electoral Count Act of 1887, ch. 90, 24 Stat. 373 (1887).

74 Foley, *Presidential Elections*, p. 6. See also "Comments of Mr. Clopton of Wednesday, October 26, 1803," 13 *Annals of Congress of the United States* (Washington, D.C.: Gales and Seaton, 1852), p. 492 ("For, sir, however respectful the public attention might have been towards the person who thus becomes Chief Magistrate of the Union, contrary to the intention of the Electors [voters], it cannot be expected that with the acquisition of the office, under these circumstances, he will receive the public confidence.").

75 Foley, *Presidential Elections*, p. 40. According to Professor Foley, "Adhering to federalism required Republicans in 1803 to retain the idea, embedded in the Electoral College of 1787, that majority rule in a federal system entails a compound majority-of-majorities. Republicanism, as a philosophy, demands majority rule at the state level. A federal majority is then formed from an overall majority of these subsidiary state-level majorities." Ibid.

During debates on the Amendment, Democratic Republicans emphasized the centrality of majority rule to our system of representative government. In particular, they warned of the danger of electing someone to the presidency who was not the choice of the voters.[76] According to Virginia congressman John Clopton, "When one person is intended for an office and another person actually obtains it, such election, if indeed it can properly be called an election, is not conformable to the will of those by whom it was made..."[77] Similarly, Maryland representative Robert Wright argued that the proposed Amendment was not a "party question." Instead, the proposal transcended party because it sought to "prevent men not intended to be chosen from being edged into power. ...to set up a man who had not a single vote..."[78] The Jeffersonians were, according to Professor Edward Foley, "much more committed to this federalist form of majoritarianism than the Philadelphia Convention delegates had ever been," because they still allowed states in which they were not a majority to allocate electoral votes based on the popular will, even after the Twelfth Amendment had been ratified.[79] Jeffersonians also believed that federalism demanded that they leave to each state the decision of how to allocate its electors. However, as usual, partisanship tended to color what would otherwise appear to be principled positions.

Importantly, the Framers of the Twelfth Amendment anticipated that each state's voting population would be organized by political parties, facilitating majoritarian principles in a way that was unthinkable in 1787.[80] The expectation that republicanism would be filtered through partisan politics was precisely why the Jeffersonians left to each state the decision of how to allocate its electors, recognizing that their party organization was dominant in enough states to secure electoral victories moving forward. As Professor Foley has observed,

> members of the Eighth Congress ...believe[d] that states would exercise their power to appoint presidential electors in a way that reflected the prevailing political perspective within each state. Once intense two-party competition emerged

[76] "Comments of Mr. Clopton of Wednesday, October 26, 1803," 13 *Annals of Congress of the United States* (Washington, D.C.: Gales and Seaton, 1852), p. 491 ("in a Government constituted as our Government is, wherein all the constituted authorities are agents of the people, the suffrages given for the election of those agents ought ever to be a complete expression of the public will").

[77] Ibid. But see "Comments of Mr. Huger of Friday, October 28, 1803," 13 *Annals of Congress of the United States* (Washington, D.C.: Gales and Seaton, 1852), p. 520 (arguing that Rep. Clopton has forgotten that "the Government under which we live is formed upon Federative no less than upon Republican principles" and the proposed amendment would lessen the power of the states).

[78] Ibid., "Comments of Mr. Wright of Friday, December 2, 1803," pp. 200–201.

[79] Foley, *Presidential Elections*, p. 30.

[80] As historian Noble Cunningham has argued, "Between the inaugurations of Washington and Jefferson, the two party system became rooted in American politics. So important had the role of parties become in the political life of the nation that the Constitution itself was soon to be amended to recognize the place of parties, whose rise had made the constitutional provisions for the election of the president and the vice president outdated and unrealistic and had led to the troublesome tie between Jefferson and Burr." Cunningham, *Jeffersonian Republicans*, p. 260.

during the elections of 1796 and 1800, politicians from both parties understood that state legislatures would select methods of appointing electors that would enable the dominant party in each state to promote its own presidential candidate.[81]

Even in a state like Maryland, where the Democratic Republicans were not a majority, they had, in 1800, been able to beat back efforts by the Federalist-dominated state legislature to use a general ticket system in the allocation of electors; that fall, Republicans were able to win five electors. The prospect of minor success in Federalist domains further reinforced that leaving the decision to the states would not imperil Republican political prospects.[82] In essence, the Twelfth Amendment embodied a type of voter-centered majority rule that conflated majoritarianism with major party preferences, rendering outcomes contrary to the relative political power of the parties in the state immediately suspect.[83]

81 Foley, *Presidential Elections*, p. 16; see also Cunningham, *Jeffersonian Republicans*, p. 189 ("it is important to emphasize that the Jeffersonians of 1803, in their Electoral College redesign, were looking forward to Jefferson's re-election of 1804 at least as much as they were looking backward to his victory in 1800. Their conception of themselves as the majority party, to be vindicated as such by the redesigned Electoral College in 1804, was based in part on the strength of their midterm victories in 1802 and their still-increasing popularity after the Louisiana Purchase. Finally, the actual voting in 1804 vindicated the Jeffersonians on this crucial point."). Not only were political parties the way to gauge which candidates enjoyed majority support among voters in a particular state, Professor Foley illustrates that the system was ill-equipped to deal with third party candidates precisely because of the difficulty that individual encounters as he (or she) attempts to amass the popular support that the Jeffersonian experiment envisioned. Foley, *Presidential Elections*, p. 117–118.

82 "Gabriel Duvall to Thomas Jefferson, 14 December 1802," *Founders Online*, National Archives, https://founders.archives.gov/documents/Jefferson/01–39–02–0142–0001. [Original source: Barbara B. Oberg (ed.), *The Papers of Thomas Jefferson*, vol. 39, 13 *November* 1802–3 *March* 1803 (Princeton: Princeton University Press, 2012), pp. 156–157.] (providing information to Jefferson as to "the probable result of a choice of Electors in Maryland by a general ticket" and concluding that district elections are unpopular but "in any rational division of the State, the Republican candidate will succeed in seven of the Eleven districts"). "John Beckley to James Madison, 5 May 1803," *Founders Online*, National Archives, https://founders.archives.gov/documents/Madison/02-04-02-0682. [Original source: Mary A. Hackett, J. C. A. Stagg, Jeanne Kerr Cross, Susan Holbrook Perdue, and Ellen J. Barber (eds.), *The Papers of James Madison*, Secretary of State Series, vol. 4, 8 *October* 1802–15 *May* 1803 (Charlottesville: University Press of Virginia, 1998), pp. 574–575.] ("N York elections are decisively democratic thro' the State, for both branches, and leave no doubt that the mode for choosing Electors in that state for the presidential Election will be such as the democrats shall prescribe").

The fact that the relative odds of Republican political success at the state level was part of the calculus behind the Twelfth Amendment was contrary to the expectations of Founders like Alexander Hamilton who thought that the proposed Amendment would both "strengthen[ ] the connection between the Foederal [sic] head and the people" and "diminish[ ] [ ] the means of party combination, in which also the burning zeal of our opponents will be generally an overmatch for our temperate flame." "Alexander Hamilton to Gouverneur Morris, 4 March 1802," *Founders Online*, National Archives, https://founders.archives.gov/documents/Hamilton/01-25-02-0300. [Original source: Harold C. Syrett (ed.), *The Papers of Alexander Hamilton*, vol. 25, July 1800–April 1802 (New York: Columbia University Press, 1977), pp. 558–560.]

83 Cunningham, *Jeffersonian Republicans*, p. 259 ("Effective organization and aggressive campaigning were keys to Republican success in the election of 1800. In their attention to party organization and machinery, the Republicans remained constantly aware of the necessity of maintaining popular

Thomas Jefferson's correspondence with Speaker of the House Nathaniel Macon regarding Democratic Republican Party success in the 1802 midterms in North Carolina illustrate this conflation of majoritarianism and majority political party rule. Although his party won 11 of the state's 12 congressional seats, Jefferson questioned the legitimacy of the election of the lone Federalist from a predominantly Democratic Republican district. According to Jefferson, "…the Republican cause is daily gaining ground with us, not only the late elections but the candid acknowledgment of many that they have been deceived fully confirm the fact; … and it is worthy of notice that the district which sends the only federalist from the state to Congress, gave a majority of votes to Republican candidates."[84]

The fact that the Federalists were still competitive in some places, contrary to what Democratic Republicans perceived to be majority sentiment, led Thomas McKean, then Governor of Pennsylvania, to note in an 1803 letter to Jefferson that, "The people do not always know their good; and when they do, it is not always pursued."[85] Yet the fact that Democratic Republicans had been successful in the last general election in Pennsylvania assured him that "their late conduct however in this State has not depreciated them, nor do I believe that it will in the next election of President."[86] He cautioned, however, that unless the Constitution was amended, the choice of vice president could still go to someone who lacked majority support. "I believe," McKean noted, "[the twenty electors] will surrender the choice of Vice-President to the Tories, unless Congress will propose an amendment to the Constitution for discriminating the characters to be voted for."[87]

The centrality of partisanship to the new Amendment was not in doubt.[88] The election of 1800 had led to the decline of the Federalist Party and, by implication,

support…. The nature of democracy made it imperative that the people should play a prominent part in party activities, and political machinery was geared to win their votes.").

84 "Nathaniel Macon to Thomas Jefferson, 3 September 1803," *Founders Online*, National Archives, https://founders.archives.gov/documents/Jefferson/01–41–02-0242. [Original source: Barbara B. Oberg (ed.), *The Papers of Thomas Jefferson*, vol. 41, *11 July–15 November 1803* (Princeton: Princeton University Press, 2014), pp. 311–312.]

85 "Thomas McKean to Thomas Jefferson, 7 February 1803," *Founders Online*, National Archives, https://founders.archives.gov/documents/Jefferson/01-39-02-0406. [Original source: Barbara B. Oberg (ed.), *The Papers of Thomas Jefferson*, vol. 39, *13 November 1802–3 March 1803* (Princeton: Princeton University Press, 2012), pp. 471–474.]

86 Ibid. (promising Jefferson that "in 1804 the twenty electors of President & Vice-President will give their unanimous vote for the present Chief Magistrate").

87 Ibid. During the Revolutionary War, "Tories" were supporters of the British Crown.

88 "DeWitt Clinton to Thomas Jefferson, 10 June 1802," *Founders Online*, National Archives, https://founders.archives.gov/documents/Jefferson/01-37-02-0464. [Original source: Barbara B. Oberg (ed.), *The Papers of Thomas Jefferson*, vol. 37, *4 March–30 June 1802*, (Princeton: Princeton University Press, 2010), pp. 573–574.] Jefferson stated that the prospects of the Republican Party in South Carolina were "very good" and, according to an editorial note, included with his missive a pamphlet entitled, *Considerations on the Propriety of Adopting a General Ticket in South-Carolina, for the Election of Representatives in Congress and Electors of President and Vice-President of the United States. Addressed to the People of South Carolina by Crito*. Ibid.

any meaningful opposition to both ratification of the Twelfth Amendment and the path to a Democratic Republican presidency.[89] As Kean wrote to Jefferson in January 1804 upon signing an Act to ratify the Amendment, "We shall, if this amendment shall be adopted by thirteen States, (which I believe it will, tho' probably no more, unless the effects of party shall in the mean time cease) have our next President and Vice-President genuine Republicans, otherwise I doubt it."[90] In elections prior to the ratification of the Twelfth Amendment, the Democratic Republicans were "endeavoring not only to beat them [the Federalists]," according to a New York partisan, but "to beat them soundly; that they may be still next Spring and not attempt to intermeddle in the Legislature which is to appoint Electors for P. U.S. & V.P."[91]

The premise that political parties should filter majority preferences in the selection of the president was not without its controversy. The Amendment was intended to make it less likely that presidential elections would be resolved by the House of Representatives, where each state delegation has one vote, and election results would be instead left to the public that was, in the words of one representative, "agitated with violent party rage."[92] By putting power back in the hands of the people, this provision reduced the likelihood that the presidency would be thrown to the House of Representatives, where all states – big and small – enjoyed equal voting power in the selection of the president and could maneuver the presidency into the

89 The fact that a bill had been introduced in Massachusetts to divide the states into districts for the purpose of choosing presidential electors in 1803 is notable, given that the state had traditionally been a Federalist stronghold. See "Joshua Danforth to Thomas Jefferson, 16 July 1803," *Founders Online*, National Archives, https://founders.archives.gov/documents/Jefferson/01-41-02-0036. [Original source: Barbara B. Oberg (ed.), *The Papers of Thomas Jefferson*, vol. 41, *11 July–15 November 1803*, (Princeton: Princeton University Press, 2014), pp. 60–61.] ("A motion will be made at the next Session of the Legislature of Massachusetts to divide the State into districts. for the Choice of electors of President&c, but it is very uncertain whether it will succeed, if it should, Massachusetts will give eight or nine Votes to the republican Candidate for President."). See also "Joseph Barnes to Thomas Jefferson, 25 March 1804," *Founders Online*, National Archives, https://founders.archives.gov/documents/Jefferson/01–43-02-0082. [Original source: James P. McClure (ed.), *The Papers of Thomas Jefferson*, vol. 43, *11 March–30 June 1804* (Princeton: Princeton University Press, 2017), pp. 86–90.] ("In fine; so highly do I approve, & so ardent is my zeal for the principles & measures of the present Administration that were my efforts necessary, and were it possible, I would *waft* myself on the wings of friendship & esteem to *Ensure* the re-election of Mr. Jefferson – however I am happy in the Opinion there will be but a *feeble* Opposition made especially as the Federalist party, from the general advice I receive, Seems daily to decline.").

90 "Thomas McKean to Thomas Jefferson, 8 January 1804," *Founders Online*, National Archives, https://founders.archives.gov/documents/Jefferson/01–42–02-0222. [Original source: James P. McClure (ed.), *The Papers of Thomas Jefferson*, vol. 42, *16 November 1803–10 March 1804* (Princeton: Princeton University Press, 2016), pp. 243–244.]

91 "Samuel Latham Mitchill to James Madison, 28 April 1803," *Founders Online*, National Archives, https://founders.archives.gov/documents/Madison/02–04–02-0660. [Original source: Mary A. Hackett, J. C. A. Stagg, Jeanne Kerr Cross, Susan Holbrook Perdue, and Ellen J. Barber (eds.), *The Papers of James Madison*, Secretary of State Series, vol. 4, *8 October 1802–15 May 1803* (Charlottesville: University Press of Virginia, 1998), p. 558.]

92 "Comments of Mr. Huger of Friday, October 28, 1803," 13 *Annals of Congress of the United States* (Washington, D.C.: Gales and Seaton, 1852), p. 492.

hands of someone not preferred by a majority of voters.[93] Delegations could only select among the top three candidates instead of the top five, thereby decreasing the likelihood that a political minority could conspire in the election of a fourth or fifth-place finisher who lacked majority support. Some representatives opposed the Amendment because of this perceived shift of authority from the states (particularly the smaller states) to the people.

Majoritarianism nonetheless served as a legitimizing function, and its reach would extend beyond the formal strictures of the Twelfth Amendment to the informal congressional nominating caucuses that selected presidential candidates. The absence of majority sentiment from the caucuses, which artificially shrunk the pool of available candidates, led to attacks on that mechanism from all corners of the political spectrum. The Federalists held a congressional nominating convention in 1800, selecting John Adams as their candidate, but abandoned the practice in subsequent elections due to their declining political strength. After the election of 1800, Federalists and Democratic Republicans alike attacked the Democratic Republican presidential caucus as undemocratic and divorced from majority rule. In the words of one of these dissidents, the caucus was "an attempt to produce an undue bias in the ensuing election of president and vice president, and virtually to transfer the appointment of those officers from the people, to a majority of the two Houses of Congress."[94] Republican principles required that the mediating institutions between the government and the people – in this context, the Electoral College – reflect the people's preferences. Some critics viewed the congressional caucuses as an additional intermediary, not sanctioned by the Constitution, that could distort this process.

Yet the congressional nominating caucus was designed to throw party support behind a consensus candidate to avoid a repeat of the election of 1800, in which the House of Representatives could potentially land on someone who – like Aaron Burr – did not have the support of the people. The value of the caucus, according to North Carolina Republican (and 1824 caucus attendee) Richard Dodds Spaight, was that it was "consonant to the opinions of the majority of the people; or because that majority, having confidence in the persons recommending, adopt it as their own…The avowed object of these recommendations has been to concentrate and unite public sentiment…"[95] However, intra-party divisions and the expansion of the electorate led to increased calls for the abolition of the congressional nominating caucus, which, over time, became increasingly unable to play its mediating role. So long as the caucus resulted in candidates who had broad support among the public, drama was mostly averted … until 1824.

93 Cunningham, *Jeffersonian Republicans*, p. 240.

94 Arthur M. Schlesinger, Jr. (ed.), *History of U.S. Political Parties*, 4 vols. (New York: Chelsea House Publishers, 1973), vol. 1, p. 264.

95 Ibid., vol. 1, pp. 270–271.

The lack of a consensus candidate in the 1824 election led to the demise of the caucus. In 1824, the presidential election was thrown to the House for the first time since 1800, an indication that the congressional nominating caucus could no longer serve the legitimizing function that it had served over the course of five election cycles (where party elites would filter, but still reflect, majority preferences). This was the first election in which the country had no Founders run for president, and a new crop of leaders were vying for the presidency – John Quincy Adams, the son of a founding father; Andrew Jackson, a hero of the War of 1812; and Henry Clay, a powerful senator and eventual leader of the Whig Party. The Whig Party would emerge as the opposition party to the Democratic Republicans (re-christened the Democratic Party after the 1824 election).

While William H. Crawford, Secretary of the Treasury under James Monroe, was considered by many to be the obvious preference of the Democratic Republican caucus leading up to the 1824 presidential election, supporters of the other candidates nominated their preferred candidates in state legislative caucuses designed to compete with the congressional caucus. In 1822, the Tennessee legislature nominated Andrew Jackson; Massachusetts followed suit by nominating John Quincy Adams in 1823. Likewise, the legislatures of Kentucky and Missouri threw their support behind Henry Clay.[96] William Crawford only received forty-one electoral votes after his selection in a caucus in which only a fraction of congressional Republicans participated.[97] The House of Representatives awarded John Quincy Adams the presidency, an outcome that many Jackson supporters decried as a "corrupt bargain" between Adams and Clay, then speaker of the House.[98] Cries of a corrupt bargain would motivate Jackson supporters up to the election of 1828.[99]

Despite the upheaval of the 1824 election, the ability of political parties to shape and redefine republicanism not only survived the death of the caucuses and the first party system, but also drastically altered the scope of federal power over voting and elections. State legislatures became more assertive in putting forward their own candidates, a splinter in the party that lead some congressional Republicans to also abandon the caucus and hasten its demise.

Federalism – ostensibly preserved by the Twelfth Amendment – could not prevent coordination between officials at each level of government in the context of presidential elections. Political parties blurred the lines between state and federal officials, creating a synergy among these individuals – originally intended to be in opposition to each other – that prevented the states' role in the composition of the federal

96 Ibid., vol. 1, p. 268.

97 Ibid., vol. 1, p. 271.

98 Marc W. Kruman, "The Second American Party System and the Transformation of Revolutionary Republicanism" (1992) 11 *Journal of the Early Republic* 509–537, 520–521

99 Jackson's supporters had great faith in him: not only did they believe that "[o]nly the election of the Old Hero [Jackson] could save the republic[,]" but also that Jackson's "victory in 1828 rescued the republic from corruption and faction[.]" Ibid., 521.

government from actually cabining federal authority.[100] These synergies rendered obsolete one of the Electoral College's intended purposes of protecting smaller states by making it less likely that presidential disputes would be resolved by the House of Representatives in which small states had equal voting power with larger states.

The increasing centrality of political parties also made it difficult for the president to maintain his (or her) independence because electors were committed to vote for the party's slate of candidates in advance of the election.[101] This remained true after the abolition of the congressional caucus and the move toward national nominating conventions. Political parties also facilitated coordination across elections that extended beyond the presidency. Just as Burr's political maneuvering in the New York state legislative elections was key to the Democratic Republicans' fortunes in the 1800 presidential election that fall, partisan presidential politics would continue to impact and shape state and federal elections moving forward. Thus, the Twelfth Amendment, by elevating the role of the parties in presidential politics, set the stage for the deployment of federal power to influence state political systems, interventions that often worked to the benefit (and detriment) of state and federal officials along partisan lines.[102]

1.3 WHAT IS A REPUBLIC? THE GUARANTEE CLAUSE, PARTISAN POLITICS, AND THE ADMISSION OF NEW STATES

Pickering's attempt to secede in late 1803 signaled the extent to which the country still lacked a national identity, and the compact of states (or little republics)[103]

[100] Compare Daryl J. Levinson and Richard H. Pildes, "Separation of Parties, not Powers" (2006) 119 *Harvard Law Review* 2312–2386 (arguing that separation of powers has to be viewed through the lens of party competition). Arguably, the same assumption applies to our system of federalism. See Malcolm M. Feeley and Edward Rubin, *Federalism: Political Identity and Tragic Compromise* (Ann Arbor: University of Michigan Press, 2011), p. 5 (offering a theory of federalism that "assume[s] the centrality of political identity").

[101] Levinson and Pildes, "Separation of Parties, not Powers," 2323; see also Larry D. Kramer, "Putting the Politics Back into the Political Safeguards of Federalism" (2000) 100 *Columbia Law Review* 215–293, 225 ("[T]he power of state legislators to pick electors could have given the states considerable leverage over the chief executive had the Electoral College stayed true to its original design. But the emergence of the popular canvass and winner-take-all rule have deprived the College of most of its significance.").

[102] Franita Tolson, "Partisan Gerrymandering as a Safeguard of Federalism" (2010) *Utah Law Review* 859–910 (arguing that states can gerrymander to maximize the number of districts that mirror (a) the partisan composition of a majority of the electorate, and (b) the majority party in the state, in order to ensure that state interests are represented nationally); Franita Tolson, "Benign Partisanship" (2012) 88 *Notre Dame Law Review* 395–456.

[103] Anti-Federalists favored establishing a confederation of what were termed "little republics" or "small republics" due to their belief that, when governments are limited in size, political corruption and oppression of citizens are less likely, and the public good can be better served. See Tom N. McInnis, "Conflict and Legitimacy in the Political Thought of the Antifederalists" (1997) 21 *Legal Studies Forum* 53–72.

concept persisted well throughout the first third of the nineteenth century. During the War of 1812, for example, northeastern Federalists again threatened secession, a threat made with little thought of the practical reality facing a handful of states outside the Union,[104] but instead reflected the belief that these states had the right to leave.[105] Voting in lockstep against the war and all war measures was the Federalists' last gasp as a national political party.[106]

Federalist governors refused to provide military support, also flirting with secession in response to the unpopular war effort. The resulting Hartford Convention, in which several northeastern states appointed delegates in the mold of the Constitutional Convention of 1787, went further than Pickering's efforts in 1803.[107] The convention failed to attract delegates from all of the northeastern states, but nonetheless flagged the extent to which the U.S. Constitution had done little to displace the view that there was no collective, only a compact; no national, only states.[108]

Politics and the rise of mass political parties helped to forge this national identity through the office of the president. The expectation that the president would be elected by a compound majority of majorities, organized by political parties, illustrated which people mattered for purposes of defining the majoritarianism inherent in republican principles – the voters. Furthermore, majoritarianism was an implicit limit on how states could define the electorate. The concepts of voter, electorate, and political community could no longer be insulated from questions of federal power since Congress had an obligation to enforce the republican guarantee. This restructuring implicitly challenged the notion of the states as the independent, self-policing bastions of republicanism central to the compact theory. Instead, Congress would more aggressively determine whether state governments were "republican in form,"[109] which became a shorthand for policing these categories.

During the antebellum era, Congress exercised its power under the Admission Clause (Article IV, Section 3 of the Constitution) to determine whether newly formed states complied with the mandate of republicanism in

104 Brian Steele, "Thomas Jefferson, Coercion, and the Limits of Harmonious Union" (2008) 74 *Journal of Southern History* 823–854, 850–851.

105 Alan Taylor, "Dual Nationalisms: Legacies of the War of 1812" in Pietro S. Nivola and Peter J. Kastor (eds.), *What So Proudly We Hailed: Essays on the Contemporary Meaning of the War of 1812* (Washington, D.C.: Brookings Institution Press, 2012), p. 81 ("During the fall [of 1814], the nation became financially bankrupt and the union seemed on the verge of collapse as Federalists in the northeast flirted with secession which would provoke a civil war.").

106 Donald R. Hickey, *The War of 1812: A Forgotten Conflict* (Urbana: University of Illinois Press, 2012), p. 261.

107 "The Harford Convention," in John P. Gordy, *Political History of the United States*, 2nd ed., 4 vols. (New York: Nabu Press, 1902), vol. 2, pp. 277–299.

108 See ibid.

109 See Charles O. Lerche, Jr., "The Guarantee of a Republican Form of Government and the Admission of New States" (1949) 11 *Journal of Politics* 578–604.

the Guarantee Clause.[110] This assessment extended beyond the question of who could vote and was an early indicator of Congress's willingness to think about the interaction between various constitutional provisions that bear on its authority over state political systems. Congress had to ensure that, in admitting new states under Article IV, these states had properly defined their political communities and structured their state governments in a manner consistent with post–Twelfth Amendment republican ideals.

The decision of which states to admit, and what forms of government might run afoul of the republican guarantee, quickly became partisan in nature. This partisanship reflected increasing polarization over the slavery issue, which led to the crystallization of the parties as more ideological and regional.[111] The politicization of this issue demonstrated that there were few, if any, explicit constitutional constraints on Congress's authority to decide whether states had republican governments.

The Northwest Ordinance of 1787[112] and the Territorial Clause of Article IV, Section 3 gave Congress two important powers regarding the territories: (1) to regulate them, and (2) to set the parameters for when they could be admitted as new states.[113] In setting up territorial governments, the ordinance required elections "[s]o soon as there shall be five thousand free male inhabitants of full age," extending the right to vote to those who own "a freehold in fifty acres of land in the district, having been a citizen of one of the states, and being a resident in the district."[114] Those elected to the territorial government served for a term of two years.[115] Most importantly, the ordinance also required that any "constitution and government so to be formed, shall be republican, and in conformity to the principles contained in these articles."[116]

Prior to the mid-nineteenth century, Congress's power to deny the admission of a new state for having an unrepublican government was mostly dormant. Had this

[110] The Admissions Clause provides:

> New States may be admitted by the Congress into this Union; but no new State shall be formed or erected within the jurisdiction of any other State; nor any State be formed by the Junction of two or more States, or Parts of States, without the Consent of the Legislatures of the States concerned as well as the Congress.

United States Constitution Art. IV, s.3.

[111] See, for example, "Comments of Mr. Garrett Davis, April 28, 1842," 27 *Congressional Globe* (Washington, D.C.: Globe Office, 1842) p. 448 (expressing astonishment that "any man who claimed to be a States Rights man should come forward and advocate the general ticket system" because "[t]he peculiar principles of the South, and every interest it cherished, were to be protected by the district system.").

[112] Ordinance for the Government of the Territory of the United States North-West of the River Ohio (1787) [hereinafter Northwest Ordinance of 1787].

[113] The Territorial Clause provides: "The Congress shall have power to dispose of and make all needful Rules and Regulations respecting the Territory or other Property belonging to the United States." United States Constitution Art. IV, s. 3.

[114] Northwest Ordinance of 1787, s. 9.

[115] Ibid., ss. 9–10.

[116] Ibid., s. 14, art. 5.

authority been broadly used, this would have suggested that the federal government had broad authority to regulate or otherwise prohibit slavery.[117] The attempt to reconcile slavery with republican principles was a persistent challenge throughout the founding era, especially given that slaveowners had constitutionally entrenched advantages within the structure of the federal government.[118]

During the Continental Congress, for example, slavery was a point of contention in debates over how the national government would finance and structure itself.[119] James Madison originally proposed that slaves count as three-fifths of a person in 1783, when Congress switched from apportioning land as a basis of taxation to using population as the tax base.[120] While this proposal failed, Madison's rhetoric on the issue of slavery, which wavered between public condemnation and private acknowledgements of its necessity,[121] did little to resolve debates in the interim over whether

117 See Gerard Magliocca, *American Founding Son: John Bingham and the Invention of the Fourteenth Amendment* (New York: New York University Press, 2013), p. 53 (discussing arguments by John Bingham and others in 1850s that "Congress had broad authority to regulate the territories under Article Four, Section Three of the Constitution, and that this included the authority to ban slavery" and noting that these arguments derived from the Northwest Ordinance of 1787).

118 Edmund Morgan, "Slavery and Freedom: The American Paradox" (1972) 59 *Journal of American History* 5–29, 6 ("Virginia at the time of the first United States census in 1790 had 40 percent of the slaves in the entire United States. And Virginia produced the most eloquent spokesmen for freedom and equality in the entire United States: George Washington, James Madison, and above all, Thomas Jefferson. They were all slaveholders and remained so throughout their lives. In recent years we have been shown in painful detail the contrast between Jefferson's pronouncements in favor of republican liberty and his complicity in denying the benefits of that liberty to blacks."); David Waldstreicher, "The Beardian Legacy, the Madisonian Moment, and the Politics of Slavery" (2013) 2 *American Political Thought* 274–282, 276 ("Why was Madison the one to forward, and perhaps even invent, the three fifths clause? Shuttling between the Virginia legislature and the Continental Congress during the early to mid-1780s, he saw that slavery's nature, and the nature of republican government, required it to be dealt with. Even before the constitution-making moments of the 1780s, there had been aspects of the imperial conflict – the ways that it centered around questions of sovereignty and taxation and representation – that tended to bring up the problem of slavery."). See also Edmund Morgan, *American Slavery, American Freedom: The Ordeal of Colonial Virginia* (New York: W.W. Norton & Company, 2003) (originally published 1975).

119 See Jeffrey Schmitt, "Slavery and the History of Congress's Enumerated Powers" (2022) 74 *Arkansas Law Review* 641–688, 648 (noting that, in addition to the Three-Fifths Clause, the "second major structural protection for slavery was the enumeration of Congress' powers. Enumeration ensured that the federal government had no power to interfere with slavery in the states."). See also Michael J. Klarman, *The Framers' Coup: The Making of the United States Constitution* (New York: Oxford University Press, 2016), p. 258 ("In 1776, as the Continental Congress debated how to apportion tax obligations and military service quotas among the states, a South Carolina delegate warned that if it was 'debated whether their [southerners'] slaves are their property, … there is an end of the Confederation.' At the Philadelphia convention of 1787, southern threats were similarly successful at extracting safeguards for slavery.").

120 Waldstreicher, "Beardian Legacy," 276. Notably, this article refers to James Madison as "theoretically antislavery." Ibid., 275. This, of course, is the historical equivalent of calling an abusive wife or husband "theoretically pacifist."

121 That Madison's views on slavery were complicated and contradictory has been documented in the literature. See, for example, Greg Weiner, "James Madison and the Legitimacy of Majority Factions" (2013) 2 *American Political Thought* 198–216, 210 (Madison was against the ban on slavery as a violation

slavery was compatible with republican principles. Instead, the Constitution struck an uneasy compromise designed to protect slavery in the immediate term, while also laying out what the Founders believed would be the groundwork for its eventual demise. Spoiler alert: it did not work.

Madison supported a revived version of the three-fifths proposal in 1787–88, insisting that the real issue was not a big state-small state problem, but rather, a free state-slave state problem.[122] The Three-Fifths Clause of Article I, Section 2, provides that, "Representatives and direct Taxes shall be apportioned among the several States which may be included within this Union, according to their respective Numbers, which shall be determined by adding to the whole Number of free Persons, including those bound to Service for a Term of Years, and excluding Indians not taxed, three fifths of all other Persons."[123] By counting "three fifths of all other Persons," this Clause ensured that slave states would receive greater representation in the national government relative to the free states by partially counting the enslaved, who were treated as people for purposes of allocating seats in the House of Representatives. In *The Federalist* 54, Madison referred to the scheme as one that recognizes the "mixed character of persons and of property," which he viewed as necessary to account for a time in which slavery would no longer be countenanced by law.[124]

For the founding generation, slavery's eventual demise would follow the constitutionally mandated abolition of the African slave trade. While Congress could tax the importation of slaves, Article I, Section 9 provided that, "The Migration or Importation of such Persons as any of the States now existing shall think proper to admit, shall not be prohibited by the Congress prior to the Year one thousand

of property rights, while at the same time advocating for "diffusionism – the belief that slavery was likelier to be abolished if it was defused"); Jack N. Rakove, "The Madisonian Moment" (1988) 55 *University of Chicago Law Review* 473–505, 487 (characterizing Madison's position on the issue of slavery, which he "abhorred … on moral grounds" as illustrative of "the difficulty or impossibility of balancing moral embarrassment over the very existence of slavery against the candid recognition that the social systems (and thus arguably the political cultures) of at least five states demanded its preservation").

122 Waldstreicher, "Beardian Legacy," 277.

123 "Representatives and direct Taxes shall be apportioned among the several States which may be included within this Union, according to their respective Numbers, which shall be determined by adding to the whole Number of free Persons, including those bound to Service for a Term of Years, and excluding Indians not taxed, three fifths of all other Persons." United States Constitution Art. I, s. 2.

124 "The federal Constitution, therefore, decides with great propriety on the case of our slaves, when it views them in the mixed character of persons and of property. This is in fact their true character. It is the character bestowed on them by the laws under which they live; and it will not be denied, that these are the proper criterion; because it is only under the pretext that the laws have transformed the negroes into subjects of property, that a place is disputed them in the computation of numbers; and it is admitted, that if the laws were to restore the rights which have been taken away, the negroes could no longer be refused an equal share of representation with the other inhabitants." Alexander Hamilton, "The Federalist 54," in Hamilton (ed.), *The Federalist*, pp. 417–418.

eight hundred and eight…"[125] Congress would give effect to this language, banning the African slave trade by statute in 1807, effective January 1, 1808.[126] In *The Federalist 42*, Madison framed the Migration and Importation Clause "as a great point gained in favor of humanity" and decried efforts to cast it as "a criminal toleration of an illicit practice."[127] Nonetheless, slave traders routinely violated federal law by importing slaves well after the ban on such practices,[128] nor was there the "considerable discouragement from the federal government" of slave importation that Madison predicted would occur in the twenty-year period prior to the ban.[129]

These ambiguities regarding the constitutional status of slavery gave ammunition to both sides to attack its compatibility with republican principles.[130] While the Northwest Ordinance had prohibited slavery in the territories,[131] debates over the admission of these territories into the Union revealed that Congress had authority to substantially shape the form of state governments, possibly extending to a ban on slavery.[132] Those who rejected the admission of Missouri as a slave state, for example, explicitly argued that slavery was fundamentally incompatible with republican principles.[133] Guided by the Northwest Ordinance, anti-slavery advocates asserted that its requirement that "the constitution and State government so to be formed

[125] United States Constitution Art. I s. 9. Article I, Section 9 provides, in its entirety, "The Migration or Importation of such Persons as any of the States now existing shall think proper to admit, shall not be prohibited by the Congress prior to the Year one thousand eight hundred and eight, but a Tax or duty may be imposed on such Importation, not exceeding ten dollars for each person."

[126] An Act to Prohibit Importation of Slaves Into Any Port or Place Within the Jurisdiction of the United States, From and After the First Day of January, in the Year of Our Lord One Thousand Eight Hundred and Eight (Act Prohibiting Importation of Slaves of 1807), ch. 22, 2 Stat. 426 (1807).

[127] James Madison, "The Federalist 42," in Hamilton (ed.), *The Federalist*, pp. 330–331.

[128] "After the federal abolition of the trade went into effect January 1, 1808, hundreds of illegal slaving voyages with American connections crisscrossed the Atlantic Ocean, bringing captives not just to the United States but also to the two largest destinations for enslaved Africans during this period, Brazil and Cuba. … After the ban, American ships smuggled around 8,000 enslaved Africans to U.S. shores, usually through the Gulf of Mexico, and sold them illicitly to cotton planters in the Deep South." Manuel Barcia and John Harris, "The Slave Trade Continued Long after It Was Illegal – With Lessons for Today," *Washington Post*, December 6, 2020. www.washingtonpost.com/outlook/2020/12/06/slave-trade-continued-long-after-it-was-illegal-with-lessons-today/.

[129] James Madison, "The Federalist 42," in Hamilton (ed.), *The Federalist*, p. 331.

[130] For an overview of the debates on this topic during this period, see "The Politics of Southern Upheaval, 1846–1853," in James L. Huston, *Calculating the Value of the Union: Slavery, Property Rights, and the Economic Origins of the Civil War* (Chapel Hill: University of North Carolina Press, 2003), pp. 164–189.

[131] Northwest Ordinance of 1787, s. 14, art. 6.

[132] Lerche, "Admission of New States," 578.

[133] During the Missouri debates, it became clear that restrictionists saw it as "axiomatic … that slavery was incompatible with a republican government[.]" William Wiecek, *The Sources of Anti-Slavery Constitutionalism in America, 1760–1848* (Ithaca: Cornell University Press, 1977), p. 119. When Missouri was admitted to the union in 1821, its constitution included the following provision: "The general assembly shall have no power to pass laws … [f]or the emancipation of slaves without consent of their owners[.]" Constitution of Missouri (1820), Art. III, s. 25.

'shall be republican,'" meant no slavery upon admission.[134] Advocates of this position turned to the Constitution's bar on migration and importation of slaves as further evidence that, after 1808, a state could no longer be republican if it joined the Union as a slave state.[135] In 1808, there were nine free states and eight slave states; consistent with this argument, the sixteen states admitted between 1808 and 1859 would have all had to be admitted as free states, arguably hastening the demise of slavery and possibly avoiding the Civil War.[136]

Not only did the Federal Constitution implicitly sanction slavery,[137] according to opponents of this view, but Tennessee (admitted 1796), Louisiana (admitted 1812), Mississippi (admitted 1817), and Alabama (admitted 1819) had already been admitted as slave states; the latter three after 1808, making it difficult to argue that republicanism could not coexist with slavery.[138] As one pro-slavery advocate noted, foreshadowing the infamous *Dred Scott* decision discussed in Chapter 3,[139] "Congress … not only has no power to impose the contemplated restriction on the State of Missouri, when admitted into the Union; but having guarantied [sic] to the owners of slaves,

134 Northwest Ordinance of 1787, s. 14, Art. 5. See also Matthew J. Festa, "Property and Republicanism in the Northwest Ordinance" (2013) 45 *Arizona State Law Journal* 409–470, 458 ("[M]any in the founding era believed that slavery was incompatible with the personal independence that formed the very core of the republican vision for society. … By precluding slavery, the Ordinance indicated the intent to have the territory settled by citizens who would have the independence and the virtue to secure a republican society in the western lands. It is possible, then to see the abolition clause of the Ordinance as part and parcel of the larger republican vision for the new territory.").

135 United States Constitution Art. I, s. 9.

136 In 1808, the free states were Pennsylvania (1787), New Jersey (1787), Connecticut (1788), Massachusetts (1788), New Hampshire (1788), New York (1788), Rhode Island (1790), Vermont (1791), and Ohio (1803). The slave states were Delaware (1787), Georgia (1788), Maryland (1788), South Carolina (1788), Virginia (1788), North Carolina (1789), Kentucky (1792), and Tennessee (1796). The states admitted between 1808 and 1859 were Louisiana (1812), Indiana (1816), Mississippi (1817), Illinois (1818), Alabama (1819), Maine (1820), Missouri (1821), Arkansas (1836), Michigan (1837), Florida (1845), Texas (1845), Iowa (1846), Wisconsin (1848), California (1850), Minnesota (1858), and Oregon (1859).

137 "Comments of Mr. Elliott of Georgia of Friday, January 11, 1820," 35 *Annals of Congress of the United States* (Washington, D.C.: Gales and Seaton, 1855), p. 130 ("the admission of involuntary servitude into a State does not affect the form of the Government, nor violate the Federal Constitution; for one-half of the States in the Union allow of it, and the Federal Constitution expressly recognises and sanctions it. Under the Constitution, then, an, State in this Union may admit involuntary servitude within its limits, in the exercise of its unquestionable right of self-government; and Congress cannot be supposed to have power to impose a restriction, which the State has authority to abrogate at pleasure").

138 "Comments of Mr. Roberts of Pennsylvania of Friday, January 11, 1820," 35 *Annals of Congress of the United States* (Washington, D.C.: Gales and Seaton, 1855), p. 125. But see "Comments of Mr. Elliott of Georgia," ibid., 130 ("The terms migration and importation are not synonymous. Migration implies volition, choice, self-direction but they belong not to a slave. He may be carried or imported, or he may abscond, but he can never migrate. The Irish, the Scotch, and the Dutch, migrate to this country, and it was probably to prevent Congress until after the year 1808, from interdicting this practice, under the authority given to that body "to establish a uniform rule of naturalization," that the word migration was introduced in this section. But importation applies to slaves.").

139 *Dred Scott v. Sandford*, 60 U.S. (19 How.) 393 (1857).

in the ceded territory, the free enjoyment of their property, that body could not, under any Territorial regulation, have imposed such a restriction."[140]

Thomas Jefferson, in a letter to John Adams in January 1821, similarly argued that Congress had no such authority to condition state admission on the ban of slavery, and that conceding such authority would precipitate violence. "If Congress has the power to regulate the conditions of the inhabitants of the states, within the states, it will be but another exercise of that power to declare that all shall be free," leading Jefferson to wonder, "Are our slaves to be presented with freedom and a dagger?"[141]

To be clear, slavery was not necessarily inconsistent with the principles of republicanism and self-government embraced by the founding generation. Republicanism was based on the idea of rule by the virtuous few (who could effectively communicate the preferences of the majority) over those who lacked the required independence to govern themselves. As historian Edmund Morgan has argued, "Whenever debt brought a man under another's power, he lost more than his own freedom of action He also weakened the capacity of his country to survive as a republic."[142] The debate over slavery similarly emphasized that independence remained important in republican theory. However, republicanism had also been premised on the presumed equality of all, despite the unfitness of some to govern, because this unfitness derived from idleness rather than one's natural predisposition.[143]

Race-based slavery brought these strands of republican thought together, by overcoming the socioeconomic barriers that divided White people and infantilizing Black people to paint them as inherently unfit to govern. As the cornerstones of civic virtue, slaveowners stressed both the absolute equality of all White people,

140 "Comments of Mr. Elliott of Georgia of Friday, January 11, 1820," 35 *Annals of Congress of the United States* (Washington, D.C.: Gales and Seaton, 1855), p. 132. And, foreshadowing the equal sovereignty argument that would be used in more than a century later in *Shelby County v. Holder*, 570 U.S. 529 (2013), pro-slavery advocates would question this particular use of the Guarantee Clause to "impose restrictions upon the States hereafter to be admitted into the Union; thereby producing an invidious inequality in the rights and privileges of the States? Will this not be to sow the seeds of jealousy and distrust?" Ibid.; see also "Comments of Mr. Barbour of Virginia of Tuesday, February 1, 1820," 35 *Annals of Congress of the United States* (Washington, D.C.: Gales and Seaton, 1855), p. 323 ("This shows that in all other respects, they were to be on an equal looting with the old States; for, had not such been the design of the Convention, as they -discriminated in the one case, they would have done so in every particular where it was intended.").

141 "Thomas Jefferson to John Adams, 22 January 1821," *Founders Online*, National Archives, https://founders.archives.gov/documents/Jefferson/03-16-02-0465. [Original source: J. Jefferson Looney et al. (eds.), *The Papers of Thomas Jefferson*, Retirement Series, vol. 16, *1 June 1820 to 28 February 1821* (Princeton: Princeton University Press, 2019), pp. 562–564.]

142 Edmund Morgan, "Slavery and Freedom: The American Paradox" (1972) 59 *Journal of American History*, 5–29, 8 ("A nation of men, each of whom owned enough property to support his family, could be a republic. It would follow that a nation of debtors, who had lost their property or mortgaged it to creditors, was ripe for tyranny.").

143 Ibid., 10 (noting that the belief that "people in the lowest condition, the dregs of society, generally arrived at that position through their own vice and misconduct, whether in ancient Rome or modern Britain, was an unexamined article of faith among eighteenth-century republicans")

leaving open the prospect of upward social mobility, and the biological inferiority of African Americans, which made them suitable for enslavement given their genetic predisposition to dependence.[144] As servitude became increasingly associated with skin color from the late seventeenth to the early eighteenth century, White yeoman farmers gained a greater voice in state legislatures, since they posed less of a threat to the ruling class. Thomas Jefferson's exhortations about the inalienable rights of man became a big tent that united White people across classes – and indeed, regions – and facilitated notions of republicanism and representative government despite the existence of chattel slavery.[145]

White supremacy became a principle that united Northerners and Southerners alike, which undermined northern attacks on the spread of slavery into the territories even if, ideologically, they opposed it.[146] Whites in the South pointed to enslavement as an appropriate station for African Americans given their inherent inferiority and lack of humanity.[147] In contrast, Northerners emphasized the inherent inferiority of Black people, independent of slavery, while painting themselves as morally superior to Southerners by advocating against slavery.[148]

Some Northerners opposed the spread of slavery because of the moral questions raised by treating people as property, and they interpreted the Constitution accordingly.[149] Others, however, wanted to put a firewall between the North and

[144] William W. Freehling, *The Road to Disunion: Secessionists at Bay*, 2 vols. (New York: Oxford University Press, 1990), vol. I, p. 40 ("The nineteenth century's newly rampart racism read blacks out of the new biological equality. Civic virtue now required superior racial genes. The slaveholder must now defer to virtuous white citizens but dictate to degraded black noncitizens."). See also Morgan, "Slavery and Freedom', 12–13 ("When Jefferson contemplated the abolition of slavery, he found it inconceivable that the freed slaves should be allowed to remain in the country. In this attitude he was probably moved by his or his countrymen's racial prejudice. But he may also have had in mind the possibility that when slaves ceased to be slaves, they would become instead a half million idle poor, who would create the same problems for the United States that the idle poor of Europe did for their states."). See also ibid., 28 ("A free society divided between large landholders and small was much less riven by antagonisms than one divided between landholders and land-less, masterless men. With the freedman's expectations, sobriety, and status restored, he was no longer a man to be feared. That fact, together with the presence of a growing mass of alien slaves, tended to draw the white settlers closer together and to reduce the importance of the class difference between yeoman farmer and large plantation owner.").

[145] Morgan, "Slavery and Freedom," 29 ("It was slavery, I suggest, more than any other single factor, that had made the difference, slavery that enabled Virginia to nourish representative government in a plantation society … slavery that made the Virginians dare to speak a political language that magnified the rights of freemen, and slavery, therefore, that brought Virginians into the same commonwealth political tradition with New Englanders. The very institution that was to divide North and South after the Revolution may have made possible their union in a republican government.").

[146] James G. Gigantino II, "Slavery and the Creation of Arkansas Territory: A Reconsideration" (2019) 78 *Arkansas Historical Quarterly*, 231–247, 241.

[147] See, e.g., *Neal v. Farmer*, 9 Ga. 555 (Ga. Sup. Ct. 1851) (holding that the killing of a slave is not murder because the common law does not apply to the slave).

[148] See Eugene H. Berwanger, "Negrophobia in Northern Proslavery and Antislavery Thought" (1972) 33 *Phylon*, 266–275.

[149] See generally Festa, "Property and Republicanism."

the South. This led them to accept political compromises that permitted slavery's spread, based on the dubious argument that diffusing the slave population across these territories would ultimately lead to its abolition.[150] In reality, the expansion of slavery into Arkansas and Missouri meant that free Black people and fugitive enslaved people continued to travel north. This sparked fears among Northerners that Black people, once they reached sufficient numbers, would rebel against the White population.[151] Abolitionist sentiments notwithstanding, this fear incentivized northern states to engage in extensive racial discrimination, arguing that Black people could never embody republican ideals.[152] Ironically, the concern about in-migration by free Black people drove much of the northern opposition to the spread of slavery in the territories, while also providing fodder for Southerners' arguments that the inferiority of Black people rendered them unfit for citizenship but fit for enslavement.[153]

Taking advantage of this incoherence, pro-slavery advocates auditioned several lines of argument in the context of admitting new states with two goals in mind: (1) to perfect the relationship between republicanism and slavery, and (2) to leave little daylight between the scope of the Guarantee Clause and the politics surrounding the slavery debate. To understand the distinction between these two goals, the first assumes that Congress's obligation to ensure republican government does not extend past the point of admission (i.e., slave states existed at ratification and must be presumptively republican); the other does not (i.e., what counts as republican government can change).

With respect to the first point, John C. Calhoun noted that Congress "in determining whether the Government of a state be, or not be republican, within the meaning of the Constitution, has no right to look beyond its admission to the Union."[154] But even if Congress has to assess whether state governments were republican in form at admission, arguably this obligation kicked in "[w]henever the States may choose to substitute other republican forms … [and] claim the federal guaranty."

150 Gigantino II, "Slavery and the Creation of Arkansas Territory: A Reconsideration," 244–245 ("When northern newspapers, targeting those representatives who had voted for permitting slavery in Arkansas, questioned why they voted to extend such a vile and inhumane system westward, Jonathan Mason, a Federalists from Massachusetts, responded that, though he understood that his constituents opposed expansion, he believed that Americans has the right to travel across the country with slaves, 'thereby lessening the evils of their condition and giving them more comfort and health.'").

151 Ibid., 241 ("The presence of free blacks represented a distinct danger to northern whites. They feared rebellion inspired by the Haitian declaration of independence…").

152 Ibid., 243.

153 Ibid., 242 ("The expansion of slavery in Arkansas and Missouri did not, in many people's imagination, promise a diffusion of the black population away from the North as some had hoped, but, quite the opposite, promised to flood the region with freed people of color. Missouri's proposed constitution included a prohibition on free blacks living in the state, raising fears that free blacks, barred from much of the South, would soon head north, or stay in the North.").

154 Clyde N. Wilson et al. (eds.), *The Papers of John C. Calhoun*, 28 vols. (Columbia: University of South Carolina Press, 1959–2003) vol. 17, p. 277.

The ever-evolving nature of republicanism during the nineteenth century, from the inchoate conceptual frame of the Enlightenment (in which republicanism embodied many forms of government) to a system of majoritarianism centered on the community of voters (facilitated by political parties), meant that this congressional assessment of republicanism also evolved. Slaveowners wanted slavery to be consistent with republicanism in either scenario, pre- or post-admission. From this perspective, even if one viewed slavery as fundamentally incompatible with republican government, the argument was that if some people could vote and participate – thereby establishing a republican government – then the duly-elected state legislature could subject the masses to unrepublican laws.[155]

Thus, Madison's position in *The Federalist* 39 – that republican government derived its power from "the great body of the people" – did not necessarily prohibit a sizeable portion of the population from being enslaved (or being disenfranchised, for that matter). Along these lines (and holding up the thirteen colonies as models), one major argument, advanced by prominent Democratic Republican William Pinkney of Maryland, was that republicanism required that the form of government be a sufficient vehicle for conveying the public good, but said nothing about the outputs of that government, once government was properly formed:

> The government of a new State, as well as of an old State, must, I agree, be republican in its form. But it has not been very clearly explained what the laws which such a government may enact can have to do with its form. The form of the government is material only as it furnishes a security that those laws will protect and promote the public happiness, and be made in a republican spirit. The people being, in such a Government, the fountain of all power, and their servants being periodically responsible to them for its exercise, the Constitution of the Union takes for granted … that every such exercise will be just and salutary. The introduction or continuance of civil slavery is manifestly the mere result of the power of making laws. It does not, in any degree enter into the form of the government.[156]

These arguments by the slavocracy tended to be less about internal consistency and offering a principled conception of congressional power, and more so about accounting for changing political circumstances. Thus, justifications ranged from Pinkney's distinction between form and outputs to arguments that Congress's authority was limited to regulating the political aspects of state government rather than "nonpolitical" issues like slavery.[157] Still others argued Congress's authority was limited to protecting state governments once established, as opposed to imposing limits on the establishment of state governments.[158]

[155] Lerche, "Admission of New States," 581.
[156] "Comments of Mr. Pinkney of Maryland of Tuesday, February 15, 1820," 35 *Annals of Congress of the United States* (Washington, D.C.: Gales and Seaton, 1855), pp. 409–412.
[157] Lerche, "Admission of New States," 583.
[158] Ibid.

With respect to this last point, there was a circularity to this argument. For example, if noncitizens could participate in the formation of the government – especially those who satisfied the independence and virtue requirements at the heart of republican theory – the fact they could later be disenfranchised through state law should pose similar theoretical concerns.[159] Whether the requirements of republican government are met, and whether Congress has an obligation to police it, cannot plausibly depend on if otherwise independent voters are excluded after government is formed or during its creation (or vice versa) – this would truly be a triumph of form over substance. Yet noncitizen voting remained a live issue in the admission of new states, as Congress repeatedly confronted the issue of whether to admit states whose constitutions extended the franchise to this group.

However inconsistent or self-serving they may have been, the arguments of slaveowners put Congress in the position of according recognition to unrepublican state governments in circumstances that had little to do with slavery, at least not directly. This reflected a deeper structural problem: there was no explicit constitutional check on Congress's authority to define the parameters of republican government.[160] *The Federalist* 43 suggested only that Congress's obligation to ensure republican government was ongoing but left the details largely to Congress.

159 This excerpt from a June 1826 speech by Mr. Hamer of Ohio described this paradox as it related to noncitizens:

> Another objection is, that aliens have aided in making this constitution, and are allowed the right of suffrage in all elections by the provisions it contains. As to the first point, it is sufficient to say that all the new States northwest of the Ohio formed their constitutions precisely in the same way. The ordinance of 1787 does not require sixty thousand *citizens* of the United States to be resident within the limits of a new State, in order to authorize a constitution and admission into the Union. It requires that number of 'free inhabitants,' and the alien who resides there, if he be a 'free inhabitant' is entitled to vote in the election of delegates to the convention; and afterwards, in deciding whether the people will accept the constitution formed by their convention. Such has been the construction and practice in all the country north of the Ohio; aid as the last census shows that there are but a few hundreds of aliens in Michigan, it would be hard to set aside their constitution, because some of these may have participated in its formation. It would be unjust to do so, if we had the power; but we have no authority to do it; for if we regard the ordinance as of any validity, it allows all 'free inhabitants' to vote in framing the State governments, which are to be created within the sphere of its influence.

"Speech of Mr. Hamer of Ohio of June, 1826," 24 *Congressional Globe Appendix* (Washington, D.C.: Globe Office, 1836), p. 607. But see Jamin B. Raskin, "Legal Aliens, Local Citizens: The Historical, Constitutional and Theoretical Meanings of Alien Suffrage" (1993) 141 *University of Pennsylvania Law Review*, 1391–1470, 1401 (noting that "[T]he War of 1812, which produced a militant nationalism and suspicion of foreigners, heralded the end of the Revolutionary period of liberal attitudes towards noncitizen voting. In 1812, beginning with Louisiana, most newly admitted states … confined the franchise to citizens.").

160 Ibid. ("No slave state was again to enter the Union without some effort to evoke the coercive power they saw residing in the guarantee. Although no modifications in practice were accomplished, the extreme positive concept of the guarantee was refined and extended in the course of later slavery debates, and when secession brought about the crisis that had been predicted in 1820 the guarantee was ready at hand as a convenient tool.").

According to Madison, "As long, therefore, as the existing forms are continued by the States, they are guaranteed by the federal constitution. Whenever the States may choose to substitute other republican forms they have a right to do so, and to claim the federal guaranty for the latter."[161] But slaveowners had outsized power in the federal government that helped their arguments carry the day. The Supreme Court compounded this problem, placing the authority to determine the nature of republican government firmly with the political branches and further cementing the partisan nature of the inquiry.[162]

The consequences extended beyond slavery, with controversy emerging over other proposed admissions: Michigan (noncitizen suffrage),[163] Minnesota (noncitizen suffrage, no periodic elections),[164] and Oregon (exclusion of free Black people from the state).[165] In each case, the question of whether a state's constitution met republican standards was entangled with larger ideological and sectional battles, revealing just how unstable and politicized the federal government's commitment to republicanism could be.

Michigan, for example, did not permit slavery, but its constitution extended voting rights to noncitizens.[166] Its admission caused significant controversy and raised

161 James Madison, "The Federalist 43," in Hamilton (ed.), *The Federalist*, p. 342.

162 See Chapter 4 (discussing *Luther v. Borden*).

163 Michigan's admission to the Union took place in 1837, at which time the state's constitution granted the right to vote to both "citizens" and "inhabitants" – specifically, "every white male citizen above the age of twenty-one years, having resided in the state six months next preceding any election," and any other white man of sufficient age "who may be a resident of this state at the time of the signing of this constitution[.]" Constitution of Michigan art. II, s. 1 (1835).

164 Minnesota's constitution at the time of its admission to the Union in 1858 provided the right to vote to four separate classes of men aged 21 and older, as follows:

> "White citizens of the United States,"
> "White persons of foreign birth, who shall have declared their intention to become citizens ... of the United States,"
> "Persons of mixed white and Indian blood, who have adopted the customs and habits of civilization," and
> "Persons of Indian blood" as long as they resided in the state and had passed an examination, issued by a state court, showing that they had "adopted the language, customs, and habits of civilization."

Constitution of Minnesota art. VII, s. 1 (1857).

Minnesota also did not provide for periodic elections; instead, any vacancies were filled by gubernatorial appointment. Constitution of Minnesota art. IV, s. 17 (1857) ("The Governor shall issue writs of election to fill such vacancies as may occur in either House of the Legislature...").

165 The constitution of Oregon that was in effect when it was admitted to the Union in 1859 included the following provision: "White foreigners who are or may hereafter become residents of this State shall enjoy the same rights in respect to the possession, enjoyment and descent of property as native born citizens. And the Legislative Assembly shall have power to restrain and regulate the immigration to this State of persons not qualified to become citizens of the United States." Constitution of Oregon art I, s. 32 (1857).

166 Michigan's 1835 constitution granted the right to vote to both "citizens" and "inhabitants" – specifically, "every white male citizen above the age of twenty-one years, having resided in the state six

questions about Congress's authority under the Clause. Was Congress empowered to alter the internal structure of the state by preventing the enfranchisement of noncitizens or merely authorized to guarantee self-government?[167] As it turned out, Michigan's admission would not resolve whether Congress's power under the Clause was limited to only ensuring self-government. However, the dispute confirmed that Congress had a role to play in the construction of the political community of voters. Congress upheld Michigan's enfranchisement of noncitizens on the grounds that the Northwest Ordinance of 1787 defined republican government to include governments formed by free inhabitants who might also be noncitizen voters.[168]

By approving Michigan's constitution on the grounds that the Northwest Ordinance sanctioned the involvement of immigrants in territorial elections by referencing "free persons," Congress was able to avoid any resolutions about the scope of its authority that would have huge political implications for slavery. According to one scholar, extending political rights to immigrants placed pro-slavery forces "in a dilemma" because "alien suffrage was contrary to their aristocratic theories of government, but to call it anti-republican would open their case on slavery to devastating assaults, since they would thus be advocating an interference with a domestic institution of a state."[169] Thus, the individuals most likely to reject Michigan's constitution were pro-slavery representatives, not the anti-slavery forces,[170] even though in opposing the state constitution they were arguably endorsing broad congressional power to impose limits on the establishment of state governments (rather than protecting state governments once established).

Like Michigan, the controversy over the constitutions of Minnesota and Oregon also cast doubt on arguments by pro-slavery advocates that the Clause allowed Congress to object to the form of government but not its legislative outputs.

months next preceding any election," and any other white man of sufficient age "who may be a resident of this state at the time of the signing of this constitution[.]" Constitution of Michigan art. II, s. 1 (1835).

167 Lerche summarized the two views as follows:

> Pro-slavery forces insisted republican government was self- government, and that there was no power in the guarantee to alter the internal arrangements of a state. On the opposite side, Representative Hard of New York took the most extreme position expressed up to this time: If Congress, then, in admitting a new State, is bound to guaranty a re- publican form of government, a duty is created which raises a corresponding right to inquire into the terms of the government founded by the State to be admitted, and a right to dictate the form of its fundamental code or constitution, with a view of rendering it consistent with such a form of government; and this it has a right to do, as a fundamental condition of its admission.

Lerche, "Admission of New States," 583.

168 Ibid., 583, 585–586. See generally ibid., 578.

169 Ibid., 585.

170 There were exceptions, of course. See Magliocca, *American Founding Son*, p.62–63 (noting that John Bingham opposed the admission of Oregon and Michigan because both territories gave noncitizens the right to vote).

Minnesota's constitution, through poor drafting, appeared to grant its first legislature life tenure. While the creation of a perpetual legislature clearly touches on the form of government, Congress ultimately accepted Minnesota's constitution because its legislators were elected by something resembling universal White male suffrage. But the notion that the Minnesota voters could legitimately ratify a government with life tenure, a concept that was clearly unrepublican, strains credulity.

The debate over Oregon's admission further established that many of the constraints on federal power were political rather than constitutional. Although seeking to enter the Union as a free state, Oregon barred the in-migration of any African Americans into the state, a fact that led some anti-slavery representatives, including John Bingham, to vote against admission.[171] Like Minnesota, Oregon's constitution was arguably anti-republican. Some representatives in Congress questioned the ability of Oregon to exclude free Black people from its borders – a law that, but for *Dred Scott*,[172] would have raised nonfrivolous legal and political issues.[173] But the point was clear: Oregon, gaining statehood in 1859, and Minnesota, in 1860, came into the Union at a time in which the slavery question was coming to a head. Concerns about federal power were poised to tear the country apart, leading Congress to stay its hand.

To some extent, congressional acquiescence over Minnesota and Oregon might have reflected the lessons learned from the admission of Kansas. The debate over the Kansas–Nebraska Act in the early 1850s and the resulting violence in the territory, discussed in the next chapter, reveal how much of Congress's power and the meaning of the republican guarantee was increasingly shaped by the national political controversy over slavery. "Bleeding Kansas," as it came to be known, was the flashpoint that illustrated that Congress's conception of its Guarantee Clause authority was shifting.

Prior to Kansas's admission, the interpretation preferred by southern pro-slavery advocates – that republicanism embraced a broad variety of governments – prevailed. During Reconstruction, the preferred interpretation became one in which Congress forced a more uniform interpretation of republicanism by requiring state political systems to comply with majoritarian principles. To facilitate this process,

171 Oregon's 1857 Constitution included the following provision: "White foreigners who are or may hereafter become residents of this State shall enjoy the same rights in respect to the possession, enjoyment and descent of property as native born citizens. And the Legislative Assembly shall have power to restrain and regulate the immigration to this State of persons not qualified to become citizens of the United States." Constitution of Oregon art I, s. 32 (1857).

172 In its 1857 *Dred Scott* opinion, the Supreme Court held that descendants of enslaved Africans were not eligible to be citizens of the United States and did not enjoy any constitutional protections. *Dred Scott v. Sandford*, 60 U.S. (19 How.) 393 (1857). Accordingly, the states were constitutionally permitted to enact laws that discriminated against them.

173 Lerche, "Admission of New States," 586–587.

Congress aggregated its Guarantee Clause authority with its power under other constitutional provisions – most notably, the Elections Clause and Article I, Section – to further challenge the limited view of federal power that had been standard prior to the Civil War. As Chapter 2 shows, Congress's use of these provisions, much like its exercise of its Guarantee Clause power, initially started out quite modestly.

2

Federalism as a Political Construct?

Federal Power under the Elections Clause and Article I, Section 5

The weather on March 4, 1849, was unexceptional in the universe of presidential inauguration days. It was slightly colder but less brisk than the weather that contributed to the death of President William Henry Harrison in 1841 after he delivered a speech – without outerwear – that clocked in at almost two hours. Nor was the day marred by the snow that forced President William Howard Taft to deliver his speech indoors in 1909. Rather, the problem with March 4, 1849, was that it was a Sunday. General Zachary Taylor absolutely refused to be sworn in as president on a Sunday, arguing that the oath of office could only be administered on business days, not the Sabbath, which he devoutly observed.[1] The problem, however, was that President Polk's term of office officially ended at noon on March 4th with no one in the role of president or vice president. In 1849, the line of succession, after the president and vice president, included the senate president pro tempore, an office held in this case by David Atchison, a powerful senator from Missouri.

"Bourbon" Dave was a pro-slavery Democrat who served in the U.S. Senate from 1843 until 1855. He is not well known for his stint as one-day president, in which he signed a few official papers in connection with the inauguration but otherwise served as a placeholder for President Taylor until noon on Monday, March 5th. This one-day president is better known for his role in precipitating Bleeding Kansas, a dispute that forced Congress into a full-throated endorsement of broad federal power over elections in the years immediately preceding the Civil War.

The shift to an increasingly aggressive federal presence was gradual. In the first half of the nineteenth century, Congress had no interest in displacing state authority over elections, at least not in a manner that would cede to the federal government any role in defining the qualifications of electors. As the prior chapter shows, the

1 John W. Townsend, "History of David Rice Atchison of Kentucky," (1910) 8 *Register of Kentucky State Historical Society* 39–44, 37, 41. See also Stacy Conradt, "David Rice Atchison, One-Day President," *Mental Floss*, September 27, 2022, www.mentalfloss.com/article/61234/grave-sightings-david-rice-atchison-one-day-president [https://perma.cc/Y6WJ-9DK7].

Guarantee Clause offered one avenue of federal intervention into the regulation of state political systems. The desire to promote republican values was colored by partisanship and disputes over the legality of slavery, which impacted debates not only over the form of government that states could establish at the point of admission but also later decisions about the allocation of political power within a state. The ratification of the Twelfth Amendment, in a sense, constitutionalized political parties and partisanship as a means of ascertaining the majority sentiment that lies at the heart of republicanism.

In some ways, the Twelfth Amendment was also an invitation for greater federal involvement over elections, given that parties operated horizontally across state government, causing tension between dueling factions, and vertically, converging the interests of partisan state and federal officials. But the use of federal power to alter state political systems remained rare. In most circumstances, Congress's commitment to a political system in which a winner was chosen from a process legitimized by clear rules and a definitive outcome generally trumped any desire to use electoral disputes as a vehicle for asserting the primacy of federal law. Even in situations in which state procedures were not ideal, Congress still deferred to state authority to promote these broader values. Early in the country's history, deference to state law, or more accurately, Congress's self-imposed "federalism" constraints, brought coherence and administrative ease to a system in which multiple states had de facto control over federal elections.[2]

While Congress was generally reticent about interfering with state power over elections, there were times in which Congress discarded its self-imposed federalism constraints when politically expedient. That body had to reassert the primacy of federal law on several occasions early in the country's history, negating any inference that the states were truly sovereign over federal elections. These displays of federal power often occurred when legislating pursuant to the Elections Clause[3] or resolving

2 These self-imposed federalism constraints were consistent with at least some views of federal power under the Clause at the country's founding. See "Ratification of the Constitution by the State of New York (July 26, 1788)," in *Documentary History of the Constitution of the United States of America, 1786–1870*, 3 vols. (Washington, D.C.: Department of State, 1894), vol. 2, p. 197 (stating "that the Congress will not make or alter any Regulation in this State respecting the times places and manner of holding Elections for Senators or Representatives, unless the Legislature of such State shall neglect or refuse to make Laws or Regulations for the purpose, or from any circumstance be incapable of making the same; and then only until the Legislature of such State shall make provision in the premises … ."). Rhode Island's proposed amendments, submitted two years after New York's, include identical language. "Ratification of the Constitution by the State of Rhode Island and the Providence Plantations (May 29, 1790)," *Documentary History*, vol. 2, p. 315. See also Franita Tolson, "Reinventing Sovereignty?: Federalism as a Constraint on the Voting Rights Act" (2012) 65 *Vanderbilt Law Review* 1195–1259, 1224–25 (discussing similar proposals in other states).

3 The "Elections Clause" reads as follows: "The Times, Places and Manner of holding Elections for Senators and Representatives, shall be prescribed in each State by the Legislature thereof; but the Congress may at any time by Law make or alter such Regulations, except as to the Places of chusing Senators." United States Constitution Art. 1, s. 4.

election disputes pursuant to Article I, Section 5.[4] In contrast to the Guarantee Clause, these provisions offered another route of intervention, but at a more micro level – now that state governments had been established as republican in form, are their rules that govern federal elections operating in a manner that is complimentary to, rather than in conflict with, the structure of the federal government? Additionally, to what extent do federalism principles constrain congressional action under the Elections Clause and Article I, Section 5? For exercises of federal power under these provisions, this chapter will show that federalism was a political construct in much the same way as republicanism had been for Congress's authority under the Guarantee Clause.

2.1 THE ELECTIONS CLAUSE AS A POST-ADMISSION LIMIT ON THE POWER OF STATE GOVERNMENTS

While the Guarantee Clause empowers Congress to police state governments based on an ill-defined concept of republicanism, the constitutional framework is straightforward in how, post-admission, political power over federal elections is allocated between the states and the federal government. An uninformed read of the original Constitution suggests that states have the power to decide who votes in federal elections (via Article I, Section 2);[5] Congress has final say about the procedural rules that govern these elections (via the Elections Clause); and Congress ultimately decides which representatives get seated post-election (via Article I, Section 5). But the system is much more fluid than this structure suggests, a point that is especially powerful considering that the constitutional framework embraces multiple layers of authority to prevent, to the best of its ability,[6] both levels of government from being sovereign in the same regulatory sphere at the same time.

The colonies inherited the concept of divided government from Great Britain.[7] The pre-Revolutionary period initially split sovereignty between the Crown and Parliament, but then Parliament became the dominant sovereign, consistent with prevailing notions that sovereignty had to be unlimited and undivided within a

4 "Each House shall be the Judge of the Elections, Returns and Qualifications of its own Members, and a Majority of each shall constitute a Quorum to do Business; but a smaller Number may adjourn from day to day, and may be authorized to compel the Attendance of absent Members, in such Manner, and under such Penalties as each House may provide." United States Constitution Art. 1, s. 5, cl. 1.

5 "The House of Representatives shall be composed of Members chosen every second Year by the People of the several States. ... When vacancies happen in the Representation from any State, the Executive Authority thereof shall issue Writs of Election to fill such Vacancies." United States Constitution Art. 1, s. 2, cl. 1 and 4.

6 Sometimes maintaining these silos is impossible and impractical.

7 See Alison L. LaCroix, *The Ideological Origins of American Federalism* (Cambridge: Harvard University Press, 2011), p. 5 (citing *U.S. Term Limits, Inc. v. Thornton*, 514 U.S. 779, 838 (1995) (Kennedy, J., concurring)) ("The Framers split the atom of sovereignty .... [T]heir idea that our citizens would have two political capacities, one state and one federal, each protected by incursion from the other....").

single polity.[8] Throughout this period, the colonies continued to exercise autonomy over areas of local jurisdiction, but Parliament was technically the locus of sovereign authority.[9] The absence of divided authority fueled many of the disputes between Great Britain and the colonists, as Parliament sought to govern the colonies with little to no input from those subject to its authority.[10]

The post-Revolutionary period reflected these concerns regarding power being concentrated in one supreme authority. The struggle over how sovereign authority should be delegated continued well after the colonists split from Great Britain. The emaciated Congress that operated under the Articles of Confederation (1783–89) was a byproduct of this fear of centralized power. The delegates to the Constitutional Convention of 1787 recognized that states had to cede more power to the federal government without undermining their sovereignty. To avoid the despotism of parliamentary sovereignty, the new constitution gave states control over local matters – including, importantly, state elections – and the federal government would exercise power only over limited areas that exceeded the scope of local competencies.[11] Sovereignty, at least from the late eighteenth century on, was not "final, unqualified, and indivisible" in only one body; instead, the power was divided between two sovereigns, each responsible for specific policy areas, with ultimate sovereignty lying with the people.[12]

The Articles of Confederation were also ineffective because of Congress's inability to control the content or direction of state laws that conflicted with its own dictates. To address this problem, Charles Pinckney proposed during the Constitutional Convention "that the National Legislature should have authority to negative all laws which they should judge to be improper."[13] Both Pinckney and James Madison believed that a congressional veto was necessary because "the States must be kept in

8 Ibid., pp. 13–15 (noting that throughout the seventeenth and eighteenth centuries, "[t]he idea that separate and equal authorities could exist within the same juridical boundaries offended contemporary understandings of the very nature of government power" and noting that some commentators stated that Parliament "hath sovereign and uncontrollable authority…").

9 See Bernard Bailyn, *The Ideological Origins of the American Revolution* (Cambridge: Harvard University Press, 1967), pp. 200, 202–203 (noting that except for certain powers England exercised over "only the outer fringes of colonial life" that "[a]ll other powers were enjoyed … by local, colonial organs of government"). In the seventeenth century, there was a dispute over where the locus of sovereignty lay – with the Crown or Parliament. By the Glorious Revolution, the theory of parliamentary sovereignty, justified by the notion that the people are supreme, was the dominant theory in England until the eve of the American Revolution. Ibid., pp. 200–201.

10 LaCroix, *American Federalism*, p. 17 (noting that the nature of sovereignty was contested and that there were "two versions of the British Constitution" – the one "in which Parliament was omnipotent" and "the colonial interpretation, premised on the belief that there were limits to Parliament's authority to legislate for the colonies") (internal citations omitted).

11 Ibid., pp. 35, 132–133.

12 See Bailyn, *American Revolution*, pp. 200–228 (discussing the progression from the idea of an absolute, unified sovereignty to the Revolutionary idea of sovereignty in the people).

13 James Madison, "Debate on the Veto of State Laws of June 8, 1787," in Ralph Ketcham (ed.), *The Anti-Federalist Papers and the Constitutional Convention Debates* (New York: Signet Classic, 2003), p. 58.

due subordination to the nation."[14] Each understood that a powerful central government was key to the nation's success. Madison had proposed the federal negative to Thomas Jefferson, Edmund Randolph, and George Washington in the months prior to the Convention, arguing that this veto power would establish the supremacy of the national government.[15] Madison envisioned it as a tool to keep the states from defeating acts of Congress, violating national treaties, and being aggressive toward each other.

Importantly, Madison believed that the congressional negative would show that power emanated from the center; he was willing, in fact, to model the negative after the one used by the very empire from which colonists had sought to escape. The federal negative mirrored "the same type of ex ante review of state legislative acts that the British Crown, through the mechanism of the Privy Council, had formerly wielded over the acts of the colonial assemblies."[16] According to legal historian Allison LaCroix, "Madison envisioned the federal negative functioning in the same manner as the Privy Council's practice of reviewing statutes ex ante, in a general posture, before they could be applied in individual cases or challenged by specific parties."[17] Congress's ability to invalidate state laws before they went into effect would have sharply limited state sovereignty and state autonomy.[18]

Some delegates rejected the congressional negative precisely because it too closely resembled the pre-Revolutionary practices of Great Britain.[19] Others expressed fears that a congressional negative over state laws placed too much power in Congress over the internal workings of the states,[20] but they indicated a willingness to support a negative in a narrower form. The congressional veto in the Elections Clause of Article I, Section 4 represented a compromise of sorts: it gave Congress the ability to veto state laws in limited, but important, circumstances – those regulations governing the time, place, and manner of federal elections. As Chapter 1 shows, the importance

14 Ibid., pp. 58–59. This provision was a part of Article VI of the Virginia Plan, which gave the national legislature the ability "to negative all laws passed by the several States, contravening in the opinion of the National Legislature the articles of the Union." James Madison, "The Virginia Plan, May 29, 1787)," in William T. Hutchinson et al. (eds.), *The Papers of James Madison*, 17 vols. (Chicago: University of Chicago Press, 1962–77 [vols. 1–10]; Charlottesville: University of Virginia Press, 1977–91 [vols. 11–17]), vol. 10, p. 16 (noting that James Madison supported "Charles Pinckney's motion for an unlimited veto over state laws").

15 LaCroix, *American Federalism*, pp. 138–139.

16 Ibid., pp. 139, 141 ("By positing that lands beyond the realm were held by the monarch alone by virtue of conquest, the doctrine of the king's dominions vested the king's council with authority to oversee colonial legislation and to review the decisions of colonial courts.").

17 Ibid., p. 145.

18 Ibid., p. 146 (noting that the negative gave "the general government the power to police both a state's relationship with its inhabitants and its relationship with its fellow states").

19 See ibid., pp. 147–154 (stating that some thought the negative looked "like little more than a rehash of imperial procedure").

20 Madison, "Debate on the Veto of State Laws of June 8, 1787," in Ketcham (ed.), *The Anti-Federalist Papers*, pp. 58–60 (stating that Mr. Williamson was concerned that a congressional negative would undermine the states' ability to set internal policies and also that Mr. Sherman believed the nature of the congressional veto should be defined).

of federal elections was a recurrent theme during the Convention. Congress's ability to veto state electoral regulations was widely seen as necessary to prevent the states from destroying the national government, but without intruding on state sovereignty to the same degree as a general negative over state laws.

Even a more limited veto over federal elections was unsurprisingly problematic for some in the founding generation. Similar to concerns raised about the Guarantee Clause, the language of the proposed Elections Clause furthered fears that the Constitution created an all-powerful national government that would introduce tyranny, despotism, and a governing aristocracy. Despite the delegates' assurances about the limited nature of the Elections Clause veto, some states were not swayed. Massachusetts and New Hampshire, for example, proposed an amendment to the Elections Clause that would allow Congress to exercise its veto power only if states either failed to call for congressional elections or passed electoral laws that subverted rights protected by the Constitution.[21] North Carolina and Virginia lodged similar objections when they ratified the Constitution.[22] South Carolina argued that the federal government's power under the Elections Clause attached where "the legislature of the States shall refuse or neglect to perform" their duties.[23]

James Winthrop, an Anti-Federalist writing under the pseudonym Agrippa, also sought to limit congressional power under the Clause. Among the fourteen conditions that Winthrop proposed as prerequisites to accepting the new constitution, he argued that, "Congress shall have no power to alter the time, place or manner of elections, nor any authority over elections, otherwise than by fining such state as shall neglect to send its representatives or senators, a sum not exceeding the expense of supporting its representatives or senators one year."[24]

21 See generally Pauline Maier, *Ratification: The People Debate the Constitution 1787–1788* (New York: Simon and Schuster, 2010), p. 448 ("All of the states that recommended amendments asked for a modification of that provision so Congress could regulate congressional elections only when states themselves did not or could not call elections. Massachusetts and New Hampshire also proposed to add a statement that would allow Congress to use its power over elections against state electoral rules that were 'subversive of the rights of the People to a free & equal representation in Congress agreeably to the Constitution.'"). See also "Report of the Committee on Privileges and Elections on the Repeal of Federal Election Laws of December 14, 1893," *Senate Reports of the 53rd Congress* (1893–95), vol. 1, report no. 113, p. 6 (arguing that Congress can invoke its Elections Clause authority "[w]here the states refuse to provide the necessary machinery for elections" and "[w]here they are unable to do so for any cause, rebellion, etc.").

22 The Virginia Convention's Form of Ratification included the following constitutional amendment: "That Congress shall not alter, modify, or interfere on the times, places, or manner of holding elections for Senators and Representatives, or either of them, except when the Legislature of any state shall neglect, refuse, or be disabled by invasion or rebellion to provide the same." Bernard Bailyn (ed.), *Debate on the Constitution: Federalist and Antifederalist Speeches, Articles, and Letters During the Struggle over Ratification*, 2 vols. (New York: Library of America and Viking Press, 1993), vol. 2, p. 564. North Carolina offered a proposed amendment with essentially the same language. Ibid., p. 571.

23 "Report of the Committee on Privileges and Elections on the Repeal of Federal Election Laws of December 14, 1893," *Senate Reports of the 53rd Congress* (1893–95), vol. 1, report no. 113.

24 See James Winthrop, "'Agrippa' XVIII, of February 5, 1888," *Massachusetts Gazette* (Boston, MA), reprinted in Bailyn (ed.), *The Debate on the Constitution*, vol. 2, pp. 155, 158.

Others expressed alarm at the veto, questioning "how can [C]ongress guarantee to each state a republican form of Government" when the "time place & Manner of chusing the Members of the Lower house is intirely [at their mercy]."[25] On this view, Congress could negate any action of the state in the context of federal elections, even those actions that comported with principles of republicanism. The argument that Congress would assert undue influence over elections, when taken to its most extreme conclusion, implied that Congress could destroy the states' ability to be independent, autonomous units.[26] As William Findley, a prominent Pennsylvania Anti-Federalist, observed, "Congress [is] to have the power of fixing the *time, place,* and *manner* of holding elections, so as to keep [the states] forever subjected to [its] influence."[27]

The promise that the veto would be used rarely and only for practical reasons[28] provided little comfort to opponents who feared that the Elections Clause not only undermined the proposed constitution's creation of a federation but also indicated the national government's intent to absorb the states. As one commentator opined:

> By sect. 4th of the 1st article, "the times, places and manner of holding elections for senators and representatives, shall be prescribed in each state by the legislature thereof; *but the Congress may at any time, by law, make or alter such regulations, except as to the place of chusing senators?*" The plain construction of which is, that when the state legislatures drop out of sight, from the necessary operation of this government, then Congress are to provide for the election and appointment of representatives and senators.[29]

25 "Letter from Joseph Spencer to James Madison of February 28, 1788, Enclosing John Leland's Objections," in Bailyn (ed.), *The Debate on the Constitution*, vol. 2, pp. 267–268. (noting the objections of John Leland, a leading Virginia Baptist.)

26 See generally Maier, *Ratification*, p. 452 (noting that Aedanus Burke proposed to limit Congress's authority over elections to "'only when any state shall refuse or neglect, or be unable, by invasion or rebellion' to make such regulation itself" as a part of the Bill of Rights); Ibid., p. 151 (discussing objections by individual towns in Massachusetts and Connecticut to Congress's power to overrule the states over the matter of elections); Ibid., p. 339 (discussing similar objections in the New York ratification debates); see also Max Farrand (ed.), *Records of the Federal Convention of 1787*, 3 vols. (New Have: Yale University Press, 1911), vol. 3, p. 597 (giving states the ability to "prescribe the time & manner of holding elections" under the Pinckney Plan submitted to John Quincy Adams).

27 "Reply to Wilson's Speech: 'An Officer of the Late Continental Army' [William Findley?], November 6, 1787," *Independent Gazetteer* (Philadelphia, PA), reprinted in Bailyn (ed.), *The Debate on the Constitution*, vol. 1, pp. 97, 100.

28 See "Samuel Holden Parsons to William Cushing: 'Our Security Must Rest in Our Frequently Recurring Back to the People,' January 11, 1788," in Bailyn (ed.), *The Debate on the Constitution*, vol. 1, pp. 748, 751 ("[I]t appears to me proper that Congress should determine the Time, our Different Legislatures have on this Subject gone into different Practices, it is necessary all Elections should be in Season to attend the federal Legislature and expedient, at least, they should be in One Day throughout the Union this can only be done by the national Authority – it may be so that the present Places of holding Elections will be impossible for the Electors to be convened at … it may happen that some one of the States in the Union may neglect or refuse to make any Law by which the Electors may be conven'd.").

29 "'Centinel' [Sameul Bryan] I: 'A Most Daring Attempt to Establish a Despotic Aristocracy, October 5, 1787'," *Independent Gazetteer* (Philadelphia, PA), reprinted in Bailyn (ed.), *The Debate on the*

Adding to these worries was the fact that representatives would be elected to two-year terms and senators to six-year terms with no term limits for either, a structure that was different from many of the state systems then in existence.[30]

In response to these objections, Federalists drew parallels between the rights that free men surrendered to their governments to protect liberty and the power that states relinquished to the central authority, also viewed as necessary to protect freedom.[31] In other words, just as individuals had to give up a portion of their individual liberty to state governments to secure peaceful enjoyment of those liberties, so too did states have to surrender some of their power to the federal government for the same purpose – to protect the people. The congressional veto in the Elections Clause, from this perspective, was simply another layer of protection for the people, the cost of which was final policymaking authority over elections would lie with the national government.[32]

Constitution, vol. 1, pp. 52, 58–59. The exception in the Elections Clause that Congress had no power to interfere with "the place of chusing senators" seemed couched in the worry that giving Congress this power would allow it to change the meeting place of the state legislature that, prior to the Seventeenth Amendment, selected the senators. See Michael T. Morley, "Remedial Equilibration and the Right to Vote under Section 2 of the Fourteenth Amendment," (2015) 2015 *University of Chicago Legal Forum* 279–329. This would give Congress too much authority to interfere with the power of the state legislature when exercising its constitutional duty to select senators. For example, it was quite possible that a congressional dictate that state legislatures meet in some small town distant from the state capitol could be the equivalent of preventing them from choosing senators as Article I, Section 2 requires.

30 Maier, *Ratification*, p. 31 ("The Constitution put no limit on the number of terms representatives and senators could serve, unlike both the Articles of Confederation and many state constitutions, which imposed terms limits to avoid … an 'inconvenient aristocracy' of entrenched officials with no immediate knowledge of the people's needs and feelings.").

31 James Madison, "The Federalist 51," in John C. Hamilton (ed.), *The Federalist: A Commentary on the Constitution of the United States* (Philadelphia, PA: J.B. Lippincott & Co., 1864), p. 400 ("In the compound republic of America, the power surrendered by the people is first divided between two distinct governments, and then the portion allotted to each subdivided among distinct and separate departments. Hence a double security arises to the rights of the people. The different governments will control each other; at the same time that each will be controlled by itself."); see also Herbert J. Storing, *What the Anti-Federalists Were For* (Chicago: University of Chicago Press, 1981), p. 11 ("[J]ust as individuals have to give up some of their natural rights to civil government to secure peaceful enjoyment of civil rights, so states must give up some of theirs to federal government in order to secure peaceful enjoyment of federal liberties." (citing multiple sources). The analogy between individual liberty/states and state liberty/federal government was a common one. See, for example, Madison, "Debate on the Veto of State Laws of June 8, 1787," in Ketcham (ed.), *The Anti-Federalist Papers*, p. 60 (comments of James Wilson) ("Federal liberty is to States, what civil liberty, is to private individuals. And States are not more unwilling to purchase it, by the necessary concession of their political sovereignty, than the savage is to purchase civil liberty by the surrender of his personal sovereignty….").

32 See generally *Foster v. Love*, 522 U.S. 67, 73 (1997) (noting that one of the reasons that Congress, pursuant to its power under the Elections Clause, passed a statute fixing the election of congressional members to the same day was to remedy "the distortion of the voting process threatened when the results of an early federal election in one State can influence later voting in other States, and with the burden on citizens forced to turn out on two different election days to make final selections of federal officers in Presidential election years….") (citing Cong. Globe, 42d Cong., 2d Sess. 141 (1871) (remarks of Rep. Butler)).

The Federalists further defended the veto as an important check on state authority since the national government, unlike the states, would be insulated from the passions of the people (at least in theory).[33] They argued that Congress would prevent the undue influence of partisan zeal that came from unchecked state control of elections.[34] The veto also mitigated the fear that the states, had they been in complete control of elections, would use this power to the detriment of their citizens, who would have little recourse.[35] Giving the states' autonomy – or the authority to set the times, places, and manner of federal elections – but not sovereignty – in that Congress can at any time make or alter these regulations – addressed these concerns.

Thus, the structure of the Clause, much like the rejected congressional negative, created a decentralized structure over federal elections where state authority would be broad, but Congress would have a veto that, even if used sparingly, still reflected a one-sovereign regime rather than a dualist or concurrent one. The existence of a source of federal power unencumbered by federalism gave Congress significant leverage, particularly in light of the slavery politics that dictated much of the nineteenth century. But the presence of this repository of federal power in the Elections Clause did not mean that Congress would aggressively use it. Coupled with its power to influence the form of state governments under the Guarantee Clause, these two provisions laid a foundation for the broad exercise of federal power over elections that would not reach its apex until almost eight decades after ratification.

2.2 PARTISANSHIP, NOT FEDERALISM: THE ELECTIONS CLAUSE IN HISTORICAL PERSPECTIVE

Congressional resolution of contested elections under Article I, Section 5 presented opportunities for that body to probe the scope of both state and federal authority under the Elections Clause.[36] Besides the text, the founding generation provided

33 See, for example, Oliver Ellsworth, "Reply to Elbridge Gerry: 'A Landholder' IV of November 26, 1787," *Connecticut Courant* (Hartford), reprinted in Bailyn (ed.), *The Debate on the Constitution*, pp. 234, 236 ("[P]erhaps it may be said, Congress have a power to control this formality as to the time and places of electing, and we allow they have: But this objection which at first looks frightful was designed as a guard to the privileges of the electors. Even state assemblies may have their fits of madness and passion, this tho' not probable is still possible.").

34 "Rebuttal to 'An Officer of the Late Continental Army': 'Plain Truth', November 10, 1787," *Independent Gazetteer* (Philadelphia, PA), reprinted in Bailyn (ed.), *The Debate on the Constitution*, p. 115 ("Congress indeed are to have control to prevent undue influence in elections, which we all know but too often happens through party zeal.").

35 See, for example, "Comments of James Madison, Thursday Aug. 9 in Convention," in James Madison, *Notes of Debates in the Federal Convention of 1787* (Athens: Ohio University Press, 1984), pp. 414, 425 (noting that the Elections Clause "was meant to give the National Legislature a power not only to alter the provisions of the States, but to make regulations in case the States should fail or refuse altogether").

36 See Derek T. Muller, "Scrutinizing Federal Election Qualifications" (2015) 90 *Indiana Law Journal* 559–612, 589 ("Congress can examine qualifications of its own members and probably those of

little guidance to either the House or the Senate regarding what Congress's power to judge elections under Article I, Section 5 actually entailed; accordingly, each body had to create its own procedures to govern the disputes. In the early years, the procedure that governed contested elections cases was inconsistent and erratic.[37] In 1798, Congress passed a code of procedure for contested elections cases, but these regulations expired in 1804.[38] From that point on, both houses operated with "chaotic irregularity," having no uniform mode of procedure or formal framework to resolve the contests until 1851.[39]

Prior to the Civil War, Congress believed that its authority under the Clause permitted, at a minimum, federal intervention if the states either failed to enact legislation governing the times, places, and manner of federal elections, or if state legislation was inadequate to permit federal elections to occur without incident.[40] Congress took a broader view of its authority in the wake of the sharp partisan conflict that emerged during the 1830s and early 1840s, thanks to the development of clearly defined and organized political parties: the Democrats and the Whigs.[41] Disagreements over slavery predominated, but there were also disputes over economic issues such as patronage at the state and local level.[42]

presidential candidates. For states, however, their roles of evaluation would look slightly different: it would occur through the context of ballot access.").

37 Charles H. Rammelkamp, "Contested Congressional Elections" (1905) 20 *Political Science Quarterly* 421–442, 424.

38 An Act to Prescribe the Mode of Taking Evidence in Cases of Contested Elections for Members of the House of Representatives of the United States and to Compel the Attendance of Witnesses, ch. 8, 1 Stat. 537 (1798).

39 Rammelkamp, "Contested Congressional Elections," p. 425.

40 James Kent, *Commentaries on American Law*, John M. Gould (ed.), 14th ed., 4 vols. (Boston: Little, Brown, and Company, 1896), vol. 1, p. 232 ("The legislature of each State prescribes the times, places, and manner of holding elections, subject, however, to the interference and control of Congress, which is permitted them for the sake of their own preservation, and which, it is to be presumed, they will not be disposed to exercise, except when any state shall neglect or refuse to made adequate provision for the purpose."). Congress did not think that its authority under the Clause extended to calling a new election even in the face of obvious fraud or disenfranchisement by the state. See, for example, "Featherston v. Cate, House Committee on Elections, 51st Congress (1889)," in Chester H. Rowell, *A Historical and Legal Digest of all the Contested Election Cases in the House of Representatives of the United States from the First to the Fifty-Sixth Congress*, 1789–1901 (Washington, D.C.: Government Printing Office, 1901; reprinted edition: Westport, CT: Greenwood Press, 1976), pp. 441, 441–442. Congress can, however, declare a seat vacant. See "Bowen v. De Large, House Committee on Elections, 42nd Congress (1871)," in Rowell, *Contested Election Cases*, p. 282 ("[I]t was impossible to determine who was elected, and the committee unanimously recommended that the seat be declared vacant.").

41 See Erik J. Engstrom, *Partisan Gerrymandering and the Construction of American Democracy* (Ann Arbor: University of Michigan Press, 2013), pp. 43–44 ("By the election of 1840, Whig and Democrat organizations were fighting on an even basis in almost every state By 1840, nearly 80 percent of the states had a competitive two-party system, compared to only 10 percent in 1824."); Richard P. McCormick, *The Second American Party System: Party Formation in the Jacksonian Era* (Chapel Hill: University of North Carolina Press, 1966), p. 341 ("In 1840, for the first time, two parties that were truly national in scope contested for the presidency.").

42 See Scott C. James, "Patronage Regimes and American Party Development from 'The Age of Jackson' to the Progressive Era" (2006) 36 *British Journal of Political Science* 39–60, 42 ("Since party policies

In thinking about the scope and nature of federal power in the first half of the nineteenth century, this period can be defined by two trends that pointed to a restrained federal government that was comfortable with the state-centered status quo: (1) as Chapter 1 showed, Congress's use of its power under the Guarantee Clause to shape the structure of state governments was constrained by slavery politics and increasing partisan polarization and (2) as Chapter 3 will show, Congress was reluctant to use its authority to remedy the disenfranchisement of individual electors wrongly disenfranchised under state law. But, as this chapter illustrates, there was also a related phenomenon that heavily shaped the narrative that federal power was conservative during this period: Congress's deferential posture toward the states with respect to the regulation of federal elections under the Elections Clause and Article I, Section 5.

Congress's state-friendly posture could not last indefinitely, for this period also laid the groundwork for the broad assertion of federal power that would start to crest in the 1850s and reach its apogee after the Civil War. This shift illustrated that the conservative use of federal power had been somewhat of a choice rather than a constitutional mandate. In fact, the 1851 law that Congress passed establishing its mode of procedure in contested elections corresponded to the increase in the number of contested election cases over the course of the nineteenth century.[43] This number averaged 3.54 cases per Congress before 1855 but rose to 13.92 cases per Congress from 1855 to 1905.[44]

While election disputes that necessitated a strong showing of federal power were relatively rare in the antebellum period, there were still instances of malfeasance that demanded federal intervention. Electoral fraud was rampant,[45] and Congress

are 'public goods' – that is, once enacted, no supporter can be excluded from enjoying their benefits – labour contributions to the party campaign should have been under-supplied. The answer of course was patronage – well-paid public jobs – a selective incentive with the power to induce participation in the otherwise profitless process of electioneering."); Peter Levine, "State Legislative Parties in the Jacksonian Era: New Jersey, 1829–1844" (1975) 62 *Journal of American History* 591–608, 600 ("Patronage and its control were critical links between legislative parties and state party organizations.").

43 An Act to Prescribe the Mode of Obtaining Evidence in Cases of Contested Elections, ch. XI, 9 Stat. 568 (1851).

44 Rammelkamp, "Contested Congressional Elections," 424. Under the 1851 law, the contestant must serve notice upon the contestee within thirty days after the result of an election was finalized. Then, the contestee has thirty days to file an answer affirming or denying the claims made in the petition and adding in any claims they had to support their victory in the election. During this sixty-day window, both contestant and contestee were assumed to be taking testimony to support their case. Theoretically, this meant that cases were brought to the House or Senate within sixty days of an election's final results for debate among the members. In 1875, Congress extended the time for taking testimony to ninety days from service of the contestee's answer. Ibid., 424–425.

45 See, for example, "Rutherford v. Morgan," in Rowell, *Contested Election Cases*, p. 48 (5th Congress (1797)) (contested election where contestant, Rutherford, argued that Morgan's election should be vacated because "money was promised by [General Morgan] or his friends for 'meat, drink, wagon hire, and other acts of bribery and corruption,' with the result that the freedom and purity of the election was greatly interfered with by disorder and carousals").

deducted fraudulent votes from the total ballots cast in very close races.[46] Even the extreme case – where Congress set aside an election in its entirety – happened on occasion if the election was conducted in a manner contrary to state law.[47]

Very rarely was any contested election case decided against the majority party. According to one study of the almost 400 contested elections in the First through Fifty-Ninth Congresses, only three challengers not of the dominant party obtained seats.[48] The partisanship of contested election decisions even led some congressmen to call for shifting the power to review elections from Congress to the federal courts.[49] By the mid-nineteenth century, however, the manipulation of electoral rules for partisan gain led Congress to be more assertive in exercising its authority over federal elections, forced by circumstances to loosen, and ultimately discard, its self-imposed federal constraints.

2.3 CREATING THE GROUNDWORK FOR BROAD FEDERAL POWER: ELECTION DISPUTES IN THE FIRST HALF OF THE NINETEENTH CENTURY

In the first Congress, Representative William Smith survived an election challenge after his opponent claimed that Smith had not been a citizen for seven years and was ineligible to keep his seat. Smith, who had been abroad studying law and was later shipwrecked for a year, was able to prevail because of "the tacit recognition of [his] citizenship by the people and legislature of the State."[50] This case set an early precedent in the House of Representatives for deferring to the states in judging its members' elections under Article I, Section 5, as well as Congress's concomitant authority under the Elections Clause to regulate the procedure of their elections.

This principle was on full display in *Barney v. McCreery*, a case arising during the tenth Congress, where the contestant, Barney, argued that the sitting Maryland

46 See, for example, "Chapman v. Ferguson," in David W. Bartlett, *Cases of Contested Elections in Congress, From 1834 to 1865, Inclusive* (Washington, D.C.: Government Printing Office, 1865), pp. 267–270 (35th Congress (1859)) (adding votes cast for "Judge Ferguson" instead of "Fenner Ferguson" to contestant's vote total and rejecting entire precinct's vote where there were "numerous evidences of illegalities and frauds practiced"); see also "Howard v. Cooper, House Committee on Elections, 36th Congress (1860)," in Rowell, *Contested Election Cases*, p. 161 (noting issue with illegal and fraudulent votes).

47 See, for example, "Taliaferro v. Hungerford, House Committee on Elections, 13th Congress (1813)," in Rowell, *Contested Election Cases*, pp. 63–64 (finding that the election was illegal and should be set aside).

48 De Alva S. Alexander, *History and Procedure of the House of Representatives* (Boston and New York: Houghton Mifflin Co., Riverside Press, 1916), pp. 313–324.

49 Vincent M. Barnett, Jr., "Contested Congressional Elections in Recent Years" (1939) 54 *Political Science Quarterly* 187–215, 192.

50 "Ramsay v. Smith, House Committee on Elections, 1st Congress (1789)," in Rowell, *Contested Election Cases*, p. 37.

congressman, McCreery, did not have the qualifications necessary to be seated.[51] Barney contended that McCreery was not "an inhabitant of his district at the time of his election," nor had he "resided therein twelve calendar months immediately before" in accordance with Maryland law.[52] McCreery moved his family to their second home in the summer months and lived in Washington, D.C, during the winter when Congress was in session.[53] The House Committee on Elections awarded the seat to McCreery because the state legislature had no authority to prescribe the qualifications of Representatives.[54] Despite finding that the state acted unconstitutionally in this instance, the Committee took a very narrow view of Congress's authority under the Elections Clause, arguing that federal intervention was warranted only when states abuse their power:

> The Federal Constitution indeed provisionally delegates to the State Legislature the authority of directing the time, place, and manner of holding elections at the discretion of Congress. It is not necessary nor convenient that the time, place, and manner of holding elections should be uniform, therefore nothing but abuses or usurpations of power by the States, can ever excite or justify Congress in assuming the exercise of it, which, however, they may do at discretion.[55]

Similarly, in an 1804 election dispute over a Pennsylvania House seat that became vacant after the representative resigned, the Committee on Elections further limited federal intervention by deferring to the state even where there was no state law to regulate how these vacancies should be filled.[56] Although the Committee was of the opinion that the state legislature should fill the vacancy, the House seated John Hoge, who won a special election that the Governor scheduled on short notice.[57] Despite the circumstances surrounding Hoge's election being less than ideal, the Committee demurred because the state was able to fill the seat with a legitimate candidate quickly and with minimum disruption.[58] Congress was deferential, even

[51] "Barney v. McCreery," in Rowell, *Contested Election Cases*, p. 56 (10th Congress (1807)) (noting that "seat was contested on the ground that [McCreery] was not a resident of the city").

[52] "Report of the Committee of Elections of Thursday, November 12, 1807," 17 *Annals of Congress of the United States* (Washington, D.C.: Gales and Seaton, 1852), pp. 870–71.

[53] Ibid.

[54] See *U.S. Term Limits v. Thornton*, 514 U.S. 779, 816–817 (1995) (examining Thomas Jefferson's letter to Joseph Cabell discussing this contested election outcome with approval because, in Jefferson's words, "to add new qualifications to those of the Constitution would be as much an alteration as to detract from them").

[55] "Remarks of Mr. Findley of Thursday, November 12, 1807," 17 *Annals of Congress of the United States* (Washington, D.C.: Gales and Seaton, 1852), p. 874.

[56] "Summary of the case of John Hoge, House Committee on Elections, 8th Congress (1804)," in Rowell, *Contested Election Cases*, p. 52.

[57] Ibid., p. 53 ("[Y]et, considering the special circumstances connected with the election of John Hoge, and particularly that the election took place on the day fixed by the State legislature for the appointment of electors for the State of Pennsylvania, the committee are of opinion that John Hoge is entitled to a seat in this House.").

[58] Ibid.

where there was a legislative vacuum that could be filled by federal legislation, so long as disputes were resolved in a reasonable and timely manner.[59]

The sedate uses of Congress's power in the early decades of the nineteenth century stood in marked contrast to its decision to implement the most intrusive piece of federal legislation then to date: the 1842 Apportionment Act, which required states to elect their congressional representatives from single-member districts.[60] Congress's decision to institute single-member districts for congressional elections in 1842, and not during prior eras in which the party in power could have used partisan legislation to cement electoral gains, might reflect the political boldness of the Whigs, or more likely, a more substantial shift in the political landscape that had cautioned against broad federal authority in earlier times.[61]

So, what changed? Recall that with the Twelfth Amendment, "We the People" became "We the Voters" in republican theory. This shift gave the federal government a greater foothold in the regulation of state and federal elections as partisan competition became increasingly nationalized.[62] Until the 1840s, nearly all state and federal election administration was regulated by the states. However, because of the Twelfth Amendment, election administration was more directly connected to constitutional grants of authority to Congress: namely, its obligation to ensure that states maintain a republican form of government by enfranchising some portion of their population to facilitate the selection of a president who reflected majoritarian preferences.

In addition, the splintering of the Jeffersonian Republican coalition, which had been dominant for over two decades, gave rise to not only a new Democratic Party but also a Whig opposition that would exploit the party form to impose partisan election legislation enacted under the guise of republican principles. With the 1840 election of the first Whig president, William Henry Harrison – who would die during his first month in office and be replaced by John Tyler – and with Whig majorities

59 See Franita Tolson, "Election Law Federalism and the Limits of the Antidiscrimination Framework" (2018) 59 *William & Mary Law Review* 2211–2284, 2246 (arguing that Elections Clause privileges the values of finality and ease of administration).

60 An Act for the Apportionment of Representation Among the Several States According to the Sixth Census (Apportionment Act of 1842), ch. 47, 5 Stat. 491 (1842).

61 See Chapter 1. See Engstrom, *Partisan Gerrymandering*, p. 48 (arguing that the Whigs, which was the party in power at the time, tended to fare better under single member districting schemes); Rosemarie Zagarri, *The Politics of Size: Representation in the United States, 1776–1850* (Ithaca: Cornell University Press, 1987), p. 130 ("What differentiated the 1842 conflict from previous debates was that several small states that still elected by general ticket came to support the districting measure.").

62 Cunningham, *Jeffersonian Republicans*, p. 256 ("The mass of evidence points to the conclusion that the Republican party was not the outgrowth of persisting state parties. Indeed, one does not find the type of ready-made state party that needed only to affiliate with a national headquarters set up by Jefferson. In some instances (e.g., New York) the new party built upon existing state factions, and elsewhere it attracted various of the old elements of political power in the several states. But the Republican party was a new growth that sprang from divisions in Congress and the national government; it was a product of national rather than state politics.").

in both houses of Congress, the Whigs leveraged the power of the federal government for political gain to intrude on an area that had long been regulated by the states. Their tour de force was the 1842 Apportionment Act,[63] requiring that members of the House of Representatives be elected from districts rather than at-large.[64]

2.4 THE FIRST PARTISAN FEDERAL ELECTION LEGISLATION: THE APPORTIONMENT ACT OF 1842 AS FEDERAL OVERREACH?

In 1839, New Jersey had a six-member congressional delegation, all elected at-large.[65] At-large elections were not outside of the norm. Many states elected their delegations in this manner, even though there was an emerging trend toward districted elections. Nonetheless, the New Jersey elections became "celebrated" and "of historical importance," according to the majority report from the House Committee on Elections, because control of that delegation (at the time disputed) would ultimately determine partisan control of the House of Representatives.[66] Two contingents – one Whig, one Democrat – each presented themselves as the duly-elected congressional delegation from New Jersey.[67]

New Jersey produced rival delegations because its 1839 elections were procedurally unusual. The county clerk refused to include vote totals from precincts in Middlesex and Cumberland counties in the official tally, claiming that noncitizens voted illegally. In reality, he excluded these votes because they would have given the Democratic candidates a statewide majority of 350 votes.[68] The governor nevertheless certified the Democratic slate, and the House Committee on Elections affirmed, noting that "votes received by election officers were prima facie legal," and "could not be thrown out until their illegality was affirmatively shown," which "must be shown to the exclusion of a reasonable doubt."[69] Rejecting other alleged irregularities, the Committee voted 101–22 to overrule the decision of the county clerk and count the returns from the contested precincts, a conclusion endorsed

63 An Act for the Apportionment of Representation Among the Several States According to the Sixth Census (Apportionment Act of 1842), ch. 47, 5 Stat. 491 (1842).

64 "Comments of Representative Clifford of Maine, April 28, 1842," 11 *Congressional Globe* (Washington, D.C.: Globe Office, 1842), appendix, p. 348 (in which Congressman Clifford suggests that Congress can only exercise its power pursuant to Article I, Section 4, if the states, "by design or accident," fail to elect Representatives).

65 "Twenty-Sixth Congress: March 4, 1839, to March 3, 1841," *Biographical Direction of the U.S. Congress, 1774–2005* (Washington, D.C.: Government Printing Office, 2005), pp. 119, 120, www.govinfo.gov/content/pkg/GPO-CDOC-108hdoc222/pdf/GPO-CDOC-108hdoc222.pdf.

66 "The New Jersey Case, House Committee on Elections, 26th Congress (1840)," in Rowell, *Contested Election Cases*, p. 109.

67 Ibid., pp. 109–10.

68 Ibid., p. 110.

69 Ibid., p. 112 (noting that "the burden was on the parties attacking the votes to show not only that the voters were foreign born, but also that they had never been naturalized").

by the full House. Accordingly, New Jersey's Democratic delegation was seated, a decision that would become a battle cry when Whigs took control of Congress and the Presidency two years later.

The New Jersey controversy laid the foundation for a partisan power move by Whigs in 1842, which fundamentally altered the relationship between the states and the federal government by eviscerating longstanding norms regarding state oversight over elections. Whether House elections should be at-large or use single-member districts would become a contentious political issue in the new Congress as Whigs sought to regain seats denied to them three years earlier. Over the course of these debates, the Whigs elevated majoritarianism, republicanism, and yes – partisanship – over federalism as values that the federal government had a role in promoting.

The shift toward nationwide uniformity implicitly raised questions about the motivation behind federal intervention, since states were arguably trending away from at-large elections on their own initiative. By 1842, only ten out of twenty-six states then in the Union elected their representatives at-large, and because three of the ten states were only entitled to one representative, there were only seven states in which the use of at-large versus districted elections made any meaningful difference.[70] Notably, of the seven states that used at-large elections and were entitled to more than one representative, four were Democratic strongholds in which Whigs were in the minority – Alabama, Mississippi, Missouri, and New Hampshire.

Unpacking the debates surrounding the Apportionment Act of 1842 reveals that federalism was the foil used to paper over a deep partisan dispute occurring at the height of the second-party system, in which the "parties had developed into large-scale electoral machines focused on winning mass-based elections and capturing control of the national government."[71] Debates were colored by one's priors regarding slavery and, by implication, the federal government's power to regulate matters traditionally left to the states. Opponents framed the legislation as overreach, and they sought to keep federal power limited vis-à-vis the states, despite a constitutional text that expressly allowed Congress "to make or alter" state regulations governing federal elections.[72] The 1842 Act was, according to Rep. John G. Floyd of New York,

70 The ten states that seated at-large representatives in the 27th Congress (1841–43) were Alabama, Arkansas, Delaware, Georgia, Michigan, Mississippi, Missouri, New Hampshire, New Jersey, and Rhode Island. "Twenty-Seventh Congress: March 4, 1841, to March 3, 1843," in *Biographical Directory of the U.S. Congress, 1774–2005* (Washington, D.C.: Government Printing Office, 2005), pp. 123–126. Of those, Arkansas, Delaware, and Michigan were only entitled to one representative. Ibid.

71 Engstrom, *Partisan Gerrymandering*, p. 43 (The "intense competition to win elections on a nation-wide scale further increased the incentives for parties to seek out every possible advantage, including manipulating the rules of the game.").

72 Martin H. Quitt, "Congressional (Partisan) Constitutionalism: The Apportionment Act Debates of 1842 and 1844" (2008) 28 *Journal of the Early Republic* 627–651, 630 ("The apportionment debates reveal the stance of both parties on the balance of power between state and national governments. At the core of these debates was the relationship between state legislatures and Congress.").

"not a question between the district system and election by general ticket; but it is a question between the General Government and the State Governments."[73]

After the New Jersey debacle, the push for nationwide uniformity for congressional redistricting gained considerable momentum. In 1841, Alabama's Democrat-controlled legislature switched from district to at-large elections, and the Democrats secured all five of the state's congressional seats.[74] The Whigs argued that the at-large election system that the Democrats used in Alabama signaled a worrisome move away from districted elections that other states would follow. Their fears generated concerns "that the large states might begin utilizing this electoral system [at-large elections] in an effort to form their own bloc within the House," thereby overwhelming the smaller states and "control[ling] the legislation of Congress."[75] Some Whigs explicitly noted that the rise of political parties made uniformity in how representatives were elected a necessity to avoid an at-large election system that disenfranchised minority parties within any given state.[76] An election by general ticket was, as the argument went, "anti-republican" because a winner-take-all system would ensure that those elected would only feel beholden to the party rather than the people.[77]

73 "Comments of Representative John Floyd, 27th Congress, Second Session, April 27, 1842," 11 *Congressional Globe* (Washington, D.C.: Globe Office, 1842), appendix, p. 320.

74 The five representatives from Alabama who served in the 27th Congress – Reuben Chapman, George S. Houston, Dixon H. Lewis, William W. Payne, and Benjamin G. Shields – were all Democrats.

75 "Comments of Representative Stanly, 27th Congress, Second Session, April 28, 1842," 11 *Congressional Globe* (Washington, D.C.: Globe Office, 1842), pp. 446–47. See also "Comments of Representative Davis of April 28, 1842," 11 *Congressional Globe* (Washington, D.C.: Globe Office, 1842), p. 448 (arguing, "If all the States adopted the general ticket system, five of the large States would have a majority on this floor. They would all be elected by the same political party; and the consequence would be, that a little more than one quarter of the people of the United States would constitute a majority and governing power in this House.").

76 "Comments of Representative Bernard of April 28, 1842," 11 *Congressional Globe* (Washington, D.C.: Globe Office, 1842), p. 454 ("Mr. B scouted the idea of conducting the Government without party; and when he heard gentlemen profess such a purpose, he thought they meant very little of what they said; it was an idle dream. And if the Government must proceed on party principles, how unfairly did the present unregulated system work. By adopting the system of general ticket, Alabama came into the House with a party strength of five votes; while New York, with forty Representatives, exerted a party force of but two votes. Was this fair? What he contended for was uniformity. Whichever way the rule might work, let us have one rule for all."). See also "Comments of Representative Bernard of April 28, 1842," 11 *Congressional Globe* (Washington, D.C.: Globe Office, 1842), p. 454 (quoting James Madison and noting that, at the time of the founding, "no such notion as that of a general ticket system had entered anybody's head; it was an afterthought, devised for party ends").

77 As Senator Kerr argued,

> The general-ticket system had always been considered revolting to every just idea of republicanism. A direct election in districts involves the only democratic principle that can be devised. A caucus representation is nothing but a farce of representation; it is no representation at all. The general-ticket system is a system of dictation by party, at last concentrated into a faction, the objects of which are attained by gerrymandering. …The time has come when people must prefer the district system, which enables them to select their Representatives at home from among those best known to them, and most capable of representing their interests.

"Comments of Senator Kerr of Monday, June 6, 1842, 27th Congress, Second Session," 11 *Congressional Globe* (Washington, D.C.: Globe Office), p. 584.

But the real rationale was less lofty. Districted elections would give Whigs a decided advantage in not only Alabama, but also the remaining Democratic strongholds, some of which gained seats after the 1840 census.[78]

Enacted pursuant to the Elections Clause, the 1842 Apportionment Act required districted elections for states entitled to more than one representative, and provided in pertinent part:

> *And be it further enacted*, That in every case where a State is entitled to more than one Representative, the number to which each State shall be entitled under this apportionment shall be elected by districts, composed of contiguous territory, equal in number to the number of Representatives to which said State may be entitled; no one district electing more than one Representative.[79]

Whether the Whigs overstepped the bounds of federal authority in enacting this legislation presented a novel question of constitutional interpretation, but the partisan nature of the proposal colored arguments about whether Congress had the power to enact it.[80] First published around the time of these debates, James Madison's *Notes of Debates in the Federal Convention*[81] heavily influenced the scope of these arguments, with Whigs focusing on the intent of the Framers of the Constitution in arguing for broad federal power that extended to mandating districted elections for the House of Representatives. For example, Senator William Alexander Graham, a Whig and later governor of North Carolina, was reported to have

> quoted several passages from the Federalist to show that the district system was the mode of electing members to the popular branch of the National Legislature, contemplated by the Founders of the Constitution. He had not been able to find, in the debates in the Convention, that any one was in favor of the adoption of the general ticket system. The district system was adopted by most of the States immediately after the ratification of the Constitution; and, among these, was the State of Virginia, in which Mr. Madison, Gen. Washington, and many of the framers of the Constitution resided. It was clear, then, that the system was considered not only undoubtedly constitutional, but most eligible.[82]

78 Engstrom, *Partisan Gerrymandering*, p. 43.

79 "Comments of Representative Clifford of Maine of April 28, 1842," 11 *Congressional Globe* (Washington, D.C.: Globe Office, 1842), appendix, p. 348.

80 Quitt, "Congressional (Partisan) Constitutionalism," 632 ("More than a half-century after ratification, most Whigs and Democrats agreed that their understanding of the Constitution should be based on historical ('contemporaneous') records. Here congressmen of both parties made clear that in interpreting the Constitution they gave greater priority to the intentions of the past than to advantages in the present.").

81 James Madison, *Notes of Debates in the Federal Convention of 1787* (Athens: Ohio University Press, 1984).

82 "Discussion of the Apportionment Bill in the Senate, 27th Congress, Second Session, Friday, June 3, 1842," 11 *Congressional Globe* (Washington, D.C.: Congressional Globe Office, 1842), p. 572.

His colleagues in the Senate likewise relied on Madison's convention notes to argue that the Act "did not go farther than was contemplated by the Framers of the Constitution," quoting extensively from the proceedings.[83]

In contrast, Democrats argued that federal power was limited, placing more weight on the debates in the state ratifying conventions than on the convention notes.[84] They framed the 1842 Apportionment Act as improperly imposing the districting system in an effort "to encroach upon the rights and sovereignty of the States."[85] Because states had traditionally determined the manner of elections, these arguments carried a lot of weight, even though the constitutional text seemed to speak to broad federal power more generally.

Democrats relied on creative arguments to cabin this authority.[86] Some contended that Congress did not have the power to order the states to draw districts

[83] "Discussion of the Apportionment Bill in the Senate, 27th Congress, Second Session, Wednesday, June 1, 1842," 11 *Congressional Globe* (Washington, D.C.: Congressional Globe Office, 1842), p. 562 (describing Senator Henderson's comments during the debate of the Apportionment Bill as follows: "to the record of debates in the Federal Convention to frame the Constitution with a view of showing that General Pinckney considered the report of the committees contemplated nothing else but the exercise of the entire control, should Congress see fit to make use of it; and the object of Mr. Pinckney's amendment was to modify the proposition so that the States should have the regulation of time, manner, and place of electing Representatives, should they think proper to exercise it. This was voted down; and General Pinckney then proposed that the next branch should be elected by the people in the manner in which the Legislature shall direct. Had this been adopted, it would have met the ideas of those who now oppose this bill. But the proposition was not adopted; and at a subsequent stage of the debate, the clause, as it now exists in the Constitution, was agreed to.").

[84] Quitt, "Congressional (Partisan) Constitutionalism," 628 ("In opposing the districting proposal… Democrats invoked a new principle of constitutional construction, stare antiquas via, where Congressional precedent should be conclusive. Thus when government usage has been 'uniform, and the acquiescence of the people general … the practice establishes the construction.' In this argument and in their emphasis on the ratifiers' expectations, Democrats embodied…'popular constitutionalism.'") (citing Larry Kramer, *The People Themselves: Popular Constitutionalism and Judicial Review* (New York: Oxford University Press, 2004)).

[85] "Debate of the Apportionment Bill in the Senate, 27th Congress, Second Session, Friday, May 27, 1842," 11 *Congressional Globe* (Washington, D.C.: Congressional Globe Office, 1842), appendix, p. 436 (comments of Senator McRoberts) (arguing that the Framers "would hardly think it possible that this could be the same General Government which [they] assisted to frame fifty-three years ago … [one which] assumes to dictate to the Legislatures of the States what they shall do in regard to their election laws") (emphasis in original); "Comments of Representative Kennedy, 27th Congress, Second Session, April 27–28, 1842," 11 *Congressional Globe* (Washington, D.C.: Congressional Globe Office, 1842), appendix, p. 317 (advising Congress "not to superinduce a struggle for existence between this Government and the States" because "[i]f that struggle ever comes, it will be fierce and deadly, and will only end in the destruction of one or the other").

[86] See, for example, "Comments of Representative Gamble, 27th Congress, Second Session, Tuesday, April 26, 1842," 11 *Congressional Globe* (Washington, D.C.: Congressional Globe Office, 1842), p. 446 (having no "no doubt that Congress had the power to district the States; but the language of the Constitution was merely permissive, not obligatory. Congress could act, if it pleased, upon the whole subject; but could not direct a State how to act. Should the amendment prevail, it would only be advisory in its effect; the States might comply or not; but when Congress aced authoritatively, it superseded the State action.").

but had to draw the districts itself, a Herculean undertaking given the twenty-seven states then in existence.[87]

Others framed the legislation as an infringement on the right to vote. For example, Representative Walter Colquitt, a Democrat from Georgia, argued that Congress could not require districted elections because, pursuant to Article I, Section 2's requirement that members be chosen by "the *people* of the several States … [e]ach voter or elector in a State is entitled under the Constitution to exercise his suffrage in the election of as many members as the State is entitled to send to Congress."[88] Likewise, Senator Arthur Bagby, an Alabama Democrat who as governor had signed a general ticket bill in 1841,[89] conceded "the power of Congress over the time, manner, and place of elections" but argued, "this power did not and could not, reach to the interference with any personal right secured to every citizen of the Constitution":

> [W]ould any gentlemen contend that it was constitutional to divide one county entitled to four members, into four districts, confining a voter to vote for only one member, and denying him the right of voting for the other three Representatives of his country? The Constitution entitles the voters of the county to vote according to their respective numbers; and the respective numbers of that county entitle it to four members. But Congress says no voter in such county shall vote for these four members: how can such an order be constitutional?… [E]very qualified voter of a State had the right to vote for every member to which such State was entitled to represent her in the House.[90]

In light of these critiques, the partisanship underlying the Act generated concern, even among Whigs. Representative William Goggin, a Virginia Whig, admitted that "Congress did possess the power to district the States," but conceded that its exercise in this instance was "a most odious use of authority."[91] Goggin then "appealed to the committee [on Elections] not to disturb a state of things which had existed so long." Other Whigs similarly argued that "this authority was given by the Constitution to the General Government, as the means of self-preservation; and that it should not be exercised until the States had entirely failed to legislate on the subject."[92]

87 Ibid., p. 452 (comments of Kennedy) ("Now, for his part, he (Mr. K) did not see any force in this objection [that Congress did not have the authority to command the States to do certain acts]; for if [the Elections Clause] did give Congress that power, it did not give the power to command the States to do it. All that it did was to give Congress the power to make the district itself, or to alter those made by the States. Though Congress might do the act, it could not order the States to do it…")

88 "Comments of Representative Colquitt, 27th Congress, Second Session, Wednesday, April 27, 1842," 11 *Congressional Globe* (Washington, D.C.: Globe Office, 1836), p. 446.

89 Mary Jane McDaniel, "Governors: Arthur P. Bagby (1837–41)," in Alabama Humanities Alliance (ed.), *Encyclopedia of Alabama*, updated August 20, 2018, www.encyclopediaofalabama.org/article/h-1446.

90 "Comments of Senator Bagby, 27th Congress, Second Session, Friday, June 3, 1842," 11 *Congressional Globe* (Washington, D.C.: Globe Office, 1836), p. 572 (referencing Article I, Section 2).

91 "Comments of Representative Goggin, 27th Congress, Second Session, Wednesday, April 27, 1842," 11 *Congressional Globe* (Washington, D.C.: Globe Office, 1836), p. 447.

92 "Comments of Representative Pendleton, 27th Congress, Second Session, Monday, May 2, 1842," 11 *Congressional Globe* (Washington, D.C.: Globe Office, 1836), p. 464.

Still others split the difference, limiting Congress's authority to circumstances in which states had "neglected or refused to perform [their authority under the Elections Clause], or to perform it in a manner satisfactory to this Government,"[93] but finding that those circumstances existed and necessitated passage of the Apportionment Act.[94] The majority of Whigs nonetheless asserted that there was no party influence motivating the passage of the legislation, arguing that the Act provides stability for this important part of our republican system.

The districted elections requirement also exacerbated the tension surrounding the appropriate ratio for the House pursuant to Article I, Section 2, which requires that "Representatives ... be apportioned among the several states ... according to their numbers..."[95] Notably, questions about the size of the House had been the focus of debate until the amendment requiring single-member districts sucked all of the air out of the room.

The single-member district provision had been introduced by Whig William Halstead, chairman of the Committee on Elections and – in a twist of fate – member of the New Jersey delegation not seated in 1839. Tinkering with the number of representatives directly affected the composition of the Electoral College, so the implications were quite far-reaching if states were denied representation because of the population-to-representative ratio. The larger the ratio, the smaller the composition of the House. Given that states could either gain or lose seats because of reapportionment, the ratio could mean the difference between an open seat and two incumbents facing off in the same district, given the ban on at-large elections under the 1842 Act.

Most importantly, the debate over the proper size of the House of Representatives revealed deep partisan divisions between Whigs and Democrats over which size ensured adequate representation for the electorate. Specifically, the conversation focused on the relationship between the size of the House and the country's republican tradition, which required that there be intermediaries between the people and

93 "Comments of Representative Bernard, 27th Congress, Second Session, Thursday, April 28, 1842," 11 *Congressional Globe* (Washington, D.C.: Globe Office, 1836), p. 447.

94 "Comments of Representative Bernard, 27th Congress, Second Session, Thursday, April 28, 1842," 11 *Congressional Globe* (Washington, D.C.: Globe Office, 1836), p. 454 (arguing that "the present mode of conducting elections in the different States was not equal or uniform"). See also "Comments of Representative Tillinghast, 27th Congress, Second Session, Tuesday, April 26, 1842," 11 *Congressional Globe* (Washington, D.C.: Globe Office, 1836), p. 446 ("The Constitution reserved to the States the right to regulate the time, place, and manner of State elections just as they pleased, until Congress should take up the subject and act upon it. Congress had not yet done this; and, until then, it had no right to direct the States how to act in, the matter. The amendment did not legislate, but called on the States to legislate, which was quite another thing").

95 Apportionment pertains to how many congressional seats each state should have whereas redistricting concerns how the boundaries within each state should be drawn, but the two are closely connected. David Butler and Bruce E. Cain, *Congressional Redistricting: Comparative and Theoretical Perspectives* (New York: Macmillan Pub. Co., 1992), p. 43 ("The task of drawing new congressional district boundaries occurs in two phases. The first is the apportionment of congressional seats to the fifty states, and the second is the adjustment of congressional district boundaries within the states after the initial state allocation has taken place.").

the levers of power that could accurately translate popular preferences into policy.[96] Liberally peppered throughout the debates were arguments that the ratio should be high to preserve the democratic nature of the House.[97] But some members were concerned that a small House would no longer be representative of the people.[98] While the disagreement between the Whigs and Democrats about the number of representatives that would best ensure meaningful discussion of policy implicated differing conceptions of republican government and meaningful representation, this contentiousness was directly linked to deep disagreements over the expansion of slavery.

Some representatives assumed that a smaller House would keep the slavery controversy at bay by limiting the election of more individuals from northern states with larger populations likely to oppose the institution.[99] For example, Congressman Elisha Allen, a Whig whose Maine district was eliminated prior to the 1842 election

96 As Sandy Levinson has noted, "'Democracy' can refer only to the numbers of people who are actually part of the decision-making pool; a 'republic,' on the other hand, requires as well a certain disposition on the part of the demos in order to assure the genuine legitimacy of the decisions reached." Sandy Levinson, "How Do Republics Die? Reflections on 'Constitutional Rot,'" *Balkanization*, February 17, 2020, 12:52 pm, https://balkin.blogspot.com/2020/02/how-do-republics-die-reflections-on.html. See also "Comments of Representative Atherton, 27th Congress, Second Session, Monday, April 25, 1842," 11 *Congressional Globe* (Washington, D.C.: Globe Office, 1836), p. 443 ("This House, Mr. A. said, embodied the Democratic principle in the Government; and it was important that that principle should be preserved in its greatest purity. The reason for establishing a representative Government was because the whole people could not assemble and determine for themselves what measures shall be adopted for their benefit; and it therefore became necessary to appoint agents to carry out their wishes. A representative Government was, therefore, the people acting through their agents; and hence it was important that there should be the freest and fullest representation.... One of the greatest blessings of a Republican Government was that measures of a doubtful character could not be hurried through, to the injury of the people. A large body of Representatives would always act promptly enough when they had public sentiment with them; and it was only when it was doubtful whether the people favored certain measures that there was difficulty in passing them.").

97 "Comments of Representative White, 27th Congress, Second Session, Tuesday, April 26, 1842," 11 *Congressional Globe* (Washington, D.C.: Globe Office, 1836), p. 444 (noting that "Mr. W. contended that a small House would destroy its representative character entirely"); "Comments of Representative Gordon, 27th Congress, Second Session, Tuesday, April 26, 1842," 11 *Congressional Globe* (Washington, D.C.: Globe Office, 1836), p. 444 (noting that "He [Gordon] contended that the sages who established our form of government were in favor of a low ratio to secure a representation of the people, and the greatest good of the greatest number").

98 This concern was not limited to Democrats. Whig Joseph White, for example, noted that "a small House would destroy its representative character entirely." "Comments of Representative White, 27th Congress, Second Session, Tuesday, April 26, 1842," 11 *Congressional Globe* (Washington, D.C.: Globe Office, 1836), p. 444.

99 It is not clear that this assumption was justified. For example, New York lost six of its 41 seats and Massachusetts lost two of its 12 seats after the 1842 Apportionment Act, but in the South, Virginia also lost six of its 21 seats and Kentucky lost three of its 13 seats. Compare An Act Providing for the Apportionment following the 1830 Census (May 22, 1832), *1830 Apportionment Results and Notes*, U.S. Census Bureau, www2.census.gov/about/history/historical-censuses-surveys/survey-census-history/decennial/legislation-1790-1830/1830-results-notes.pdf, with An Act Providing for the Apportionment following the 1840 Census (June 25, 1842), *1840 Apportionment Results and Notes*, U.S. Census Bureau, www2.census.gov/about/history/historical-censuses-surveys/survey-census-history/decennial/legislation-1840-1880/1840-results-notes.pdf.

because of the state's population decrease, accused South Carolina Senator John C. Calhoun (a staunch advocate of both slavery and states' rights) of trying to decrease the size of the House for this very reason, by pushing for a larger ratio/smaller House so as to mitigate the effect of the increasing split in public support over slavery.[100] A larger House would reveal the diversity of public opinion about – and likely broad objection to – the institution.

Others were more explicit about the effects of the slavery question on the House as compared to the Senate, noting that the size of the House must account for the fact that deliberation in the branch was susceptible to being sidetracked by the passions of the people, passions that had arguably been inflamed by the slavery question.[101] In other words, a smaller House was another way to stem the "excesses of democracy."[102] A House of reduced size would enable the Whig leadership to better moderate debate, thereby avoiding comparisons to the then unruly and unmanageable British House of Commons.[103]

Finally, some members were concerned about the impact of the ratio on the allocation of power between the states and the federal government. On one hand, a smaller House reflected that the states were the primary sources of positive law and Congress should play a much more limited role in law-making, even with regards to exercising those powers the Constitution has delegated to it.[104] But a smaller House

[100] Here, Congressman Allen argued,

> Everyone knows that, for the last eight or ten years, the public mind has been deeply agitated upon questions of the highest moment to the liberties of the country. I do not say that any blame on this account lies at this or that man's door. I speak of the fact merely; and of the additional fact, that the same state of feeling which pervades the public mind has displayed itself among the Representatives of the people of the United States in Congress assembled.

"Comments of Senator Allen, 27th Congress, Second Session, May 26, 1842," 11 *Congressional Globe* (Washington, D.C.: Congressional Globe Office, 1842), appendix, p. 409.

[101] According to Senator Archer, "Because, for a considerable time past, there has been more than usual excitement throughout the country upon various political questions; and this excitement is naturally impaired imparted to the popular branch of the Legislature, producing angry discussion and excited feeling; and, notwithstanding the high character which undoubtedly exists … their proceedings scarcely deserve the name of legislation." "Comments of Senator Archer, 27th Congress, Second Session, May 27, 1842," 11 *Congressional Globe* (Washington, D.C.: Congressional Globe Office, 1842), appendix, p. 437.

[102] For a description of what the Founders viewed as the potential pitfalls of the "excesses of democracy," see Alexander Hamilton, "The Federalist 15," in Hamilton (ed.), *The Federalist*, pp. 138–46.

[103] "Mr. U[nderwood] argued in favor of having a House of limited numbers, as more favorable to cool and intelligent legislation. … He deprecated any large increase of members, as leaning toward a mob government, by confusion, crowing like cocks, braying like asses, shuffling with feet, coughing, and other similar expedients now pursued in the House of Commons in England." "Comments of Representative Underwood, 27th Congress, Second Session, Thursday, April 21, 1842," 11 *Congressional Globe* (Washington, D.C.: Globe Office, 1842), p. 436.

[104] According to Senator Buchanan,

> That the country is vast, none will pretend to deny; but after all, the legitimate duties of Congress under the Constitution are confined to but a few subjects.… The people look to their State Governments for all the legislation of a municipal character… I am one of those who believe

would leave a large portion of the population without adequate representation, a complication in what was supposed to be the democratic branch of government and the voice of the majority that sits at the apex of republican theory.[105]

Indeed, a smaller House, particularly if some portion was elected at-large, would all but ensure that many people would lack sufficient representation, and that legislation unpopular with the masses would likely become law. Some Whigs warned of the deleterious effects of such a system:

> [T]here never was a more aristocratic, anti-republican measure than…the general ticket system…. If they adopted the general ticket system, they would have nearly one and a half million inhabitants of New York unrepresented on this floor. Was that right, just, or republican? Republicanism was, to have the greatest possible number represented here. … [T]he general ticket system … would result in the ultimate ruin of this country and the prostration of liberty. The general ticket system would introduce the caucus system universally throughout the country [106]

Harkening back to a time in which the president was chosen by congressional caucus, a system that was assailed for decades as impermissibly removing the choice of president from the people, Whigs similarly warned that, "If the general ticket system prevailed … [t]he nominations of the Representatives would be regulated exclusively by caucuses, conventions, and cabals, and the voice of the people would be completely stifled."[107]

As these debates illustrate, the passage of legislation and the function of representatives as intermediaries for the people cannot be understood without the lens of party politics. The advent of political parties all but ensured that republicanism, federalism, and other notions of representative government could no longer be considered neutral principles that constrained federal power in any meaningful way, and partisanship would shape exercises of federal authority in the area of elections for decades to come.

> that the preservation and peace of this Union require that Congress should never extend their powers by construction and should interfere with State legislation as little as possible.

"Comments of Senator Buchanan, 27th Congress, Second Session, Thursday, May 26, 1842," 11 *Congressional Globe* (Washington, D.C.: Globe Office, 1842), appendix, p. 411. See also "Comments of Representative Stanly, 27th Congress, Second Session, Wednesday, April 27, 1842," 11 *Congressional Globe* (Washington, D.C.: Globe Office, 1842), p. 447; "Comments of Representative Houston, 27th Congress, Second Session, Wednesday, April 27, 1842," 11 *Congressional Globe* (Washington, D.C.: Globe Office, 1842), p. 448 ("If Congress had the same power the States had, the power was concurrent in every part and parcel, with the solitary exception of the places where the Senators shall be chosen; but when Congress thought proper to act, her action overruled that of the States…. The language of the Constitution was, that Congress shall have the power at any time to amend or alter such regulations as were made by the States").

105 "Comments of Representative Atherton, 27th Congress, Second Session, Monday, April 25, 1842," 11 *Congressional Globe* (Washington, D.C.: Globe Office, 1842), p. 443

106 "Comments of Representative Sampson H. Butler, 27th Congress, Second Session, Tuesday, May 3, 1842," 11 *Congressional Globe* (Washington, D.C.: Globe Office, 1842), p. 471.

107 "Comments of Representative Garrett Davis, 27th Congress, Second Session, Tuesday, May 3, 1842," 11 *Congressional Globe* (Washington, D.C.: Globe Office, 1842), p. 448.

2.5 DON'T THROW OUT THE BABY WITH THE BATHWATER: THE AFTERMATH OF THE 1842 APPORTIONMENT ACT

The 1842 Apportionment Act revealed several fault lines surrounding the exercise of federal authority over elections, but over the course of the next decade, politics and custom, rather than federalism, dictated a return to a more limited view of federal power.[108] Indicative of this backsliding was a dispute during the twenty-eighth Congress (1843–45), where the House had to determine whether representatives from the four states that held at-large elections, in violation of the 1842 Apportionment Act, could take their seats.[109] Seating representatives contrary to the Act could be perceived as a concession that states had complete constitutional freedom to choose the manner of congressional redistricting with virtually no federal oversight.[110] As the majority report from the House Committee on Elections described the dispute, "[t]here is not only a conflict of law [between the respective state laws and the 1842 Act], but a conflict of right, of power, of sovereignty, between the Federal Government and four of the independent States of this Union."[111]

Framing the controversy as implicating issues of federalism, as opposed to a naked partisan power grab by the ruling party, was likely deliberate. Following the enactment of the 1842 Act, political winds almost immediately shifted, with the Whigs suffering massive losses in the 1844 elections.[112] Democrats, now back in power, did not want to relinquish the authority that Congress had gained from the Whigs' partisan move. The House Committee on Elections, now composed primarily of Democrats, reaffirmed that federal authority over redistricting was paramount, but provided a detailed blueprint for congressional intervention that had been absent from prior disputes:

> Under the Constitution the State legislatures are *required* to prescribe the times, places, and manner of holding elections for Senators and Representatives, but Congress is *permitted* at any time to "make or alter such regulations." The State

[108] Early in the country's history some elected officials argued that at-large elections were constitutionally mandated, implicitly suggesting that a return to this type of redistricting was inevitable, but the fact that districted elections survived the expiration of the 1842 Apportionment Act demonstrates the extent to which this view was not universally adopted. See Zagarri, *Politics of Size*, pp. 109–11 (discussing constitutional debate between proponents of at-large and district elections). See also ibid., p. 131 ("Although the 1842 act expired within ten years, the principle of district elections had been firmly established. The legal tradition for the method had won approval. Districting laws were passed in 1862, 1872, and throughout the early years of the twentieth century.").

[109] See "Members Elected by General Ticket, House Committee on Elections, 28th Congress (1843)," in Rowell, *Contested Election Cases*, pp. 117, 117–120 (debating whether representatives from Georgia, Mississippi, Missouri, and New Hampshire could take their seats).

[110] See ibid., p. 118 (noting issue was whether federal government or states have freedom in determining manner of elections).

[111] Ibid., p. 117.

[112] Engstrom, *Partisan Gerrymandering*, p. 54 (noting House representation of Whigs "plummeted from 59 percent to 36 percent").

> legislatures have an imperative duty in this matter, but they are intrusted [sic] with an unlimited discretion in the manner of its performance. But – [t]he privilege allowed Congress of altering State regulations or of making new ones, if not in terms is certainly in spirit and design dependent and contingent. If the legislatures of the States fail or refuse to act in the premises or act in such a manner as will be subversive of the rights of the people and the principles of the Constitution, then this conservative power interposes, and, upon the principle of self-preservation, authorizes Congress to do that which the State legislatures ought to have done.[113]

Half a century after Massachusetts and New Hampshire sought to restrict Congress to exercising its power under the Clause only if states failed to call for congressional elections,[114] a congressional committee revived this argument to put some constraints on Congress's newly expanded role over elections that had been endorsed by the Whigs two years earlier.

The Committee's view can be summed up as follows: Congress has a narrow role ("If the legislatures of the States fail or refuse to act …"), but federal power is broad once action is warranted ("If the legislature … fail[s] or refuse[s] to act … this conservative power … authorizes Congress to do that which the State legislatures ought to have done."). On this view, congressional power under the Elections Clause, when invoked, must completely displace state election regulations. Arguably, the Democrats wanted to impose principled limitations on the exercise of federal power that would allow for, in the immediate term, the seating of mostly Democratic representatives elected via at-large elections, while, in the long term, protecting the slaveholding states, which had been concerned about *any* broad interpretation of federal power.[115] Yet Democrats also wanted to take advantage of their majority status by reaffirming the more expansive interpretation of federal authority embraced by the Whigs through the 1842 Act by allowing Congress to completely displace state law (as opposed to simply replacing certain aspects of the state's regulatory regime) when states fail to act.

The cognitive dissonance of this position – that Congress has to legislate broadly and cannot tailor its response to the actual problem – led to a somewhat confused and ultimately untenable interpretation of the Elections Clause. When faced with the decision of whether to seat representatives elected in violation of federal law, or to exclude them (and, by implication, subordinate state power to federal authority), Congress adopted a compromise position.

113 "Members Elected by General Ticket, House Committee on Elections, 28th Congress (1843)," in Rowell, *Contested Election Cases*, pp. 117, 118.

114 See generally Maier, *Ratification*, p. 448.

115 See, for example, Robert P. Forbes, *The Missouri Compromise and Its Aftermath: Slavery and the Meaning of America* (Chapel Hill: University of North Carolina Press, 2007), p. 21 ("If the Constitution empowered Congress to build roads and canals, warned one [Republican], it could 'with more propriety' be invoked to 'free all the slaves in the U.S.'").

The House Committee on Elections concluded that the provision of the 1842 Act mandating single-member districts was invalid because it "[did] not provide the districts in which the election [was] to be held or furnish any of the necessary regulations."[116] Essentially, the 1842 Act was unlawful because it was not broad enough. The law failed to provide a complete code for federal elections, which, in this case, would have included drawing the congressional districts for those states that adhered to at-large elections. The full House agreed with the Committee's report and seated the representatives elected at-large in violation of federal law.[117]

By inviting significantly broader uses of federal authority under the Elections Clause, the twenty-eighth Congress's approach was arguably more intrusive of state sovereignty than simply mandating single-member districts, as Congress would essentially eliminate any role for the states in the more consequential act of drawing the districts. Given that the twenty-eighth Congress was dominated by pro-slavery Democrats, this was likely unintentional and a product of political opportunism.

While Congress's all-or-nothing approach embraced a thicker interpretation of federal power in some respects, it did not completely displace the self-imposed federalism limits that were at odds with the text and purpose of the Elections Clause. First, the Committee's argument that Congress must provide a full regulatory scheme for federal elections, capable of being executed without further state legislation, was arguably a procedural hurdle that would protect the regulatory authority of the states. But this requirement created tension with Congress's authority, under the Clause, to "alter" state regulations.[118] As the minority report recognized:

> Congress has power to *alter* State regulations, and it is upon this power that the validity of the second section of the apportionment act rests. No State can prevent or circumscribe the action of Congress in this respect. Congress may alter the State regulations to any extent it chooses, leaving those parts not altered still in force.[119]

[116] "Members Elected by General Ticket, House Committee on Elections, 28th Congress (1843)," in Rowell, *Contested Election Cases*, pp. 117, 118.

[117] See "Phelps and Cavanaugh, House Committee on Elections, 35th Congress (1857)," in Rowell, *Contested Election Cases*, pp. 154, 155 ("The fact that the election was by general ticket did not invalidate it, as the second section of the apportionment act of 1842 only applied to that apportionment, and even where it applied the House had refused to recognize or enforce it.").

[118] "Members Elected by General Ticket, House Committee on Elections, 28th Congress (1843)," in Rowell, *Contested Election Cases*, pp. 117, 120 (describing the minority position that, "The Constitution itself, from which the legislatures derive their authority, commands them to enact regulations; and if Congress so exercises its authority to alter State regulations as to render further legislation necessary before the laws as altered can form a complete and practicable system, the command for the enactment of such legislation comes not from Congress, but from the Constitution. The law, then, not being contrary to the Constitution, is valid and binding in all the States … .").

[119] Ibid., p. 119. The minority view would play a central role in validating the scope of Reconstruction-era voting rights legislation. See Chapters 5 and 6. See also *Ex parte Yarbrough*, 110 U.S. 651, 660–661 (1884) (discussing favorably Congress's various exercises of authority under Elections Clause including enactment of 1842 Apportionment Act); *Ex parte Siebold*, 100 U.S. 371, 383 (1879) ("If Congress

Second, the Committee failed to appreciate that the affected states also recognized the supremacy of federal law in this context and were relying solely on political capital to resist the requirement of single-member districts.[120] The Alabama general ticket legislation was short lived,[121] and the three remaining outlier states – New Hampshire, Mississippi, and Missouri – switched to single-member districts in 1846 while under Democratic control.[122]

Professor Erik Engstrom attributed these shifts to the fact that the "Democrats in the holdout states likely discerned that national political tides had turned against them and, fearing that their delegations would not be seated, preemptively switched to districts."[123] The single-member district requirement arguably breached the political norms of the day, but many political elites, even those who resisted the change from at-large to single-member districts, did not seriously question Congress's constitutional authority to institute this mandate.[124] By 1846, only four years after the Act was implemented, the reasoning of the minority report challenging those representatives elected at-large had, for all practical purposes, attained majority status.

The Committee's diminished and somewhat misleading conception of congressional power to enact the 1842 Act was not all in vain, however. The decade before the Civil War would bear out an important aspect of its theory about federal power. The Committee's assertion that Congress could intervene in federal elections when states "act in such a manner as will be subversive to the rights of the people and the principles of the Constitution" was especially path-breaking,[125] as it opened the door for a wide-ranging interpretation of the Clause that became dominant during the dispute over slavery in the territories that would usher the country into war.

does not interfere [with state election regulations], of course they may be made wholly by the State; but if it chooses to interfere, there is nothing in the words [of the Constitution] to prevent its doing so, either wholly or partially. On the contrary, their necessary implication is that it may do either. It may either make the regulations, or it may alter them."). And this approach is also consistent with how we view federal power today. See *United States v. Windsor*, 570 U.S. 744, 764–765 (2013) (noting the "general principle that when the Federal Government acts in the exercise of its own proper authority, it has a wide choice of mechanisms and means to adopt").

120 Engstrom, *Partisan Gerrymandering*, p. 55 (noting that Democrats finally adopted districts when they viewed them as politically advantageous).

121 McDaniel, "Arthur P. Bagby" ("The General Ticket Bill was enacted in January 1841, but Whig outrage forced the legislature to include a rider that required a popular referendum on the bill in August.... The public voted in the August referendum to restore the district system, and in November 1841 the legislature repealed the general ticket legislation.").

122 Ibid.

123 Ibid. (discussing why districting took hold under Democrats despite their success under general-ticket elections).

124 Tolson, "Partisan Gerrymandering," 884.

125 "Members Elected by General Ticket, House Committee on Elections, 28th Congress (1843)," in Rowell, *Contested Election Cases*, pp. 117, 118.

2.6 BLEEDING KANSAS, SLAVERY POLITICS, AND THE EXPANSION OF FEDERAL POWER

Congress's somewhat state-protective stance with respect to the regulation of federal elections was short lived, and conflicts over slavery, the Kansas–Nebraska Act, and later, the Supreme Court's decision in *Dred Scott v. Sandford*,[126] all pushed Congress toward a broader reading of its authority than in the preceding decades. The Kansas–Nebraska Act, enacted in May 1854, was especially important in this regard, as it allowed the people in those territories to decide whether they wanted to enter the Union as slave or free states, implicating Congress's power under the Guarantee Clause. Also in 1854, a series of violent confrontations over slavery in the territory of Kansas and neighboring Missouri – setting off a series of events that became known as Bleeding Kansas – forced Congress to also use its authority under the Elections Clause and Article I, Section 5 to resolve the legitimacy of Kansas' territorial elections.[127]

The Kansas–Nebraska Act showcased a political rivalry in neighboring Missouri that was a microcosm of the national debate over the expansion over slavery. This rivalry featured two U.S. Senators from Missouri: Bourbon Dave Atchison, who served in the Senate from 1843 to 1855, and Thomas Hart Benton, a Senator who served from 1821 to 1851. Benton was a colorful character who ended up losing his Senate seat after three decades of service due to the escalating controversy over slavery.[128]

Although both were members of the Democratic Party, Benton and Atchison were at odds during their overlapping service in the Senate. As the politics in Missouri

[126] 60 U.S. (19 How.) 393 (1857) (holding that Black people whose ancestors had been imported into the United States for the purposes of being enslaved were not American citizens and, accordingly, did not have standing to bring a lawsuit in federal court).

[127] See John B. Gates, "Partisan Realignment, Unconstitutional State Policies, and the U.S. Supreme Court, 1837–1964," (1987) 31 *American Journal of Political Science* 259–280, 264–265 (discussing how the Kansas-Nebraska Act and the *Dred Scott* decision resulted in the restructuring of political parties); Rebecca E. Zietlow, "The Ideological Origins of the Thirteenth Amendment" (2012) 49 *Houston Law Review* 393–458, 403 ("The Kansas-Nebraska Act … allowed the residents of Kansas and Nebraska to vote on whether or not they wanted slavery[.]").

[128] In 1849, Benton, a slaveowner, declared that he no longer supported the institution during a debate over legislation that would ultimately become the Compromise of 1850. In his remarks on the subject, he made it clear that he opposed "the extension of slavery" and believed that it should not be "plant[ed] … in new regions where it [did not then] exist," because of the "the incurability of the evil" of the institution. "Mr. Clay's Plan of Slavery Compromise: Mr. Benton's Speech against It: Extracts," in *Thirty Years' View, or A History of the Working of the American Government for Thirty Years, from 1820 to 1850*, 2 vols. (New York: D. Appleton and Company, 1856), vol. 2, p. 759. This declaration, as well as Benton's increasingly combative exchanges with other senators in the chamber over this issue, led Mississippi Senator Henry Foote to pull a gun on Benton on the senate floor. United States Senate, "On This Day: April 17, 1850," available at www.senate.gov/artandhistory/history/anecdote/days/015week_0417.htm. Benton survived the attempt on his life after other senators wrestled Foote to the floor and disarmed him. Ibid. After losing his Senate seat in 1851, Benton served two years in the House of Representatives (1853–1855), a tenure cut short by his opposition to slavery.

became increasingly fraught, the slavery issue became a holy grail for Atchison. Slave state Missouri, surrounded on two sides by free states, had a vested interest in ensuring that Kansas entered the Union as a slave state to prevent Missouri slaves from having another free state into which they could escape.

Atchison hoped that passage of the Kansas–Nebraska Act would ensure a Democratic victory in the Kansas state elections during the summer of 1854. But the passage of the Kansas–Nebraska Act did little to assuage the concerns of slaveowners in western Missouri that Kansas would enter into the Union as a slave state, leaving Atchison vulnerable heading into the 1854 election. The disintegration of the Whig Party in Missouri, the corresponding rise of the xenophobic American Party (or "Know Nothings"),[129] and the failure of Benton Democrats to coalesce behind Atchison left the state legislature with no party in control of the chamber and cast doubt on Atchison's re-election to the Senate.[130] Securing the institution of slavery in the state was, of course, essential to Atchison's re-election prospects, but Atchison's fervor over slavery and its expansion transcended politics. In the words of one historian, Kansas territory had become "a southern firewall that Atchison was determined to defend."[131]

Atchison decided to challenge the entire notion of popular sovereignty underlying the Kansas–Nebraska Act by capturing the political apparatus in Kansas and pushing a pro-slavery agenda.[132] Urging those living in western Missouri to take up temporary residency in eastern Kansas, Bourbon Dave asked for 500 volunteers to make the one-day journey to participate in the Kansas election for a nonvoting delegate to Congress.[133] More than three times the number requested heeded Atchison's call for one-day-Kansans, with 1700 Missouri residents casting ballots in the November 1854 Kansas race, compared to the 1100 permanent Kansas voters.[134]

[129] "At its height in the 1850s, the Know Nothing party, originally called the American Party, included more than 100 elected congressmen, eight governors, a controlling share of half-a-dozen state legislatures from Massachusetts to California, and thousands of local politicians." Lorraine Boissoneault, "How the 19th-Century Know Nothing Party Reshaped American Politics," *Smithsonian Magazine*, January 26, 2017, www.smithsonianmag.com/history/immigrants-conspiracies-and-secret-society-launched-american-nativism-180961915/. Unlike the other political parties of the period, the main concern of their platform was not slavery, but immigration. Ibid. They believed that only native-born white protestant men were deserving of privileges and rights: "[w]omen's suffrage was abhorrent and unnatural, Catholics were a threat to the stability of the nation, and German and Irish immigrants undermined the old order established by the Founding Fathers." Ibid.

[130] Alice E. Malavasic, *The F Street Mess: How Southern Senators Rewrote the Kansas-Nebraska Act* (Chapel Hill: University of North Carolina Press, 2017), pp. 144–145.

[131] Ibid., p. 146.

[132] William W. Freehling, *The Road to Disunion: Secessionists Triumphant 1854–1861*, 2 vols. (Oxford: Oxford University Press: 1990), vol. II, pp. 80–81.

[133] Ibid.

[134] Ibid. The first voter eligibility rules were set by Governor Reeder, including the requirement that prospective voters intend to live in the state permanently. See Matthew Reeves, "Andrew Horatio Reeder," *Civil War on the Western Border: The Missouri-Kansas Conflict, 1854–1865*, available at civilwaronthewesternborder.org.

The winner of that 1854 election, John W. Whitfield, a pro-slavery Democrat who resided in Independence, Missouri, as late as 1853, was set to become Kansas's first delegate to Congress.

Atchison became so focused on his pro-slavery efforts in Kansas that he lost his re-election battle for his U.S. Senate seat in 1854. Democrats in the Missouri legislature split between Atchison and Benton, their divergent positions on the Kansas–Nebraska Act essentially dividing the party.[135]

The next elections in March 1855 were for the Kansas Territorial Legislature. Once again, Missouri voters overwhelmed the balloting, thanks to same-day registration and geographic proximity. Kansas, which at the time only had 2,905 permanent residents eligible to vote, had 4,968 one-day Kansans (from Missouri) and 1,210 permanent Kansans participate in the election.[136] Five days prior to the election, Atchison led over eighty armed men over the border into Kansas, foreshadowing the violence between anti-slavery and pro-slavery forces that would follow for the next two years.

The political fallout of Bleeding Kansas led the House of Representatives, which was in the midst of the disintegration of the second-party system, to build on the Whigs' 1842 blueprint by using Congress's authority under both Article I, Section 5 and the Elections Clause to strengthen federal oversight of House elections, further reflecting the sharp divide over the slavery issue.[137] Congress established the House Committee on Kansas Affairs to investigate the 1854 and 1855 Kansas elections, including the congressional seat won by John W. Whitfield.

Agreeing with the free staters, the Committee (operating in a Congress that, as of the summer of 1856, was a body in which no party commanded a majority) deemed the 1854 and 1855 elections illegitimate, noting the "unlawful interference" of "leading citizens of Missouri" who had "crossed into the Territory." Indicative of this fraudulent behavior, the seventh district had 53 voters registered for the November 1854 election, but 604 votes were cast.[138] Similarly, of the 105 votes cast in the sixth district, only 25 were from Kansas voters.[139] And so it went in one district after

[135] Malavasic, *The F Street Mess*, p. 147 ("Atchison and Benton had taken opposing sides on the Kansas-Nebraska Act, each believing his position on the act would assure his victory in the Senate election. Both had been wrong.").

[136] Freehling, *Road to Disunion*, vol. II, pp. 74–75 (discussing the plague of one-day Kansans in the 1855 election). See also James Henry Lane, "Gen. Lane's Answer to the President's Message, Published in the Lawrence Republican Extra on 13 February 1858," in Kansas Historical Society, *Kansas Memory*, available at www.kansasmemory.org/item/90447. After the 1855 elections, Governor Reeder invalidated elections in seven districts because of fraud. Malavasic, *The F Street Mess*, pp. 147–148.

[137] The Democrats suffered heavy losses in the 1854 and 1855 congressional elections, losing ground to the xenophobic Know Nothings who were largely agnostic on the slavery question. Democrats retook the House in the 1856 congressional elections. See David M. Potter, *The Impending Crisis: America before the Civil War, 1848–1861* (New York: Harper & Row, 1976), pp. 238–240.

[138] "Report of the House Committee on Kansas Affairs of July 2, 1856," *House Reports of the 34th Congress* (1855–56), vol. 2, report no. 200, p. 5.

[139] Ibid.

another, leading Governor Reeder to call for new elections for several districts with obviously fraudulent results.[140]

According to the Committee, "*every election* has been controlled, not by the actual settlers, but by citizens of Missouri; and, as a consequence, every officer in the Territory, from constable to legislators, except those appointed by the president, owe their positions to non-resident voters."[141] Moreover, "[n]o law exists in Kansas for the election of a delegate to Congress … and no territorial law for such an election can be enacted, for the plain reason that the law-making power of that Territory has been subverted by usurpation" because of the fraud in the 1855 legislative elections.[142] The Committee observed that "[i]t is undoubtedly competent for the Congress of the United States to enact a law under which a legal election of a delegate from Kansas could be effected."[143] This view was consistent with the determination of the 1844 House Committee on Elections which, in resolving the seats of those elected in violation of the 1842 Apportionment Act, established that Congress could legislate in this manner as long as it (1) did so comprehensively and (2) provided a complete code of regulations to govern the election.

The Committee also found that, consistent with this earlier position, if Congress refused to enact this law, it could accept the candidate who received the most votes, and disregard that the election was governed by laws enacted by a legislature that

140 Ibid., pp. 6–9 (detailing frauds in the eleventh, fourteenth, fifteenth, and sixteenth districts).

141 Ibid., p. 2. As the Committee's report colorfully detailed the November 1854 elections: "The election in the 2d district was held at the village of Douglas, near fifty miles from the Missouri line. On the day before the election large companies of men came into the district in wagons and on horseback, and declared that they were from the State of Missouri, and were going to Douglas to vote. On the morning of the election they gathered around the house where the election was to be held. Two of the judges appointed by the governor did not appear, and other judges were selected by the crowd; all then voted. In order to make a pretence [sic] of right to vote, some persons of the company kept a pretended register of squatter claims, on which any one could enter his name, and then assert he had a claim in the Territory. A citizen of the district, who was himself a candidate for delegate to Congress, was told by one of the strangers that he would be abused, and probably killed, if he challenged a vote. (4) He was seized by the collar, called a-damned abolitionist, and was compelled to seek protection in the room with the judges. About the time the polls were closed these strangers mounted their horses and got into their wagons and cried out, 'All aboard for Westport and Kansas City.' A number were recognized as residents of Missouri, and among them was Samuel H. Woodson, a leading lawyer of Independence. Of those whose names are on the poll-books, 35 were resident settlers and 226 were nonresidents." Ibid., p. 4. See also ibid. (discussing the 7th district).

142 "Reeder v. Whitfield, House Committee on Elections, 34th Congress (1856)," in Bartlett, *Cases of Contested Elections*, pp. 185, 203 (first case)(discussing the findings of the Committee regarding the 1855 Kansas legislative elections). There were two disputed election contests between Reeder and Whitfield in the 34th Congress, which I identify as "first case" and "second case," respectively. See also "Report of the House Committee on Kansas Affairs of July 2, 1856," *House Reports of the 34th Congress* (1855–56), vol. 2, report no. 200, pp. 9–10 ("By an organized movement … companies of men were arranged in irregular parties and sent *into every council district in the Territory* and *into every representative district but one*").

143 "Reeder v. Whitfield, House Committee on Elections, 34th Congress (1856)," in Bartlett, *Cases of Contested Elections*, pp. 185, 203 (first case).

was an "illegally constituted body, [that] had no power to pass valid laws, and their enactments are, therefore, null and void."[144]

But Congress did neither, radically departing from its earlier stance by rejecting John Whitfield's 1855 victory outright and declaring the seat vacant. Notably, Whitfield's election was challenged from the floor of the House, despite "the usual custom in admitting Delegates on prima facie evidence."[145] Using Article I, Section 5 to aggressively enforce the principles of republican government, the House decided that the election, as conducted under rules adopted by the state legislature, could not stand because "[t]o admit the legality of the so-called territorial legislature of Kansas would be to sanction fraud, violence, and perjury…."[146]

Congress also did not award the seat to Whitfield's opponent, former governor Andrew Reeder, even though Reeder received more lawful votes than Whitfield. In August 1855, President Pierce had removed Governor Reeder from office, citing official misconduct. In October 1855, free staters held their own election and selected Reeder as their territorial delegate. Because the election was held in the context of a party convention rather than a "state" sanctioned election, however, Congress declined to award Reeder the seat because the election "was not held in pursuance of law."[147]

Notably, Congress's willingness to set aside the election and to deem the state government illegitimate represented a more expansive view of federal power than, for example, that embraced by the eighth Congress, which deferred to a state legislature that filled a vacancy through a procedurally problematic special election,[148] or, alternatively, when Noah Webster denied, in a debate over apportionment in the twenty-second Congress, that Congress has the authority to weigh in on whether the representative power of a state was allocated fairly.[149]

But the political fallout over the events that came to be known as "Bleeding Kansas"– and the corresponding questions this controversy raised about the scope

[144] Ibid., p. 202.

[145] Asher C. Hinds, *Hinds' Precedents of the House of Representatives of the United States*, 5 vols. (Washington, D.C.: United States Government Printing Office, 1907), p. 1072.

[146] Ibid. See also "Reeder v. Whitfield, House Committee on Elections, 34th Congress (1856)," in Bartlett, *Cases of Contested Elections*, pp. 215, 216 (first case). To be clear, Congress has broad authority over the territories, see United States Constitution Art. IV, s. 3., and it is an open question whether the outcome would be different had Kansas already been a state. The Reconstruction Acts, discussed in Chapter 6, suggest that Congress has an ongoing obligation to police a state's political system under the Guarantee Clause, post-admission.

[147] "Report of the Select Committee Concerning the Constitution Framed at Lecompton, in the Territory of Kansas, of May 11, 1858," *House Reports of the 35th Congress*, 3 vols. (1857–58), vol. III, report no. 377, p. 67.

[148] "Summary of the case of John Hoge, House Committee on Elections, 8th Congress (1804)," in Rowell, *Contested Election Cases*, p. 52.

[149] "Davidson vs. Gilbert, House Committee on Elections, 56th Congress (1901)," Rowell, *Contested Election Cases*, p. 605 (quoting Webster for the proposition that, "Whether the subdivision of the representative power within any State, if there be a subdivision, be equal or unequal, or fairly or unfairly made, Congress can not know and has no authority to inquire. It is enough that a State presents her own representation on the floor of Congress in the mode she chooses to present it.")

of federal power – was not limited to the disputed territorial and congressional elections. There was also significant controversy over the drafting of the constitution that had to be submitted for the territory to formally become a state. At issue in Kansas were four competing constitutions, with the pro-slavery Lecompton document and the anti-slavery Topeka Constitution generating the most controversy. In 1857, a pro-slavery delegation met at Lecompton and drafted a constitution that, under an article entitled "Slavery," recognized "[t]he right of property is before and higher than any constitutional sanction" and provided that the legislature "shall have no power to pass laws for the emancipation of slaves without the consent of the owners."[150]

Slaveowners drafted this document as a counterproposal to the 1855 Topeka Constitution, which was the first constitution written for Kansas territory. The Topeka Constitution provided that, "[t]here shall be no slavery in this state, nor involuntary servitude, unless for the punishment of crime."[151] Free-state voters had approved the Topeka Constitution after Missouri voters had overwhelmed the ballot boxes and undermined Kansas's November 1854 territorial elections. They also elected a territorial legislature under the new constitution, seeking to displace the pro-slavery government that had triumphed in Kansas's March 1855 territorial elections.

President Pierce condemned the Topeka Constitution as a violation of republican principles, treating the decades long fight over whether slavery was compatible with republicanism as settled. But it was far from settled. In May 1856, Representative Preston Brooks of South Carolina beat Massachusetts Senator Charles Sumner with a cane after Sumner criticized Southerners who defended slavery.[152] Also in 1856, the Whig Party disbanded and the xenophobic Know Nothing Party declined, leaving a power vacuum in which the Republican Party emerged as an anti-slavery alternative to the Democrats. Amid these massive changes in the political structure in the country, President Pierce declared the Topeka government to be in open rebellion in January 1856 and treated the pro-slavery Lecompton Constitution as the only legitimate governing document for the Kansas territory.

Pro-slavery Democrats regained control of the House of Representatives after the August 1856 elections,[153] and its majority status allowed it to paint the dispute in terms most favorable to the slave power. While normally eschewing broad federal authority, pro-slavery Democrats in Congress had a change of heart once back in control. Like President Pierce, Congress rejected the Topeka Constitution on the grounds that the Topeka government had not lawfully convened and had no authority to draft a constitution. According to the Committee on Territories,

150 Lecompton Constitution of the Territory of Kansas, Art. VII (1857).

151 The Constitution of the Topeka Kansas Territory, s. 6 (1855).

152 Joanne B. Freeman, *The Field of Blood: Violence in Congress and the Road to the Civil War* (New York: Farrar, Straus, and Giroux, 2018).

153 Of the 237 seats in the House of Representatives, Democrats controlled 132 seats; Republicans controlled 90 seats; the Know Nothings controlled 14 seats; and there was 1 independent. See Congressional Profile, 35th Congress, https://history.house.gov/Congressional-Overview/Profiles/35th/).

> The societies had previously sent out the worst part of the spurious population of Kansas for the professed and avowed object of excluding slavery from the Territory. That attempt was justly regarded as offensive to the southern States. The people of' the United States, through their representatives in Congress, established the principle of strict non-intervention on the subject of slavery in the Territories and States. The Supreme Court subsequently sustained, by a solemn decision [in *Dred Scott v. Sandford*], the same principle.[154]

Consistent with this position, a special select Committee reviewing the Lecompton Constitution concluded that it, unlike the Topeka Constitution, was republican in form because "No State ever before applying [for admission] exhibited greater regularity in her proceedings."[155] The Committee sustained the Lecompton Constitution, despite the fact that it had not been ratified by popular vote, because the power of the people to make a constitution can be delegated to "conventions or intermediate bodies," a principle at the heart of representative government.[156]

Efforts to save the pro-slavery government would subsequently dictate the manner in which the Democratic controlled Congress used its power under Article I, Section 5 to resolve these disputes. The territorial government – the same one deemed illegal by the House – held another election in October 1856 in which John Whitfield, the winner of the previously invalidated election, emerged as the *unanimous* winner of the seat.[157] This time, however, the majority Democratic House decided to seat Whitfield, ignoring the irregularities surrounding his election (and despite a recommendation from the House Committee on Elections that the seat be declared vacant).[158]

When the dust settled, the Kansas–Nebraska dispute left us with the city of Atchison, Kansas, so named after Bourbon Dave and his band of one-day Kansans. Atchison boasts a county museum with the "World's Smallest Presidential Library," in honor of Atchison's one-day stint as President of the United States. But the undeserved honorific to Atchison should not obscure that this controversy over slavery, at a time in which all politics was slavery politics, ultimately forced the House to more assertively frame its authority to "alter" regulations pursuant to the Elections Clause and its authority to police republican government as a failsafe triggered when states have overstepped their constitutional authority and subverted the rights of the

[154] "Report of the Committee on Territories, to Accompany Bill S. 161, of February 18, 1858," *Senate Reports of the 35th Congress*, 3 vols. (1857–58), vol. I, report no. 82, p. 2.

[155] "Report of the Select Committee Concerning the Constitution Framed at Lecompton, in the Territory of Kansas, of May 11, 1858," *House Reports of the 35th Congress*, 3 vols. (1857–58), vol. III, report no. 377, p. 3.

[156] Ibid., p. 4.

[157] "Reeder v. Whitfield, House Committee on Elections, 54th Congress (1856)," in Rowell, *Contested Election Cases*, pp. 145–146 (second case).

[158] Ibid. See also Joshua A. Chafetz, *Democracy's Privileged Few: Legislative Privilege and Democratic Norms in the British and American Constitutions* (New Haven: Yale University Press, 2007), pp. 181–182.

people. And this approach, contrary to early assertions that federal power was limited to providing a full regulatory alternative to state law, represented the broadest presentation of federal power under the Clause to date: that Congress could expressly and explicitly invalidate contrary state pronouncements without replacing the state's regulatory framework in its entirety.[159]

[159] Compare "Barney v. McCreery, House Committee on Elections, 10th Congress (1807)," in Rowell, *Contested Election Cases*, pp. 56–57 (invalidating state election law without dictating replacement provisions).

See also "Fouke v. Trumbull, House Committee on Elections, 34th Congress (1856)," in Rowell, *Contested Election Cases*, p. 141. Lyman Trumbull, who would go on to become a prominent conservative Republican during Reconstruction, was the subject of an election challenge in 1856 after he won the seat in the eighth congressional district of Illinois. His opponent claimed that Trumbull, then a state supreme court judge, violated an Illinois law that provided that "[t]he judges of the supreme and circuit courts shall not be eligible to any other office of public trust or profit in this State, or the United States, during the term for which they are elected, nor for one year thereafter." Ibid. In rejecting this challenge, the House Committee on Elections treated the Illinois law as an impermissible attempt to add to the list of congressional qualifications: "[I]t is equally clear that a State of the Union has not the power to super add qualifications to those prescribed by the Constitution for representatives, to take away from "the people of the several States" the right given to them by the Constitution to choose, "every second year," as their representative in Congress, any person who has the required age, citizenship, and residence." Ibid., p. 168.

In finding that Trumbull was entitled to his seat, the Committee viewed the Illinois law as an affront not only to the people's authority under Article I, Section 2, but also to congressional power under the Elections Clause:

> By the plain letter of the Constitution Congress may prescribe the time, place, and manner of holding elections for representatives; and at such time and place, and in the manner thus prescribed, every second year, the people of each State may choose as representative in Congress any person having the qualifications enumerated in that Constitution. The power attempted to be asserted by the State of Illinois in the cases before us is in direct contravention of the letter, as also of the spirit, true intent, and meaning of these provisions of the federal Constitution, and absolutely subversive of the rights of the people under that Constitution.

Ibid., p. 169 (finding that votes given to Trumbull not void "because they were given by electors having the qualifications prescribed by the Constitution of the United States, and at the time and place and in the manner prescribed by law"). Article I, Section 2 of the Constitution provides that the qualifications for federal electors should be the same as the electors for the most numerous branch of the state legislature. See United States Constitution Art. I, s. 2.

PART II

From Madison's Republic to Jackson's Democracy

The Constitution of Political Rights and the Evolution of Political Communities

1839 was not the first time that all eyes were fixated on New Jersey's congressional elections. At the very outset, New Jersey distinguished itself in notable ways, most famously by trying to make its elections perpetual. New Jersey law set February 11, 1789, as its first election day under the newly ratified U.S. Constitution.[1] On the ballot were candidates vying to fill the state's four seats in the House of Representatives.[2] The law failed, however, to specify when the election would end, leading to intense partisan wrangling over those counties that had yet to report their results as of March 3rd, which was the day that state law set to canvass the election returns. Essex County (home to Newark) kept its polls open well into March, hoping to secure two of the four congressional seats for Anti-Federalist candidates.[3] The governor refused to include Essex County in the final tally, certifying the results without it and declaring that candidates from the Federalist Party had won all four seats in the state's delegation.[4] Had Essex county been included in the tally, two of the four seats would have gone to the Anti-Federalists.

In one of its first contested election cases, Congress backed New Jersey's governor, finding that he had discretion to certify the election without the Essex County

1 Richard P. McCormick, "New Jersey's First Congressional Election, 1789: A Case Study in Political Skullduggery" (1949) 6 *William and Mary Quarterly* 237–250 (citing Acts of the General Assembly of the State of New Jersey, Thirteenth Session, First Sitting (Trenton, 1788), Acts of November 21, 29, 1788).

2 Edward Foley, *Ballot Battles: The History of Disputed Elections in the United States* (New York: Oxford University Press, 2016), p. 34.

3 Ibid., p. 35.

4 Ibid.

votes to ensure that New Jersey had representation in the House of Representatives once that body reached a quorum.[5] The decision to back the governor was not uncontroversial, as some representatives believed that he was obligated to wait for all of the election returns given the ambiguity in the New Jersey statute.

The governor's actions, and Congress's support of his decision, should not obscure that Congress decided not only whether voters in Essex County would be disenfranchised, but also, by implication, which political party would control New Jersey's delegation. While the states set voter qualifications and the rules regarding how votes are certified, this authority has been constrained by Congress's power to assess the vote tallies ex-post.

Partisan considerations arguably shaped Congress's decision to intervene. A win for the Anti-Federalists would have brought the margin in the House of Representatives much closer, a 35–30 split in favor of the Federalists rather than 37–28. Furthermore, the Federalists' control of the chamber was arguably tenuous. By 1793, they lost the majority they had achieved only four years earlier.

At the very outset of our country's history, Congress has shaped the structure of state political systems and influenced the outcome of state and federal elections. As Part I shows, slavery influenced the framework in which politics was deployed, discussed, and implemented into policy, including the federal government's forays into election regulation through the Constitution of Political Structure (or the Guarantee Clause, the Elections Clause, and Article I, Section 5). By the 1840s, slavery politics was all politics, necessitating greater federal intervention into state political systems as the controversy came to a head.

The breadth of federal authority was also contingent upon the Constitution of Political Rights, or those provisions of the Constitution that directly and indirectly regulate the political rights that stand at the apex of republican political theory. The rights-based Constitution – the focus of this Part – pertains to the vehicles through which the majority that legitimizes republican government can express their will – either through the right to vote, or alternatively, the right to alter or abolish government.

Of course, the latter option was still technically available to the disenfranchised voters in Essex County, had they chosen to use it. The right to alter or abolish government was the "right of revolution" that the colonists invoked against the British during the Revolutionary War. It provided a mechanism, outside of suffrage, for the people writ large to express their sovereign authority vis a vis the government.

This Part highlights these aspects of the Constitution of Political Rights, laying the foundation for its interplay between the structural Constitution and the subsequent expansion of federal authority during the Reconstruction period that is the focus of Part III. At the center of the rights–bearing constitution has always been an

5 Ibid., p. 39.

incessant struggle between two competing political communities and the rights to which they are entitled: that of the voters, and that of the people, writ large.

The Founders, through our governing documents, created the broader community of "We the People," or those whom the federal government is required to protect. But the government also delegated substantial authority to the states through Article I, Section 2, which empowers them to define the state and federal electorates. These electorates are the true sovereigns who hold political power translated through the medium of representative government.

The delineation between "We the People" and "we the Voters" was based on a theory of republicanism that prioritized the needs of the community and emphasized an independent concept of the public good.[6] In the storied narrative of "We the People," the public will trumped individual participation – the hallmark of liberal constitutional thought – such that propertied White men were the only individuals deemed to have the competence and independence sufficient to responsibly exercise the right to vote on behalf of the entire polity.[7] Republican political thought conceptualized rights like suffrage as constructs subject to the existing political will of the governing majority (of White men) as opposed to a product of liberalism's natural rights tradition;[8] thus, those who lacked independence and were subject to arbitrary control from others could be denied the right to vote.[9]

6 Frank I. Michelman, "Conceptions of Democracy in American Constitutional Argument: Voting Rights" (1989) 41 *Florida Law Review* 443–490, 445 ("[R]epublicanism affirms, while liberalism denies, the notion of a statewide substantive common interest or good ... the special mark of republican constitutional thought is affirmation of 'an autonomous public interest independent of the sum of individual interests.'") (citing Morton J. Horwitz, "Republicanism and Liberalism in American Constitutional Thought" (1987) 29 *William & Mary Law Review* 57–74, 67). See also Chapter 1.

7 See Robert J. Steinfeld, "Property and Suffrage in the Early American Republic" (1989) 41 *Stanford Law Review* 335–376, 342–343, 344 (describing this as a tension between English republicanism and liberal individualism). As Steinfeld observes, "In both of these early modern movements ... there was considerable tension between the abstract norm of self-government and its elaboration in the detailed arrangements of social life. English republicanism, for example, celebrated personal independence as the virtue which made genuinely human community possible and vilified dependence as a source of corruption. Yet at the same time, it took for granted that self-government could not be the lot of all mankind. It relegated the propertyless to the degraded status of permanent dependence ... Liberal individualism celebrated the norm of self-government in a different way. The liberal universe was composed of equal, separate, and autonomous individuals. In this universe, all men by nature were assumed to be equally free and independent ... [but] some individuals, such as women and children, were thought to lack the basic capacity to govern themselves." Ibid., 349–350. See also Joseph Fishkin and William E. Forbath, *The Anti-Oligarchy Constitution: Reconstructing the Economic Foundations of American Democracy* (Cambridge: Harvard University Press, 2022), pp. 32–33 (arguing that republicanism required economic equality among white men).

8 Michelman, "Conceptions of Democracy," 446.

9 Under the doctrine of civic republicanism, "the paramount republican value is political liberty, understood as non-domination or independence from arbitrary power." "Republicanism," *Stanford Encyclopedia of Philosophy*, revised June 29, 2002, https://plato.stanford.edu/entries/republicanism/. Philosopher Philip Pettit, "who has done more than anyone else to develop this republican concept of freedom philosophically," posits that such freedom comes from "rightly-ordered laws, institutions, and norms ... in a well-ordered self-governing republic of equal citizens under the rule of law[.]" Ibid.

These elites carved out their own subcommunity of "We the Voters" to make all important policy decisions on behalf of "We the People." They treated the right to vote as akin to a property right and viewed universal suffrage as an unjustifiable socialist endeavor, imbuing the undeserving with a share of the political power.[10] They limited suffrage to property owners to avoid a natural rights conception of voting that would lead to an allocation of resources inuring almost entirely to the benefit of those who, as Alexis de Tocqueville argued almost two centuries ago, "are possessed of no property upon which taxes can be imposed ... [yet in which] all the money which is spent for the community appears to be spent to their advantage, at no cost of their own."[11]

The poor well outnumbered the rich, all but insuring that, if allowed to vote, the poor would set the legislative agenda and jeopardize the interests of wealthy White male property owners.[12] And other groups similarly excluded from the political community, including African Americans, Native Americans, and women, likewise threatened the interests of these elites because of their perceived dependence and unsuitability for the ballot.

Over the course of the nineteenth century, states expanded the electorate to give substance to the egalitarian ideals of the period.[13] While scholars often point to the election of Andrew Jackson and the development of mass political parties as the genesis of almost universal White male suffrage, some states enfranchised 70 percent of White men in the two decades before Jackson won the White House.[14] Even after the abolishment of property requirements for voting, however, property owners protected their interests, not only by retaining property qualifications for referenda on issues related to local government finance, but also by giving property owners the right to vote wherever they owned qualifying property.[15] Americans borrowed the technique of carving out sub-categories within the political community from the British crown, which would charter boroughs or vestries – essentially new political communities – to create both a source of revenue and a means of giving

[10] See generally Steinfeld, "Property and Suffrage" (arguing that pauper restrictions were integral to how earlier generations conceived of a republican political community which was why, in the nineteenth century, pauper restrictions were being added while property restrictions were being eased.)

[11] Alexis de Tocqueville, *Democracy in America*, Arthur Goldhammer (trans.) (New York: Library of America, 2004), p. 11.

[12] Tocqueville, *Democracy in America*, p. 12; Kenneth N. Vines and Henry R. Glick, "The Impact of Universal Suffrage: A Comparison of Popular and Property Voting" (1967) 61 *American Political Science Review* 1078–1087, 1078.

[13] Sean Wilentz, *The Politicians and the Egalitarians: The Hidden History of American Politics* (New York: W.W. Norton & Company, 2016).

[14] These states included New Hampshire, Massachusetts, Pennsylvania, New York, and North Carolina. Andrew W. Robertson, "Afterword: Reconceptualizing Jeffersonian Democracy" (2013) 33 *Journal of the Early Republic* 317–344.

[15] Vines and Glick, "Universal Suffrage," 1078; see also Donald Ratcliffe, "The Right to Vote and the Rise of Democracy, 1787–1828" (2013) 33 *Journal of the Early Republic* 219–254, 233.

discrete groups more direct political control over local government.[16] The democratizing impulse that triggered an aggressive growth in the electorate was therefore still tempered by attempts to carve out enclaves unsullied by the march toward a more universal suffrage.

Indeed, as states gradually loosened voting restrictions in the first half of the nineteenth century, the desire to exclude individuals along racial, gender, and wealth dimensions complicated the push for a broader electorate. Once admitted to the Union, states exercised their authority over voter qualifications without direct federal oversight, exercising free rein over "We the Voters." However, a state's decision to enfranchise a portion of its population did not mean that these individuals became a part of the community of "We the People." *Dred Scott*, for all its infamy, established that the federal government has exclusive authority over defining the community of "We the People."[17]

While suffrage was not enough to establish American citizenship, "We the Voters" and "We the People" were not siloed. Not only was there substantial overlap – most voters were citizens even if all citizens were not voters – the notion of a small electorate became anathema in a country with Democratic impulses that began to emerge well before the Age of Jackson.

State governments attempted to balance the requirements of republicanism, in which the preferences of the majority were supposed to hold sway, with their desire for a narrow electorate by arguing that all people retained their fundamental right to alter or abolish governments. The right, at least in theory, belonged to all of those in "We the People" including nonvoters such as women, African Americans, and property-less White men.[18]

The nominal availability of the right to alter or abolish government to all individuals within the category of "We the People" notwithstanding, the Guarantee

[16] Chilton Williamson, *American Suffrage: From Property to Democracy, 1760–1860* (Princeton: Princeton University Press, 1960), pp. 8–9 (noting that boroughs would extend voting privileges to those allowed to "engage in trade" or those "who were not paupers" while vestries might allow "all householders, male rate-payers, or inhabitants" to vote).

[17] *Dred Scott v. Sandford*, 60 U.S. (19 How.) 393 (1856).

[18] Compare the United States Declaration of Independence, para. 2 (1776) (decreeing that "whenever any Form of Government becomes destructive of these ends, it is the Right of the People to alter or to abolish it, and to institute new Government, laying its foundation on such principles and organizing its powers in such form, as to them shall seem most likely to effect their Safety and Happiness"), with the Constitution of the State of Pennsylvania art. V (1776) ("[T]he community hath an indubitable, unalienable and indefeasible right to reform, alter, or abolish government in such manner as shall be by that community judged most conducive to the public weal."), Virginia Constitution s. 3 (1776) ("[A] majority of the community hath an indubitable, inalienable, and indefeasible right to reform, alter, or abolish [government], in such manner as shall be judged most conducive to the public weal."), and James Madison, "The Federalist 40," in John C. Hamilton (ed.), *The Federalist: A Commentary on the Constitution of the United States* (Philadelphia: J.B. Lippincott & Co., 1864), p. 815 (invoking the "transcendent and precious right of the people to 'abolish or alter their governments'" as a justification for the new constitution).

Clause, with its focus on preventing "domestic violence," made it difficult for "We the People" to use violent means to exercise this right. Delegates descending on Philadelphia on the heels of Shays' Rebellion sought to design a government that pushed the public toward suffrage to ensure republican government, rather than using the alter or abolish right to give voice to their complaints. It was difficult, however, to incentivize states to embrace a more inclusive (but not too inclusive) suffrage, even if the prospect of having federal troops available to quell domestic violence resulting from robust use of the alter or abolish right was an attractive proposition. Nevertheless, the Guarantee Clause – and its focus on representative government – limited the ability of elected officials to disenfranchise those rightfully belonging to the community of "We the Voters," at least not without rendering the notion of republican government meaningless.

The ability to define and shape these communities would slowly evolve to become issues of federal concern over the course of the nineteenth century. While this was contrary to the expectations of the original Constitution, it was not inconsistent with the post–Twelfth Amendment alterations that linked majoritarianism to presidential politics. The volatility of alter or abolish as an unspoken threat to the written Constitution ultimately enhanced congressional power relative to the states. In other words, Congress's role in enforcing republican principles in service of "We the Voters," and imposing limits on the natural right to alter or abolish government retained by "We the People" intruded on the state's authority to unilaterally define their electorates and keep these political communities separate.

Given this tension, there was play in the joints regarding the practical implementation of republican principles, particularly in a society in which states had broad power to define the electorate, yet all sovereign authority technically derived from the people, not the government. As states rejected the right of their citizens to invoke alter or abolish, these refutations of the right punched holes in the theory that all sovereignty remains with the people, even if most cannot vote, precisely because they retain the right to alter or abolish government.

For example, Rhode Island was still governed by its royal charter well into the nineteenth century. Through what became known as the Dorr Rebellion,[19] the people of Rhode Island exercised their right to alter or abolish their state government because the legislature was unwilling to expand the electorate beyond the landed gentry. Rhode Island's charter illustrated the relatively amorphous nature of the republican guarantee, in which republicanism could derive from principles laid out by the very government that the colonists sought to escape.

Invoking the Guarantee Clause, the state government sought federal assistance to quell the rebellion, placing the natural right to alter or abolish government on

[19] The Dorr Rebellion took root in 1842, when the state of Rhode Island effectively had two governments. Robert W. Coakley, *The Role of Federal Military Forces in Domestic Disorders, 1789–1878* (Washington, D.C.: Center of Military History, U.S. Army, 1988), pp. 119–120. See also Chapter 4.

a collision course with notions of republican government. The dispute that culminated in the Dorr Rebellion became yet another casualty of the slavery controversy – where federal intervention would insinuate that the national government had broad authority to interfere with state political systems and, by implication, with slavery. This fear stymied efforts to enforce the Guarantee Clause, either on behalf of the state or those seeking to challenge the political system that excluded them. The relatively nonviolent rebellion significantly weakened the alter or abolish right, while simultaneously undermining the ability of political elites to rely on the right as a justification for a narrowly defined electorate – a customary defense of an electorate defined primarily by property ownership.

Once the Confederacy invoked alter or abolish to secede from the Union, the right completed its descent into desuetude.[20] The South's secession, based on some combination of compact theory and alter or abolish, forced President Abraham Lincoln to develop new theories under the Guarantee Clause to legitimate invocations of the right that inured to the benefit of the Union (namely with the admission of West Virginia) while condemning others (namely southern secession).

Lincoln firmly rejected the legality of secession because he believed that the South's departure, premised on the notion of the Union as a compact that states could leave voluntarily (just as individuals could dissolve their bond with government in invoking alter or abolish), was not "consensual or pursuant to a morally justified revolution," whereas pro-Unionists in West Virginia needed to be protected from "insurrectionists."[21]

Given the status of alter or abolish as a natural right, the distinction between a "morally justified revolution" and "illegal secession" was of utmost importance. Lincoln's circumscription of the right was designed to bring it in line with a requirement of moral justification and, ultimately, federal consent. However, this unintentionally created a conundrum; specifically, the narrowing of the right led to an increasing number of arguments that republicanism now required universal male suffrage rather than simply the option of revolution. Conflict gave the federal government a starring role in this transition.

The exigencies created by the Civil War, which required the federal government to alternate between carving out new states to further Republican dominance and

[20] Herman Belz, "Lincoln, Secession, and Revolution: The Civil War Challenge to the Founding," in Paul D. Moreno and Johnathan G. O'Neill (eds.), *Constitutionalism in the Approach and Aftermath of the Civil War* (New York: Fordham University Press, 2013), p. 81 ("In political life, to question the desirability or necessity of the survival of the political community implicates the crime of treason. Similarly, conflict over the internal structure of the political community, including the question of who should rule the society, implicates the danger of Civil War.").

[21] Peter Radan, "Lincoln, the Constitution, and Secession," in Don H. Doyle (ed.), *Secession as an International Phenomenon: From America's Civil War to Contemporary Separatist Movements* (Athens: University of Georgia Press, 2010), p. 56 ("For Lincoln, the unilateral secessions of the eleven southern states lacked any legitimacy because they were not accompanied by either of these two conditions.").

ensuring the political participation of those loyal voters residing in the Confederacy, expanded federal power over voting and elections in ways that would have been inconceivable only a few years earlier. Furthermore, the demise of strong assertions of the alter or abolish right, now firmly aligned with (and sullied by) the Confederacy, made the turn toward a more inclusive suffrage – and broader federal power – inevitable. By the end of the war, the alter or abolish right was replaced by a right to vote that had transitioned from a quasi-property right of the elites to a political right tied to notions of democracy and representation, available to a broader swath of "We the People."[22] And Congress was no longer an understudy in American democracy but was now in the lead role.

[22] See Akhil R. Amar, "The Consent of the Governed: Constitutional Amendment Outside Article V" (1994) 94 *Columbia Law Review* 457–508, 458; Christian G. Fritz, "Recovering the Lost Worlds of America's Written Constitutions" (2005) 68 *Alabama Law Review* 261–293, 268.

3

Constructing "We the People" and "We the Voters"

A Tale of Two Polities

For four years, Dred Scott traveled with his rather sickly owner, Dr. John Emerson, through several states that today comprise parts of the Midwest and the South. Emerson was in the United States Army and worked as an army surgeon. From 1834 until 1836, Scott and Emerson lived on an army base called Fort Armstrong, located in a sparsely populated area north of St. Louis. In 1836, they moved to Fort Snelling in Upper Louisiana Territory, close to the future home of St. Paul, Minnesota, and importantly, where the Missouri Compromise prohibited slavery.[1] During this time, both Scott and Emerson married. In 1838, Dred and Harriet Scott briefly joined Dr. Emerson and his new bride at Fort Jessup in Louisiana, but the entire group returned to Fort Snelling that fall. After Dr. Emerson was transferred to Florida, Mrs. Emerson and the Scotts settled in St. Louis to await his return. Upon Dr. Emerson's discharge from the army in 1842, the families relocated to Davenport in Iowa Territory, where Dr. Emerson died prematurely in December 1843 and, notably, where slavery was illegal.[2]

Dr. Emerson named his wife's brother, John F.A. Sandford, the executor of his will; Sandford also served as the defendant in the litigation that led to the Supreme Court's decision in *Dred Scott v. Sandford* on behalf of his sister.[3] Between 1843 and 1846, the Scotts were loaned out to Sandford, an army captain stationed in Florida, and they tried unsuccessfully to purchase their freedom from Mrs. Emerson during this time. In April 1846, Dred and Harriet Scott sued for their freedom in state court

1 "[I]n all that territory ceded by France to the United States, under the name of Louisiana, which lies north of thirty-six degrees and thirty minutes north latitude, not included within the limits of the state, contemplated by this act, slavery and involuntary servitude, otherwise than in the punishment of crimes, whereof the parties shall have been duly convicted, shall be, and is hereby, forever prohibited[.]" An Act to authorize the people of the Missouri Territory to form a constitution and state government, and for the admission of such state into the Union on an equal footing with the original states, and to prohibit slavery in certain territories, ch. 22, 3 Stat. 545 (1820), s. 8.

2 See *In the Matter of Ralph (a Colored Man,) on Habeas Corpus*, 1 Morris 1 (Iowa 1839) (declaration of the Iowa Supreme Court that the Missouri Compromise of 1820 established that slavery was illegal in the Iowa Territory).

3 *Dred Scott v. Sandford*, 60 U.S. (19 How.) 393 (1857).

in St. Louis, claiming that Mrs. Emerson had severely mistreated them. Dred Scott also claimed that he was being held as a slave despite being a "free person."[4] The lawsuit was not unprecedented, and slaves bringing such "freedom suits" had routinely been successful in Missouri courts.[5] Despite the pedestrian nature of the case, at least in terms of Missouri law as it existed in 1846, the litigation became the face of a political issue that had long caused controversy on the national stage: Congress's power to regulate slavery in the territories.

Coincidentally, the Scotts sued for their freedom the very same year that David Wilmot, a young member of the House of Representatives from Pennsylvania, introduced his controversial proviso that prohibited slavery in any territories acquired from the Mexican American War (which include the modern-day states of California, Nevada, Utah, New Mexico, Arizona, Colorado as well as parts of Texas, Oklahoma, Kansas, and Wyoming).[6] The proviso spearheaded a national debate over slavery and rendered Congress impotent for four years until reaching a deal in 1850 that, among other things, admitted California as a free state, allowed Utah and New Mexico to decide whether to be slave or free, and permitted slaveowners to enlist the federal government to aid in the return of fugitive slaves.

The Compromise of 1850 did not settle the slavery issue and, instead, inflamed passions on both sides. Its controversial fugitive slave provision infuriated Northerners, who were increasingly convinced that the institution of slavery was immoral, while also failing to pacify Southerners, who felt judged and were certain that the Wilmot Proviso would make another appearance in federal legislation.[7] The controversy over slavery in the territories not only infected Congress and the Supreme Court, it also fueled the judges, juries, and litigants involved in *Dred Scott v. Sandford*. This case, which came to define the 1850s and likely hastened the start of the Civil War, reflected that the public's appetite for freedom suits like the ones brought by the Scotts had disappeared.[8]

[4] Paul Finkelman, *An Imperfect Union: Slavery, Federalism, and Comity* (Union: Lawbook Exchange, 2000), p. 49 (noting that Dred sought to establish that he had been free since at least 1834 so that he could claim twelve years of back wages).

[5] Don E. Fehrenbacher, *The Dred Scott Case: Its Significance in American Law and Politics* (New York: Oxford University Press, 1978), p. 252 ("Again and again, the highest court of the state had ruled that a master who took his slave to reside in a state or territory where slavery was prohibited thereby emancipated him. To be sure, military service at an army post was somewhat different than taking up residence, but the court had disposed of this special problem in Rachel v. Walker (1836).").

[6] Rolander G. M'Clellan, *Republicanism in America: A History of the Colonial and Republican Governments of the United States of America from the Year 1607 to the Year 1869* (San Francisco: R. J. Trumball & Company, 1869), pp. 143–146 (describing the introduction of and the discussion surrounding the Wilmot Proviso in Congress).

[7] See William B. Hesseltine, *The South in American History* (New York: Prentice-Hall, 1943), pp. 309–312.

[8] Fehrenbacher, *The Dred Scott Case*, p. 257 ("Down until 1850, the Scott case attracted little attention beyond the circle of those persons directly involved in the litigation. It had no political implications, and the legal precedents seemed to be all in Scott's favor. These circumstances were already

For eleven years, the Scotts litigated their cases through the lower courts, and it was a mixed bag at best. They initially lost on technical issues, but later received a favorable verdict granting them freedom, at least temporarily. By the time the case reached the Missouri Supreme Court, however, the Scotts became casualties of a much larger fight between the slavery and anti-slavery forces within the state.

As historian Don Fehrenbacher has documented,[9] the states' pro-slavery Supreme Court justices sought to use Scott's case to undermine the political position of Thomas Hart Benton, U.S. Senator from Missouri and celebrated foe of Bourbon Dave Atchison, due to Benton's moderate position on slavery. Pro-slavery Democrats surged in the 1850 elections and sought to secure their political position in the state. In January 1851, the heavily Democratic, pro-slavery state legislature declined to reappoint Benton to the Senate seat that he had held for thirty years. In addition, the once-appointed state Supreme Court became an elected body that year, with only one justice allied with Benton surviving re-election. A pro-slavery justice assumed the role of presiding judge of the court after winning in a landslide during the 1850 election.

Just as this environment generated calls from Bourbon Dave for "one-day Kansans" to stop anti-slavery forces from preventing the spread of slavery into new territories, it also enabled the Missouri Supreme Court to revisit cases holding that the act of taking slaves into a free state liberated them.[10] As early as 1847, the court backed away from precedents that encouraged the presence of free African Americans in the state, fearing the threat these individuals posed to slavery. Pro-slavery forces made further gains in the 1851 elections, which cemented the view that jurisprudence favorable to freedom suits was anathema. In March of 1852, the Missouri Supreme Court, in a 2–1 decision, ruled against the Scotts and reversed the judgment of the trial court.[11]

Five years later, the United States Supreme Court famously (or infamously) affirmed the decision of the Missouri Supreme Court in finding that Dred Scott's travel to a free jurisdiction did not change his status as a slave.[12] The Court went further than its Missouri counterpart, holding that, not only did Congress lack

beginning to change, however, and during the next two years his prospects were adversely affected by the recent course of national politics, by a peculiar crisis in Missouri politics, and by a decision of the United States Supreme Court."). See also ibid., p. 258 ("Geography and history made Missourians especially sensitive to the rising temperature of the sectional quarrel over slavery. Their state was in an exposed position, bordered on three sides by free territory … Furthermore, Missouri was unlike most other slaveholding states in having an articulate antislavery minority, whose presence and utterances heightened the feeling of insecurity among slave-owners in the state.").

9 Ibid., p. 259.

10 Ibid., p. 262 ("The Missouri precedents for the Dred Scott case had been set by liberal-minded judges who were predisposed to favor freedom and whose opinions seemed to reflect the older view of enlightened southerners that slavery was, at best, a necessary evil.").

11 *Scott v. Emerson*, 15 Mo. 576 (1852).

12 *Dred Scott v. Sandford*, 60 U.S. (19 How.) 393, 454 (1857).

authority to prohibit slavery in the territories,[13] but that a "negro of African descent, [whose] ancestors were of pure African blood, and were brought into this country and sold as negro slaves"[14] could not ever claim the mantle of citizenship.[15] Because Dred Scott could never be a citizen, he could not enjoy the rights guaranteed in the Constitution's Privileges and Immunities clause, which included the right to invoke the Court's diversity jurisdiction.[16]

The Court's discussion of citizenship centered on the idea that a citizen is one who, upon the ratification of the Constitution, became a member of the political community created by the Constitution, or "We the People":

> It is true, every person, and every class and description of persons, who were at the time of the adoption of the Constitution recognized as citizens in the several States, became also citizens of this new political body, but none other; it was formed by them, and for them and their posterity, but for no one else.[17]

Yet the Court denied that enslaved people who had been brought into the United States from Africa and their descendants were ever members of this political community because the founding documents intended to exclude them. The Fugitive Slave Clause and the ban on importation of slaves after 1808 confirmed their inferior status.[18] Likewise, the reference to free inhabitants and White inhabitants in the Articles of Confederation was, in the Court's view, further evidence that Black people were outsiders.[19] Even the Declaration of Independence, revered for its admonition that all men are created equal with certain inalienable rights, did not establish the humanity of the Black population, but the opposite: If the Founders meant the Declaration to apply to them, then it would have precluded holding them in slavery.[20]

For all its infamy, the *Dred Scott* decision introduced the idea that the Federal Constitution had a role to play that rivaled that of the states in shaping the boundaries of the political community of "We the People," and this authority would set the terms of federal intervention in the protection of political rights. For example, one of the main points of contention between the majority and the dissent was the status of free Black people during this period. For the majority, the heavy regulation of free Black people illustrated that they, like the enslaved, were not bona fide members of the political community. The law had continually reinforced their inferior status by regulating their movement, their travel, and their employment.

[13] Ibid., 452.
[14] Ibid., 397.
[15] Ibid., 406.
[16] Ibid.
[17] Ibid.
[18] Ibid., 411.
[19] Ibid., 418.
[20] Ibid., 410.

Despite Justice Taney's position that the Founders never intended Black people, regardless of status, to be a part of "We the People," it was not entirely clear that skin color was intended to be the legal disability that it would ultimately become, where race – as opposed to wealth or status – equated to automatic exclusion. As Alexander Hamilton observed in *The Federalist* 54,

> [I]t is only under the pretext, that the laws have transferred the negroes into subjects of property, that a place is denied to them in the computation of numbers; and it is admitted that if the laws were to restore the rights which have been taken away, the negroes could no longer be refused an equal share of representation with the other inhabitants.[21]

Similarly, Justice Curtis, in dissent, pointed to suffrage as one of the clearest indicia that Black people could be citizens, illustrating that race was not automatically disqualifying. The fact that free African Americans in New Hampshire, Massachusetts, New York, New Jersey, and North Carolina exercised the right to vote at the founding was, in his view, sufficient to illustrate their citizenship.[22] Rather than provide clarity, the existence of African American suffrage during the earliest days of the republic complicated the legal questions surrounding the construction of the political community of "We the Voters." The small subset of states identified by Justice Curtis allowed African Americans to vote in their elections, subject to the same property restrictions as all voters, but it is contestable what inferences about federal citizenship can be drawn from enfranchisement of these voters at the state level.[23]

To make this point concrete, consider that foreign-born individuals were not citizens but might be voters. Importantly, the colonies did not list citizenship as a prerequisite for voting,[24] and the practice of allowing noncitizens to vote continued well

[21] Alexander Hamilton, "The Federalist 54," in John C. Hamilton (ed.), *The Federalist: A Commentary on the Constitution of the United States* (Philadelphia: J.B. Lippincott & Co., 1864), p. 418.

[22] "To determine whether any free persons, descended from Africans held in slavery, were citizens of the United States under the Confederation, and consequently at the time of the adoption of the Constitution of the United States, it is only necessary to know whether any such persons were citizens of either of the States under the Confederation, at the time of the adoption of the Constitution. Of this there can be no doubt. At the time of the ratification of the Articles of Confederation, all free native-born inhabitants of the States of New Hampshire, Massachusetts, New York, New Jersey, and North Carolina, though descended from African slaves, were not only citizens of those States, but such of them as had the other necessary qualifications possessed the franchise of electors, on equal terms with other citizens." *Dred Scott v. Sandford*, 60 U.S. (19 How.) 393, 572–573 (1856) (Curtis, J., dissenting).

[23] See generally Robert J. Dinkin, *Voting in America: A Study of Elections in the Original Thirteen States, 1776–1789* (Westport: Greenwood Press, 1982). See also Alexander Keyssar, *The Right to Vote: The Contested History of Democracy in the United States* (New York: Basic Books, 2000), p. 24.

[24] See, e.g., Constitution of the State of New York (1777) (defining an elector as one who "shall have been a freeholder, possessing a freehold of the value of twenty pounds, within the said county, or have rented a tenement therein of the yearly value of forty shillings, and been rated and actually paid taxes to this State"); Constitution or System of Government, Agreed to and Resolved Upon by the Representatives in Full Convention of the Delaware State (1776) ("One of the branches of the

past the ratification of the Constitution.[25] Queries about the connection between citizenship and voting did not happen in earnest until after the War of 1812, which generated a suspicion of noncitizens and led many states to change their qualifications to require citizenship as a prerequisite for voting.[26] Even as citizenship requirements became more widespread, noncitizens – unlike African Americans – could be naturalized,[27] or vote in some jurisdictions if they stated their intention to become citizens.[28] The enfranchisement of both foreign-born electors and African Americans suggested that, while states have significant control over the composition of "We the Voters," the decision to be inclusive cannot alter the boundaries of "We the People," which was under federal control.

This ambiguity provided an opening for Justice Taney to be unequivocal that the inferior status of both enslaved and free Black people rendered them ineligible for American citizenship. It was irrelevant that a state might choose to clothe these individuals with some of the privileges and immunities associated with being a citizen because "no State can, by any act or law of its own … introduce a new member into the political community created by the Constitution of the United States."[29] Or, put differently, states could voluntarily give rights to Black people, but they could not bring Black people within the community created by the Federal Constitution if that inclusion was contrary to that document's intent.

Legislature shall be called, 'The House of Assembly,' and shall consist of seven Representatives to be chosen for each county annually of such persons as are freeholders of the same."). See also Jamin B. Raskin, "Legal Aliens, Local Citizens: The Historical, Constitutional and Theoretical Meaning of Alien Suffrage" (1993) 141 *University of Pennsylvania Law Review* 1391–1470, 1399 ("The practice of noncitizen voting first appeared in the colonies, which generally required only that voters be local 'inhabitants or residents,' and not British citizens.").

25 Raskin, "Alien Suffrage," 1400 ("Alien suffrage survived the Revolution in 1776 as many states granted foreigners state 'citizenship,' a status which was 'given extraterritorial consequences by the privileges and immunities clause of the Articles of Confederation.'").

26 Ibid., 1404 ("In 1812, beginning with Louisiana, most newly admitted states, including Indiana (1816), Mississippi (1817), Alabama (1819), Maine (1820), and Missouri (1821), confined the franchise to citizens. Meanwhile, a number of early states which had permitted alien suffrage, revoked the practice during this same period.").

27 *Dred Scott v. Sandford*, 60 U.S. (19 How.) 393, 417 (1856) ("And this power granted to Congress to establish a uniform rule of naturalization is, by the well-understood meaning of the word, confined to persons born in a foreign country, under a foreign Government. It is not a power to raise to the rank of a citizen any one born in the United States, who, from birth or parentage, by the laws of the country, belongs to an inferior and subordinate class.").

28 See Raskin, "Alien Suffrage," 1406 ("The framers of Wisconsin's Constitution adopted a modified form of alien suffrage, extending full voting rights only to so-called declarant aliens – '[those] White persons of foreign birth who shall have declared their intention to become citizens, conformably to the laws of the United States on the subject of naturalization.' … [T]his provision took advantage of federal naturalization law, which since 1795 had required aliens seeking citizenship to 'first declare under oath to a competent court their intention to apply subsequently for citizenship …'"); see also *Minor v. Happersett*, 88 U.S. 162, 177 (1874) (citing the constitutions of Alabama, Arkansas, Florida, Georgia, Indiana, Kansas, Minnesota, Missouri, and Texas).

29 *Dred Scott v. Sandford*, 60 U.S. (19 How.) 393, 405 (1857).

One can therefore draw an important inference from *Dred Scott*: There was a political community of citizens, separate and distinct from the community of voters, that states do not have authority to define. Some groups qualified for admission into one community but not the other. The most obvious example of those within this category of citizens, but not voters, were disenfranchised women and White men who were obviously citizens but failed to meet the property requirements to become electors. Yet few contested the disenfranchisement of these individuals despite their citizenship status because of a belief that they lacked the requisite independence to be voters.[30]

Instead of suffrage resolving the issue of citizenship, as Justice Curtis asserted, the decision of some states, but not others, to enfranchise certain groups illustrated only that suffrage might sometimes be relevant, but was not indispensable, to becoming a member of the political community of "We the People." But if this group does not automatically have the right to vote, then what rights does it have as a "political" community?

Because citizenship did not necessarily signal that one held rights, the disenfranchised – citizen or not – asserted their political will through the natural right to alter or abolish government, which, as a natural right, belonged to everyone under the jurisdiction of the sovereign: women, property-less men, noncitizen foreigners, and noncitizen free Blacks.[31] Because this was a right commonly situated in violence, however, federal power was inevitably triggered when "We the People" sought to change the political structure outside of official channels.[32]

The interaction between the alter or abolish right and the right to vote is an important chapter in American political history. Attempts to set boundaries on the use of alter or abolish by both the states and the federal government irrevocably shaped the community of voters under state control. On the federal side, the Guarantee Clause limited the ability of the people to radically alter the political community

30 Keyssar, *The Right to Vote*, p. 174 ("That women throughout the nation lacked the right to vote in 1848 reflected beliefs and values long embedded in the politics and culture of the United States and western Europe. Although women were regarded as intelligent adults, they were viewed as having capacities different from those of men, capacities appropriate to private life and the domestic sphere rather than the public world of politics. More decisively perhaps, women – who were envisaged and treated in law as members of families rather than as autonomous individuals – were excluded from the polity for the same reason that the poor and propertyless were disfranchised in the late eighteenth century: they purportedly lacked the 'independence' necessary for participation in electoral politics.").

31 This concept created a lot of dissonance with slavery in which one might argue that slaves were exercising their alter or abolish rights during insurrections. See generally Jill Lepore, *These Truths: A History of the United States* (New York: W.W. Norton & Co., 2019). But the fact, consistent with the Guarantee Clause, that the federal government was obligated to come to the aid of states facing slave insurrections suggests that slaves did not have a natural right to alter or abolish government.

32 See Manisha Sinha, *The Slave's Cause: A History of Abolition* (New Haven: Yale University Press, 2016), p. 47 ("African Americans, slave and free, participated in the crowd action against British rule as early as the Stamp Act crisis. They were part of the revolutionary mob led by the Sons of Liberty that took down King George III's statue in New York. Even in the heart of slavery in the Deep South, Charleston, South Carolina, African Americans marched to the revolutionary slogan 'Liberty.'").

of "We the People" and "We the Voters" through violence and, importantly, served as a constraint on the form of government that the state could adopt. Similarly, the Elections Clause and Article I, Section 5, empowered Congress to reject election outcomes that skirted principles of majoritarianism and that impermissibly intruded on Congress's authority to ensure a republican form of government. Together, these provisions promoted an ideal of republicanism that would ultimately serve as the basis for the Reconstruction project.

3.1 THE POLITICAL COMMUNITY OF "WE THE PEOPLE"

In 1787, there were consistent refrains from the Federalists that if the new constitution was "found defective or inconvenient, two-thirds of both houses of Congress or the application of two-thirds of the legislatures, may open the door for amendments."[33] But there was little doubt that the people had the ultimate power to discard the document altogether, at least rhetorically.[34]

Noah Webster, while advocating for Article V amendment as the solution to Constitution's shortcomings, conceded that the people had the power to resist unjust and unconstitutional laws outside of Article V because, "The supreme power in American cannot enforce unjust laws by the sword; because the whole body of the people are armed, and constitute a force superior to any band of regular troops that can be, on any pretence [sic], raised in the United States."[35] The idea that the people can resist unjust laws through collective violence persisted throughout the debates on the Constitution. According to "A Citizen of Philadelphia," there should be little to fear about Congress abusing its power because "Congress can never get more power than the people will give, nor hold it longer than they will permit; for should they assume tyrannical powers, and make incroachments [sic] on liberty without the consent of the people, they would soon atone for their temerity, with shame and disgrace, and probably with their heads."[36]

Some of the Founders viewed the alter or abolish right as a last resort that should only be used in the most extreme circumstances where the people have lost faith in

33 A Citizen of America [Noah Webster], "An Examination into the Leading Principles of the Federal Constitution, Philadelphia, October 17, 1787," in Bernard Bailyn (ed.), *The Debate on the Constitution: Federalists and Antifederalists Speeches, Articles, and Letters During the Struggle over Ratification*, 2 vols. (New York: Library of America and Viking Press, 1993), vol. 1, pp. 129, 162.

34 Formally, the people play an indirect role in ratifying amendments proposed by Congress which, under Article 5, have to be ratified by three-fourths of the state legislatures (who are directly elected by the people) or state conventions (whose delegates are also typically elected). The people cannot directly propose amendments.

35 A Citizen of America [Noah Webster], "An Examination into the Leading Principles of the Federal Constitution, Philadelphia, October 17, 1787," in Bailyn (ed.), *The Debate on the Constitution*, pp. 129, 155.

36 A Citizen of Philadelphia [Pelatiah Webster], "Congress Can Never Get More Power than the People Will Give," in Bailyn (ed.), *The Debate on the Constitution*, pp. 176, 183–184.

the government, such as what occurred under the Articles of Confederation and during the Revolution. The *Federalist* 39 implied such a limit on alter or abolish, noting that the Constitution was not "wholly national nor wholly Federal" because "were it wholly national, the supreme and ultimate authority would reside in the majority of the people of the Union; and this authority would be competent at all times, like that of a majority of every national society, to alter or abolish its established government."[37]

This passage did not treat alter or abolish as inherently incompatible with republicanism; elsewhere, the *Federalist Papers* noted that the "fundamental principle of republican government … admits the right of the people to alter or abolish the established Constitution, whenever they find it inconsistent with their happiness," yet denied that it should be "inferred from this principle, that the representatives of the people, whenever a momentary inclination happens to lay hold of a majority of their constituents incompatible with the provisions in the existing Constitution, would, on that account, be justifiable in a violation of those provisions."[38]

The idea that there were limits on the people's ability to invoke their right to alter or abolish government was consistent with Lockean notions that, while men are free in a state of nature, this freedom is divested when man consents to become part of a political community in exchange for "their comfortable, safe, and peaceable living one amongst another, in a secure enjoyment of their properties, and a greater security against any, that are not of it."[39] This political community is governed based on the consent of the majority, and is "impowered [sic] to act by positive laws," because the individual is "understood to give up all the power, necessary to the ends for which they unite into society."[40] In turn, the legislative power of the community includes "a right to direct how the force of the commonwealth shall be employed for preserving the community and the members of it."[41] For Locke, the right to exclude – and, in doing so, protect the property interests and rights of the insiders – was, by definition, part and parcel of the commonwealth's coercive authority. Once the people act to constrain their freedom by joining together, the community boundaries cannot be easily disregarded (either from dissenters within or by outsiders who hope to join its ranks).

37 Madison, "The Federalist 39," in Hamilton (ed.), *The Federalist*, pp. 301, 307.

38 Hamilton, "The Federalist 78," in Hamilton (ed.), *The Federalist*, p. 580.

39 John Locke, *Two Treatises on Government* (London: Butler, Reid, Sharpe, and Bumpus, 1821), book 2, ch. VIII, § 95, p. 269. See also John Milton, *The Tenure of Kings and Magistrates* (London: Matthew Simmons, 1650), pp. 8–9 ("No man who knows ought, can be so stupid to deny that all men naturally were borne free, being the image and resemblance of God himself, and were by privilege above all the creatures, born to command and not to obey…Till from the root of Adams transgression, falling among themselves to do wrong and violence, and foreseeing that such courses must needs tend to the destruction of them all, they agreed by common league to bind each other from mutual injury, and joyntly [sic] to defend themselves against any that gave disturbance or opposition to such agreement.").

40 Locke, *Two Treatises on Government*, book 2, ch. VIII, § 99, p. 272.

41 Ibid., book 2, ch. XII, § 143, p. 313.

Political community, as a theoretical concept, has played an important role in determining not only community membership based on shared characteristics and the rights to which members are entitled, but also the sovereign to which members owe their allegiance and that must, concomitantly, be held accountable as the trustee of power that ultimately belongs to the people within the community. Our Constitution places the onus on the states to create these commonwealths that would protect the rights of insiders.

In *Reynolds v. Sims*, for example, the Supreme Court allowed states to depart from the rule of absolute population equality for state legislative districts to preserve political subdivisions with shared characteristics that should be uniformly represented.[42] Similarly, in *District of Columbia v. Heller*, the Court resolved the issue of whether the Second Amendment right to bear arms belonged to the broader community of gun owners or the smaller subset of the militia.[43] By framing the case in these terms, *Heller* was no different from other precedents in which the determination of who were the appropriate rightsholders turned on the boundaries of the relevant political community.

Likewise, *Holt Civic Club v. City of Tuscaloosa* concerned both physical boundaries and the scope of individual rights, with the Court holding that the City of Tuscaloosa could exclude people who lived in its police jurisdiction from voting in its elections because they did not live within city limits.[44] The Court found that geography could limit rights such that the case did not actually present a controversy over whether those outside of city limits could vote in municipal elections; instead, the case's resolution turned on whether there was a rational basis for Alabama statutes that gave extraterritorial force to city ordinances that affected individuals outside of city limits.[45] Geography and rights were, therefore, central attributes of defining the political community.

Political communities also aligned constituencies with the appropriate sovereigns. Some law professors, for example, have presented *McCulloch v. Maryland*[46] as a powerful (though woefully misunderstood) endorsement of broad federal power,[47] while others argue that it represented a misguided or, even worse, erroneous embrace of a nationalist constitutional vision.[48] The decision invalidated a state

42 *Reynolds v. Sims*, 377 U.S. 533 (1964).

43 *District of Columbia v. Heller*, 554 U.S. 570 (2008).

44 *Holt Civic Club v. City of Tuscaloosa*, 439 U.S. 60 (1978).

45 Ibid., p. 70.

46 *McCulloch v. Maryland*, 17 U.S. 316, 327 (1819).

47 See, e.g., David S. Schwartz, "McCulloch v. Maryland and the Incoherence of Enumerationism" (2021) 19 *Georgetown Journal of Law & Public Policy* 25–71; David S. Schwartz, *The Spirit of the Constitution: John Marshall and the 200-Year Odyssey of McCulloch v. Maryland* (New York: Oxford University Press, 2019). See also Franita Tolson, "What is 'Appropriate' Legislation?: McCulloch v. Maryland and the Redundancy of the Reconstruction Amendments" (2020) *Arkansas Law Review* 111–118.

48 See, e.g., Kurt Lash, "John Marshall's Effort to Bury Madisonian Federalism" (2020) 73 *Arkansas Law Review* 119–128; Richard E. Ellis, *Aggressive Nationalism: McCulloch v. Maryland and the Foundation of Federal Authority in the Young Republic* (New York: Oxford University Press, 2007).

tax on the Bank of the United States, famously holding that "the power to tax is the power to destroy."[49] But also central to understanding *McCulloch* is the fact that a tax imposed by constituents of one state against a bank chartered for the good of the people of the United States allowed Maryland to "act[ ] upon institutions created, not by their own constituents, but by people over whom they claim no control."[50] In other words, the people of Maryland sought to deploy the coercive power of the state against constituents not within its borders.

Maryland's attempt to tax a bank intended to benefit citizens of the United States, writ large, shows that political communities overlap in ways that can color the stakes of a particular dispute. The questions surrounding these overlapping political communities have presented very complex legal issues. For example, should Morris Kramer, a thirty-one-year-old stockbroker who lived with his parents, be allowed to vote in school board elections even though he did not own taxable real estate or have children enrolled in public schools, as state law required?

In *Kramer v. Union Free School District No. 15*, the Supreme Court reasoned that, while Kramer himself might not present a persuasive case for enfranchisement, there were others similarly situated, as they neither own nor lease property, who should not be denied the right to vote in school board elections, such as parents with young children or children enrolled in private schools.[51] Notably, Justice Stewart, in a dissenting opinion, argued that Kramer's exclusion was permitted since he could vote for members of the state legislature and was, therefore, part of the political community responsible for promulgating the substantive policies that governed the school board.[52] For Justice Stewart, Kramer's exclusion from one political community, but inclusion in another, mitigated any potential harm that arose from his not being able to participate in school board elections that did not directly affect him.[53]

As these cases show, some of the Supreme Court's most famous individual rights cases were not solely about the individual or federalism, as such. Instead, they concerned the boundaries of the political community. Political community is a concept that defines the scope of rights that any person within its boundaries is entitled to at any given time. Communities can be fluid and enduring; after all, "We the People" is well over two centuries old. While communities can be destroyed (such as the demise of the powerful planter class in the wake of the Civil War), they have also been created on a much smaller scale outside of the ebbs and flows of constitutional change. Each state is a political community, and so is each city and town, and the various jurisdictions in between. For our purposes, any group that exercises power and possesses rights is a political community. Historically, political communities have had a certain complexion (in that they tend to be overwhelmingly White,

49 *McCulloch*, 17 U.S. at 327.
50 Ibid., 435.
51 *Kramer v. Union Free School Dist. No. 15*, 395 U.S. 621, 630 (1969).
52 Ibid., 639 (Stewart, J., dissenting).
53 Ibid.

male, and privileged), and many of the fault lines that have emerged have stemmed from attempts to expand the boundaries of these communities to include those who were previously excluded.

There has not been a perfect overlap between the political communities of "We the People" and "We the Voters" because these communities serve very different sovereigns. Despite the expansion of the franchise over the course of the eighteenth and nineteenth centuries, the structure of the federal government as described by the U.S. Constitution is not populist in the same way as state governments. The Constitution could only be amended by way of formal procedures under Article V and limited the direct involvement of the people to selecting members of the House of Representatives. Accordingly, the text delegated to the states the authority to determine the qualifications of those who would vote on behalf of the people which, in the Founders' view, was just as good as the people exercising power for themselves. As James Madison noted in *The Federalist* 39, "[t]he house of representatives will derive its powers from the people of America, and the people will be represented in the same proportion, and on the same principle, as they are in the Legislature of a particular State."[54]

The Constitution's division of power among the federal government, the states, and the people reflected the selective use of popular sovereignty to validate the new powers of the national government, while relegating majoritarianism to the state level.[55] Given this structure, it is unsurprising that there is no mechanism for direct democracy at the federal level, nor does the Constitution contain an alter or abolish provision similar to those that existed in state constitutions during the founding.

Yet there was still a belief among the founding generation that the natural right to alter or abolish held by "We the People" survived the ratification of the Constitution. In *Notes on Suffrage*, James Madison struggled to reconcile the inherent tension between limiting voting to property owners, a category in which most people could never realistically belong, and creating a society "in which an equal voice in making the laws might be allowed to every individual bound to obey them."[56] For Madison,

[54] James Madison, "The Federalist 39," in Hamilton (ed.), *The Federalist*, p. 302.

[55] See Akhil R. Amar, "Of Sovereignty and Federalism," (1987) 96 *Yale Law Journal* 1425–1520, 1436 ("[A]s sovereign, the People need not wield day-to-day power themselves, but could act through agents on whom they conferred limited powers.... So long as the People at all times retained the ability to revoke or modify their delegations, such agency relationships were in no sense a surrender or division of ultimate sovereignty."); see also Cass R. Sunstein, *The Partial Constitution* (Cambridge: Harvard University Press, 1994), p. 21 ("[The Framers] attempted to carry forward the classical republican belief in virtue ... but to do so in a way that responded realistically, not romantically, to likely difficulties in the real world of political life.... We might understand the Constitution as a complex set of precommitment strategies, through which the citizenry creates institutional arrangements to protect against political self-interest, factionalism, failures in representation, myopia, and other predictable problems in democratic governance ... .").

[56] James Madison, "Note on Suffrage, December 1829," National Archives, *Founders Online: Madison Papers*, https://founders.archives.gov/documents/Madison/99-02-02-1922.

resolving this tension did not require this "unfavoured [sic] class of the community" receive a share of the political power because "the proportion being without property, or the hope of acquiring it, cannot be expected to sympathize sufficiently with its rights to be safe depositories of power over them."[57] Extending suffrage to the impoverished was too risky, Madison warned, cautioning that universal suffrage was "dangerous to all parties and to liberty itself."[58]

Madison rationalized that enfranchising only a small subset of the political community was justified because the disenfranchised could invoke their natural right to alter or abolish government, which was a better reflection of the sovereignty of the people than broad access to political rights. Indeed, the Federal Convention of 1787 was treated by attendees as itself a manifestation of the people's right to alter or abolish the Articles of Confederation.[59] According to Madison, "The people were in fact the fountain of all power, and by resorting to them, all difficulties were got over. They could alter constitutions as they pleased. It was a principle in the [state] bills of rights, that first principles might be resorted to."[60]

State constitutional revision during the Confederation period of 1776–87 reflected this view that the people were both the rulers and the ruled such that they could adopt, amend, and abolish their constitutions at will.[61] Yet a coherent definition of who constituted "the people" entitled to wield this tremendous power created difficulties for a highly stratified political system in which property owners exercised direct political power while the people retained the arguably greater power to alter or abolish the government. Locke himself did not envision the alter or abolish right extending to the impoverished, instead envisioning a system of compulsory labor that uncomfortably mirrored that of slavery.[62]

57 Ibid.

58 Ibid.

59 See, e.g., Michael Coenen, "The Significance of Signatures: Why the Framers Signed the Constitution and What They Meant By Doing So" (2010) 119 *Yale Law Journal* 966–1010, 999 (noting that "at the Pennsylvania ratifying convention, James Wilson countered charges that the Constitution violated the Articles of Confederation by reading out loud the Declaration's recognition of 'the Right of the People to alter or abolish' ineffective governments") (citing "Debates from the Pennsylvania Ratification Convention," in Jonathan Elliott (ed.), *Debates in the Several State Conventions on the Adoption of the Federal Constitution*, 2nd. ed, 4 vols. (Washington, D.C.: Jonathan Elliott, 1881), vol. 2, p. 457).

60 James Madison, "Comments of Tuesday, August 31, 1787," in *Notes of Debates in the Federal Convention of 1787* (Athens: Ohio University Press, 1984), p. 448.

61 Christian G. Fritz, "Out from under the Shadow of the Federal Constitution: An Overlooked American Constitutionalism" (2010) 41 *Rutgers Law Journal* 851–880, 868–869.

62 Edmund Morgan, "Slavery and Freedom: The American Paradox" (1972) 59 *Journal of American History* 5–29, 9–10 ("John Locke, the classic explicator of the right of revolution for the protection of liberty, did not think about extending that right to the landless poor. Instead, he concocted a scheme of compulsory labor for them and their children.... And many of Locke's intellectual successors, while denouncing slavery in the abstract, openly preferred slavery to freedom for the lower ranks of laborers."). See Sinha, *The Slave's Cause*, p. 35 ("To the English thinker John Locke slavery was abominable and outside the social contract but the enslavement of Africans was legitimate, a condition of prisoners taken in a 'just war.'").

The founding generation did not explicitly endorse the view that poverty should automatically result in enslavement, but concerns remained about the prospect of alter or abolish being invoked by those who lacked independence yet sought upward mobility contrary to their station and by enslaved people seeking to contest their enslavement. Indeed, Bacon's Rebellion – a 1676 Virginia uprising by populists against the British governor[63] – featured an alliance between Black and White Virginians that was the embodiment of these concerns. To the founding generation, slaves forfeited any claim to natural rights by virtue of their condition and subsequent lack of independence, including the right to alter or abolish government;[64] however, the ghost of Bacon's Rebellion reminded the landed gentry to also be prudent in limiting the circumstances in which alter or abolish could be invoked as a basis for grassroots political action among White men.[65]

One such person who played an integral but unintended role in the domestication of the alter or abolish right was a thirty-nine-year-old farmer from Massachusetts named Daniel Shays. Shays was a Revolutionary War veteran who saw action in some of the most famed battles of the conflict including Bunker Hill, Lexington, and Saratoga. When he returned to civilian life, however, he experienced the limitations of the Articles of Confederation firsthand and, in particular, the lack of federal aid to alleviate the debt burden in places like Shays' home

63 Bacon's Rebellion was spearheaded by Nathaniel Bacon, Jr., who had been shipped off to Virginia from England in 1670 after angering his father, a member of the English nobility, with his choice of a wife. Julian A.C. Chandler and Travis B. Thames, *Colonial Virginia* (Richmond: Times-Dispatch Company, 1907), p. 226. The younger Bacon eventually became a plantation owner. Ibid., p. 229. When his plantation came under armed threats from Native Americans, Bacon sought a commission from the Virginia governor, Sir William Berkeley, to fight against them, which Berkeley denied. Ibid. This led to a prolonged battle between Bacon (and his amassed supporters) and Berkeley, with Berkeley accusing Bacon of armed rebellion. Ibid. Bacon issued a manifesto in response to this treatment, in which he accused Berkeley of

> raising unjust taxes for the advancement of favorites, … not having provided for the colony fortifications, towns or trade, … having rendered the majesty of the law contemptible by placing ignorant favorites in responsible positions, … having assumed the monopoly of the beaver trade, and … having refused to protect the people of Virginia against the invasions and murders committed by the Indians.

Ibid., p. 234. Bacon died in 1676, and his rebellion died with him. Ibid., pp. 236–237.

64 Sinha, *The Slave's Cause*, p. 35 (noting that "Locke's notion of property as a natural right also bolstered slaveholder's claims…Racial slavery was a material basis of the growth of white republicanism in Virginia. But belief in republican principles also posed a threat to slavery, which in turn weakened commitment to revolutionary ideals.").

65 Morgan, "Slavery and Freedom," 22 ("Virginia's poor had reason to be envious and angry against the men who owned the land and imported the servants and ran the government. But the rebellion produced no real program of reform, no ideology, not even any revolutionary slogans. It was a search for plunder, not for principles. And when the rebels had redistributed whatever wealth they could lay their hands on, the rebellion subsided almost as quickly as it begun."); Ibid. ("It had been a shattering experience, however, for Virginia's first families. They had seen each other fall in with the rebels in order to save their skins or their possessions or even to share in the plunder.").

state of Massachusetts.[66] The Articles restricted Congress's ability to raise revenue, address foreign policy concerns, and force the states to comply with federal law and treaty obligations.[67] Congress attempted to enact a comprehensive revenue plan that would spread the burden of national expenses among the states and force them to levy taxes designated exclusively for federal use, but the plan ultimately failed because all of the states did not agree to it, as required by the Articles.[68]

The financial crisis in the post–Revolutionary War period was further exacerbated by Congress's inability to protect the country's commercial interests abroad.[69] Great Britain, presumably still peeved about their defeat, closed their ports to American ships while British exporters flooded American markets with goods that had not been attainable during the war. Congress did not have the power under the Articles of Confederation to punish the British for these retaliatory policies.[70] Nor did Congress have the power to punish states that violated the Treaty of Paris, which ended the Revolutionary War, when states refused to permit British citizens and American loyalists to recover property confiscated during the war.[71] This noncompliance led Great Britain to violate the treaty as well, specifically by refusing to vacate the northwestern forts after the war.[72] Congress submitted proposals to the states between 1784 and 1786 requesting amendments to the Articles that would give Congress more authority over foreign commerce, but like Congress's revenue

66 See David P. Szatmary, *Shay's Rebellion: The Making of an Agrarian Insurrection* (Amherst: University of Massachusetts Press, 1980).

67 Jack Rakove, *Original Meanings: Politics and Ideas in the Making of the Constitution* (New York: A.A. Knopf, 1996), p. 25; Gordon S. Wood, *The Creation of the American Republic, 1776–1787* (Chapel Hill: University of North Carolina Press, 1998), p. 395.

68 Rakove, *Original Meanings*, p. 25 (noting that the plan had three major elements including "an impost lasting twenty-five years," "the appropriation by the states of supplemental taxes dedicated to federal use," and "a revision of the formula in Article VIII … for apportioning national expenses among the states").

69 Ibid., p. 26 (describing this as a "crucial defect" because it was "widely assumed that American relations with Europe would be commercial rather than political in nature").

70 Ibid. ("Congress could neither devise nor impose a uniform set of restrictions on British ships. And this constitutional debility in turn diminished the prospects for advancing American trading interests through the negotiation of a satisfactory commercial treaty with Britain … .").

71 Ibid., p. 27 (noting that Congress can only recommend that the states "permit British subjects and American loyalists to sue for the recovery of confiscated property" even though the treaty with Britain required it).

72 Ibid. See also Gordon S. Wood, *Empire of Liberty: A History of the Early Republic, 1789–1815* (Oxford: Oxford University Press, 2009), p. 15 ("Britain refused to send a minister to the United States and ignored its treaty obligations to evacuate from American territory in the Northwest."); John J. Gibbons, "The Eleventh Amendment and State Sovereign Immunity: A Reinterpretation" (1983) 83 *Columbia Law Review* 1889–2004, 1900 ("Article VII of the Treaty imposed two obligations on the British: to evacuate all military posts within American territory, and to leave behind the slaves. The British, however, honored neither obligation") (internal citation omitted). Sensing the weak new government, other European governments also refused to honor American sovereignty. Wood, *Empire of Liberty*, p. 15 (noting that in the southwest, Spain "refused to recognize American claims to the territory between Florida and the Ohio River" and attempted to "close the Mississippi to American trade").

plan, these proposals floundered because of the requirement of unanimous assent by the states.[73]

Massachusetts floundered after the war, during which it had amassed a debt of $14 million. As a result, the state was forced to levy high property taxes and head taxes to cover the deficit.[74] The Massachusetts government ignored requests that emerged from county conventions seeking to alleviate the burdens that these taxes imposed on yeoman farmers. The conventions put forth proposals calling for "a reduction in government salaries, increased power for the towns, a tender law, … a moratorium on civil cases … removing the government from Boston, changes in judicial organization, and, ultimately, a statewide convention to amend the Massachusetts Constitution."[75]

On August 29, 1786, Shays led 1,500 men in a revolt that closed the courts, preventing foreclosures on the impoverished and embittered population.[76] As historians have recognized, his rebellion, which was fundamentally a violent response to excessive taxation, followed a similar track as the events leading to the Revolutionary War.[77] Yet the rebellion did not invoke the same sense of urgency and justified outrage that prompted the declaration, in 1776, that circumstances had deteriorated such that it was "necessary for one people to dissolve the political bands which have connected them with another."[78] For almost ten months, Shays' Rebellion played out in a series of scattered skirmishes and, in the process, revealed the impotence of the Massachusetts government and the financial constraints of the Confederation.

In the wake of Shays' Rebellion, which formally ended one month after delegates descended on Philadelphia in May 1787, newspaper editorials did not defend the alter or abolish right that lie at the heart of the rebellion, but instead favored a stronger national government better equipped to quell revolt.[79] While the rebellion was not the singular cause of the Constitutional Convention, it was one element that not only reinforced the need for a more powerful central government, but also reflected a hardening of sentiment toward the right of revolution.[80] It was easy to

73 Wood, *Empire of Liberty*, p. 15.

74 Rachel R. Parker, "Shay's Rebellion: An Episode in American State-Making," 34 *Sociological Perspectives* 95–113, 100.

75 Ibid., 100.

76 Ibid.

77 Ibid.

78 Ibid.

79 Ibid., 103 (noting that "During the first three months [of Shays' Rebellion], 88 percent of statements [in seven newspapers studied from the time period] specified that Massachusetts should manage the revolt. By the following May, a majority of statements designated the Confederation as the authority obliged to deal with the problem.").

80 Compare Wood, *Empire of Liberty*, p. 31 ("In addition to correcting the deficiencies of the Articles of Confederation, the Constitution was intended to restrain the excesses of democracy and protect minority rights from overbearing majorities in the state legislatures"), with Christian G. Fritz, *American Sovereigns: The People and America's Constitutional Tradition before the Civil War* (New York: Cambridge University Press, 2008), pp. 8–9 ("[W]e assume from Wood's description of the rise of a more constrained proceduralism [through the adoption of Article V] that the constitutionalism

overlook that Shays and others had attempted to call a Constitutional Convention in Massachusetts but were rebuked; for many in this camp, rebellion was the only option, and they felt justified in exercising it. And for good reason.

Several states that drafted constitutions during the Revolutionary War included alter or abolish provisions that mirrored the traditional, and sometimes violent, version of this right;[81] despite Shays' Rebellion, states continued to adopt these provisions upon entry into the Union post-ratification, even while being remarkably reluctant to sanction its exercise.[82] For example, Ethan Allen and his Green Mountain Boys relied on the alter or abolish right to break away from New York and form Vermont in 1777, but leaders from the Continental Congress rejected this attempt as "untenable."[83] After fourteen years as a de facto republic, Vermont was successful in its quest to become independent of New York in 1791, but it was not clear what distinguished Allen's invocation of alter or abolish from that of Daniel Shays, other than gradual public acceptance of Vermont's cause.[84] In fact, Shays and his followers modeled themselves after the Green Mountain Boys, who had started Vermont's push toward eventual statehood ten years earlier.

of the early revolutionary period has been dead for over two centuries. But the … records of nearly a hundred constitutional conventions after 1787 belie the assumption that non-procedural constitutionalism died with the birth of the Federal Constitution…. In the years following the Constitution's adoption, Americans continued to dispute, both at the federal and state level, whether constitutional procedures could limit the powers of the sovereign – the people – who created those constitutions.").

81 Fritz, "Out from under the Shadow," 871.

82 See ibid. ("The constitutional logic of recognizing the people as sovereign may have suggested that the right of revolution no longer applied in America. This did not develop instantly or uniformly after the establishment of American governments. Some of the first state constitutions included 'alter or abolish' provisions that mirrored the traditional right of revolution. [discussing Maryland] Other state constitutions adopted different versions of this right to 'alter or abolish' that did not sound like the traditional right of revolution. [discussing Virginia] Increasingly, however, as Americans included it in their state constitutions, the right of revolution came to be seen as a constitutional principle permitting the people as sovereign to control government and revise their constitutions without limit.").

83 See Ethan Allen, *A Vindication of the Opposition of the Inhabitants of Vermont to the Government of New York and of their Right to Form an Independent State: Humbly Submitted to the Consideration of the Impartial World* (Dresden, VT, i.e. Hanover, NH: Alden Spooner, 1779); Fritz, *American Sovereigns*, p. 55 (noting that "Americans could 'alter or abolish' their governments but congressional leaders faced a quandary" because "maintaining the status quo of newly established American governments was a more pressing concern than extending the logic of the Revolution's principles that might challenge those governments"); Aaron T. Knapp, "Law's Revolutionary: James Wilson and the Birth of American Jurisprudence" (2014) 29 *Journal of Law and Politics* 189–307, 233 ("In the decade after Independence, the intellectual tides increasingly turned against the more radical articulations of popular power that had debuted in the heady days of revolution – a trend that began as early as 1778 and which culminated in an oft-expressed fear of anarchy in the wake of Shays' Rebellion.").

84 See James M. Greene, "Ethan Allen and Daniel Shays: Contrasting Models of Political Representation in the Early Republic" (2013) 48 *Early American Literature* 125–151, 140 ("The Massachusetts protestors likely imagined themselves as part of the same stream of local resistance as the residents of Vermont since both groups had used collective action to block the proceedings of a legal system they believed favored wealthy, metropolitan interests at the expense of rural communities. The protestors in western Massachusetts even adopted the same visual symbolism used by the Green Mountain Boys, with members of both groups placing a sprig of evergreen in their hatbands to show affiliation.").

These similarities, notwithstanding, Allen distanced himself from Shays, whose cause had failed to cultivate similar public support.[85] According to historian James Greene, "The Framers imagined popular political violence as a legitimate revolution only when it emerged from the unified will of the body of the people to replace a corrupt government."[86] Thus, the lack of public support for Shays' Rebellion proved detrimental to the exercise of this power, even if Shays was presumably exercising a natural right in circumstances similar to that of the Revolution.[87]

Despite the controversy in Massachusetts, the right to alter or abolish government remained vibrant throughout the founding and antebellum periods, albeit in a more watered-down form. Many state leaders recognized that alter or abolish could be dangerous, but did not believe they had the authority to eliminate it outright because of its connection to the "right of revolution" in the Declaration of Independence.[88] State constitutions adopted during this period circumscribed this authority in two ways: by adding mechanisms by which state constitutions could be formally amended, and by delegating significant authority to the people to revise their state constitutions at will.[89] During this period, the people used the alter or abolish right to displace state laws with which they disagreed;[90] to hold constitutional conventions independent of the legislature;[91] to revise their state constitutions

85 Ibid., 126.

86 Ibid., 127.

87 Ibid., 126–127.

88 See Akhil R. Amar, "Philadelphia Revisited: Amending the Constitution Outside Article V" (1988) 55 *University of Chicago Law Review* 1043–1103, 1050 (describing the people's alter or abolish power as an "inalienable legal right – that is, a right that [the people] were incapable of waiving, even if they tried").

89 State constitutions at the founding constantly evolved because drafters looked to the constitutions of sister states in writing, revising, and creating their own constitutions. See Marsha L. Baum and Christian G. Fritz, "American Constitution-Making: The Neglected State Constitutional Sources" (2000) 27 *Hastings Constitutional Law Quarterly* 199–242, 207–208 ("Compilations [of existing state constitutions] facilitated the first wave of constitution-making after the Revolution and produced an enduring trait of American constitution-making: a clear instinct for comparison, modeling, and borrowing. Newspapers regularly published the texts of state constitutions, which were subjected to close analysis and scrutiny by revolutionary constitution-makers"); see also John J. Dinan, *The American State Constitutional Tradition* (Lawrence: University Press of Kansas, 2009), p. 3 ("[T]he drafters of the federal Constitution established a rigid amendment and revision process, [but] state convention delegates have almost uniformly rejected this approach and adopted relatively flexible procedures for constitutional change…."); Fritz, *American Sovereigns*, p. 242 ("With one exception, every state between 1820 and 1842 holding a constitutional convention inserted a provision for amendment if one did not already exist in its constitution.").

90 See generally Larry D. Kramer, *The People Themselves: Popular Constitutionalism and Judicial Review* (New York: Oxford University Press, 2004).

91 Richard L. Mumford, "Constitutional Development in the State of Delaware, 1776–1897," 108–109 (1968) (unpublished PhD dissertation, University of Delaware) (on file with author) (noting that Delaware's 1776 Constitution "did not include any mode of calling a convention [but] [i]t was called on the assumption that the people retained an inherent right to change their frame of government").

without official ratification;[92] and, as in the case of Vermont, to form new states.[93] The right was not contingent on wealth, status, or intellect, and because the people could exercise it at any time, government was still based on the consent of the governed, even if much of the population could not vote.[94]

3.2 FROM "WE THE PEOPLE" TO "WE THE VOTERS": POLITICAL COMMUNITY AND THE CREATION OF AN ELECTORATE

Over a century after Dred Scott made the winding journey upon which his claim for freedom was predicated and two centuries after Daniel Shays closed the courts to stall the economic downfall of his countrymen – both in their own way hoping to redefine the terms upon which one could be a part of "We the People" – Jim Blumstein sought to assert the rights given to those who belong in the political community of "We the Voters."

Excited to start his job as an assistant professor at Vanderbilt Law School, Blumstein moved to Nashville on June 12, 1970. He arrived with the intention of relocating permanently, and over five decades later, Professor Blumstein still calls Nashville home. Currently the director of Vanderbilt's Health Policy Center, Blumstein has had a distinguished career, eventually rising to the level of university professor because of his path-breaking work in health law and medicine.[95] But he has also made his mark in other ways, notably as the named plaintiff in one of the most important voting rights cases in U.S. history: *Dunn v. Blumstein*.

92 See Amar, "Philadelphia Revisited," 1051–1052 (arguing that Massachusetts, Pennsylvania, and Maryland legally ratified the U.S. Constitution – even though its adoption effectuated a change to their existing state constitutions by a procedure not explicitly mentioned in those documents – because the natural right to alter or abolish government gave "a bare majority of the People … a legal right to amend their constitution" outside of its formal strictures); Christian G. Fritz, "Fallacies of American Constitutionalism" (2004) 35 *Rutgers Law Review* 1327–1370, 1352 ("Studies have long documented numerous instances – if not a tendency toward – constitutional revision bypassing established constitutional procedures.").

93 See James Q. Dealey, *Growth of American State Constitutions: From 1776 to the End of the Year 1914* (Boston: Ginn and Company, 1915), p. 50 (noting that, in eight of the states that entered the Union between 1831 and 1860, "the inhabitants, in their eagerness for statehood, called a convention on their own account and then petitioned Congress for admission"); Fritz, "Fallacies," 1352 ("[O]nly one of the seven constitutions that formed states out of the Northwest Territory between 1802 and 1830 was [submitted to a constitutional convention and] ratified by the people" and "of the 119 constitutions created between 1776 and 1900, 45 constitutions (roughly 38%) were adopted without [constitutional convention and] popular ratification ….").

94 See Locke, *Two Treatises on Government*, book 2, ch. II, § 9, p. 194 ("Those who have the supreme power of making laws in England, France, or Holland are, to an Indian, but like the rest of the world – men without authority … I see not how the magistrates of any community can punish an alien of another country, since, in reference to him, they can have no more power than what every man naturally may have over another.").

95 James F. Blumstein, "Vanderbilt Law School Faculty Directory," https://law.vanderbilt.edu/bio/james-blumstein [https://perma.cc/D2ZT-4FH6], last visited March 15, 2023.

Professor Blumstein's excitement upon arriving in his new city on that June day in 1970 was significantly dampened when he appeared at the Davidson County office of the Registrar-at-large on July 1, 1970. Election supervisors informed him that he could not register, despite his intent to become a permanent Nashville resident, because he had not been a resident of Davidson County for the three-month period preceding the election nor had he been a resident of the State of Tennessee for a full year preceding the same election. Outraged, Blumstein demanded a provisional ballot that he filled out on the spot, something that federal law would not require for another two decades.[96]

The state of Tennessee decided that Blumstein had not proven that he was a member of the political community entitled to exercise the right to vote in its elections. In litigation brought following his disenfranchisement, Blumstein – a Yale graduate not yet admitted to the Tennessee bar but the first in his class to argue a case before the U.S. Supreme Court – successfully showed that Tennessee's exclusionary rules were indefensible, given the importance of voting. As the Supreme Court observed in the case that shares Blumstein's name, preserving "the purity of the ballot box" and "preventing fraud" were not state interests furthered by expansive regulation that affects both temporary and bona fide residents.[97]

To be clear, the issue was not whether Tennessee could limit voting to bona fide state residents. Tennessee and its citizens had defined their political community based on Lockean notions of government by consent. As a newcomer, Blumstein was a trespasser in the eyes of the state, seeking a share of the political power though he had not yet established that he was entitled to be a member of either Tennessee's political community or the smaller political community of Davidson County. Instead, the issue was whether Tennessee could require individuals to live in the state for a year and the County for three months to prove that they were bona fide residents. This was the requirement that the Supreme Court found wanting.[98]

[96] Grace Renshaw, "A New York Yankee in Tennessee Court" (2012) 40 *Vanderbilt Lawyer*, https://law.vanderbilt.edu/alumni/lawyer-vol40num2/blumstein.php [https://perma.cc/H59G-REHT, last visited March 15, 2023.

[97] *Dunn v. Blumstein*, 405 U.S. 330, 345 (1972).

[98] Ibid., 347 ("Even if durational residence requirements imposed, in practice, a pre-election waiting period that gave voting officials three months or a year in which to confirm the bona fides of residence, Tennessee would not have demonstrated that these waiting periods were necessary. At the outset, the State is faced with the fact that it must defend two separate waiting periods of different lengths. It is impossible to see how both could be 'necessary' to fulfill the pertinent state objective."). A one-year residency requirement was not unusual, historically. See *Williams v. Whiting*, 11 Mass. 424 (1814) (finding that one who had not resided in the town for one year prior to a congressional election, as required by law, was not entitled to cast a ballot). The goal was to separate bona fide residents from transient populations. See *Putnam v. Johnson*, 10 Mass. 488 (1813) (holding that a college student who lived in the area on his own for three years and paid taxes was a resident who was entitled to vote); *Custis v. Lane*, 17 Va. 579 (1813) (voter properly disenfranchised in Virginia elections because the county in which he was domiciled was ceded to Washington, D.C.).

As Professor Blumstein experienced firsthand, our relationship with democracy is and always has been complicated. This complication arises because the question of who should be entitled to vote as a bona fide member of the political community – regardless if we are referring to the electorate of Davidson County or Tennessee or the more ubiquitous American people – is intimately connected to decisions about the composition of the "majority" that should be able to deploy the coercive power of the state. And for most of our first century, the decision of who the majority would be was a decision made solely by the states, making it very difficult to conceive of "We the Voters" in a way that would give the federal government any significant power over the state-level decisions that ultimately defined "We the People" in the aggregate.

In fact, had Professor Blumstein sued even ten years earlier, the Supreme Court would have likely found that Tennessee still possessed the power to exclude him on the basis of residency, the failure to pay a poll tax, or an inability to read a provision of the state constitution.[99] In the years since Reconstruction, states reasserted a vision of voting that was closely aligned to its colonial and antebellum era status; specifically, as a property right to be enjoyed by those who showed the requisite independence and virtue that we infer from qualities such as wealth, literacy, and status within the political community. *Dunn v. Blumstein* happened to be litigated during a broader federal intervention into the electoral apparatus of the states taking place just that decade, resolved by constitutional provisions that had long lain dormant.

The fact that federal power to directly regulate and shape the electorate could lay mostly quiet for decades was notable. Arguably, the Court's decision in *Dunn* – that the Federal Constitution has implications for the construction of state electorates – was not foreordained because of several factors: our country's fraught history of politically- and racially-motivated violence; a constitutional text and structure that, in its first iteration, allowed states to define the electorates for almost all elections; and a federal government that was bearish on confronting these restrictions, no matter how unconstitutional.

But the existence of federal authority must be distinguished from its exercise. As Part I of this book showed, Congress could have intervened, for example, by changing the registration rules for federal elections pursuant to the Elections Clause. Or, to foreshadow Part III, Congress could have found that Tennessee's restrictive registration regime constituted an abridgment of the right to vote under Section 2 of the Fourteenth Amendment. Yet the post-Reconstruction-era was one in which the political norms again favored state authority over elections, a throwback to the antebellum period.

Prior to the Civil War, states created political communities that placed the political power in the hands of propertied White men. This foundation would prove

[99] See "Voting Restrictions in Special Districts: A Case Study of the Salt River Project" (1969) *Law and the Social Order* 636–677, 641–643 (providing background on several Supreme Court decisions, issued during the 1960s, related to voting restrictions enforced by the states).

difficult to dislodge, even as property restrictions for voting declined. Majority rule was both an ideal and a dilemma for a society that, while touting itself as egalitarian, sought, with few exceptions, to enfranchise only a limited number of White men. Benjamin Franklin was an early advocate of eliminating property requirements for electors, an idea consistent with a majority that is more representative of society being able to keep elected officials accountable. In 1769, Franklin remarked that "they who have no voice nor vote in the electing of representatives do not enjoy liberty; but are absolutely enslaved to those who have votes and to their representatives."[100] Ethan Allen also regarded suffrage as a right that should be broadly available beyond the propertied, leading Vermont to become the first state to adopt voter qualification standards free of property or tax-paying restrictions.[101] Franklin and Allen endorsed a brand of republicanism that required the underlying community to extend beyond the wealthy to give meaning to the idea of a government that rules with the consent of the governed.

In contrast, most in the founding generation looked to either property ownership, or a tax-paying requirement, as necessary to ensure that government would continue to exist primarily to protect property rights; on this view, property owners should wield all of the political power from which voting derived.[102] Property ownership had long signaled the independence and virtue thought to be a prerequisite for both electors and elected officials, and those who possessed property were deemed qualified to speak on behalf of those who did not.[103]

[100] Dinkin, *Voting in America*, p. 29:

> Benjamin Franklin, while colonial agent in English in 1770 wrote that the franchise should be "the common right of [all] freemen." ... The majority of men in authority, primarily from well-to-do backgrounds did not readily embrace these views. Most Patriot leaders still thought that political participation should be reserved for those who had a "common interest with, and an attachment to the community." The right to vote, therefore, should be limited to individuals with a financial "stake in society," for they alone could make competent, reasonable judgments. They alone could be trusted in making decisions involving the use and disposal of property.

As Alexander Keyssar argued in his seminal study of the right to vote, "The idea that voting was a right, even a natural right, had become increasingly widespread in the eighteenth century (its ancestry dated to antiquity) and was embraced by many small farmers and artisans, as well as by the most radical leaders of the revolution such as Franklin, Thomas Young of Pennsylvania, and Ethan Allen of Vermont." Keyssar, *The Right to Vote*, p. 12; see also "Comments of Tuesday, August 31, 1787," in Madison, *Notes of Debates*, p. 354 (comments of Benjamin Franklin) (arguing that "the elected [did not have] any right in any case to narrow the privileges of electors"). See also Cassius (pseud) (Aedanius Burke?), *Rights of Suffrage* (Philadelphia 1783).

[101] Williamson, *American Suffrage*, p. 98.

[102] Keyssar, *The Right to Vote*, p. 13.

[103] William Blackstone, *Commentaries on the Laws of England: Book the First of the Rights of Persons* (Oxford: Clarendon Press, 1765), p. 172 (noting that "And it is essential to the very being of parliament that elections should be absolutely free, therefore all undue influences upon the electors are illegal, and strongly prohibited..."). See also Robert J. Steinfeld, "Property and Suffrage in the Early American Republic," (1989) 41 *Stanford Law Review* 335–376, 340–341 ("But by the time of the Revolution only South Carolina retained a taxpaying qualification for the vote. In all other colonies,

Indeed, some Founders echoed sentiments expressed by the British against colonists during the Revolutionary War that those with property would represent the interests of those who were not freeholders through virtual representation. John Adams, for example, argued that voters who lacked property "talk and vote as they are directed by some man of property who has attached their minds to his interests," making them "to all intents and purposes as much dependent upon others, who will please to feed, clothe and employ them, as women are upon their husbands, or children on their parents."[104]

Even Plato, in defining his republic, thought that "no one whose property falls below the amount fixed [should] have any share in the government."[105] The community as a narrowly defined political construct, based on wealth, allowed states to navigate competing notions of voting as a natural right, a concept that would demand almost universal suffrage, and voting as property, to be exercised only by those of sufficient financial means, so long as property ownership remained an attainable ideal.[106]

State laws enacted during the revolutionary era and in the first decade of the new republic reflected this tension between equality ideals that entitled all men to be rightsholders of some sort,[107] and the idea that voting was a right properly exercised by elites. This period represented an awakening for the average citizen who, according to historian Robert Dinkin, had "passively accepted rule by the rich and well-born [but] was no longer willing to do so."[108] These new-age voters were less

election laws excluded the propertyless from the suffrage without distinction. … The political community simply could not trust such men with the important task of selecting magistrates or legislative representatives because they could never exercise independent judgment. They would always be compelled to do the bidding of the wealthy.").

104 John Adams, "Letter to James Sullivan of May 26, 1776," in Charles F. Adams (ed.), *The Works of John Adams, Second President of the United States*, 10 vols. (Boston: Little and Brown, 1850–56), vol. 9, pp. 376–377.

105 Plato, *The Republic: Book VIII*, Benjamin Jowett (trans.) (London: Sirius Publishing, 2020), p. 249.

106 See, e.g., William Goddard, *An Address to the People of Rhode Island, Delivered in Newport, on Wednesday, May 3, 1843* (Providence: Knowles and Vose, 1843), p. 42 (defending a limited suffrage in Rhode Island, noting that "At the commencement of the popular movement in this State, which ultimately terminated in a resort to force, the question of suffrage was drawn largely into question. We maintained then, and we maintain now, that the right of suffrage is a political and not a natural right; and that this important political right is to be established and regulated by the persons composing the body politic, and possessing the right to exercise political power, and according to their judgment of what the general welfare may demand.").

107 See Thomas Paine, *Common Sense* (1776), reprinted in William M. Van Der Weyde (ed.), *The Life and Works of Thomas Paine*, 10 vols. (New Rochelle: Thomas Paine National Historical Association, 1925), vol. 6, pp. 107–108 ("The representatives of the nation … who are the legislative power, originate in and from the people by election, an inherent right in the people, as an inherent right of the people. In England it is otherwise; and this arises from … its monarchy….").

108 Dinkin, *Voting in America*, p. 5. See also ibid., p. 6 ("As deferential politics declined, the overall function of voting started to expand. Until this time, the voter's role had by custom been limited to choosing the best man among rival candidates without any thought of influencing him in regard to future policy or legislation. But during the Revolutionary era many people came to the conclusion

concerned about electing the best-qualified individuals and more focused on influencing and changing policy.

For this reason, the Revolutionary Era had poorly defined political parties that tended to be issue oriented. Despite the fact that these early parties, known as the Conservatives, or "Commercial Cosmopolitans," and the Radicals, or "Agrarian-Localists," were relatively haphazard compared to the organized parties that would come to dominate the mid-to-late nineteenth century, this did not prevent political participation among White men from being fairly widespread.[109] As precursors to the Federalists and Anti-Federalists, these early parties prompted the common man, who had been traditionally deferential to the elites, to take his own positions and be more politically active in his own right.[110]

In response to this cultural shift, states enfranchised a significant number of White men who could not meet the property requirements.[111] For example, a 1760 North Carolina law required that, in addition to establishing his residency, "[E]very person who, *bona fide*, hath an Estate real for his own Lifetime, or the Life of another, or any Estate of greater Dignity of a sufficient Number of Acres in the County, which by the Law enables him to vote, or be a Candidate for such County, shall be accounted a Freeholder within the Meaning of this Act."[112] In 1776, this law was amended to allow taxpayers who did not own property to vote in

that their representative, instead of being a free agent, should be made to reflect the views of those electing him.").

109 Donald Ratcliffe, "The Right to Vote and the Rise of Democracy, 1787–1828" (2013) 33 *Journal of the Early Republic* 219–254, 221 (noting that "the abundance and availability of land in North America meant that large numbers of colonists satisfied [property requirements]").

110 Dinkin, *Voting in America*, p. 7:

> As Jackson T. Main has demonstrated, two relatively continuous and cohesive legislative parties appeared sooner or later in almost every state during the Revolutionary era.... The first [the Commercial-Cosmopolitans] comprised chiefly business and professional men who resided in or near urban settings. Sometimes, they allied themselves with large landowners who had similar economic interests. Many of these individuals were well educated, had considerable worldly experience, and possessed a broad or "continental" outlook. In contrast, [the Agrarian-Localist] were usually small farmers who produced relatively little for distant markets. The latter lived mostly in isolated rural areas far from trade and cultural centers. Unlike the Cosmopolitans, they often lacked formal education and worldly experience and displayed a narrow or provincial outlook.

111 See Williamson, *American Suffrage*, pp. vii, 42. See also Dinkin, *Voting in America*, p. 27 ("To be sure the franchise was already quite extensive in the late provincial period. Not all obstacles to eligibility before 1776 were insurmountable. Despite the existence of stringent regulations regarding race, religion, residence, citizenship, and especially property holding, a major part of the adult white males – perhaps 50 to 80 percent – had acquired suffrage. Nonetheless, a substantial number of free white men (20 to 50 percent), not to mention other segments of the population such as blacks and women, failed to meet all the requirements. Noncitizens and recent settlers in a particular colony were generally denied the vote. Members of minority religious sects found themselves barred in certain regions. Clearest in evidence among the unqualified males were those of little property – agricultural laborers and tenant farmers in the rural areas, and unskilled workers in large coastal cities.").

112 Ch. I, Art. III (1760), in *Complete Revisal of All the Acts of Assembly, of the Province of North-Carolina, Now in Force and Use* (Newbern: James Davis, 1773), p. 248. Article IV of the same act permitted residents to vote as follows:

elections for the General Assembly, although only freeholders could vote in elections for the state senate.[113] Likewise, in 1709, New Jersey enacted a statute that limited its elections to "every Free-holder having One Hundred Acres of Land in his own Right, or be worth Fifty Pounds, current Money of this Province, in Real or Personal Estate."[114] In 1776, the state relaxed this requirement to allow taxpayers worth at least fifty pounds to vote in its elections.[115]

Complaints from disenfranchised members of the military would be another catalyst for expanded suffrage during this period. As would be the case for much of the next two centuries, men who fought in America's wars, regardless of their socioeconomic status, refused to fight unless granted access to the ballot.[116] States responded to these criticisms by loosening voting restrictions immediately after the Revolutionary War, most directly by expanding access to the ballot to taxpayers, defining "freeholder" broadly, or by explicitly extending suffrage to those who served in the militia.[117] For example, New York, once one of the most undemocratic states in the Union, explicitly extended voting to those who served in the militia in 1821.[118]

Further expansion of the voter base was also a foreseeable consequence of loosening the prerequisites to be a candidate for public office, forcing at least some

> [N]o person shall be hereafter be admitted to give his Vote in any Election of a Member or Members to sit in General Assembly for any County within this Province, unless he hath been an Inhabitant of this Province Six Months, and hath been possessed of a Freehold, within the Meaning of this Act, of Fifty Acres of Land, at least Three Months before he gives his Vote, and is also of the full Age of Twenty-one Years: And that hereafter, no Person shall be deemed qualified, or admitted to sit and vote in the General Assembly, unless he hath been one full Year an Inhabitant of this Province, and possessed of a Freehold, within the Meaning of this Act, of at least One Hundred Acres of Land in the County for which he shall be elected or chosen, and is also of the full Age of Twenty-one Years at the time he is chosen

Ibid., Art. IV.

113 Dinkin, *Voting in America*, p. 32.

114 Ch. IV, Preamble (1709), in Samuel Nevill (ed.), *The Acts of the General Assembly of the Province of New-Jersey, from the Time of the Surrender of the Government in the Second Year of the Reign of Queen Anne, to This Present Time* (Philadelphia: W. Bradford, 1752), p. 7.

115 Dinkin, *Voting in America*, p. 33.

116 Michael J. Klarman, *From Jim Crow to Civil Rights: The Supreme Court and the Struggle for Racial Equality* (Oxford: Oxford University Press, 2004), p. 202 (arguing that military service prompted African Americans to demand voting rights after World War I and II).

117 Ibid., pp. 352–353 (noting that "the Revolution had also spawned ideas and generated movements which began to make the close identification of political rights with property ownership deeply problematic. Almost as soon as the Revolution broke out, groups of artisans and mechanics began to agitate for suffrage reform. They claimed the maxim "[t]hat all men are by nature equally free and independent, and have certain inherent rights" for themselves. And under the banner of equality of right, they began to insist that property owning qualifications betrayed the fundamental precepts of the Revolution.").

118 Williamson, *American Suffrage*, p. 201. See also Robertson, "Jeffersonian Democracy," 322 (noting that the 1821 amendments to the state constitution would also enfranchise those "possessed than £20 freehold or a 40-shilling yearly tenancy").

parity between the qualifications of candidates and the qualifications of voters.[119] Although some states retained freehold requirements for voters in the early decades of the nineteenth century,[120] state officials liberalized candidacy laws much earlier, allowing almost anyone to run for office in both state and federal elections.[121] For example, New Jersey law provided that "it shall … be lawful for every Inhabitant of this State, who is or shall be qualified to vote for Members of the State Legislature, to nominate four Candidates to the Choice of the People, as Representatives in the said Congress of the United States, by writing on one Ticket or Piece of Paper the Names of four Persons … at least thirty Days previous to the Day of Election … ."[122]

Thus, New Jersey limited who could vote, but not who could be a candidate, as long as the individual met the age, residency, and citizenship requirements of the U.S. Constitution.[123] While its 1776 state constitution required its legislators to be freeholders, New Jersey's 1787 election law, implemented after the state ratified its Constitution, did not impose this requirement on House and Senate candidates.[124]

Similarly, New York's election law divided the state into six districts and gave the people in each district the authority to elect one representative without articulating any constraints on who could be nominated outside of those criteria specifically mentioned in the U.S. Constitution.[125] Connecticut likewise provided that "each [Freeman shall] give his Votes or Suffrages for a number not exceeding twelve

119 Numerous scholars have noted the connection between who can be on the ballot and who can participate in the election. See Samuel Issacharoff and Richard H. Pildes, "Politics as Markets: Partisan Lockups of the Democratic Process" (1998) 50 *Stanford Law Review* 643–718, 714–715. However, the practical reality is that it is difficult for the state to allow anyone to be a candidate while circumscribing that candidate's support amongst the electorate through restrictive voter registration requirements.

120 See Gordon DenBoer et al. (eds.), *The Documentary History of the First Federal Elections, 1788–1790*, 4 vols. (Madison: University of Wisconsin Press, 1976–89), vol. 3, p. 365 (quoting freehold requirements in the 1787 New York Constitution).

121 It was not clear in the nineteenth century that states were barred from adding to the qualifications outlined in the Constitution for House and Senate candidates. Compare *U.S. Term Limits v. Thornton*, 514 U.S. 779, 783 (1995) (holding that states do not have this authority), with Roderick M. Hills, Jr., "A Defense of State Constitutional Limits on Federal Congressional Terms" (1991) 53 *University of Pittsburgh Law Review* 97–152, 101 (arguing that "the states' power under Article I, Section Two, to set qualifications for voters for the House of Representatives implies a power to set qualifications for federal representatives as well"). See also "Voter and Officeholder Qualifications," (2006) 119 *Harvard Law Review* 2230–2251, 2233 ("At the time of the Convention, almost every state imposed property qualifications on state elected officials, and many also imposed religious qualifications and term limits. Even after the Constitution defined federal officeholder qualifications, numerous states retained property qualifications for their state office.").

122 DenBoer et al. (eds.), *First Federal Elections*, vol. 3, p. 16.

123 See United States Constitution Art. I, s. 2, cl. 2.

124 Constitution of New Jersey s. III (1776); DenBoer et al. (eds.), *First Federal Elections*, vol. 3, pp. 16–18. New Jersey might have opted not to have explicit criteria because a large percentage of its white men were freeholders. Dinkin, *Voting in America*, p. 37 ("A recent sampling of tax lists from the mid 1770s discloses that roughly 50 to 75 percent of the adult male inhabitants were freeholders.").

125 DenBoer et al. (eds.), *First Federal Elections*, vol. 3, pp. 361–362 (listing the same qualifications as Article I, Section 2 of the U.S. Constitution).

Persons whom he Judges Qualified to stand in nomination for Representatives of the People of this State to the Congress of the United States."[126] Delaware also placed few constraints on who could be nominated for Congress, allowing voters to name "two persons" for the one congressional seat, subject only to the limitation that "one of whom at least shall not be an Inhabitant of the same County with themselves."[127] Arguably, any nonlandowning candidate who managed to win election in these states had proven to his peers that he was sufficiently virtuous to hold office such that his lack of wealth was irrelevant. Virginia, by contrast, was one of the more restrictive states and allowed voters to name one person for the office so long as that person was "a freeholder and … a bona fide resident for twelve months."[128]

This virtually unfettered ability to nominate candidates "of the people," once conceived as an aspect of the people's sovereign authority to choose the representatives exercising power on their behalf,[129] made the slide toward broad access to the ballot inevitable. The change was gradual at first, with Delaware eliminating its property qualification for voting in 1792 and Maryland right after the turn of the century.[130] Then, Massachusetts and New York allowed broader access to the ballot in the 1820s, with Virginia and North Carolina doing the same in the 1850s.[131] Between 1830 and 1855, six states abolished the poll tax,[132] and no state admitted after 1790 required electors to be freeholders.[133] In turn, state legislatures compelled municipalities to adopt more liberal voting regulations for local elections, leading to a convergence between state and local regulations that governed voter qualifications by the 1850s.[134] The relationships of dependency that had defined the pre-Revolutionary era began to give way to a nascent and developing concept of popular sovereignty that would make a larger portion of "We the People" the ultimate source of governing authority.[135]

126 DenBoer et al. (eds.), *First Federal Elections*, vol. 2, p. 24.

127 Ibid., p. 71

128 Ibid., p. 294.

129 Samuel Adams, "Letter to John Adams of November 20, 1790," in Adams (ed.), *The Works of John Adams, Second President of the United States*, vol. 4, pp. 420–421 (arguing that the people exert their sovereignty when "they delegate the exercise of the powers of government to particular persons, who, after short intervals, resign their powers to the people, and they will reelect them, or appoint others, as they see fit"); see also Hills, "State Constitutional Limits," 123 (defending the ability of state citizens to add qualifications for federal legislators as an aspect of popular sovereignty).

130 Keyssar, *The Right to Vote*, p. 29.

131 Ibid., p. 31.

132 Ibid.; see also Kramer, *The People Themselves*, pp. 191–192 ("Wealth restrictions on voting by white men were abandoned in many states even before the 1820s, and other majority-restrictive devices were similarly replaced during these years. By the time of Andrew Jackson's first election in 1828, significant property or tax-paying requirements for voting existed in no more than two or three states, and only in South Carolina were presidential electors not popularly chosen.").

133 Keyssar, *The Right to Vote*, p. 29.

134 Ibid.

135 Steinfeld, "Property and Suffrage," 350–351.

This progress does not mean that the relaxation of suffrage restrictions was linear. Some states tightened the criteria necessary to run for office, such as imposing property ownership requirements (especially for candidates for the state senate) and making local offices appointive (a move common in the southern states).[136] Other states, such as Virginia and New York, relaxed some requirements while keeping other restrictions in place.[137]

In the end, concerns about the independence of the impoverished lingered, as experience had taught those in power that potential voters tended to be swayed by the opinions of powerful benefactors. The structure of the early modern republic deliberately created the circumstances that necessitated such relationships through exploitive economic systems in which the poor depended on the rich for rent, jobs, and daily sustenance.[138] Delaware, for example, disenfranchised paupers in 1831, reflecting the persistent belief that those who sought poor relief were insufficiently independent to exercise the right to vote.[139] Their inability to own a freehold or pay taxes illustrated that they could not be trusted with another form of property: namely, the ballot. A world in which the poor were beholden to those who served as landlord, employer, or banker placed these individuals outside of the political community of "We the Voters," on equal footing with others who lacked a political identity such as enslaved people and women.[140]

In many cases, these restrictions were not limited to the poor but also extended to groups deemed unfit for membership in the political community of voters for other reasons. States like New York and South Carolina imposed more stringent property requirements for some groups during the Revolutionary period, particularly for Tories (British sympathizers), Catholics, and Jewish people.[141] Competitive elections in most states in the 1780s, not only over issues such as the treatment of the

[136] Ratcliffe, "Right to Vote," 233.

[137] Ibid., 234 ("Virginia in 1776 held to its basic freehold qualification of 25 acres of improved land, but then in 1785 lowered the alternative requirement for freehold owners of unimproved land from 100 to 50 acres"); ibid., p. 225 ("The 1777 [New York] constitution opened the qualification to vote for the house to both those who owned a £20 freehold (previously £50) and tenants who paid 40 shillings annual rent and state taxes" but nothing that "[t]hese terms continued to exclude many of New York's tenant farmers and laborers."). See also Robertson, "Jeffersonian Democracy," 322 (noting that participation in state senate elections required individuals to own at least £100 of property).

[138] "Explicit relationships of dependence were a common feature of social life at all levels, both in Europe and America. In late colonial New York City, for example, a system of personal loyalty and 'economic clientage' was well established. [Numerous artisans] were beholden to merchants, lawyers, and urban landholders who controlled their rents, job opportunities, credit, and even personal affairs.... Such dependence frequently translated into political loyalty. Even with secret balloting many artisans cast their votes as their patron desired, for it was not easy to hide one's political preferences." Steinfeld, "Property and Suffrage," 342–344.

[139] Ibid., 362.

[140] But see Ratcliffe, "Right to Vote," 234–235 (noting that the secret ballot was the norm in most states in the early republic despite assumptions by historians that viva voice voting was the dominant mode that allowed the affluent to monitor the votes of less wealthy men).

[141] Williamson, *American Suffrage*, pp. 112, 118–119; Dinkin, *Voting in America*, pp. 36–37.

Tories, but also over taxes, paper money, and payment of British debts, raised the stakes in elections that had previously been uncontroversial.[142] As such, concerns about election fraud led fewer individuals to contest the reemergence of voting restrictions during this decade.[143] In time, however, most states moved away from the restrictive voter qualifications of the colonial and Confederation periods.[144]

3.3 VOTING AS PROPERTY? THE COMPLICATED NATURE OF POLITICAL RIGHTS

While founding fathers like Benjamin Franklin and Ethan Allen pushed back against the idea of a limited suffrage, restrictions on the right to vote were not necessarily inconsistent with Lockean notions of government prominent at the time – that the purpose of government is to protect antecedent natural rights like property rights.[145] But these debates over whether voting was a natural right persisted because the category of natural rights was itself conceptually incoherent. Traditional property rights, under Lockean theory, existed independently of the legal regime, which had the sole purpose of ensuring their protection and continued validity.[146] Unlike traditional property rights, the right to vote did not exist in nature but courts still treated it as "property like," meaning that it was protected by positive law and could not be taken away without due justification, in accordance with the implicit understanding that suffrage was socially constructed and could not exist separate from the political regime in which one sought to exercise it.[147] Suffrage was therefore entitled to

142 Wood, *Creation of the American Republic*, pp. 462–464; Jackson T. Main, *The Antifederalists: Critics of the Constitution*, 1781–1788 (Chapel Hill, University of North Carolina Press, 1961). pp. 7–8, 73; Wood, *Empire of Liberty*, p.16.

143 Dinkin, *Voting in America*, Chapter 1. See also Tracy Campbell, *Deliver the Vote: A History of Election Fraud, an American Political Tradition*, 1742–2004 (New York: Carroll & Graf, 2006).

144 Williamson, *American Suffrage*, 121.

145 But see Keyssar, *The Right to Vote*, 12 (discussing how the notion of voting as a natural right had gained a foothold in post-revolutionary America because "it meshed well with the Lockean political theory popular in eighteenth-century America, it had a clear antimonarchical thrust, and it had the virtue of simplicity," but such arguments never became dominant because "there was no way to argue that voting was a … natural right without opening Pandora's box"). The Supreme Court implicitly rejected the natural right argument in its 1849 decision in *Luther v. Borden*, which is famous for holding that the power to determine whether a state government has been lawfully established is a political question. See *Luther v. Borden*, 48 U.S. 1, 42 (1849). The case also involved a challenge to the voting provisions of the Rhode Island Constitution because, according to the petitioners, the property requirements excluded half of the state's population of white males from voting.

146 Howard J. Graham, "The Early Antislavery Backgrounds of the Fourteenth Amendment," (1950) *Wisconsin Law Review* 610–661, 613 (noting that one of the principles of the antislavery movement, later embraced by the Fourteenth Amendment, was that "governments were instituted for purposes of protection and 'derived their just powers from the consent of the governed'").

147 For example, in 1865, Maryland's highest court, citing earlier decisions from itself and courts of other states in support, held that "[t]he Franchise of voting is property. The right of voting is recognized by law as an inalienable right of property sui generis, and cannot be impugned without injury[.]" *Anderson v. Baker*, 23 Md. 531, 539 (Md. 1865) (citing *Wheeler v. Patterson*, 1 N.H. Rep. 88 (N.H. 1817),

some protections, like other natural rights, but tying it to the underlying legal regime meant that access could be restricted, making voting not very "natural" at all.[148]

These conceptual difficulties did not prevent the founding generation from treating voting as property by aligning suffrage with property ownership and holding out the promise of enfranchisement, while effectively limiting the number of undesirables who could exercise it. After all, if *anyone* could own property, then technically anyone could become an elector. Throughout the eighteenth and nineteenth centuries, voting's evolution from a right that was property adjacent (and thus not natural) to a property right without any meaningful distinction from traditional property would become critical in discussions over the scope of the political community (and, later, the federal government's authority to protect that community).

Thus, rhetoric like that from Blackstone, who spoke of suffrage as a natural right while advocating for a restricted ballot, was not obviously contradictory; the right to vote properly conferred on an elector by the state as a matter of positive law was treated as a species of property based on Lockean notions that each man has a right to "enjoy life, liberty, and property."[149] Using traditional property ownership as a proxy, the question of who was most invested in society such that they should be entitled to vote assumed the utmost importance. These conversations were the first step in carving out a community of voters, entitled to both direct and utilize the coercive power of the state, from the broader community of "We the People." When Alexander Hamilton described voting as the manner in which citizens exercised their "share in the sovereignty of the State," it was less about everyone being able to cast a ballot and more about its importance as a vehicle for the expression of the people's sovereign authority.[150] This demand for sovereign power, in the form of representation in the halls of Parliament and not just in local governments, prompted the Revolutionary War, so it is unsurprising that suffrage became a key tenet in the republicanism platform, putting further distance between the American experiment and more monarchial forms of government.[151]

Jenkins v. Waldron, 11 Johns. 114 (N.Y. 1814), and *Bevard v. Hoffman*, 18 Md. Rept. 480 (1862)). There is also a long tradition of treating violations of the right to vote as a common law tort, with the American Law Institute recognizing common law tort liability for actors who, "by consciously wrongful act, intentionally deprives the person of the lawful right to vote in a public election." Restatement (Third) of Torts, Miscellaneous Provisions (2025).

148 See, e.g., *Harper v. Virginia State Board of Elections*, 383 U.S. 663 (1966) (a case in which the state equated the restrictions that it had placed on the right to vote, for which it required payment of a poll tax in order to be exercised, as akin to requiring "an equal fee for a driver's license").

149 *Somerset v. Stewart*, (1772) 98 Eng. Rep. 499 (K.B.).

150 "A share in the sovereignty of the State, which is exercised by the citizens at large in voting at elections is one of the most important rights of the subject; and in a Republic ought to stand foremost in the estimation of the law. It is that right by which we exist as a free people." Alexander Hamilton, "Letters from Phocion to the Considerate Citizens of New York, on the Politics of the Times, in Consequence of the Peace, of 1784," in Henry C. Lodge (ed.), *The Works of Alexander Hamilton* (Federal Edition), 12 vols. (New York: G.P. Putnam's Sons, 1904), vol. 4, p. 270.

151 William M. Wiecek, *The Guarantee Clause of the U.S. Constitution* (Ithaca: Cornell University Press, 1972), p. 41.

Because the ballot manifested the sovereign power of the state, possessed by an elector who would determine the officials entitled to wield that power, state law protected the elector from being impermissibly deprived of his voting rights. Once deemed properly qualified to vote under state law, an elector could sue for damages resulting from abridgments of this right by elected officials.[152] Colonial laws also punished sheriffs for disenfranchising someone who state law had properly designated as an elector or for otherwise affecting the election results while executing their duties. Such interference undermined the notion that government is "for the preservation of every man's right and property."[153]

[152] See, e.g., *Kilham v. Ward*, 2 Mass. 236 (Mass. 1806) (holding that someone born in the colonies, but absent during the Revolutionary War, was an American citizen and could not be denied the right to vote); *Stewart v. Foster*, 2 Binn. 110 (Pa. 1809) (holding that an alien who has paid taxes and lived in the borough for one year preceding an election for borough officers was entitled to vote because of his "common interest with other inhabitants"); *Lincoln v. Hapgood*, 11 Mass. 350 (Mass. 1814) (temporary absence from town did not render ineligible one who met all of the prerequisites for voting); *Catlin v. Smith*, 2 Ser. & Rawl 267 (Pa. 1816) (finding that the plaintiff was not impermissibly disenfranchised where he failed to pay his taxes at least six months before the election, as required by law). See also Dinkin, *Voting in America*, p. 4 ("In the past, sheriffs and other officials in the colonies had often interfered with the voting process, stifling the popular will.").

[153] Blackstone recognized that elected officials who failed to discharge their duty could be fined by law: "Undue influence being thus … guarded against, the election is to be proceeded to on the day appointed; the sheriff or other returning officer first taking an oath against bribery, and for the due execution of his office. The election being closed, the returning officer in boroughs returns his precept to the sheriff, with the persons elected by the majority: and the sheriff returns the whole, together with the writ for the county and the knights elected thereupon, to the clerk of the crown in chancery; before the day of meeting, if it be a new parliament, or within fourteen days after the election, if it be an occasional vacancy; and this under penalty of 500 (pounds?) if the sheriff does not return such knights only as duly elected, he forfeits, by the old statutes of Henry VI, 100 (pounds); and the returning officer in borough for a like false return." Blackstone, *Commentaries on the Laws of England*, p. 174.

Some colonies, and later states, penalized the sheriff for failing to discharge their election duties, which ranged from failing to return poll books and bribing electors to taking action that resulted in the disenfranchisement of an otherwise qualified elector. For example, the statute enacted by North Carolina in 1760 to regulate elections included the following language:

> And be it further Enacted, by the Authority aforesaid, That if the Sheriff of any County, or in his Absence the Under-Sheriff, shall refuse to take the Poll, or take it in any other Manner than is herein directed, or shall refuse or neglect to give a Copy of the Poll as aforesaid [Art IX], within Ten Days after such Election, or shall not regularly and in Time return the Writ of Election, or shall make a false Return thereof, every such Sheriff or Under-Sheriff as aforesaid offending herein, or any of these Cases respectively, shall forfeit and pay the Sum of Fifty Pounds, Proclamation Money[.]

Ch. I, Art. XI (1760), in *Complete Revisal of All the Acts of Assembly, of the Province of North-Carolina, Now in Force and Use* (Newbern, NC: James Davis, 1773), p. 249.

New Jersey's election regulation statute, enacted in 1725, includes similar language: "And be it further enacted by the Authority aforesaid, That every Sheriff or other Officer, to whom the Execution of any Writ for the Electing any Member or Members to serve in the General Assembly of this Province, shall belong, that shall act contrary or otherwise than by this Act is directed, or shall return any Person not duly elected by the Majority of the Freeholders, every such Officer shall forfeit the Sum of Three Hundred Pounds[.]" Ch. XL, Art. 2 (1725), in Nevill (ed.), *The Acts of the General Assembly of the Province of New-Jersey*, p 144.

Lawsuits challenging one's wrongful exclusion from voting were not uncommon, and courts drew on a 1702 British case, *Ashby v. White*, to develop a framework in which voters could successfully challenge their disenfranchisement. Matthew Ashby sought to vote in the parliamentary election of 1700 but was denied the opportunity by election supervisor William White. Ashby sued challenging his exclusion.

Ashby lost his suit, but Judge Holt of the King's Bench argued forcefully in dissent that a disenfranchised elector was entitled to a remedy from elections officials who wrongfully denied him a ballot, even though there was no governing statute that provided a remedy for this violation.[154] While a majority of his colleagues disagreed, finding in favor of the election official, Holt's position was later vindicated when the House of Lords overturned the judgment and awarded damages to Ashby.[155] Other cases would also vindicate claims by electors that they were wrongfully denied the ballot, although courts in both England and the United States would later read *Ashby* to require a plaintiff to show the election supervisor acted with malice or willfulness in denying the right to vote.[156]

3.4 THE LIMITS OF VOTING AS PROPERTY: AFRICAN AMERICAN AND WOMEN'S SUFFRAGE DURING THE ANTEBELLUM ERA

As the *Ashby* controversy indicates, there were protections in place against wrongful disenfranchisement for those within the community of voters. Nonetheless, courts heavily policed the boundaries of this political community, favoring exclusion

On the eve of the adoption of the Constitution, Virginia law established a regime that significantly regulated and penalized elected officials who failed to discharge their duties in the context of elections: "Any sheriff or deputy sheriff refusing to take the poll, when he shall be required by a candidate or person qualified to vote for persons to the general assembly, or taking it in other manner than is herein before prescribed, or making or signing a false certificate or return of election, as herein before directed, or making any erasure or alteration in the poll books, or refusing to suffer any candidate or person qualified to vote, at his own expense to take a copy of the poll books, shall forfeit and pay one hundred pounds, which penalties may be recovered with costs in action of debt, by any person who will sue for the same; one half to his own use, and the other half to the use of the commonwealth." "Act Concerning Election of Members of General Assembly (1779)," in William W. Henning (ed.), *Statutes At Large; Being a Collection all the Laws of Virginia from the First Session of the Legislature in the Year 1619*, 13 vols. (New York: R. & W. & G. Bartow, 1819–1823), vol. 12, Ch. LV, Art. X, p. 127.

[154] *Ashby v. White*, 92 Eng. Rep. 126 (QB) (1702). See also Ted Sampsell-Jones, "The Myth of Ashby v. White," (2010) 8 *University of St. Thomas Law Journal* 40–59.

[155] *Ashby v. White*, (1703) 1 Eng. Rep. 417 (H.L.).

[156] See *Cullen v. Morris*, 171 Eng. Rep. 741 (K.B.) (1819) (finding against the plaintiff because the defendants did not act with malice in denying him the right to vote); *Harman v. Tappenden*, 102 Eng. Rep. 214 (ICE) (1801) (same); *Jenkins v. Waldron*, 11 Johns 114 (N.Y. 1812); *Swift v. Chamberlain*, 3 Conn. 537 (1821). See also Sampsell-Jones, "Myth of *Ashby*," 56 (noting that the holding of *Ashby* is ambiguous because Judge Holt relied on the ubi jus principle that for every right there must be a remedy while the House of Lords emphasized the fact that the defendants acted with malice in finding for the plaintiff).

rather than inclusion and further perpetuating the hierarchical relationships that defined society.[157] In fact, courts were aggressive about excluding undesirables from the franchise even when state law technically allowed them to vote. The malice requirement meant that plaintiffs rarely prevailed in voting lawsuits, but the possibility of legal liability for denying an otherwise eligible voter the ballot reinforced the insularity of the community. On this view, it was better for courts to err in impermissibly excluding an otherwise qualified elector than to allow one who should be excluded to come within the confines of the community.[158]

This preference for exclusion had racial and gender undertones. If John Locke was correct that the purpose of government was for the protection of private property that would otherwise be vulnerable in a state of nature, then Black people and women who had achieved property ownership should, at least theoretically, be able to share in the political power that derives from their membership in the community of the enfranchised. In conferring the right to vote on property owners and giving the right itself the status of property, protectable in a court of law, this suggested that those who could cast a ballot owned a tangible share of political power that could not be impermissibly withdrawn even on the basis of race or gender.

Like property-less White men, women could, but did not have to be, members of "We the Voters," a fact that perversely reinforced the distance between citizenship and voting. While the Founders may have signaled the exclusion of African Americans from the political community through the Constitution's textual and structural accommodations of slavery, this was not true for women who arguably came within the ambit of "We the People."[159]

Women, like African Americans, could vote in some places at the founding. After the Revolutionary War, widows were permitted to vote in Rhode Island, Connecticut, and Delaware if they owned property.[160] Suffrage would be more accessible to women as America expanded west.[161] Yet women became victims of a system invested in establishing the inferiority of Black people across all dimensions to create a moral and societal need for slavery. The subjugation of women helped to cement the narrative of African American inferiority by holding out political power

157 See, e.g., *Parker v. Lovejoy*, 3 Mass. 565 (1795) (holding that residents of unincorporated plantations were not entitled to vote in state elections because the state constitution refers to "towns" in discussing the jurisdictions in which voting is supposed to take place).

158 See *Rail v. Potts & Baker*, 27 Tenn. 225 (1847) (conceding that the plaintiff was legally entitled to vote, but noting that holding defendants liable for denying him the ballot without any showing of malice "was opposed to all principles of justice"); *Sparrow v. Wood*, 16 Mass. 457 (1820) (finding that the defendant was not liable for preventing the plaintiff from casting a ballot because of an error in the list of tax assessments that determined which electors could vote).

159 See *Minor v. Happersett*, 88 U.S. 162 (1874).

160 Ratcliffe, "The Right to Vote," 229.

161 Campbell Curry-Ledbetter, "Women's Suffrage in New Jersey 1776–1807: A Political Weapon," (2020) 21 *Georgetown Journal of Gender and the Law* 705–724, 707.

as an unattainable good, even for a group fit for citizenship and otherwise qualified to be electors.[162]

In the mid-nineteenth century, the women's suffrage movement had not yet earned the title of movement, but its inception held out the prospect of long-term structural change. While some had advocated for women's suffrage in the early nineteenth century, the turning point came in 1848. A group of prominent individuals met in Seneca Falls, New York – including Elizabeth Cady Stanton, Lucretia Mott, and Frederick Douglass – for the first national convention demanding universal suffrage, jumpstarting the movement that would take shape over the subsequent decades.[163] Importantly, the movement was not just about voting rights. It also represented a demand for equality that would give women a legal identity separate and distinct from their husbands.

The quest for expanded political rights often coincided with demands by women for property rights. The late 1840s and early 1850s witnessed a number of states revoking gendered restrictions over property ownership.[164] If women had property rights, then it was much more difficult to argue that they lacked the independence to be electors. Yet political elites resisted this argument, even though voting had, by the middle of the nineteenth century, been held out as a form of property entitlement protectible in a court of law.

Instead, states were more willing to give women traditional property rights, viewing this concession as less controversial than granting universal enfranchisement.[165] Part of the reason lies in the framing – legislators cast married women's property rights as a bulwark against a careless or irresponsible husband, rather than as an indication that women had demonstrated the civic virtue that enabled them to act in the best interests of the whole.[166] But even more practically, property restrictions had declined over the course of the nineteenth century, which meant that property ownership did not necessarily come with voting rights.

Coinciding with the 1848 Seneca Falls Convention, New York became the first state to give married women the right to own property separate from their

[162] Jan E. Lewis, "What Happened to the Three-Fifths Clause: The Relationship between Women and Slaves in Constitutional Thought, 1787–1866," (2017) 37 *Journal of the Early Republic* 1–46, 2 (arguing that "women's assumed political incapacity was used to anchor a system of representation that rested on enslavement").

[163] Rosalyn Terborg-Penn, *African American Women in the Struggle for the Vote, 1850–1920* (Bloomington: Indiana University Press, 1998), p. 14 (arguing that "free Black women who lived in the upstate New York area – perhaps in cities like Rochester – attended the meeting along with male abolitionists of color"). See also Chapter 7.

[164] Holly J. McCammon, Sandra C. Arch, and Erin M. Bergner, "A Radical Demand Effect: Early U.S. Feminists and the Married Women's Property Acts" (2014) 38 *Social Science History* 221–250, 226 (noting that New York, Wisconsin, New Jersey, Maine, Massachusetts, Michigan and Kansas all passed laws allowing women to own property from 1848 until 1858).

[165] Ibid., 222.

[166] Ibid., 232.

husbands,[167] yet women remained disenfranchised in that state. In 1846, suffragists had pressed for the right to vote at the New York Constitutional Convention, but the failure of this effort – and the success of abolishing gender-based property restrictions two years later[168] – showed that the status of suffrage as a property right (or something property-like that can nonetheless be denied) depended very heavily on who sought to exercise it. In other words, the space between voting and more traditional property rights varied depending on the demographic who sought access.[169]

But when these efforts to prove that they were deserving of the vote through property ownership in the 1840s and 1850s failed, women appealed to principles of democratic theory, government, and human rights to argue for their enfranchisement. In one example, women suffragists convened in Ohio in May of 1850 and offered resolutions that challenged their disenfranchisement as a denial of human rights and contrary to natural law. They argued that disenfranchisement prevented them from proving that they are worthy of wielding political power and relegated them to a quasi-slave-like status.[170] In line with the Convention's resolutions, many women challenged the notion that men and women were so different such that women could not govern; instead, as Lucy Stone would argue in a letter to the Convention, women were deserving of the vote, in some cases more than men (Black, noncitizen, or otherwise):

> The lowest drunkard may come up from his wallowing in the gutter, and, covered with filth, reel up to the ballot box and deposit his vote, and his right to do so is not questioned! The meanest foreigner who comes to our shores, who cannot speak his mother tongue correctly, has secured for him the right of suffrage.

[167] Ibid., 225.

[168] Nancy A. Hewitt, "From Seneca Falls to Suffrage? Reimagining a 'Master' Narrative in U.S. Women's History," in Nancy Hewitt (ed.), *No Permanent Waves: Recasting Histories of U.S. Feminism* (New Brunswick: Rutgers University Press), pp. 15, 20.

[169] McCammon, Arch, and Bergner, "Radical Demand Effect," 229 (arguing that delegates viewed property ownership "as a more moderate demand" and demands for suffrage "far more radical").

[170] See "Resolutions Adopted at the Women's Convention Held in Salem, Ohio April 19 and 20, 1850: Resolution 6," in Florence E. Allen and Mary Welles (eds.), *The Ohio Woman Suffrage Movement: "A Certain Unalienable Right": What Ohio Women Did to Secure It* (Cleveland, Ohio: Committee for the Preservation of Ohio Woman Suffrage Records, 1952), p. 12 ("Resolved, That in those laws which confer on Man the power to control the property and person of Woman, and to remover from her at will the children of her affection, we recognized only a modified code of the slave plantation; and that thus we are brought more nearly in sympathy with the suffering slave, who is despoiled of all his rights."). As scholars of the nineteenth century women's movement have observed, it was no accident that women were fighting for their property interests, their interests within marriages, and their right to vote all at the same time. Women during this period viewed these battles as part of the larger fight for their basic human rights on their own terms, rather than the terms dictated to them by male-dominated society. See, e.g., Ellen C. DuBois, "Outgrowing the Compact of the Fathers: Equal Rights, Woman Suffrage, and the United States Constitution, 1820–1878" (1987) 74 *The Journal of American History* 836–862, 842 ("As the demand for woman suffrage became linked with a widely held republican faith, it also expressed the desire of some women for a radically different position in society than a women's traditional one. Woman suffrage carried with it the unmistakable message of women's desire for independence, especially from men within the family").

> The negro, crushed and degraded as if he were not a brother man – made the lowest of the low – even he, in some of the States, can vote; but woman, in every State, is plunged in a degradation lower than his lowest deep.[171]

Notably, Stone's appeals to racism and xenophobia were not critiques that had been confined to the ranks of men. The notions of deservedness that punctuated the antebellum period were fundamentally centered in notions of White supremacy, which meant that women of color were painted as equally undeserving as Black men. As a number of scholars have persuasively documented, the women's suffrage movement, despite its lofty goals, was punctuated with racism and classism against nonwhite women.[172] White elites sought to exclude women of African American, Native American, and Mexican American backgrounds, as well as immigrants and poor women, from the movement's political agenda.[173]

Instead of challenging the antebellum framework, women tried to exploit the same ethnic and racial distinctions that had permitted the initial exclusion of Black men from the community of "We the Voters," painting educated White women as a barrier of protection against the "mongrelization" of the ballot by Black men who had not proven worthy of exercising political power.[174]

The elitist and exclusionary attitudes that pervaded the movement had not been inevitable. Many of those who attended the 1848 Seneca Falls meeting started as abolitionists, arguing not only for emancipation but also for full racial equality.[175]

171 "Letter from Lucy Stone, April 10, 1850," in Robert W. Audretsch (ed.), *The Salem, Ohio Women's Rights Convention Proceedings* (Salem, OH: Salem Area Bicentennial Committee and Salem Public Library, 1975), p. 35.

172 Martha S. Jones, *Vanguard: How Black Women Broke Barriers, Won the Vote, and Insisted on Equality for All* (New York: Basic Books, 2021); Terborg-Penn, *African American Women*.

173 See Hewitt, "From Seneca Falls to Suffrage?," p. 16. According to Hewitt, "Historians, like suffragists, have hailed the West as the vanguard of the movement. Yet the story becomes complicated if we focus on the racial dimensions of these campaigns. Asian American, Mexican American, and American Indian women were often denied the rights accorded native-born white women in western states and territories. Idaho, for instance, supposedly granted women full suffrage in 1896 but specifically excluded the insane, felons and convicts, bribe takers, polygamists, persons of Chinese descent, and Indians. In the Southwest, Mexican American women were denied the vote, alternately, as Mexicans and as women. Arizona granted the vote to women in 1912 but denied it to most people of Mexican descent, women or men. In neighboring New Mexico, Mexican Americans could vote, but not women, whatever their race. For Indians, federal laws created a confusing array of possibilities – the most blatant division being that between 'civilized' and 'uncivilized' Indians." Ibid., p. 29.

174 Kate Masur, *Example for All the Land: Emancipation and the Struggle over Equality in Washington, D.C.* (Chapel Hill: University of North Carolina Press, 2012), p. 174 (noting that "a group of activists led by Elizabeth Cady Stanton and Susan B. Anthony adopted new idioms of civilizational hierarchy and ethnic and racial difference and argued that white women – or sometimes educated or 'intelligent' women-would exert a purifying or reforming influence on a degraded electorate"). See generally Jones, *Vanguard*; Terborg-Penn, *African American Women*.

175 Hewitt, "From Seneca Falls to Suffrage?," p. 21 (arguing that the inception of the women's suffrage movement was not Seneca Falls 1848 but rather earlier activists such as Frances Wright, a Scottish immigrant, and Maria Stewart, a free born black woman, who advocated for racial and gender justice in the 1820s and 1830s).

It is unclear whether women of color were present at Seneca Falls, but their advocacy in church conferences and churchwomen's societies helped the nascent social movement gain steam beyond the upper class White women who dominated its ranks.[176] Like their White counterparts, they, too, were persistent in their demands for equality, undeterred by the twin evils of racism and sexism that complicated what would otherwise be natural alliances.[177]

In addition to navigating the prejudice that tended to undermine natural alliances, property-owning African Americans faced their own unique challenges during the colonial period. As noted previously,[178] free Black people voted on and off in many states during the eighteenth and nineteenth centuries. Some of these states had very robust slave cultures, including Virginia, where African Americans voted until they were disenfranchised in 1723, and in North Carolina, where they were allowed to vote between 1734 and 1836.[179] South Carolina permitted African American freeholders to cast ballots from 1701 to 1716, and Georgia did not confine voting to White men until 1761. Kentucky also had a short time frame in which African Americans could vote, from 1792 to 1799, and Tennessee permitted African American suffrage under its 1796 constitution. Delaware and Maryland enfranchised them until the mid-eighteenth century.[180]

In many southern colonies, property ownership was sufficient to overcome the perceived handicap of race in determining who should be a part of the political community of voters. Sometimes, their inclusion was the result of poor legislative drafting that was corrected in later iterations of the law.[181] Not always – an early draft of the 1780 Massachusetts Constitution initially disenfranchised Black people – but the final version made no racial distinctions. And free Black men continued to vote in some states after the ratification of the U.S. Constitution, overwhelmingly

[176] See Terborg-Penn, *African American Women*, p. 14 (noting that "[n]o African American women appear to have been present at the meeting if we rely on the records kept by the major players" but "speculat[ing] that free Black women who lived in the upstate New York area … attended the meeting along with the male abolitionists of color"); Jones, *Vanguard*, p. 10 ("black women did not attend the 1848 women's convention at Seneca Falls, but at the same moment in church conferences, they demanded rights equal to those of men.").

[177] Jones, *Vanguard*, pp. 10–11.

[178] See discussion of *Dred Scott*, Chapter 3.

[179] W.E.B. Du Bois, *Black Reconstruction in America: 1860–1880* (New York: Russel & Russel, 1935), p. 6.

[180] Ibid., pp. 7–8.

[181] Dinkin, *Voting in America*, p. 41. As Robert Dinkin observed:

> Several states allowed free Negroes to possess the franchise for the first time, though often due to inadvertence, confusion, or haste in constitution-making, rather than to conscious design. In Pennsylvania, North Carolina, and New York, free blacks became members of the electorate on the same terms as whites. Of course, the latter state's property qualification continued to serve as a barrier to many. Maryland's constitution (1776) permitted voting for the lower house without color discrimination, but a statute in 1783 denied the ballot to anyone manumitted after that date.

Ibid.

supporting the Federalist Party. As that party's fortunes declined, so too would those of African American voters.[182]

But the voting-as-property framework presented several difficulties, particularly when states sought to exclude women and Black property owners from the franchise while simultaneously treating the disenfranchisement of those rightfully entitled to be in the political community of voters as the equivalent of a government taking of property. Litigation by African Americans challenging their disenfranchisement squarely presented the question of whether Lockean principles regarding the benefits of property ownership, such as the right to vote, extended to all who could meet the prerequisites set by law. *Ashby v. White's* malice requirement, stringently imposed in cases of racial disenfranchisement, generally limited the success of most of these suits.[183]

In the case of *Jenkins v. Waldron*,[184] decided by New York's high court in 1812, an African American plaintiff attempted to vote in an 1811 election for members of the New York General Assembly but was turned away by defendant election inspectors. Under New York law at the time, "the inspectors may challenge persons who offer to vote, and may tender them the oaths prescribed, and inquire into their qualifications."[185] Nonetheless, these officers could still be liable "if they go beyond their powers, or exercise them in an improper, illegal or oppressive manner."[186]

The plaintiff had successfully voted for members of the General Assembly in the prior eight elections. In this instance, however, the inspectors rejected his ballot on the grounds that the judge who certified that he was a freeman eligible to vote, rather than a slave, was improperly commissioned. The court did not reach the question of whether the judge was properly commissioned, instead holding that the plaintiff was not entitled to recover against the defendants.[187] Drawing on *Ashby*, the court stated that the plaintiff failed to prove that the defendants acted with fraud or malice, which was a prerequisite to establishing that the inspectors exceeded their authority. At no point did the court question, however, the propriety of free Black voters participating in elections for the New York General Assembly.

[182] Alan Taylor, "Dual Nationalisms: Legacies of the War of 1812," in Pietro S. Nivola and Peter J. Kastor (eds.), *What So Proudly We Hailed: Essays on the Contemporary Meaning of the War of 1812* (Washington, D.C.: Brookings Institution Press, 2012), p. 70 (noting that "Jefferson's Republicans cared primarily for the rights of free white men, who along could vote in most of the states...The paternalism of the Federalists led them to offer a little more protection for the rights of free blacks and a little more room for women to express themselves in politics. Because free blacks generally voted for the Federalists, they usually lost the franchise when Republicans rewrote state constitutions.").

[183] For a discussion of *Ashby*, see Chapter 3.3.

[184] *Jenkins v. Waldron*, 11 Johns 114, 117 (N.Y. 1812).

[185] Ibid.

[186] Ibid.

[187] Ibid. ("[A]s to the validity of the certificate granted by Judge Edmonds; it is sufficient, if he was even a judge, de facto, at the time he gave it. His acts would be valid. All judicial and ministerial acts done by an officer, de facto, who comes into his office by color of title, are good, as they concern the public, or the rights of third persons.").

Other courts were less strategic, explicitly arguing that Black people could be disenfranchised because their inferior status meant that they could never be members of the political community of "We the Voters." While the *Jenkins* court recognized the validity of the plaintiff's claim, even if it ultimately determined that he lost on the merits, Pennsylvania courts engaged in a decades long endeavor to prevent African Americans from exercising any political rights in the state.

In the 1809 case of *Stewart v. Foster*, for example, the court interpreted a statute that enfranchised "freeholders, housekeepers, and other inhabitants" to exclude African Americans because these words were not meant to be "understood in their most extensive import; for if they were so understood," according to the court, "not only alien friends and alien enemies might be included, but also women, minors, apprentices, slaves and servants for years."[188]

In another Pennsylvania case, *Hobbs v. Fogg*,[189] the plaintiff – either a free Black person or mulatto (mixed ancestry) – argued that he met all the requirements to be a qualified elector under Pennsylvania law, yet he was turned away from the polls. Similar to *Stewart v. Foster*, the court rejected the argument that an African American was "a freeman in the common acceptance of the term … [because] freedom signifies nothing but exemption from involuntary servitude."[190] The court turned to English law to establish that "freeman" was a legal term of art, distinct from those who were "inhabitants, neither planters nor taxable, who, though free as the winds, might be unsafe depositories of popular power; and the design was to admit no man to the freedom of the province who had not a stake in it."[191] The term "freeman" was, in the court's view, "like the term citizen, which supplanted it, to denote one who had a voice in public affairs."[192]

One can therefore be a freeman in the sense of being free of bondage or one can be a freeman in the sense of having a political identity; African Americans were in the former group but not the latter.[193] And the plaintiff's status as free did not erase the fact that African Americans arrived in the United States as slaves, which negated any possibility of his becoming a citizen.[194]

188 *Stewart v. Foster*, 2 Binn. 110, 117, 121 (Pa. 1809).

189 *Hobbs v. Fogg*, 6 Watts 553 (Pa. 1837).

190 Ibid., 556.

191 Ibid., 557.

192 Ibid.

193 Ibid., 558 ("it is difficult to discover how the word freeman, as used in previous public acts, could have been meant to comprehend a coloured [sic] race. As well might it be supposed that the declaration of universal and unalienable freedom in both our constitutions, was meant to comprehend it. Nothing was ever more comprehensively predicated, and a practical enforcement of it would have liberated every slave in the state; yet mitigated slavery long continued to exist among us in derogation of it.").

194 "Whence an unconquerable prejudice of caste, which has come down to our day, insomuch, that a suspicion of taint still has the unjust effect of sinking the subject of it below the common level. Consistently with this prejudice, is it to be credited that parity of rank would be allowed to such a race? Let the question be answered by the statute of 1726, which denominated it an idle and a slothful people; which directed the magistrates to bind out free negroes for laziness or vagrancy; which

Hobbs v. Fogg was not only *Dred Scott* before *Dred Scott*, but *Hobbs* also previewed what was at stake in the latter case, which was about more than defining who can be a citizen or settling the difficult issues surrounding congressional power to regulate slavery in the territories. According to *Hobbs*, African Americans could never be, and were not intended to be, members of the political community of Pennsylvania voters because they could never escape the original taint of slavery, even as freemen.[195] *Dred Scott* would apply this principle twenty years later to exclude African Americans from the broader community of "We the People."

Jenkins, *Stewart*, and *Hobbs* illustrated the yawning chasm between the rhetoric of republicanism – centered on virtue, the public good, and suffrage – and its reality, which was less inclusive, less good, and significantly less virtuous for many groups. The disenfranchisement of African Americans brought republican thought in line with the racialization of chattel slavery and the stamp of inferiority attributed to black skin. The Revolutionary War, initially holding out the promise of abolition due to the incongruence of slavery with the notion that "all men are created equal," ultimately cemented the exclusion of free Black people and enabled the spread of slavery.[196] As Michael Klarman has noted,

> Slave owners had been a relatively small minority in an empire where local laws were subject to regulatory vetoes by an imperial government in which they had no direct representation. After independence, however, they constituted the political and economic elite that governed nearly half of a nation in which control of "domestic" institutions such as slavery was relegated to local governance.[197]

Over time, not only did race become formalized as a marker of inferiority, but voting became a foil to understand the political construction of whiteness.[198]

forbade them to harbour [sic] Indian or mulatto slaves, on pain of punishment by fine, or to deal with negro slaves, on pain of stripes; which annexed to the interdict of marriage with a white, the penalty of reduction to slavery; which punished them for tippling, with stripes, and even a white person with servitude for intermarriage with a negro. If freemen, in a political sense, were subjects of these cruel and degrading oppressions, what must have been the lot of their brethren in bondage." Ibid., 558–59.

195 Note that the court glossed over the fact that the Pennsylvania legislature refused to qualify freemen with the word "white" in the statute, and at least one member worried that "respectable men of dark complexion would often be insulted at the polls, by objections to their colour." Ibid., 559. The court dismissed this argument, noting that the word "freemen" itself excludes African Americans by definition. Ibid.

196 Sinha, *The Slave's Cause*, pp. 47, 53.

197 Klarman, *Jim Crow to Civil Rights*, pp. 317–318 ("Adding to the clout of slave owners was the continuing growth in the slave population of the United States, which increased by more than 50 percent during the 1770s and 1780s.").

198 Professor Cheryl I. Harris suggests that the passage of the Naturalization Act of 1790, which "broadened [the franchise] to extend voting rights to unpropertied white men at the same time that Black voters were specifically disenfranchised" represented an intentional adjustment to the property ownership requirements for suffrage "from land to whiteness." Cheryl I. Harris, "Whiteness as Property" (1993) 106 *Harvard Law Review* 1707–1791, 1744. White men enjoyed this exclusive symbol of their social and political advantage for as long as they alone had the right to vote. It has been observed that,

The post-ratification disenfranchisement of free Black people illustrated how notions of republicanism had become racialized – arguably, they could not exhibit the requisite independence required of an elector because they had the same stamp of inferiority (skin color) that rendered Blacks suitable for slavery.

Because the notion of the "public" good meant catering to everyone, even those outside of the community of voters (like African Americans and women), the Founders believed that elites could still speak for the disenfranchised so long as elected officials remained responsive to societal needs. Those excluded from the body politic could cultivate virtue in other ways.[199]

The founding generation was also well aware that either bad behavior by officials elected to act in accordance with the public trust, or alternatively, the development of policies that predominantly served elites and not the masses, could lead the people to exercise their natural right to alter or abolish government, as the colonists had in 1776. Thus, the prospect of access to suffrage – and, by definition, membership into the political community of voters at the heart of republican constitutional thought – would become especially important in keeping these masses at bay.

well into the nineteenth century, "one of the most important ways in which men in particular could perform whiteness was … through the exercise of … performance acts of citizenship" such as voting. Ariela J. Gross, "Litigating Whiteness: Trials of Racial Determination in the Nineteenth-Century South" (1998) 108 *Yale Law Journal* 109–188, 113.

[199] Wood, *Creation of the American Republic*, p. 56 ("Of course even the most radical English Whigs admitted that the people might sometimes mistake their own interests and might often be unable to effect even when they did correctly perceive it. Most Americans therefore assumed that the people, in their representational expression of their collective liberty in the houses of representatives, could not run the whole government."). See also ibid., p. x ("Classical virtue had flowed from the citizen's participation in politics; government had been the source of his civic consciousness and public spiritedness. But for many in the eighteenth century, virtue now flowed from the citizen's participation in society, not in government, which the most enlightened increasingly saw as the source of the evils of the world…It was society, not politics, the bred the new domesticated virtue of politeness. Mingling in drawing rooms, clubs, coffeehouses and even counting houses – partaking of the innumerable interchanges of the daily comings and goings of modern life, including those of the marketplace – created affection, fellow feeling, credit, and trust that bound people together in the natural harmony of the social world that was as marvelous to the eighteenth century as the discovery of the force of gravity in the physical world.").

4

The Fight to Expand the Boundaries of "We the Voters"

From Alter or Abolish to the Right to Vote

If Black people were "unsafe depositories of popular power" such that they could be denied the right to vote,[1] were they entitled to invoke the alter or abolish authority on the same terms as disenfranchised White people? The initial impulse was to answer this question in the affirmative. For example, Crispus Attucks, a person of African and Native American ancestry and the first person killed in the Boston Massacre, was arguably asserting his natural right to alter or abolish governing in rebelling against the British.[2] But Attucks' race likely had very little salience in resolving whether African Americans could explicitly invoke the alter or abolish right,[3] given that his interests happen to align with those of political elites seeking to be free of British rule.

Fifteen years after Attucks laid down his life for the promise of liberty, an uprising in the French colony of Saint-Domingue led by former slave Toussaint-Louverture was the first real test of whether the alter or abolish right was truly colorblind and also – consistent with the prevailing sentiment – a natural right. While the Haitian Revolution initially started as a slave rebellion, it shared a common theme with the American Revolution that resonated with many in the founding generation: namely, the desire to break away from a foreign power and establish a sovereign nation.

Prominent Federalists like Alexander Hamilton and Timothy Pickering supported the rebellion throughout many of its iterations. Toussaint-Louverture's forces battled France, Britain, and Spain at various points, all of which sought to gain or regain

[1] *Hobbs v. Fogg*, 6 Watts 553, 558 (Pa. 1837).

[2] Manisha Sinha, *The Slave's Cause: A History of Abolition* (New Haven: Yale University Press, 2016), p. 33 (noting that "Attucks thought he had a stake in the fight. He had the temerity to write to Gov. Thomas Hutchinson charging him with crimes against the 'people in general.'").

[3] Rogers M. Smith, *Civic Ideals: Conflicting Visions of Citizenship in U.S. History* (New Haven: Yale University Press, 1997), p. 64 ("By increasingly making African descent or dark skin color a basis for legal restrictions, they established by positive law a racially defined gulf in the status of human beings so vast that in 1772, the highest common law court in England disavowed it.") (citing *Somerset v. Stewart*).

control of the colony.[4] When the treasonous Benedict Arnold escaped across enemy lines during the Revolutionary War, the fact that former slaves ejected Arnold and other British troops from Guadeloupe during the Haitian Revolution likely induced many smiles among the ranks of these Federalists.[5] Support also came from official quarters. For example, President John Adams appointed Edward Stevens as consul-general to build diplomatic relations with Saint-Domingue and encourage trade between the two nations.[6]

Unsurprisingly, Thomas Jefferson was not a fan of the uprising. Slaves in Saint-Domingue overthrew a plantation system similar to that which formed the backbone of the American South. In a letter to the Revolutionary War hero Marquis de Lafayette, then-Secretary of State Jefferson voiced support for the French Revolution while warning that the French colonies "will be lost if not more effectively succoured. Indeed, no future efforts you can make will ever be able to reduce the blacks."[7] Jefferson worried more generally that the insurrection in the Caribbean "ha[s] given a considerable impulse to the minds of the slaves in different parts of the U.S." and could lead to violence on America's shores.[8]

4 Robin Blackburn, "Haiti, Slavery and the Age of the Democratic Revolution" (2006) 63 *William & Mary Quarterly* 643–674, 646. See also Timothy Pickering, "Letter to John Adams, 24 September 1798," National Archives, *Founders Online: Adams Papers*, https://founders.archives.gov/documents/Adams/99-02-02-3023; Timothy Pickering, "Letter to John Adams, 12 July 1799," National Archives, *Founders Online: Adams Papers*, https://founders.archives.gov/documents/Adams/99-02-02-3749.

5 Blackburn, "Haiti, Slavery," 646.

6 Saint Domingue maintained some connection with France until 1804, but acted independently in many ways, prompting Napoleon's invasion in 1802. Ibid., 647 ("Toussaint-Louverture insisted that Saint Domingue remained French, yet he dealt with Britain and the United States as a sovereign power … . In 1801 he drew up a constitution for the colony that declared in the first article that it was part of the French Empire but subject to 'special laws.'"); see also Timothy Pickering, "Letter to John Adams, 1 May 1797," National Archives, *Founders Online: Adams Papers*, https://founders.archives.gov/documents/Adams/99-02-02-1954. Toussaint-Louverture undoubtedly garnered support in the U.S. because he prevented any invasion of southern states, which had been rumored to be imminent at various points throughout the Revolution. See Gerald Horne, "Haitian Revolution and the Central Question of African American History" (2015) 100 *Journal of African American History* 26–58, 31 ("It was Stevens who in 1799, when control of the island remained unclear, reported that a plan had been hatched on the island to 'invade both the Southern States of America and the Island of Jamaica,' a design that was to be bruited repeatedly in coming years. Toussaint won plaudits from the U.S. consul when, it was reported, Toussaint was 'determined to prevent this Expedition….'").

7 Thomas Jefferson, "Letter to Marquis de Lafayette, 16 June 1792," National Archives, *Founders Online: Jefferson Papers*, https://founders.archives.gov/documents/Jefferson/01-24-02-0079.

8 Thomas Jefferson, "Letter to William Moultrie, 23 Dec 1793," National Archives, *Founders Online: Jefferson Papers*, https://founders.archives.gov/documents/Jefferson/01-27-02-0544 ("A French gentleman, one of the refugees from St. Domingo, informs me that two Frenchmen, from St. Domingo also, of the names of Castaing, and La Chaise, are about setting out from this place for Charleston with a design to excite an insurrection among the negroes. He says that this is in execution of a general plan formed by the Brissotine party at Paris, the first branch of which has been carried into execution at St. Domingo. My informant is a person with whom I am well acquainted, of good sense, discretion and truth, and certainly believes this himself."). See also Paul Finkleman, *Slavery and the Founders: Race and Liberty in the Age of Jefferson* (New York: Routledge, 2014).

Jefferson was not alone. In the early days of the Haitian Revolution, Southerners worried that "the 'flame' of sedition [would] spread northward."[9] Jefferson would have been well aware of how the dramatic increase in the slave trade in America created the conditions ripe for revolution – enslaved Black people in Saint-Domingue well outnumbered the White people on the island, which was also true in South Carolina in 1780s. Other southern states also had significant numbers of enslaved Black people, in some instances comprising over 30 percent of their populations and generating similar fears of insurrection.

In 1802, Napoleon Bonaparte, with support from both the Jefferson Administration and Great Britain, sent troops to Saint-Domingue to retake the colony and reestablish slavery (even though the practice was outlawed throughout the French colonies in 1794).[10] While officially following a policy of neutrality, Jefferson opposed Toussaint-Louverture's regime and curbed the trade with Saint-Domingue that had thrived during the Adams Administration.[11] However, his refusal to send resources and aid undermined French efforts to retake the island. While the French captured Toussaint-Louverture, their invasion failed and, in 1804, the island was renamed the Republic of Haiti. The new Haitian Constitution not only extended citizenship to everyone on its shores, it also permanently outlawed slavery.[12]

As a Southerner and a slaveowner, Jefferson's opposition to the Republic of Haiti – a majority-Black nation of formerly enslaved people who wrestled control from White planters and rebuffed foreign superpowers – was not surprising, but it was a position that was hard to coherently defend given the reverence accorded to the natural right to alter or abolish government. Political community, if you will recall, was about protecting liberty in the Lockean sense, and the formerly enslaved in Saint-Domingue exercised the right to alter or abolish – just as the Americans and the French did during their revolutions – to establish a community that would recognize and sanction their freedom.[13]

The prevailing sentiment that enslaved Black people could not be in the political community because they were neither independent nor the holders of rights

[9] Horne, "Haitian Revolution," 28 ("the recently born United States, birthed not least because of its desire to maintain slavery in the face of abolitionist pressure from London, was then confronted by a threatening slave revolt not far from its shores, which created enormous leverage for Britain to wield against its former colony.").

[10] Blackburn, "Haiti, Slavery," 647.

[11] Tim Matthewson, "Jefferson and the Nonrecognition of Haiti" (1996) 140 *Proceedings of the American Historical Society* 22–48, 26.

[12] Ibid. (noting that the constitution declared that "all citizens were legally black, probably an attempt to forestall conflict between black and mulatto groupings").

[13] See Thomas Jefferson, "Letter to Thomas Mann Randolph, Jr., 7 August 1791," National Archives, *Founders Online: Jefferson Papers*, https://founders.archives.gov/documents/Jefferson/01-22-02-0010 (arguing that "A decree of the National assembly of France, giving the rights of citizenship to the free people of colour of St. Domingo, has thrown that colony into a dangerous fermentation.").

was inapplicable;[14] the people in the new republic of Haiti, including the communities of the formerly enslaved, free Black people, and mulatto people, had cleared this bar time and time again, beating back armies from three different sovereign nations seeking to curb this freedom. It was clear that the problem, for Jefferson and others, was not the emergence of a new state; rather, it was the emergence of a free Black state, which threatened to disrupt the plantation system in the American South.[15]

By the turn of the nineteenth century, the rules for establishing those who retained the "natural" right to alter or abolish government were starting to crystallize and, in the process, conflict with the very notion of natural rights as a concept that defied both positive law and custom. Slavery, and the lack of independence requisite for that condition, provided further justification for denying the enslaved the right to alter or abolish government, even if women and property-less men (who otherwise lacked a certain level of independence) retained it. But the Haitian Revolution would set the true outer limit for the scope of the right, due to its implications for both race and slavery. Like Bacon's Rebellion a century earlier, which led to the racialization of slavery in the Americas,[16] the natural right to alter or abolish, nominally retained by everyone who could claim to be a "free" person, would also become racialized.

But, as the discussion of the Dorr Rebellion in this chapter shows, the right posed such an existential threat to the institution of slavery that White people had trouble successfully invoking the right as well.[17] Thomas Pickering, Daniel Shays, and Ethan Allen established that invocations of the right required some level of public support. And over the course of the nineteenth century, the right to alter or abolish government lost its position as the fallback justification for a narrow electorate, and its invocation by the Confederates in 1860 would pave the way for the right to vote to

[14] Blackburn, "Haiti, Slavery," 649 (noting that the Declaration of Independence's assertion that "all men are created equal" was "easier to reconcile with the enslavement of blacks than might be thought, since the rights it asserted could only be claimed by members of a people with their own properly organized government. Natural rights doctrines had traditionally declared that all men were born free but qualified this notion immediately by insisting that liberty could only be realized in specific communities organized by the law of the peoples").

[15] Horne, "Haitian Revolution," 30 ("[T]he Haitian Revolution created a general crisis for the system of slavery that could only be resolved with its collapse. The avid 20th century racialist T. Lothrop Stoddard found it necessary to study the Haitian Revolution intensely and emerged with the conclusion that 1791–1804 marked 'the first great shock between the ideals of white supremacy and race quality,' a confrontation that compelled a retreat of the racialized slavery that had given rise to the slaveholding republic in the first instance.") (internal citations omitted).

[16] See Chapter 3.

[17] Mathewson, "Nonrecognition of Haiti," 22 ("Because the Haitian rebels defeated British, French, and Spanish armies sent against them, and eliminated the former colony's planter class, the slave revolution cast a conservative pall over subsequent emancipations in the Atlantic world. It encouraged a reaction against antislavery and the libertarian trends of the eighteenth century, especially in the southern United States.").

take its place as the primary political right. By the end of the war, the admission of West Virginia would illustrate how alter and abolish had become a political, rather than a natural, right.

4.1 SLAVERY AND REPUBLICANISM: ALTER OR ABOLISH AS A WHITES ONLY PROPOSITION

In January 1649, England's Rump Parliament cut off King Charles I's head,[18] effectively severing the bonds of kinship between king and subject. This extraordinary move was defended, according to historian Quentin Skinner, "as an act of self-liberation on the part of an enslaved people who had thereby succeeded in regaining their birthright of freedom."[19] Invoking the language of slavery to refer to the sovereign's violation of the fundamental rights of the subjects over which he held dominion reflected a basic duality common in the seventeenth century: people were either slaves or they were free. The term "slave" had not yet become racialized. Importantly, this was a concept of slavery that extended beyond the physical restraints of the chattel slavery common in the American South and across the Caribbean. To be an enslaved person was not simply to be in bondage but was defined as being subject to another's will.[20] A state of slavery also existed when one's rights were contingent on the grace of another person. As Thomas Hobbes noted in *The Leviathan*, "A Freeman, is he, that in those things, which by his strength and wit he is able to do, is not hindered to do what he has a will to."[21]

The physical condition and subjugation of enslaved Africans deprived them of any of the indicia of independence that denoted freedom, at least as defined by political theorists of the time. And their right to rebel against their condition, not as a matter of moral principle but as a matter of natural right, was also circumscribed by positive law. Regardless of the reference to the right as "natural," it was almost impossible for the right to alter or abolish the government to exist independent of conflicting positive law. Notably, the Guarantee Clause, in addition to holding out the promise of republican government to each state, also vowed to protect such government from domestic violence, a provision referring to the prospect of slave rebellions.[22] As the Haitian Revolution demonstrated in clear terms, respect for

[18] "Pride's Purge, 'the Rump' and Regicide," in UK Parliament, *About Parliament*, www.parliament.uk/about/living-heritage/evolutionofparliament/parliamentaryauthority/civilwar/overview/prides-purge/ [https://perma.cc/ZY6B-F3HP].

[19] Quentin Skinner, *Visions of Politics*, 3 vols. (Cambridge: Cambridge University Press, 2002), vol. 2 (*Renaissance Virtues*), p. 287.

[20] Ibid., p. 289.

[21] Thomas Hobbes, *Leviathan, or the Matter, Form and Power of a Commonwealth, Ecclesiastical and Civil*, 4th ed. (London: George Routledge and Sons, 1894), ch. XXI, p. 100.

[22] Paul Finkelman, "The Root of the Problem: How the Proslavery Constitution Shaped American Race Relations" (2003) 4 *Barry Law Review* 1–20, 8.

invocations of the alter or abolish right by the formerly enslaved was not accorded as a matter of moral authority, but as a result of their military success. Might, as is often the case, was right.

The fact that, for Black people, their natural rights were respected only at the end of a sword further illustrated the perniciousness of the *Dred Scott* decision.[23] By finding that this group, regardless if enslaved or free, could never be citizens of the United States, the decision relegated free Black people to the same station as the enslaved, even though the former held at least some rights that signified independence and civic virtue in republican thought.[24] While "freedom" required that one possess some subset of rights that are not controlled by a third party,[25] for African Americans, their race would render freedom presumptively unattainable.[26]

In contrast, there was a presumption that White people did not inherently exist in a state of slavery, although there were differences of opinion about when this status had befallen them. Even property-less White men[27] and women[28] in America had legal rights to which they could point as a sign that they had achieved some level of independence. Indeed, the emphasis on civic virtue during the founding era was, in some ways, an attempt to distinguish the enslaved from those who were free, especially among White people.

King Charles, before he lost his head, tried to argue that the decision of what rights should be given to his subjects was his prerogative. Hobbes, writing two years after King Charles' execution, agreed, arguing that subjects give up their rights to avoid perpetual war. For Hobbes, the conditions establishing the political community

[23] *Dred Scott v. Sandford*, 60 U.S. (19 How.) 393 (1856).

[24] Henry L. Chambers, Jr., "Slavery, Free Blacks, and Citizenship" (2013) 43 *Rutgers Law Journal* 487–514, 502.

[25] John Milton, *The Tenure of Kings and Magistrates* (London: Matthew Simmons, 1650), p. 41.

[26] *Dred Scott v. Sandford*, 60 U.S. (19 How.) 393 (1856).

[27] Of all those who were not granted the right to vote at the founding, landless white men with jobs were viewed to be at the pinnacle of citizenship and the logical first in line to eventually be granted suffrage: the "[g]rowth of the market economy, the transition from apprenticeship to wage labor, and migration to cities created a large population of white men who lived off wages and rented homes." Corinne T. Field, *The Struggle for Equal Adulthood: Gender, Race, Age, and the Fight for Citizenship in Antebellum America* (Greensboro: University of North Carolina Press, 2014), p. 55. That these men worked as laborers was key to this status: "in antebellum America the worker-citizen had become a central ideal that would fuel the quest for extending citizenship protections beyond the polls to other political, civil, and social rights for the white male worker, and eventually for women and minorities." James W. Fox Jr., "Citizenship, Poverty, and Federalism: 1787–1882" (1999) 60 *University of Pittsburgh Law Review* 421–578, 476.

[28] "[W]omen began to gain some – even if marginal – level of property rights and participation in the early industrial workforce from the colonial period through the middle of the nineteenth century." Fox, Jr., "Citizenship, Poverty, and Federalism," 472. In 1848, New York was the first state to enact a married women's property rights statute, one of more than forty such laws enacted by states in the nineteenth century. Holly J. McCammon, Sandra C. Arch, and Erin M. Bergner, "A Radical Demand Effect: Early U.S. Feminists and the Married Women's Property Acts" (2014) 38 *Social Science History* 221–250, 226, 227.

were permanent, and the people ceded authority to the sovereign, whose rule essentially could not be challenged. Hobbes' position that a new government could not supersede the old meant, by definition, that Parliament could not depose the King because the King could never breach the covenant between ruler and ruled unless he failed to ensure peace within the polity. Obedience for peace.[29]

But the idea that there were legal rights not based on the whims of a king made it possible for a republic to exist alongside a monarchy, and attempts to circumscribe those rights were treated as an attempt to relegate subjects to a condition of servitude.[30] John Milton, also reflecting on the deposing of King Charles, emphasized how important it was that the sovereign honor the temporary sacrifice that the people made in ceding some of their power to him. As Milton noted,

> since the King or Magistrate holds his autoritie of the people, both originally and naturally for their good in the first place, and not his owne, then may the people as oft as they shall judge it for the best, either choose him or reject him, retaine him or depose him though no Tyrant, meerly by the libertie and right of free born men to be govern'd as seems to them best.[31]

Hobbes' extreme absolutism with respect to the authority of the sovereign did not embrace Milton's equivalence of slavery with the absence of rights. Hobbes did not treat the covenant between the King and subject as contingent. He also framed the subject's obligation as one of absolute obedience. This meant that his conception of slavery was significantly narrower than that of Milton and other contemporaries. Slaves, according to Hobbes, "have no obligation at all, but may break their bond or the prison, and kill or carry way captive their master, justly."[32] But for Hobbes, a slave was one who was subject only to physical restraint.[33] For this reason, Hobbes was more likely to accept the validity of the Haitian Revolution, an uprising of the truly enslaved (at least theoretically), than the 1649 English Civil War, an uprising of those who still enjoyed freedom from physical constraint. "Physical liberty," according to theorist David Luban, "is simply a sign of the trust between master and servant resulting from the covenant, and it is this covenant that explains why the servant has obligations toward the master, but the slave does not."[34]

Americans increasingly accepted a version of republicanism that was more Hobbes than Milton: that the social contract was permanent; that the absence of rights was not necessarily enslavement; and that the citizen's primary obligation was

[29] Hobbes, *Leviathan*, chs. 13–15.
[30] Skinner, *Visions of Politics*, pp. 291–293.
[31] Milton, *The Tenure of Kings and Magistrates*, pp. 14–15.
[32] Hobbes, *Leviathan*, ch. XX, p. 97.
[33] Daniel Luban, "Hobbesian Slavery" (2018) 46 *Political Theory* 762–748, 734 (noting that, based on Hobbes' argument, "if the only true restrictions on freedom are physical impediments, this implies that the only truly unfree people are those who are 'imprisoned or restrained with walls and chains'").
[34] Ibid., 735.

to obey. However, White Americans would come to discover that the "right of free born men to be govern'd as seems to them best" had as little purchase for them as it did for free Black people, for their rights would also be subject to the whims of the slavery politics of the mid-nineteenth century.

4.2 ALTER OR ABOLISH FOR ME BUT NOT THEE: THE DORR REBELLION AS PARADIGM

In 1842, Luther Borden and several of his comrades broke into Martin Luther's Rhode Island home. Sort of. Well, it really depends on who you ask. Luther argued that Borden's action constituted trespass, while Borden claimed that, as a militiaman, he was authorized to arrest Luther; his actions, sanctioned by the state legislature, could not constitute trespass.[35] Whether Borden and the other infantry officers working for the General Assembly committed trespass when they entered the home of Martin Luther to arrest him, or were insulated from sanction as officials acting under color of law, turned on which of two factions constituted the legal government of Rhode Island.

Disaffected citizens had called a constitutional convention in Rhode Island, setting their new government on a collision course with the preexisting one. The legality of Borden's actions depended on whether Thomas Dorr was the rightful governor, elevated to the office by populist sentiment after running on a platform of universal male suffrage, or if that title belonged to Samuel King, the choice of propertied elites who preferred the existing government.[36] In *Luther v. Borden*, the Supreme Court held that the controversy presented a nonjusticiable political question, resolvable by the political branches and not the courts.[37]

The Court's refusal to intervene was inextricably tied to polarization over slavery, with the Court ceding to the political branches a power that they had steadfastly refused to exercise in any meaningful way. President Tyler also declined to act, finding that the relatively nonviolent revolution did not present grounds for federal

35 "It is an action of trespass brought by Martin Luther, the plaintiff in error, against Luther M. Borden and others, the defendants, in the Circuit Court of the United States for the District of Rhode Island, for breaking and entering the plaintiff's house. The defendants justify upon the ground that large numbers of men were assembled in different parts of the State for the purpose of overthrowing the government by military force, and were actually levying war upon the State; that, in order to defend itself from this insurrection, the State was declared by competent authority to be under martial law; that the plaintiff was engaged in the insurrection; and that the defendants, being in the military service of the State, by command of their superior officer, broke and entered the house and searched the rooms for the plaintiff, who was supposed to be there concealed, in order to arrest him, doing as little damage as possible. The plaintiff replied that the trespass was committed by the defendants of their own proper wrong, and without any such cause; and upon the issue joined on this replication, the parties proceeded to trial." *Luther v. Borden*, 48 U.S. 1, 35 (1849).

36 Ibid., 37–38.

37 Ibid., 47–48.

intervention.[38] Given the range of opinions over slavery, the issue also generated significant controversy in Congress.[39]

Southerners favored the incumbent government even if most of its constituents rejected it. If the federal government could decide the lawful government of Rhode Island, consistent with its obligations under the Guarantee Clause, Southerners feared that it could make a similar determination should a conflict arise between pro-slavery and anti-slavery factions in their own states (or, as with Bleeding Kansas, in the territories).[40] Just as Southerners resisted challenges to the admission of Michigan, Minnesota, and other states, deeming broad federal authority in this area anathema to the slavery cause, so too would the controversy over the Dorr Rebellion fall victim to slavery politics. But importantly, the conflict would also raise questions about the rights that citizens retain against an unresponsive government.

Over the course of the nineteenth century, expanded access to the franchise helped bridge the gap between the nonprocedural lawmaking of the people's alter or abolish right and formal amendment procedures present in state and federal constitutions. This access to political power, however, was accompanied by rapid industrialization that pitted rural towns against rapidly expanding, yet impoverished, industrial centers, a conflict that tested the resilience of governing elites.

Rhode Island, in particular, felt the brunt of industrialization that defined the Northeast after 1820 (and that, subsequently, brought these political disputes to a head).[41] Between 1790 and 1860, four-fifths of the state's population was condensed in the northern counties, populated with immigrants and factory workers, while the southern and western counties remained mostly agricultural.[42] Almost every state adopted a new constitution during the Revolutionary (1775–83) and Confederation (1781–89) periods. However, Rhode Island's 1663 charter functioned as its governing document in the mid-nineteenth century,[43] making its political structure nonresponsive to both population shifts and to the national tide that had led many other states to move closer to universal White male suffrage in the 1820s and 1830s.

Under the charter, suffrage was limited to "freemen,"[44] leaving many of the property-less factor workers disenfranchised as this term was defined by the General

[38] John Tyler, "Letter to Governor Samuel King of Rhode Island of April 11, 1842," in Lyon G. Tyler (ed.), *The Letters and Times of the Tylers*, 2 vols. (Richmond: Whittet & Shepperson, 1885), vol. 2, pp. 194–196.

[39] Michael A. Conron, "Law, Politics, and Chief Justice Taney: A Reconsideration of the *Luther v. Borden* Decision" (1967) 11 *American Journal of Legal History* 377–388, 381–383.

[40] Ibid., p. 381.

[41] William Wiecek, "'A Peculiar Conservatism' and the Dorr Rebellion: Constitutional Clash in Jacksonian America" (1978) 22 *American Journal of Legal History* 237–253, 241.

[42] Ibid., 238–239; Robert E. Shalhope, "The Radicalism of Thomas Dorr: Review of *The Dorr Rebellion: A Study in American Radicalism: 1833–1849*, by Marvin E. Gettleman" (1974) 2 *Reviews in American History* 383–389.

[43] Rhode Island replaced its 1663 charter with a constitution in 1842.

[44] Rhode Island Royal Charter of 1663.

Assembly,[45] and Rhode Island's legislature was severely malapportioned, with the northern counties electing less than one-third of its representatives despite their substantial populations.[46] Seth Luther distinguished himself as a spokesperson for these workers,[47] but the movement was ultimately taken over by upper-middle-class elites committed to a complete restructuring of Rhode Island's political system.

The Dorr of the "Dorr Rebellion" referred to Thomas Wilson Dorr, a wealthy elite who, prior to the rebellion, advocated for a new constitutional convention in 1834 to enfranchise taxpayers and those in the military rather than just property owners.[48] The General Assembly could amend the charter by statute, but wealthy rural landowners who benefited from both a limited suffrage and a malapportioned legislature rejected even the most moderate proposals.[49] This precursor to the Dorr Rebellion, the so-called Constitutionalist Movement, petered out and disbanded by 1837, having accomplished none of the goals that its organizers hoped for.[50]

The movement was reborn in 1840 with the creation of the Rhode Island Suffrage Association, a more radical organization led by Dorr that relied on the natural right to alter or abolish government to push for universal White male suffrage.[51] Invoking the right, the Suffrage Association argued that the disenfranchised called a convention to elect delegates in response to a resistant and nonresponsive General Assembly.[52] The convention was tasked with drafting a more representative constitution than the 1663 charter, which was then submitted to the people for approval.[53] Should the people ratify this new constitution, referred to as the "People's Constitution," then this document would become the governing charter for a new government that would replace the General Assembly.

45 William Goddard, *An Address to the People of Rhode Island, Delivered in Newport, on Wednesday, May 3, 1843* (Providence: Knowles and Vose, 1843), p. 42 (noting that under the charters of 1644 and 1663, "[n]either of these charters regulated the right of suffrage, or the admission of persons into the body politic. They left all power over this matter to be exercised by the representatives of the people.").

46 Wiecek, "A Peculiar Conservatism," 241 (noting that Rhode Island "retained a substantial freehold qualification, as well as a special provision allowing the eldest sons of freeholders to vote, an even less defensible exception to a bad rule. The apportionment of the lower house was rigid: each town, no matter what its population, sent two representatives, except that Providence, Portsmouth, and Warwick sent four and Newport six.").

47 Not to be confused with Martin Luther of *Luther v. Borden* fame.

48 See Erik J. Chaput, "Proslavery and Antislavery Politics in Rhode Island's 1842 Dorr Rebellion" (2012) 85 *New England Quarterly* 658–694, 661–662.

49 William Wiecek, *The Guarantee Clause of the U.S. Constitution* (Ithaca: Cornell University Press, 1972), pp. 87–88.

50 Chaput, "Proslavery and Antislavery Politics," 663.

51 Ibid.; see also Wiecek, *Guarantee Clause*, p. 89 ("The Constitutionalists had sought only taxpayer-militia suffrage and had contented themselves with petitioning the General Assembly, but the Suffrage Association insisted that a majority of the male adults in a state had the right to change or abolish their government if it was oppressive. The reformers now advocated for a type of majoritarian democracy, at least for the original ratification of a new state constitution.").

52 Chaput, "Proslavery and Antislavery Politics," 659.

53 Wiecek, *Guarantee Clause*, p. 90.

The General Assembly did not go quietly. They called a constitutional convention, known as the Freeholders Convention, which drafted a constitution that retained the freehold requirements of the original charter, while also addressing some of the malapportionment issues that had persisted under the 1663 charter.

The People's Constitution, which was submitted to a broader swath of the population because its suffrage restrictions were based on sex, race, and citizenship, but not on property ownership, was ratified 14,000 to 52, while the Freeholder's Constitution, which was submitted only to voters enfranchised under the original charter, failed 8,689 to 8,013.[54] After the failure of their constitution, the General Assembly attacked the legitimacy of the People's Constitution, rejecting the argument that republicanism required majority rule and emphasizing the anarchy associated with exercising the alter or abolish power.[55]

In a pamphlet that would eventually become famous, *An Address to the People of Rhode Island, Delivered in Newport, on Wednesday, May 3, 1843*, William Giles Goddard, a professor at Brown University, attacked the Suffrage Association's reliance on the right of revolution to justify universal suffrage.[56] In his view, suffrage was not an essential element of republican government because it was a political right, not a natural one.[57] He defined the "People" of Rhode Island as those who spoke through the enfranchised gentry and their elected representatives, rather than those seeking to exercise the alter or abolish right.[58]

By recognizing only a narrowly defined "We the Voters of Rhode Island" and denying that there was a "We the People of Rhode Island" to whom elected officials must also be accountable, Goddard sought to delegitimize efforts by the Suffrage Association to paint the General Assembly as a band of aristocrats. He instead positioned the Assembly as the duly elected representatives of the state that the Suffrage Association had no right – constitutional or natural – to remove through the People's Constitution. As Goddard observed,

> [I]t was reserved for sage politicians in 1841, to discover that Rhode Island had not a republican form of government, but was an aristocracy so oppressive as to justify

54 Ibid., p. 91.

55 In his speech to the people of Rhode Island on this topic, William Goddard reminded them that "the People's Constitution has no validity" and that they had "been saved from the terrific calamities incident to a state of anarchy" when it was not implemented. Goddard, *People of Rhode Island*, p. 45; see also Chaput, "Proslavery and Antislavery Politics," 660.

56 Goddard, *People of Rhode Island*, p. 43.

57 "[T]he right of suffrage is a political and not a natural right[.]" Ibid., p. 42.

58 "More than a hundred years ago, the people of this State, by their representatives in the General Assembly, provided that none but Freeholders should be entitled to the right of suffrage, or should be admitted members of the body politic. Those who admit the sovereignty of the people are bound to admit the right of the people of this State so to make and constitute this portion of their fundamental law, were, in a constitutional sense, the people of Rhode-Island; that no other persons had a right to change the law in this respect, or to exercise those constitutional powers which belong to the people." Ibid., p. 42.

> a Revolution! A Revolution by whom? Had those who by the fundamental laws of the State had no right to the exercise of political power, a right to destroy the body politic, that they might erect another upon its ruin? Whence did they derive this right? Not certainly from the law. The social compact makes no provision for such a right, and cannot recognize such a right. The law denies to all those who are not legal people, the right to exercise any political power in the State. It must, therefore, a fortiori, deny their right to revolutionize the body politic.[59]

Ignoring that the source of disagreement was the unduly narrow electorate, Goddard denied that this was an appropriate use of the right of revolution which, in his words, was "preposterous to claim for the majority in a free State," and contended that. "[w]hatever grievances they may chance to suffer, can be redressed at the ballot-box …"[60] According to Goddard, once the people settled on a form of government, the people were bound to change that government by the terms laid out in its governing documents.[61]

Other supporters of the General Assembly took a less aggressive stance than Goddard with respect to the right to alter or abolish government. Congressman Elisha Potter, for example, disavowed any intent to diminish the right of revolution, arguing, "we do not wish to be understood as denying what may be called the right of revolution, or the right of any portion of the people who are oppressed to redress their grievances by force, after having tried all peaceable means without effect."[62] Yet, like Professor Goddard, he agreed that a majority of the population could never exercise this power: "But this is a right which belongs not to majorities only, but to any number of citizens, however small, who are oppressed, where the oppression is sufficient to justify it, and there is no mode of redressing it but by a revolution."[63] Since the majority adopted the means by which government could be amended in the 1663 charter, a majority cannot then seek to change government through revolutionary means since they have the numbers to change it through formal amendment.[64]

Emphasizing the importance of amendment through formal mechanisms, Potter drew on the U.S. Constitution to illustrate the risk of interpreting alter or abolish expansively:

> if the majority of the people of Rhode Island have a right to change their own government in this manner, they have an equal right to throw off the government

59 Ibid., p. 43.

60 Ibid., p. 44.

61 "Had those who by the fundamental laws of the State had no right to the exercise of political power, a right to destroy the body politic, that they might erect another upon its ruins? Whence did they derive this right? Not certainly from the law." Ibid., p. 43.

62 Elisha R. Potter, *Considerations on the Questions of the Adoption of a Constitution, and Extension of Suffrage in Rhode Island* (Boston: Thomas H. Webb & Co., 1842), p. 22.

63 Ibid.

64 Ibid.

> of the Union; for they both stand upon the same foundation, a compact made by our forefathers … never legally adopted, and is not legally binding, for a majority of the whole people never assented to it…[65]

The fear that invoking the right to alter or abolish government could lead not only to a reversion back to the state of nature, but also to unfettered chaos, was a powerful rhetorical device. The pamphlets by Goddard and Potter also raised questions about how one should go about identifying the relevant political community that can exercise the sovereign power of the state and, importantly, determining whether the sovereignty exercised by this community could be limited to a written constitution.[66] The propertied elites rejected any exercise of political power centering on pure majoritarianism that could manifest outside of a written document, which they viewed as an aspect of democracies, not constitutional republics.[67] In contrast, for Dorr and his followers, "The establishment of any mode of convenience, for amending a Constitution through the action of the Legislature, cannot impair the general unalienated & inalienable right of the People at large to make alterations in their organic laws in any other mode, which they may deem expedient."[68]

After the rejection of the Freeholder's Constitution, it became apparent that these were two very different communities vying for power in Rhode Island: the state-level microcosm of "We the People" seeking a greater share of the political power versus the community of "We the Voters" that existed under the 1663 charter. The General Assembly sought to perpetuate the privileged subset that had traditionally defined "We the Voters," but "We the People" sought to force discussions of meaningful political power and representation beyond this community and, notably, beyond the scope of the traditional right to vote.

While the Suffrage Association's explicit goal was White male suffrage, women played a large part in both the organization and the resulting rebellion, signifying that the alter or abolish right was important in providing access to public discourse for women and others deemed unqualified to vote. Among these early suffragettes was Catharine Read Williams, a confidante to Thomas Dorr, who held numerous events to raise money for Dorrites who were fired from their jobs for joining the rebellion.[69] Frances H. Whipple, a well-known poet, writer, and

65 Ibid., p. 24.

66 Wiecek, *Guarantee Clause*, p. 92.

67 In a 1978 article about the Dorr Rebellion, William Wiecek outlined the entire catalog of the political views of Rhode Island conservatives during this period, all of which sat in direct opposition to the majoritarianism favored by the Dorrites. Wiecek, "A Peculiar Conservatism," 237–253, 245–250.

68 Wiecek, *Guarantee Clause*, p. 95 (referencing a letter from Dorr to Nathan Clifford, January 24, 1848) (internal citation omitted).

69 Frank L. Grzyb and Russell J. DeSimone, *Remarkable Women of Rhode Island* (Charleston, SC: The History Press, 2014), pp. 21–22; Susan Graham, "'A Warm Politition and Devotedly Attached to the Democratic Party': Catharine Read Williams, Politics, and Literature in Antebellum America" (2010) 30 *Journal of the Early Republic* 253–278, 253–254.

editor of *The Wampanoag, and Operatives Journal*, wrote a book, *Might and Right*, in support of Dorr and the suffrage movement under the pseudonym "A Rhode Islander."[70] Two other women – Ann Parlin and Abby Lord – were directly involved in the rebellion, forming benevolent associations that provided funds for Dorrite families.[71]

Notably, African Americans in Rhode Island were also huge supporters of the Dorr Rebellion. Disenfranchised since 1822, those in the state's small Black community were active members of Dorr's Suffrage Party.[72] The voter qualifications to participate in delegate elections for the constitutional convention in August 1841 conspicuously did not mention race, although there were accounts of African Americans being turned away from the polls on election day.[73]

Black people consistently challenged Dorr and the People's Party, not only asserting that they were legitimate holders of rights, but importantly, challenging the racialization of the alter or abolish right that had persisted since the Haitian Revolution. Throughout the 1830s and 1840s, the Black community had established their own schools and churches, purchased their own homes, and otherwise liberated themselves from the White community in ways that established their independence.[74] Dorr openly favored enfranchising Black men, but lost this fight because others in the party viewed African American enfranchisement as a political liability that could lead the public to support Governor King and the General Assembly.[75]

Against the backdrop of these internal disagreements about the scope of suffrage rights, the conflict between the rival governments intensified, igniting a series of confrontations throughout 1841–42. The Suffrage Association held elections under their new constitution in April 1842, despite a state law enacted by the General Assembly that prohibited the formation of a new government (the so-called "Algerine laws").[76] As a result, Rhode Island had two governors during this period:

70 "A Rhode Islander" [Frances H. Whipple], *Might and Right* (Providence, RI: A.H. Stillwell, 1844). Whipple dedicated the book to Dorr, calling him a "tried and true patriot" and a "fearless defender of human rights." Ibid., p. v. In it, she provides a rich and detailed history of Rhode Island politics during the Dorr Rebellion period, describing the rise of the suffrage movement, the conventions and their resulting constitutions, and the state legislature's passage of the Algerine laws.

71 Grzyb and DeSimone, *Remarkable Women*, pp. 22–23.

72 Chaput, "Proslavery and Antislavery Politics," 665.

73 Ibid., 668.

74 Ibid., 665.

75 For example, People's Constitution advocate Dutee Pearce, in opposition to extending suffrage to African Americans, "asserted the practicalities of the historical moment," insisting that "[p]erceived notions of black inferiority … ensured that the People's constitution would not be ratified without a whites-only clause[.]" Ibid., 669.

76 On April 2, 1842, the Rhode Island legislature passed "the Act in relation to offences against the sovereign power of the State, better known as the ALGERINE LAWS … by a majority of 60 to 6." Whipple, *Might and Right*, p. 178. Section 1 of this legislation declared that "All town, ward or other meetings of the freemen, inhabitants or residents of this state, or of any portion of the same, for the election of any town, county or state officer or officers, called or held in any town, of this state or in the city

Dorr, who was elected in the 1842 election, and Samuel King, who was the choice of the landed gentry.

The involvement of President John Tyler in the Rhode Island dispute provided an occasion to define the scope of the federal guarantee that each state should have a republican government. After the elections in April 1842, Governor King wrote to President Tyler, invoking the Guarantee Clause and requesting federal intervention to quiet the threat that Dorr posed to his government.[77] King's request put Tyler in a bind. Some Southerners supported the General Assembly, but federal intervention in a state-level dispute that had yet to erupt into violence at the time of King's letter could contravene the two-decade effort by southern states to protect slavery by limiting federal power under the Clause.[78] Relying heavily on the Guarantee Clause's reference to "domestic violence," President Tyler rejected Governor King's request, arguing that "there must be an actual insurrection, manifested by lawless assemblages of the people, or otherwise, to whom a proclamation may be addressed, and who may be required to betake themselves to their respective abodes."[79]

Tyler's framing of the Clause as permitting federal intervention only upon "actual insurrection, manifested by lawless assemblages of people" created inevitable conflict with at least some legitimate exercises of the alter or abolish right.[80] While the people can exercise this power peacefully – for example, by calling a constitutional convention outside of the legislature as Dorr and others had in 1841 – it mostly manifested in not so peaceful ways, such as the colonists' revolution against the British and Shays' Rebellion. While Tyler's position was inconsistent with violent exercises of the right, he did not think that Governor King and the General Assembly could ignore the Dorrites' demands, because acknowledging them would indicate that peaceful exercises of the right still retained some validity.[81] Since the Suffragists were demanding political rights, a reasoned response by those in power should obviate the need for violence and force political disagreement through the aegis of the state rather than around it.

Nonetheless, Tyler's interpretation of the Clause largely inured to the benefit of the established government, rather than to the people seeking better political representation. Limiting federal intervention to cases of violent uprising meant that the federal government would come to the assistance of the recognized state

of Providence, except in the manner, for the purposes, at the times, and by the freemen by law prescribed, are illegal and void[.]" Ibid., p. 179.

77 Wiecek, *Guarantee Clause*, p. 101 ("King's specific request was moderate enough: he wanted a proclamation from Tyler (contents unspecified) and one United States Army officer. King seemed to have felt that a mere gesture of support by the President would be enough to persuade the Dorrites to disband.").

78 Ibid., pp. 102–103.

79 Tyler, "Letter to Governor Samuel King of Rhode Island of April 11, 1842," in Tyler (ed.), *The Letters and Times of the Tylers*, vol. 2, pp. 194–196.

80 Ibid., p. 195.

81 Wiecek, *Guarantee Clause*, p. 106.

government, rather than the faction seeking to overthrow it. Perhaps contradictorily, Tyler viewed his duty in this situation as nondiscretionary, in that "the President is not free to choose the group that he will aid on the basis of his own notions of republicanism."[82]

The idea that there was some abstract definition of republicanism that should dictate the President's actions here is a nonstarter; after all, if sovereignty lies with the people, the People's Constitution had received overwhelming endorsement. And even if republicanism is consistent with the idea of a more limited suffrage, such as that embraced by the Freeholder's Constitution, that document was rejected when put to a vote in late 1841. In some ways, Tyler's background as a Southerner partially explained his very limited view of the Guarantee Clause.[83] But he also recognized the power of the alter or abolish right and sought to preserve its core by implying that the federal government would respond (only) in the event of violence.

The situation in Rhode Island came to a head in June 1842, with a violent uprising in which Dorr's troops were defeated and he was forced to flee the state.[84] The rebellion ended with a whimper but established an important baseline for federal intervention in state political disputes.[85] The Dorr Rebellion eventually became

82 Ibid., p. 105. See also Tyler, "April 11, 1842 Letter to King," p. 195 ("the executive could not look into real or supposed defects of the existing government, in order to ascertain whether some other plan of government proposed for adoption was better suited to the wants and more in accordance with the wishes of any portion of her citizens").

83 John Tyler was born in Virginia in 1790 and served that state as a member of the House of Representatives between 1816 and 1821. White House Historical Association, "John Tyler: Tenth President of the United States," www.whitehouse.gov/about-the-white-house/presidents/john-tyler/. A lawyer who believed in a strict interpretation of the Constitution, he "joined the states' rights Southerners in Congress who banded with Henry Clay, Daniel Webster, and their newly-formed Whig party" in opposition to President Jackson and was elected as vice president in 1840. Ibid. Tyler became the president upon the death of William Henry Harrison, who passed away after only a few weeks in office. Ibid.

84 Wiecek, *Guarantee Clause*, pp. 97–98.

85 Compare Alabama Governor George Wallace's request to President Johnson for federal intervention during the Selma Marches in 1965, which were "organized to protest the blocking of Black Americans' right to vote by the systematic racist structure of the Jim Crow South." "Selma Marches," National Archives, *African American Heritage*, www.archives.gov/research/african-americans/vote/selma-marches. During the first two marches, which took place on March 7 and March 9, there were violent attacks on the marchers by members of law enforcement and the Ku Klux Klan. Ibid. The third march began on March 21 and lasted four days. Ibid. Prior to the third march, Governor Wallace requested federal assistance in controlling the march. Ibid. President Johnson described his fulfillment of this request as follows: "It is not a welcome duty for the Federal Government to ever assume a State Government's own responsibility for assuring the protection of citizens in the exercise of their constitutional rights. It has been rare in our history for the Governor and the legislature of a sovereign State to decline to exercise their responsibility and to request that duty be assumed by the Federal Government. Governor Wallace and the legislature of the State of Alabama have now done this. I have responded both to their request and to what I believe is the sure and the certain duty of the Federal Government in the protection of constitutional rights of all American citizens. I have called selected elements of the Alabama National Guard into Federal Service. Additionally, I have military police put in position at both Selma and Montgomery, Alabama. In addition, we have

a distant memory, but it raised two (maybe three) important questions. First, was there a definition of republicanism in the abstract that defined the terms upon which the people could change or overthrow government before triggering federal involvement? And second, what were the circumstances under which Congress could preempt or forbid the exercise of the alter or abolish right altogether? In other words, was President Tyler right in asserting that the Guarantee Clause required federal intervention to ensure a republican form of government in the event of a violent uprising, even at the cost of circumscribing the people's right to alter or abolish government?

In some ways, these were questions that well predated the Dorrites. A half century before Thomas Dorr was expelled from Rhode Island, Daniel Shays lost his battle but almost certainly won the war. Following Shays' Rebellion, Massachusetts voters removed Governor James Bowdoin and his allies from office, penalizing them for their ineptitude in handling the uprising.[86] The new government not only pardoned Shays but made some accommodations to address the malcontent that led to the rebellion.[87]

Despite the absence of support from "official" corners and contested views regarding the legality of Shays' actions,[88] the rebellion succeeded in altering the terms of the relationship between the Massachusetts government and its citizens. These changes almost certainly vindicated the alter or abolish right as an appropriate method of dispute resolution that Americans carried into the new nation. It was, according to Professor Richard D. Brown, a response to "ruinous policies" for Americans unaccustomed to partisan electoral competition that could similarly address conflict between government and the governed.[89]

The rise of partisan politics in the first half of the nineteenth century had a domesticating effect on alter or abolish, relegating its invocation to times in which the governed became enslaved in a Hobbesian sense or when they lacked the rights

Federal marshals, FBI agents on duty in that area at this time." "The President's News Conference at the LBJ Ranch of March 20, 1965," in *Public the Presidents of the United States: Lyndon B. Johnson*, 2 books (Washington, D.C.: United States Government Printing Office, 1966), book 1, speech 117, pp. 299–300.

86 Sean Wilentz, *The Politicians and the Egalitarians: The Hidden History of American Politics* (New York: W.W. Norton & Company, 2016), p. 31.

87 Following the events of Shays' Rebellion, "the state laws were modified and reforms were undertaken which resulted in the abolition of imprisonment for debt and other oppressive practices – together with measures which included a complete overhauling of the unjust tax system, with the purpose of relieving the towns and polls of some of the burden and placing it on trade." Walter A. Dyer, "Embattled Farmers" (1931) 4 *New England Quarterly*, 460–481, 478. Shays was pardoned in the summer of 1788. Ibid., 479.

88 Richard D. Brown, "Shays's Rebellion and Its Aftermath: A View from Springfield, Massachusetts, 1787" (1983) 40 *The William and Mary Quarterly* 598–615, 598. ("Interpretations of the uprising and its suppression, have varied, depending on the sympathies of the writer, the credence given to the triumphant friends of government, who characterized the Shaysites as a despicable rabble, and the confidence placed in the veracity of the defeated underdogs.").

89 Ibid., 599.

that Milton believed integral to freedom. In early modern America, "[r]iots and rebellions were often calmly accepted as a constant and even necessary element of free government."[90] Even where their actions were condemned, there was usually sympathy with the mob's plights and an assumption that violence would be kept to a minimum.[91] Yet the Dorr Rebellion – the sedate affair that it was, undertaken for the sympathetic purpose of expanding the electorate – was unsuccessful despite its consistency with popular sentiments surrounding "appropriate" mob action.

Sectional politics also killed official support for Dorr's cause on both sides of the political spectrum. What was once a natural right had become a political zero-sum game. Just as Governor King turned to President Tyler for help suppressing the insurrection, Thomas Dorr turned to northern Democrats to promote it.[92] The fact that Democrats in the North, rather than the South, voiced support for Dorr was notable. While there were members of both wings of the party who endorsed Dorr's efforts, southern Democrats feared that supporting the principles of majoritarianism inherent in Dorr's position could require extending rights to African Americans.[93]

Although the word "White" became a prerequisite to being an elector in the People's Constitution, these debates crystallized the risk to White supremacy and slavery attendant to supporting Dorr and his cause.[94] Paradoxically, Dorr's belief in colorblind popular sovereignty could have disrupted the balance between slave and free states that had existed since the Missouri Compromise in 1820. Some southern Democrats had been willing to support Dorr so long as "the people" remained White and male,[95] but the ability to bypass official channels to establish a new government posed a threat to all states, making Dorr's cause anathema even in friendly corners.[96]

Dorr, like Shays, would go on to win the war despite losing the battle. Samuel King retired from the governorship in 1843, even though the federal government had recognized his right to hold that office, paving the way for a more liberal state constitution that broadened the electorate.[97] This sequence of events simultaneously

90 Pauline Maier, "Popular Uprisings and Civil Authority in Eighteenth-Century America" (1970) *William and Mary Q.* 27, 3–35, 24.

91 Ibid.

92 John B. Rae, "Democrats and the Dorr Rebellion" (1936) 9 *New England Quarterly* 476–483, 476.

93 Ibid.; Chaput, "Proslavery and Antislavery Politics," 659 ("Northern abolitionists understood that if President John Tyler intervened in Rhode Island's constitutional crisis he would set a precedent, a precedent of federal government involvement in state affairs that might lay the groundwork for future antislavery measures.").

94 Ibid., 678 ("Reflecting on his expertise in Washington in a later to Walter Burgess, Dorr state that he now understood that his Jeffersonian doctrine of the people sovereignty could be construed to include all men and thus had given white Southerners the impression that he meant to include slaves in his definition of 'the people.'").

95 Ibid., 679.

96 Ibid., 672 (nothing that the majority of northeastern abolitionists opposed the People's Constitution).

97 William Goddard provided a thorough record of the May 1843 ceremony in Newport that transferred the governorship from King, who Goddard describes as "the last Governor under the Charter of

reinforced and undermined a competing notion that had always been in tension with alter or abolish, even during its height in the age of the Revolutionary War: that "[t]he people, as a political entity, existed only on election days."[98] Yet the changes that "the people" initiated – from forcing King's retirement to triggering a new constitution – were unlikely to have happened without the Dorr Rebellion.

Nonetheless, the nationalization of politics had rendered populist eruptions of discontent inherently suspect. Dorr had failed to garner popular support for his cause outside of his home state, but the relatively developed politics of the 1840s added another complication that had not been an issue for Daniel Shays over half a century earlier.[99] The prospect of being able to "vote them out," particularly as voter qualification standards became more liberalized and the electorate expanded nationally, meant that the status of the right of revolution was less secure in 1842 than it was in 1787.

In addition, the prospect of an election or formal constitutional amendment, as both Elisha Potter and Professor Goddard argued in 1842, negated the existence of a collective right to alter or abolish government asserted by a majority of citizens rather than a minority. A majority, in other words, could never resort to mob action, a proposition that would outlive the relatively bloodless conflict and be tested again in 1860.

4.3 A RIGHT IN DECLINE: THE THIN LINE BETWEEN ILLEGAL SECESSION AND THE RIGHT OF REVOLUTION

Congressman Elisha Potter's argument that the Dorr Rebellion was improper because the right of revolution belonged to oppressed minorities rather than democratic majorities who can use formal channels to impose their will suffered from a clear logical fallacy.[100] The obvious problem with this position was that the state

1663," to James Fenner. Goddard, *People of Rhode Island*, pp. 75–80. It was during this same month that Rhode Island's new constitution went into effect, in which "[t]he right of suffrage [was] vested in all male native citizens of the United States, who have resided in the state two years, and in the town where they propose to vote, six months; who have been registered in the town clerk's office at least seven days before the election; have paid within one year a tax of one dollar, or have done military duty within the preceding year; likewise, in all male citizens (naturalized foreigners) of the United States, who in addition to the preceding qualifications, possess real estate in the town or city, worth $134 over all incumbrances, or which rents for $7 per annum." Samuel Medary, *The New Constitution* (Columbus: S. Medary, 1849), issue 11, p. 170.

[98] Wilentz, *Politicians and the Egalitarians*, p. 8 ("If the unelected had any other political voice, it came in the form of extralegal mob violence and crowd disturbance – forms of protect condoned and even instigated by established political leaders when it suited their political advantage.... Whether commanded from above or organized on their own, these tumults affirmed that the mass of ordinary citizens had no regular, legal, permanent involvement in the making of decisions, the actual stuff of government and politics.").

[99] Chaput, "Proslavery and Antislavery Politics," 660.

[100] Potter, *Considerations*, p. 22.

legislature had limited the ability of democratic majorities to use formal channels by defining the relevant electorate narrowly. Nevertheless, there was something intuitive about Potter's broader assumption that the grievances of the People's Party could be redressed at the ballot box. Even for numerical minorities, the opportunity to have your views judged by the entire electorate in a free and fair election, governed by previously agreed-upon rules, would seem to negate the moral legitimacy of alter or abolish as a subsequent avenue for recourse should one's views fail to carry the day in that free election.

The election of 1860 became a litmus test for this proposition. The conventional wisdom was that the South seceded from the Union because of the threat that a Lincoln administration would pose to the institution of slavery, but the divides were actually more complicated. For slaveowners, their revulsion to the still fledgling, but increasingly dominant, Republican Party reflected an emerging partisan divide of which slavery was a core part; their aversion to the Party reflected the belief that Republican policies would be so devastating for the nation that, in their mind, its very existence was on the ballot in 1860.[101]

Notably, Republicans campaigned against the Democrats on an anticorruption platform, rather than the slavery issue: to do otherwise would make the regionalism of their party evident.[102] In making the anticorruption argument, Republicans focused on how President Buchanan tried to bribe reluctant Democrats in the House to admit Kansas as a slave state under the fraudulent Lecompton Constitution, a move that infuriated Republicans and some Democrats alike.[103] The Republicans, by focusing on non-slavery issues, did not want to be known simply as a northern abolitionist party, even though it was no secret that the party opposed the spread of slavery beyond where it already existed.

In fact, of the four major contenders for the presidency in 1860, only John C. Breckinridge insisted on the centrality of the slavery issue to the election, while

[101] In the lead-up to the 1860 election, fears grew among Southerners about a Republican presidential administration led by Abraham Lincoln. "Lincoln, southern leaders predicted, would not enforce the Fugitive Slave Law. He would appoint Republicans to federal posts in the South and build a Republican party there. Under a Lincoln administration, first in the Border South and then in the Middle and Lower South, slave escapes would multiply.... [N]onslaveholders would turn against slaveholders, and white supremacy would crumble." Stanley Harrold, *Border War: Fighting over Slavery before the Civil War* (Chapel Hill: University of North Carolina Press, 2010), p. 195. Fearmongering of this nature was taking place throughout the South well before the Confederacy was established: "Even before the creation of the Confederacy, the seceding states sent commissioners to the Middle and Border South states to argue they must secede to avoid the danger Lincoln, Republicans, and the North in general posed to them and the white South." Ibid., p. 196.

[102] Michael F. Holt, *The Election of 1860: A Campaign Fraught with Consequences* (Lawrence: University Press of Kansas, 2017), p. xiii ("Ousting Democrats from power and restoring honesty to the federal government – not stopping slavery's spread, let alone demanding its abolition – was the central theme of the Republican campaign and, so far as campaign issues determined the election's outcome, by far the major reason why Abraham Lincoln was elected.").

[103] Ibid., p. 33.

literally everyone else knew that the issue didn't play well politically.[104] Those on the other end of the political spectrum joined Breckinridge in trying to force slavery to the forefront. Many abolitionists were excited about the Republican Party's chances of winning the presidency in 1860 yet refused to voice their support publicly because of the party' failure to endorse slavery's abolition.[105] Frederick Douglass, who had thrown his support behind John C. Fremont in 1856 and, at least initially, was poised to support the Republicans, attacked the party for its lukewarm stance on slavery, deeming it "as good a southern party as either wing of the old Democratic Party."[106] Abolitionists became significantly less excited when the relatively unknown Abraham Lincoln secured the Republican nomination rather than William Seward, a known quantity whose antislavery bona fides were well established.[107]

The tenor of the 1860 presidential race revealed the one issue that was not on the table that year – the morality of slavery as a general matter (hence the anger of many abolitionists)[108] – both for the Republicans, who were against slavery's expansion in sparsely populated territories rather than its existence writ large,[109] and for Democrats, who were looking for more affirmative support for the institution on the federal stage. Meanwhile, the bloody events in Kansas,[110] along with the violent caning of antislavery Senator Charles Sumner,[111] helped precipitate the rise of the Republican Party as an anti-slavery force.

[104] Ibid., p. 11 ("John Bell's Constitutional Union supporters in both the North and the South, where the largest slaveholders usually backed him, consistently declared that territorial slavery extension was a mooted question, a phony issue, since slaveholders had no interest whatsoever in moving into any of the remaining territories in the United States.... Ultimately the Douglas camp, like the Constitutional Union Party, maintained that the fate of the nation, not the fate of slavery or slavery extension, was what was at stake in the 1860 race."); Ibid., p. 21 ("Republican leaders in 1854 and 1855 knew all too well that many northern voters worried more about Catholics, immigrants, and booze than they did about slavery extension.").

[105] James M. McPherson, *The Struggle for Equality: Abolitionists and the Negros in the Civil War and Reconstruction*, updated ed. (Princeton: Princeton University Press, 2015), p. 9 ("For the first time, an avowedly antislavery party had an excellent chance of winning the presidency. This intoxicating prospect was too much for some Garrisons ... who also forsook the antipolitical tradition of the movement and gave positive support for Abraham Lincoln. A majority of Garrisons, however, remained true to their principles, refused to give an explicit endorsement to the Republican party (though hoping for its victory), and criticized the party sharply for its antislavery shortcomings.").

[106] Ibid., p. 32.

[107] Ibid., p. 11 ("Abolitionists were understandably perplexed about this man Lincoln. He was plainly against slavery, but he was just as plainly not for its immediate and total abolition.").

[108] Holt, *The Election of 1860*, p. 18 ("Only a tiny minority of Republicans demanded the immediate abolition of slavery in the South."); McPherson, *Struggle for Equality*, p. 12 ("The Republican Party made careful efforts to keep the slavery question in bounds, to make it appear that the issue was not one of racial equality but of the extension of slavery into the territories.").

[109] Holt, *The Election of 1860*, p. 19 ("...virtually every public pronouncement by the party denied that Republicans would interfere with slavery where it legally existed...").

[110] See Chapter 2.6.

[111] In 1856, Democratic Congressman Preston Brooks of South Carolina attacked Republican Senator Charles Sumner of Massachusetts with a cane and left him "bleeding and unconscious." Harrold, *Border War*, p. 159. Brooks was the cousin of Andrew P. Butler, a senior senator from South Carolina.

With the defeat of the Lecompton Constitution in August 1858, the Republican Party lost the one political issue that had driven the party's growth for two years: Bleeding Kansas.[112] Yet Lincoln's "House Divided" speech in 1858, in which he forcefully argued that the "government cannot endure, permanently half slave and half free,"[113] as well as an 1858 speech by William Seward, in which he made a claim similar to that of Lincoln about the instability of the divisions over the slavery issue,[114] reignited fears that the Republican Party would abolish slavery in its entirety should they gain control of the levers of government.[115] The presidential election of 1860 was, in many ways, a fight over the same core issues that had divided the nation in the prior three decades, but with one central difference. This election was the first since 1824 in which the planter class faced the prospect of losing their iron grip on the presidency, where one of their own, or someone sympathetic to their interests, would not occupy the office.[116]

Given that the morality of slavery as an institution was not a campaign issue in 1860, what gave secession the moral legitimacy usually required for successful invocations of alter or abolish? The short answer was nothing. The longer answer was that southern secession was a political act, rather than a moral one, because slaveowners feared that confining slavery to the South would undermine their power to control the federal government, as free states would inevitably overshadow slave states in representation as more and more states were admitted.[117]

So while secession still centered on the issue of slavery, it brought to the fore longstanding disputes over the Constitution's inequitable allocation of power that enhanced the authority of slaveowners on the national stage.[118] The slave states'

Brooks' attack on Sumner was motivated by a speech that Sumner gave in which he ridiculed Senator Butler and South Carolina, which Brooks believed "insult[ed] the honor of his state and family." Ibid.

112 Holt, *The Election of 1860*, p. 37 ("With the final defeat of the Lecompton Constitution on August 2, 1858, and with it the last realistic possibility of slavery expansion into existing territories, the justification for an exclusively northern party like the Republicans had seemingly disappeared.").

113 "Speech of Hon. Abraham Lincoln, At Springfield, June 17, 1858," in *Political Debates between Hon. Abraham Lincoln and Hon. Stephen A. Douglas, In the Celebrated Campaign of 1858, in Illinois* (Columbus, OH: Follett, Foster and Company, 1860), p. 1.

114 "The Irrepressible Conflict: A Speech by William H. Seward," Delivered at Rochester, Monday, October 25, 1858 (New York: New York Tribune, 1858).

115 Holt, *The Election of 1860*, p. 46.

116 The following men were president during this timeframe: John Quincy Adams (1825–29), Andrew Jackson (1829–37), Martin Van Buren (1837–41), William Henry Harrison (1841), John Tyler (1841–45), James K. Polk (1845–49), Zachary Taylor (1849–50), Millard Fillmore (1850–53), Franklin Pierce (1853–57), and James Buchanan (1857–61).

117 Edward Foley, *Presidential Elections and Majority Rule: The Rise, Demise, and Potential Restoration of the Jeffersonian Electoral College* (New York: Oxford University Press, 2020), p. 81 ("In so far as the south in 1860 was now repudiating Lincoln's election, it was Southerners – not Lincoln and his supporters in the North – who were attempting to undo the conception of a federally appropriate president made part of the Constitution by the adoption of the Twelfth Amendment. Accordingly, if the Electoral College was a cause of the Civil War, it was only because the South was unwilling to abide by the terms of the federal arrangement embodied in the Electoral College in 1803.").

118 Robert Elder, *Calhoun: American Heretic* (New York: Basic Books, 2021), pp. 16–17 ("South Carolina's delegation soon made it clear that slavery's existence and protection was a nonnegotiable position…").

relative standing in relation to the free states required a steady stream of new slave states, lest they be eclipsed by the free North not only in the Senate, but also, because of the Three-Fifths Clause, the Electoral College and the Presidency. Few slaveowners had argued that slavery was morally acceptable, further illustrating that its salience as a political issue was deeply tied to the power that the South had wielded in Congress and over the presidency for decades thanks to the compromises in the U.S. Constitution rather than any broad defense of the institution as a moral good.[119]

Despite their efforts to distance themselves from the controversy over slavery's expansion, this was, as historian Michael Holt has argued, the Republican Party's "most concrete policy position" that not only distinguished themselves from their competitors but on the most important national issue. President Buchanan's machinations to garner the pro-slavery outcome in *Dred Scott* made it even more difficult for Republicans to distance themselves from the issue's political dimensions, with the president seeking to influence the justices to fulfill his "top priority upon taking office … [which] was to reverse the growth of the Republican Party."[120]

The fact that slavery and secession were political rather than moral issues, sufficient to place them in the mold of legitimate uses of the right of revolution, was also illustrated in the split among Democrats themselves, hence their failure to present a united pro-slavery front against the Republicans in the 1860 election. The party was splintered because some Democrats were concerned about the corruption of the Buchanan Administration.[121] Others opposed Democratic presidential candidate and Illinois Senator Stephen Douglas for his failure to support Kansas' admission as a slave state in accordance with his theory of popular sovereignty, which required that the decision be left to the *actual* residents of the territory (rather than one day Kansans).[122] Still others, including President Buchanan, threw their support behind John C. Breckinridge because he supported federal protection for slavery in the territories.[123] The Constitution Union Party, a fringe group of former Whigs, nominated John Bell, a Tennessee planter and politician who ran on a platform that

[119] Ibid., p. xiii ("Parting with an earlier generation of Southerners who viewed slavery as a necessary evil, as a U.S. Senator during the 1830s Calhoun formulated a defense of the peculiar institution as a 'positive good' in a white democracy and became the foremost advocate of slaveholders right to carry their peculiar form of property into the new territories added by American imperialism in Mexico and the West.").

[120] Holt, *The Election of 1860*, p. 13 ("Buchanan's top priority upon taking office as president in March 1857 was to reverse the growth of the Republican Party, which, he correctly perceived, jeopardized the Union. That goal is why he persuaded Robert Grier, a Pennsylvania associate justice on the Supreme Court, to join five southern justices in support of the *Dred Scott* decision, which by clear implication ruled Republicans' most concrete policy proposal – congressional prohibition from all federal territories – unconstitutional.").

[121] William W. Freehling, *The Road to Disunion: Secessionists Triumphant 1854–1861*, 2 vols. (Oxford: Oxford University Press: 1990), vol. II, p. 105.

[122] Holt, *The Election of 1860*, p. 50.

[123] Elbert Smith, *The Presidency of James Buchanan* 112–13 (Lawrence: University of Kansas Press, 1975).

sought to deemphasize the slavery issue. Unsurprisingly, Bell's nomination further splintered the Democratic vote.

In November 1860, this crowded field produced a Lincoln victory. He won with less than 40 percent of the vote but garnered enough electoral college votes to secure the presidency even though none came from southern states.[124] As Edward Foley has persuasively argued, Lincoln was the legitimate winner of the 1860 election, despite his support being concentrated above the Mason-Dixon line, because he competed and won under the rules as established by our constitutional system.[125] He secured a majority of the popular votes in those states that delivered his Electoral College victory, giving Lincoln the endorsement of the relevant majority of voters central to the Jeffersonian post–1804 Electoral College.[126] For legitimacy under this version of republicanism, the geographic spread of the states mattered less than securing majority support among those states required to reach the threshold to secure the presidency.[127] Because the Electoral College operated precisely as intended, southern secession from the Union – following a free and fair election – was illegitimate, both morally and under the terms of the U.S. Constitution.[128]

Secession also pushed the right of revolution into its death throes. The Civil War forced elected officials to confront the legitimacy of alter or abolish, since the Confederate states relied on this authority as one of the main legal arguments justifying secession.[129] The Confederacy asserted that the U.S. Constitution was a compact that was breached twofold: first, by the federal government, due to its failure to

124 Foley, *Presidential Elections*, pp. 79–80.

125 Ibid., p. 78 (noting that "mere national popularity – without regard to its distribution among states – was irrelevant to the Jeffersonian quest for a federally appropriate winner" and concluding that "[Stephen] Douglas [unlike Abraham Lincoln] was not a genuinely Jeffersonian candidate in 1860" because he "was incapable of assembling the kind of compound majority-of-majorities necessary for federal legitimacy").

126 Ibid., p. 80.

127 Ibid. ("The Jeffersonians specifically anticipated in 1803 that a presidential candidate, perhaps even Jefferson himself in 1804, might win an Electoral College majority without any support from one specific region of the federal union. In 1804, a candidate could lose all of New England's 45 electoral votes and still have far more than the majority needed for an Electoral College victory.").

128 Adam I.P. Smith, "Beyond the Realignment Synthesis: The 1860 Election Reconsidered," in Gareth Davies and Julian E. Zelizer (eds.), *America at the Ballot Box: Elections and Political History* (Philadelphia: University of Pennsylvania Press, 2015), pp. 59–74, 61.

129 States that explicitly relied on the alter or abolish right as a basis for secession were South Carolina, Mississippi, Georgia and Texas. See Confederate States of America – Declaration of the Immediate Causes Which Induce and Justify the Secession of South Carolina from the Federal Union (1860) [hereinafter South Carolina Secession Declaration]; A Declaration of the Immediate Causes which Induce and Justify the Secession of the State of Mississippi from the Federal Union (1861) [hereinafter Mississippi Secession Declaration]; Republic of Georgia, Ordinance of Secession, Passed Jan'ry 19, 1861, With the Names of the Signers (1861) [hereinafter Georgia Secession Declaration]; A Declaration of the Causes Which Impel the State of Texas to Secede from the Federal Union (1861) [hereinafter Texas Secession Declaration]. See also G. Edward White, "Recovering the Legal History of the Confederacy" (2011) 68 *Washington and Lee Law Review* 467–554, 480–481.

allow slavery in territories acquired in the first half of the nineteenth century,[130] and second, by non-slave-holding states, due to their refusal to return fugitive slaves.[131]

The argument that states could secede based on contract theory was often followed by the claim that there existed an inherent, natural right to overthrow the federal government.[132] The right of the people to alter or abolish the government appeared in six of the eleven Confederate state constitutions prior to the Civil War, as well as in the constitutions of the contested border states of Missouri and Kentucky.[133] Jefferson Davis, who served as the first and only president of the Confederate States of America, framed secession as not only natural, but at least partially derived from the Declaration of Independence:

> Our present political position has been achieved in a manner unprecedented in the history of nations. It illustrates the American idea that governments rest on the consent of the governed, and that it is the right of the people to alter or abolish them at will whenever they become destructive of the ends for which they were established.... In this [the Confederate states] merely asserted the right which the Declaration of Independence of July 4, 1776, defined to be "inalienable."[134]

Beyond the implicit threat of a Lincoln presidency to the institution of slavery, vindicating the right to alter or abolish government – here, the notion that White men could not be forced to acquiesce in a government that threatened their interests – pushed Virginia and the remaining, somewhat reluctant, southern states into the Confederacy.[135] This argument, rooted in the Declaration of Independence, convinced moderately pro-slavery states to support secession even though they were not otherwise swayed by claims of breach of contract or protecting the property rights of

[130] Mississippi Secession Declaration ("In 1819–20, [the U.S.] deprived the South of more than half the vast territory acquired from France.").

[131] South Carolina's secession declaration included the following language: "Thus was established, by compact between the States, a Government with definite objects and powers, limited to the express words of the grant .... We hold that ... the mode of its formation subjects it to ... the law of compact. We maintain that in every compact between two or more parties, the obligation is mutual; that the failure of one of the contracting parties to perform a material part of the agreement, entirely releases the obligation of the other; and that where no arbiter is provided, each party is remitted to his own judgment to determine the fact of failure, with all its consequences." South Carolina Secession Declaration. The declaration of secession issued by Georgia included similar language. See Georgia Secession Declaration.

[132] Jefferson Davis, "Inaugural Address of the President of the Provisional Government of February 18, 1861," in James D. Richardson (ed.), *A Compilation of the Messages and Papers from the Confederacy*, 2 vols. (Nashville: United States Publishing Company, 1905), pp. 32–36.

[133] Constitution of the State of Alabama art. I, s. 2 (1819); Constitution of the State of Arkansas art. II, s. 2 (1836); Constitution or Form of Government, for the People of Florida art. I, s. 2 (1838); Constitution of the Commonwealth of Kentucky art. 13, s. 4 (1850); Constitution of the State of Mississippi art. I, s. 2 (1832); Constitution of the State of Missouri art. 8, s. 2 (1820); Constitution of the State of Tennessee art. I, s. 1 (1835); Constitution of the State of Texas art. I, s. 1 (1845).

[134] Davis, "Inaugural Address," Confederacy Papers, p. 32.

[135] See Freehling, *Road to Disunion*, vol. II, pp. 527–528.

slaveowners as justification for outright rebellion.[136] As the Mississippi declaration of secession put it, "[f]or far less cause … our fathers separated from the Crown of England."[137]

President Lincoln's first inaugural address tried to carefully thread the needle with respect to the South's exercise of the right of revolution. He argued that "the Union is perpetual" and "no State upon its own mere motion can lawfully get out of the Union," but "the people retain their right to alter or abolish government."[138] To underscore his point, President Lincoln insisted that, "This country, with its institutions, belongs to the people who inhabit it."[139] Lincoln had long disputed that the South could legally secede, viewing the United States as one indissoluble nation in which its citizens theoretically retained their individual right to alter or abolish government, as opposed to treating the country as a compact of nation states in which each state possessed a legal right of secession.[140]

Lincoln emphasized that the right to alter or abolish government belonged to the people, in their individual capacity, and not the formal apparatus of the state. Republicans in Congress appreciated how this distinction could legitimize invocations of alter or abolish by Unionists living in Confederate states. This conception of alter or abolish was very different from one in which invocations were reserved for overthrowing or subduing a sovereign that has violated its obligation to the people. If anything, the fact that the admission of West Virginia did not align with the previously established rules governing the admission of new states signaled that its admission was a (completely understandable but nonetheless) purely partisan move, rather than a moral or philosophical decision justifying alter or abolish.

4.4 ETHAN ALLEN OR DANIEL SHAYS? ALTER OR ABOLISH AND THE ADMISSION OF "WEST" VIRGINIA

West Virginia was the first state to seek admission to the Union post-secession. Its claim to statehood was primarily rooted in Lincoln's conception of alter or abolish as belonging to the people within a state rather than the state itself. Unlike

136 See ibid.

137 Mississippi Secession Declaration.

138 Abraham Lincoln, "First Inaugural Address: March 4, 1861," in *Inaugural Addresses of the Presidents of the United States: From George Washington 1789 to Richard Milhous Nixon 1973*, H. Doc. 93–208 (Washington, D.C.: United States Government Printing Office, 1974), pp. 121–122.

139 Ibid., p. 125.

140 Herman Belz, "Lincoln, Secession, and Revolution: The Civil War Challenge to the Founding," in Paul D. Moreno and Johnathan G. O'Neill (eds.), *Constitutionalism in the Approach and Aftermath of the Civil War* (New York: Fordham University Press, 2013), pp. 82–83 ("Although on several occasions political minorities threatened disunion to secure their ends, such threats were not proof that a constitutional and legal right of secession existed. Should the necessity arise, the natural right of revolution, not a constitutionally privileged right of state secession, was in the founders' view the ultimate ground of resistance against unjust and abusive government.").

Elisha Potter or William Goddard in Rhode Island, Lincoln did not seem to care if the right was exercised by a majority of the population, as was argued during the Dorr Rebellion. Virginia seceded from the Union in early 1861, but many residents in its western counties rejected the legality and necessity of secession.[141] Northwestern Virginia had always been culturally, economically, and politically distinct from the rest of the state;[142] it not only had a quarter of the state's free population, but it also was home to few slaves.[143] The planter class who governed the state gave preference to slaveholders through large tax-breaks at the expense of the northwest;[144] the east region also received the benefit of internal improvements withheld from those in the northwest. Other restrictions on landownership also favored the East.[145] During the critical 1860 presidential election, Virginia delegates at the Democratic National Convention endorsed a platform that demanded full federal protection for slavery, which further contributed to the unrest in the state.[146]

In fact, the Civil War was not the first time there was a deadly split between Virginia's western and eastern halves. Recall Bacon's Rebellion, the 1676 uprising in which poor White servants and farmers, free Black people, and the enslaved violently rebelled against the planter class.[147] This conflict was a direct result of these cultural, economic, and political differences, in which the planters, by maintaining an iron grip on the levers of government, sought to create a permanent underclass separated only by racial animosity.[148]

In the wake of the rebellion, the Virginia Assembly enacted laws that expanded the rights of White servants while simultaneously creating hereditary racial slavery, thereby preventing any future alliances between the two groups.[149] While what became known as the Slave Codes made it impossible for White yeoman farmers

[141] Otis K. Rice and Stephen W. Brown, *West Virginia: A History*, 2nd ed. (Lexington: University Press of Kentucky, 1993), p. 117 (noting that, after the ordinance of secession was adopted, "[n]umerous officials [in the western counties] resigned their posts, and civil government began to disintegrate in many counties. Bands of armed men, taking advantage of the confusion, roamed the countryside and intimidated peaceful citizens. Sensing a great moment in history, farmers left their plows, blacksmiths their anvils, and merchants their shops to gather and discuss the uncertainties of the future and courses of action.").

[142] See William A. Link, "'This Bastard New Virginia': Slavery, West Virginia Exceptionalism, and the Secession Crisis" (2009) 3 *West Virginia History* 37–56, 39–40.

[143] Vasan Kesavan and Michael S. Paulsen, "Is West Virginia Unconstitutional?" (2002) 90 *California Law Review* 291–400, 297.

[144] Ibid., 298; see also Link, "Bastard New Virginia," 40–41, 43.

[145] Kesavan and Paulsen, "West Virginia," 298.

[146] Rice and Brown, *West Virginia*, p. 111.

[147] See Chapter 3.

[148] Heather C. Richardson, *How the South Won the Civil War: Oligarchy, Democracy, and the Continuing Fight for the Soul of America* (New York: Oxford University Press, 2022), pp. 17–20.

[149] Ibid., p. 20 ("As leaders bound African Americans more tightly into slavery, they courted white Virginians into joining the cultural and social world from which they had previously been excluded.").

to align themselves with enslaved and free Black people,[150] the faux equality that rich planters sought to cultivate between themselves and their less prosperous, non-slaveholding White brethren never really took hold on matters outside of some nominal agreement in the perceived racial superiority of the White man.[151] Despite efforts by rich planters to convey a sense of equality among White people in the state on economic and cultural issues – held together, as it were, by a belief that all White men had the capacity for upward mobility – Virginia had been, for all intents and purposes, two states for almost two centuries.

Unsurprisingly, the northwestern voters rejected the secession of Virginia from the Union approximately three-to-one.[152] Delegates from the region called a convention at Wheeling in May 1861 to condemn secession and, at a second June convention, declared themselves to be the proper authorities of Virginia.[153] After deeming the secessionist-Confederate legislature illegal, they established their own government by requiring all officials and legislators to swear an oath of loyalty to the U.S. Constitution and declare it the supreme law of the land.[154] The delegates explicitly relied on the right to alter or abolish government as the foundation for the new state, arguing in a June 13th resolution, that the state government had betrayed its people:

> The true purpose of all governments is to promote the welfare and provide for the protection and security of the governed, and when any form of organization of government proved inadequate for, or subversive to this purpose, it is the right, it is the duty of the latter to alter or abolish it.[155]

Seeking a firm break with its eastern brethren, delegates also introduced resolutions "forbidding the entry of additional slaves into West Virginia once the constitution was adopted and providing gradual emancipation for those already in the state."[156]

150 Ibid., p. 19 ("The Slave Codes made it costly for white colonists to fraternize across race lines. People of color could not own white Christians, which meant that if any master married a person of color, his white servants would immediately become free. Any white person attempting to marry across race lines would be fined and sent to jail, and the minister performing such a marriage would be fined an astonishing price of ten thousand pounds of tobacco. White servant women who had mixed-race children either had to pay a whopping fine or have their term of service extended for five years. The child would be a slave until he or she was thirty-one years old.").

151 Ibid., p. 29.

152 Richard O. Curry, *A House Divided: A Study of Statehood Politics and the Copperhead Movement in West Virginia* (Pittsburgh: University of Pittsburgh Press, 1964), p. 17 ("Twenty-four of the thirty-five counties of northwestern Virginia gave substantial majorities for the Union … the region as a whole was predominantly Unionist, perhaps by as much as three to one.")

153 Ibid., pp. 27–29.

154 Kesavan and Paulsen, "West Virginia," pp. 293, 300.

155 Memorial of the Commissioners Appointed by the Convention of West Virginia, Praying For the Admission of That State Into the Union, S. Misc. Doc. No. 99, 37th Congress, 2d Session (May 31, 1862). p. 6; see also "Western Virginia: Declaration of Independence and Plan for Reorganization," *New York Times*, June 20, 1861, p. 2, www.nytimes.com/1861/06/20/archives/western-virginia-declaration-of-independence-and-plan-for.html.

156 Rice and Brown, *West Virginia*, p. 145.

The final constitution barred African Americans from the state, providing that "no slave shall be brought, or free person of color permitted to come into the State for permanent residence."[157]

President Lincoln and Congress soon recognized the new pro-Unionist government as the lawful government of Virginia, and Congress quickly seated its two senators and three House members. However, northwestern Virginians did not stop at assembling a new state government for Virginia, and in October 1861 they called a third convention to propose the creation of the new state. In the wake of this convention, both the vote on the statehood referendum and the new constitution were approved by a landslide.[158] It would prove to be a challenge, however, to reconcile this use of alter or abolish with the express text of the Constitution.

Under Article IV, Section 3 of the Constitution, a new state may not be admitted by Congress into the Union from within the jurisdiction of another state without the consent of Congress and the legislators of both states.[159] This new state – West Virginia – was carved from Virginia, which had seceded from the Union and did not consent to the parceling of its jurisdiction. To get around the potential constitutional problems, the formerly "restored" legislature of Virginia, controlled by those in the northwest, passed an act consenting to the new state of West Virginia.[160]

Despite these constitutional gymnastics, the admission of West Virginia placed President Lincoln in a bit of a quandary. In acknowledging the right of these citizens to abolish their ties with the state of Virginia, does this accord implicit recognition of the right of the southern states to leave the Union? Lincoln resoundingly rejected this premise, concluding that Virginia's secessionist convention had not received the consent of the people.[161] This failure of popular ratification illustrated that the secessionist government was not the lawful government of Virginia and required Lincoln, acting pursuant to the Guarantee Clause, to protect the citizens of the state from the insurrectionists.[162]

[157] Ibid.

[158] Ibid., pp. 300–301.

[159] "Comments of Representative Conway, 37th Congress, Second Session, December 17, 1861," 32 *Congressional Globe* (Washington, D.C.: Globe Office, 1862), pt. 1, p. 86. ("A government for the State of Virginia made its appearance last May, and claimed to be entitled to consideration, because, as it was said, the people west of the mountains had instituted it. It received the recognition of the President, which was construed to bind the other branches of the Government....[T]he people of Western Virginia having created a government for the whole State, of which the needed recognition was afforded, and having now created their new State of Kanawha, have only to give to the latter, through the former, the necessary assent, to secure the requisite compliance with the terms of the Constitution, and be doubly admitted into the Union – thus becoming invested with the constitutional powers of the old State of Virginia, besides those which will belong to the new State of Kanawha, including, of course, two United States Senators for each. I conceive this to be a gross outrage upon the constitutional rights of all the other States.").

[160] Kesavan and Paulsen, "West Virginia," p. 301.

[161] Ibid., p. 311–312.

[162] Ibid.

But a second argument was also at play here, challenging the notion that secession could be legal if ratified by popular vote. Secession, in Lincoln's view, was unconstitutional without the consent of the United States, and no consent had been forthcoming.[163] Ignoring that the restored government was populated by those only from the northwestern counties,[164] Lincoln believed the federal government had the power to recognize alternative state governments created by loyal citizens "in resistance to insurrectionary regimes that have taken over the usual governing machinery of their states."[165] In sum, the counties in northwestern Virginia validly invoked the alter or abolish right so as to preserve republican government recognized by the U.S. Constitution.

President Lincoln signed a proclamation admitting West Virginia to the Union on December 31, 1862.[166] Notably, emancipation was a condition of admission but universal male suffrage, regardless of race, was not. West Virginia officially became a state on June 20, 1863, the voters having ratified its new constitution in April 1862.[167] In navigating West Virginia's path to statehood, Lincoln was, through his rhetoric, able to conceptualize appropriate uses of the alter or abolish right, consistent with the Guarantee Clause, while establishing that the Confederacy consisted of states still in the Union (although in rebellion) that had not properly invoked the right. Thus, the Civil War was not only about slavery, but it was also about restoring republican government, as defined by the federal government, to these wayward states.

Despite the legal uncertainty surrounding reconstituted Virginia and newly admitted West Virginia, Congress legitimized only those elections held in accordance with state law, at least initially. For example, the House of Representatives refused to seat S. Ferguson Beach, who claimed that he won an 1860 congressional election despite the armed occupation by Confederates in most of the district.[168] Given that the district was occupied by enemy forces, the majority of qualified voters could not vote in the election.[169] The failure of a majority of the district to elect the representative meant that the election was not held in conformity with Virginia

[163] Ibid., pp. 308–309, 311–312.

[164] Ibid., p. 315 (conservatives argued that the new legislature was a legal fiction that precluded the admission of West Virginia as a state). But see ibid., p. 318 (moderates argued that West Virginia could be admitted because the new, consenting government represented at least three-fourths of the loyal population of Virginia).

[165] Ibid., p. 313.

[166] Abraham Lincoln, "Proclamation Admitting West Virginia into the Union, April 20, 1863," in Arthur B. Lapsley (ed.), *The Writings of Abraham Lincoln*, Fed. Ed., 8 vols. (New York: G.P. Putnam's Sons, 1905–06), vol. 6, p. 282.

[167] Kesavan and Paulsen, "West Virginia," pp. 300–301.

[168] "Beach, House Committee on Elections, 37th Congress (1861–1863)," in Chester H. Rowell, *A Historical and Legal Digest of all the Contested Election Cases in the House of Representatives of the United States from the First to the Fifty-Sixth Congress, 1789–1901* (Washington, D.C.: Government Printing Office, 1901; reprinted edition: Westport: Greenwood Press, 1976), pp. 176–177.

[169] Ibid.

law; therefore, the claimant was not entitled to his seat.[170] Despite secession, compliance with established state law remained one of the most important factors in determining whether a claimant would be seated.[171]

State law did not always resolve the disputed election before Congress. For example, the House initially refused to seat Joseph Segar after the election was held in one precinct where twenty-five votes were cast.[172] Another election was subsequently held in two counties and one additional precinct, in which about 1,000 votes were cast, despite the fact that the usual vote total from the district's seventeen counties was around 8,000.[173] Despite these discrepancies, the House admitted Segar to the seat following this second election. Key to this decision was the fact that the President and Congress had recognized the provisional government formed by those from the western counties. Since Segar was certified by Governor Pierpont, then recognized as the legitimate governor of the State of Virginia, Congress was, in its view, obligated to recognize his official act by certifying Segar as the congressional representative from the first congressional district of Virginia.[174]

Subsequent ratification by the governor or the legislature was not always sufficient to validate an election held in violation of state law. In another Virginia congressional election during this period, the governor of soon-to-be West Virginia issued writs of election, but authorized persons to change the date of election if necessary.[175] The House Committee on Elections found that the power to fix the election date could not be delegated.[176] The reconstructed Virginia legislature subsequently passed an act that legalized the election, but the Committee found that this act affecting West Virginia's elections was beyond the power of the

170 Ibid.

171 See, e.g., "McCloud and Wing, House Committee on Elections, 37th Congress (1861–1863)," in Rowell, *Contested Elections Cases*, pp. 182–183 (finding that an election was held in disregard of state law where the required notice was not given, the qualification of voters was inconsistent with state law, and only four of eleven counties participated in the election).

172 "Segar, House Committee on Elections, 37th Congress (1861–1863)," in Rowell, *Contested Elections Cases*, p. 179.

173 Ibid., p. 181.

174 "Comments of Representative Maynard, 37th Congress, Second Session, February 12, 1862," 32 *Congressional Globe* (Washington, D.C.: Globe Office, 1862), pt. 1, p. 751 ("It has been settled by all of the departments of the government in recognition of the provisional government which is now there in operation. We have recognized Mr. Pierpoint as the legitimate and legal Governor of the State of Virginia; and the authority he exercises as being the true gubernatorial authority of the State. Having so recognized it, then we must accept his official acts as such. One of his official acts is to certify the present applicant as a Representative to this House from the first congressional district of Virginia. This is not, as has been well said, a contested-election case. Nobody is here controverting the fact of the election. No person comes here and claims … to occupy a seat as a Representative in the district. It is simply a naked proposition whether we shall recognize and act upon the credentials presented by Mr. Segar or not.").

175 "McKenzie, House Committee on Elections, 37th Congress (1861–1863)," in Rowell, *Contested Elections Cases*, p. 183.

176 Ibid.

Virginia legislature.[177] Finally, the Committee determined that, because only two of the nine counties in the district were under Union control and participated in the election, the "winner" of the election was not entitled to the seat.[178]

Outside of the unique situation presented by Virginia and West Virginia, both the House and the Senate repeatedly confronted the question of whether to seat representatives and senators elected from Confederate states during the Thirty-Seventh (1861–63) and Thirty-Eighth (1863–65) Congresses.[179] Loyal voters in those states continued to hold congressional elections, often in contravention of state law, and winners of these elections petitioned Congress to take their seats. During the antebellum era, people who were elected in violation of state law were not seated. On the eve of the Civil War, however, Congress seated some of these claimants, even though there was not yet an armed insurgency or the official outbreak of war. In most cases, the primary determinant of whether a claimant was entitled to the congressional seat turned on Congress's ability to discern whether legal votes had been cast as opposed to whether the election itself was held in contravention of state law.[180]

For example, Tennessee passed an ordinance of secession from the United States, and an election was held for members of the Confederate Congress.[181] Voters loyal to the Union disregarded the ordinance as a violation of the U.S. Constitution and cast their votes for representatives to the United States Congress. Although the Tennessee governor refused to grant a certificate of election and sheriffs refused to return the votes cast as state law required, the claimant, Andrew J. Clements, proved that he had received sufficient legal votes to claim the seat.[182] The House of Representatives agreed, and Clements was seated.[183]

177 Ibid. ("The legislature of Virginia had subsequently passed an act which, it was contended, legalized this election, but…[i]f this act had had the intention claimed, it would have been beyond the power of the legislature to legalize an election not legal at the time it was held.").

178 Ibid. See also "Grafflin, House Committee on Elections, 37th Congress (1861–1863)," in Rowell, *Contested Elections Cases*, p. 184 (Because the election was held in only a small part of the district, the claimant was not entitled to a seat).

179 "Ten times in the Senate and more than thirty times in the House of Representatives, during the Thirty-seventh and Thirty-eighth Congresses, was application made for admission by men claiming to represent some portion of the territory then in insurrection against the national government." Frederick W. Moore, "Representation in the National Congress from the Seceding States, 1861–65" (1897) 2 *American Historical Review* 279–293, 279.

180 "The House committee was very free in going behind the returns and examining into the character of the election. It sought for conformity to law of the polling places. … In many cases reported with the recommendation to reject, the committee had been unable to satisfy themselves that any votes at all had been legally cast and counted." Ibid., 287.

181 "Clements, House Committee on Elections, 37th Congress (1861–1863)," in Rowell, *Contested Elections Cases*, p. 174.

182 Moore, "Seceding States," 284–285. The committee, after examining the evidence that Clements put forward, found that he was "unmistakably the choice of the Union men of the whole district[,]" and that "the refusal of the governor to grant a certificate did not prejudice [his right], which in other respects they found satisfactory." Ibid., 285.

183 Ibid.

Where the claimant failed to prove that votes had been legally cast for him, however, Congress did not permit the person to hold the seat. In 1862, voters in a Tennessee congressional district that was relatively free of Confederate influence held a convention, during which they determined that they would hold an election on a fixed date unless another date was chosen by the governor.[184] Governor Andrew Johnson (who would later become the nation's seventeenth president) then issued writs of election for a later date, but Confederate loyalists heard about these writs, invaded the district, and prevented the election from being held.[185] The Union general occupying the area postponed the election, but some polls were still open and about 1,900 votes were cast, although the only proof of these votes was unsworn letters and statements.[186] The Committee on Elections found that the claimant, Alvin Hawkins, was not entitled to the seat because it would set a dangerous precedent to accept unsworn statements and letters as legal ballots.[187]

The inability to discern "legal" votes was also at issue in other contests. When Virginia seceded from the Union and suspended congressional elections, one candidate, Charles H. Upton, announced his candidacy for Congress and set up "side polls" for voting.[188] Just like the elections held by loyal voters in Tennessee, these "side polls" were not established in conformity with state law; the sheriff did not deliver any returns; and the results were not certified. In addition, almost all of the votes that Upton claimed were cast in support of his candidacy could not be substantiated.[189] In fact, the Committee on Elections went out of its way to distinguish the Clements case – where there were enough legal votes to select a winner – noting that, "The case was not analogous to that of Clements, because in that case some 2,000 votes were legally cast, and several hundred of them were legally returned and canvassed. In this case there was no proof that these 10 votes had been legally cast, and they were not returned or canvassed at all."[190] Similarly, the House rejected a claim to a South Carolina congressional seat after no regular election was held anywhere, and the claimant, Charles Henry Foster, asked to be seated based on papers signed by a few citizens expressing him as their choice.[191] The committee rejected

[184] Ibid., 289–290.
[185] Ibid., 290.
[186] "Hawkins, House Committee on Elections, 37th Congress (1861–1863)," in Rowell, *Contested Elections Cases*, p. 185.
[187] Ibid.
[188] "Upton, House Committee on Elections, 37th Congress (1861–1863)," in Rowell, *Contested Elections Cases*, p. 174
[189] Ibid. ("[Upton] claimed that 95 persons had voted for him at 'side polls,' but 85 of these were shown merely by the signatures of the voters to unauthenticated papers, and he did not base his claims on them. But the poll book of one precinct (the election was viva voce) showed, of 51 votes cast, 10 which were cast for claimant as Representative. But the election officers whose oaths were appended to it were only sworn to conduct the election for State officers.").
[190] Ibid.
[191] "Foster, House Committee on Elections, 37th Congress (1861–1863)," in Rowell, *Contested Elections Cases*, p. 180.

Foster's claim, holding that there were no legal votes upon which his right to a seat could be based.[192]

The fact that Congress honored legally cast votes from loyal voters in states that were in rebellion, provided that the claimant could verify the authenticity of the ballots, further signaled that secession did not mean state suicide. People, but not states, could claim the protections of the alter or abolish right, a fact that remained true even if people within a state departed the Union in numbers sufficient to effectively dismantle a state's political system.

The "restoration" of Virginia and admission of West Virginia, as well as disputes during the Civil War over who could represent loyal citizens in Congress, was the culmination of an eight-decade debate over the validity and scope of the alter or abolish right. The obvious tension between northern claims that secession was illegal and the accepted use of alter or abolish among pro-Union sympathizers in Virginia created a cognitive dissonance in the doctrine that became almost impossible to reconcile. Similar to arguments made by those who opposed the Dorrites in Rhode Island, one could say that Lincoln recognized the claims of only the minority, not the majority, to resist their governing coalition. But it may be more accurate to say that Lincoln believed the right to alter or abolish government cannot be exercised by the state itself, no matter how many citizens represented themselves as its corporeal form.

Nonetheless, the dispute over West Virginia, and the issue of federal consent as a basis for alter or abolish – rather than as a natural right that belonged to everyone – ironically reaffirmed a core premise from the *Dred Scott* decision.[193] Lincoln corroborated that the federal government's authority to shape the boundaries of the political community of "We the People" trumped the will of the states, similar to the Supreme Court's holding, in *Dred Scott*, that African Americans cannot be part of "We the People" even if a state desired otherwise. During this period, Congress relied on this authority to exercise greater control over federal elections and the construction of all political communities.

4.5 FROM PROPERTY RIGHT TO POLITICAL RIGHT: REDEFINING THE COMMUNITY OF "WE THE VOTERS"

The Confederacy's exercise of the right to alter or abolish government, regardless if the decision to do so was valid, pushed the boundaries of the political communities of both "We the People" and "We the Voters." In fact, the Civil War field-tested antebellum conceptions of both independence and civic virtue, long thought to be essential qualities of the ideal elector. Similar to other periods, military voters

192 Ibid.

193 *Dred Scott v. Sandford*, 60 U.S. (19 How.) 393 (1856).

challenged their exclusion from the polls, arguing that independence and virtue could be proven through military service and not just through property ownership.[194]

The voting rights of those disloyal to the United States would also come under fire, paving the way for broad federal intervention in state elections. In 1861, the Lincoln Administration faced the possibility that residents in border states might cast votes that could push these states into the Confederacy. General John Dix, the Union general overseeing New York and Pennsylvania, had to confront this threat head on when he learned that Confederate soldiers would be returning home to the border state of Maryland to vote in the November 1861 elections.[195] On November 1, 1861, General Dix issued an order mandating the arrest of all disloyal persons "in any of the election districts or precincts in which they may appear at the polls to effect [sic] their criminal attempt to convert the elective franchise into an engine for the subversion of the Government, and for the encouragement and support of its enemies."[196]

Using military authority to prevent individuals who were otherwise eligible to vote under state law from casting their ballots was an unprecedented use of federal authority. But loyalty to the Union, imposed by either the federal government or under state law, would become an important factor in determining the eligibility of voters during the war. On June 12, 1862, a convention of loyal Missouri Unionists adopted an ordinance providing that all voters had to take a loyalty oath to vote, implementing this requirement out of fear that individuals aligned with the Confederacy would cast potentially decisive ballots in state elections.[197]

Other states were similarly concerned that disloyalty would lead to violence and deter turnout in state and federal elections. In 1863, the Delaware legislature made

194 Larry T. Balsamo, "'We Cannot Have Free Government without Elections': Abraham Lincoln and the Election of 1864" (2001) 94 *Journal of the Illinois State Historical Society* 181–199, 196.

195 Edward McPherson, *The Political History of the United States of American during the Great Rebellion*, 2nd ed. (Washington, D.C.: Philp & Solomons, 1865), p. 308. General Dix argued that the order was necessary because,

> Information has come to my knowledge that certain individuals formerly resided in this State, and who are known to have been recently in Virginia bearing arms against the authority and the forces of the United States, have returned to their former homes with the intention of taking part in the elections of the 6th of November instant, ths carrying out at the polls the treason that they have committed in the field. There is reason also to believe that other individuals lately residents of Maryland, who have been engaged in similar acts of hostility to the United States … are about to participate in the election for the same treacherous purpose, with the hopes of carrying over the State by disloyal votes to the cause of rebellion and treason.

Ibid.

196 Ibid.

197 Ibid., p. 314. At this time, Missouri had two governments – one loyal to the Union and the other loyal to the Confederacy. William R. Geise, "Missouri's Confederate Capital in Marshall, Texas" (1962) 66 *Southwestern Historical Quarterly* 193–207, 193. Although the Confederate government sent representatives to the Confederate Congress, it was never able to control much territory within the state and had to govern from Marshall, Texas. Ibid.

it a felony for any soldiers to be at a polling place for purposes of interfering in state elections.[198] Similarly, Kentucky stripped all Confederates of state citizenship and further provided that, "whenever a person attempts or is called on to exercise any of the constitutional or legal rights and privileges belonging only to citizens of Kentucky," the person would have to submit to a loyalty oath.[199] The Governor of Kentucky argued that this law was necessary for "the purity of the elective franchise."[200] The Union colonel overseeing Kentucky went further, issuing an order mandating the imprisonment of all Kentucky voters who had been stripped of their citizenship but showed up to the polls to vote.[201]

Notably, the Lincoln administration mandated such oath requirements even in the absence of any state regulation, paving the way for conflict between state and federal officials. In the 1861 elections, for example, General Dix explained that arresting the disloyal at the polls would be less intrusive than requiring people of doubtful loyalty to offer "an oath to support the Constitution of the United States," because "the constitution and laws of Maryland provide for the exercise of the elective franchise by regulations with which I have no right to interfere."[202]

But it is clear that the Administration's position had changed by the 1863 elections, when General Robert C. Schenck, who oversaw Maryland, ordered all "provost marshals and other military officers" to require "an oath of allegiance to the United States, as a test of citizenship of any one whose vote may be challenged on the ground that he is not loyal."[203] Schenck issued this order despite the fact that Governor Bradford of Maryland contested the legality of the loyalty oath; in Bradford's opinion, "It is the judgment of the judges of election alone [and not military personnel], founded upon the provisions of the constitution and laws of the State, that must determine the right to vote of any person offering himself for that purpose."[204]

President Lincoln recognized that an oath requirement risked federal interference with state voter qualification standards but emphasized to Governor Bradford that the military order "assure[d] the right of voting to all loyal men."[205] Lincoln was dismissive of the federalism questions raised by imposing an oath requirement

198 McPherson, *Political History of the United States*, p. 312. Generals Schenck and Tyler issued orders in support of this law; in his, General Tyler declared that "the whole object of the order of the Commanding General is to preserve peace at the places of voting, to sustain the judges or inspectors of election, to protect loyal voters, and to prevent from voting disloyal and traitorously disposed persons, who refuse to take the oath of allegiance." Ibid.

199 Ibid., p. 313.

200 Ibid.

201 Ibid., p. 314.

202 Ibid., p. 308.

203 Ibid., p. 309. See also William E. Gienapp, "Abraham Lincoln and the Border States" (1992) 13 *Journal of the Abraham Lincoln Association* 13–46, 20.

204 McPherson, *Political History of the United States*, p. 310.

205 Ibid.

outside of the strictures of state law, instead focusing on its importance to the war effort: "In this struggle for the nation's life, I cannot so confidently rely on those whose election may have depended on disloyal votes."[206] State voter qualification standards must yield, in Lincoln's view, to the exigencies of war.

Not everyone agreed with the president. In January 1864, Senator Lazarus Powell, a Kentucky Democrat who survived an 1862 attempt to expel him from the Senate because of allegations that he was a secret confederate sympathizer, introduced a bill "to prevent officers of the army and navy, and other persons engaged in the military service, from interfering in elections in the States."[207]

The federal government did not use the failure of this particular bill, or even the excuse of war, to completely displace state authority over elections. Indeed, its deference was reflected in the fact that it was the states – and not Congress – that needed to make the changes necessary to enfranchise military voters. President Lincoln, for example, urged General William Sherman to furlough troops hailing from the crucial battleground state of Indiana because the state had made no provisions for absentee voting by members of the military.[208] Similar orders had been issued for Maryland soldiers for the 1861 and 1863 elections.[209] In time for the 1864 elections, a number of states allowed soldiers to vote where they were stationed.[210]

Military service and loyalty to the Union also challenged the racist assumptions that African Americans had a genetic predisposition toward laziness, biological inferiority, and suitability for enslavement, beliefs that had long justified their exclusion from the community of voters.[211] But the solicitude shown to White men did not extend to African American men who served the nation militarily, even though this service had exposed them to freedoms that had been denied to them prior to the war. For example, in military courts, African Americans could testify in their own

[206] Ibid. Lincoln argues that if the Governor approves of Missouri's loyalty oath, then he should approve of such oaths in Maryland, even if not explicitly required by state law because it reaches "precisely the same end." Ibid.

[207] Ibid. p. 315.

[208] Jonathan W. White, *Emancipation, the Union Army, and the Reelection of Abraham Lincoln* (Baton Rouge: Louisiana State University Press, 2014), p. 104 (noting that the vast majority of union soldiers voted for Lincoln but challenging the premise that this vote signaled support for Republican policies).

[209] The 1861 order was from Simon Cameron, Secretary of War, to General George McClellan. McPherson, *Political History of the United States*, p. 309.

[210] Oscar O. Winther, "The Soldier Vote in the Election of 1864" (1944) 25 *New York History* 440–58.

[211] See generally Eugene H. Berwanger, "Negrophobia in Northern Proslavery and Antislavery Thought" (1972) 33 *Phylon* 266–275; Jacob K. Cogan, "The Look Within: Property, Capacity, and Suffrage in Nineteenth-Century America" (1997) 107 *Yale Law Journal* 473–498, 489–491; Wilhelmena S. Robinson, "Changing the African-American Image through History" (1970) 33 *Negro History Bulletin*, 44–46; Stephen B. Weeks, "The History of Negro Suffrage in the South" (1894) 9 *Political Science Quarterly* 671–703. See also Le'Trice D. Donaldson, *Duty beyond the Battlefield: African American Soldiers Fight for Racial Uplift, Citizenship, and Manhood, 1870–1920* (Carbondale: Southern Illinois University Press, 2020).

defense when facing court martial or other punishment for alleged crimes committed while enlisted.[212] Outside of this context, Black men waited for moderate Republicans – then the dominant wing of the party – to set the timing and pace on the suffrage issue. Similar to the enfranchisement of military voters, the prevailing view was that the states should set voter qualifications.

This state-centered view dominated early Reconstruction policy. In December 1863, President Lincoln issued his Proclamation of Amnesty and Reconstruction, also known as the Ten Percent Plan, which restored to the Union any seceding states when at least 10 percent of the state's qualified voters – as of 1860 – swore an oath of loyalty to the Union.[213] Presidential reconstruction firmly segregated the issue of the permanent eradication of slavery and the equality of African Americans before the law from questions surrounding the restoration of the former Confederate states.[214] It would fall to the benevolence of leaders in the reconstructed southern states to extend suffrage to African Americans, and views of who was fit to be part of the community of "We the Voters" continued to be governed by antebellum conceptions of independence and civic virtue that had once been at the heart of republican theory.

The reconstruction of Louisiana, Tennessee, and Arkansas during the Civil War proved that local elites, even those backed by the U.S. government, could not be trusted to provide equal political rights to African Americans. Black people in New Orleans, for example, testified against White people in certain criminal and civil cases in courts set up by the Union army in the spring of 1862.[215] However, there were limits to the willingness of White people to fully embrace African American equality before the law. In February 1864, Louisiana held an election prior to writing a new constitution, effectively limiting suffrage to those White people already enfranchised under state law and refusing to abolish slavery in the state.[216] Michael Hahn, the Lincoln-backed moderate who won the governorship, opposed African

212 Melissa L. Milewski, *Litigating across the Color Line: Civil Cases between Black and White Southerners from the End of Slavery to Civil Rights* (New York: Oxford University Press, 2018), p. 30. See also Eric Foner, "Rights and the Constitution in Black Life during the Civil War and Reconstruction" (1987) 74 *Journal of American History* 863–883, 864 ("For the first time in American history, large numbers of blacks were treated as equals before the law– if only before military law. In army courts blacks could testify against whites (something unheard of throughout the South and in much of the North as well). It was in the army that those former slaves first learned to read and write, either from teachers employed by the military or in classrooms and literary societies established and funded by the soldiers themselves."). See also ibid., p. 865 ("From the army would come many of the black political leaders of Radical Reconstruction, including at least forty-one delegates to state constitutional conventions, sixty legislators, and four congressmen.").

213 Abraham Lincoln, "Proclamation of Amnesty and Reconstruction, December 8, 1863," in Lapsley (ed.), *The Writings of Abraham Lincoln*, p. 28.

214 Balsamo, "Abraham Lincoln and the Election of 1864," 182 (noting that "those swearing such an oath would receive amnesty, resumption of all rights, and guaranteed return of all property except slaves").

215 Milewski, *Litigating across the Color Line*, p. 30.

216 McPherson, *Struggle for Equality*, pp. 251–255.

American enfranchisement.[217] General Nathaniel P. Banks, who oversaw wartime reconstruction of Louisiana, also opposed Black suffrage.[218]

In March 1864, President Lincoln wrote Hahn, urging him to enfranchise African Americans who had served in the military: "Now you are about to have a [constitutional] Convention which, among other things, will probably define the elective franchise. I barely suggest for your private consideration, whether some of the colored people might not be let in – as, for instance, the very intelligent and especially those who have fought gallantly in our ranks."[219] In the end, this plea fell on deaf ears and the 1864 Louisiana Constitution did not enfranchise Black men.[220]

On May 31, 1864, Republicans who were critical of President Lincoln's handling of the Civil War and sought stronger action on the issues of both abolition and universal male suffrage met in convention in Cleveland. Abolitionist Wendell Phillips, who was unable to attend, sent a strongly worded letter that was read aloud to the attendees, in which he noted, with more than a little acrimony, that, "Mr. Lincoln's model of reconstruction is the experiment in Louisiana, which puts all power into the hands of the unchanged White race, soured by defeat, hating the laboring classes, plotting constantly for antidemocratic institutions."[221] Phillips further charged that, "Such reconstruction makes the freedom of the negro a sham, and perpetuates slavery under a softer name," and concluded that, "There is no plan of reconstruction possible within twenty years, unless we admit the black to citizenship and the ballot, and use him, with the White, as the basis of States."[222]

Governor Hahn's refusal to embrace colorblind suffrage reflected that antebellum notions of voting, notably the perception of who should be able to vote as determined by the states and not the federal government, continued to persist just as claims of innate black inferiority – and their perceived lack of fitness to be electors – held sway among southern White people, even those aligned with the Lincoln Administration.[223] African Americans, arguing that they were entitled to vote in the 1864 Louisiana elections, presented a petition citing high literacy and property ownership among their ranks as evidence of their fitness.[224] They sought to prove that

[217] Ibid., pp. 243–244.

[218] Foner, "Rights and the Constitution in Black Life," 868.

[219] Abraham Lincoln, "Letter to Michael Hahn, March 13, 1864," in Roy P. Basler (ed.), *The Collected Works of Abraham Lincoln*, 9 vols. (New Brunswick: Rutgers University Press, 1953–55), vol. 7, p. 243. See also Eugene H. Berwanger, "Lincoln's Constitutional Dilemma: Emancipation and Black Suffrage" (1983) 5 *Papers of the Abraham Lincoln Association* 25–38, 36.

[220] Berwanger, "Lincoln's Constitutional Dilemma," 36 ("[Louisiana's] constitutional convention failed to enfranchise any blacks but instead referred the question to the state legislature, meaning that suffrage never would be granted in Louisiana.").

[221] "Letter from Wendell Phillips to the Cleveland Convention, dated May 27, 1864," in McPherson, *Political History of the United States*, p. 412.

[222] Ibid.

[223] McPherson, *Struggle for Equality*, p. 244.

[224] The force behind the petition was "the free blacks of New Orleans, [for whom] enfranchisement was an especially urgent concern." Larry E. Nelson, "Black Leaders and the Presidential Election

they deserve the ballot through the same gatekeeping criteria that had long defined access: literacy and property ownership.

Even in northern states, these criteria continued to be the vehicles through which African Americans established their civic virtue. Nonetheless, inequality persisted because the belief in the fundamental inferiority of African Americans was as much a part of the northern legacy as in the South, despite the gradual emancipation of slaves that had occurred in the region during the first half of the nineteenth century.[225] New York, for example, outlawed slavery in 1799, yet still required African Americans, but not White people, to own property to vote.[226] And in reconstructed Louisiana, where African American suffrage enjoyed some limited support, the possibility of imposing property restrictions was not enough to convince newly elected Governor Hahn, a political moderate, to enfranchise them.

The expansion of federal authority in the area of voting and elections moved slowly, even as state officials rejected incremental movement toward a qualified suffrage for Black men. Like Louisiana, the states of Tennessee and Arkansas, also reconstructed during the war, refused to extend voting rights to this group. Congress did very little to counter this resistance. For example, the Wade–Davis Reconstruction bill required that 50 percent of the White male voters take a loyalty oath prior to reestablishing the state government.[227] The bill sought to enlarge Congress's role in Reconstruction at the expense of presidential power, but it did so by sacrificing universal suffrage.[228] Large majorities in both houses of Congress defeated efforts

of 1864" (1978) 63 *Journal of Negro History* 42–48, 45. This demographic "owned property of considerable value, played a vital role in the urban economy as artisans and merchants, and were frequently well-educated." Ibid. In support of this initiative, "One thousand blacks signed the petition which recounted their record of federal military service, affirmed their loyalty to the Union, and declared that they were gainfully employed and tax paying citizens of the United States and residents of Louisiana." Ibid. That their appeal to President Lincoln was unsuccessful "was disappointing to many blacks in New Orleans, and his refusal to intervene decisively in their favor had negative repercussions among Negroes later in the presidential campaign." Ibid.

225 Milewski, *Litigating across the Color Line*, p. 31.

226 McPherson, *Struggle for Equality*, p. 244 ("This idea of a qualified Negro suffrage was gaining considerable support in the North. But most abolitionists wanted no qualifications which were not applied equally to both races.") (internal citations omitted).

227 The Wade-Davis Reconstruction bill was drafted by Senator Benjamin F. Wade of Ohio and Representative Henry Winter Davis of Maryland and submitted to the House on February 15, 1864. "Wade-Davis Bill (1864)," National Archives, *Milestone Documents*, www.archives.gov/milestone-documents/wade-davis-bill. The bill "would have abolished slavery, but it also required that 50 percent of a state's White males take a loyalty oath to the United States (and swear they had never assisted the Confederacy) to be readmitted to the Union." Ibid. Although it was passed by both houses of Congress, it was vetoed by President Lincoln. Ibid.

228 Mary K. Strong, "Post-War Congressional Elections" (1946) 10 *Current History* 435–441, 436 ("Congress instantly passed the Wade-Davis Manifesto, which received a pocket veto from the President. This brutal denunciation of Lincoln's reconstruction plan claimed that Lincoln was usurping legislative power, that Congress alone had the authority to reconstruct the southern states. This bill raised the number of pardoned necessary to form a new government to 51 per cent, and disqualified all those

to amend the bill to enfranchise African Americans.[229] Lincoln ultimately vetoed the Wade–Davis bill, ensuring the continuation of presidential Reconstruction in the near term, but also guaranteeing the continued disenfranchisement of African Americans by leaving the decision to the states as a matter of federal policy.

4.6 THE 1864 ELECTION AND THE INCREASING PROSPECT OF BLACK SUFFRAGE

President Lincoln's decision to stand for re-election in November 1864 as the Union remained splintered by war was risky. True, there were victories available for him to tout after years of what could, at best, be referred to as a stalemate – the Union army having repelled Confederate General Robert E. Lee's forces at Gettysburg in July 1863, and Union General Ulysses S. Grant's taking of Vicksburg, a Confederate stronghold, that same year. State elections were also a useful barometer for determining the strength of the Republican Party, which had rebranded itself as the "National Union Party" to appeal to pro-union Democrats, as it headed into the 1864 elections.[230] The rebranded Republican Party had significant victories that fall in gubernatorial elections in Ohio and Pennsylvania, making the case for a second Lincoln term.[231]

While these successes and others helped to cement Lincoln's re-election, to call the situation an ideal time to hold an election would be folly. Increasingly, two-term presidents had fallen out of favor.[232] The Republican Party was also marked by splits within its own coalition. "Radical" Republicans were consistently critical of Lincoln over the course of the war, dismayed by his failure to be decisive on the slavery issue.[233]

Mirroring his ambivalence four years earlier, Frederick Douglass would once again waver in his support of President Lincoln's 1864 re-election campaign. For reasons similar to those held by the radicals, he nursed complex emotions about Lincoln well after the latter's death. For example, Douglass once referred to Lincoln

who had borne arms against the federal government, which left very few eligible. But, which is significant, not even this bill insisted upon Negro suffrage.")

229 McPherson, *Struggle for Equality*, pp. 245–246.

230 By the end of 1863, the party of Lincoln had taken to "calling itself the National Union Party in order to broaden its appeal[.]" Balsamo, "Abraham Lincoln and the Election of 1864," 181.

231 "In October in Ohio John Brough was elected Governor by a margin of 100,000 votes over the always controversial 'Copperhead' Democrat Clement Vallandigham. Also in October in Pennsylvania incumbent Governor Andrew Curtin won re-election over the Democrat George Woodward, a State Supreme Court Justice." Ibid., pp. 181–182.

232 "For decades the country had been served by a succession of one-term presidents. The last chief executive elected to a second term was Andrew Jackson in 1832. Between that election and 1864 only one incumbent president had been renominated by his own party, and that president, Martin Van Buren, had been soundly defeated by William Henry Harrison in the famous 'Hard Cider' campaign of 1840." Ibid., p. 182.

233 Ibid.

as "a White man's president" because of Lincoln's early view that slavery was constitutionally protected,[234] but Douglass later anointed Lincoln "one of the greatest and best men ever produced by this country" because of his role in ending slavery.[235] Douglass' comments about Lincoln, occurring long after Lincoln's assassination, nonetheless captured the position of the war-weary country in the fall of 1864. While it was clear to abolitionists and radicals that successful completion of the war could not exist alongside the institution of slavery, President Lincoln was slow in coming around, not only on the issue of slavery, but also on the rights of the formerly enslaved once they became free.

The 1864 election was thus a referendum on Lincoln's conservative Reconstruction policy and an assessment of his stance on the African American suffrage issue.[236] Among the northern states that Lincoln won in the presidential election four years earlier was New York, which he carried with a healthy margin of fifty thousand votes. On the ballot that November was also a provision that would eliminate the $250 property qualification for African American voters in the state, a provision that was defeated by a margin of almost two to one.[237]

Black suffrage continued to be unpopular during the war, and Black people were left to make the case for their enfranchisement based on antebellum conceptions of deservedness. Abolitionists urged the explorer John C. Fremont to run for president in 1864 on a "Radical Democrat" ticket backing African American suffrage and southern land redistribution.[238] But efforts to replace Lincoln as a candidate and add a platform that promised African American suffrage failed.

234 "It must be admitted, truth compels me to admit, even here in the presence of the monument we have erected to his memory, Abraham Lincoln was not, in the fullest sense of the word, either our man or our model. In his interests, in his associations, in his habits of thought, and in his prejudices, he was a white man. He was preeminently the white man's President, entirely devoted to the welfare of white men. He was ready and willing at any time during the first years of his administration to deny, postpone, and sacrifice the rights of humanity in the colored people to promote the welfare of the white people of this country." Frederick Douglass, "Oration Delivered on the Occasion of the Unveiling of the Freedmen's Monument, In Memory of Abraham Lincoln, in Lincoln Park, Washington, D.C., April 14, 1876," in *Life and Times of Frederick Douglass* (Hartford: Park Publishing Co., 1882), pp. 492–493.

235 Frederick Douglass, "Address," in *Services Commemorative of the Seventy-Ninth Anniversary of the Birth of Abraham Lincoln*, February 12, 1888, by Republican National League (Washington, D.C.: Gibson Bros., 1888), p. 14

236 McPherson, *Struggle for Equality*, pp. 267–268.

237 Ibid., p. 25.

238 McPherson, *Struggle for Equality*, pp. 267, 269; see also William F. Zornow, "The Unwanted Mr. Lincoln" (1952) 45 *Journal of the Illinois State Historical Society* 146–163, 163 ("General John C. Fremont had a small following of abolitionists and German radicals who nominated him at Cleveland on May 31, as the candidate of an ephemeral party known as Radical Democracy."). Fremont had a long history of sympathizing with the abolitionist movement. Vernon L. Volpe, "The Fremonts and Emancipation in Missouri" (1994) 56 *The Historian* 339–354. While serving in the Union Army as the commander of the Western Department in 1861, he issued a proclamation that, in the state of Missouri, "property of rebel supporters would be seized and their slaves freed." Ibid., 340. This proclamation had two effects: it caused him to be removed from command of his unit, while also endearing him to radical abolitionist groups. Ibid., 348–350. His nomination to the top of the Radical

The Republican Party re-nominated Lincoln, who ended up running on a platform that promised only to pass a constitutional amendment barring slavery and did not offer any guarantees regarding suffrage.[239] In political debates that year, arguments that the country was not ready for universal male suffrage were especially pronounced. While this would become a theme that would play out for years to come, in the immediate term the debate highlighted the differences between Wendell Philips, William Lloyd Garrison (another prominent abolitionist), and the mainstream Republican Party.[240] That African American suffrage was a nonstarter as a potential wedge issue was clearly evident by the Union victory in Atlanta in August 1864, after which both radicals and mainstream Republicans fell in line behind President Lincoln.

Despite the capitulation of Radical Republicans in 1864, Lincoln nonetheless contemplated whether Congress could enfranchise African Americans on a more limited basis, given the state level resistance to this option. In the fall of 1864, at the height of his re-election campaign, he expressed a willingness to sign a bill that would extend the vote to African Americans in the military but vetoed one such bill after Radical Republicans inserted language that would have enfranchised all African American men.[241]

This law, if passed, would have caused a sea change in state political systems. As historian Eric Foner has noted, "By the war's end some 180,000 blacks had served in the Union army – over one-fifth of the adult male black population of the United States below the age of forty-five."[242] The enfranchisement of these individuals, absent any other legislative action on the question of citizenship, would have brought voting closer to the status of a natural right, for if the right could not be denied to these individual noncitizens tainted by slavery, then it would be significantly more difficult to deny the vote to women who were similarly situated to men in every respect except for gender, or men who had served in the military yet failed to meet the age restriction set by most state legislatures to cast a ballot.[243]

Democracy Party's ticket, while not necessarily favored by every abolitionist in the Republican Party, "won warm support from [antislavery activists], including Wendell Phillips, Elizabeth Cady Stanton, and Susan B. Anthony." Ibid., 351.

239 See "Republican Party Platform of 1864," American Presidency Project: Republican Party Platforms, www.presidency.ucsb.edu/documents/republican-party-platform-1864.

240 McPherson, *Struggle for Equality*, pp. 271, 279–280 (noting that Fremont and his supporters had aligned themselves with war Democrats, making abolitionists question their commitment to African American equality).

241 See Berwanger, "Lincoln's Constitutional Dilemma," 36.

242 Foner, "Rights and the Constitution in Black Life," 864.

243 During a House debate on the topic of suffrage in the District of Columbia, Representative Kasson offered the following comment comparing equality before the law and equality in suffrage rights in the United States up until that point:

> Now, sir, in prescribing these qualifications, if you will look to the history of the country, you will find that women have not been permitted to vote, even after they have attained the age of twenty-one years, although they might be unmarried, are taxed and even hold offices under the Government of the United States and are, in all other respects, equal before the law with

Lincoln was committed to some limited form of African American suffrage until his death. In April of 1865, he delivered his last public speech, shocking the small audience of approximately 3,000 onlookers because of his support for Black suffrage. Many of those present were expecting a celebratory and rousing address on the heels of the successful completion of the Civil War. The President was instead practical and strategic in his remarks, using the speech to chart a path forward for the conquered South and treating the moment as an opportunity, not to shame or criticize the vanquished, but to provide a rough blueprint for what the Reconstruction project would look like during peacetime.[244] He urged support for the newly reconstituted government in Louisiana, which had outlawed slavery and would go on to support the Thirteenth Amendment.[245] Most importantly, he publicly committed to the idea that those African Americans who had fought in the war should be enfranchised.[246] This was a radical change for a person who had, just a few short years earlier, refused to press the issue of Black suffrage with Louisiana's governor.

John Wilkes Booth, who had been present for – and outraged by – Lincoln's comments on African American enfranchisement,[247] assassinated Lincoln before he could implement many of these plans. Nevertheless, Lincoln's nascent and underdeveloped ambitions of a more inclusive suffrage marked a turning point in the evolution of federal power over elections, the use of which was often controversial in the years leading up to the Civil War. Lincoln likely envisioned a redefined electorate, shaped largely by the actions of state legislatures, but instead, he initiated a conversation about the federal role in determining the composition of the post–Civil

> the men. You will find that equality before the law does not mean the exercise of the right of suffrage. Even service in the Army of the country does not give this right, for one fourth of the gallant men composing the armies of the United States at one time were men of less than twenty-one years of age. If qualification to exercise the right of suffrage is to be determined as a natural right, and to secure equality before the law, you must let all of them vote, whether twenty-one years of age or not. For a man old enough to fight for his country ought to be old enough to vote for his country.

"Comments of Representative Kasson, 39th Congress, First Session, January 15, 1866," p. 36 *Congressional Globe* (Washington, D.C.: Congressional Globe Office, 1866), part 1, p. 238. See also the comments by Representative Kelley during that same debate, ibid., pp. 237–238.

244 Regarding the states that had joined the Confederacy, he reminded the crowd that, when those states "[find] themselves safely at home, it would be utterly immaterial whether they had ever been abroad." Abraham Lincoln, "Last Public Address, April 11, 1865" in Basler (ed.), *The Collected Works of Abraham Lincoln*, vol. 8, p. 399. Instead, he suggested, "Let us all join in doing the acts necessary to restoring the proper practical relations between these States and the Union, … [as if] they [had never] been out of it." Ibid.

245 Ibid., pp. 400–401.

246 Regarding African American suffrage, Lincoln recognized that it was "unsatisfactory to some that the elective franchise is not given to the colored man." Ibid., p. 400. On this issue, Lincoln offered the following: "I would myself prefer that it were now conferred on the very intelligent, and on those who serve our cause as soldiers." Ibid.

247 Manisha Sinha, "Did He Die an Abolitionist? The Evolution of Abraham Lincoln's Antislavery" (2015) 4 *American Political Thought* 435–454, 451.

War electorate that was much broader than he ever could have imagined. Looming large over this conversation was, of course, the Supreme Court's decision in *Dred Scott v. Sandford*,[248] which not only challenged African American citizenship and enfranchisement, but the authority of the federal government to have any role in defining these political communities in a manner the de-centered the propertied White man as the governing ideal.

[248] *Dred Scott v. Sandford*, 60 U.S. (19 How.) 393 (1856).

PART III

Reconstruction

For many Americans, secession is a perfectly southern concept, a reference to that region's efforts to expand the reach of slavery at the threat of destroying the Union. But the first secessionist movement did not originate in the South. Instead, it was of northern origin as the Federalist Party became increasingly dismayed at the dominance of the Jeffersonian Republicans and the slaveocracy on the national stage. After a contentious battle for the presidency, Thomas Jefferson, during his inauguration on March 4, 1801, ridiculed those who thought secession a plausible response to his election, noting, "If there be any among us who would wish to dissolve the Union ... let them stand as monuments of the safety with which error of opinion may be tolerated when reason is left free to combat it."[1]

Yet Jefferson's acquisition of the Louisiana Purchase, which opened up new lands to the spread of slavery, convinced many northern Federalists that secession was the only path forward.[2] Influential Federalists like Alexander Hamilton[3] and

[1] Eberhard P. Deutsch, "The Real Origin of the Secession Movement" (1969) 55 *American Bar Association Journal* 1134–1140, 1134 (noting that Federalist leaders warned that "every year will add power & influence to the south & to the west at the expense of the east…Must New England support and submit to a government directed by *slave-holders*?").

[2] The marginalization of the nonslaveholding North was a legitimate fear. Because of the three-fifths clause of Article I, Section 2, "a Southern planter who owned fifty slaves had, in effect, as much voice in federal affairs as thirty Northern freemen." Ibid., 1135.

[3] Hamilton considered the idea "that a party to a compact could revoke that contract," especially in the context of the Confederation, to be "gross heresy." David F. Houston, *Critical Study of Nullification in South Carolina* (New York: Longmans, Green, and Co., 1896), p. 21. See also Daniel Webster, "Letter to J.A. Hamilton and Others, Westchester, New York, of January 27, 1851," in Daniel Webster

John Adams[4] opposed secession, causing the movement to peter out. The calls for secession, less than two decades after the drafting of the Constitution, nonetheless raised the alarm about the fact that political community and political identity were closely tied to one's state of residence, and each state's defining feature was whether it permitted slavery. The American Revolution, itself a secessionist movement that did not turn on these demarcations and instead involved colonists advancing a nationalist identity distinct from their British overlords, evaded many of the hard questions about the sub-communities within America who could claim the right of revolution.[5]

The post–Civil War period presented an opportunity for Congress to answer this question as well as other, in some ways more pressing, questions about the scope of its authority to determine the boundaries of and the rights belonging to these communities. In approaching these issues, Congress aggregated its power, relying on multiple sources of authority from the Constitution of Political Structure to not only reconceptualize "We the People" and "We the Voters" but also to completely redefine the right to vote protected by the Constitution of Political Rights. Reconstruction is, and was, the golden era of multi-clausal federal authority that persisted until federalism-inspired political arguments, emerging from the ashes of the antebellum era, made adherence to this program untenable.

A quarter century after dueling factions sought federal recognition as the rightful government of Rhode Island, the Reconstruction Congress relied on the Guarantee Clause to craft new political communities in the wake of the Civil War. Congress sought to replace the old communities that had been governed by a planter class defined by their identity as slaveholders with a much more egalitarian political order that – importantly – was governed by *national* ideals. Congress facilitated this process by declaring the governments of the former Confederate states unrepublican in form, requiring each to adopt new constitutions that minimized the right to alter or abolish government in favor of broad suffrage rights as the preferred mechanism for the people to express their dissatisfaction with government. And through the Reconstruction Amendments, Congress completely reworked the Constitutions of Political Rights and Political Structure by elevating this right to vote, enshrined in state constitutions, as the primary vehicle for popular sovereignty that Congress was legally obligated to protect.

Republicans in the Thirty-Ninth Congress created an extensive and complicated regulatory regime to ensure that the right to vote was broadly extended to the newest

(ed.), *The Works of Daniel Webster*, 6 vols. (Boston: Charles C. Little and James Brown, 1851), vol. VI, p. 583 ("Where the blood of Alexander Hamilton fills the veins, or his example and patriotic services are remembered, the language of separation, secession, and disunion will find no utterance[.]")

4 Sean Wilentz, *The Rise of American Democracy: Jefferson to Lincoln* (New York: W.W. Norton and Company, 2005), p. 139.

5 There were, of course, some exceptions, most notably the Tories (or British loyalists) as well as escaped slaves who fought on behalf of the British.

entrants into the political community of "We the People" and "We the Voters." Congressional Republicans' explicit aim, through Section 2 of the Fourteenth Amendment, was to bring African American men into this community with the help of enabling legislation, such as the Civil Rights Act of 1866,[6] the Military Reconstruction Act of 1867,[7] and the various Enforcement Acts that would guarantee their position.[8]

Section 2 – then considered the "crown jewel" of the Fourteenth Amendment – was designed to penalize states that failed to comply with the Guarantee Clause's guiding principle of majoritarianism. This provision sought to accomplish this goal through a fairly draconian penalty – by reducing the state's delegation in the House of Representatives for abridging the right to vote in violation of the republican ideal.

With the ratification of the Thirteenth Amendment,[9] African American men became a part of the broader political structure entitled to representation and, as such, a constituency in which the right to vote could not be abridged or denied, in accordance with the Guarantee Clause. Because the Clause did not provide an express penalty for state governments constructed in violation of its terms – the provision triggered federal action only "on Application of the [state] Legislature, or of the Executive (when the Legislature cannot be convened)" – Section 2 of the Fourteenth Amendment imposed an ongoing obligation on Congress to penalize states for abridgments of the right to vote that could undermine the Guarantee Clause's requirement of republican government.

However, Section 2 rejected an explicit link between voting and citizenship that would have further expanded the boundaries of the political community of "We the Voters." While Republicans repudiated *Dred Scott*'s holding that African Americans could not be citizens,[10] they nonetheless continued to embrace that decision's notion of political community defined by affirmative government act, as illustrated by their acquiescence in the ongoing disenfranchisement of women, Native Americans, and other out-groups after the ratification of the Reconstruction Amendments.[11]

6 An Act to Protect All Persons in the United States in their Civil Rights, and Furnish the Means of Their Vindication, ch. 31, 14 Stat. 27 (1866).

7 An Act to Provide for the More Efficient Government of the Rebel States, ch. 153, 14 Stat. 428 (1867).

8 See Howard K. Beale, *The Critical Year: A Study of Andrew Johnson and Reconstruction* (New York: F. Ungar Pub. Co., 1958).

9 The Thirteenth Amendment reads as follows:

> Section 1. Neither slavery nor involuntary servitude, except as a punishment for crime whereof the party shall have been duly convicted, shall exist within the United States, or any place subject to their jurisdiction.
> Section 2. Congress shall have power to enforce this article by appropriate legislation.

United States Constitution Amend. XIII.

10 *Dred Scott v. Sandford*, 60 U.S. (19 How.) 393 (1856).

11 See, e.g., *Elk v. Wilkins*, 112 U.S. 94, 99 (1884) (rejecting the argument that "an Indian, born a member of one of the Indian tribes within the United States, is, merely by reason of his birth within the United States, and of his afterwards voluntarily separating himself from his tribe and taking up

Since the states still retained substantial authority over defining their community of voters through their control over voter qualification standards, Section 2 of the Fourteenth Amendment was an important inducement for states to enfranchise African American men.[12] Yet Congress, by refusing to extend the amendment's protections to other out-groups, laid the groundwork for the disenfranchisement of the very population of Black men that it had hoped to protect. Section 2 embraced this duality of inclusion and exclusion with devastating consequences.

Section 2 of the Fourteenth Amendment was also the culmination of a long-standing feud between the executive and legislative branches of the federal government about the new constitutional order. For its part, presidential reconstruction had impressed upon both the North and the South that the right to vote was not a right that had to be protected for either the formerly enslaved or White Unionists in the Confederacy.[13] Between the end of the war in April 1865 and December 1865, when Congress reconvened, President Andrew Johnson readmitted the former Confederate states on the condition that at least 10 percent of the White population take a loyalty oath, ratify the Thirteenth Amendment, disavow the Confederate debt, and repeal the ordinances of secession.[14] He fully expected that constitutional conventions reorganizing southern governments would be guided by White men, with the only explicit exclusions from participation being former Confederate leaders and the most prosperous slaveowners.

Triggering outrage among congressional Republicans and in most of the northern states, President Johnson's quick readmission of the South revealed several important things about the post–Civil War constitutional order. Despite the Guarantee Clause's requirement of republicanism, a threshold that was clearly not met regarding the states readmitted in mid-to-late 1865, the Clause was not self-executing. The laxness of presidential reconstruction also escalated the mistreatment of African Americans at the hands of former Confederates after they realized that the penalty for waging war on the United States would be the equivalent to a smack on the hand.

Former masters wanted African Americans who had abandoned the plantations to return to the fields. This would allow the recently treasonous to capitalize on high cotton prices and define what freedom would look like in the post-war era; in other words, like slavery. As historian Michael Fitzgerald has observed, "slavery had given whites such a strong conviction of racial incapacity that any alternative view looked mad, like defying gravity. Someone in authority simply had to monitor the freed people's behavior, either the state or employers, and preferably both."[15]

his residency among white citizens," a citizen within the meaning of Section 1 of the Fourteenth Amendment and therefore entitled to vote).

12 *Dred Scott v. Sandford*, 60 U.S. (19 How.) 393 (1856).

13 Michael Fitzgerald, *The Union League Movement in the Deep South: Politics and Agricultural Change during Reconstruction* (Baton Rouge: LSU Press, 2000).

14 Ibid.

15 Ibid.

Any new political order would therefore have to be backed by force and continuous federal oversight, and the first order of business was to create a framework that could lead to the equal legal status and enfranchisement of some subset of the formerly enslaved. With the adoption of the Reconstruction Amendments – and the accompanying changes to the American system of federalism – the Elections Clause of Article I, Section 4 and Congress's power to judge the elections of its members under Article I, Section 5 became formidable sources of federal authority.

Congress used these provisions collectively to not only advance its vision of a broader and more inclusive electorate, but also to police the boundaries of the political community of "We the Voters" post-election. Republican majorities in the House used their authority under Article I, Section 5 to alter or set aside elections that violated the Fourteenth and Fifteenth Amendments as well as other provisions of state and federal law. In election disputes, the House rarely required the state to hold another election when it determined that the winner of a specific seat was selected in error; through its Committee on Elections, the House simply resolved the contests based on evidence presented by the two candidates.

The House's authority under Article I, Section 5 ultimately became an invaluable source of power to combat racial discrimination in voting, particularly in light of the fact that the coalition that favored broad nondiscriminatory access to the franchise would dissipated by the mid-1870s.[16] Yet, even when race discrimination was absent, the House set aside votes cast by electors who were otherwise not qualified under state law, or alternatively, added votes from electors illegally disenfranchised under state and federal law, illustrating that this authority went well beyond the confines of enforcing the Reconstruction Amendments.

[16] See Paolo E. Coletta, "The Democratic Party 1884–1910," in Arthur M. Schlesinger (ed.), *History of U.S. Political Parties*, 4 vols. (New York: Chelsea House Publishers, 1973), vol. II, p. 987 ("Once the southern states were readmitted to the Union, the Democrats staged a strong comeback, winning the House of Representatives in 1874, the popular vote for the presidency in 1876 and the Senate in 1878.").

5

Reinventing Federalism?

The Shift toward a National Conception of Voting and Elections

We do not see in those amendments any purpose to destroy the main features of the general system. Under the pressure of all the excited feeling growing out of the war, our statesmen have still believed that the existence of the states with powers for domestic and local government, including the regulation of civil rights – the rights of person and of property – was essential to the perfect working of our complex form of government, though they have thought proper to impose additional limitations on the states, and to confer additional power on that of the Nation.

The Slaughter-House Cases (1872)[1]

The text and structure of the Fourteenth Amendment reflected the absolute messiness and insurmountable disorder of post–Civil War politics. The provision was neither the invitation to discriminate that its opponents claimed nor was it evidence of the triumph of conservative Republicans who sought to preserve state authority over elections. Instead, it was the foundation for hugely consequential changes to our federal system and a roadmap for a more radical vision of Reconstruction. Because of events that happened after the Fourteenth Amendment's passage in Congress, one might say that it was the Radicals who were ultimately able to prevail for a time, victorious in part because the complete split between Republicans and the President foreclosed any need to appease the executive.[2]

The split was inevitable. On February 19, 1866, President Johnson vetoed the Freedman's Bureau bill, which would have extended the life of the unit tasked with providing food, shelter, and other necessities in the war-torn South. Johnson refused to approve any Reconstruction legislation unless the southern delegates were seated.[3] Despite this veto, the Joint Committee on Reconstruction continued along the path of presidential appeasement, for example, voting six to five in committee to

1 *Slaughter-House Cases*, 83 U.S. 36, 82 (1872).

2 Michael Les Benedict, *A Compromise of Principle: Congressional Republicans and Reconstruction, 1863–1869* (New York: W. W. Norton, 1974), pp. 156–157.

3 Ibid., p. 156.

reject Rep. George Boutwell's motion requiring Tennessee to adopt universal male suffrage prior to readmission into the Union.[4] Republicans also removed the general prohibition on discrimination in the Civil Rights Act of 1866 prior to placing the bill on the President's desk, seeking to head off the critique that civil rights could be construed to cover voting.[5]

With his veto of the Civil Rights Act, alienating both conservatives and moderates, President Johnson broke with the party and opened the door fully for congressional Reconstruction. The willingness of conservatives and moderates to part ways with the President and – by implication, eschew his positions against Black enfranchisement, Black civil rights, and even Black citizenship – bode well for the prospects of African Americans.[6] The Freedmen's Bureau bill became law in July 1866, enacted over presidential veto. The Civil Rights Act was also enacted over Johnson's veto, enlarging the field of potential Republican voters by extending citizenship, a common prerequisite to voting in many states, to "all persons born in the United States and not subject to any foreign power."[7]

In crafting the language that would become Section 2 of the Fourteenth Amendment, congressional Republicans faced two – once unthinkable – options. They could eliminate the distance between voting and citizenship by making all (or most) citizens into voters. This reconceptualization would elevate the right to vote to the status of a natural right – a view endorsed by some founding fathers – such that suffrage could not be denied to any citizen (man or woman[8]) without just cause. Alternatively, Republicans could create a new category of federally protected political rights derived from the Guarantee Clause's requirement of majority rule and the right to vote protected by state constitutions. This approach would allow

4 Ibid., p. 159.

5 Ibid., p. 162.

6 See Andrew Johnson, "Veto Message of February 19, 1866," in James D. Richardson (comp.), *Compilation of the Messages and Papers of the Presidents*, 10 vols. (Washington, D.C.: Government Printing Office, 1896–97), vol. 6, pp. 403–04 ("I cannot but add another very grave objection to this bill. ... At the time ... of the consideration and passing of this bill there was no Senator or Representative in Congress from the eleven States which are to mainly affected by its provisions. ... At present the people of eleven States are excluded – those who were most faithful during the war not less than others.").

7 An Act to Protect All Persons in the United States in their Civil Rights, and Furnish the Means of Their Vindication, ch. 31, 14 Stat. 27 (1866) [1866 Civil Rights Act].

8 During the Reconstruction period, "The belief that the right to vote was the individual's natural right made the case for woman suffrage much stronger, more self-evident than it had ever been." Ellen C. DuBois, "Outgrowing the Compact of the Fathers: Equal Rights, Woman Suffrage, and the United States Constitution, 1820–1878" (1987) 74 *Journal of American History* 836–862, 845. The problem that women faced was, "[g]iven the Republican party's determination to draw the line at [B]lack suffrage, ... the political claims of women and of freedmen were increasingly antagonistic." Ibid., 847. In the end, "[t]he failure of the universal suffrage campaign in the face of the political realities of Reconstruction can be read in the language of the Fourteenth Amendment. The amendment included the first reference in the Constitution to the distinction of sex and to the inferiority of women by specifying the number of 'male citizens' as the basis of congressional representation." Ibid.

states to continue to heavily police the boundaries of a redefined and expanded political community entitled to exercise these new rights, but with federal oversight. The debate over the 1866 Civil Rights Act and early versions of the Fourteenth Amendment highlighted the struggle between these two views.

5.1 CIVIL RIGHT OR POLITICAL RIGHT? DEFINING SUFFRAGE IN THE POST–CIVIL WAR ERA

In the 1850s, residents of Wisconsin felt like their state was under invasion from the federal government. This feeling emerged in no small part because of the Fugitive Slave Act of 1850, and one famous incident in particular – when slave catchers came into the state to recapture an escaped slave named Joshua Glover. Glover had escaped from a Missouri farm in 1852, finding refuge in Racine, Wisconsin where he was able to live in relative peace until federal marshals showed up at his door two years later. Glover was beaten and dragged out of his cabin, and then transported to a Milwaukee, Wisconsin jail to await legal proceedings that would resolve his legal status.[9]

The Fugitive Slave Act of 1850 laid out a legal process by which slaveowners could offer evidence that the person in custody was enslaved but had fled. A substantial number of Northerners denied the Act's lawfulness, which often resulted in outright defiance of its terms. Among its more outrageous provisions, the law empowered a federal commissioner to determine the status of the person in custody, for which he received a five-dollar fee if he ruled in favor of the alleged fugitive and ten dollars if he found in favor of the slaveowner.[10]

Given this, it was not surprising that federal marshals crossed into Wisconsin to collect Glover under the authority of the Fugitive Slave Act of 1850, only to be met with outrage and federalism-based claims by Wisconsinites alleging that federal officials had violated the state's sovereignty by crossing into state lines to commit an illegal kidnapping in violation of the anti-slavery state constitution. A state court judge issued a writ of habeas corpus demanding Glover's release, which came about – not because of the court order – but because a crowd of residents broke Glover out of the Milwaukee jail. While Glover ultimately escaped into Canada and was never recaptured, his case led to the famous Supreme Court decision in *Ableman v. Booth*,[11] which held that states cannot nullify federal law or impede federal officials in executing federal law.

The notion that federal officials could "invade" states where slavery was prohibited to "kidnap" residents, potentially with the assistance of local officials who were "forced" to assist in these efforts, and then subject these victims to a process

9 Allison LaCroix, *The Interbellum Constitution: Union, Commerce, and Slavery in the Age of Federalisms* (New Haven: Yale University Press, 2024), pp. 393–394.

10 Ibid., pp. 389–390.

11 62 U.S. 506 (1859).

that incentivized their re-enslavement, raised federalism concerns not unlike those voiced by Southerners concerned about a federal government trying to regulate slavery within their borders. In the view of Wisconsinites, state law prohibited slavery, yet its courts, officials, and residents were impressed into enforcing a contrary federal regulation at the behest of southern states who had captured the lawmaking apparatus of the federal government. The 1850 Fugitive Slave Law triggered the northern version of states' rights arguments, articulated by free states against the slave states that usually invoked this language.[12]

But just as northern states could not be trusted to enforce federal slave laws in 1850s, neither could the South be trusted to enforce the federal laws that would emerge out of Reconstruction to protect the formerly enslaved. Federalism would again become the political foil that would be raised, time and time again, to object to federal laws that sought to redefine the rights and privileges to which a person was entitled in the face of a contrary state law.

Unironically, the enforcement provisions of the Civil Rights Act of 1866 were modeled after the Fugitive Slave Law of 1850 – most notably through the use of commissioners who enforced statutory terms in exchange for payment of a fee – triggering the same federalism and states' rights arguments that had been levied against the latter act almost two decades earlier. "Surely we have the authority to enact a law as efficient in the interests of freedom, now that freedom prevails throughout the country, as we had in the interest of slavery when it prevailed in a portion of the country," Senator Lyman Trumball, the bill's chief sponsor, argued.[13]

Maybe, maybe not. But borrowing an enforcement regime from a controversial law that had essentially been nullified by Wisconsin officials and residents through outright defiance (indeed, one might even say this nullification of federal law was an exercise of the right to alter or abolish government[14]) meant that federalism – and in

[12] LaCroix, *The Interbellum Constitution*, p. 386 ("The slaveholding interests that had long dominated their own numerous states, with the apparent acquiescence of a large portion of the rest of the American electorate, now seemed to be extending their grasp beyond the boundaries of their own localities and inserting their will into the domain of other states. To the outrage of Wisconsinites, the weapon of this attack was a federal statute. To this invasion they objected.").

[13] Patrick W. Riddleberger, *1866: The Critical Year Revisited* (Lanham: University Press of America, 1979), pp. 88–89.

[14] The Wisconsin Legislature passed a resolution criticizing *Ableman v. Booth* that invoked arguments similar to those raised by the southern states during the secession crisis. According to historian Allison LaCroix.

> The Constitution, the legislators maintained, was the fruit of a "compact among parties" having "no common judge" but rather leaving each party with "an equal right to judge for itself." Not "the party which now rules in the councils of the nation" but rather the Constitution itself was the proper judge of the scope of the general government's powers. The "several states which formed that instrument, being sovereign and independent, have the unquestionable right to judge of its infraction." The "rightful remedy" for "all unauthorized acts done or attempted to be done under color of" the Constitution was "a positive defiance" by the sovereign states.

LaCroix, *The Interbellum Constitution*, pp. 417–418 (internal citations omitted).

particular the focus on states' rights – would remain a political obstacle to the more expansive version of Reconstruction that could have been possible. Trumball handed the bill's opponents ready-made and battle-tested arguments about federal overreach. And in the context of the Civil Rights Act of 1866, this controversy played out not only on the enforcement side but also in the debates over whether the Act can and should enfranchise African Americans, or if this was a matter that should be left to the states.

Part of this ambiguity over the source of political rights, triggered by debates over the Civil Rights Act of 1866, can be distilled from disagreements among members of the Thirty-Ninth Congress (1865–67) about three key questions: First, what kind of right is the right to vote? Hoping to decisively shape the federal government's Reconstruction response as broad or as narrow as they deem necessary, many of the representatives discussed political rights, civil rights, and the privileges and immunities of citizenship as separate concepts, while others conflated these terms.[15] While one can debate the nature of each of these categories individually, it was beyond dispute that, as of 1866, the right to vote owed much of its scope and structure to state law, creating uncertainty about the category in which suffrage belonged.

Second, what is the right to vote's relationship to the republican form of government requirement? And, given this relationship, what is the federal government's obligation to extend and protect voting rights in the states? As these debates will show, carving out political rights as a subset of civil rights, or as their own unique category, was less about setting the right to vote apart from traditional rights in a categorical sense – after all, the influential *Corfield v. Coryell* opinion had defined privileges or immunities to include voting.[16] Rather, these distinctions were important for defining the terms of federal intervention in enforcing the republican guarantee. Tying rights, however labeled, to citizenship relieved Congress of the obligation of affirmatively defining their scope, which could be particularly useful in the context of a right to vote that had been defined almost exclusively by the states.

Initially, disaggregating voting and citizenship had been crucial to refuting the idea that voting was a natural right that African Americans and women were entitled to exercise.[17] But, as illustrated by cases litigated during the antebellum period,

15 See, e.g., "Comments of Senator Clark, 39th Congress, First Session, February 9, 1866," 36 *Congressional Globe* (Washington, D.C.: Congressional Globe Office, 1866), part 1, p. 832 ("We propose to elevate the freedmen to all the dignities and privileges of a citizen, and to make him the equal of other men in regard to political privileges."); "Comments of Representative Newell, 39th Congress, First Session, February 15, 1866," 36 *Congressional Globe* (Washington, D.C.: Congressional Globe Office, 1866), part 1, p. 867 (referring to the right to vote as the most "sacred" of the privileges and immunities).

16 "Treating voting as a fundamental right requires some theory of the representation necessary in a constitutional democracy. And that sort of theory took a long time to work itself pure. *Corfield* was the first case to anticipate that development, if only in passing." Gerard N. Magliocca, "Rediscovering *Corfield v. Coryell*" (2019) 95 *Notre Dame Law Review* 701–726, 721.

17 "According to [gradual emancipation laws], the children of enslaved mothers were to achieve full emancipation on reaching the age of majority (twenty-five for males). This meant that in the years

conceiving of voting as property presented a host of problems, especially when these groups were able to obtain the level of property ownership required by law to become electors yet were still excluded from the political community. Thus, the question (but not the answers!!) in the wake of the Civil War was simple: What kind of "right" is the right to vote?

In the 1850s, debates over the *Dred Scott* decision, the still developing political ideology of the nascent Republican Party, and the increasing dissension over the slavery issue had consistently reaffirmed that the right to vote was not inalienable or natural, but a political construct. Indeed, Abraham Lincoln, as an 1858 candidate for the Senate, defended himself against charges that he sought equal rights for African Americans by employing this distinction between political rights and natural rights:

> I have no purpose to introduce political and social equality between the white and the black races.... But I hold that...there is no reason in the world why the negro is not entitled to all the natural rights enumerated in the Declaration of Independence, the right to life, liberty, and the pursuit of happiness.[18]

Just as Lincoln denied that he was "in favor of making voters or jurors of negroes,"[19] he also disaggregated voting and citizenship, consistent with *Dred Scott*'s discussion of the two as circles that do not perfectly overlap.[20] Lincoln resisted the idea that the federal government should grant citizenship to African Americans, advocating

between 1805 and 1829 – twenty-five years from the passage of the first gradual emancipation law, by Pennsylvania, in 1780, and from the last, by New Jersey, in 1804 – a generation of African American males came of age with the expectation of a measure of real freedom, including such rights of citizenship as an education, the vote, and the freedom to make a living. It is hardly coincidental that these years coincided with the rise of laws to restrict black citizenship in the North, of extralegal white action against blacks, and of colonization." Robert P. Forbes, *The Missouri Compromise and Its Aftermath: Slavery and the Meaning of America* (Chapel Hill: University of North Carolina Press, 2007), pp. 30–31.

18 Reuben M. Wanamaker, *The Voice of Lincoln* (New York: Charles Scribner's Sons, 1920), pp. 205–206. Moderate Republicans followed Lincoln's lead on this issue. Kate Masur, "Civil, Political, and Social Equality after Lincoln: A Paradigm and a Problematic" (2010) 93 *Marquette Law Review* 1399–1406, 1401 ("Lincoln and many other moderate Republicans had long distinguished between civil equality and political equality, supporting the former but not the latter.").

19 "Fourth Joint Debate, At Charleston, September 18, 1858: Mr. Lincoln's Speech," in *Political Debates between Hon. Abraham Lincoln and Hon. Stephen A. Douglas, In the Celebrated Campaign of 1858, in Illinois* (Columbus: Follett, Foster and Company, 1860), p. 164.

20 President Lincoln's thoughts on this topic were cited by Representative Kasson during his remarks on the House floor on January 15, 1866:

> Now, sir, I have for myself thought it proper that we should fall back upon the declarations of Mr. Lincoln and Thomas Jefferson upon this subject. Mr. Lincoln's opinions are well known, that the intelligent negro and the fighting negro, of proper age, should be allowed to vote, the first for his intelligence, the second for his military service. Secondly, I would add the taxpayer, because with taxation should go representation.

"Comments of Representative Kasson, 39th Congress, First Session, January 15, 1866," 36 *Congressional Globe* (Washington, D.C.: Congressional Globe Office, 1866), part 1, p. 238.

instead for the repatriation of Black people to Africa.[21] Unlike the *Dred Scott* majority, however, Lincoln thought that states could confer citizenship on this group.[22] During the Lincoln–Douglas debates at Charleston, he argued that, "different States have the power to make a negro a citizen under the Constitution of the United States, if they choose," but denied that the state of Illinois should ever exercise that power.[23]

The notion that states could confer citizenship was not an unusual premise, particularly in a federalist system. As Professor Gerald Neuman has argued, "[c]itizenship in the individual states was the dominant concept in the immediate post-revolutionary period," and while the Constitution "added a concept of national citizenship…[it] did not specify the intended relationship between citizenship in a state and in the nation."[24] This question of whether the federal government has exclusive authority to confer citizenship for immigrants was not resolved until decades later,[25] but *Dred Scott* signaled "even thereafter the possibility of state

[21] Manisha Sinha, "Did He Die an Abolitionist? The Evolution of Abraham Lincoln's Antislavery" (2015) 4 *American Political Thought* 435–454, 443; see also David F. Forte, "Spiritual Equality, The Black Codes, and the Americanization of the Freedmen" (1998) 43 *Loyola Law Review* 569–612, 570–571 (discussing "forced recolonization" of formerly enslaved Black people "back to Africa or the Caribbean" as a favored option among "moderate opponents of slavery"); "Intelligent Colored Suffrage," *New York Times*, January 16, 1866, p. 4 (In response to the national conversation at the time about forcing any states to enfranchise Black men, asking "Why not provide a country for freedmen – a country which they can inhabit and govern? This would simply be in accordance with Divine wisdom, for the Creator gave Africa to the African.").

[22] Sinha, "Did He Die an Abolitionist?," 446 (noting that Lincoln's argument at Charleston "repudiated the proslavery logic of the *Dred Scott* decision that denied that blacks could ever be citizens of the United States; most of the New England states, he well knew, gave black men the right to vote, yet he did not adopt the abolitionist demand for black citizenship.").

[23] "Fourth Joint Debate, At Charleston, September 18, 1858: Mr. Lincoln's Rejoinder," in *Political Debates between Hon. Abraham Lincoln and Hon. Stephen A. Douglas*, p. 187.

[24] Gerald L. Neuman, "We Are the People: Alien Suffrage in German and American Perspective" (1992) 13 *Michigan Journal of International Law* 259–335, 292–293.

[25] For those who immigrate to the United States and seek citizenship, Congress's power over immigration undoubtedly affects the ability of states to confer citizenship on those who are not United States citizens. The Supreme Court has generally determined that the power to regulate immigration has been granted to Congress through the Commerce Clause, the Naturalization Clause, as well as Congress's power over foreign affairs and war, which has resulted in "federal courts afford[ing] significant deference to Congress when evaluating state laws for federal preemption[.]" Stephen L. Nelson, Jennifer L. Robinson, and Kara H. Glaubitz, "States Taking Charge: Examining the Role of Race, Party Affiliation, and Preemption in the Development of In-State Tuition for Undocumented Immigrant Students" (2014) 19 *Michigan Journal of Race & Law* 247–286, 277–278. The Supreme Court issued several opinions in support of this determination in the late nineteenth century. Ibid., 278 (citing *Chae Chan Ping v. United States*, 130 U.S. 581 (1889); *Ekiu v. United States*, 142 U.S. 651 (1892); and *Fong Yue Ting v. United States*, 149 U.S. 698 (1893)). For U.S. citizens who move from one state to another, the validity of state conferred citizenship is somewhat in flux. See, e.g., Peter Schuck, "Citizenship in Federal Systems," 48 *American Journal of Comparative Law* 195–226, 223 (noting that "the precise nature and significance of state citizenship remain uncertain" because the "14th Amendment's Citizenship Clause made state citizenship a matter of federal constitutional law, defining it simply as residence in a state … but a state presumably retains the power, within constitutional limits, to define what conduct constitutes 'residence'") (discussing *Saenz v. Roe*, 526 U.S. 489 (1999)).

conferral of state citizenship."[26] State conferral – and state removal – of citizenship remained possible in the years leading up to the Civil War.[27]

If states regulate access to state citizenship, then surely, as Lincoln recognized, states could also expand the scope of their electorates to include African Americans. While Lincoln adhered to the antebellum framework in which citizenship and suffrage were treated as separate categories, the boundaries of both of these categories had traditionally been left to the discretion of the states (most of which were not predisposed to creating Black voters).[28]

Ultimately, the Fourteenth Amendment was not only an explicit rejection of *Dred Scott*'s holding regarding African American citizenship, but it and its sister Amendments also rejected pre–Civil War conceptions of the right to vote as a species of property discriminately doled out by the states. As Republicans went about their work in early 1866, they recognized that there had to be some parameters on the power of states to set voter qualification standards. They also understood the difficulties of imposing these boundaries within a natural rights framework that might lean too far in the direction of creating an absolute entitlement to voting.

The test of whether voting was a natural right, entitled to be exercised by everyone, or a right of unknown stature, subject to regulation by the states and the federal government, was a focal point during the debates over the Civil Rights Act of 1866. The 1866 Act, enacted in April in the midst of discussions over the text of the Fourteenth Amendment, presented one of the first opportunities for Republicans to effectuate Lincoln's sentiment, on the eve of his death, that some limited form of suffrage should be available to African Americans.

On January 5, 1866, Senator Lyman Trumbull, chairman of the Judiciary Committee, introduced Senate Bill 61, which would "protect all persons in the United States in their civil rights and furnish the means of their vindication."[29] Among the rights protected by the Act were those "to make and enforce contracts, to

26 Neuman, "We Are the People," 293.

27 Some states prohibited African Americans from entering their borders, suggesting that this group could never qualify for state citizenship. See, e.g., Constitution of Oregon, Art. I, s. 1, cl. 32 (1857) ("White foreigners who are or may hereafter become residents of this State shall enjoy the same rights in respect to the possession, enjoyment, and descent of property as native born citizens. And the Legislative Assembly shall have the power to restrain and regulate the immigration to this state of persons not qualified to become citizens of the United States."); An Act to Prevent the Immigration of Free Negroes into This State, Laws of the State of Illinois, 18th Gen Assem, 1853, §1 ("Be it enacted by the people of the State of Illinois, represented in the General Assembly, that if any person or persons shall bring or cause to be brought into this State any negro or mulatto slave, whether said slave is set free or not, shall be liable to an indictment….").

28 During the debates on Reconstruction, "[t]he issue of suffrage was [very] ambiguous. With so many northern states denying [B]lack suffrage, it was hard to argue that citizenship necessarily required the right to vote. But the radicals in Congress realized that the absolute denial of suffrage meant that there was no political protection available to the freedman in the enjoyment of the attributes of citizenship." Forte, "Spiritual Equality," 591.

29 "Bills Introduced, 39th Congress, First Session, January 5, 1866," 36 *Congressional Globe* (Washington, D.C.: Congressional Globe Office, 1866), part 1, p. 129.

sue, be parties, and give evidence, to inherit, purchase, lease, sell, hold, and convey real and personal property, and to full and equal benefit of all laws and proceedings for the security of person and property, as is enjoyed by white citizens."[30]

In theory, Republicans could have opted to treat voting as a civil right under the Act, making the abridgment of which subject to criminal penalty. Its inclusion in the 1866 Act would have met three important objectives: (1) elevating the right from property right to natural right; (2) furthering the Republican's partisan and egalitarian goals of protecting their coalition in the southern states; and (3) expanding federal power over voting and elections. But it was not to be.

Senator Trumbull did not view the Act as a vehicle for enfranchising African Americans. Instead, he framed the Act as a means of enforcing the Thirteenth Amendment by responding to the discriminatory laws that undermined the civil rights of the formerly enslaved in the post-war period.[31] Trumbull also believed that Congress had the power to grant citizenship to Black people through its authority to provide uniform rules of naturalization under Article I, Section 8, Clause 4 of the Constitution; thus, the bill also provided that "all persons born in the United States and not subject to any foreign power, excluding Indians not taxed, are hereby declared to be citizens of the United States."[32] In articulating the civil rights that belonged to every citizen, Trumbull drew on the famous language from *Corfield v. Coryell*,[33] detailing the privileges and immunities protected by Article IV, Section 2, such as the right to contract and the right to sell and lease property. He was clear, however, that the 1866 Act did not extend to political rights, stating that it only extended to "rights as should appertain to every free man."[34]

30 1866 Civil Rights Act.

31 "Comments of Senator Trumball, 39th Congress, First Session, January 29, 1866," 36 *Congressional Globe* (Washington, D.C.: Congressional Globe Office, 1866), part 1, p. 474 ("I regard the bill to which the attention of the Senate is now called as the most important measure that has been under its consideration since the adoption of the constitutional amendment abolishing slavery. That amendment declared that all persons in the United States should be free. This measure is intended to give effect to that declaration and secure to all persons within the United States practical freedom. There is very little importance in the general declaration of abstract truths and principles unless they can be carried into effect, unless the persons who are to be affected by them have some means of availing themselves of their benefits.").

32 1866 Civil Rights Act. See also "Comments of Senator Trumball, 39th Congress, First Session, January 29, 1866," 36 *Congressional Globe* (Washington, D.C.: Congressional Globe Office, 1866), part 1, pp. 474–475 (arguing that individuals do not have to be foreign born in order to be naturalized by Congress).

33 *Corfield v. Coryell*, 6 F. Cas. 546 (C.C.E.D. Pa. 1825) (No. 3230).

34 "Comments of Senator Trumball, 39th Congress, First Session, January 29, 1866," 36 *Congressional Globe* (Washington, D.C.: Congressional Globe Office, 1866), part 1, p. 476 ("This bill has nothing to do with the political rights or status of parties. It is confined exclusively to their civil rights, such rights as should appertain to, every free man."). But see "Comments of Representative Wilson, 39th Congress, First Session, January 10, 1866," 36 *Congressional Globe* (Washington, D.C.: Congressional Globe Office, 1866), part 1, pp. 173–174 (arguing that natural rights became civil rights and political rights with the creation of civil government).

The Act, which would give Congress a critical and imperative role in enforcing rights long thought to be within the province of the states, received significant criticism within that body.[35] In particular, there was strong opposition to Senator Trumbell's argument that Congress's power over naturalization allowed it to confer citizenship by statute.[36]

However, the Act's conferral of citizenship made good political sense, given that citizenship had long been a requirement for voting in many southern states prior to the Civil War.[37] Settling the question of citizenship helped to define the political identity of the formerly enslaved, once considered property in the eyes of the law. As Senator Morrill later observed during debates over the Fourteenth

35 James Wilson, the bill's sponsor on the House side, that the Thirteenth Amendment provided authority for the Act. "Comments of Representative Wilson, 39th Congress, First Session, March 1, 1866," 36 *Congressional Globe* (Washington, D.C.: Congressional Globe Office, 1866), part 2, p. 1118 ("A man who enjoys the civil rights mentioned in this, bill cannot be reduced to slavery. Anything which protects him in the possession of these rights insures him against reduction to slavery. This settles the appropriateness of this measure, and that settles its constitutionality.").

36 "Comments of Senator Van Winkle, 39th Congress, First Session, January 29, 1866," 36 *Congressional Globe* (Washington, D.C.: Congressional Globe Office, 1866), part 1, p. 497 ("I think, sir, that we have now at last got to the beginning of all these questions in reference to the negro race. I think it needs a constitutional amendment to make these people citizens of the United States. I am not satisfied with the reasons given by the Senator from Illinois yesterday for doing it under the clause of the Constitution authorizing Congress to pass uniform laws of naturalization. I think it is one of the gravest subjects that ever could be sub-mitted to the people of the United States, and it involves not only the negro race, but other inferior races that are now settling on our Pacific coast, and perhaps involves a future immigration to this country of which we have no conception…"). See also "Comments of Senator Cowan, 39th Congress, First Session, January 29, 1866," 36 *Congressional Globe* (Washington, D.C.: Congressional Globe Office, 1866), part 1, p. 499 (arguing that Section 2 of the Thirteenth Amendment only gave Congress the power to "break[] the bond by which the negro slave was held to his master" and was "not intended to overturn this Government and to revolutionize all the laws of the various States everywhere. It was intended, in other words, and a lawyer would have so construed it, to give to the negro the privilege of *habeas corpus*; that is, if anybody persisted in the face of the constitutional amendment in holding him a slave, that he should have an appropriate remedy to be delivered. That is all."); "Comments of Representative Bingham, 39th Congress, First Session, March 9, 1866," 36 *Congressional Globe* (Washington, D.C.: Congressional Globe Office, 1866), part 2, p. 1290 (questioning Congress's authority to pass the 1866 Act and proposing various remedies to address this defect). But see "Comments of Representative Shellabarger, 39th Congress, First Session, March 9, 1866," 36 *Congressional Globe* (Washington, D.C.: Congressional Globe Office, 1866), part 2, p. 1293 ("I do not understand that there is now any serious doubt anywhere as to our power to admit by law to the rights of American citizenship entire classes or races who were born and continue to reside in our territory or in territory we acquire. I stated the other day some of the cases in which we naturalized races, tribes, and communities in mass, and by single exercises of national sovereignty. … There can, therefore, be no doubt as to our right to enact that part of this section which confers citizenship upon all our native people.").

37 See Jamin B. Raskin, "Legal Aliens, Local Citizens: The Historical, Constitutional and Theoretical Meaning of Alien Suffrage" (1993) 141 *University of Pennsylvania Law Review* 1391–1470, 1409 (noting that, "During the period of the 1850s and 1860s, alien suffrage played a growing role in the struggle between north and south, with Southerners trying to reduce and Northerners trying to expand the political influence of immigrants, who were overwhelmingly hostile to slavery (if not necessarily friendly to [B]lacks)").

Amendment – a draft of which was reported out of the Joint Committee on Reconstruction only weeks after the Civil Rights Act became law – the task of bringing these individuals, who lacked a political identity, "within the pale of the Constitution" was not only about rights but also status and identity:

> What shall we do with the everlasting, inevitable negro? Is the question which puzzles all brains and vexes all statesmanship. Now, as a definition, this amendment settles it. Hitherto we have said that he was a nondescript in our statutes; he had no status; he was ubiquitous; he was both man and thing; he was three fifths of a person for representation and he was a thing for commerce and for use. In the highest sense, then, in which any definition can ever be held, this bill is important as a definition. It defines him to be a man and only a man in American politics and in American law; it puts him on the plane of manhood; it brings him within the pale of the Constitution. That is all it does as a definition, and there it leaves him.[38]

The status of African Americans had remained in flux after the Thirteenth Amendment as they continued to be excluded from the body politic despite emancipation.[39] Citizenship would bring African Americans within the scope of "We the People" by erasing the "taint" of slavery as their origin story, which had long prevented all Black people, even those who were not enslaved, from exercising the full cache of rights enjoyed by White people.

But it was not clear if citizenship would be enough to bring them into the community of "We the Voters," or, more pointedly, into the state and federal electorates. Throughout the debates, both opponents and supporters of the Act continuously connected citizenship with political power.[40] Senator Trumbull might have been

38 "Comments of Senator Morrill, 39th Congress, First Session, February 1, 1865," 36 *Congressional Globe* (Washington, D.C.: Congressional Globe Office, 1866), part 1, p. 570.

39 See, e.g., "Comments of Senator Johnson, 39th Congress, First Session, February 9, 1866," 36 *Congressional Globe* (Washington, D.C.: Congressional Globe Office, 1866), part 1, p. 768 ("There are certain rights which belong to a freeman. He has a right to contract; he has a right to support himself; he has a right to do everything necessary to make him a freeman, or rather to enable him to enjoy life as a freeman, that any other freeman can do; but he is just as much a freeman without having the right to exercise the political right of franchise as he is with the right; for otherwise the result would follow which I have just stated, that there are a great many who are not freemen now in Massachusetts. The whole female sex not only are not, but never have been, free women. The whole object of this clause is not to give to Congress the right to interfere with the power of the States over the political status of their population, but to prevent the States from interfering with the right of one who has been a slave and remains in the State, to do what a white man can do under the general laws.").

40 See, e.g., "Comments of Senator Cowan, 39th Congress, First Session, January 29, 1866," 36 *Congressional Globe* (Washington, D.C.: Congressional Globe Office, 1866), part 1, p. 499 ("The identical question came up in my State – the question whether the negro was a citizen, and whether he possessed political power in that State – and it was there decided that he was not one of the original corporators, that he was not one of the freemen who originally possessed political power, and that they hail never, by any enactment, or by any act of theirs, admitted him into a participation of that power, except so far as to tax him for the support of government.").

a bit of an outlier, endorsing the view that if the national government protected the former slaves' exercise of civil rights, then voting rights became less critical.[41]

Despite Trumbull's protestations to the contrary, however, many in Congress recognized that the Act could be read broadly enough to directly require enfranchisement. As mentioned prior, among the privileges that Justice Bushrod Washington mentioned in his famous *Corfield* opinion – which Trumbell relied on to show a consensus surrounding the meaning of "civil rights" – was "the elective franchise, as regulated and established by the laws or constitution of the State in which it is to be exercised."[42] Because voting had property-like characteristics in the antebellum era, the bill's guarantee of "full and equal benefit of all laws and proceedings for the security of person and property" could potentially encompass the right of nondiscriminatory access to the ballot.[43] In fact, the bill's opponents lamented that the Act gave "the right of voting, not only to the freedmen, but to the whole race of negroes."[44]

Moderate Republican Representative John Bingham, who opposed the bill on the grounds that it exceeded the scope of Congress's enforcement authority under the Thirteenth Amendment, also thought that the term civil rights encompassed "every right that pertains to the citizen under the Constitution, laws, and Government of this country" including political rights:[45]

> A distinction is taken, I know very well, in modern times, between civil and political rights. I submit with all respect that the term "political rights" is only a limitation of the term "civil rights," and by general acceptance signifies that class of civil rights which are more directly exercise by the citizen in connection with the government of his country. If this be so, are not political rights all embraced in the term "civil rights," and must it not be of necessity so interpreted?[46]

41 Les Benedict, A *Compromise of Principle*, p. 147 ("Protect the blacks by national action, [Trumball] believed, and black suffrage and well-disposed southern governments became less critical.").

42 "Comments of Senator Trumball, 39th Congress, First Session, January 29, 1866," 36 *Congressional Globe* (Washington, D.C.: Congressional Globe Office, 1866), part 1, p. 475; see also *Corfield v. Coryell*, 6 F. Cas. 546 (C.C.E.D. Pa. 1825) (No. 3230).

43 "Comments of Senator Saulsbury, 39th Congress, First Session, January 29, 1866," 36 *Congressional Globe* (Washington, D.C.: Congressional Globe Office, 1866), part 1, p. 478 ("What is property? It has been judicially decided that the elective franchise is property. Leaving out the question of voting, however, as a question of property, is it not true that under our republican form and system of government the ballot is one of the modes of securing property, one of the means by which property is secured? Your bill gives to these person every security for the protection of person and property which a white man has. Under our system of government … one of the strongest and most efficient means for the security of person and property is a participation in the selection of those who make the laws. It is therefore that I thought that the honorable Senator when he framed this bill meant to give these persons the right of voting; and I should still think so, but for his personal disclaimer of any such subject.")

44 "Comments of Senator Saulsbury, 39th Congress, First Session, January 29, 1866," 36 *Congressional Globe* (Washington, D.C.: Congressional Globe Office, 1866), part 1, p. 477 (noting that "civil rights" is a "generic term which in its most comprehensive significance includes every species of right that man can enjoy").

45 "Comments of Representative Bingham, 39th Congress, First Session, March 9, 1866," 36 *Congressional Globe* (Washington, D.C.: Congressional Globe Office, 1866), part 2, p. 1290.

46 Ibid., p. 1291.

Bingham found support for the interchangeability of political and civil rights from William Blackstone, who treated the terms "civil liberty" and "political liberty" as synonyms.[47] With his focus on political rights as a subset of civil rights that relate "to … all the rights of the citizen," Bingham connected the right to vote with a conception of political community defined by citizenship.[48]

He also believed that Congress had limited authority to determine how states define the relevant community, be it by citizenship or otherwise, and the rights that should be accorded to that community, be they civil, political or both.[49] In his view, the 1866 Act would "reform the whole civil and criminal code of every State government by declaring that there shall be no discrimination between citizens on account of race or color in civil rights or in the penalties prescribed by their laws," which was not power that Congress had in times of peace.[50]

The imposition of criminal penalties for disenfranchisement was perceived as especially egregious. "By the constitution of my own State neither the right of the elective franchise nor the franchise of office can be conferred upon any citizen of

47 Ibid., p. 1291 ("Blackstone, whose Commentaries on the common law are so exact in definition, uses in that class of the law the terms "civil liberty" and "political liberty" everywhere as synonymous. It never occurred to him that there was a colorable distinction between them."). See also "Comments of Representative Wilson, 39th Congress, First Session, January 10, 1866," 36 *Congressional Globe* (Washington, D.C.: Congressional Globe Office, 1866), part 2, p 173 ("I do not claim that the right of suffrage is a natural right to which every person subject to human government is entitled. It is not a natural right, for where natural rights alone obtain there is no right of suffrage. But this state of things can only exist in the absence of properly adjusted civil government, the right of suffrage is a political right, and is the attendant of civil government. This, however, renders it no less sacred than it would be if it were a natural right. We always class it among the rights. We speak of it as the *right* of suffrage, and never give it the more doubtful designation of the *privilege* of suffrage.") (emphasis in the original).

48 "Comments of Representative Bingham, 39th Congress, First Session, March 9, 1866," 36 *Congressional Globe* (Washington, D.C.: Congressional Globe Office, 1866), part 2, p. 1291.

49 One of the reasons that Bingham opposed the statutory conferral of citizenship through the Act was because such conferral would allow Congress to determine that aliens should be excluded from both the body politic and from the broader protections of life, liberty and property guaranteed by Due Process Clause of the Fifth Amendment. "Comments of Representative Bingham, 39th Congress, First Session, March 9, 1866," 36 *Congressional Globe* (Washington, D.C.: Congressional Globe Office, 1866), part 2, p. 1292. See also Gerard Magliocca, *American Founding Son: John Bingham and the Invention of the Fourteenth Amendment* (New York: New York University Press, 2013), p. 119 (noting that Bingham opposed the Civil Rights Act, in part, because "the Freedmen's Bureau bill, which contained a catalog of rights similar to the Civil Rights Act, applied to unreconstructed states and expressly disclaimed the power to do the same in the loyal states as this bill would.").

50 "Comments of Representative Bingham, 39th Congress, First Session, March 9, 1866," 36 *Congressional Globe* (Washington, D.C.: Congressional Globe Office, 1866), part 2, p. 1293. Instead, Bingham proposed that the language be amended to "give citizens of every race or color … the same right in every State and Territory of the United States to make and enforce contracts, to sue, be parties and give evidence, to inherit…" and to eliminate any criminal penalties for violating its terms because he did not believe Congress had the power to require states to eliminate racial distinctions in their laws. Ibid., p. 1291 ("The law in every State should be just; it should be no respecter of persons. It is otherwise now, and it has been otherwise for many years in many of the States of the Union. I should remedy that not by an arbitrary assumption of power, but by amending the Constitution of the United States, expressly prohibiting the States from any such abuse of power in the future.").

the United States save upon a white citizen of the United States," Bingham argued. "What do you propose to do by this bill? You propose to make it a misdemeanor."[51] While Bingham conceded the legal wrong of discriminating with respect to civil and political rights, he denied that Congress, then lacking the enforcement power of the Fourteenth Amendment, had the authority to force states to extend civil and political rights (long protected by state law) under threat of federal penalty.[52]

Some representatives interpreted Bingham's criticism of the 1866 Act as disingenuous because civil and political rights had never been perfectly overlapping categories that sat beyond the purview of federal authority. As James Wilson observed,

> He [Bingham] knows, as every man knows, that this bill refers to those rights which belong to men as citizens of the United States and none other; and when he talks of setting aside the school laws and jury laws and franchise laws of the States by the bill now under consideration, he steps beyond what he must know to be the rule of construction which must apply here, and the result of which this bill can only relate to matters within the control of Congress.[53]

In other words, the 1866 Act would not enlarge Congress's ability to directly regulate the franchise because voting remained a state matter.

Criticism that the 1866 Act, if enacted, would enfranchise African Americans ignored that Senators Trumbull and Wilson had a powerful political incentive to punt on the suffrage question and, instead, lay the groundwork for future enfranchisement (preferably by the states) by extending citizenship to this group.[54] Republicans were well aware of the current unpopularity of the suffrage issue among voters in the northern states, and supporters of the Act sought to distance themselves from this topic by defining civil rights as natural rights that "have no relation to the establishment, support, or management of government."[55] This approach was possible because none of the legislative accomplishments of 1866, including the Fourteenth Amendment, technically enfranchised anyone.[56]

51 "Comments of Representative Bingham, 39th Congress, First Session, March 9, 1866," 36 *Congressional Globe* (Washington, D.C.: Congressional Globe Office, 1866), part 2, p. 1291.

52 Ibid., p. 1291 (citing the text of the proposed bill and noting that, "I should remedy that not by an arbitrary assumption of power, but by amending the Constitution of the United States, expressly prohibiting the States from any such abuse of power in the future.").

53 Ibid., p. 1294.

54 See Les Benedict, *A Compromise of Principle*, pp. 39, 147–148.

55 "Comments of Representative Wilson, 39th Congress, First Session, March 1, 1866," 36 *Congressional Globe* (Washington, D.C.: Congressional Globe Office, 1866), part 2, p. 1117 (defining a civil right as "the natural rights of man" and an immunity as the right of "equality in the exemptions of the law"). He went on further to describe the Act as "establishing no new right, declaring no new principle." Ibid.

56 Leslie H. Fishel, Jr., "Northern Prejudice and Negro Suffrage 1865–1870" (1954) 39 *Journal of Negro History* 8–26, 17 ("Section two of the proposed amendment left the decision on suffrage with the states, its framers fearing the adverse Northern reaction to a direct enactment.").

The omission of voting from the list of rights protected by the 1866 Act should not obscure the fact that one of its primary purposes was to help incorporate the freedmen into the political community of "We the People," a necessary prerequisite in most states to joining the community of "We the Voters."[57] The Act thus became a vehicle to declare that African Americans were, contrary to *Dred Scott*, citizens, but in doing so the law muddied the definition of civil and political rights (and, by implication, the rights that citizens were entitled to beyond those listed in the Act). In the end, the Act sacrificed theoretical and conceptual clarity in exchange for progress – any progress – in answering the question of what to do "with the everlasting, inevitable negro."[58]

Both the 1866 Act and, later, the Fourteenth Amendment would prove to be imperfect and deeply flawed vehicles for constitutional change. The 1866 Act targeted those civil rights that Congress believed it could protect with minimum political blowback, and drawing a distinction between civil and political rights allowed them to delineate this universe of rights in a politically feasible way.[59] The Act also reflected Congress's political limitations and lofty aspirations by simultaneously omitting the right to vote as a civil right within the scope of the Act while creating a class of citizens eligible to exercise the franchise. Thus, the task of Section 2 of the Fourteenth Amendment was to finish what the 1866 Act started: make suffrage one of the "matters within the control of Congress" that can be extended to the individuals whom the 1866 Act has primed to be welcomed into the body politic through its grant of citizenship.

57 "Comments of Senator Van Winkle, 39th Congress, First Session, January 29, 1866," 36 *Congressional Globe* (Washington, D.C.: Congressional Globe Office, 1866), part 1, p. 497 (describing a citizen as "one who is an integer of the body politic or community").

58 "Comments of Senator Morrill, 39th Congress, First Session, February 1, 1866," 36 *Congressional Globe* (Washington, D.C.: Congressional Globe Office, 1866), part 1, p. 570.

59 For example, it is not clear that the Act would outlaw anti-miscegenation statutes provided that they applied equally to Black and White people. See Peggy Pascoe, *What Comes Naturally: Miscegenation Law and the Making of Race in America* (New York: Oxford University Press, 2010). In addition, the focus on civil rights while excluding voting seemed opportunistic to many of the Act's opponents. "Comments of Senator Saulsbury, 39th Congress, First Session, January 29, 1866," 36 *Congressional Globe* (Washington, D.C.: Congressional Globe Office, 1866), part 1, p. 477 ("But here you use a generic term which in its most comprehensive signification includes every species of right that man can enjoy other than those the foundation of which rests exclusively in nature and in the law of nature. Now, I ask the honorable Senator to show me, if he can, any origin of a right he has or can have that, is not derived either from nature or from government. I shall enter into no discussion or argument in reference to what are the rights man has by nature; they are familiar to the legal mind and to the thoughtful student. The rights which a man has under government are defined in the fundamental or other law of the Government under which he lives. How do I possess the right of voting in the State of Delaware? Is that a civil right? A civil right I define to be a right belonging to the citizenship. I know of no clearer definition of civil rights than that, the rights which I have by reason of the law of the State under which I live, whether they be rights secured by the fundamental law, the constitution of the State, or be secured by enactments of the Legislature.").

Nevertheless, the question "What kind of right is the right to vote?" remained unanswered throughout the early months of 1866 as Congress grappled with the failure of the traditional (though ill-defined) conception of natural/civil/political rights to graft easily onto the rights that they wanted the formerly enslaved to exercise in the post-War era.[60] These difficulties necessitated the creation of a new conception of the right to vote subject to federal regulation.

This redefined right presented a challenge to the states' authority over voter qualification standards. Congress sought to set parameters for the right to vote through a mix of direct and indirect coercion to enforce the mandate of republicanism required by the Guarantee Clause, while leaving states with plenary control over voter qualifications in times of good behavior. While the Fourteenth Amendment did not require states to enfranchise their populations directly, Congress sought to redefine republicanism to require enfranchisement of those who were rightfully within the political community of "We the Voters." Many representatives, including Civil Rights Act opponent John Bingham, recognized that connecting Section 2 of the Fourteenth Amendment to the Guarantee Clause's requirement of republicanism would be key to justifying the exercise of federal power in an area traditionally regulated by the states.

5.2 THE ROAD TO SECTION 2 AND A NEW CONCEPTION OF THE RIGHT TO VOTE

The broad resistance to enfranchising African Americans pursuant to the Civil Rights Act was an issue that was being debated in the same time frame as a more permanent solution to the suffrage question; in other words, a constitutional amendment that had the end goal of indirectly enfranchising Black men while punishing southern states that resisted this change. More importantly, a constitutional amendment would definitively resolve the questions of what Congress was empowered to do in protecting the formerly enslaved.

On December 5, 1865, Representative Thaddeus Stevens introduced a bill to apportion representatives based on "legal voters," a term that excluded, according to Stevens, those "who are not either natural-born citizens or naturalized

[60] Simply stated, "[d]uring Reconstruction, the concept of civil rights was employed to demand equal treatment by the government in civil and criminal matters." *Travis Crum, "The Superfluous Fifteenth Amendment?"* (2020) 114 *Northwestern Law Review* 1549–1630, 1580. What fell under the category of "political rights" was quite different, and included "the rights to vote, to hold office, and to sit on juries." Ibid. There was also a third category, designated as "social rights," which was "a broad category" that essentially encompassed participation in society and included access to public transportation and accommodations. Ibid. As the Reconstruction period wore on, "the political center of the Republican Party shifted to support [B]lack suffrage and the enforcement of social rights," which had only, up until that point, been combined into a single set of rights by Radical Republicans. Ibid., 1581.

foreigners."[61] Not only would the focus on legal voters incentivize southern states to enfranchise African American men,[62] Stevens also cautioned that the current formula, if not changed, would result in the election of eighty-three additional southern representatives without imposing any requirement that the region enfranchise the previously enslaved.[63] The added representation would give the former Confederacy a numerical advantage in Congress and the Electoral College, which,

[61] "Apportionment of Representation: Introduction of a Joint Resolution by Representative Stevens, 39th Congress, First Session, December 5, 1865," 36 *Congressional Globe* (Washington, D.C.: Congressional Globe Office, 1866), part 1, p. 10. The language of Representative Stevens' resolution that he submitted to the Joint Committee on Reconstruction reads as follows: "Representatives shall be apportioned among the several States, which may be included within this Union, according to the number of their respective legal voters; and for this purpose none shall be considered as legal voters who are not either natural born or naturalized citizens of the United States, of the age of twenty-one years." Benjamin B. Kendrick, *The Journal of the Joint Committee of Fifteen on Reconstruction: 39th Congress, 1865–1867* (New York: Columbia University, 1914), p. 41. Representatives Robert C. Schenck of Ohio and John M. Broomall of Pennsylvania also introduced bills that would also apportion representatives based on the number of legal voters in the states. "Apportionment of Representation: Introduction of a Joint Resolution by Representative Schenck, 39th Congress, First Session, December 5, 1865," 36 *Congressional Globe* (Washington, D.C.: Congressional Globe Office, 1866), part 1, p. 9; "Basis of Congressional Representation: Introduction of a Joint Resolution by Representative Stevens, 39th Congress, First Session, December 5, 1865," 36 *Congressional Globe* (Washington, D.C.: Congressional Globe Office, 1866), part 1, p. 10. Representative Sloan of Wisconsin also made a similar proposal on January 23, 1866:

> Mr. Speaker, I desire to call the attention of the House to a proposition which I had the honor to submit at the last session of the Thirty-Eighth Congress in relation to this subject. That proposition provides that the right of representation in this House shall be based upon the right of suffrage upon the numbers who are allowed the right to vote in the respective States. The amendment which has been reported by the committee is intended to apply the same principle, but not to adopt it directly. It is an indirect attempt to adopt that principle and incorporate it in the Constitution.

"Comments of Representative Sloan, 39th Congress, First Session, January 23, 1866," 36 *Congressional Globe* (Washington, D.C.: Congressional Globe Office, 1866), part 1, p. 378.

[62] "By one of the so-called compromises in the Constitution … representation in Congress was based upon slaves equal to three-fifths of their number. Stevens always contended that this was wrong; but it was in the Constitution, and he showed that sort of willingness to abide by it which springs out of compulsion. But after emancipation had raised the negro above the dignity of property, and had transformed him from chattel into a man, Steven very justly contended that this dumb representation should end[.] … He therefore proposed … to divide the representatives among the States according to their legal voters[.] … Under this provision, which was to have universal application throughout the Union, any State which saw fit to exclude black men or any other men from the suffrage would do so at the expense of its representation in the national House. If excluded classes could not have representatives of their own choosing, they were to have none chosen by someone else." Samuel W. McCall, *Thaddeus Stevens* (Boston: Houghton, Mifflin and Company: 1899), pp. 294–295; see also Xi Wang, "Black Suffrage and the Redefinition of American Freedom, 1860–1870" (1996) 17 *Cardozo Law Review* 2153–2224 (citing Stephens' characterization of this proposed requirement as an "penalty" that would endure until the southern states "corrected [their] actions.").

[63] "[Stevens] estimated that [the Southern] States would have eight-three representatives, if the blacks were counted, and forty-six if there were excluded, and that the opportunity to multiply their representation almost by two would induce them to confer the suffrage upon the negro." McCall, *Thaddeus Stevens*, pp. 263–264.

ironically, would make them better off politically than they had been prior to the war. Stevens warned that the easy readmission of the southern states without securing some protection for African American suffrage would inevitably lead to "[a]ssumption of the rebel debt or repudiation of the Federal debt" as well as "[t]he oppression of the freedmen; the re-amendment of their State constitutions, and the reestablishment of slavery…"[64]

Stevens' proposal to change the basis of apportionment was one of the first signs that the political and legal norms had completely shifted around representation and voting, illustrating that "true" republicanism could no longer tolerate a system in which men who exercised the indicia of citizenship (including, but not limited to, taking up arms on behalf of their country), could be disenfranchised.[65]

This proposal linked representation and voting in an unprecedented way. Under Article 1, Section 2, the enslaved counted as three-fifths of a person. Everyone else, including women and children, counted as whole people for purposes of determining representation, even though some were disenfranchised and therefore excluded from the political community of "We the Voters." The Voter Qualification Clause of this provision further distinguished representation and voting, leaving the states with virtually unfettered authority to choose the qualifications of their voters. This authority could be exercised to disenfranchise (or enfranchise) those who counted for representation purposes. Since the states in the former Confederacy (as well as many northern states) had no intention of enfranchising African Americans or women,[66] a standard based on legal voters would cost them numerically in Congress.

While a formula based on total voters fundamentally reflected the idea that political power and representation should overlap,[67] there was substantial

64 "Comments of Representative Stevens, 39th Congress, First Session, December 18, 1865," 36 *Congressional Globe* (Washington, D.C.: Congressional Globe Office, 1866), part 1, p. 74.

65 Stevens found an unlikely ally in President Andrew Johnson, who thought that reapportioning based on total voters would reward military voters who "for the most part were men who were subject to draft and enlistment when it was necessary to repeal invasion, suppress rebellion, and quell domestic violence and insurrection." See "The Present Agitation of the Negro Suffrage Question Deprecated," *New-York Daily Tribune*, January 29, 1866, p. 5, https://chroniclingamerica.loc.gov/lccn/sn83030213/1866-01-29/ed-1/seq-5/. Others linked enfranchisement to military service. For example, Rep. Shellabarger proposed that apportionment be based on "the number of male citizens… above the age of twenty-one years having the qualifications requisite for electors of the most numerous branch of the state legislature" because "it invites the States to adjudge every one whom the law deems fit to bear arms for his country also fit to be counted as an elector of his country." "Comments of Representative Shellabarger, 39th Congress, First Session, January 24, 1866," 36 *Congressional Globe* (Washington, D.C.: Congressional Globe Office, 1866), part 1, p. 406.

66 In order to prevent the South "from profiting on its treason[,] … all states would have [to be] incentivized to enfranchise voters they were currently excluding," including both women and African American men, "something that a number of states, particularly in New England, were loath to do." Jan E. Lewis, "What Happened to the Three-Fifths Clause: The Relationship between Women and Slaves in Constitutional Thought, 1787–1866" (2017) 37 *Journal of the Early Republic* 1–46, 36.

67 See "Comments of Representative Lawrence, 39th Congress, First Session, January 24, 1866," 36 *Congressional Globe* (Washington, D.C.: Congressional Globe Office, 1866), part 1, p. 403 (criticizing

opposition to Stevens' plan, particularly among representatives from the Northeast. Representative James G. Blaine of Maine, the most prominent opponent of this proposal, warned that apportionment based on registered voters would result in "an unseemly scramble in all the States during each decade to increase by every means the number of voters, and all conservative restrictions, such as the requirement of reading and writing now enforced in some of the States, would be stricken down in a rash and reckless effort to procure an enlarged representation in the national councils."[68] Much of the gender-based disparity in prospective voters stemmed from the large number of disenfranchised women in the northeast as compared to the western states,[69] and also from the variations in voter qualifications across states.[70] As Blaine recognized, disparities in voters, even among states with comparable populations, could lead to widely divergent representation in Congress.[71]

the proposal based on total population because it "perpetuates the very political evil which to some extent it remedies. It gives representation to women, children, and unnaturalized foreigners, all declared by the laws of the States unsafe or unnecessary depositaries of political power. It disregards the fundamental idea of all just representation, that every voter should be equal in political power all over the Union.").

68 "Comments of Representative Blaine, 39th Congress, First Session, January 8, 1866," 36 *Congressional Globe* (Washington, D.C.: Congressional Globe Office, 1866), part 1, p. 141. Representative Blaine endorsed an amendment to Article I, Section 2 that would have excluded "those to whom civil or political rights or privileges are denied … on account of race or color" from the basis of apportionment. Ibid., 141–142. Representative Shellabarger also proposed an amendment to Article I, Section 2 that would base reapportionment on "the number of male citizens … above the age of twenty-one years having the qualifications requisite for the electors of the numerous branch of the State Legislature," which would, in his words, "prevent[] a race as between the States for cheapening the elective franchise by giving it to persons to whom experience has shown it not to be best to give it." "Comments of Representative Shellabarger, 39th Congress, First Session, January 24, 1866," 36 *Congressional Globe* (Washington, D.C.: Congressional Globe Office, 1866), part 1, pp. 405–406.

69 "Exchange between Representatives Stevens and Blaine, 39th Congress, First Session, January 8, 1866," 36 *Congressional Globe* (Washington, D.C.: Congressional Globe Office, 1866), part 1, p. 141.

70 James G. Blaine, *Twenty Years of Congress: From Lincoln to Garfield, with a Review of the Events Which Led to the Political Revolution of 1860*, 2 vols. (Norwich: The Henry Bill Publishing Company, 1886), vol. 2, p. 195 ("The only mode of getting at the number of voters was by the ballots cast at general elections, and the relative ratio was varied by so many considerations that it did not correctly represent the actual number of voters in each State. But the facts presented by Mr. Blaine and elaborated by other speakers turned the attention of the House away from an apportionment based on voters.").

71 "Comments of Representative Blaine, 39th Congress, First Session, January 8, 1856," 36 *Congressional Globe* (Washington, D.C.: Congressional Globe Office, 1866), part 1, p. 141 As Blaine argued, "The ratio of voters to population differs widely in different sections…For example, California has a population of 358,110, and Vermont 314,369, and each has three Representatives on this floor to-day. But California has 207,000 voters and Vermont has 87,000. Assuming voters as the basis of apportionment, and allowing to Vermont three Representatives, California would be entitled to eight. The great State of Ohio, with nearly seven times the population of California, would have but little more than two and a half times the number of Representatives; and New York, with quite eleven times the population of California, would have in the new style of apportionment less than five times as many members of this House."

Representative Roscoe Conkling of New York similarly noted,

> If voters alone should be made the foundation of representation, the actual ratio would vary infinitely among the different States. One State might let women and minors vote. Another might – some of them do – give the ballot to those otherwise qualified who have been residents for only ten days. Another might extend suffrage to aliens. This would lead to a strife of unbridled suffrage.[72]

Stevens' proposed language opened the door to the issues that emerged every time there was a census, raising questions about the formula and how fractions should be handled. And changing the basis of population only complicated these questions. In the end, the Republicans shied away from endorsing any formula that would alienate the Northeast, especially after the issue of African American suffrage had failed so miserably in the 1865 elections.[73]

72 "Comments of Representative Conkling, 39th Congress, First Session, January 22, 1866," 36 *Congressional Globe* (Washington, D.C.: Congressional Globe Office, 1866), part 1, p. 357. It was disputed whether the disproportionate number of women in the North would have had an adverse effect on the basis of population such that the North, and in particular New England, would lose representatives. Roscoe Conkling visualized this point, producing a chart that took the total representative population of all the states, divided it by 233 (the total number of representatives then in the House) and divided the representative population of the state by the resulting ratio. From this, Conkling was able to divine that no New England state would lose a single representative if total voters, instead of total population, was used as the basis of population; instead, Ohio (−1), Illinois (−1), and Pennsylvania (−2) emerged as the big losers and California would come out ahead (+3). "Comments of Representative Conkling, 39th Congress, First Session, January 22, 1866," 36 *Congressional Globe* (Washington, D.C.: Congressional Globe Office, 1866), part 1, p. 358.

There is some dispute over the accuracy of Conkling's estimates, and Blaine countered with his own chart that, in his view, proved that certain Northern states would lose representation relative to other states in the same region. "Comments of Representative Blaine, 39th Congress, First Session, January 22, 1866," 36 *Congressional Globe* (Washington, D.C.: Congressional Globe Office, 1866), part 1, p. 358 ("I hold in my hand a table which was prepared with very great care by my estimable friend on the Committee of Ways and Means, [Mr. Morrill,] in which upon a basis of white males above twenty-one years of age, upon a representation of two hundred and forty members [note: Conkling used a baseline of 233 members], New York would have thirty-five and five tenths members, or in a close struggle for the fraction she would have thirty-six; Pennsylvania would have twenty-four and two tenths, and be confined to twenty-four members. Today New York has thirty-one members and Pennsylvania twenty-four; giving New York now twenty-eight and a half per cent more representation than Pennsylvania. But upon the basis upon which the table is calculated New York would be entitled to fifty per cent more Representatives than Pennsylvania. I admit that Pennsylvania would not absolutely lose one of her Representatives, but relatively she would lose by the representation of New York being increased.").

Debate in the House on this issue continued later in the week, with others pointing out the challenges of establishing accurate numbers. See, e.g., "Comments of Representative Cook, 39th Congress, First Session, January 24, 1866," 36 *Congressional Globe* (Washington, D.C.: Congressional Globe Office, 1866), part 1, p. 411. See also "Comments of Representative Conkling, 39th Congress, First Session, January 22, 1866," 36 *Congressional Globe* (Washington, D.C.: Congressional Globe Office, 1866), part 1, p. 357; "Comments of Representative Sloan, 39th Congress, First Session, January 23, 1866," 36 *Congressional Globe* (Washington, D.C.: Congressional Globe Office, 1866), part 1, p. 379.

73 During the Reconstruction period, Republicans had to act with caution, as "[r]espectable Northerners who had once supported the Republican policy began to charge that Congress had inflicted

In early 1865, Republicans had instituted a propaganda machine designed to steer northern sentiment favorably toward political rights for the recently emancipated freedmen.[74] At that time, Connecticut was the only northern state that explicitly barred African Americans from voting, and an October special election that year placed the suffrage issue squarely before the voters. Republicans, recognizing that African American suffrage was key to the success of the Reconstruction enterprise, lobbied Connecticut voters heavily, only to lose the vote 33,489 to 27,217.[75] This loss led Republicans in states such as Ohio and Pennsylvania to abandon or ignore Black enfranchisement in their party platforms,[76] and prompted other northern politicians to advocate for a more qualified suffrage to make it palatable to northern voters.[77] Throughout the fall of 1865, voters uniformly rejected every referendum designed to enfranchise Black people. In Republican-controlled Colorado, the proposal went down 476 to 419.[78] Wisconsin voters defeated the measure 55,454 to 46,629, despite the fact that Republicans were able to secure the governorship during the same election by 12,000 votes.[79] African American suffrage continued to be an unpopular issue on the ballot throughout 1866, 1867, and 1868.[80]

undeserved penalties on southern whites and had bestowed unearned rights on uncomprehending southern blacks." Larry Kincaid, "Victims of Circumstances: An Interpretation of Changing Attitudes toward Republican Policy Makers and Reconstruction" (1970) 57 *Journal of American History* 48–66, 48. Regarding voter rejection of African American suffrage during the elections of 1865, see Fishel, "Northern Prejudice," 9–15.

74 Fishel, "Northern Prejudice," 11 ("The Radicals depended to some extent on humanitarian propaganda to whip up sentiment for the Negro voter, and publicists like Theodore Tilton, Increase Taxbox, Gerrit Smith, Frederick Douglass, John Langston, and Lydia Maria Child worked diligently to this end. Behind the scenes, men who engaged in politics scurried about to bring the North into line behind the Radical program.").

75 Ibid., 12–13; see also William Gillette, *The Right to Vote: Politics and the Passage of the Fifteenth Amendment* (Baltimore: Johns Hopkins University Press, 1969), pp. 25–26.

76 See, e.g., Fishel, "Northern Prejudice," 13 ("Thaddeus Stevens … explained to Charles Sumner that the Republican convention at Harrisburg had passed over the question [of African American suffrage] 'as heavy and premature.' The New York State Republican platform, like its Democratic counterpart, ignored the issue.").

77 Ibid., 13–14 ("In New Jersey, Republicans in convention decisively defeated a resolution endorsing it while Democrats went on record opposing it. Indiana's governor, Oliver P. Morton, stated the position of his state organization: freedmen should wait for fifteen or twenty years before receiving the franchise….Charles A. Dana, writing to Charles Sumner early in September [1865], warned that only a reading and writing qualification would make Negro suffrage palatable to voters in Illinois, Wisconsin and Michigan.").

78 Gillette, *The Right to Vote*, pp. 25–26 (noting that "During 1865 five jurisdictions voted down Negro suffrage in popular referendums.").

79 Ibid.

80 In the following excerpt, Gillette provides election return data for several states between the period of 1866 and 1868:

> In June 1866, settlers in the northern-oriented Nebraska territory defeated Negro suffrage in a close vote, for the majority against the discriminatory state constitution in question was only 100 (3,938 to 3,838). During 1867 the elections were more significant, but the result was the same in Kansas, where the majority against was 9,071 or 55.05 per cent while again the vote was closer in Minnesota, where the majority against was only 1,298. But in the most important referendum

Concerns over the competency of African American voters, after a lifetime of enslavement, would be a consistent theme throughout congressional debates in 1866.[81] After a generation in which property restrictions on the right to vote declined, there was serious consideration of whether property and educational qualifications should be reinstituted as prerequisites to voting. Many representatives were reluctant to return to the days in which property qualifications routinely determined who could exercise a ballot.[82] For its part, the 1866 Civil Rights Act temporarily bypassed

in Ohio in the same year, voters decisively rejected Negro suffrage in a vote actually cast by a majority of 38,353, while twelve counties voted Republican for governor but opposed Negro suffrage. Ohio was the acid test and the answer was negative. Michigan in April, 1868, rejected the proposed state constitution, which provided for Negro suffrage – although the issue was not a separate question in the referendum – by a vote of 71,733 to 110,852, or a negative majority of 38,849. Missouri also in 1868 struck down Negro suffrage by a majority of 18,817 or 57.27 per cent. New Yorkers followed the national trend by rejecting the issue in 1869 by a majority of 32,601.

In Iowa and Minnesota only, voters accepted Negro suffrage on November 3, 1868, with Minnesotans favoring it by 56.80 per cent, Iowans by 56.50 per cent – a majority of 24,265. Significantly, victory came on a presidential election day in but two solidly Republican states, and with the use of sharp tactics in Minnesota: placing the suffrage question on the presidential ballot to discourage ticket splitting, and concealing the issue by labeling the question not 'Negro suffrage' but rather 'revision of section 1, article 7.'

Ibid., 26.

81 For example, in objecting to enfranchising African Americans as a bridge too far that the recipients of the right could not handle anyway, Representative Chanler had the following to say on the House floor on January 12: "It seems to me, sir, that freedom from slavery and equality before the law are as full a reward as we can justly grant the negro for his recent service in arms. The right to vote carries with it too many and too weighty responsibilities[.]" "Comments of Representative Chanler, 39th Congress, First Session, January 12, 1866," 36 *Congressional Globe* (Washington, D.C.: Congressional Globe Office, 1866), part 1, p. 217. Representative Harding of Kentucky employed similar language during a speech on the House floor on January 26, while also implying that even those of his colleagues who favored African American suffrage did not believe that African Americans were entirely fit to exercise that right: "We [in Kentucky] are to have a dense negro population who are unfit to control themselves as you say; there must be a Freedmen's Bureau to control them. You want to force us in Kentucky, for example, either to enfranchise all these negroes or give up part of our representation? Is that fair? Is that just?" "Comments of Representative Harding, 39th Congress, First Session, January 26, 1866," 36 *Congressional Globe* (Washington, D.C.: Congressional Globe Office, 1866), part 1, p. 449. Later in his speech, Representative Harding doubled-down: "So long as this system of negro equality is enforced by military power, you may hold up the negro beyond his natural position[.] … Nature has made the white man the superior of the negro; and that superiority will eventually assert itself, in spite of all your efforts to crush down the white man to a level with the negro." Ibid., p. 450.

82 "Comments of Representative Baker, 39th Congress, First Session, January 23, 1866," 36 *Congressional Globe* (Washington, D.C.: Congressional Globe Office, 1866), part 1, p. 385 ("… large numbers of persons might be excluded from the franchise, and yet be counted in the basis of representation if only they were excluded on some other account than color or race. This, it appears to me, is too narrow a foundation to rest the proposed remedy upon. For in my opinion, there are other grounds upon which men may be disfranchised, which are quite as odious and quite as dangerous to liberty as disfranchisement on account of race or color. A property qualification is one, the whole strength of which was tested by Franklin's question. A man owns an ass today and he votes. Tonight, his ass dies, and tomorrow he cannot vote. 'Now,' said Franklin, 'who has the vote – the man or the ass? At all events, the right to the vote died with the ass. … No State should reserve in her basis of representation persons disfranchised and not represented, no matter' on what ground she so excludes them").

the political toxicity of the suffrage issue but bolstered the cause indirectly by providing African Americans with citizenship and an opportunity to achieve economic independence through nondiscriminatory access to property ownership.

In the end, apportionment based on total voters proved to be an untenable solution. Although neatly sidestepping the issue of African American suffrage (at least on the surface), the proposal incentivized a race to the bottom with respect to voter qualification standards.[83] Congress would be forced to set voter qualifications to avoid this problem, which some viewed as an intolerable affront to our system of federalism in which states traditionally exercised this authority.[84] Just as the Founders refused to set voter qualifications for federal elections eight decades earlier, the Framers of the Fourteenth Amendment were similarly unwilling to tie the hands of the states by imposing uniform criteria beyond certain categories (citizenship, age, and gender) that White elites viewed as mostly uncontroversial.

As a counterproposal, Blaine offered that apportionment be determined by "taking the whole number of persons except those to whom civil or political rights or privileges or denied or abridged by the constitution or laws of any State on account of race or color."[85] But this proposal also had its detractors. The *Chicago Tribune*, for example, accused Blaine of giving states "direct and express permission and encouragement to deprive not only the colored people, but persons of foreign birth, of their political rights and privileges."[86]

Blowback to Blaine's proposal foreshadowed the broader criticism of what would eventually become the final text of Section 2 of the Fourteenth Amendment, in which its failure to establish an affirmative right to vote was viewed in some corners as a sanction for discrimination (so long as states were willing to suffer the penalty of reduced representation). But the focus on reducing the basis for apportionment, rather than enshrining a federal right to vote, was also a reflection of deep reservations among Republicans about completely displacing antebellum and founding-era norms regarding state power over elections. For some, the upside of Blaine's proposal was that it operated within a framework in which Congress already had substantial authority because that body controlled the allocation of congressional representation among the several states.

83 "Comments of Representative Conkling, 39th Congress, First Session, January 22, 1866," 36 *Congressional Globe* (Washington, D.C.: Congressional Globe Office, 1866), part 1, p. 357.

84 During debates in the House, a significant number of representatives resisted the notion that Congress had this authority. See "Exchange between Representatives Marshall and Kelley, 39th Congress, First Session, January 25, 1866," 36 *Congressional Globe* (Washington, D.C.: Congressional Globe Office, 1866), part 1, p. 412. This was not a universal position, as some representatives thought it appropriate for Congress to exercise this authority. See "Comments of Representative Jenckes, 39th Congress, First Session, January 23, 1866," 36 *Congressional Globe* (Washington, D.C.: Congressional Globe Office, 1866), part 1, p. 386.

85 "Comments of Representative Blaine, 39th Congress, First Session, January 8, 1866," 36 *Congressional Globe* (Washington, D.C.: Congressional Globe Office, 1866), part 1, p. 141.

86 "Blaine's Amendment to the Constitution," *Chicago Tribune*, January 10, 1866, p. 2, https://chroniclingamerica.loc.gov/lccn/sn82014064/1866-01-10/ed-1/seq-2/.

Unsurprisingly, the journey from reapportionment based on legal voters, subject to reductions for the denial of political rights, to reapportionment based on total population, less any who suffer abridgment of these rights, was quite sinuous during the first six months of 1866. Eight days after Stevens proposed apportionment based on legal voters, Congress formed the Joint Committee of Fifteen on Reconstruction, a group of nine representatives and six senators tasked with developing the language of the Fourteenth Amendment, which, among other things, would enshrine in the constitutional text birthright citizenship and attempt to induce states to enfranchise their African American populations or face a penalty of reduced representation in Congress.[87]

Early in its deliberations, the Committee rejected several proposals centered on legal voters, including Thaddeus Stevens' original plan, with every member from New England voting against the proposition.[88] While rejecting apportionment based on total voters, the Committee almost universally embraced the idea that race discrimination would be the trigger for the penalty of reduced representation in the text.

In early January 1866, the Committee entertained four alternatives to Stevens' initial proposal:

- Representatives and direct taxes shall be apportioned among the several States, which may be included within this Union, according to their respective numbers of persons, deducting therefrom all of any race or color, whose members or any of them are denied any of the civil or political rights or privileges[89] ("Morrill Proposal").
- Representatives and direct taxes shall be apportioned among the several States of the Union according to their respective numbers, excluding negroes, Indians, Chinese, and all persons, not white, who are not allowed the elective franchise by the Constitutions of the States in which they respectively reside[90] ("Williams Proposal").
- Representatives and direct taxes shall be apportioned among the several States, which may be included within this Union, according to their respective numbers, counting the whole number of citizens of the United States; provided that

87 "Motion of Representative Stevens of December 4, 1865," in Kendrick, *Journal of the Joint Committee of Fifteen*, p. 37. The members of the Committee included: William P. Fessenden (Maine), James W. Grimes (Iowa), Ira Harris (New York), Jacob M. Howard (Michigan), Reverdy Johnson (Maryland), and George H. Williams (Oregon) from the Senate, and Thaddeus Stevens (Pennsylvania), Elihu B. Washburne (Illinois), Justin S. Morrill (Vermont), Henry Grider (Kentucky), John A. Bingham (Ohio), Roscoe Conkling (New York), George S. Boutwell (Massachusetts), Henry T. Blow (Missouri), and Andrew J. Rogers (New Jersey) from the House. Ibid., pp. 38–39.

88 George D. Zuckerman, "A Consideration of the History and Present Status of Section 2 of the Fourteenth Amendment" (1961) 30 *Fordham Law Review* 93–136, 96.

89 Kendrick, *Journal of the Joint Committee of Fifteen*, p. 43.

90 Ibid., pp. 43–44.

whenever in any State civil or political rights or privileges shall be denied or abridged on account of race or color, all persons of such race or color shall be excluded from the basis of representation or taxation[91] ("Conkling Proposal").

- Representatives and direct taxes shall be apportioned among the several States, which may be included within this Union, according to the respective number of citizens of the United States in each State; and no State shall make any distinction in the exercise of the elective franchise on account of race or color[92] ("Boutwell Proposal").

Despite efforts to preserve the pre–Civil War federalist system, many of these proposals required some displacement of antebellum norms regarding the state's authority over elections; that system could not be preserved in its entirety if Congress would be empowered to punish states for exercising their authority as they had in the past.

These proposals also tell a powerful story about how key members of Congress conceived of sectionalism and partisan politics in 1866. For example, the inclusion of the "race or color" language would exclude almost all northern states from the penalty given the small number of racial minorities who resided there; that most of the proposals included some variation of this language was also a sober recognition of the deep unpopularity of African American suffrage across the North. However, the reference to "race or color," without any citizenship limitation, would extend the penalty to the disenfranchisement of Chinese people, much to the ire of representatives from the Western states that had long denied voting rights to this population.[93] Indeed, the Williams proposal would explicitly do so. The Conkling and Boutwell proposals, by conditioning reduced representation on citizenship, would continue to exclude Native Americans from both taxation and representation similar to the existing system.[94] All of these proposals would bring African Americans granted citizenship through the Civil Rights Act into the realm of "We the Voters."

91 Ibid., p. 44. See also "Submission of Resolution by Representative Conkling, 39th Congress, First Session, January 15, 1866," 36 *Congressional Globe* (Washington, D.C.: Congressional Globe Office, 1866), part 1, p. 233.

92 Kendrick, *Journal of the Joint Committee of Fifteen*, p. 44.

93 For example, when Oregon was admitted to the Union in 1859, non-citizens, if they met certain qualifications, were permitted to vote. Kirk H. Porter, *A History of Suffrage in the United States* (Chicago: University of Chicago Press, 1918), p. 131. This right was expressly prohibited to "Chinamen" who, along with "negroes and mulattoes[,] were specifically excluded from the suffrage." Ibid. Indeed, in the period prior to the Civil War, "[o]n the Pacific Coast the Chinaman was excluded [from enfranchisement] with violent indignation." Ibid. Hostility toward granting people of Chinese descent the right to vote continued, on the federal level. The Burlingame Treaty of 1868 sanctioned immigration between the U.S. and China; however, in 1870, Congress barred Chinese immigrants from obtaining citizenship. See Chapter 7.

94 A discussion on the topic of voting rights for both Native Americans and people of Chinese descent (who were, unfortunately, derogatorily referred to as "coolies") took place between Representatives Brooks and Stevens on the House floor on January 23, 1866:

Two of the four proposals – the Morrill proposal and the Conkling proposal – would have reduced representation based on the exclusion of political *and* civil rights, further muddying the waters regarding whether these categories were treated interchangeably (as Bingham contended during debates over the 1866 Civil Rights Act) or distinctly (as Trumbull argued). Treating these categories as encompassing separate, but not overlapping, suites of rights meant that denial could trigger reduced representation in significantly more circumstances. As Blaine argued, "make it so that a State shall not count in her basis of representation any race to which 'civil or political rights and privileges' are denied or abridged....[T]he phraseology 'civil or political rights and privileges' is more inclusive than the phrase 'elective franchise' because the exclusion from holding real estate would be a denial of civil rights or privileges."[95]

Importantly, this language also signaled that political rights encompassed a broader swath of rights beyond exercising the right to vote.[96]

> Mr. Brooks. Let me put a question. The proviso reads that whenever the elective franchise shall be denied or abridged in any State on account of race or color, all persons therein of such race or color shall be excluded from the basis of representation. There are in California and Oregon something like one hundred thousand coolies. They are increasing and going into the western States to build railroads. Are they included?
>
> Mr. Stevens. I understand that if they are excluded by the laws of California because they are Chinese, these amendment operates upon them because they are excluded on account of race.
>
> Mr. Brooks. They will not be counted in the basis of representation.
>
> Mr. Stevens. Not at all; it was so intended; the word "race" was inserted for that purpose.
>
> Mr. Brooks. One other question. Why exclude the Indian? Is he not a man and a brother.
>
> A Member. The Constitution now excludes him.
>
> Mr. Stevens. "Excluding Indians not taxed."
>
> Mr. Brooks. We exclude them at this time, but are not Indians our brethren?
>
> Mr. Stevens. The Constitution of the United States has always excluded them.
>
> Mr. Brooks. Why not, as we are amending the Constitution, embrace the Indian as a man and a brother?
>
> Mr. Stevens. Because they are a tribal race, have their own separate governments, and, as a general rule, are not citizens.

"Exchange between Representatives Stevens and Brooks, 39th Congress, First Session, January 23, 1866," 36 *Congressional Globe* (Washington, D.C.: Congressional Globe Office, 1866), part 1, p. 376.

95 "Comments of Representative Blaine, 39th Congress, First Session, January 23, 1866," 36 *Congressional Globe* (Washington, D.C.: Congressional Globe Office, 1866), part 1, p. 377.

96 See, e.g., Alfred Avins, "The Right to Hold Public Office and the Fourteenth and Fifteenth Amendments: The Original Understanding" (1967) 15 *University of Kansas Law Review* 287–306, 287 ("The dichotomy in the mind of Representative John A. Bingham of Ohio, the Radical-Republican lawyer who drafted the first section of the fourteenth amendment, between "natural rights" or what later would be called "civil rights," and "political rights" including the right to hold public office, pre-dated the Civil War."); Kate Masur, "Civil, Political, and Social Equality," 1401 ("During the postwar debate about equality, whenever radicals pushed the bounds of racial equality – for example, by demanding the equal right to vote, hold office, or enjoy access to public schools or public accommodations – opponents charged them with seeking something that just about everyone professed to despise: social equality"); Crum, "The Superfluous Fifteenth Amendment?," 1580 ("During Reconstruction, the concept of civil rights was employed to demand equal treatment by government in civil and criminal matters. By contrast, political rights were defined as the rights to vote, to hold office, and to sit on juries. The Reconstruction vision of citizenship intersected with this hierarchy of rights.").

Finally, the proposals varied on the issue of proportionality – should Congress reduce the basis of population by the number of people who were actually denied civil and/or political rights, or should the basis be reduced by the entire class of persons if any of their number were denied civil and/or political rights? The Williams proposal embraced the former, whereas the Morrill and Conkling proposals endorsed the latter. Notably, the Boutwell proposal imposed no penalty at all for racially discriminatory abridgments of the right to vote, and likely would have had no real effect without an enforcement provision in the text of the Fourteenth Amendment. His proposal provided for apportionment based on citizenship, and then separately barred discrimination in voting on the basis of race.

The Committee was able to narrow down the proposals to two possible alternatives as well as a separate enforcement provision. The first proposal was a variation of the Boutwell proposal, providing that:

> Representatives and direct taxes shall be apportioned among the several States within the Union, according to the respective numbers of citizens of the United States in each State; and all provisions in the Constitution or laws of any State, whereby any distinction is made in political or civil rights or privileges, on account of race, creed or color, shall be inoperative and void.

This language extended beyond Boutwell's original text that prohibited discrimination in voting. However, like his proposal, the updated text did not impose a penalty on those states that violated its terms. Instead, Congress could, presumably, render such laws inoperative and void through the proposed enforcement provision.

The second alternative tracked more closely to the language from the Conkling, Morrill, and Williams proposals, linking vote denial to a reduction in representation:

> Representatives and direct taxes shall be apportioned among the several States which may be included within this Union, according to their respective numbers, counting the whole number of citizens of the United States in each State; provided that, whenever the elective franchise shall be denied or abridged in any State on account of race, creed or color, all persons of such race, creed or color, shall be excluded from the basis of representation.[97]

The sub-committee recommended that the Committee submit one of these two proposals to Congress, in addition to this enforcement provision: 'Congress shall have power to make all laws necessary and proper to secure to all citizens of the United States, in every state, the same political rights and privileges and to all persons in every State equal protection in the enjoyment of life, liberty and property."

With this, the connection between the apportionment provision of Section 2 and the enforcement provision of Section 5 made its first appearance, illustrating that

97 Kendrick, *Journal of the Joint Committee of Fifteen*, pp. 50–51.

(at least from the prospective of the sub-committee) that Section 2, in whatever form it would take, might need enabling legislation. However, on Monday, January 15, 1866, Thaddeus Stevens made a motion to separate the enforcement provision from the substantive proposal.[98] The Committee voted ten to four to consider draft Section 5 alone, and eleven to three to adopt the second proposal as the language for draft Section 2.

The Committee then voted eleven to three, on Roscoe Conkling's motion, to change "citizens" to "persons," an edit that signaled Congress's multi-clausal approach to incorporating African Americans into the communities of "We the People" and "We the Voters." While the Civil Rights Act would grant the citizenship necessary to bring this group into "We the People" and provide a necessary prerequisite to becoming members of "We the Voters," Conkling took to the floor of the House during the debate over suffrage in the District of Columbia to clarify that this change from "citizens" to "persons" was important for punishing those states that would deny African Americans their lawful citizenship status to exclude them from "We the Voters." Conkling argued that,

> [t]he entire object is to devise such a mode of adjusting representation that if race or color is made a ground for withholding political or civil rights the consequence shall be to deduct the whole of that race from the enumeration upon which political power is based. Its excellence, if it has any, consists in the fact that it prevents evasion, and insures the nation against votes to be cast in Congress in future on account of those who in truth have no political status in the country.[99]

[98] Ibid., p. 51.

[99] "Comments of Representative Conkling, 39th Congress, First Session, January 17, 1866," 36 *Congressional Globe* (Washington, D.C.: Congressional Globe Office, 1866), part 1, p. 278 (arguing that, although his original proposal referred to citizens, this language was "in the copy sent up only *pro forma*" but his own "preference and judgment are for 'persons,' not 'citizens,' in this connection.").

Conkling, who would later argue that he advocated that "citizens" be changed to "persons" to protect corporations, initially seemed focused on how the term "citizen" could be used to undermine the rights of African Americans:

> I beg to say, therefore, first, that the purpose is not at all to restrict the basis of representation to citizens. No such point as that was considered at all as the object aimed at in preparing the amendment. That question is foreign from the spirit of the amendment; entirely independent of it. The use of the word "person" or the word "citizen" disposes of that question in all amendments on this subject alike; and the one basis or the other does not enter into the motive or object of my proposition. The idea is wholly different. My sole purpose is to get rid of the present injustice and inequality of representation between different sections of the country, arising from the fact that four million people who have now no political rights are, in the present condition of things, to be represented in Congress whenever southern Representatives shall be admitted to seats.

Ibid. See also Adam Winkler, *We the Corporations: How American Businesses Won Their Civil Rights* (New York: Liveright Publishing, 2018).

Arguably, the use of "persons" instead of "citizens" and the severity of the penalty reflected hopes that Section 2, in conjunction with the citizenship granted by the Civil Rights Act (and later reaffirmed by Section 1 of the Fourteenth Amendment), would function as the equivalent as an affirmative grant of suffrage.

On January 22, 1866, Representative Stevens reported a resolution (H.R. No. 51) out of the Joint Committee that, as modified and reintroduced by the Committee on January 31st, contained the following proposed language:

> Representatives shall be apportioned among the several States which may be included within this Union according to their respective numbers, counting the whole number of persons in each State, excluding Indians not taxed: *Provided*, That whenever the elective franchise shall be denied or abridged in any State on account of race or color, all persons therein of such race or color shall be excluded from the basis of representation.[100]

The draft of Section 2 that was introduced to the House and debated over this eight day period seemed to signal that, if states were willing to pay a fairly draconian price, they could discriminate in voting on the basis of race. Again, creating a regime in which states were incentivized, but not required, to enfranchise African Americans was a relic of an earlier time. Like Lincoln, who pleaded with reconstructed Louisiana to enfranchise those Black men who had served in the military, but did not demand it of the state, Section 2 also did not appear to be anything other than a forceful request.[101] Indeed, some representatives noted that limiting the penalty in Section 2 to abridgments on the basis of race could be circumvented by the states because "property qualifications could easily get around the Reconstruction Committee's bill, though not depriving Negroes of the right to vote because of race or color."[102]

In a speech on the House floor, Representative Stevens offered a few reasons why the Committee settled on this language. Specifically, he reiterated that Section 2

[100] "Comments of Representative Stevens, 39th Congress, First Session, January 31, 1866," 36 *Congressional Globe* (Washington, D.C.: Congressional Globe Office, 1866), part 1, pp. 535. The amended resolution introduced on January 31st removed the language apportioning both representatives and direct taxes "among the several States" and made Section 2 solely about representation. Ibid., p. 351. See also George P. Smith, "Republican Reconstruction and Section Two of the Fourteenth Amendment," (1970) 23 *The Western Political Quarterly* 829–853, 839. The final version of H.R. 22 was criticized for "separating taxation and representation. It would reduce the representation of a state refusing to enfranchise the Negro, yet total population would remain the standard for allocating direct, federal taxes," resulting in the affected states having less representation but a larger tax base. Ibid., 841.

[101] At least one of the nation's newspapers, *Freedom's Champion* of Atchison, Kansas, viewed the proposal as a forceful request that would, in the end, likely work to bring the southern states around. In a January 18, 1866 editorial, the paper declared that: "The Southern States will not lose any power or any officers if they can help it. And rather than be deprived of twenty-two Congressmen they will quickly give the blacks the right to vote. The South loves power and place more than it hates the negroes." "The Right Way," *Freedom's Champion* (Atchison, Kansas), January 18, 1866.

[102] Zuckerman, "History and Present Status of Section 2," 97–98.

would offer a severe punishment sufficient to deter states from abusing their power over voter qualifications.[103] Key to the success of this proposal, in his view, was the lack of proportionality in the amendment. Stevens argued that, without it, White elites would extend suffrage to only those African Americans who lacked sufficient independence to exercise the vote wisely, while disenfranchising all others:

> They will give the suffrage to their menials, their house servants, those they can control, and elect whom they please to make our laws. That is not the kind of increase of suffrage I want. I want all such men cut off from it. But when they have said to all the freedmen, to the former slaves, "You are men and you shall be represented," then let them come here. I shall not be here to see them, as I did their masters, who a few years since drew pistols and daggers upon me when I was making such a speech as this, yet a free people will be here represented, and they will take care of themselves.[104]

While Stevens was a strong advocate of universal male suffrage, it was clear that the independence of the elector continued to be an animating principle in determining which individuals deserved the franchise, despite earlier signs that this norm was waning.[105] During the Civil War, this principle had come under assault because the usual indicia of independence – property ownership or taxpaying ability – excluded from suffrage those risking their lives on the country's battlefields. The military service of African American soldiers demonstrated that they were deserving of the franchise because of their loyalty to the Union.[106]

[103] "Comments of Representative Stevens, 39th Congress, First Session, January 31, 1866," 36 *Congressional Globe* (Washington, D.C.: Congressional Globe Office, 1866), part 1, p. 535 ("I say no more strong inducement could ever be held out to them, no more severe punishment could ever be inflicted upon them as States. If they exclude the colored population they will lose at least thirty-five Representatives in this Hall. If they adopt it they will have eighty-three votes….Their eighty-three votes, with the Representatives of the Five Points and other dark corners, would be sufficient to overrule the friends of progress here, and this nation would be in the hands of secessionists at the very next congressional election and at the very next presidential election."). But see William W. van Alstyne, "The Fourteenth Amendment, the 'Right' to Vote, and the Understanding of the 39th Congress" (1965) *Supreme Court Review* 33–86, 57 n.72 ("The announced secondary objective, to induce the states to extend the franchise in order to maintain full representation in Congress, could scarcely have been taken seriously by any member of the Joint Committee. During practically the whole time that H.R. No. 51 was under consideration, the Joint Committee was holding hearings on conditions in the South … Almost none of the witnesses interrogated on this point … felt that the states would extend the franchise rather than suffer a loss in representation.").

[104] "Comments of Representative Stevens, 39th Congress, First Session, January 31, 1866," 36 *Congressional Globe* (Washington, D.C.: Congressional Globe Office, 1866), part 1, p. 536.

[105] See generally Fishel, "Northern Prejudice"; see also Stephen B. Weeks, "The History of Negro Suffrage in the South" (1894) 9 *Political Science Quarterly* 671–703, 680–690 (describing the manifestations, with less-than-ideal results, of fears that African American men newly granted the right to vote would fall victim to the undue influence of white "adventurers" throughout the South).

[106] As part of a larger conversation about Reconstruction, by early 1866, discussions about suffrage for Black men, especially for those who had served in the Union army, were reported on in the press. For example, on January 3, 1866, the *Lowell (Massachusetts) Daily Citizen* newspaper reported on a

Not coincidentally, African Americans, once deemed inherently unfit to exercise the vote, began to challenge their exclusion from the political community of voters in like terms – first with free Black people illustrating that their community could achieve the independence key to antebellum republicanism and later, through the service of Black people, enslaved and free, in the military.[107] Their loyalty to the Republican Party would also be a key factor in the debate over whether they should be enfranchised during presidential, and later, congressional, reconstruction.

H.R. 51 was introduced in the Senate on Monday, February 5th, after the House passed it by a vote of 120 to 46 six days earlier.[108] While much of the House debates focused on the proportionality of the penalty, the debate that occurred in the Senate raised a slightly different, but in some ways, more important, issue: whether Section 2 would confer upon the states authority *that they never had, i.e.*, the power to disenfranchise those entitled to be in the political community of "We the Voters."

Because the 1866 Civil Rights Act would have, once enacted, conferred citizenship and the ability to contract and own property, it removed the barriers that might otherwise keep African Americans from the community of "We the People" and "We the Voters," at least based on antebellum conceptions of these communities. The transformation in legal status offered by the Act made it difficult to leave in place discriminatory state action – potentially legitimized by the structure of Section 2 as a penalty but not a prohibition – that would deprive African Americans of recognition as full members of these political communities.

lecture by General Carl Schurz, a German immigrant who led Union troops during the Civil War and eventually served in the Senate. General Schurz was strongly in favor of granting the right of suffrage to African American men, especially those who had, "[i]n the service of the Union, … learned to fight." "General Carl Schurz on 'Reconstruction,'" *Lowell Daily Citizen*, January 3, 1866. General Schurz argued that free Black people in the South would be under significant threat from the White leadership in the states of the former Confederacy, and that "they must be allowed to protect themselves by having the right to vote." Ibid. See also Richard M. Re and Christopher M. Re, "Voting and Vice: Criminal Disenfranchisement and the Reconstruction Amendments" (2012) *Yale Law Journal* 1584–1670, 1602–1603 ("…if valiant citizens could earn enfranchisement through military service, then the logic of formal equality suggests that disloyalty should trigger punitive exclusion from the body politic…. With the Civil War not yet formally concluded and the Thirteenth Amendment still pending ratification, the political philosophy underlying American abolitionism was already being redirected towards the right to vote.").

107 During a speech to the Equal Suffrage Association of Washington on January 21, 1866, Representative Boutwell of Massachusetts specifically cited the training that 150,000 Black soldiers had received while serving in the Union army as having given them the skills they would need to "render rebellion and insurrection, war and bloodshed, throughout the slave states" if they were denied the franchise. "Mr. Boutwell on Equal Suffrage," *Lowell Daily Citizen*, January 10, 1866. In other words, Boutwell believed it was folly for the southern states "to ask [the federal government] to pursue a policy by which these people are to be deprived of all share in the government[,]" because adopting this policy would "consign these eleven states to civil and social war for an indefinite period of time." Ibid.

108 "Apportionment of Representation," 36 *Congressional Globe* (Washington, D.C.: Congressional Globe Office, 1866), part 1, p. 644. See also Smith, "Republican Reconstruction," 339.

Thus, the Senate debate took a broader view of congressional authority, analyzing Section 2 in light of not only the changes to the status of the formerly enslaved under the pending Civil Rights Act, but also the authority that the Constitution already conferred on Congress to regulate suffrage. The fact that states would be willing to pay the price of reduced representation was immaterial if, as some argued, disenfranchising those entitled to be within the political community violated the Guarantee Clause. At least that was the position of the most famous of radicals – Charles Sumner – a character who would loom large among those opposed to the adoption of Section 2.

5.3 IS SECTION 2 NECESSARY? DISAGREEMENTS OVER FEDERAL POWER TO PREVENT DISENFRANCHISEMENT

Senator Charles Sumner's commitment to full equality for African Americans before the law had very little parallel among his contemporaries in the Thirty-Ninth Congress. Yes, there were other radicals. But few were willing to go as far in advocating for the civil and political rights of Black people, and Sumner felt the distance between him and his colleagues on these issues during the debates over the Fourteenth Amendment.[109]

Sumner had always been ahead of his time. As early as 1862, he had repeatedly argued that the Civil War was a war against slavery, a framing that the Lincoln administration initially resisted, despite the Confederacy's unambiguous statements that they were prosecuting the war to preserve that institution.[110] In the post-war era, Sumner's commitment to equality challenged the antebellum conception of the states as the primary guarantors of civil and political rights; in his view, no longer should the federal government stay its hand in protecting the formerly enslaved. For Sumner, both the war and the newly ratified Thirteenth Amendment abolishing slavery changed both the status of African Americans and the very fabric of our system of federalism by rejecting outright antebellum norms regarding federal deference to state control over voting and elections.

109 Masur, "Civil, Political, and Social Equality," 1401 ("In part because of disagreements among Republicans over the definition of civil rights, Congress's two major statements about civil rights in 1866 – the Civil Rights Act and the Fourteenth Amendment – left considerable ambiguity about the boundaries of federally enforceable civil rights.").

110 In 2001, nearly 100 historians signed a brief article authored by their colleague, Charles Joyner, which declared their rejection of so-called revisionist history of the Civil War and that "[t]he historical record … clearly shows that the cause for which the South seceded and fought a devastating war was slavery." Charles Joyner, "The Flag Controversy and the Causes of the Civil War: A Statement by Historians" (2001) 24 *Callaloo* 196–198, 197. Among the evidence provided in the article in support of this belief was that "as President and Vice President of the Confederate States of America, Jefferson Davis and Alexander H. Stephens each candidly acknowledged that their new nation was created for the specific purpose of perpetuating slavery." Ibid., 196. See also David H. Donald, *Lincoln* (New York: Simon & Schuster, 1995).

Sumner's strategy was to marshal the resources of the federal government to force states to incorporate fully the Black population in their respective political communities. Accordingly, he introduced three provisions that would endow Black people with equal rights: (1) a constitutional amendment, providing that, "No State, in prescribing the qualifications requisite for electors therein shall discriminate against any person on account of race or color;"[111] (2) a statute "to declare that all men were equal before the law, and that there could be no denial of rights, civil or political;"[112] and (3) a resolution providing that, "there shall be no oligarchy, aristocracy, caste, or monopoly, invested with peculiar privileges and powers, and there shall be no denial of rights, civil or political, on account of color or race anywhere within the limits of the United States, or the jurisdiction thereof."[113]

By bringing forth these proposals, Sumner sought to counter the Fourteenth Amendment, which, in his view, would be a compromise with the former slavocracy and an abandonment of moral principles such that other alternatives were needed.[114] He argued that the Amendment, and Section 2 in particular, would undermine progress toward racial equality by "acknowledging that states were entitled to limit suffrage on racial grounds."[115] While Section 2 would provide a penalty for disenfranchisement, according to Sumner, it nonetheless countenanced the South's ability to discriminate in voting on the basis of race or color by not directly forbidding it.[116]

This argument – that Section 2 permitted racial discrimination – would later be used to the challenge the validity of the Fifteenth Amendment during the Redemption and Restoration periods.[117] During Redemption, which began in the 1870s but became much more formalized and widespread by the 1890s, White supremacists cemented their control of southern state governments by manipulating elections through force and violence, widespread fraud, and enacting discriminatory

[111] "Discussion of the Apportionment of Representation Issue in the Senate, 39th Congress, First Session, February 7, 1866," 36 *Congressional Globe* (Washington, D.C.: Congressional Globe Office, 1866), part 1, p. 702.

[112] "Comments of Senator Sumner, 39th Congress, First Session, February 7, 1866," 36 Congressional Globe (Washington, D.C.: Congressional Globe Office, 1866), part 1, p. 704.

[113] "Comments of Senator Fessenden, 39th Congress, First Session, February 7, 1866," 36 *Congressional Globe* (Washington, D.C.: Congressional Globe Office, 1866), part 1, p. 707.

[114] "Comments of Senator Sumner, 39th Congress, First Session, February 7, 1866," 36 *Congressional Globe* (Washington, D.C.: Congressional Globe Office, 1866), part 1, pp. 704–706.

[115] Eric Foner, *Reconstruction: America's Unfinished Revolution, 1863–1877* (New York: Harper & Row, 1988), pp. 253, 255.

[116] Ibid., see also Joseph B. James, *The Framing of the Fourteenth Amendment* (Urbana: University of Illinois Press, 1965), p. 73 (noting that Sumner objected "to bringing inequalities into the language of the Constitution;" that the amendment "sanctioned taxation without representation;" and finally, it "made concessions to states' rights" while compromising "human liberty" on the basis of color).

[117] Michael Perman, *Struggle for Mastery: Disfranchisement in the South, 1888–1908* (Chapel Hill: University of North Carolina Press, 2001), p. 10–11 (describing Reconstruction, Redemption, and Restoration as the "Three Phases in the History of Black Suffrage in the Southern States since the Civil War").

state laws; during Restoration, tactics shifted to holding state constitutional conventions across the South from 1890 to 1908 to permanently enshrine disenfranchisement after decades of undermining Reconstruction.[118]

In thinking about what Section 2 would change about the preexisting allocation of state and federal power over elections (and if, as its opponents argued, it countenanced discrimination), there were questions about whether an amendment was needed in the first place given that aggregating congressional authority across already existing provisions could conceivably provide sufficient authorization for federal action. Sumner did not think that a new amendment was required for Congress to be proactive on these issues, and certainly not one – like Section 2 – that could arguably undermine progress.

In a now famous speech, Sumner argued that Congress could, pursuant to the Guarantee Clause and the Thirteenth Amendment, protect the formerly enslaved from discrimination at the hands of their former masters.[119] His counterproposals explicitly relied on these provisions as a source of authority to enfranchise African Americans and rebuild the governments of the southern states in a republican mold.[120]

[118] See Chapter 9. See also "Comments of Congressman Bowie," reprinted in "The 14th and 15th Amendments," *Nashville Tennessean*, August 15, 1904 ("…that amendment [Fifteenth Amendment] prohibited any state from denying the suffrage to any citizen because of race, color or previous condition of servitude. The thing then which was permitted by the Fourteenth Amendment under a certain condition was prohibited altogether by the 15th. The two amendments were not only inconsistent; they are totally antagonistic to each other.").

[119] Sumner argued that Congress had four options for doing this: (1) the "necessity of the case;" (2) the "Rights of War;" (3) "the constitutional injunction to guaranty a Republican Form of Government;" and (4) "the constitutional amendment by which Congress … is empowered to 'enforce' the abolition of slavery 'by appropriate legislation.'" "Comments of Senator Sumner, 39th Congress, First Session, February 6, 1866," 36 *Congressional Globe* (Washington, D.C.: Congressional Globe Office, 1866), part 1, p. 674. Sumner described the combined effect of these powers as follows: "From four specific fountains they flow – each one sufficient for the purpose – all four swelling into an irresistible current … [which] lead[s] to the jurisdiction of Congress over this whole subject. No matter which road you take, you arrive at the same point." Ibid.

[120] At Sumner's request, the following proposed joint resolution was read to the Senate during his speech on February 6, 1866:

> Whereas it is provided in the Constitution that the United States shall guaranty to every State in the Union a republican form of government; and whereas by reason of the failure of certain States to maintain governments which Congress might recognize, it has become the duty of the United States, standing in the place of guarantor, where the principal has made a lapse, to secure to such States according to the requirement of the guarantee, governments republican in form; and whereas further, it is provided in a recent constitutional amendment that Congress may "enforce" the prohibition of slavery by "appropriate legislation," and it is important to this end, that all relics of slavery should be removed, including all distinction of rights on account of color: Now, therefore, to carry out the guarantee of a republican form of government and to enforce the prohibition of slavery, Be it resolved by the Senate and House of Representatives of the United States of America in Congress assembled, That there shall be no Oligarchy, Aristocracy, Caste, or Monopoly invested with peculiar privileges and powers, and there shall be no denial of rights, civil or political, on account of color or race anywhere within the limits of the United States or

In defining the republic that should emerge from the ashes of the war, Sumner explicitly rejected definitions offered by a number of philosophers who applied this label to a wide variety of governments that allowed broad disenfranchisement. Instead, Sumner argued that the republican form of government embraced by the Guarantee Clause was a distinctly American concept. It prohibited taxation without representation, and disenfranchising those who pay taxes would impose that very harm.[121] The notion of taxation without representation undermined the principle of majority rule underlying the American republic, and harkened back to the primary grievance of the American colonies: all laws passed by a non-representative body that operated by using the taxes of its powerless constituents were illegitimate.[122] The idea that, post–Thirteenth Amendment, African Americans would now be subject to taxation as full persons governed by the U.S. Constitution, while at the same time being denied the right to vote, went against the very heart of the American project.

The Guarantee Clause gave Congress two options to address this untenable situation. That provision required states to either "reform their governments to the satisfaction of Congress," or "Congress, in performance of the 'guarantee,' and according to the plenary authority 'for carrying into execution the powers vested in the Government of the United States,' … [can] place the Equal Rights of All under the guardianship of National Law."[123]

Sumner found support among some of his colleagues for the proposition that the Constitution, as then constituted, was sufficient to address racial discrimination in voting. For example, Representative Michael Kerr argued that existing provisions of the Constitution authorized Congress to regulate voter qualifications, and the Elections Clause could be used to rectify electoral inequality in the states and remedy voter disenfranchisement.[124] Others believed that Congress had such power as a war measure, viewing secession as the termination of a state's legal status, which left

> the jurisdiction thereof; but all persons therein shall be equal before the law, whether in the court-room or at the ballot-box. And this statute, made in pursuance of the Constitution, shall be the supreme law of the land, anything in the Constitution or laws of any State to the contrary notwithstanding.

"Reading of the Joint Resolution by the Secretary during the Comments of Senator Sumner, 39th Congress, First Session, February 6, 1866," 36 *Congressional Globe* (Washington, D.C.: Congressional Globe Office, 1866), part 1, p. 674.

121 According to Senator Sumner, to allow the state governments to establish elector "qualifications" that are beyond "those requirements of personal condition which are regarded as essential to the security of the franchise[,]" especially if those qualifications are "permanent or insurmountable[,]" would be "equivalent to a deprivation of suffrage – in other words, it is the tyranny of taxation without representation." "Comments of Senator Sumner, 39th Congress, First Session, February 6, 1866," 36 *Congressional Globe* (Washington, D.C.: Congressional Globe Office, 1866), part 1, p. 684.

122 Several times during his February 6 speech, Senator Sumner cited what he referred to as a Revolutionary-era battle cry: "Taxation without Representation is Tyranny." See ibid., pp. 679–682.

123 Ibid., p. 684.

124 Ibid., pp. 454–455.

that state "unorganized, ungoverned territory ... to be governed and disposed of by us at our sovereign will."[125]

Sumner was not the first to voice concern about the potentially disenfranchising effects that Section 2, once ratified, would have, or relatedly, whether Section 2 would undermine Congress's existing power to remedy discrimination.[126] Weeks earlier, Representative William Higby of California had argued that Section 2 would amend the Guarantee Clause, empowering states to disenfranchise half their populations and, in the process, modify the concept of majoritarianism the Clause embodied.[127] He questioned the ability of a state to exclude "a whole class on account of race or color," no longer enslaved, and suffer only the penalty of reduced representation as the cost of maintaining a government that was essentially unrepublican in form.[128] As Higby observed, disenfranchising African Americans would result in the disenfranchisement of many, and in some cases, most of the state's residents.[129] It was difficult to reconcile any definition of republicanism with the notion that states can disenfranchise the majority of their citizens, especially after the removal of the one

125 "Comments of Representative Raymond, 39th Congress, First Session, January 29, 1866," 36 *Congressional Globe* (Washington, D.C.: Congressional Globe Office, 1866), part 1, pp. 484, 486. See also "Comments of Senator Lane, 39th Congress, First Session, February 8, 1866," 36 *Congressional Globe* (Washington, D.C.: Congressional Globe Office, 1866), part 1, p. 736 (echoing the idea that the Confederacy was, effectively, a foreign power with member states that "have abdicated and forfeited every right; they are no longer to be recognized as a governing power under the Constitution of the United States.").

126 See, for example, "Comments of Representative Eliot, 39th Congress, First Session, January 24, 1866," 36 *Congressional Globe* (Washington, D.C.: Congressional Globe Office, 1866), part 1, p. 406 (arguing that draft Section 2 was "impliedly saying that States may disfranchise because of race or color if they are content to pay the penalty; that they may disfranchise men of color if they are content to have them excluded from the basis of representation".

127 "Now Mr. Speaker, when we are attempting to amend another portion of the Constitution in the first section of it, I say that we are making a direct attack on the Constitution. I say it; I do not know how many say it. I say it, without fear or favor, that that amendment will allow any State government in its organization to exclude one half of its population from the right of suffrage; and I say such State governments will not be republican in form." "Comments of Representative Higby, 39th Congress, First Session, January 25, 1866," 36 *Congressional Globe* (Washington, D.C.: Congressional Globe Office, 1866), part 1, p. 427.

128 "Comments of Representative Higby, 39th Congress, First Session, January 25, 1866," 36 *Congressional Globe* (Washington, D.C.: Congressional Globe Office, 1866), part 1, p. 427 ("I do not believe that any State which excludes any class of citizens on account of race or color is republican in form."). Higby went as far as to argue that the constitution of his own state (California) was not republican in form.

129 "Comments of Representative Higby, 39th Congress, First Session, January 25, 1866," 36 *Congressional Globe* (Washington, D.C.: Congressional Globe Office, 1866), part 1, p. 427 ("The State of South Carolina, in 1860, had within its limits 291,388 white people and 402,406 slaves – more of the colored race than of the white race. I will give you another instance, an instance in which this proposed amendment of the Constitution would directly apply, and would give the State governments the power to exclude more than half of their population from the elective franchise. The State of Mississippi had 353,901 white population and 436,681 slave population. Why, sir, I can find right here on this table other instances where they were nearly one half of the population in 1860. There was not one of the slave States where a large proportion of the population was not black.").

disability – slavery – that had long justified the exclusion of African Americans from the political communities of "We the People" and "We the Voters."

Representative Shellabarger likewise criticized Section 2 for "authoriz[ing] the States to wholly disenfranchise entire races of its people, and that, too, whether that race be white or black, Saxon, Celtic, or Caucasian, and without regard to their numbers or proportion to the entire population of the State."[130] He further noted,

> [I]t has never been held, so far as I know, that it is within the power of the States *ad libitum* to disfranchise races as such; and this, I think, or at least fear, will be the effect of the clause as reported by the committee; it will, I apprehend, be construed as giving authority to the States to disfranchise races as such at pleasure, and that without regard to color …

In other words, if states can liberally disenfranchise Black people then no man, of whatever race, was safe.[131]

But Sumner, Shellabarger, and Higby were in the minority, and many of those serving in Congress at the time thought that they were ignoring the practical barriers to enfranchising the formerly enslaved. Senator Fessenden admitted he too "would prefer … a distinct proposition that all provisions in the constitution or laws of any State making any distinction in civil or political rights, or privileges, or immunities whatever, should be held unconstitutional, inoperative and void, or words to that effect."[132] But he conceded that there were obstacles to this approach as

> no man looks at the question dispassionately and calmly could contend that the great mass of those who were recently slaves … and who have been kept in ignorance all their lives, oppressed, more or less forbidden to acquire information, are fit at this day to exercise the right of suffrage, or could be trusted to do it, unless under such good advice as those better able might be prepared to give them.[133]

While the Thirteenth Amendment had negated the institution of slavery and eliminated it as a justification for the exclusion of Black people from the community of "We the People," the badges and incidents of slavery remained barriers that continued to

[130] "Comments of Representative Shellabarger, 39th Congress, First Session, January 24, 1866," 36 *Congressional Globe* (Washington, D.C.: Congressional Globe Office, 1866), part 1, p. 405. Shellabarger also complained that Section 2 "is a declaration made in the Constitution of the only great and free Republic in the world that it is permissible and right to deny to the races of men all their political rights." Ibid.

[131] Ibid., p. 406. During that same discussion, Representative Banks of Massachusetts, in support of Shellabarger, argued that the Thirteenth Amendment is a restriction on the states' ability to disenfranchise on the basis of race, and that Section 2 "reestablish[es] that power which has come to an end by virtue of the abolition of slavery." "Comments of Representative Banks, 39th Congress, First Session, January 24, 1866," 36 *Congressional Globe* (Washington, D.C.: Congressional Globe Office, 1866), part 1, p. 406.

[132] "Comments of Senator Fessenden, 39th Congress, First Session, February 7, 1866," 36 *Congressional Globe* (Washington, D.C.: Congressional Globe Office, 1866), part 1, p. 704.

[133] Ibid.

impede the incorporation of the members of this community into "We the Voters." Just as a lack of independence kept many White men from the franchise during the antebellum era and most women from the franchise until the twentieth century, this norm would persist during Reconstruction for Black men. Emancipation would not be enough to guarantee one's position in the community of "We the Voters," and elector independence would continue to be a factor in the price of admission.

Ironically, Senator Sumner's proposal was also attacked for not going far enough to ensure the equality of the formerly enslaved. Senator Fessenden argued that Sumner's statutory and constitutional proposals would have less impact than the proposal generated by the Joint Committee, noting that he [Fessenden] was

> unaware how far two measures so entirely distinct can go together, one an amendment to the Constitution to endure for all time, and which lies at the bottom as a foundation principle, the other an act of Congress that may be repealed tomorrow, and which provides no sanction, nor penalty, no measure, no machinery, nothing but a reenactment of the Constitution itself in language not half so forcible.[134]

But Sumner's broader purpose in proposing these measures was clear – the war and the Thirteenth Amendment had brought the nature of republican government front and center, creating an opportunity to redefine this term in a more egalitarian manner. But Sumner failed to appreciate the extent to which draft Section 2 provided a clear answer to at least some of these questions.

The Guarantee Clause, thanks in part to Sumner's efforts in bringing this provision to the forefront, played a prominent role in constructing a political theory of Section 2 that allowed Congress to actively enforce rights and to define who was entitled to be a part of the political community of "We the Voters." The Clause became a prominent feature of Republican discourse as they searched for constitutional support for the Reconstruction program.[135] Of course, arguments based on the Guarantee Clause ran into a problem of historical importance – none of the original thirteen states enfranchised all segments of their populations who were, at least theoretically, qualified to vote. While one can argue that disenfranchising half of the state's population is inconsistent with majoritarianism – the criticism that Higby lodged against the potential scope of Section 2 – it did not necessarily follow that republicanism required states to enfranchise everyone who could cast a ballot.[136]

[134] Ibid., pp. 704–705.

[135] Les Benedict, *A Compromise of Principle*, pp. 74–75 (noting that the Guarantee Clause "was the only constitutional basis for Reconstruction which could promise the national government permanent power, even after the rebel states were restored to normal relations").

[136] "Exchange between Representatives Hale and Farnsworth, 39th Congress, First Session, January 23, 1866," 36 *Congressional Globe* (Washington, D.C.: Congressional Globe Office, 1866), part 1, p. 383. See also "Comments of Representative Lawrence, 39th Congress, First Session, January 24, 1866," 36 *Congressional Globe* (Washington, D.C.: Congressional Globe Office, 1866), part 1, p. 406 (arguing that Section 2 would not "disturb or impair the undoubted power of Congress and the President to determine whether a State government is republican in form, and if not to interpose and guaranty such government.").

Instead, proponents of the view that the Guarantee Clause prohibited broad disenfranchisement framed the harm as one of malapportionment, where the disenfranchisement of African Americans in one state, but not in others, undermined that provision's requirement, not of nondiscrimination, but of the "absolute political equality" to which African Americans were now entitled.[137] This was a question of not just voting rights, but also a question of status, community, and representation.

Senator Sumner's disapproval of Section 2 notwithstanding, his critique raised a fundamental question about the scope of state authority over voter qualifications in the years prior to the Civil War, and what Reconstruction would change about that authority. While we know that the inclusion of the penalty in Section 2 was itself an enlargement of federal power, questions remained about the other ways in which Section 2 fundamentally changed the relationship between the states and the federal government.

Was Section 2 an endorsement of state authority to disenfranchise their populations as they saw fit, even though the existence of this authority prior to the war was questionable? Sumner and a select few thought this surely to be the case. But the proponents of Section 2 would hang their hat on a very different question: Does Section 2 provide a penalty for that which is already prohibited – disenfranchisement of those within the political community – and in doing so give Congress the power to regulate suffrage? In other words, how much did Section 2 change about Madison's Constitution of 1787? For these individuals, the answer was that Section 2 and the legislation needed to enforce its terms would create a new political community, a community that would be unrecognizable to those in the founding generation, now protected by Congress.

5.4 AMENDING THE GUARANTEE CLAUSE THROUGH SECTION 2

The definition of federalism during the antebellum period was determined by the political disputes of the day – be they slavery, congressional reapportionment, the admission of new states, etc. – but the need to recreate the country's political communities in the wake of the war necessitated that Congress revisit the basic federal structure that had been so easily manipulated by politics in decades prior. Section

[137] See "Comments of Representative Shellabarger, 39th Congress, First Session, January 24, 1866," 36 *Congressional Globe* (Washington, D.C.: Congressional Globe Office, 1866), part 1, p. 406 ("The pending proposition of the committee is a radical departure from the principles of representative republican government, in this, that it does not provide for nor secure the absolute political equality of the people, or, relatively, of the States. It does not secure to each vote throughout the Government absolute equality in its governing force. It, for example, permits twenty-five thousand votes in New York City to elect two members of Congress, provided one half of its population should happen to be foreigners unnaturalized and not electors of the State, whom the law deems unfit to vote; whereas twenty-five thousand votes in Ohio would elect but one member of Congress, provided her citizens were all Americans instead of foreigners.").

2 became a vehicle for revisiting the norms around voting that existed prior to the Civil War, that is, answering important questions such as: How were states constrained in their determinations of who was within the community of "We the Voters"? Relatedly, what was Congress's role in policing those determinations?

With respect to the first question, Thaddeus Stevens, refuting Sumner's view that Section 2 would encourage discrimination if enacted, argued that, as the law then stood, states could withdraw the franchise from half of their population, *without penalty*.[138] This does not mean that Section 2, by penalizing the wrong of race-based voting discrimination, ratified or legalized the prior exercise of that wrong before its enactment. The existence of a penalty was about constraining future behavior rather than sanctioning prior exercises of the contested practice.

The crux of Stevens' argument was, at least when it comes to race, states had previously been unconstrained in crafting their electorates because federal law had been absent on the issue of voter qualifications prior to Reconstruction. This was why, in *Dred Scott*, it was not outcome determinative to the question of African American citizenship that some Black people were voters in the antebellum era. The existence of Black voters simply indicated that the threshold for what constituted republican government would vary unless, and until, Congress intervened to set the floor. Section 2 was that intervention.

But absent federal intervention, there was still a distinction between a sovereign having the power to undertake an action versus being authorized to do so, a theme that many of Stevens' congressional colleagues would echo in defending Section 2. While states might have the power to disenfranchise segments of their population, that did not mean that such actions were legal (just that there was no mechanism to prohibit it).[139] Thus, Section 2, by providing a penalty for such actions, was a

[138] See "Exchange between Representatives Stevens, Higby, and Farnsworth, 39th Congress, First Session, January 25, 1866," 36 *Congressional Globe* (Washington, D.C.: Congressional Globe Office, 1866), part 1, p. 428. To Representative Farnsworth's contention that, "can it not be implied from language not so clear, not so strong, that by this amendment a State is given the right to disfranchise the half of her people?" Stevens responded, "Nobody understood it so; everybody understood that without that prohibition they had the right, and with that prohibition it was restrained from a certain time; nothing more." Ibid.

To understand Representative Stevens' argument, pretend that murder is not a crime punishable by death or imprisonment in a specific jurisdiction; instead, there are social norms against the commission of murder but nothing else. If the jurisdiction adopts a statute subjecting any murders to the penalty of death, the statute does not recognize a preexisting right to commit murder simply by penalizing those who now decide to engage in the practice.

[139] Senators Fessenden and Yates argued this point during the Senate's discussion of the apportionment joint resolution on March 9, 1866:

> Mr. FESSENDEN. They have the power to do it. I am not speaking of the right; I am speaking of the power.
>
> Mr. YATES. Under the Constitution they cannot do it.
>
> Mr. FESSENDEN. What constitution?
>
> Mr. YATES. The clause of the Constitution which I have just read [Article I, Section 2].
>
> Mr. FESSENDEN. How are you going to interfere?

constraint on that power without implicitly sanctioning any preexisting authority or right of states to engage in unlawful disenfranchisement.

Stevens' views about Section 2 enjoyed broader support than those of Sumner; very few believed that Section 2 endorsed disenfranchisement or that the Guarantee Clause alone was enough to prevent it.[140] Nonetheless, Sumner found support from an unlikely source on the issue of whether the Guarantee Clause alone prohibited states from disenfranchising substantial swaths of their populations: Representative John Bingham, who explicitly linked Section 2 with the principles of republicanism underlying the Clause.[141]

> Mr. YATES. "The people" are to elect the Representatives.
>
> Mr. FESSENDEN. I know that, but who decides who shall be "the people" to elect the members of the lower branch of the Legislature?
>
> Mr. YATES. That is the objection I make to this amendment. You say it shall be decided by the States now, which would exclude that portion of the people who were made free by the constitutional amendment.
>
> Mr. FESSENDEN. The Senator is entirely mistaken. [Section 2] says no such thing....
>
> Mr. YATES. That admits that it may be denied.
>
> Mr. FESSENDEN. I say that that is nothing in the world but a limitation upon the Constitution as it stands. The Senator says it admits the right of the State to exclude them. I say it admits no such right; it denies the right.
>
> Mr. YATES. It suffers it.
>
> Mr. FESSENDEN. No, sir; it denies the right of the State to exclude them. It does not deny the power, for you cannot deny the power. The power exists under the Constitution. The power is there.
>
> Mr. YATES. I do not deny the power to violate the Constitution, of course.

"Exchange between Senators Fessenden and Yates, 39th Congress, First Session, March 9, 1866," 36 *Congressional Globe* (Washington, D.C.: Congressional Globe Office, 1866), part 2, p. 1279.

140 See, e.g., the comments of Senator Johnson on February 9, during which he stated that:

> There was not a State in the Union when the Constitution was adopted that was republican, if the honorable member's definition of a republican government is the one now to be relied upon. A property qualification was required in all at that time. Negroes were not allowed to vote, although free, in most of the States. In the southern States the mass of the negroes were slaves, and of course were not entitled to vote.

"Comments of Senator Johnson, 39th Congress, First Session, February 9, 1866," 36 *Congressional Globe* (Washington, D.C.: Congressional Globe Office, 1866), part 1, p. 767.

Senator Johnson then shifted his focus from the specifics of the states' voting laws to their republican character in general:

> If the absence of the universal right of suffrage proves that the government is not republican, then there was not a republican government within the limits on the United States when the Constitution was adopted; and yet the very object of the clause to guaranty a republican government – and the honorable member's citations prove it – was to prevent the existing governments from being changed by revolution. It was to preserve the existing governments; and yet the honorable member would have the Senate and the country believe that in the judgment of the men who framed the Constitution there was not a republican form of government in existence.

Ibid.

141 Representative Bingham expressly cited the Guarantee Clause in his remarks during the House's discussion of the basis of representation issue on January 24:

The fact that Sumner and Bingham agreed on this point was notable.[142] Bingham is considered one of the chief architects of the Fourteenth Amendment; Sumner opposed it. Bingham – moderate, Sumner – radical. On the Guarantee Clause implications of African American suffrage, however, they were mostly aligned. Sumner and Bingham found consensus on the idea that the Guarantee Clause endorsed a communitarian principle that treated the impermissible exclusion of individuals from the political community as detrimental to society as a whole but disagreed about whether the Guarantee Clause was self-executing.

Bingham did not share Stevens' belief that states could disenfranchise their residents in the absence of Section 2, even if not explicitly empowered to do so; like Sumner, Bingham did not rely on such distinctions between power and authority.[143] In response to the assertion that Section 2 would amend the Guarantee Clause to

> I have endeavored to show that the words of the Constitution, the people of 'the States shall choose their Representatives,' is an express guarantee that a majority of the free male citizens of the United States in every State of this Union, being of full age, shall have the political power subject to the equal right of suffrage in the minority of free male citizens of full age. There is a further guarantee in the Constitution, of a republican form of government to every State, which I take to mean that the majority of the free male citizens in every State shall have the political power.

"Comments of Representative Bingham, 39th Congress, First Session, January 24, 1866," 36 *Congressional Globe* (Washington, D.C.: Congressional Globe Office, 1866), part 1, p. 431.

142 See van Alstyne, "The Fourteenth Amendment, the 'Right' to Vote, and the Understanding of the 39th Congress", 43 ("§ 2 was primarily the handiwork of Thaddeus Stevens, a man of quite different temperament and purpose from Bingham, the principal author of § 1.").

143 "Comments of Representative Bingham, 39th Congress, First Session, January 24, 1866," 36 *Congressional Globe* (Washington, D.C.: Congressional Globe Office, 1866), part 1, p. 432 During his lengthy speech on that day, Bingham rejected the assertion that, "a law which inflicts a penalty or works a forfeiture for doing an act, by implication authorizes the act to be done for doing which the penalty is inflicted." Ibid. In response, he noted:

> You place upon your statute book a law punishing the crime of murder with death. You do not thereby, by implication, say that anybody may, of right, commit murder. You but pass a penal law. You do not prohibit murder in the Constitution – you guaranty life in the Constitution. You do not prohibit the abuse of power by the majority in the Constitution in express terms, but you guaranty the equal right of all free male citizens of full age to elect Representatives; and by the proviso you inflict a penalty upon a State which denies or abridges that right on account of race or color. In doing that we are not to be told that we confer a power to override the express guarantees of the Constitution. We propose the penalty in aid of the guarantee, not in avoidance of it.

Ibid.

Bingham then went on to say that,

> There cannot be such a construction of the proviso. It is a penalty. It says in terms that if any of the States of the United States shall disobey the Constitution; that if they shall make distinctions in violation of the second section of the first article of the Constitution, that as a penalty such State shall lose political power in this House, to the extent of the whole class or race against any part of whom the unjust discrimination has been made.

Ibid. He concluded that such violations would run afoul of "every principle of Republican government." Ibid.

permit disenfranchisement,[144] for example, Bingham asserted that draft Section 2 did nothing more than impose a penalty for actions already prohibited by the Guarantee Clause and Article I, Section 2, which states that the "House of Representatives shall be composed by members chosen every year by the people of the several states":

> I have endeavored to show that the words of the Constitution, the people of the States shall choose their Representatives, is an express guarantee that a majority of the free male citizens of the United States in every State of this Union, being of full age, shall have the political power subject to the equal right of suffrage in the minority of free male citizens of full age. There is a further guarantee in the Constitution, of a republican form of government to every State, which I take to mean that the majority of the free male citizens in every State shall have the

[144] During an exchange with Representative Hill on January 25, Representative Higby explained his belief that the requirements of the Guarantee Clause evolve over time:

> Mr. HIGBY. … I have stated that in two states in the Union there has been a palpable violation of the principles contained in the Constitution. I will ask the gentleman if he thinks that those States that have excluded and disfranchised more than half of their native population have a republican form of government?
>
> Mr. HILL. The gentleman has propounded to me a question, and I will answer it by saying that in my opinion, when the framers of the Constitution placed in that instrument the declaration or the provision that the Government of the United States would guaranty to each State a republican form of government, they spoke with reference to such governments as then existed, and such as those same framers recognized for a long time afterward as republican governments. That is my answer.
>
> Mr. HIGBY. Well, that is a very good answer. It is an answer from a standpoint seventy-five-years ago. I speak from the standpoint of the present time.

"Exchange between Representatives Higby and Hill, 39th Congress, First Session, March 9, 1866," 36 *Congressional Globe* (Washington, D.C.: Congressional Globe Office, 1866), part 1, p. 426. Rep. Higby further observed that,

> no State is republican in form that excludes from the suffrage any portion of its citizens on account of race or color, I do not care how few the number. That was my answer. I do not know but that some of these States may have their constitutions republican in form, but I must confess that their practice under their constitutions has been very different from the precepts contained in them. I judge by their action and practice.

"Comments of Representative Higby, 39th Congress, First Session, January 24, 1866," 36 *Congressional Globe* (Washington, D.C.: Congressional Globe Office, 1866), part 1, p. 428. This assertion, based on the idea that the requirements of the Guarantee Clause has evolved "from seventy-five years ago" sheds light on the willingness of some representatives to remove the entire class of African Americans from the basis of representation regardless of the number of individuals actually disenfranchised. But it was not clear if this evolution applied outside of the protected classes explicitly mentioned in the text of draft Section 2. See "Comments of Representative Eliot, 39th Congress, First Session, January 24, 1866," 36 *Congressional Globe* (Washington, D.C.: Congressional Globe Office, 1866), part 1, pp. 405–407 (arguing that Section 2 would limit Congress's ability to determine whether a state's government is republican, even in cases where property restrictions "exclude multitudes of all classes of citizens, making the State no longer republican but oligarchical," because "this amendment as reported by the committee admits by implication that although a State may so legislate as to exclude these multitudes of men, not on account of race or color, but on account of property, yet, nevertheless, she would have a republican form of government, and that Congress will not and ought not to interfere.").

> political power. I submit to my friend that this proviso [Section 2] is nothing but a penalty for a violation on the part of the people of any State of the political right of franchise guaranteed by the Constitution to their free male fellow-citizens of full age.[145]

For Bingham, Sumner and others, once the Thirteenth Amendment barred slavery, then African American men became a part of the "majority of free male citizens in every State [who] shall have political power." Thus, the issue was not whether the Guarantee Clause prohibited broad disenfranchisement – it plainly did – the issue was whether Congress had the authority to penalize states who failed to comport with this republican ideal. Simply put, Section 2 would make Congress's obligation to enforce the republican guarantee ongoing, rather than active only at the point of admission.

During the antebellum era, there was controversy surrounding whether states with narrowly defined electorates, noncitizen voters, and potentially perpetual legislatures satisfied the requirement of republicanism,[146] but the question of whether Congress had a post-admission obligation to oversee state political systems was decidedly novel. The extent of this obligation was in some dispute. For example, Senator Reverdy Johnson, a Democrat who voted for the Thirteenth Amendment and would go on to support the 1867 Military Reconstruction Act (which reorganized the southern states pursuant to the Guarantee Clause), argued that the Clause did not give Congress the power to regulate suffrage even if the guarantee of republicanism was subject to federal enforcement. Johnson argued that "the very object of the clause was to secure by force of the guarantee the existing governments, and nothing else."[147] Like Senator Johnson, Representative Welker did not define the republican ideal that Congress was tasked with enforcing, arguing instead that Section 2 was necessary because it provided a penalty for the disenfranchisement of legal voters without forcing Congress to define how many "must be disenfranchised before it [a State] ceases to be republican," which he viewed as an impossible task.[148]

145 "Comments of Representative Bingham, 39th Congress, First Session, January 25, 1866," 36 *Congressional Globe* (Washington, D.C.: Congressional Globe Office, 1866), part 1, p. 431 ("The guarantee in the first article of the second section of the Constitution rightly interpreted is, as I claim, this, that the majority of the male citizens of the United States of full age in each State shall forever exercise the political power of the State with this limitation, that they shall never by caste legislation impose disabilities upon one class of free male citizens to the denial or abridgment of equal rights. The further provision is that the United States shall guaranty to each State a republican form of government, which means that the majority of male citizens of full age in each State shall govern, not, however, in violation of the Constitution of the United States or of the rights of the minority.").

146 See Chapter 2.

147 "Comments of Senator Johnson, 39th Congress, First Session, February 9, 1866," 36 *Congressional Globe* (Washington, D.C.: Congressional Globe Office, 1866), part 1, p. 767.

148 "Comments of Representative Welker, 39th Congress, First Session, February 9, 1866," 36 *Congressional Globe* (Washington, D.C.: Congressional Globe Office, 1866), part 1, p. 767.

In contrast, John Bingham treated questions of republicanism as a matter of shoring up the constitutional structure rather than protecting individual rights. He believed that the proposed Fourteenth Amendment would not "take away from any State any right that belongs to it, or from any citizen of any State any right that belongs to him under that Constitution."[149] Bingham thought that federal legislation should proceed from the default that states form the first line of defense in the protection of political rights; if they fail, Congress had no choice but to enforce Section 2's penalty to ensure republican government. This early articulation of the state failure thesis, embraced by the Supreme Court in a much more rigid form in the *Civil Rights Cases*,[150] was, in Bingham's view, more faithful to Madison's original framework than allowing Congress to directly regulate rights that owe their substantive content to state law.

Notably, Bingham did not consider voting to be one of the "privileges or immunities" that the Fourteenth Amendment would ultimately protect. With the "privileges or immunities" language, Bingham sought to create a parallel set of national rights, independent of state law and insulated from state interference, which did not include the right to vote but instead focused on incorporating the Bill of Rights against the states.[151]

In the *Slaughter-House Cases* and *Minor v. Happersett*, the Supreme Court endorsed a more extreme version of Bingham's position that privileges and immunities does not include voting, holding that the Privileges or Immunities Clause only extended to those rights that were incidental to national citizenship, such as the right to use the navigable waters of the United States; the right to peaceably

149 "Comments of Representative Bingham, 39th Congress, First Session, February 27, 1866," 36 *Congressional Globe* (Washington, D.C.: Congressional Globe Office, 1866), part 2, pp. 1088–1090. See also "Comments of Representative Bingham, 39th Congress, First Session, May 10, 1866," 36 *Congressional Globe* (Washington, D.C.: Congressional Globe Office, 1866), part 3, p. 2542 ("No State ever had the right, under the forms of law or otherwise, to deny to any freeman the equal protection of the laws or to abridge the privileges or immunities of any citizen of the Republic[.]").

150 *Civil Rights Cases*, 109 U.S. 3, 11 (1883) ("[T]he last section of the amendment invests Congress with power to enforce it by appropriate legislation. To enforce what? To enforce the prohibition. To adopt appropriate legislation for correcting the effects of such prohibited State laws and State acts, and thus to render them effectually null, void, and innocuous. This is the legislative power conferred upon Congress, and this is the whole of it. It does not invest Congress with power to legislate upon subjects which are within the domain of State legislation, but to provide modes of relief against State legislation, or State action, of the kind referred to."). But see Magliocca, *American Founding Son*, p. 161 ("Bingham rejected the idea that there was a rigid 'state action' limitation in the Fourteenth Amendment, explaining that Congress could legislate against the denial of rights by states…as well as against the unlawful acts of combinations and conspiracies against the rights of the people.'").

151 See Jacobus tenBroek, *Equal under Law* (originally published as *The Antislavery Origins of the Fourteenth Amendment*) (Berkeley: University of California Press, 1951), pp. 214–225; Michael K. Curtis, *No State Shall Abridge: The Fourteenth Amendment and the Bill of Rights* (Durham: Duke University Press, 1986), pp. 57–66.

assemble and petition for redress of grievances; and the right of habeas corpus.[152] It was unlikely that Bingham was thinking of the rights protected by the Privileges or Immunities Clause as narrowly as the Court, but he did not intend for the right to vote to fall under its auspices.

Importantly, Bingham believed that, with respect to *all* rights (both civil and political), only a constitutional amendment could bring "[a right] within the control of Congress."[153] This distinction explained his later endorsement of Section 2. For even if Congress retained the authority to regulate the right to vote under the Guarantee Clause, as some contended in denying that suffrage was a civil right subject to the 1866 Act,[154] Bingham argued that there was still need for a constitutional amendment to empower Congress to enforce the protections of the Guarantee Clause with respect to suffrage. Section 2 assuaged many of Bingham's federalism-based concerns because, unlike the 1866 Act, Section 2 empowered Congress to police suffrage, with the caveat that states would still be primarily responsible for shaping their electorates. Congressional power, in other words, kicked in when states failed in their duties.

In contrast, President Andrew Johnson invoked a narrow view of federal power over voting and, in the process, corroborated Charles Sumner's fears about the provision's potentially disenfranchising effect. In comments to the *New York Daily Tribune*, Johnson argued that Section 2 permitted race-based discrimination because such discrimination was necessary to avoid "contention

152 *Slaughter-House Cases*, 83 U.S. 36, 79–80 (1872); *Minor v. Happersett*, 88 U.S. 162 (1875).

153 Representative Bingham emphasized that,

> the care of the property, the liberty, and the life of the citizen, under the solemn sanction of an oath imposed by your Federal Constitution, is in the States, and not in the Federal Government. I have sought to effect no change in that respect in the Constitution of the country. I have advocated here an amendment which would arm Congress with the power to compel obedience to the oath, and punish all violations by State officers of the bill of rights, but leaving those officers to discharge the duties enjoined upon them as citizens of the United States by that oath and by that Constitution.

"Comments of Representative Bingham, 39th Congress, First Session, March 9, 1866," 36 *Congressional Globe* (Washington, D.C.: Congressional Globe Office, 1866), part 2, p. 1292.

154 See, for the example, the remarks of Representative Wilson of Iowa, in which he noted that the Act

> provides for the equality of citizens of the United States in the enjoyment of "civil rights and immunities." What do these terms mean? Do they mean that in all things civil, social, political, all citizens, without distinction of race or color, shall be equal? By no means can they be so construed. Do they mean that all citizens shall vote in the several States? No; for suffrage is a political right which has been left under the control of the several States, subject to the action of Congress only when it becomes necessary to enforce the guarantee of a republican form of government. Nor do they mean that all citizens shall sit on the juries, or that their children shall attend the same schools.

"Comments of Representative Wilson, 39th Congress, First Session, March 1, 1866," 36 *Congressional Globe* (Washington, D.C.: Congressional Globe Office, 1866), part 2, p. 1117.

and strife between the two races," and "a war between them."[155] Johnson further noted that,

> Such an amendment would remove from Congress all issues in reference to the political equality of the races. It would leave the States to determine absolutely the qualifications of their own voters with regard to color, and thus the number of Representatives to which they would be entitled in Congress would depend upon the number upon which they conferred the right of suffrage.[156]

For all his shortcomings (and there were many), the President was right to a limited degree. By leaving discretion with the states to define voter qualifications yet punishing states that exercised this authority in contravention of republican principles, Section 2 maintained some of the remnants of the state-centered regime that existed during the antebellum era. Yet President Johnson's comments ignored the fact that Section 2, by amending the Guarantee Clause and empowering Congress to penalize abridgments of the republican ideal, substantially upended elements of the prior regime. Not only would Section 2's penalty serve as a powerful inducement to enfranchise African American men, but its final language would extend to all abridgments and denials of the right to vote, rather than only race-based abridgments, thereby empowering Congress in ways unimaginable under the original Madisonian framework.

5.5 REDUCED REPRESENTATION AS AN INDUCEMENT TO BROAD ENFRANCHISEMENT

The President's statements about the need for race-based disenfranchisement were reflective of a fairly common belief that states were best equipped to determine when African Americans had reached sufficient independence to be electors.[157] While Johnson was doubtful that Black people could ever be electors, Section 2 sought more of a balance. While states could still determine when African Americans had

155 "The Present Agitation of the Negro Suffrage Question Deprecated," *New-York Daily Tribune*, January 29, 1866, p. 5, https://chroniclingamerica.loc.gov/lccn/sn83030213/1866-01-29/ed-1/seq-5/.

156 Ibid.

157 See, e.g., "Comments of Representative McKee, 39th Congress, First Session, January 25, 1866," 36 *Congressional Globe* (Washington, D.C.: Congressional Globe Office, 1866), part 1, p. 452 ("And it rests entirely with them whether they enfranchise one race or another. On the general question of suffrage for the negro I need make no explanation. My views are on the record. I voted against the bill allowing negro suffrage in the District of Columbia. I did not believe then, nor do I believe now, that this race, coming immediately out of bondage, is fit for all the rights of citizens. When they develop sufficient fitness for that purpose I will be the last man to withhold the right of suffrage from them."). See also "Comments of Representative Wright, 39th Congress, First Session, February 9, 1866," 36 *Congressional Globe* (Washington, D.C.: Congressional Globe Office, 1866), part 1, p. 459 ("It is not simply the emancipation of the colored race, but it contemplates their entire enfranchisement, elevating them without regard to necessity or capacity to a political, and necessarily to a personal and social equality with the white race. I most respectfully aver that this result would promote an injustice.").

reached the threshold of readiness sufficient to exercise political power, Section 2 restructured our system of federalism by incentivizing states to recognize their fitness sooner rather than later through the penalty of reduced representation.

The version of Section 2 that emerged from the House of Representatives in February 1866 would have removed all African Americans from the basis of population if even one eligible Black man was disenfranchised, and the demographics of the southern states explain why Congress believed that the penalty would be a powerful inducement. In 1860, a quarter of the population of the Confederacy was enslaved;[158] thus, states who refused to enfranchise African American men prior to the 1870 census faced a substantial reduction in their congressional seats. In the post–Civil War era, most states had restrictions on the right to vote, so Section 2 could potentially work a sea change in the existing regimes, depending on the size of the state's African American population.[159] States with large Black populations would have no way of offsetting the population losses that came from disenfranchising Black men, if the entire population of Black men was removed from the denominator.[160]

The removal of the entire group from the basis of population, if even one is disenfranchised, was viewed as both necessary for the regime of indirect coercion to work and as a proper punishment for the treasonous South. Representative Blaine, for example, highlighted its draconian nature in noting that the penalty would apply even if a state used criteria with which some subset of the targeted group could comply:

> the proposed amendment excludes all of a race until the last one of that race shall be enfranchised; that is to say, if the people of the South choose to impose an educational qualification upon the elective franchise among the negroes, by which all the negroes shall be permitted to vote but one-tenth of them, the provision of the committee will exclude not only that one-tenth, but the other nine tenths also.[161]

Given its severity, the penalty – in all its proposed forms – was not without controversy. As Representative Rogers complained, Section 2's unprecedented structure "pours out the vials of despotic wrath so profusely upon the heads of the people of the southern States."[162]

158 Avidit Acharya, Matthew Blackwell, & Maya Sen, *Deep Roots: How Slavery Still Shapes Southern Politics* (Princeton: Princeton University Press, 2018), p. 8.

159 "How many States in the Union now admit the colored man to the exercise of the right of suffrage? Only six. In every State except Maine, Vermont, New Hampshire, Massachusetts, Rhode Island, there is a distinction in regard to suffrage on the ground of color." "Comments of Senator Johnson, 39th Congress, First Session, February 9, 1866," 36 *Congressional Globe* (Washington, D.C.: Congressional Globe Office, 1866), part 1, p. 764.

160 See "Comments of Representative Blaine, 39th Congress, First Session, January 23, 1866," 36 *Congressional Globe* (Washington, D.C.: Congressional Globe Office, 1866), part 1, p. 377.

161 "Comments of Representative Blaine, 39th Congress, First Session, January 25, 1866," 36 *Congressional Globe* (Washington, D.C.: Congressional Globe Office, 1866), part 1, p. 433.

162 "Comments of Representative Rogers, 39th Congress, First Session, January 22, 1866," 36 *Congressional Globe* (Washington, D.C.: Congressional Globe Office, 1866), part 1, p. 354.

In response to these critiques, the Senate coalesced behind language that would increase the exposure that states face under federal law, but subject to a less aggressive penalty. First, full removal of the entire group if one was disenfranchised was replaced, as many of the Senators favored proportional reduction of the group to better correlate the penalty to the harm and be less intrusive of the states' ability to both define their electorates and how people should be represented.

By removing an entire subset of individuals from the basis of representation for rights violations, the draft of Section 2 that emerged out of the House complicated the Revolutionary-era theory of virtual representation that had remained popular as applied to women and children, and now, post–Thirteenth Amendment, could have applied to Black people. As the Supreme Court had held less than a decade earlier, African Americans – both enslaved and free – had never been entitled to any legal acknowledgment of their existence.[163] While physically present in a state and partially counted in the basis of representation, they nonetheless remained outside the community of "We the People." Unlike women and children, they were inhabitants but not citizens;[164] they constituted both people and property; and they lacked an individual political identity yet remained structurally important to the American polity – politically, legally, and economically.

Thus, African Americans were uniquely situated relative to other groups, testing the boundaries of any preexisting concept of representation, virtual or otherwise. Roscoe Conkling recognized the paradox that Black freedom presented to the theory of representation that had long defined the American political project.[165] With respect to immigrants, for example, the Constitution left to both the states and Congress the "power to clothe foreigners with full political rights as fast as they should be prepared to assume them" but, as Conkling noted, "[t]he political disability of aliens was not for this purpose counted at all against them, because

163 *Dred Scott v. Sandford*, 60 U.S. (19 How.) 393 (1857). As Representative Conkling stated during the House discussion on January 22,

> The slaves of the South were not members of that political society which formed the Constitution of the United States. They were without personal liberty, and therein they were without a natural right, not a political right; but they were also without political rights, and therefore they were not members of the political community. From this it followed that political power was not to be apportioned by treating them as political persons.

"Comments of Representative Conkling, 39th Congress, First Session, January 22, 1866," 36 *Congressional Globe* (Washington, D.C.: Congressional Globe Office, 1866), part 1, p. 356.

164 *Dred Scott v. Sandford*, 60 U.S. (19 How.) 393 (1857) (noting that "Women and minors, who form a part of the political family, cannot vote; and when a property qualification is required to vote or hold a particular office, those who have not the necessary qualification cannot vote or hold the office, yet they are citizens.").

165 "Comments of Representative Conkling, 39th Congress, First Session, January 22, 1866," 36 *Congressional Globe* (Washington, D.C.: Congressional Globe Office, 1866), part 1, p. 356 ("This emancipated multitude has no political status. Emancipation vitalizes only natural rights, not political rights.").

it was certain to be temporary, and they were admitted at once into the basis of apportionment."[166]

The recently emancipated presented a different issue, mandating a more creative solution than traditionally applied to those who were, in his words, a "political nonage."[167] According to Conkling, "The slave alone was the anomaly and the nondescript. A man, and not a man. In flesh and blood, alive; politically, dead. A native, an inhabitant, a producer, but without recognized political attributes or prerogative; the representative in the system of nothing but value. What could be done with him? He was nowhere."[168]

With the ratification of the Thirteenth Amendment, African Americans were no longer "political nonage[s]" who could be ignored, and while freedom did not automatically confer political rights, it was not clear that they should automatically suffer the same political disabilities as women and children. The Civil Rights Act of 1866 made representation a necessity by conferring citizenship on this group, but it was Section 2 that gave African American men a definitive political identity that necessitated more than virtual representation.[169]

Nevertheless, the Senate's change to the penalty, from full to proportional reduction, left some discretion to the states to determine the appropriate representation for African Americans (virtual or otherwise) whose rights had not been abridged. This edit reinforced that, in the postbellum era, states retained some authority to exclude from their political community certain nonvoters who, in turn, would be adequately represented in the state legislature even if they cannot cast a ballot. Full reduction, by removing the entire category of African American men from the denominator if the voting rights of even one African American man was abridged, would have eliminated this authority.

Second, the Senate removed the "race or color" language from Section 2, thereby extending the reach of the sanction to race-neutral abridgments. Collectively, these changes resulted in a less severe penalty, but a broader basis upon which the penalty could be imposed. Notably, the new language forced northern states to have some skin in the game. The prior version, as some Senators recognized, would have all

166 "Comments of Representative Conkling, 39th Congress, First Session, January 22, 1866," 36 *Congressional Globe* (Washington, D.C.: Congressional Globe Office, 1866), part 1, p. 356.

167 Ibid.

168 Ibid.

169 During his remarks on January 23, Representative Donnelly explained why he was "vot[ing] for it, cheerfully, as a step in the right direction":

> It follows as a logical conclusion that if men have no voice in the national Government, other men should not sit in this Hall pretending to represent them. … In fact, I cannot see how any northern man can vote against this measure unless he wishes to perpetuate an injustice to his section, because the effect of it will clearly be to increase the representation of the North and decrease that of the South; and this, too, upon a basis of undoubted justice. It means simply that those who do not take part in the Government shall not be represented in the Government.

"Comments of Representative Donnelly, 39th Congress, First Session, January 23, 1866," 36 *Congressional Globe* (Washington, D.C.: Congressional Globe Office, 1866), part 1, p. 378.

but insulated the North from any impact of its penalty, even though these states also had discriminatory laws.[170] Even if these states disenfranchised one African American man on account of race, with the effect of removing all of them from the basis of representation, this would have had no effect on their representation in Congress. In fact, their representatives would emerge more powerful because they would have to answer to fewer constituents.

Just as the Guarantee Clause served as a bulwark against arguments that states could disenfranchise at will, the Clause also served as a justification for why the insulation of northern states from the penalty was impermissible. If no state in which African American men were denied the ballot could be republican, then it cannot be "an evil, if it be one, without remedy" in the northern states.[171] The fact that the former Confederacy had no representation in the Thirty-Ninth Congress, and could not weigh in on the proposed amendment, only served to bolster the argument that the North had to be subject to the same constraints as the South under its terms.[172]

The best way to ensure that the North was similarly affected by Section 2 was by extending the penalty of reduced representation to any abridgment of the right to vote. This change would permit Congress to protect all electors but do so without having to police criteria that had long been accepted as prerequisites to voting under state law (yet could be applied in a discriminatory manner).

For example, Representative Roscoe Conkling argued that both property and educational qualifications remained permissible "if framed to operate impartially on both races,"[173] implying that neutral criteria discriminately applied could trigger

170 "Comments of Senator Conness, 39th Congress, First Session, February 9, 1866," 36 *Congressional Globe* (Washington, D.C.: Congressional Globe Office, 1866), part 1, p. 764. Senator Conness, for example, made the following observation about how the North would benefit if the language of Section 2 remained race-based:

> Massachusetts has a white population of 1,221,961, and a colored population of only 9,602. New York has a white population of 8,831,730, and a colored population of 49,005; Vermont a white population of 319,889, and a colored population of 709. The State of New Hampshire…has a white population of 325,579 and a colored population of 424. The experiment is quite a safe one for them. They will not be affected by it injuriously. They will lose no Representative, but on the contrary they gain, not in the number of Representatives perhaps, but they gain the relative influence of the Representatives that they will have on the floor.

Ibid.

171 Ibid., pp. 764–765.

172 "My objection to the adoption of the proposed amendment to the Constitution I base simply upon the fact that the States in part to be affected by it, and the States hereafter to conform to it as the fundamental law of the country, are not here present to participate in the consideration and the action by which it is to become the law of the land. We are without the Representatives from eleven States, and it is proposed to make this binding upon them as a part of the Constitution of the country." "Comments of Representative Randall, 39th Congress, First Session, February 27, 1866," 36 *Congressional Globe* (Washington, D.C.: Congressional Globe Office, 1866), part 2, p. 1057.

173 James, *The Framing of the Fourteenth Amendment*, pp. 61–62. See also ibid., p. 133 (noting that Senator Sherman found Section 2 of the proposed Fourteenth Amendment "as the most objectionable feature because under it intelligence tests as a voting qualification would be discouraged").

the penalty of Section 2, while still adhering to antebellum notions of deservedness and exclusion by sanctioning such criteria.[174] Representative Thaddeus Stevens likewise stuck to this framing, noting that men lacking in intelligence should be "cut off from [the franchise]," and suggesting, somewhat naively, that intelligence could be a race-blind criterion to define those who belong in the political community of "We the Voters."[175]

Also, recall that proposals were rejected that would "prohibit States from denying civil or political rights to any class of persons," because this broad prohibition "trenches upon the principle of local sovereignty" and "denies to the people of the Several States the right to regulate their own affairs in their own way."[176] As Conkling observed,

> Every State will be left free to extend or withhold the elective franchise on such terms as it pleases, and this without losing anything in representation if the terms are impartial to all. Qualifications of voters may be required of any kind – qualifications of intelligence, of property, or of any sort whatever, and yet no loss of representation shall thereby be suffered.[177]

The very decision to let the states decide the complexion of their political identity, subject to the penalty of reduced representation, was a deliberate nod to the system of federalism that had existed prior to the Civil War.[178] Contrary to some of

174 But see "Comments of Representative Eliot, 39th Congress, First Session, January 24, 1866," 36 *Congressional Globe* (Washington, D.C.: Congressional Globe Office, 1866), part 1, p. 406 (suggesting that the inclusion of property restrictions violates the Guarantee Clause because such restriction "enables a State, consistently with its provisions, by making the right to vote depend upon a property qualification, to exclude large classes of men of both races. A State may legislate in such way as to be in fact an oligarchy, and not a republican State.").

175 See "Comments of Representative Stevens, 39th Congress, First Session, January 31, 1866," 36 *Congressional Globe* (Washington, D.C.: Congressional Globe Office, 1866), part 1, p. 536.

176 As Conkling noted:

> The second plan mentioned, the proposition to prohibit States from denying civil or political rights to any class of persons, encounters a great objection on the threshold. ... It meddles with a right reserved to the States when the Constitution was adopted, and to which they will long cling before they surrender it. No matter whether the innovation be attempted on behalf of the negro race or any other race, it is confronted with the genius of our institutions. But more than this. The northern States, most of them, do not permit negroes to vote. Some of them have repeatedly and lately pronounced against it. Therefore, even it were defensible as a principle for the General Government to absorb by amendment the power to control the action of the States in such a matter, would it not be futile to ask three quarters of the States to do for themselves and all others, by ratifying such an amendment, the very thing which most of them have already refused to do in their own cases?

"Comments of Representative Conkling, 39th Congress, First Session, January 22, 1866," 36 *Congressional Globe* (Washington, D.C.: Congressional Globe Office, 1866), part 1, p. 358.

177 "Comments of Representative Conkling, 39th Congress, First Session, January 22, 1866," 36 *Congressional Globe* (Washington, D.C.: Congressional Globe Office, 1866), part 1, p. 358.

178 For example, during his remarks of January 24, Representative Lawrence noted that "[e]ach State enjoys the political right of deciding for itself who shall and who shall not vote. The amendment

its detractors, this should not be viewed as a concession that states had preexisting authority to discriminately halve their electorate; instead, the amendment provided clarity on sequencing – who decides and when. Structurally, the states would remain the primary drivers of constructing the electorate, but subject to congressional oversight that assesses the credibility of the state's choices with the option of imposing proportional deductions.

With the removal of race or color as a trigger for the penalty, the principles of majoritarianism underlying republican government would prevent race-neutral criteria from becoming the foil through which states artificially restricted their electorates. As Representative Cook observed:

> It is said that the southern States may impose a property qualification, and so exclude the negroes, not on account of race or color, but for want of a property qualification, or that they might provide for a qualification of intelligence, and so disfranchise the negroes because they could not read or write, and still enumerate them. To do this they must first repeal all the laws now denying suffrage to negroes; and second, provide qualifications which will disfranchise half their white voters; two things neither of which will, in any human probability, occur. And in the event that it was possible that both these measures should be adopted, and all the blacks and half the whites disqualified, it would become a grave question whether the provision of the Constitution which requires the United States to guaranty to each State a republican form of government would not authorize the Government to rectify so gross a wrong.[179]

Thus, it was the Guarantee Clause, and not just Section 2, that would prohibit state-enacted abridgments of the right to vote that were either race-based on their face, or race-neutral and applied discriminately. Congress's ability to invoke multiple constitutional provisions, both as a justification and a source of authority for its actions, allowed it to impose limitations on states that would have otherwise been able to evade the penalty through creative, nondiscriminatory means.[180]

under consideration does not propose to disturb the enjoyment of that right. But it does affirm that one class of men shall not have political power on behalf of a race declared by their laws unfit to exercise it." "Comments of Representative Lawrence, 39th Congress, First Session, January 24, 1866," 36 *Congressional Globe* (Washington, D.C.: Congressional Globe Office, 1866), part 1, p. 404.

179 "Comments of Representative Cook, 39th Congress, First Session, February 9, 1866," 36 *Congressional Globe* (Washington, D.C.: Congressional Globe Office, 1866), part 1, p. 411.

180 See "Comments of Representative Farnsworth, 39th Congress, First Session, January 23, 1866," 36 *Congressional Globe* (Washington, D.C.: Congressional Globe Office, 1866), part 1, p. 384 (urging his colleagues to consider "adopt[ing] a provision which shall put it out of the power of these States to circumvent it, and by any shift, or trick to get round it that by declaring if this class of people of African descent are not allowed the elective franchise in any State, no matter upon what pretext, whether it is because of lack of intelligence, or because of lack of property qualification, or any other; if they are debarred the right of exercising the elective franchise, then they shall not be counted in the basis of representation"). See also "Comments of Representative Baker, 39th Congress, First Session, January 23, 1866," 36 *Congressional Globe* (Washington, D.C.: Congressional Globe Office, 1866), part 1, p. 385 ("State might deny or abridge the elective franchise, not on account of race or color,

After robust debate, and even with the naysayers within the Republican Party, the Fourteenth Amendment as a whole passed both chambers of Congress on June 13, 1866. The final version of Section 2 of the Fourteenth Amendment, now substantively broader than earlier versions, read:

> Representatives shall be apportioned among the several States according to their respective numbers, counting the whole number of persons in each State, excluding Indians not taxed. But when the right to vote at any election for the choice of electors for President and Vice-President of the United States, Representatives in Congress, the Executive and Judicial officers of a State, or the members of the Legislature thereof, is denied to any of the male inhabitants of such State, being twenty-one years of age, and citizens of the United States, or in any way abridged, except for participation in rebellion, or other crime, the basis of representation therein shall be reduced in the proportion which the number of such male citizens shall bear to the whole number of male citizens twenty-one years of age in such State.

The Fourteenth Amendment was later ratified by three-fourths of the states then in the Union,[181] and it went into effect on July 28, 1868.

In the end, Section 2 reshaped and redefined republicanism to establish a more concrete link between political rights and principles of majority rule that, prior to the war, had only existed in theory.[182] But the new consensus that Congress could, through Section 2, intervene to enforce the principles of the Guarantee Clause did not answer difficult, second-order questions that would arise about whom this majority included beyond some subset of age-eligible African American men. Further federal action would be needed to settle the remaining disagreements about the scope of federal power to limit the states' authority to define their new electorates.

but on some other account-as, for instance, property or intelligence-and in such case though very large numbers of her people might be disfranchised, yet under the operation of this amendment, they would all be counted in the basis of her representation, which would be highly unjust in itself, besides potentially leaving the identical obnoxious thing standing in our representative system which it is the object of this amendment to extirpate!"). The removal of the "race or color" language in the Senate version of Section 2 responded to these concerns voiced in earlier House debates.

181 There is a literature on whether the ratification of the Fourteenth Amendment was legal, which is beyond the scope of this book but is nonetheless useful for shedding light on how we conceive of political community. See, generally, John Harrison, "The Lawfulness of the Reconstruction Amendments" (2001) *University of Chicago Law Review* 375–462; Thomas B. Colby, "Originalism and the Ratification of the Fourteenth Amendment" (2013) 107 *Northwestern University Law Review* 1627–1688; Douglas H. Bryant, "Unorthodox and Paradox: Revisiting the Ratification of the Fourteenth Amendment" (2022) 53 *Alabama Law Review* 555–581.

182 This view is consistent with Akhil Amar's argument that the central meaning of republican government is popular sovereignty which, he equates to the numerical majority of the residents in the state, or put more simply, majority rule. See Akhil R. Amar, "The Central Meaning of Republican Government: Popular Sovereignty, Majority Rule, and the Denominator Problem" (1994) 65 *Colorado Law Review* 749–786.

6

"In Whom Is the Right of Suffrage?"

Reconstruction Legislation as Political Community Redefined

In 2014, Sue Evenwel and Edward Pfenninger filed suit in federal district court, challenging the manner in which Texas had drawn the state legislative districts in which they resided.[1] At the heart of their case was a single, powerful claim: that Texas's system of apportioning legislative districts based on total population, which includes undocumented immigrants, children, and prisoners, violated the Equal Protection Clause of the Fourteenth Amendment.[2] In their view, only eligible or registered voters should count when drawing district lines given that the practice, according to Evenwel, of relying on total population for reapportionment gave "equal representation to a block of undocumented people who are not eligible or registered to vote."[3] Represented by the Project on Fair Representation, which describes its mission as litigating "racial and ethnic classifications and preferences in state and federal courts."[4] Evenwel, the chairperson for the Titus County Republican Party, and Pfenninger, a Christian fundamentalist with an extensive YouTube presence,[5] challenged the use of total population as a basis for apportionment all the way to the U.S. Supreme Court.

In *Evenwel v. Abbott*, the Supreme Court held that the Fourteenth Amendment's principle of one person, one vote did not require states to draw their state legislative districts based on eligible voters.[6] Instead, states are permitted to construct districts based on total population figures because doing so is consistent with the Court's precedent, longstanding practice, and constitutional history.[7] In reaching this

1 *Evenwel v. Abbott*, 578 U.S. 54, 62 (2016).

2 Ballotpedia, "Evenwel v. Abbott," https://ballotpedia.org/Evenwel_v._Abbott.

3 Stephanie Mencimer, "Meet the Brains behind the Effort to Get the Supreme Court to Rethink Civil Rights," *Mother Jones*, March/April 2016, www.motherjones.com/politics/2016/04/edward-blum-supreme-court-affirmative-action-civil-rights/.

4 Ballotpedia, "Project on Fair Representation," https://ballotpedia.org/Project_on_Fair_Representation.

5 Stephanie Mencimer, "The Craziest Thing about This Supreme Court Case Isn't That One Plaintiff Believes Unicorns Are Real," *Mother Jones*, December 4, 2015, www.motherjones.com/politics/2015/12/evenwel-abbott-supreme-court-redistricting/.

6 *Evenwel v. Abbott*, 578 U.S. 54, 73–75 (2016).

7 Ibid., 75 (noting that "Texas, like all other States, draws its legislative districts on the basis of total population.").

conclusion, Section 2 of the Fourteenth Amendment figured prominently in the Court's analysis, with particular attention being paid to the rejection of an apportionment standard based on total voters in the Thirty-Ninth Congress.[8]

Notably, the *Evenwel* Court referred to Section 2 as a "theory of the Constitution" that "underlies not just the method of allocating House seats to States; it applies as well to the method of apportioning legislative seats within States."[9] According to the Court, Section 2 stands for the broad proposition that states can reapportion based on total population because elected officials represent everyone, including the disenfranchised. In other words, the government is required to respect even those who do not have a political identity, a finding that is consistent with the proportional (rather than full) reduction of representation that the Thirty-Ninth Congress embraced over a century earlier that would allow states to recognize the interests of legally disenfranchised individuals through virtual representation.

Justice Alito concurred, but wrote separately to challenge the Court's conception of the "theory of the Constitution" underlying Section 2.[10] He argued that Section 2 was "power politics, not Democratic theory," and as such, did not preclude the reapportionment of districts based on total voters.[11] Instead, many of its Framers were concerned that a focus on total population alone would penalize the loyal states and reward the South, which stood to gain a substantial amount of representation with the repeal of the Three-Fifths Clause.[12] For Justice Alito, the "bottom line is that in the leadup to the Fourteenth Amendment, claims about representational equality were invoked, if at all, only in service to the real goal: preventing southern States from acquiring too much power in the National Government."[13]

What does framing Section 2 as a "theory of the Constitution" illuminate about the scope of federal power? A lot, as it turns out. Justice Alito's myopic view about the motivations underlying the adoption of Section 2 ignored that members of the Thirty-Ninth Congress used this provision as a vehicle to facilitate goals tangentially related to power politics that were important in their own right.

First, as discussed in Chapter 5, Section 2 provided a political identity for those who had previously lacked one. Second, this provision clothed those who met certain age, citizenship, and gender requirements with the designation of potential voter entitled to federal protection. Section 2 also brought this constituency within the ambit of federal law, allowing Congress to legislate broadly on their behalf using a multiclausal approach that included the Guarantee Clause, Section 5 of the Fourteenth Amendment and, as we will see, the Elections Clause; Article I, Section 5; and the Fifteenth Amendment. While the intentions of the Fourteenth Amendment's drafters

8 Ibid., 73.
9 Ibid., 65–67.
10 Ibid., 81–82 (Alito, J., concurring).
11 Ibid., 99 (Alito, J., concurring).
12 Ibid., 99–102 (Alito, J., concurring).
13 Ibid., 102 (Alito, J., concurring).

certainly varied, few would deny that their goal of incorporating African Americans into the political community was just as important as preventing the reemergence of a southern political structure with White supremacy at its foundation.

The conferral of citizenship by the Fourteenth Amendment and the Civil Rights Act of 1866 was a crucial second step – after the eradication of slavery – in bringing African Americans within the political community of "We the People." But just because one was entitled to the sovereign's protection does not mean that one has rights that the sovereign was bound to respect. The provision that Justice Alito dismissed as "power politics" gave Congress a more explicit role in defining the scope of the political community and the rights to which those within its confines were entitled.

After the Civil War, many people remained outside of the political community as defined by Article I, Section 2, which established the electorate for state and federal elections.[14] While North Carolina was the last state to abolish property qualifications for voting in 1856, tax-paying qualifications in many states continued to disenfranchise large swaths of the population.[15] Most states continued to disenfranchise women, although they enjoyed limited rights in Kentucky, and there was soon a movement in western states like Wyoming and Utah to give women the vote.[16] Thus, suffrage was far from universal, even after the war between the states. For the disenfranchised, they nominally retained their right to alter or abolish government, yet the reliance by the Confederacy on that right had significantly diminished it. In the end, the disenfranchised were left with few political rights, either in fact or theory, due to the need to sideline the alter or abolish right in the wake of the war.

Thus, the story of the Fourteenth Amendment, and in particular, Section 2 of that provision, is not only about the quest to give the right to vote national significance.

14 Outside of uniform federal action, states could only bring African Americans and women within the ambit of their local political communities. See *Dred Scott v. Sandford*, 60 U.S. (19 How.) 393, 422 (1856). In *Corfield v. Coryell*, Justice Bushrod Washington listed suffrage among the privileges of citizenship protected by Article IV. *Corfield v. Coryell*, 6 F. Cas. 546, 552 (C.C.E.D. Pa. 1825) (No. 3230). Despite *Corfield*'s language, however, no one believed that states were obligated to enfranchise a woman or African American who could vote in a sister jurisdiction. Justice Washington was referring to a default political community – white men who are citizens over the age of 21 – able to vote in every jurisdiction subject to whatever restrictions the state imposed within this category. One could say that the eradication of slavery meant that African Americans became a part of this political community by default. But the desire to keep some groups out of the political community – women, other minority populations, etc. – incentivized Republicans to continue to disaggregate citizenship and voting. Thus, citizenship – even in Justice Washington's formulation – is necessary, but not sufficient for voting.

15 Stanley L. Engerman and Kenneth L. Sokoloff, *The Evolution of Suffrage Institutions in the New World* (Cambridge: National Bureau of Economic Research, 2001).

16 "The first victory for [woman] suffrage on the American continent came by action of the Wyoming territorial legislature in 1869. The Utah territorial legislature enacted woman suffrage the following year. Woman suffrage was provided in the constitutions of both of these states when they were admitted to the union, Wyoming in 1890 and Utah in 1896." David R. Berman, "Male Support of Woman Suffrage: An Analysis of Voting Patterns in the Mountain West" (1987) 11 *Social Science History* 281–294, 292 fn 1. See also T.A. Larson, "Woman Suffrage in Wyoming" (1965) 56 *The Pacific Northwest Quarterly* 57–66, 57.

Importantly, it is also a story about the convergence of two different communities: (1) those who could exercise the traditional right to alter or abolish government, a natural right that had belonged to every (White?) person on the eve of the war, and (2) those who could exercise the right to vote, which was a political right belonging only to a subset of the population. Section 2 extended federal protection to the right to vote, encouraging the transition from violent exercises of the alter or abolish power to the more peaceful process of voting in elections. In promoting the right to vote as the core expression of sovereign authority, Section 2 also represented the creation of a new political community that was built on nondiscriminatory access to the ballot that would be exercised in biracial political systems in which African American men would be key participants entitled to a share of the political power.

For this reason, Section 2 is, in fact, a "theory of the Constitution," in the sense that it fundamentally redefined the contours of "We the Voters" and altered the conditions upon which states could grant entry into that category. It constructively amended the Constitution of Political Structure – including the Guarantee Clause – and enhanced congressional power under others – notably, the Elections Clause and Article I, Section 5. Because of Section 2, the general wisdom about what constituted republican government and how Congress could police it underwent a significant transition. It truly gave meaning to the concept of multi-clausal congressional power over elections. But it was unclear in 1868 whether Section 2's regime of indirect coercion would be enough to prevent disenfranchisement on a massive scale, particularly if Southerners were willing to pay the price of reduced representation.[17] Standing alone, Section 2 left too much of the antebellum framework in place and ignored the unpredictability of politics. Despite these shortcomings, this provision empowered Congress to enforce a particular theory of representation – or the idea that he who has a political existence, as defined by federal (and not state) law, was entitled to representation.

Most importantly, Section 2 was supposed to be an integral part of a multi-year, multi-step process designed to safeguard the civil and political rights of the formerly enslaved and, together with subsequent legislative enactments, function as a structural reset for both republican government and congressional power.[18] The Fifteenth

17 "Comments of Senator Wilson, 40th Congress, Third Session, January 28, 1869," 40 *Congressional Globe* (Washington, D.C.: Congressional Globe Office, 1869), part 1, p. 672. ("The crowning act of emancipation, the great constitutional amendment, was sternly resisted. The fourteenth article of amendment to the Constitution, the civil rights bill, the Freedman's Bureau bill, every measure that we have passed to enlarge the rights of privileges of that emancipated race, to protect them, to life them, has encountered not only the sternest opposition of those who were against us politically, but it has encountered the prejudices of a portion of those who ordinarily vote with us."); Eric Foner, *Reconstruction: America's Unfinished Revolution, 1863–1877* (New York: Harper & Row, 1988), pp. 412–459 (discussing how some Southern Democrats tried to convince the nation that they were beyond racial issues, but that most still refused to accept the reality of Reconstruction and African American suffrage).

18 See generally Bruce Ackerman, *We the People, Volume 2: Transformations* (Boston: Harvard University Press, 1998) (discussing how select moments – the Founding, Reconstruction, and the

Amendment further defined the terms of federal intervention, laying out specific restrictions that states were bound by under the revamped Constitution of Political Rights.[19] The Amendment, ratified two years after the Fourteenth, cemented the political identity of African Americans and the independent federal significance of the right to vote. It definitively answered the question, left open by Section 2, of whether states retained the authority to discriminate on the basis of race if they were willing to pay the penalty of reduced representation with a resounding no.

And federal legislation enacted contemporaneously with and pursuant to these Amendments – from the Military Reconstruction Act of 1867[20] to the Enforcement Acts of 1870[21] and 1871[22] – remade the South (and, to a lesser extent, the North) into the majoritarian societies to which the Guarantee Clause had alluded and the Second Founding sought to manifest.[23]

The new state governments created through the Military Reconstruction Act of 1867, which was enacted pursuant to the Guarantee Clause, provided a clean slate

New Deal – were pivotal in constitutional history because they realigned the body politic with the "fundamental values that are usually taken as the constitutional baseline in normal political life.").

19 The text of the Fifteenth Amendment reads as follows: "Section 1. The right of citizens of the United States to vote shall not be denied or abridged by the United States or by any state on account of race, color, or previous condition of servitude. Section 2. The Congress shall have power to enforce this article by appropriate legislation." United States Constitution Amend. 15.

20 An Act to Provide for the More Efficient Government of the Rebel States, ch. 153, 14 Stat. 428 (1867) (enacted March 2, 1867) [Military Reconstruction Act I]. There were four federal statutes altogether that comprise what became known as the "Military Reconstruction Acts." The other three are: An Act supplementary to an Act entitled "An Act to provide for the more efficient Government of the Rebel States," passed March 2nd, 1867, and to facilitate Restoration, ch. 6, 15 Stat. 2 (1867) (enacted March 23, 1867) [Military Reconstruction Act II]; An Act supplementary to an Act entitled "An Act to provide for the more efficient Government of the Rebel States," passed March 2nd, 1867, and the Act supplementary thereto, passed on the 23rd day of March, 1867, ch. 30, 15 Stat. 14 (1867) (enacted July 19, 1867) [Military Reconstruction Act III]; and An Act to amend the Act passed March 23rd, 1867, entitled "An Act supplementary to 'An Act to provide for the more efficient Government of the rebel States,' passed March second, eighteen hundred and sixty-seven, and to facilitated their Restoration," ch. 25, 15 Stat. 41 (1868) (enacted March 11, 1868) [Military Reconstruction Act IV].

21 An Act to enforce the Rights of Citizens of the United States to vote in the several States of the Union, and for other Purposes, ch. 114, 16 Stat. 140 (1870) [Enforcement Act of 1870].

22 An Act to amend an Act approved May 31, 1870, entitled "An Act to enforce the Rights of Citizens of the United States to vote in the several States of this Union, and for other Purposes," ch. 99, 16 Stat. 433 (1871) [Enforcement Act of 1871].

23 "Comments of Representative Farnsworth, 39th Congress, First Session, January 23, 1866," 36 *Congressional Globe* (Washington, D.C.: Congressional Globe Office, 1866), part 1, p. 383. ("I deny that a State has the right to disfranchise a majority, or even a minority of its citizens because of class or race. And I say that that provision of the Constitution which makes it the duty of the General Government to 'guaranty to every State in this Union a republican form of government' ought to be taken into consideration by this Congress and enforced. Does a State that denies the elective franchise to one half of its citizens possess a republican form of government? Where a large portion of the citizens of a State-the men who are required to pay taxes and perform military duty, to contribute their money and their strength in support of the Government-are denied the elective franchise, is that a republican form of government? I say that it is a libel upon republicanism; it is not a republican form of government; it is neither republican in form nor in substance.").

for biracial democracy. The Act not only presented an opportunity to gauge the country's temperament on the issue of universal suffrage, but Thaddeus Stevens and others believed that the Act would sufficiently address concerns that Section 2 did not go far enough in inducing suffrage because it did not confer an affirmative right to vote.[24] Instead, the biracial state constitutional convention delegates elected in the wake of the Military Reconstruction Act would be tasked with constructing new state constitutions to address the discriminatory voting requirements that Section 2, once ratified, would prohibit.

Through the Reconstruction Acts of 1868 to 1872, the former Confederate states were brought back into the Union under new terms. Each state was required to adopt a new constitution as a condition of readmission, one that reflected the values of the post-war order and embraced multi-racial democracy.[25] These constitutions expanded voting rights and tempered the once-powerful provisions allowing citizens to "alter or abolish" their governments, and in the process, made watershed changes to the very concept of republican government that demonstrated that they were more than simply administrative revisions.

Congress, wary of backsliding, sought to protect these fragile, multi-racial political coalitions through a sweeping set of federal laws: the Enforcement Acts of 1870 and 1871, passed under the combined authority of the Fourteenth Amendment, the Fifteenth Amendment, and the Elections Clause.[26] These provisions cemented

[24] William Gillette, *The Right to Vote: Politics and the Passage of the Fifteenth Amendment* (Baltimore: Johns Hopkins University Press, 1969), p. 31 ("The climax of the suffrage drama in the Thirty-ninth Congress was the decision to adopt the fifth section of the First Reconstruction Act of March 2, 1867. Congress now required Negro suffrage as a condition for readmitting the former Confederate states to the Union and seating their representatives in Congress.").

[25] An Act to admit the State of Arkansas to Representation in Congress, ch. 69, 15 Stat. 72 (1868); An Act to admit the States of North Carolina, South Carolina, Louisiana, Georgia, Alabama, and Florida to Representation in Congress, ch. 70, 15 Stat. 73 (1868); An Act authorizing the Submission of the Constitutions of Virginia, Mississippi, and Texas, to a Vote of the People, and authorizing the Election of State Officers, provided by the said Constitutions, and Members of Congress, ch. 17, 16 Stat. 40 (1869); An Act relating to the State of Georgia, ch. 299, 16 Stat. 363 (1870); An Act to admit the State of Virginia to the Representation in Congress of the United States, ch. 10, 16 Stat. 62 (1870).

[26] In addition to the Enforcement Acts, Section 3 of the Fourteenth Amendment also provided important protection for these new state governments by preventing former Confederates from being reelected to state or federal office. This provision, also known as the Disqualification Clause, reads as follows:

> No person shall be a Senator or Representative in Congress, or elector of President, or hold any office, civil or military, under the United States, or under any State, who, having previously taken an oath, as a member of Congress, or as an officer of the United States, or as a member of any State legislature, or as an executive or judicial officer of any State, to support the Constitution of the United States, shall have engaged in insurrection or rebellion against the same, or given aid or comfort to the enemies thereof. But Congress may by a vote of two-thirds of each House, remove such disability.

a new vision of political community, one in which "We the Voters" and "We the People" truly included those once excluded.

This ambitious legal and political architecture reflected a web of constitutional and statutory provisions intended to work in concert to elevate voting rights as the cornerstone of legitimate governance. States and state officials that illegally disenfranchised voters could be penalized under Section 2, through criminal penalties in the Enforcement Acts, or by Congress's refusal to seat their representatives under Article I, Section 5 of the Constitution. This winding labyrinth of federal constitutional and statutory provisions – representing new iterations of the Constitutions of Political Rights and Structure – would set an important precedent for the use of expanded federal power, aggregated across multiple constitutional provisions, but nonetheless, fall far short of what was needed to create the new society that congressional Republicans envisioned.

6.1 A CLEAN SLATE: THE MILITARY RECONSTRUCTION ACT, THE DECLINE OF ALTER OR ABOLISH, AND THE RISE OF A NEW ELECTORATE

The battlefields of the Civil War extended well beyond the halls of Appomattox, where Generals Grant and Lee came to terms on the end of the war.[27] Bloodshed continued in the cotton and tobacco fields of the South, littered with the bodies of

United States Constitution Amend. 14, s. 3. By disqualifying former confederates from state and federal office, Section 3 also protected the newly formed southern governments from being usurped by the former confederates. For more on this provision, see Gerard N. Magliocca, "Amnesty and Section Three of the Fourteenth Amendment" (2021) 36 *Constitutional Commentary* 87–130 (providing a descriptive account of Section 3's adoption and enforcement); William Baude and Michael S. Paulsen, "The Sweep and Force of Section 3" (2024) 172 *University of Pennsylvania Law Review* 605–745 (arguing that Section 3 of the Fourteenth Amendment is a self-executing part of the Constitution that should be enforced by every federal or state official who judges candidate qualifications for elected office).

27 The meeting at which Robert E. Lee surrendered to Ulysses S. Grant took place on April 9, 1865, in a parlor of the Appomattox, Virginia home of Wilmer McLean. According to David C. Ward, Senior Historian of the National Portrait Gallery,

> the occasion was awkward, and the two generals exchanged small talk until Lee reminded Grant why they were there. Grant, who had the ability for swift and clear written expression, quickly drafted the terms of surrender, which focused only on military matters. Lee asked that the Southerners be allowed to keep their horses, which they owned; Grant agreed. Grant also agreed to distribute rations to the hungry Confederate army.

David C. Ward, "Lee Surrendering to Grant at Appomattox," facetoface: A Blog from the National Portrait Gallery, https://npg.si.edu/blog/lee-surrendering-grant-appomattox. Ward's remarks on the topic, published in connection with the exhibit of a portrait commemorating the occasion, which shows the two generals in a small, simple room with only a few aides, concluded as follows: "In retrospect, the surrender at Appomattox has become invested with nostalgia in part because of the dignified and humane conduct of both Grant and Lee in this final act of a heroic and tragic year of war between America's two greatest generals." Ibid.

Black people who refused pseudo-slavery, exploitive work contracts, or worse, who had dared to vote.[28] Josiah T. Walls went even further than those who had lost their lives for less – he sought to serve.

Walls was a distinguished Black man who became a political force in Florida, eventually serving as the mayor of Gainesville, a county commissioner, a state senator, and Florida's first Black congressional representative. Born into slavery in 1842, Walls was forced to join the Confederate army, but later voluntarily joined the United States Colored Troops in 1863 after he was captured by the Union Army.[29]

After completing his army service with the rank of corporal, he retired to Florida where he became very active in state politics.[30] In 1868, he served as a delegate to the state constitutional convention and was also elected to the Florida House of Representatives that year, among the first cohort of Black men to serve in legislatures in the former Confederate states during Reconstruction.[31] The danger that a Black man faced in running for office cannot be understated. In October 1869, the Ku Klux Klan brutally beat Abram Colby, an African American member of the Georgia House of Representatives.[32] White men also lynched Robert Burke, a Black state legislator from South Carolina, in August 1870.[33]

The exemplary and courageous service of Walls and others willing to risk their lives to engage in political participation and activism directly raised the question of who should be part of the new majority in the post–Thirteenth Amendment era. Congress used its authority under the Guarantee Clause to enact the Military Reconstruction Act of 1867 and suspend southern governments that deprived African

28 This mistreatment was codified in southern states in what were known as the Black Codes. These laws "recognized the legal act of emancipation, but placed the Negro in a vague limbo between slavery and freedom," and, under them, "the state legislatures compelled the Freedmen to work under a contract system of labor." Patrick Sowle, "The Abolition of Slavery" (1968) 52 *The Georgia Historical Quarterly* 237–255, 251. Some states' Black Codes "restricted the Negroes to certain occupations, usually agriculture" and reflected what was viewed by southern whites as "the inferiority of the colored man, [as the] words 'master' and 'servant' appear repeatedly in them." Ibid. In addition to the systemic violence against the formerly enslaved embodied in the Black Codes, southern Black people also dealt with localized violence during the postbellum period. "Random violence was often used to discourage political participation…[and] was also a method of labor control." Pete Daniel, "The Metamorphosis of Slavery, 1865–1900" (1979) 66 *Journal of American History* 88–99, 97. When Black people dared "[t]o question a planter's books, to complain about a settlement, to shirk work[,]" all of those actions "became excuses for violence [against them]." Ibid.

29 United States House of Representatives, "Biography of Josiah Thomas Walls," https://history.house.gov/People/Detail/23324; Paige Fry, "A Forgotten Obituary: The Life of Josiah T. Walls," *The Independent Florida Alligator*, April 23, 2019, www.alligator.org/article/2019/04/a-forgotten-obituary-the-life-of-josiah-t-walls.

30 Ibid.

31 Peter D. Klingman, "Josiah T. Walls and the Black Tactics of Race in Post Civil War Florida" (April/May 1974) 37 *Negro History Bulletin* 242–247, 243–244.

32 Equal Justice Initiative, *Slavery in America: The Montgomery Slave Trade* (Montgomery: Equal Justice Initiative, 2018), pp. 64–65, https://eji.org/reports/slavery-in-america/.

33 Equal Justice Initiative, *Reconstruction in America: Racial Violence after the Civil War, 1865–1876* (Montgomery: Equal Justice Initiative, 2020), p. 31, https://eji.org/report/reconstruction-in-america/.

Americans of civil and political rights as non-republican in form, thereby allowing individuals like Walls – the formerly enslaved – to serve in public office. Proposed by Thaddeus Stevens on May 28, 1866, the Act created a blueprint for state governance, paving the way for the most racially diverse governments with the broadest electorates in United States history.[34]

In its preamble, the first Military Reconstruction Act expressly declared that "[n]o legal state governments or adequate protection for life or property exists in the rebel States of Virginia, North Carolina, South Carolina, Georgia, Mississippi, Alabama, Louisiana, Florida, Texas and Arkansas; and whereas it is necessary that peace and good order should be enforced in said States until loyal and republican state governments can be legally established."[35] The Act suspended the governments of the southern states that had been established under President Johnson's reconstruction plan until they met three requirements viewed as essential to republican government: (1) ratify the Fourteenth Amendment; (2) hold constitutional conventions staffed by delegates "elected by the male citizens of said state, twenty-one years old and upward, of whatever race, color, or previous condition"; and (3) adopt constitutions that "provide that the elective franchise shall be enjoyed by all such persons as have the qualifications herein stated for electors of delegates…"[36] Disenfranchisement, according to the statute, was only appropriate for those who "participat[ed] in the rebellion or for felony at common law."[37]

34 See "Comments of Representative Cullom, 40th Congress, Third Session, January 27, 1869," 40 *Congressional Globe* (Washington, D.C.: Congressional Globe Office, 1869), part 1, p. 651 ("On the 2d of March, 1867, Congress, by a law passed over the President's veto, declared the State governments of the rebel States only provisional, gave military protection to all the people, and clothed all the male citizens of those States – except felons and those rendered ineligible to hold office under the fourteenth amendment – without regard to race, color, or previous condition, with the right to vote, with the right to proceed in the work of establishing civil government. By this Congress struck the foundation stone upon which republican government must be built, if built to stand."). These new governments became the vehicles for Black people to firmly assert their new political identities given that, as historian Eric Foner has argued, by 1867, "politics emerged as the principal focus of black aspirations." Eric Foner, "Rights and the Constitution in Black Life during the Civil War and Reconstruction" (1987) 74 *Journal of American History* 863–883, 874. Foner describes the period immediately after the Civil War as a time of political awakening for formerly enslaved Black people throughout the country and especially in the south, observing that, "[w]hen not deterred by violence, blacks eagerly attended political gatherings and voted in extraordinary numbers; their turnout in many elections exceeded 90 percent." Ibid., 878.

35 An Act to Provide for the More Efficient Government of the Rebel States, ch. 153, 14 Stat. 428 (1867) [Military Reconstruction Act I].

36 An Act to Provide for the More Efficient Government of the Rebel States, ch. 153, 14 Stat. 428, 429 (1867) [Military Reconstruction Act I]. Not all representatives agreed that voting should be limited to males. See "Comments of Representative Ashley, 39th Congress, First Session, May 29, 1866," 36 *Congressional Globe* (Washington, D.C.: Congressional Globe Office, 1866), part 3, p. 2879 ("It will be noticed, that in prescribing the qualifications of electors, I omit the word 'male' and use the words 'all citizens of the United States above the age of twenty-one years.' I did this purposely, as I am unwilling to prohibit any State from enfranchising its women if they desire to do so.").

37 Ibid., s. 5.

In these requirements, one sees a framework for republican government that includes a state constitution adopted through majoritarian processes by an electorate defined by age, residency, citizenship, and felony status, rather than by race.[38] Once readmitted, the reconstructed states would provide the baseline for republican government, as referenced in the Guarantee Clause, from that point forward. So long as their governments failed to meet these objectives, however, Congress had no obligation to seat representatives elected from those states.[39] Toward this end, representatives and senators from the former Confederacy seeking to take their seats had their credentials referred to the Joint Committee on Reconstruction.[40]

Republican-led constitutional conventions amended alter or abolish provisions in state constitutions and barred ex-confederates from assuming elected office, reflecting a shift from a natural rights framework to a political rights regime that featured an expanded electorate and an expectation that governmental change would happen through orderly processes.[41] Given its unpopularity, African American suffrage had proven difficult to implement through direct federal mandate – hence the structure of Section 2[42] – but voting became a natural replacement for the more robust alter or abolish provisions that had once existed. This change could be implemented at the state level, from the ground up, even if done at the behest of the federal government. The former Confederacy ultimately became a blueprint for a new republican ideal.

38 And not just any felony, but a felony at common law. See Franita Tolson, "'In Whom Is the Right of Suffrage?': The Reconstruction Acts as Sources of Constitutional Meaning" (2021) *University of Pennsylvania Law Review* 2014–2060.

39 "Resolution offered by Representative Spalding, 39th Congress, Second Session, December 10, 1866," 37 *Congressional Globe* (Washington, D.C.: Congressional Globe Office, 1866), part 1, p. 48 ("Resolved, That the committee on reconstruction be requested to inquire into the expediency of passing a joint resolution declaratory of the purpose of Congress in the reception of Senators and Representatives from the rebellious States, respectively, upon the ratification by them of the constitutional amendment and the establishment of republican forms of government not inconsistent with the Constitution of the United States.").

40 See, e.g., "Presentation of Representative Cooper, 39th Congress, Second Session, December 12, 1866," 37 *Congressional Globe* (Washington, D.C.: Congressional Globe Office, 1866), part 1, p. 86 (presenting the credentials of Benjamin H. Epperson, second congressional district of Texas); "Presentation of the Speaker of the House, 39th Congress, Second Session, December 11, 1866," 37 *Congressional Globe* (Washington, D.C.: Congressional Globe Office, 1867), part 1, p. 66 (referring Alexander H. Jones, Seventh Congressional District of North Carolina); "Presentation of Representative Cooper, 39th Congress, Second Session, December 13, 1866," 37 *Congressional Globe* (Washington, D.C.: Congressional Globe Office, 1867), part 1, p. 109 (presenting the credentials of J. Caleb Wiley, second district of Alabama).

41 See, e.g., Constitution of the State of Alabama art. VII, s. 3 (1867) ("[T]he following classes of persons shall not be permitted to register, vote or hold office: 1st, Those, who, during the later rebellion, inflicted, or caused to be inflicted, any cruel or usual punishment upon any soldier … of the United States, or who, in any other way, violated the rules of civilized warfare. 2d, Those who may be disqualified from holding office by the proposed amendment to the Constitution of the United States, known as 'Article XIV' …."). See also United States Constitution Amend. XIV s. 3.

42 See generally Foner, *Reconstruction* (discussing the challenges faced by the ex-slaves in gaining political and civil rights during Reconstruction).

The shift from alter or abolish to voting also reflected the view that the vehicle for expressing this sovereignty had to be tempered by values of republicanism, which now included expansive suffrage rights policed by state and federal law. Republicanism, and the majoritarian principles that underlie it, trumped the alter or abolish right invoked by the Confederates because the war established that the Union was indissoluble.[43] The right had already been on shaky ground prior to the war as incidents – at home and abroad – demonstrated that it was not, in fact, a natural right available to everyone (see, e.g., Shays' Rebellion,[44] the Dorr Rebellion,[45] the Haitian Revolution,[46] etc.). Thus, it was not surprising that the natural right to alter or abolish government ultimately yielded to positive law.

And yield it did. States that had alter or abolish clauses prior to the war, such as Arkansas, Texas, and Florida, instituted provisions that were less far reaching than their predecessors of the 1830s while simultaneously increasing political protections in their post-war constitutions. Only two of the state constitutions adopted in the former Confederacy, Virginia[47] and North Carolina,[48] added alter or abolish provisions during Reconstruction. But all of these provisions – both the newly added and the preexisting clauses – were qualified in favor of federal power and extensive protection of individual rights.[49]

For example, Arkansas's 1868 Constitution contained a provision that allowed citizens to alter or reform government, but it limited their ability to dissolve their connection with or rebel against the federal government.[50] In contrast, its 1836 and 1864

43 See *Texas v. White*, 74 U S. 700, 726 (1869) (holding that the ordinances of secession "were absolutely null" and "utterly without operation in law").

44 See Chapter 4.

45 Ibid.

46 Ibid.

47 Virginia's constitution constrained this power by referencing federal law and disavowing a right of secession. See Constitution of Virginia art. I, s. 5 (1870) (adding an alter or abolish provision); ibid., art. 1, s. 2 (stating that "all attempts, from whatever source or upon whatever pretext, to dissolve said Union or to sever said nation, are unauthorized"); Ibid, art. 1, s. 3 ("That the Constitution of the United States, and the laws of Congress passed in pursuance thereof, constitute the supreme law of the land, to which paramount allegiance and obedience are due from every citizen, anything in the Constitution, ordinances or laws of any State to the contrary notwithstanding.").

48 Like Virginia's constitution, North Carolina's constitution constrained this power by referencing federal law and disavowing a right of secession. See Constitution of the State of North Carolina art. I, s. 3 (1868) (adding an alter or abolish provision); Ibid., art. I, s. 4 ("That this State shall ever remain a member of the American Union; that the people thereof are part of the American nation; that there is no right on the part of this State to secede, and that all attempts from whatever source or upon whatever pretext, to dissolve said Union, or to sever said nation, ought to be resisted with the whole power of the State.").

49 Notably, Georgia did not have an alter or abolish provision prior to the Civil War, and adopted language in its 1861 Constitution that would limit the ability of the people to change the government. See Constitution of the State of Georgia art. I, s. 2 (1861) ("God has ordained that men shall live under government; but as the forms and administration of civil government are in human, and therefore, fallible hands, they may be altered, or modified whenever the safety or happiness of the governed requires it. No government should be changed for light or transient causes; nor unless upon reasonable assurance that a better will be established.").

50 Constitution of the State of Arkansas art. I, s. 1 (1868).

Constitutions gave the people an unqualified right to alter or abolish government at will.[51] Arkansas's 1836 Constitution also provided "[t]hat all elections shall be free and equal,"[52] and granted voting rights to "[e]very free white male citizen ... who shall have attained the age of twenty-one years, and who shall have been a citizen of this State six months."[53] Like Alabama, these criteria were expanded in 1868 to eliminate the race requirement and exclude former Confederates from officeholding, consistent with the penalty in Section 3 of the Fourteenth Amendment for those who engaged in "rebellion, or other crime."[54]

Texas's 1836 Constitution likewise granted the right to vote to every citizen, defining citizens as "all free white persons,"[55] and "who [have] attained the age of twenty-one years."[56] However, the right to vote described in the state's 1869 constitution was more expansive than its predecessor, enfranchising those "twenty-one years and upwards, not laboring under the disabilities named in this Constitution, without distinction of race, color or former condition."[57]

This section was markedly different than the suffrage provision of the 1866 Texas Constitution that Congress rejected, which limited voting to "[e]very free male person" rather than "[e]very male citizen."[58] The reference to "free" male persons invited discretion to disenfranchise Black men who had been relegated to a status of pseudo-slavery following the Black codes adopted across the South in the wake of the Civil War. The 1866 Texas Constitution also did not disenfranchise former Confederates,[59] and it retained the same broad alter or abolish language as its 1836 counterpart.[60] In addition to more expansive voting rights and penalties for former Confederates, the 1869 Constitution eliminated the alter or abolish provision and added a preamble to its Bill of Rights, declaring, "That the heresies of nullification and secession, which brought the country to grief, may be eliminated from future political discussion."[61]

Florida also had an alter or abolish provision in its constitution at the time of secession,[62] but it amended this provision in 1868 to subordinate the people's alter

[51] Constitution of the State of Arkansas art. II, s. 2 (1864) ("That all power is inherent in the people; and all free governments are founded on their authority .... For the advancement of these ends, they have, at all times, an unqualified right to alter, reform or abolish their government, in such manner as they may think proper."); Constitution of the State of Arkansas art. II, s. 2 (1836) (same).

[52] Constitution of the State of Arkansas art. II, s. 5 (1836).

[53] Ibid., art. IV, s. 2.

[54] Constitution of the State of Arkansas art. VIII, ss. 2–5 (1868). See also United States Constitution Amend. XIV, s. 3.

[55] Constitution of the Republic of Texas art. VI General Provisions s. 6 (1836).

[56] Ibid., art. VI, s. 11.

[57] Constitution of the State of Texas art. VI, s. 1 (1869).

[58] See ibid.; see also Constitution of the State of Texas art. III, s. 1 (1866).

[59] Constitution of the State of Texas art. III, s. 1 (1866).

[60] Ibid., art. I, s. 1 ("All political power is inherent in the people, and all free governments are founded on their authority, and instituted for their benefit; and they have at all times the unalienable right to alter, reform or abolish their form of government, in such manner as they may think expedient.").

[61] Constitution of the State of Texas art. I (1869).

[62] Constitution or Form of Government, for the People of Florida art. I, s. 2 (1838).

or abolish power to "the paramount allegiance of every citizen" to the federal government and to circumscribe the ability of the people "to dissolve their connection therewith."[63] Like Arkansas, the 1838 Florida Constitution provided for "free and equal" elections, extending the vote to every "[e]very free white male person of the age of twenty-one years and upwards" who was a U.S. citizen, but subject to a lengthy residency requirement of "two years next preceding the election at which he shall offer to vote."[64] Florida kept the alter or abolish language from its 1838 Constitution in the document submitted to Congress in 1865 as a condition of readmission, but Congress rejected it.[65] Notably, the rejected 1865 constitution retained its predecessor's voter qualification standards, limiting suffrage to free White males.[66] Thanks to Josiah Walls and other Republican allies, the 1868 constitution was significantly more inclusive, extending voting rights to "[e]very male person of the age of twenty-one years … of whatever race, color, nationality, or previous condition, who shall … be a citizen," and it reduced the residency requirement from two years to one year.[67]

Other Reconstruction-era constitutions did not have traditional alter or abolish provisions, but Congress nonetheless rejected them for lacking adequate protection for the voting rights of the formerly enslaved.[68] For example, Congress vetoed South Carolina's 1865 Constitution on these grounds, but approved a revised constitution three years later that was much more conciliatory toward voting rights.[69] Unlike the 1865 Constitution, the 1868 Constitution gave the people the right to "at all times … modify their form of government,"[70] but subject to the caveat that "[n]o power, civil or military, shall at any time interfere to prevent the free exercise of the right of voting in this State."[71]

63 Constitution Adopted by the [Florida] Convention of 1885, Declaration of Rights, s. 2 (1885); Constitution of the State of Florida, Declaration of Rights, s. 2 (1868).

64 Constitution or Form of Government, for the People of Florida art I, s. 4; art. VI, s. 1 (1838).

65 Compare Constitution of the State of Florida art. 1, s. 2 (1868) (removing alter or abolish language), with Constitution or Form of Government for the People of Florida art. I, s. 2 (1865) (including alter or abolish language). See also Jerrell H. Shofner, "Custom, Law, and History: The Enduring Influence of Florida's 'Black Code'" (1976) 55 *Florida Historical Quarterly* 1–22.

66 Constitution or Form of Government for the People of Florida art. VI, s. 5 (1865).

67 Constitution of the State of Florida art. XIV, s. 1 (1868).

68 See W. Lewis Burke, "Killing, Cheating, Legislating, and Lying: A History of Voting Rights in South Carolina after the Civil War," (2006) 57 *South Carolina Law Review* 859–888, 861–862.

69 South Carolina did not have an alter or abolish provision in its constitution at the time of the Civil War, although political power was said to derive from the people. Specifically, the constitution stated: "All power is originally vested in the people; and all free governments are founded on their authority, and are instituted for their peace, safety, and happiness." Constitution of the State of South Carolina art. 9, s. 1 (1790). This provision remained essentially unchanged in the constitutions of 1861 and 1865. Constitution of the State of South Carolina art. 9, § 1 (1861); Ibid., art. 9, § 1 (1865).

70 Compare Constitution of the Commonwealth of South Carolina art I, s. 3 (1868) ("All political power is vested in and derived from the people only; therefore, they have the right, at all times, to modify their form of government"), with Constitution of the State of South Carolina art. 9, s. 1 (1790), Constitution of the State of South Carolina art. 9, s. 1 (1861), and Constitution of the State of South Carolina art. 9, s. 1 (1865) ("All power is originally vested in the people; and all free governments are founded on their authority, and are instituted for their peace, safety, and happiness.").

71 Constitution of the Commonwealth of South Carolina art. II, s. 2 (1868).

Like South Carolina, the Alabama Constitution of 1868 gave its citizens the right to "change" but not abolish the government.[72] In contrast, the 1819 Alabama Constitution had given the people "a right to alter, reform, or abolish their form of government, in such manner as they may think expedient."[73] This document similarly provided that "[e]very white male person of the age of twenty one years, or upwards, who shall be a citizen of the United States, and shall have resided in this State one year next proceeding an election, and the last three months within the county, city, or town in which he offers to vote, shall be deemed a qualified elector."[74] The state's 1868 constitution eliminated the race restriction, reduced the required residency to six months instead of a year,[75] and added a requirement that all electors, prior to registering to vote, take an oath to "support and maintain the Constitution and laws of the United States"; "never countenance or aid in the secession of this State from the United States"; and "accept the civil and political equality of all men."[76]

Tennessee kept its alter or abolish provision in both its 1835 and 1870 Constitutions, but its 1870 Constitution specifically limited the circumstances under which this power could be exercised to majoritarian political processes:

> The Legislature shall have the right, at any time by law, to submit to the people the question of calling a Convention to alter, reform or abolish this Constitution, and when upon such submission, a majority of all the votes cast shall be in favor of said proposition, then delegates shall be chosen, and the Convention shall assemble in such mode and manner as shall be prescribed.[77]

Some states added alter or abolish provisions back into their constitutions in the 1870s, after removing them at the behest of Congress. And the return of alter or abolish often signaled the end of pro-democracy reforms that had defined the post–Civil War period.

For example, Texas amended its constitution in 1876, reinstating its alter or abolish provision, but subject to "the preservation of a republican form of government" rather than returning to the inalienable "right to alter, reform, or abolish their government" that had existed under the 1836 Constitution.[78] By 1876, Texas had

[72] Constitution of the State of Alabama art. I, s. 3 (1867) ("That all political power is inherent in the people, and all free governments are founded on their authority, and instituted for their benefit; and that, therefore, they have, at all times, an inherent right to change their form of government, in such manner as they may deem expedient."); see also Constitution of the State of Alabama art. I s. 2 (1901) (same); Constitution of the State of Alabama art. I, s. 3 (1875) (same).

[73] Constitution of the State of Alabama art. I, s. 2 (1819).

[74] Ibid., art. III, s. 5.

[75] Constitution of the State of Alabama art. VII, s. 2 (1867)

[76] Ibid., art. VII, s. 4.

[77] Constitution of the State of Tennessee art. IX, s. 3 (1870). The 1835 constitution, although it contained an alter or abolish provision similar to the 1870 version, did not provide a vehicle for abolishing the constitution through official means. See Constitution of the State of Tennessee art. XI, s. 3 (1835) (including a process for amending, but not abolishing, the constitution).

[78] Constitution of the State of Texas art. I, s. 2 (1876).

already embarked on what would be a decades-long effort to disenfranchise African American and Latino voters, so the expectation was that all political power would be in the hands of White, Democratic voters and that election-related violence would be localized.[79]

In Arkansas, Reconstruction ended in 1874, spearheaded by a constitutional convention dominated by former Confederates and Democrats who rolled back the reforms of the 1868 constitution. Arkansas reinstituted the alter or abolish provision that existed in its 1836 and 1864 Constitutions, giving citizens the right to "alter, reform or abolish … [government] in such manner as they may think proper,"[80] although this right was qualified by an expansive requirement of free elections:

> Elections shall be free and equal. No power, civil or military, shall ever interfere to prevent the free exercise of the right of suffrage; nor shall any law be enacted, whereby the right to vote at any election shall be made to depend upon any previous registration of the elector's name; or whereby such right shall be impaired or forfeited, except for the commission of a felony at common law, upon lawful conviction thereof.[81]

The reinstitution of alter or abolish provisions in the mid-1870s reflected attempts by insurgent Democrats to recapture of the machinery of southern governments, create an all-White electorate, and maintain this electorate through force and violence. Effectively, the Arkansas provision can be read as free and fair elections for White male voters, disenfranchisement through force and fraud for everyone else.

Prior to these attempts by Southern Redeemers to recapture their Confederate past, Congress used the Reconstruction Acts to solidify a new foundation for republican government, an opportunity created by the Military Reconstruction Act's relegation of southern governments to conquered provinces that could be remade in a new republican ideal. Between 1868 and 1872, the new republicanism took shape in state constitutions that not only removed broad "alter or abolish" provisions but also extended voting rights to Black men, marking a significant shift in the structure of southern governments. By memorializing these governments in law, Congress

79 During the late nineteenth century, White Texans restricted non-whites from voting and participating in politics by establishing "clubs, unions, and associations … under the banner of the Democratic party" that "restricted membership to white citizens." Darlene C. Hine, "The Elusive Ballot: The Black Struggle against the Texas Democratic White Primary, 1932–1945" (1978) 81 *The Southwestern Historical Quarterly* 371–392, 371–372. The goal of these organizations, achieved through "hold[ing] primary elections to select [White] Democratic candidates" who would go on to run unopposed in general elections, was to turn Texas into "a one-party state with the Democratic party reigning supreme." Ibid., 372. Additionally, "in an effort to make Texas politics as white as possible, a poll tax amendment was added to the state's constitution in 1902." Ibid.

80 Constitution of Arkansas art. II, s. 1 (1874); Constitution of the State of Arkansas art. II, s. 2 (1864); Constitution of the State of Arkansas art. II, s. 2 (1836).

81 Constitution of Arkansas art III, s. 2 (1874).

was trying to stave off the evitable tide of Redemption that, as Arkansas and Texas foreshadowed, eventually engulfed the entire South.[82]

6.2 THE RECONSTRUCTION ACTS OF 1868–1872: THE NEW SOUTHERN GOVERNMENTS AS REPUBLICAN PARADIGMS

After states in the former Confederacy changed their constitutions to meet congressional specifications, Congress passed a series of Reconstruction Acts readmitting these states into the Union. These Reconstruction Acts provided, in relevant part:

> [T]he constitutions of neither of said States shall ever be so amended or changed as to deprive any citizen or class of citizens of the United States of the right to vote in said State, who are entitled to vote by the constitution thereof herein recognized, except as a punishment for such crimes as are now felonies at common law, whereof they shall have been duly convicted under laws equally applicable to all the inhabitants of said State....[83]

In passing these statutes, Congress sought to cement the political rights that African Americans obtained in the wake of the Civil War by making these new southern governments permanent. Congress made Black suffrage a condition of readmission, complimenting Section 2's penalty by setting the perimeters of "lawful" disenfranchisement and emphasizing the republican principle of majority will. Importantly, these provisions also suggest that Congress had an ongoing obligation, post-readmission, to ensure that southern states did not alter their constitutions to disenfranchise voters whom Congress had deemed to be eligible.[84] Under the Reconstruction Acts, each of the former Confederate states were required to have "framed constitutions of State government which are republican,"[85] a requirement that now had a different meaning than at ratification.

82 "By 1873, many white Southerners were calling for 'Redemption' – the return of white supremacy and the removal of rights for blacks – instead of Reconstruction. This political pressure to return to the old order was oftentimes backed up by mob and paramilitary violence, with the Ku Klux Klan, the White League, and the Red Shirts assassinating pro-Reconstruction politicians and terrorizing Southern blacks." National Endowment for the Humanities, "Reconstruction vs. Redemption," February 11, 2014, www.neh.gov/news/reconstruction-vs-redemption.

83 An Act to admit the States of North Carolina, South Carolina, Louisiana, Georgia, Alabama, and Florida to Representation in Congress, ch. 70, 15 Stat. 73, 73 (1868). See also Tolson, "In Whom Is the Right of Suffrage?," 2014–2060.

84 See, e.g., "Comments of Senator Howard, 40th Congress, Third Session, February 26, 1869," 40 *Congressional Globe* (Washington, D.C.: Congressional Globe Office, 1869), part 3, p. 1625 (arguing, in the context of the readmission of Virginia, that Congress can grant the right to vote through ordinary legislation and bind states into perpetuity).

85 An Act to admit the States of North Carolina, South Carolina, Louisiana, Georgia, Alabama, and Florida to Representation in Congress, ch. 70, 15 Stat. 73, 73 (1868).

In 1787, it was unclear whether the majoritarianism that James Madison and other founding fathers advocated as central to republicanism (and embraced by the Guarantee Clause) had to reflect either the will of a majority of the people of the state or a majority of its voters.[86] During the antebellum period, Congress assessed whether territories seeking admission as new states were republican in form, yet slavery politics dictated the rigor with which Congress policed these political systems.[87] The Twelfth Amendment had provided some clarification, by constructing a regime in which the president would be the preference of a majority of the voters within the state, either by selecting electors through popular election or appointment by a popularly elected state legislature.[88]

By 1868, Congress's position on this issue was clear – majoritarianism had to reflect the will of a majority of the *voters* within the state, and Congress would take an active role in defining the parameters of this community. The readmission of the former Confederate states was the first time that Congress clearly articulated the requirements of republicanism, free from the albatross of slavery and against the backdrop of more expansive suffrage requirements, first with Section 2 of the Fourteenth Amendment and then, in short order, with the Fifteenth Amendment. In the post–Civil War era, majoritarianism now required that civil and political rights be extended to all eligible individuals on a nondiscriminatory basis.

The limitations that the Reconstruction Acts imposed on southern states with respect to their citizens' voting rights shed light on the reach of Section 2 of the Fourteenth Amendment and, importantly, the universe of crimes for which one can be disenfranchised. Section 2, by its terms, permits states to disenfranchise "for participation in rebellion or other crime."[89] Clarifying this provision, the Acts readmitting Arkansas, North Carolina, South Carolina, Louisiana, Georgia, Alabama, Florida, Virginia, and Mississippi all contain similar language specifying that these states can disenfranchise their residents only for "punishment for such crimes as are now felonies at common law" rather than the hundreds of disenfranchising offenses that currently exist in these jurisdictions.[90] The Reconstruction Acts, by prohibiting

86 See Chapter 1.2 (arguing that the controversy over the election of 1800 and the subsequent adoption of the Twelfth Amendment helped clarify the centrality of voters to republican theory).

87 See Chapter 1.3 ("The debate over the Kansas-Nebraska Act in the early 1850s and the resulting violence in the territory reveal how much of Congress's power as well as the meaning of the republican guarantee was increasingly shaped by the national political controversy over slavery.").

88 See United States Constitution Amend. XII.

89 United States Constitution Amend. XIV, s. 2.

90 See An Act to admit the States of North Carolina, South Carolina, Louisiana, Georgia, Alabama, and Florida to Representation in Congress, ch. 70, 15 Stat. 73, 73 (1868) (conditioning state readmission on the requirement that the constitutions of these States never be amended to deprive a citizen the right to vote "except as a punishment for such crimes as are now felonies at common law"); An Act to admit the State of Arkansas to Representation in Congress, ch. 69, 15 Stat. 72, 72 (1868) (including a similar provision while readmitting Arkansas); An Act to admit the State of Virginia to the Representation in Congress of the United States, ch. 10, 16 Stat. 62, 63 (1870) (including a similar provision while readmitting Virginia); An Act to admit the State of Mississippi to Representation in the Congress

states from amending their constitutions to disenfranchise otherwise eligible voters for crimes not felonies at common law, reflected yet another shift of authority from the states to Congress over voting and elections.

The expansion of the writ of habeas corpus during Reconstruction also served as an informal check on jurisdictions that skirted these principles. Notably, the Habeas Corpus Act of 1867 allowed individuals to challenge their convictions under state and federal law in federal court on the grounds that the state had committed a federal constitutional or statutory violation.[91] Prior to the 1867 Act, the writ was only available for pretrial review of actions by executive officials and not post-trial conviction to challenge the actions of state courts.[92] The Act, by allowing collateral review of bogus state convictions that targeted the formerly enslaved,[93] provided a vehicle for negating convictions that would otherwise disenfranchise this population.[94]

Congress also used its authority under Article I, Section 5 to review the elections of its members to enforce the terms of the Reconstruction Amendments.[95] For example, in 1868, the Senate Committee on the Judiciary reviewed the credentials of two prospective Senators from Georgia. The question before the Committee was whether Georgia had complied with a provision of the Reconstruction Act of June 25, 1868 (governing the state's readmission) that prohibited any person disqualified under Section 3 of the Fourteenth Amendment from holding office.[96]

of the United States, ch. 19, 16 Stat. 67, 68 (1870) (including a similar provision while readmitting Mississippi). See also Tolson, "In Whom Is the Right of Suffrage?," 2014–2060.

91 This statute empowered federal judges "to grant writs of habeas corpus in all cases where any person may be restrained of his or her liberty in violation of the constitution[.]" An Act to amend "An Act to establish the judicial Courts of the United States," approved September 24th, 1789, ch. 28, 14 Stat. 385 (1867) [Habeas Corpus Act of 1867].

92 William M. Wiecek, "The Great Writ and Reconstruction: The Habeas Corpus Act of 1867" (1970) 36 *The Journal of Southern History* 530–548, 531. See also Lewis Mayers, "The Habeas Corpus Act of 1867: The Supreme Court as Legal Historian" (1965) 33 *University of Chicago Law Review* 31–59.

93 Those in Congress who supported the 1867 Habeas Corpus Act "sought to reach vagrancy, which the Black Codes punished as a criminal offense, with penalties including corporal punishment and forced servitude on plantations. Only by extending habeas corpus to permit review of state criminal convictions could Congress ameliorate the egregious harm perpetuated under state Black Codes." Michael P. O'Connor, "Time Out of Mind: Our Collective Amnesia about the History of the Privileges and Immunities Clause" (2004) 93 *Kentucky Law Journal* 659–736, 712.

94 At the conclusion of the habeas corpus proceedings, if the judge determines "that the petitioner is deprived of his or her liberty in contravention of the constitution or laws of the United States, he or she shall forthwith be discharged and set at liberty." An Act to amend "An Act to establish the judicial Courts of the United States," approved September 24th, 1789, ch. 28, 14 Stat. 385, 386 (1867) [Habeas Corpus Act of 1867].

95 United States Constitution Art. I, s. 5.

96 "Whiteley and Farrow vs. Hill and Miller of Georgia," in George S. Taft, *Compilation of Senate Election Cases from 1799 to 1885*, 3rd ed. (Washington, D.C.: Government Printing Office, 1903), p. 343. The Reconstruction Act of June 25, 1868, provided that, "no person prohibited from holding office under the United States or any State by section 3 of the proposed amendment to the

In the cases of Joshua Hill and H.V.M. Miller, the Committee found that members of the Georgia state legislature who appointed them to the Senate were themselves disqualified from serving in the state legislature.[97] The legislature had expelled its Black members in September 1868,[98] following the state's constitutional convention and legislative elections, replacing them with White men who had not only lost at the polls but were also constitutionally ineligible for office.[99] Four state senators admitted their prior affiliation with the Confederacy,[100] and there were allegations that up to thirty to forty members of the legislature were disqualified under Section 3.[101] U.S. Senate candidate Miller, in particular, had served as a surgeon in the Confederate army.[102] Thus, the Committee refused to seat Hill and Miller because they were selected pursuant to a flawed process that included the participation of disloyal individuals.[103]

Once Georgia was reorganized and entitled to representation, however, the Committee allowed Hill and Miller to take their seats in 1871 after each took a loyalty oath.[104] The Committee made similar determinations in other contested election cases, finding that individuals appointed after the state had been duly

Constitution of the United States, known as article 14, shall be deemed eligible to any office in said State unless relieved from disability as provided in said amendment." An Act to admit the States of North Carolina, South Carolina, Louisiana, Georgia, Alabama, and Florida to Representation in Congress, ch. 70, 15 Stat. 73 (1868).

97 "Whiteley and Farrow vs. Hill and Miller of Georgia," in Taft, *Compilation of Senate Election Cases from 1799 to 1885*, pp. 345–346.

98 See John M. Matthews, "Negro Republicans in the Reconstruction of Georgia" (1976) 60 *The Georgia Historical Quarterly* 145–64, 152; Jack B. Scroggs, "Southern Reconstruction: A Radical View" (1958) 24 *The Journal of Southern History* 407–429, 420.

99 Representative Payne's presentation on January 28, 1869, to the House, on behalf of Committee on Reconstruction, included the following report of the Georgia Legislature's activities: "[T]he Legislature of Georgia has expelled the colored members thereof and admitted to their seats white men who received minorities of votes at the polls, … and … twenty-seven white men [now] hold seats in said Legislature in violation of the fourteenth amendment of the Constitution and the reconstruction acts of Congress[.]" "Comments of Representative Paine, 40th Congress, Third Session, January 28, 1869," 40 *Congressional Globe* (Washington, D.C.: Congressional Globe Office, 1869), part 1, p. 674.

100 Ibid.

101 Ibid., p. 345. Notably, Section 3 would only disenfranchise those who were "officer[s]" who took an oath to uphold the U.S. Constitution, leaving many people who sympathized or supported the Confederacy eligible to vote and run for office. United States Constitution Amend. XIV, s. 3 (disqualifying only those who "having previously taken an oath, as a member of Congress, or as an officer of the United States, or as a member of the State legislature, or as an executive or judicial officer of any State, to support the Constitution of the United States…"). See also Miles S. Lynch, "Disloyalty & Disqualification: Reconstructing Section 3 of the Fourteenth Amendment" (2021) 30 *William and Mary Bill of Rights Journal* 153–220, 158 (noting that Section 3 applies to "any office that falls within Article VI in addition to officers of the uniformed services…").

102 "Whiteley and Farrow vs. Hill and Miller of Georgia," in Taft, *Compilation of Senate Election Cases from 1799 to 1885*, p. 343.

103 Ibid., pp. 346–347.

104 Ibid., pp. 363–369.

readmitted pursuant to the Reconstruction Acts to be entitled to their seats.[105] These post-readmission state legislatures were no longer the racial monoliths of their pre–Civil War predecessors. Instead, these bodies were the most racially diverse in our country's history.

The Fifteenth Amendment was supposed to complete this process by ensuring that formerly enslaved Black men, who now served as legislators thanks to the Reconstruction Acts and who had been admitted to the community of "We the Voters" pursuant to state and federal law, could never be removed from these communities on the basis of race.

6.3 GOING ALL IN ON BLACK SUFFRAGE: THE FIFTEENTH AMENDMENT AS A BLUEPRINT FOR "WE THE VOTERS"

Because the Military Reconstruction Act relegated southern states to conquered provinces, the federal government had to oversee voter registration in the former Confederacy. Facilitated by the Bureau of Civil Affairs – an organ of the Freedmen's Bureau – Black people served alongside White people as election registrars, providing many of the first interactions that either race had ever had with Black officeholders.[106]

In April 1867, General John Pope, who oversaw Georgia, Florida, and Alabama, divided each state into districts and allowed individuals to register to vote for fall elections that would select delegates to each state's respective constitutional conventions.[107] Each district also selected a board of registration to oversee the voting process; notably, Pope required that each board have at least one Black member.[108] This quota created biracial boards that registered formerly enslaved Black men and poor White men in numbers that challenged the very fabric of the White supremacy that had been the hallmark of pre–Civil War southern society.

Unsurprisingly, many of the White unionists who became election registrars were not necessarily progressive on issues of race, and their response to the presence of Black registrars was not uniform.[109] The Black registrars generated resentment because those selected tended to be more socioeconomically privileged than many of the formerly enslaved. According to historian Edmund Drago,

[105] "Hart v. Gilbert (1870)," in Asher C. Hinds, *Hinds' Precedents of the House of Representatives of the United States*, 5 vols. (Washington, D.C.: United States Government Printing Office, 1907), pp. 353–354; "Reynolds v. Hamilton (1871)," in Hinds, *Hinds' Precedents of the House of Representatives of the United States*, p. 395.

[106] Edmund L. Drago, "Georgia's First Black Voter Registrars during Reconstruction," (1994) 78 *The Georgia Historical Quarterly* 760–793, 761.

[107] Ibid., 762–763.

[108] Ibid., 763.

[109] Ibid., 772 (noting that "The registration process was a dynamic one. On one hand, white Georgians, who never envisioned black officeholders, found themselves extolling the virtues of freedmen they nominated for federal registrars. On the other, there were Republicans, white and black who were leery of black registrars so highly praised by conservative Republicans and Democrats.").

> Most of the black registrars were more literate, wealthier, and lighter-skinned than the bulk of the freedmen.... As expected, the literacy rate was high among them. A large number was described by the 1870 federal census takers as "mulatto" rather than "black." In 1870, nineteen black registrars had $29,045 in real estate worth an average of $1,529 while twenty-five possessed $9,740 in personal property making an average of $390. Of the ten in agriculture, six owned land.... Some of the black registrars were retailers. Not surprisingly, a number were ministers, teachers and artisans...[110]

The presence of Black registrars notwithstanding, there were efforts to intimidate Black men to prevent them from voting. Election Day in November 1868 was marred by the murder and assault of many Black men who dared to cast a ballot.[111] The Ku Klux Klan, founded by Nathan Bedford Forrest – a former Confederate general who oversaw the murder of 300 Black soldiers at Fort Pillow in 1864[112] – replicated this carnage across the South in the early 1870s.[113] It quickly became apparent that the Fourteenth Amendment, and its penalty of reduced representation that had yet to be implemented,[114] would be insufficient to counter both the vigilantes who were

110 Ibid., 770. According to a Pew Research Center study on multiracial Americans throughout the history of the census, "the first census in 1790 had only three racial categories: free whites, all other free persons and slaves. 'Mulatto' was added in 1850, and other multiracial categories were included in subsequent counts." Pew Research Center, *Multiracial in America: Proud, Diverse and Growing in Numbers* (Washington, D.C.: Pew Research Center, 2015), p. 20. Multiracial classifications were incorporated into the census in the nineteenth century because "race scientists and public officials believed it was important to know more about groups that were not 'pure' white or black." Ibid., p. 23. For the 1870 census, the definition of "mulatto" included "quadroons, octoroons and all persons having any perceptible trace of African blood." Ibid., p. 24. "This definition had been refined by the 1890 census: 'a mulatto was defined as someone with "three-eighths to five-eighths black blood,' a quadroon had 'one-fourth black blood' and an octoroon had 'one-eighth or any trace of black blood'." Ibid.

111 This voter suppression was largely unsuccessful:

> Despite an effort by staunch conservatives to boycott the election and in some incidents to intimidate blacks, 106,410 out of 188,671 registered voters came out to the polls. Of this turnout, about 36,500 were white (38.3 percent of registered white voters); the remaining 69,910 were black (74.8 percent of registered black voters). By an overwhelming vote of 102,283 to 4,127, Georgians, white and black, called for a constitutional convention.

Drago, "Georgia's First Black Voter Registrars," 787.

112 The details of the battle at Fort Pillow were reported on heavily in the press for weeks afterward, which resulted in "the name of Nathan Bedford Forrest in the North [being] synonymous with the murder of Black troops." Kenneth B. Moore, "Fort Pillow, Forrest, and the United States Colored Troops in 1864" (1995) 54 *Tennessee Historical Quarterly* 112–123, 114. The battle at Fort Pillow served to inspire Black Union soldiers. Prior to an engagement with Confederate troops in June 1864, two of the Union army's Colored Infantries prepared by "[taking] an oath on their knees to show the Confederates no mercy," and entered the battle "[wearing] black badges that read 'Remember Fort Pillow.'" Ibid., 116.

113 Richard T. Schaefer, "The Ku Klux Klan: Continuity and Change" (1971) 32 *Phylon* 143–157, 145.

114 John M. Mathews, *Legislative and Judicial History of the Fifteenth Amendment*, rep. ed. (New York: Da Capo Press, 1971), p. 13 ("In the decade immediately preceding 1867 numerous propositions involving impartial negro suffrage had been submitted to the popular decision in such States as New York, Connecticut, Ohio, Wisconsin, Minnesota, and Kansas, but they had been invariably voted

terrorizing Black people into staying home on Election Day and the local election officials who discarded their votes at the polls.[115]

On March 30, 1870, President Ulysses S. Grant sent the following message to Congress: "A measure which makes at once 4,000,000 people voters, who were heretofore declared by the highest tribunal of the land not citizens of the United States, nor eligible to become so … is indeed a measure of grander importance than any other one act of the kind from the foundation of our free Government to the present day."[116]

Given the violence across the South, Grant's message could not be timelier and more welcome. Yet the obstacles to what would become the Fifteenth Amendment were substantial. Roundly rejected across the North in the 1865 elections, the issue of Black suffrage never achieved anything approaching majority support.

There were a few bright spots, however. Congressional Republicans, over presidential veto, enfranchised Black men in the District of Columbia and Nebraska territory in January and February of 1867.[117] Minnesota voters approved Black suffrage in 1868 after rejecting it a year earlier.[118] Iowa voters enfranchised African Americans that year as well.[119] Other states were well ahead of the curve. For example, Vermont had long permitted African Americans to vote (since 1777) and elected the first Black legislator in U.S. history – Alexander Lucius Twilight – to its state legislature in 1836.[120]

down. It was in view of these circumstances that the Joint Committee on Reconstruction had come to the conclusion that three fourths of the States could not be induced to grant the right of suffrage, even in any degree or under any restriction, to the colored race.").

115 Xi Wang, *The Trial of Democracy: Black Suffrage and Northern Republicans, 1860–1910* (Athens: University of Georgia Press, 1997), p. 60 (noting that Senate Republicans "saw the real obstacle to black suffrage not in the election laws of southern states but in the actual process of practicing registration and voting, where the terrorism of the Ku Klux Klan proved far more dangerous than any statute").

116 Ulysses S. Grant, "Proclamation to the Senate and the House of Representatives on the Ratification of the Fifteenth Amendment," in James D. Richardson (ed.), *A Compilation of the Messages and Papers of the Presidents, 1789–1897*, 10 vols. (Washington, D.C.: Government Printing Office, 1896), v. 7, pp. 55–56.

117 Gillette, *The Right to Vote*, pp. 30–31.

118 "In 1868, Minnesota adopted racial inclusion as a formal public policy when voters passed a statewide referendum that extended full suffrage rights to black males." William D. Green, "'Critical Mass is Fifteen Colored's!' De Fact & De Jure Policies of Racial Isolation in St. Paul's Schools and Housing Patterns during the 19th Century, and Beyond" (1996) 17 *Hamline Journal of Public Law and Policy* 299–322, 315.

119 Of all the state referenda on the issue of Black male suffrage in 1868, Iowa's was unique, in that it "adopted franchise extension by means of a single, uncomplicated referendum," thereby making it the only state in which this cause achieved a "straightforward victory." Robert R. Dykstra and Harlan Hahn, "Northern Voters and Negro Suffrage: The Case of Iowa, 1868" (1968) 32 *Public Opinion Quarterly* 202–15, 205. This election result also represented a fundamental shift in public opinion on this issue in the state whereas a similar measure on the state's 1857 ballot only won 14.6 percent of the vote, the approval rate for Black suffrage had jumped to 66.5 percent in 1868. Ibid., 207.

120 "Comments of Representative Woodbridge, 39th Congress, First Session, January 11, 1866," 36 *Congressional Globe* (Washington, D.C.: Congressional Globe Office, 1866), part 1, p. 202

But Congress's passage of the Fourteenth Amendment only inflamed the politics surrounding Black suffrage, although many Republicans were ultimately swayed by the moral and political case for enfranchising Black people (and disenfranchising Confederates).[121] Even the Radical Republicans' attempt at indirect enfranchisement through Section 2, constructed to avoid northern backlash, underestimated the contempt that northern White people felt toward Black voters. In 1867, voters in Kansas, Minnesota, and Ohio all defeated referendums seeking to enfranchise African Americans in very close votes.[122] This pattern would continue well into 1868, with Michigan, Missouri, and New York voters all rejecting Black suffrage that year.[123] While New York had technically allowed Black men to vote since 1821, most could not meet the $250 property requirement imposed on Black, but not White, voters, which effectively functioned as bar to enfranchisement.[124] Republicans internalized this warning from northern voters, memorializing it in the party's 1868 platform with a suffrage plank that affirmed, "[t]he guaranty by Congress of equal suffrage to all loyal men at the South" but was intentionally silent on northern discrimination.[125]

The promises of universal male suffrage offered by Section 2 of the Fourteenth Amendment, enforced against the backdrop of new southern governments created by the Military Reconstruction Act, felt elusive as the Republican Party paid, and would continue to pay, a steep electoral price across the North for showing any solicitude to Black suffrage, limited or otherwise. White people not only resisted the idea of Black voters, but northern states also resented congressional efforts to foist

("The gentleman from New Jersey says we are imposing upon the District of Columbia that which no State in the Union has imposed upon herself. Allow me to state, on behalf of Vermont, that black men vote there with white men."); Constitution of the State of Vermont chap. I, s. VIII (1777) ("That all elections ought to be free; and that all freemen having a sufficient, evident, common interest with, and attachment to the community, have a right to elect officers, or be elected into office."). Alexander Lucius Twilight, an 1823 graduate of Middlebury College, was not only the first Black person to serve in any state legislature, he was also the first African American to earn a bachelor's degree from an institution of higher education. See Danielle Rougeau and Rebekah Irwin, *Alexander Twilight Day, or Happy 225th Birthday*, available at www.middlebury.edu/library/news/alexander-twilight-day-or-happy-225th-birthday.

121 Richard M. Re and Christopher M. Re, "Voting and Vice: Criminal Disenfranchisement and the Reconstruction Amendments" (2012) 121 *Yale Law Journal* 1584–1671, 1594–1595 (noting that Radical Republicans "embraced formal equality," "challenged entrenched status-based legal classifications," and "found support for expanded voting rights in Christian scripture…"); Gillette, *The Right to Vote*, p. 31 ("…the congressional record on Negro suffrage between 1865 and 1868 indicates that a very substantial Republican majority, except for those northeastern and middle western advocates of universal Negro suffrage, was completely opposed to Negro voting immediately after the war. During 1866, however, this position cracked in the House of Representatives, though border state and some older middle west Republicans remained actively hostile").

122 Gillette, *The Right to Vote*, p. 26.

123 Ibid.

124 James McPherson, *Struggle for Equality: Abolitionists and the Negro in the Civil War and Reconstruction* (Princeton: Princeton University Press, 2014), p. 25.

125 "Republican Party Platform of 1868," American Presidency Project: Republican Party Platforms, www.presidency.ucsb.edu/documents/republican-party-platform-1868.

Black suffrage on states that had demonstrated their loyalty, in resources and blood, to the Union.[126]

Democrats, like Republicans, also walked a fine line on the suffrage issue. The Democratic Party platform used federalism as its foil, denouncing any congressional efforts to regulate suffrage on the grounds that this authority belonged to the states.[127] But their platform did not explicitly endorse or refute Black suffrage, allowing the party's candidates in some states to successfully recruit these voters. Southern Democrats, in particular, were able to recruit approximately 50,000 Black voters, some of whom provided the margin of victory in at least one competitive 1868 congressional race.[128]

Yet the overwhelming evidence was that Black voters were firmly in the Republican camp during that election cycle, with 450,000 southern Black men voting for President Ulysses S. Grant, who ultimately won the presidency by 300,000 votes.[129] The Democrats could have potentially been victorious in 1868 but for serendipitous circumstances coupled with small margins in a few key states that spanned all corners of the country.[130]

After losing ground in the election of 1868, Republicans in Congress had a similar realization about northern voters as they had years earlier about White Southerners: first, many people in the North would never accept African American suffrage, and

[126] Ibid.; see also Gillette, *The Right to Vote*, p. 33 ("In Ohio, for example, Republicans won ten out of nineteen congressional districts in 1866, but the Republican state ticket in 1867 carried three districts. Because of the size of the turnout in Ohio and because referendums on Negro suffrage went down in decisive defeat in Ohio, Kansas, and Minnesota, not to mention the discussion of it elsewhere, Republican losses were widely interpreted as repudiating extension of Negro suffrage in the North.").

[127] "Democratic Party Platform of 1868," American Presidency Project: Republican Party Platforms, www.presidency.ucsb.edu/documents/1868-democratic-party-platform ("…ever since the people of the United States threw off all subjection to the British crown, the privilege and trust of suffrage have belonged to the several States, and have been granted, regulated, and controlled exclusively by the political power of each State respectively, and that any attempt by congress, on any pretext whatever, to deprive any State of this right, or interfere with its exercise, is a flagrant usurpation of power, which can find no warrant in the Constitution.").

[128] Gillette, *The Right to Vote*, p. 41 ("Southern Democrats and conservatives were able to recruit roughly 50,000 Negro voters in the South … the Democrats were successful in the second Congressional district, which 'has a large majority of colored voters…'").

[129] Ibid., p. 40. Grant won the electoral college by a 126 electoral vote margin, capturing several southern states including Florida, Georgia, North and South Carolina, Tennessee, and Arkansas. Ibid.

[130] According to William Gillette,

> Three southern states did not participate in the [1868] election and six others voted under so-called carpetbag regimes, which prevented many whites from voting. Republican majorities were uncomfortable in Indiana, New Hampshire, North Carolina, and Pennsylvania. In Alabama, Arkansas, and Connecticut the majorities were slight, whereas in the western states of Nevada and California, Grant's majority was infinitesimal. Had the Democrats nominated a stronger candidate, they might have won, since a small shift in the popular vote of a few key states would have changed the outcome. In any event, Democrats made gains in the new House of Representatives.

Ibid.

second, Republicans would have difficulty holding on to power without Black voters in the South. The Fourteenth Amendment – with its nominal applicability to the North – was insufficient to crystallize a universal conception of colorblind republican government that centered on "We the Voters." Just as Lincoln had warned that a house divided could not stand, two visions of republicanism – one northern, one southern – also could not coexist.[131]

In addition, the close margins were not the only point of concern for the Republican Party, with growing violence in the South cutting into Republican turnout.[132] Force and fraud in Southern elections made the Democratic Party more competitive, significantly diminishing the Republicans' leverage in Congress.[133] Many former Confederate leaders remained defiant, despite the dictates of the Fourteenth Amendment and restrictions in their state constitutions, stubbornly refusing to grant Black Americans even the most basic civil rights.[134]

The architects of Reconstruction had hoped that Section 2 of the Fourteenth Amendment – with its threat of reducing a state's representation in Congress if it denied the vote to Black citizens – would serve as a powerful incentive for compliance. But in practice, this indirect form of coercion could still fall short. Some states, even those with large Black populations, could suppress the Black vote and still hold on to all of their seats in the House of Representatives In the end, Republicans worried that Section 2's penalty was too mild, its enforcement too uncertain, and the resistance too deeply rooted.[135]

131 See, e.g., "An Exposure of the Fourteenth Amendment," *Detroit Free Press*, September 1, 1868 (criticizing Section 2 because it "tears up by the root … the proportionate equality of the States, for although in terms it applies all of them, in practical operation it bears very unequally.") (quoting jurist George Ticknor Curtis). See also Mathews, *Fifteenth Amendment*, p. 18 (noting that some Framers argued that the disparate treatment of the North and the South with respect to suffrage would offend, to quote both Bingham and Conkling, "the theory of equality of the States").

132 Mathews, *Fifteenth Amendment*, p. 41 ("Republicans were more worried about southern Negroes who might desert the polls rather than mutiny by supporting Democrats. They were told that Negroes had been coerced to stay away from the polls by bribery, threats, superstition, and violence…").

133 Ibid., p. 20 ("Now that most of the ex-Confederate States had been in large measure rehabilitated [by 1868], it was realized that the practically complete control which Congress had exercised over them was gradually slipping away and must eventually come to an end. When this should happen, the only remaining security for negro suffrage in the South lay in the extent to which fundamental conditions of readmission had rendered the reconstruction constitutions unalterable in respect to suffrage. Confidence in the validity of these conditions was now perceptibly on the wane.").

134 Republicans waited until after the election of 1868 to propose the Fifteenth Amendment, so that it would not be an election year issue, but they believed the Amendment was necessary because, as one scholar noted, "the attitude of southern whites left no doubt that if … no additional warrant should exist for the further interference of Congress in the Southern States, negro suffrage would be doomed." Ibid., pp. 20–21.

135 "The Fourteenth Amendment – Is it Part of the Constitution? – Its Effect," *Louisville Courier Journal*, July 24, 1868 ("The black population of the State has not for years been one-fifth of the whole population … it is not at all certain then, in view of the increase of our white population and the known decrease of the black, that this Constitutional amendment will even deprive Kentucky of a single representative."). See also "Operation of the Fourteenth Amendment," *Louisville Courier Journal*,

To protect their political fortunes, congressional Republicans knew the solution was to not to retreat – especially since the cost of intervention was already being extracted across the north.[136] Growing chatter that the Fourteenth Amendment had not been lawfully adopted only further fueled sentiments that more action was needed.[137] The solution was to fully commit to Black suffrage, and in the process, create a cache of Republican voters that would endure for generations. Thus, it was both the sobering political reality and a moral imperative that led Republicans to start drafting the Fifteenth Amendment, even though the ink was barely dry on documents certifying the ratification of the Fourteenth.[138]

The Fifteenth Amendment not only offered a uniform prohibition on racial discrimination in voting that would apply nationwide, but it also placed the Republican Party firmly behind the issue of Black suffrage, banking the party's future on nationwide Black enfranchisement.[139] The new amendment eschewed the compromises that had been required of the Fourteenth, bringing aboard a new coalition of Republicans who had wished for more drastic action. Conservative

January 11, 1869. ("Under the operation of the amendment the Kentucky [9 member] delegation would be cut down to seven, or at most, eight."). See also Raoul Berger, "Fourteenth Amendment: Light from the Fifteenth" (1979) 74 *Northwestern University Law Review* 311–371, 321–323.

[136] Prior to the enactment of the Fifteenth Amendment, Republican politicians "retreated from the vigorous defense of equal rights without wholly abandoning the fight." Stephen A. West, "Remembering Reconstruction in Its Twilight" (2020) 10 *Journal of the Civil War Era* 495–523, 496. To these Republicans, protecting African American voting rights not only "[did] justice to the formerly enslaved[,]" but it also represented an important "counterbalance [to] the political influence" of Southern rebels who had violently threatened the unity of the nation. Ibid. That said, there were political risks involved. Republican politicians engaged in cost-benefit analyses related to the issue of voting rights for African Americans for several decades following the end of the Civil War. Even during the post-Reconstruction period, "Republican presidents and congressmen remained committed to the protection of black voting rights, though northern opinion was increasingly divided on the efficacy of federal intervention, and the use of military force to protect black suffrage was no longer politically practicable." Michael Klarman, "The Plessy Era" (1998) *The Supreme Court Review*, 303–314, 307–308.

[137] "The Fourteenth Amendment – Is it Part of the Constitution? – Its Effect," *Louisville Courier Journal*, July 24, 1868 (calling ratification into question because two states – Ohio and New Jersey – rescinded their endorsement and six southern states have "illegally constituted" legislatures). See also John Harrison, "The Lawfulness of the Reconstruction Amendments" (2001) 68 *University of Chicago Law Review* 375–462.

[138] See Herman Belz, *A New Birth of Freedom: The Republican Party and Freedmen's Rights, 1861–1866* (New York: Fordham University Press, 1976).

[139] "Comments of Representative Boutwell, 40th Congress, Third Session, January 23, 1869," 40 *Congressional Globe* (Washington, D.C.: Congressional Globe Office, 1869), part 1, p. 561. ("Having given to the colored people in several of the States the power to vote we have put into the politics of the country an element by which the amendment itself can be carried ... There are one hundred and fifty thousand citizens of the United States who by this bill will be entitled to the elective franchise but who are now disenfranchised – seventeen hundred in Connecticut, ten thousand in New York, five thousand in New Jersey, fourteen thousand in Pennsylvania, seven thousand in Ohio, twenty-four thousand in Missouri, forty-five thousand in Kentucky, four thousand in Delaware, thirty-five thousand in Maryland – who will rally to the support of this constitutional amendment if by the law they are enfranchised.").

Republicans, initially hoping to avoid alienating President Johnson, had downplayed any intent to make Black suffrage the centerpiece of Reconstruction efforts,[140] whereas Charles Sumner, hoping for full civil and political rights for this group, did not think the Fourteenth Amendment went far enough.[141] Thaddeus Stevens, although a strong supporter of the Fourteenth Amendment, viewed it as the best that could be accomplished at the time.[142] The Fifteenth Amendment represented the full commitment to Black suffrage that seemed impossible only months earlier.

The primary goals of the Fifteenth Amendment were the enfranchisement of Black people in the North and to provide a permanent guarantee of voting rights to those who lived in the South.[143] As ratified in 1870, the first section of the Fifteenth Amendment provides that, "The right of citizens of the United States to vote shall not be denied or abridged by the United States or by any State on account of race, color, or previous condition of servitude."[144] The second section gave Congress broad enforcement authority. Taken together with the federal statutes that readmitted the former Confederate states back into the Union, the Fifteenth Amendment prevented post–Reconstruction state governments from altering their state constitutions to abridge the right to vote on the basis of race.[145]

Most importantly, the Fifteenth Amendment was less dependent on the fluidity and unpredictability of politics than Section 2 of the Fourteenth.[146] Partisan

140 See Wang, *Trial of Democracy*, p. 2 ("Grounding their arguments on the principle of equality inscribed in the Declaration, these radical Republicans argued that the existence of slavery and legal discrimination against blacks contradicted the republican principle that government was founded on the consent of the governed.... The more conservative Republicans viewed the party's historical mission differently. More concerned with preventing the Union from falling apart over sectional disputes than with defending individual rights denied because of color and race, conservative Republicans suggested that the party avoid taking any firm positions advocating civil and political equality for blacks...").

141 See Section 5.3.

142 Joseph B. James, *The Framing of the Fourteenth Amendment* (Urbana: University of Illinois Press, 1965), p. 39.

143 Gillette, *The Right to Vote*, p. 46

144 United States Constitution Amend. XV, s. 1.

145 Notably, Professor David Currie argued that, although the Military Reconstruction Act emerged from Committee with the Fourteenth Amendment, the Act was likely unconstitutional. See David Currie, "The Reconstruction Congress" (2008) 75 *University of Chicago Law Review* 383–496, 412–414 ("Congress has no right to coerce a state into ratification – or into an extension of voting rights – by denying the right to representation in the House and Senate (or the right to its own republican government) until it complies with congressional desires."). It is difficult to square this argument with Congress's power, under the Guarantee Clause, to determine what constitutes a republican government, as it did with the Military Reconstruction Act.

146 See Paolo E. Coletta, "The Democratic Party 1884–1910," in Arthur M. Schlesinger (ed.), *History of U.S. Political Parties*, 4 vols. (New York: Chelsea House Publishers, 1973), vol. II, p. 987 ("Once the southern states were readmitted to the Union, the Democrats staged a strong comeback, winning the House of Representatives in 1874, the popular vote for the presidency in 1876 and the Senate in 1878."). The Republicans secured a huge victory in 1872, winning both the presidency and 196 of 281

politics were a real barrier, as implementation of Section 2's penalty depended on both houses of Congress having a Republican majority; the Fifteenth Amendment helped to fill this gap. While its final language would ultimately be a more direct guarantee of race-neutral suffrage than Section 2 of the Fourteenth Amendment, it was notable that the text of the Fifteenth Amendment derived, in part, from proposals that were rejected during the debates over Section 2.[147]

Two proposals before the Joint Committee in early 1866 would have prevented, or alternatively, penalized states for denying the right to vote on the basis of race or color. The first proposal, put forth by Senator Fessenden of Maine, provided that:

> All provisions in the Constitution or laws of any State whereby any distinction is made in political … rights or privileges on account of race … or color shall be inoperative and void.[148]

In contrast, the Blaine proposal stated that:

> [W]henever the elective franchise shall be denied or abridged on account of race … or color, all persons of such race … or color shall be excluded from the basis of representation.[149]

The text of the Fifteenth Amendment drew on Fessenden's proposal,[150] while Blaine's proposal was closest to the text adopted by the House as the basis for Section 2's indirectly coercive method of extending the franchise to African Americans.[151] Ultimately, the Fourteenth and Fifteenth Amendments, with their different enforcement mechanisms, gave Congress options in how it could protect the right to vote. But, importantly, these provisions also clarified the scope of state power

congressional races that year, but this win could be attributed to votes from the ex-slaves in the former confederacy. Indeed, the size of the Republican victory masked a split in the party between prominent Republican leaders and President Ulysses S. Grant over alleged corruption and economic policy that would ultimately lead to huge losses for Republicans in the 1874 mid-term elections. See Michael F. Holt, *By One Vote: The Disputed Presidential Election of 1876* (Lawrence: University Press of Kansas, 2008), p. 17.

147 See Mathews, *Fifteenth Amendment*, pp. 11–12 (arguing that section 2 of the Fourteenth Amendment is consistent with the Fifteenth Amendment); Franita Tolson, "The Constitutional Structure of Voting Rights Enforcement" (2014) 89 Washington Law Review 379–439 (same). But see Gabriel J. Chin, "Reconstruction, Felon Disenfranchisement, and the Right to Vote: Did the Fifteenth Amendment Repeal Section 2 of the Fourteenth Amendment?" (2004) 92 *Georgetown Law Journal* 259–326 (arguing that the Fifteenth Amendment superceded Section 2 of the Fourteenth Amendment).

148 Ibid., 11.

149 Ibid., 11–12.

150 The Fifteenth Amendment provides: "The right of citizens of the United States to vote shall not be denied or abridged by the United States or by any State on account of race, color, or previous condition of servitude." United States Constitution Amend. XV; see also Mathews, *Fifteenth Amendment*, p. 12 ("The Fessenden plan, which involved the idea that finally took definite shape in the Fifteenth Amendment, was intended to secure the right of suffrage to negroes by a direct guarantee."). But see Chin, "Reconstruction, Felon Disenfranchisement, and the Right to Vote," 261.

151 Mathews, *Fifteenth Amendment*, p. 12 ("The Blaine plan … aimed at the same object [as the Fessenden plan] by the indirectly coercive method of minatory inducements.").

over elections and voter qualifications by putting to rest the issue of whether the Fourteenth Amendment implicitly recognized that states had preexisting authority to disenfranchise voters on the basis of race.[152]

Around this time, new proposals emerged that shed light on a deeper purpose behind the Fourteenth and Fifteenth Amendments. These draft bills were not just about securing the rights of Black voters – they were also part of a broader effort to define where state power ended and federal authority began. For example, in January of 1869 – about a month before Congress settled on the final language of the Fifteenth Amendment – George Boutwell introduced both a statute and a constitutional amendment that prohibited discrimination on the basis of race.[153] His proposed bill, H.R. 1667, or "A bill to secure equal privileges and immunities to citizens of the United States, and to enforce the provisions of article fourteen of the amendments to the Constitution,"[154] provided in relevant part:

> [N]o State shall abridge or deny the right of any citizen of the United States to vote for electors of President and Vice-President of the United States, or for Representatives in Congress, or for members of the legislature of the State in which he may reside, by reason of race, color or previous condition of slavery; and any provisions in the laws or constitution of any State inconsistent with this section are hereby declared to be null and void.[155]

Contrary to many of his colleagues, Boutwell believed that Congress could prohibit racial discrimination in voting under the Privileges and Immunities Clause of the Fourteenth Amendment. H.R. 1667 would be enabling legislation enacted under Section 5,[156] allowing Congress to criminalize race-based disenfranchisement until

152 See, for example, "Comments of Representative Cullom, 40th Congress, Third Session, January 27, 1869," 40 *Congressional Globe* (Washington, D.C.: Congressional Globe Office, 1869), part 1, p. 651 ("While, as I say, some of [the Fourteenth Amendment's] provisions are of great value, a portion of the amendment should never have been adopted, if, as is alleged by some, it recognizes the right of each State to abridge or deny to any portion of its people without cause the exercise of the elective franchise. A State has the right to disfranchise its felons, but it has no right to disfranchise its citizens on account of race, color, or previous condition of slavery. The amendment was the best that could be done, but I would be much better satisfied with it if it were clearer on that point. Today, sir, we are at work to patch up the work which we failed at that time to do correctly, as we should.").

153 See Travis Crum, "The Superfluous Fifteenth Amendment?" (2020) 114 *Northwestern Law Review* 1549–1630, 1604–1605.

154 "H.R. 1667: A Bill to secure equal privileges to the citizens of the United States, and to enforce the provisions of article fourteen of the amendments to the Constitution," recommended to the House Committee of the Judiciary on January 11, 1869, https://memory.loc.gov/cgi-bin/ampage?collId=llhb&fileName=040/llhb040.db&recNum=5255.

155 Ibid.

156 Ibid. ("It is here provided [in section 1] that there shall be no abridgment of the privileges and immunities of citizens; and in the second section there is a penalty provided for a State that disregards the inhibition … It was uncertain when Congress would exercise the power conferred by the fifth section of the fourteenth amendment, and in order that the States should not take advantage of their own wrong during the period while Congress might be inactive a penalty was provided.").

the penalty of reduced representation could be implemented.[157] But, most importantly, he saw the connection between the recently ratified Fourteenth Amendment and what Congress intended the proposed Fifteenth Amendment to accomplish; from his perspective, "By the second section [of the Fourteenth Amendment] there is a political penalty for doing that which in the first section [of the proposed Fifteenth Amendment] it is declared the State has no right to do."[158]

Designed to ensure that Congress would fulfill its ongoing obligation to guarantee that state governments remained republican in form,[159] H.R. 1667 would have also expanded the disqualification provisions of Section 3 of the Fourteenth Amendment.[160] Under the bill, those who were disqualified by Section 3 but served as election administrators (which was not a disqualification-eligible office) would be subject to stringent penalties should they "willfully refuse to register the name, or to receive, count, return, or otherwise give the proper legal effect to the vote of any citizen entitled to vote for any officer … on account of race, color, or previous condition of slavery of such citizen…"[161]

Given that H.R. 1667 could be repealed in the future,[162] only a constitutional amendment could make permanent one of its most important goals of establishing that race discrimination in voting rendered a government unrepublican in form, at least as it relates to the disenfranchisement of Black men.[163] There were

[157] See Chapter 5. The party was split on a lot of these questions. See Earl M. Maltz, "Radical Politics and Constitutional Theory: Senator Jacob M. Howard of Michigan and the Problem of Reconstruction" (2006) 32 *Michigan Historical Review* 19–32, 27 ("At the level of pure political theory, Radicals often contended that the right to vote was either a natural right or an inherent right of citizenship" but noting that not all Radicals approached these issues through this lens and were willing to acknowledge the political limitations of this view).

[158] "Comments of Representative Boutwell, 40th Congress, Third Session, January 23, 1869," 40 *Congressional Globe* (Washington, D.C.: Congressional Globe Office, 1869), part 1, p. 559.

[159] Ibid., p. 556.

[160] "H.R. 1667: A Bill to secure equal privileges to the citizens of the United States, and to enforce the provisions of article fourteen of the amendments to the Constitution," recommended to the House Committee of the Judiciary on January 11, 1869, https://memory.loc.gov/cgi-bin/ampage?collId=llhb&fileName=040/llhb040.db&recNum=5255.

[161] Ibid.

[162] "Comments of Representative Boutwell, 40th Congress, Third Session, January 23, 1869," 40 *Congressional Globe* (Washington, D.C.: Congressional Globe Office, 1869), part 1, p. 561 ("If we rely exclusively upon a bill which when enacted is merely a law, and subject to congressional control and to all the vicissitudes of politics and changes of opinion, we cannot be assured of its fate in some future Congress.").

[163] Some representatives pointed to Section 2 as evidence that the states retained their authority over the qualification of electors and therefore Congress could not prohibit states from altering their state constitutions to disenfranchise African Americans by statute. "Comments of Senator Henderson, 40th Congress, Second Session, May 27, 1868," 40 *Congressional Globe* (Washington, D.C.: Congressional Globe Office, 1868), part 3, p. 2606 (making this point); "Comments of Senator Conkling, 40th Congress, Second Session, May 28, 1868," 40 *Congressional Globe* (Washington, D.C.: Congressional Globe Office, 1868), part 3, p. 2665 (same). But see "Comments of Senator Stewart, 40th Congress, Second Session, May 27, 1868," 40 *Congressional Globe* (Washington, D.C.: Congressional Globe Office, 1868), part 3, p. 2606 (denying that Section 2 expressly authorizes states to deny its citizens the

serious doubts among Boutwell's colleagues as to whether Congress had constitutional authority to pass H.R. 1667 under Section 5 of the Fourteenth Amendment or, indeed, any other provisions of the Constitution.[164] Enacting a constitutional amendment would explicitly address this concern.

Other proposals, in the quest to protect the newly enfranchised citizens, also sought to draw new lines regarding the balance of power between the states and the federal government. For example, John Bingham proposed the following:

> No State shall make or enforce any law which shall abridge or deny to any male citizen of the United States, of sound mind, and over twenty-one years of age, the equal exercise of the elective franchise at all elections in the State wherein he shall have naturally resided for a period of one year next preceding such election, except such of said citizens as shall hereafter engage in rebellion or insurrection, or who may have been or shall be duly convicted of treason or other crime of the grade of felony at common law.[165]

Besides the fact that there is no explicit mention of disenfranchisement on the basis of race or color, Bingham's proposed amendment differed from the final language of the Fifteenth Amendment in several important ways. First, Bingham's amendment acknowledged the legitimacy of certain prerequisites to voting – residency requirements, age, citizenship, and mental competence – but not others, including property and literacy requirements. But the fact that this provision – like Section 2 – set a default baseline for legitimate voter qualification standards was notable given that this had been solely within the purview of state power.

Second, the proposed amendment treated the violence that continued in the South at the hands of the Ku Klux Klan and others as a continuation of the Civil War, specifically through the text's prospective, rather than retroactive use of the terms "rebellion or insurrection." Whereas Section 3 of the Fourteenth Amendment disqualified those seeking certain elective offices for past action, this language would allow the disenfranchisement of those individuals who continued to labor and commit violence under the banner of what would eventually become known as the Lost Cause.[166]

right to vote). See also Travis Crum, "The Superfluous Fifteenth Amendment?," 1554 (arguing that a constitutional amendment, rather than a statute, was the only politically viable option).

164 "Comments of Representative Eldridge, 40th Congress, Third Session, January 27, 1869," 40 *Congressional Globe* (Washington, D.C.: Congressional Globe Office, 1869), part 1, pp. 642–643 (arguing that neither Article I, Section 2 nor Article I, Section 4 empowered Congress to enact H.R. 1667.). See also "Comments of Representative Kerr, 40th Congress, Third Session, January 27, 1869," 40 *Congressional Globe* (Washington, D.C.: Congressional Globe Office, 1869), part 1, pp. 657–658.

165 "Comments of Representative Bingham, 40th Congress, Third Session, January 27, 1869," 40 *Congressional Globe* (Washington, D.C.: Congressional Globe Office, 1869), part 1, p. 638.

166 The "Lost Cause" was a "southern view of [the Civil] [W]ar [that] held that secession had just been a reaction to an increasingly oppressive federal government." Richard D. Starnes, "Forever Faithful: The Southern Historical Society and Confederate Historical Memory" (1996) 2 *Southern Cultures* 177–194, 177. Further, this belief embodied the idea that "[t]he Confederate attempt at southern

Third, and notably, Bingham's amendment, like the Reconstruction Acts that readmitted the former Confederate states, acknowledged that the universe of disenfranchising crimes should be the equivalent of treason, rebellion, insurrection, or a felony at common law.[167]

In the end, the resulting language of the Fifteenth Amendment would be much more limited. Contemporaneous with Boutwell's proposal, the House Judiciary Committee reported the following text:

> The right of any citizen of the United States to vote shall not be denied or abridged by the United States or any State by reason of the race, color, or previous condition of slavery of any citizen or class of citizens of the United States.[168]

Four days later, on January 15, 1869, the Senate Judiciary Committee reported its variation of this language:

> The right of citizens of the United States to vote and hold office shall not be denied or abridged by the United States or by any State, on account of race, color, or previous condition of servitude.[169]

Even though a constitutional amendment would be permanent in a way that legislation never could be, Republicans were still well aware of the limits of these proposals. The language of both provisions, seeking to protect the formerly enslaved from race-based voting discrimination, was chosen in lieu of an amendment that would have guaranteed universal suffrage.

Language that would have entitled "all male citizens…an equal vote in all elections" was also overwhelmingly defeated. So too was language that would have placed a general veto in Congress to "abolish or modify any restrictions on the right to vote," essentially giving Congress the authority to create a federally protected right to vote, free of state law or the state constitution. With its open-endedness, this proposal would have subjected the right to vote to the volatility of party politics and

nationalism had reflected a noble experiment, which was constitutionally and morally right." Ibid. According to this worldview, "[t]he South had done everything in its power to fight for the cause, but in the end it had succumbed to superior northern resources." Ibid. This "Lost Cause" mythology became an "integral part" of the history of the Ku Klux Klan, which was seen as the "savior of the South" in post-Reconstruction America, during which, as White Southerners saw it, "ignorance and corruption dominated politics, the indolence of African Americans hampered the economic system, and crime threatened all parts of white southern society." Michael Lewis and Jacqueline Serbu, "Commemorating the Ku Klux Klan" (1999) 40 *The Sociological Quarterly* 139–158, 143.

167 Compare "Comments of Representative Shellabarger, 40th Congress, Third Session, January 27, 1869," 40 *Congressional Globe* (Washington, D.C.: Congressional Globe Office, 1869), part 1, p. 639 (offering an amendment that would allow disenfranchisement for "insurrection or rebellion against the United States, and to such as shall be duly convicted of treason, felony, or other infamous crime.").

168 "Reading of Joint Resolution H.R. No. 402, 40th Congress, Third Session, January 11, 1869," 40 Congressional Globe (Washington, D.C.: Congressional Globe Office, 1869), part 1, p. 286.

169 "Reading of the Amendment Reported by the Committee on the Judiciary, 40th Congress, Third Session, January 27, 1869," 40 *Congressional Globe* (Washington, D.C.: Congressional Globe Office, 1869), part 1, p. 638.

regional differences and had the potential to completely displace state sovereignty over voter qualifications; it was, unsurprisingly, rejected by a large margin.[170]

Most radicals actually preferred the amendment, offered by Senator Henry Wilson, that would have prohibited a denial of voting rights based on race and "nativity, property, education, [and] religious belief" as well.[171] But federalism norms still held enormous sway. In addition to concerns about this proposal intruding too far into state sovereignty, there was still substantial suspicion about any proposal that would enfranchise everyone equally, given that there were groups – women, Chinese people, the mentally disabled – that Democrats and, importantly, some Republicans sought to exclude.[172]

Ironically, the premise of an inclusive political community that Congress would be empowered to protect was undermined by Congress's desire to preserve the states' authority to exclude people from the franchise. For example, both the proposed and final language of the Fifteenth Amendment offered by the House and Senate Judiciary Committees would not prevent states from imposing property qualifications as a condition of voting.[173] Additionally, Republicans were well aware that, because the text only prohibited disenfranchisement on the three specified grounds (race, color, or previous condition of servitude), the Fifteenth Amendment might be inadequate to address the ingenious ways in which states could potentially disenfranchise African Americans.[174]

170 Maltz, "Radical Politics and Constitutional Theory," 30.

171 Ibid., 28.

172 See Chapter 7.

173 See Mathews, *Fifteenth Amendment*, pp. 33–34 (discussing the public firestorm over a proposed amendment that would have prohibited "the imposition of tests on the grounds of 'race, color, nativity property, education, or creed.'"). See ibid., p. 45 ("To provide in the Constitution that the States should not disenfranchise for the three specified causes [race, color, previous condition of servitude] was impliedly to authorize them to disenfranchise for all other conceivable causes. Thus the Amendment would operate as a virtual legalization of disfranchisement. Under it an aristocracy of property, of intellect, or of sect might be established. Although the animus of the Amendment was a desire to protect and enfranchise the colored people, yet it was anticipated that under it nine tenths of them might be prevented from voting by the requirement on the part of the States of intelligence or property qualifications."). See also "Comments of Representative Boutwell, 40th Congress, Third Session, January 23, 1869," 40 *Congressional Globe* (Washington, D.C.: Congressional Globe Office, 1869), part 1, p. 561 (denying that the Fifteenth Amendment would prevent states from requiring a property or educational qualification). Arguably, this interpretation of the Fifteenth Amendment is avoided if it is read in conjunction with Section 2 of the Fourteenth Amendment, with its prohibition on abridging the right to vote on grounds beyond race discrimination. See also "Comments of Representative Cullom, 40th Congress, Third Session, January 27, 1869," 40 *Congressional Globe* (Washington, D.C.: Congressional Globe Office, 1869), part 1, p. 652 (noting that "[t]he language [of the Fifteenth Amendment] should be such as to cover the case and not require amending again when in a short time some other injustice grows up among the people not based upon the question of race, color, or previous condition of slavery" and observing the potential for property and educational qualifications to disenfranchise Black men.).

174 Mathews, *Fifteenth Amendment*, p. 45 ("Williams of Oregon thought that if a State should pass disenfranchising legislation not based on any of the three specified grounds it would be valid legislation as far as the Amendment was concerned … . The white people of a State might decide that the negroes

There was also the view that the Fifteenth Amendment shifted enforcement responsibility from Congress to the courts, an argument endorsed by both James Blaine in his memoirs, almost twenty years after the congressional debates, and John Sherman, almost thirty years after. As Blaine noted,

> Before the adoption of the Fifteenth Amendment, if a state should exclude the negro from suffrage, the next step would be for Congress to exclude the negro from the basis of apportionment. After, if a state should exclude the negro from suffrage, the next step would be for the Supreme Court to declare that the act was unconstitutional, and therefore null and void.[175]

This framing suggests that Section 2 was supposed to be a temporary fix – a band aid – until a court could invalidate a contrary law under the Fifteenth Amendment.[176] Blaine's argument also provided fodder for the argument that the Fifteenth Amendment repealed the Fourteenth Amendment, which partially explained the race-neutral (rather than race-based) disenfranchising regimes that became prevalent during Redemption and Restoration.[177] For Southerners, the Fifteenth Amendment remained of concern, the Fourteenth Amendment less so.

The expectation at the time of the adoption of the Fifteenth Amendment, at least among most Republicans not named Blaine or Sherman, was that the apportionment requirements of Section 2 of the Fourteenth Amendment would continue to play an enforcement role because they would reach qualifications that were race-neutral on their face, yet had a discriminatory effect.[178] The public – and some prominent radicals like Blaine – might have questioned whether Section 2's

were disloyal, or were disturbers of the public peace, and on that account should not be allowed to vote."); see also ibid., pp. 46–47 ("Conkling of New York also considered the Amendment utterly inadequate and ineffective on account of its omissions. One obvious method by which it could be evaded, he said, was the full power which it allowed any State to provide by law that 'disingenuousness of birth' [i.e., birth out of wedlock] should be deemed a disqualification to exercise the right to vote.").

175 James G. Blaine, *Twenty Years of Congress: From Lincoln to Garfield*, 2 vols. (Norwich: The Henry Bill Publishing Company, 1886), vol. 2, pp. 418–419.

176 Ibid. (arguing that the Fifteenth Amendment eroded the effectiveness of Section 2 because it "took away absolutely from the State the power to exclude the negro from suffrage, and therefore the second section of the Fourteenth Amendment can refer only to those other disqualifications never likely to be applied…"). See also John Sherman, *Recollections of 40 years in the House, Senate and Cabinet*, 2 vols. (Chicago: The Werner Company, 1895), vol. 1, p. 450 (suggesting that Section 2 of the Fourteenth Amendment remained a congressionally enforceable penalty, but the Fifteenth Amendment undermined its effectiveness).

177 See Remarks of Rep. Sydney Bowie, reprinted in "The Fourteenth and Fifteenth Amendment," *The Nashville Tennessean*, August 15, 1904 ("Mr. Blaine claimed that the Fifteenth Amendment, being of a later date and inconsistent therewith, repealed the second section of the Fourteenth Amendment related to reduction of representation. Whether it did so entirely or not may be open to some question, but it undoubtedly emasculated it since the only just occasion for its enforcement, if it had any just one at all, was rendered impossible.").

178 See Travis Crum, "The Unabridged Fifteenth Amendment" (2024) 133 *Yale Law Journal* 1039–1161, 1109 (noting that, during the ratification debates over the Fifteenth Amendment, Republican legislators in border states urged support for the Amendment because otherwise "these States would likely

penalty would "amount to anything of importance" for abridgments other than those based on race or color, which was a question put forth in a November 1869 editorial in the *Chicago Tribune*. But there was little dispute that the penalty would be most felt "in those States where the voter is required to be able to read and write."[179] And Blaine, writing his memoirs in the decade before Restoration, would have had no way of knowing that facially neutral qualifications would become the dominant means by which southern states would disenfranchise African Americans after 1890.

While there may have been some disagreement about its scope,[180] most of those who supported the proposed Fifteenth Amendment viewed it as a compliment to the protections already enshrined in Section 2 of the Fourteenth Amendment. During these debates, supporters of the Fifteenth Amendment made two interrelated arguments illustrating the continued validity of Section 2. First, of course, was Boutwell's assertion in the debate over H.R. 1667 that Section 1 and Section 2 of the Fourteenth Amendment, when viewed together, "declared [that] the State has no right" to "abridge or deny to a citizen the right to vote."[181] In other words, his declaration that "[b]y the second section there is a political penalty for doing that which in the first section it is declared the State has no right to do" supported the view that Section 2 was still intended to be operative.[182] Later efforts to enforce Section 2 – in 1872 (the same year that the Fifteenth Amendment was ratified), 1899, and 1901 – were probably the most concrete evidence that this provision survived the ratification of the Fifteenth Amendment.[183]

Second, the language of the Fifteenth Amendment, substantively narrower but remedially broader than Section 2 of the Fourteenth, was yet another attempt to

lose representation in the House and the Electoral College following the 1870 Census," when the penalty of Section 2 of the Fourteenth Amendment was supposed to be applied).

179 "The Fourteenth Amendment," *The Chicago Tribune*, November 30, 1869. See also Blaine, *Twenty Years of Congress* (conceding that Section 2 of the Fourteenth Amendment could apply to other forms of discrimination even though its target was racial discrimination in voting in the southern states).

180 Some Republicans believed that the use of proxies in and of themselves could be discrimination based on race in violation of the Fifteenth Amendment. "Comments of Senator Howard, 41th Congress, Second Session, May 20, 1870," 42 *Congressional Globe* (Washington, D.C.: Congressional Globe Office, 1870), part 4, p. 3655 (noting that some courts may construe the Fifteenth Amendment narrowly because it "forbids a certain thing to be done … and that thing is denial or abridgment of the right to vote on account of race, color, or previous condition of servitude" and "[t]hat is all there is of it"). Similarly, some scholars have argued that the amendment not only bans proxies but also guarantees a right to hold office on a nondiscriminatory basis. See Travis Crum, "The Unabridged Fifteenth Amendment," 1050."

181 "Comments of Representative Boutwell, 40th Congress, Third Session, January 23, 1869," 40 *Congressional Globe* (Washington, D.C.: Congressional Globe Office, 1869), part 1, p. 559. Representative Boutwell noted, "If the right to vote for certain officers be denied or abridged, then certain political consequences follow [under Section 2]; but in the first section there is a distinct declaration this cannot lawfully be done." Ibid.

182 Ibid.

183 See Chapters 7 and 8.

strike a federalism balance between the states' authority to choose voter qualifications and federal protections for the political community of "We the Voters."[184] Its text directly intruded on the ability of states to choose the qualification of electors for both state and federal elections,[185] but unlike the substantive provisions of Section 2, the proposed Fifteenth Amendment did not contain the broad language that prohibited states from abridging the right to vote on almost any grounds.[186] It was, nonetheless, a necessary measure given that the margins in the 1868 elections across the North were tight enough that the African American votes in those states, no matter how small, had become integral to Republican success.

Given this, supporters viewed Section 2 of the Fourteenth Amendment and Section 1 of the Fifteenth Amendment as two halves of a whole: under Section 2, Congress could reduce representation for almost any abridgment whereas under Section 1, Congress could impose a broader range of penalties for abridgment on three specified grounds – race, color, or previous condition of servitude.[187]

[184] In addition to the Framers of the Fourteenth and Fifteenth Amendments, Republicans who later attempted to enforce Section 2 held a similar belief about its compatibility with the Fifteenth Amendment. See "Comments of Representative Crumpacker, 56th Congress, Second Session, January 7, 1901," 34 *Congressional Record* (Washington, D.C.: Congressional Globe Office, 1901), appendix, p. 69 ("It was not at first expected that they would be given the right of suffrage, and the fourteenth amendment was intended to give them citizenship and leave the question of their political privileges entirely with the States, but if any State should disfranchise them its representation should be reduced accordingly. That was the original plan of reconstruction. It was supposed that the importance of an increased share of political power in the Government that would result would induce the insurrectionary States to prepare the negro for suffrage and accord him the right as rapidly as they could do so without injury to their local affairs. But the fear was still entertained that the negro would be held in political bondage, notwithstanding the provisions of the fourteenth amendment, and in the light of unjust and barbarous laws enacted by some of those States, aimed at the colored race, that fear was well founded. The result was the fifteenth amendment.").

[185] "Comments of Representative Ward, 40th Congress, Third Session, January 23, 1869," 40 *Congressional Globe* (Washington, D.C.: Congressional Globe Office, 1869), part 1, p. 558 ("I find by reference to the bill now before the House that it proposes to affect the question of suffrage not only in reference to the election of members of Congress, but also in reference to the election of the presidential electors. I have no difficulty in relation to members of Congress, for I believe that we possess that power. But I would ask the gentleman whether this bill is not in violation of that provision of the Constitution which prescribes that presidential electors shall be appointed in such manner as the Legislatures of the several States may respectively direct?").

[186] "Comments of Senator Davis, 41st Congress, Second Session, May 20, 1870," 42 *Congressional Globe* (Washington, D.C.: Congressional Globe Office, 1870), part 4, p. 3665 (making this point); see also "Comments of Senator Casserly, 41st Congress, Second Session, May 20, 1870," 42 *Congressional Globe* (Washington, D.C.: Congressional Globe Office, 1870), appendix, p. 472 (noting that the Fifteenth Amendment "is more limited in its language" than the Thirteenth or Fourteenth Amendments).

[187] The legal scholarship is split on whether Section 2 was intended to be operative after the ratification of the Fifteenth Amendment. See Chin, "Reconstruction, Felon Disenfranchisement, and the Right to Vote," 259–316, 263 (conceding that "Section 2 could still have an independent role if it were construed to cover suffrage restrictions other than race" but concluding that it cannot play this role because it has been narrowly interpreted by the courts). But see William W. Van Alstyne, "The

The history of the Fourteenth and Fifteenth Amendments indicates that the Framers had a number of concerns including, but not limited to, expanding federal power to encompass the north (and possibly the west[188]), securing partisan advantage, and protecting the formerly enslaved;[189] they were not, however, trying to limit their authority by replacing Section 2 of the Fourteenth Amendment with Section 1 of the Fifteenth.

Indeed, the power of the Fifteenth Amendment would come in its tailored focus on race as a criterion that was irrelevant to being an elector. This was a view that had, to that point, been implicit in Section 2 and, post–Thirteenth Amendment, the Guarantee Clause as well. The Fifteenth Amendment, which passed Congress on February 26, 1869 with text remarkably similar to the Senate version (sans the right to hold office), served as confirmation and support for the principles of the Fourteenth Amendment and helped further refine the republican form of government requirement.[190]

Just as the Thirteenth Amendment deemed that slavery was no longer consistent with the republican ideal, even if compatible with republicanism at the founding, the Fifteenth Amendment explicitly deemed racial discrimination in voting incompatible with republican principles, even if states retained the authority to disenfranchise potential voters for permissible reasons. Prior to the Fifteenth Amendment, there was no way for Congress to ensure the success of Reconstruction and guarantee Republican dominance.[191] Even with the ratification of the Fifteenth Amendment, additional steps would be needed.

Fourteenth Amendment, the 'Right' to Vote, and the Understanding of the Thirty-Ninth Congress," (1965) *Supreme Court Review* 33–70; Franita Tolson, "Constitutional Structure of Voting Rights Enforcement," (2014) 89 *Washington Law Review* 379–439.

188 See Chapter 7. See also Crum, "The Unabridged Fifteenth Amendment," 1109–10 ("Because Section Two penalized only the disenfranchisement of citizens, the continued disenfranchisement of Chinese immigrants would not be penalized. Put differently, the Western States would continue to benefit in the House for their noncitizen population, but they would not be penalized for disenfranchising them.").

189 Earl M. Maltz, *Civil Rights, the Constitution, and Congress, 1863–1869* (Lawrence: University Press of Kansas, 1990), p. 135 (noting that moderate and conservative Republicans endorsed a "constitutional amendment dealing with suffrage [that] would admittedly be an infringement on states' rights, but at the same time, it could be a narrowly defined federal encroachment that would leave the balance of power between the state and the federal governments otherwise unaltered"). A number of opponents of the Fifteenth Amendment accused Republicans of treading on the sovereignty of the states to secure partisan advantage. See, e.g., "Comments of Representative Eldridge, 40th Congress, Third Session, January 27, 1869," 40 *Congressional Globe* (Washington, D.C.: Congressional Globe Office, 1869), part 1, p. 645 (noting that "these measures have their origin and support in the most intense partyism").

190 The final language of the Fifteenth Amendment was also very similar to Boutwell's proposed legislation, H.R. 1667, in which he invoked, among other provisions, the Guarantee Clause as authorization because it "empower[s] the federal government to prevent the establishment of an aristocracy" which was established in "any state that disenfranchised any class of men." See Crum, "The Superfluous Fifteenth Amendment?," 1607. See also ibid., 1605–1610, 1616 n. 467.

191 By 1869, the Republicans were only five years (or two elections) away from losing control of the House of Representatives. Coletta, "Democratic Party," p. 987.

6.4 THE PATCHWORK OF FEDERAL ENFORCEMENT: THE ENFORCEMENT ACTS AS BAROMETERS OF CONSTITUTIONAL MEANING

The new southern governments created in the wake of the Military Reconstruction Act ensured the ratification of the Fifteenth Amendment. As a condition of readmission, Congress required Texas, Virginia, Mississippi, and Georgia to ratify, securing the three-fourths of states needed to make the Fifteenth Amendment a part of the Constitution on March 30, 1870.[192] On paper, at least, African American men had achieved the political equality that had been in flux since emancipation, but in practice, this equality would prove to be difficult to maintain, and eventually, prove illusory altogether.[193]

Between 1870 and 1872, Congress enacted five laws to ensure that the Constitution's newest political community would be protected by more than mere parchment barriers. Two of these laws, the Enforcement Acts of 1870[194] and 1871,[195] created a nationwide system of oversight for federal elections and punished malfeasance by state election officials. A third Enforcement Act, the Ku Klux Klan Act of 1871,[196] gave the president the authority to deploy the military and suspend the writ of habeas corpus, and would help to counter the terrorism of White vigilante groups wreaking havoc across most of the South.[197]

This sweeping set of laws, collectively known as "the Force Acts," showed just how far Congress was willing to go to assert its power to remake the American electorate. Rather than relying on a single constitutional provision, lawmakers pulled from

[192] Wang, *Trial of Democracy*, p. 50. See also Travis Crum, "The Lawfulness of the Fifteenth Amendment" (2022) 97 *Notre Dame Law Review* 1543–1618.

[193] Gabriel J. Chin, "The 'Voting Rights Act of 1867': The Constitutionality of Federal Regulation of Suffrage During Reconstruction" (2004) *North Carolina Law Review* 1581–1652, 1582 (arguing that the "Reconstruction Acts had a much greater impact on African-American suffrage in the South than the Fourteenth or Fifteenth Amendments" but "[t]hey failed to prevent the political, cultural, and economic tragedy of Jim Crow … because the fundamental condition – unalterable suffrage requirements – was not honored.").

[194] An Act to enforce the Rights of Citizens of the United States to vote in the several States of the Union, and for other Purposes, ch. 114, 16 Stat. 140 (1870) [Enforcement Act of 1870].

[195] An Act to amend an Act approved May 31, 1870, entitled "An Act to enforce the Rights of Citizens of the United States to vote in the several States of this Union, and for other Purposes," ch. 99, 16 Stat. 433 (1871) [Enforcement Act of 1871]. This provision is also known as the second Force Act. See United States Senate, "The Enforcement Acts of 1870 and 1871," www.senate.gov/artandhistory/history/common/generic/EnforcementActs.htm.

[196] An Act to enforce the Provisions of the Fourteenth Amendment to the Constitution of the United States, and for other Purposes, ch. 22, 17 Stat. 13 (1871) [Ku Klux Klan Act].

[197] Congress also enacted two other laws during this period that had provisions enforcing the Fourteenth and Fifteenth Amendments. Wang, *Trial of Democracy*, p. 57 (noting that these laws dealt with immigration and appropriations). These laws are beyond the scope of this project, which focuses on the first three laws enacted in 1870–71 – the Enforcement Acts of 1870 and 1871, the Ku Klux Klan Force Act – collectively referred to as the "Force Acts." See United States Senate, "The Enforcement Acts of 1870 and 1871," www.senate.gov/artandhistory/history/common/generic/EnforcementActs.htm.

several sources of authority – including the Fourteenth and Fifteenth Amendments and the Elections Clause – as the foundation for these formidable pieces of legislation that were designed to protect the new political community of "We the Voters," created by the Military Reconstruction Acts, the Guarantee Clause, and the new state constitutions mandated by the Reconstruction Acts.

On Monday, February 21, 1870, less than three weeks after the ratification of the Fifteenth Amendment, Representative John Bingham introduced House Bill 1293 to "enforce the right of citizens of the United States to vote in the several States of this Union who have hitherto been denied that right, on account of race, color, or previous condition of servitude."[198] Although framed as an effort to enforce the mandates of the new amendment, it was clear from the scope of the bill, the debates over its language, and the law's final form that the Enforcement Act of 1870 went beyond prohibiting abridgments or denials of the right to vote on the basis of race.[199] The law not only reached discriminatory voter qualification standards, but also enforced the disqualification provisions of Section 3 of the Fourteenth Amendment; imposed criminal penalties for wayward election officials; empowered the federal government to supervise congressional elections; and expanded the jurisdiction of federal courts to resolve election disputes, among other things.[200]

Importantly, the Enforcement Act of 1870 clarified the scope of congressional power over elections now that the last of the Reconstruction-era amendments had been ratified. At the outset, the Act guaranteed nondiscriminatory access to the ballot.[201]

198 "Introduction of Suffrage Bill by Representative Bingham, 41st Congress, Second Session, February 21, 1870," 42 *Congressional Globe* (Washington, D.C.: Congressional Globe Office, 1870), part 2, p. 1459.

199 See, e.g., Richard M. Vallely, "Partisan Entrepreneurship and Policy Windows," in Stephen Skowronek and Matthew Glassman (eds.), *Formative Acts: American Politics in the Making* (Philadelphia: University of Pennsylvania Press, 2007), p. 130 (describing the Enforcement Acts of 1870 and 1871 and the Immigration and Naturalization Act of 1870 as a reaction to "the largest fraud ever devised in American electoral history – the production by Tammany Hall of sixty thousand naturalization papers a month before the 1868 elections in New York state, which tainted 16 percent of the state's presidential vote").

200 See, for example, "Comments of Representative Bingham, 41st Congress, Second Session, May 27, 1870," 42 *Congressional Globe* (Washington, D.C.: Congressional Globe Office, 1870), part 5, p. 3871. ("[T]he Senate amendment contained various provisions for the enforcement of certain sections of the fourteenth article of the amendments to the Constitution. It contained also a provision authorizing the President of the United States to employ the [military] at his discretion, in elections.... And it contained further, a provision giving jurisdiction to the district and circuit courts of the United States, concurrently with the State courts, in all contested elections, save elections of members of Congress and elections of members of the State Legislatures."). Sections 14 and 15 of the Enforcement Act sought to enforce the disqualification provisions of Section 3 of the Fourteenth Amendment. An Act to enforce the Rights of Citizens of the United States to vote in the several States of the Union, and for other Purposes, ch. 114, 16 Stat. 143–144, ss. 14 and 15 (1870) [Enforcement Act of 1870].

201 An Act to enforce the Rights of Citizens of the United States to vote in the several States of the Union, and for other Purposes, ch. 114, 16 Stat. 140, s. 2 (1870) [Enforcement Act of 1870]; ibid., 16 Stat. 145–146, s. 22. See also Pamela Brandwein, *Rethinking the Judicial Settlement of Reconstruction* (New York: Cambridge University Press, 2011) (arguing that the President and Congress, not the Court, were the ones to abandon racial minorities during Reconstruction).

Section 1 stated that all citizens of the United States can vote "without distinction of race, color, or previous condition of servitude,"[202] superseding any state law stating otherwise. With the Fifteenth Amendment and, now, the first Force Act, there were no credible arguments remaining that Section 2 of the Fourteenth Amendment permitted states to disenfranchise their voters if they were willing to pay the penalty of reduced representation.

States retained their authority to impose certain prerequisites to voting, but all citizens, pursuant to Section 2 of the Enforcement Act, must have equal opportunity to show that they meet the qualifications.[203] Controversially, Section 2 criminalized violations of state law when those violations were aimed at denying an individual's voting rights on the basis of race.[204] This was a dramatic expansion of federal authority, linking state law enforcement directly to the protection of federal rights.

Sections 3 and 4 addressed election administrator malfeasance, penalizing those who obstructed an otherwise qualified voter from casting a ballot. Election officials could be charged under federal law if they "hinder, delay, prevent, or obstruct, any citizen from doing any act required to be done to qualify him to vote or from voting at any election."[205] These provisions offered protection for the right to vote as a federally protected right, independent of state law.

Section 5 protected individuals from retaliation by private parties who sought to deter them from voting by, for example, threatening to terminate employment contracts and leasing arrangements.[206] This section complimented the Civil Rights Act of 1866, which gave individuals the right "to make and enforce contracts…and to inherit, purchase, lease, sell…real and personal property."[207]

Notably, the Enforcement Act of 1870 also reached actions by private individuals, a clear warning to the Ku Klux Klan, the Knights of the White Camelia, and other White supremacist paramilitary organizations who had terrorized Black people across the South.[208] Section 6 penalized two or more individuals who acted with the intent to prevent a citizen's "free exercise and enjoyment of any right or

[202] An Act to enforce the Rights of Citizens of the United States to vote in the several States of the Union, and for other Purposes, ch. 114, 16 Stat. 140, s. 1 (1870) [Enforcement Act of 1870].

[203] Ibid., s. 2.

[204] See *Ex parte Clarke*, 100 U.S. 399, 408 (1879) (Field, J., dissenting) (arguing that the incorporation of state law offenses into federal law unconstitutionally expanded the scope of federal power).

[205] An Act to enforce the Rights of Citizens of the United States to vote in the several States of the Union, and for other Purposes, ch. 114, 16 Stat. 141, s. 4 (1870) [Enforcement Act of 1870]. This particular provision was invalidated in *United States v. Reese*, 92 U.S. 214 (1876), because of its failure to criminalize only race-based disenfranchisement. But see Tolson, "Voting Rights Enforcement," 424 (arguing that *Reese* was wrongly decided).

[206] An Act to enforce the Rights of Citizens of the United States to vote in the several States of the Union, and for other Purposes, ch. 114, 16 Stat. 141, s. 5 (1870) [Enforcement Act of 1870].

[207] Wang, *Trial of Democracy*, p. 67 (noting that the Act "gave substance to the Fifteenth Amendment and identified the connection between civil and political rights").

[208] Robert C. Byrd, *The Senate, 1789–1989: Addresses on the History of the United States Senate*, 4 vols. (Washington, D.C.: United States Government Printing Office, 1988), v. 1, p. 300.

privilege granted or secured to him by the Constitution or laws of the United States," providing a layer of protection from private infringement.[209]

The remedies that the federal government could marshal under the 1870 Act to protect voters from state action and private violence were similarly impressive. Section 16 of the Act (the precursor to what is now 42 U.S.C. § 1981) gave individuals the right to enforce the protections of the Civil Rights Act of 1866 (to enforce contracts, give evidence, sue and be sued, sell property, etc.).[210] The law also gave federal district courts jurisdiction over cases brought pursuant to its provisions; empowered federal marshals and district attorneys with investigative authority; and authorized the president to use the military to prevent violence at the polls.[211]

Indeed, the ability to remove cases from state to federal court became an important mechanism for enforcing the provisions of the respective Force Acts.[212] Section 7 of the Habeas Corpus Act of 1867 made the writ available to any individual held in custody for "for any act done, or omitted to be done, in pursuance of a law of the United States ...."[213] This provision guaranteed that federal officials tasked with enforcing the Force Acts could, if detained by state authorities, collaterally challenge their detention.

The Enforcement Act of 1870 was the first time that, legislatively, congressional focus shifted north. The Democratic Party had rebounded quickly in the post–Civil War era, even winning the state of New York in the presidential election of 1868. But part of the party's success was due to electoral fraud in which immigrants were provided with false naturalization papers to cast ballots in northern elections.[214] Thus, the Enforcement Act's goals were not only to protect southern Black people from the Ku Klux Klan's terrorism and secure their voting rights, but also to deal with election fraud in the North. Coupled with the Naturalization Act of 1870, which sought to curb the use of false naturalization papers by recent immigrants seeking to vote, the Enforcement Act of 1870 stood as a nationwide commitment by congressional Republicans to free and fair elections.[215]

[209] An Act to enforce the Rights of Citizens of the United States to vote in the several States of the Union, and for other Purposes, ch. 114, 16 Stat. 141, s. 6 (1870) [Enforcement Act of 1870].

[210] Ibid., 16 Stat. 144, s. 16. See also Civil Rights Act of 1991, Pub. L. No. 102–166, 105 Stat. 1071 (1991), codified at 42 U.S.C. § 1981; *Johnson v. Railway Express Agency, Inc.*, 421 U.S. 454 (1975) (holding that private employers can be sued for racial discrimination under Section 1981).

[211] Wang, *Trial of Democracy*, p. 66

[212] See, e.g., An Act to amend an Act approved May 31, 1870, entitled "An Act to enforce the Rights of Citizens of the United States to vote in the several States of this Union, and for other Purposes," ch. 99, 16 Stat. 433, ss. 14, 17 (1871) [Enforcement Act of 1871].

[213] Wiecek, "The Great Writ," 535.

[214] Albie Burke, "Federal Regulation of Congressional Elections in Northern Cities, 1871–94" (1970) 14 *American Journal of Legal History* 17–34, 21–22; Andrew Gumbel, "Election Fraud and the Myths of American Democracy" (2008) 75 *Social Research* 1109–34, 1117.

[215] Wang, *Trial of Democracy*, p. 68.

The Enforcement Act of 1871, with its nineteen sections, went further than the Enforcement Act of 1870.[216] Not only did the 1871 Act reiterate the criminal penalties for voter fraud from its 1870 counterpart,[217] the law also instituted a system of federal oversight for congressional elections. Section 2 of the 1871 Act empowered federal judges to appoint two election supervisors, one from each of the major political parties, to oversee congressional elections in areas with a population of at least twenty thousand people.[218] Section 4 required that the supervisors be present "at all times and places fixed for the registration of voters,"[219] and, under Section 13, federal judges could "require of the supervisors of election, where necessary, lists of the persons who may register and vote … and to cause the names of those upon any such list whose right to register or vote shall be honestly doubted to be verified by proper inquiry and examination…."[220] The 1871 Act also established stiff penalties for those who harassed these officials.[221]

The breadth of the Enforcement Acts of 1870 and 1871 reflected the belief that fraud had become inextricably intertwined with not only disenfranchising Black voters but also suppressing support for the Republican Party among White voters.[222] Because it was not clear that the Fourteenth and Fifteenth Amendments, as then interpreted, were broad enough to address this problem, arguments arose regarding the constitutionality of both of these statutes.

Opponents argued, for example, that the 1870 Act was unconstitutional because regulations such as voter registration requirements and poll taxes do not fall within

216 An Act to amend an Act approved May 31, 1870, entitled "An Act to enforce the Rights of Citizens of the United States to vote in the several States of this Union, and for other Purposes," ch. 99, 16 Stat. 433 (1871) [Enforcement Act of 1871]; see also ibid., 16 Stat. at 433–434, s. 2 ("[W]henever in any city or town having upward of twenty thousand inhabitants, there shall be two citizens … of different political parties … who shall be designated as supervisors of election."); 16 Stat. at 434–435, s. 5 ("That it shall be the duty of the said supervisors of election, and they, and each of them, are hereby authorized and required … to challenge any vote offered by any person whose legal qualifications the supervisors … shall doubt"); 16 Stat. at 436, s. 8 (designating marshals to protect the election supervisors and to arrest individuals who violate the Act). See also An Act to enforce the Rights of Citizens of the United States to vote in the several States of the Union, and for other Purposes, ch. 114, 16 Stat. 145–146, ss. 20–22 (1870) [Enforcement Act of 1870].

217 An Act to amend an Act approved May 31, 1870, entitled "An Act to enforce the Rights of Citizens of the United States to vote in the several States of this Union, and for other Purposes," ch. 99, 16 Stat. 436, s. 10 (1871) [Enforcement Act of 1871].

218 Ibid., 16 Stat. 433, s. 2 ("[W]henever in any city or town having upward of twenty thousand inhabitants, there shall be two citizens … of different political parties … who shall be designated as supervisors of election.").

219 Ibid., 16 Stat. 434, s. 4.

220 Ibid., 16 Stat. 437–438, s. 14.

221 Ibid., 16 Stat. 435–437, ss. 7, 9, 10, 11.

222 Wang. *Trial of Democracy*, p. 68 ("Although the primary object of the Enforcement Act of May 31, 1870, was to protect southern black voters from Klan terrorism, several sections of the act also dealt with fraudulent practices in northern elections. True, the Fifteenth Amendment neither addressed election fraud nor specifically authorized Congress to provide legislation to correct it. But the reality that northern fraud could hurt the party as much as southern black disenfranchisement, and eventually hurt the whole system of congressional elections, alarmed Republicans.").

the scope of the Fifteenth Amendment, since they are "applicable alike to citizens of all colors, races, and conditions ...."[223] Other representatives did not limit themselves to attacking the 1870 Act as beyond the terms of the Fifteenth Amendment, arguing that it exceeded the scope of the Elections Clause as well.[224] What sounded the alarm loudest among Democrats, however, was that the Enforcement Acts reflected a structural shift over the regulation of federal elections from the states to the federal government, grounded in both the Reconstruction Amendments and constitutional provisions that predated the Civil War, like the Elections Clause, but had long been an underutilized source of federal power.[225]

Through the Enforcement Acts, Congress asserted the right to oversee not only the qualifications of voters but also the administration of federal elections, a move that cast a long shadow over state election practices. To many Democrats, this was not just legislation; instead, it was a structural reimagining of who controlled American democracy. For example, the appointment of federal supervisors who oversaw the election process from registration to certification of the winner made it difficult to commit fraud or disenfranchisement in any local, state, or federal election.[226] Many of the 1871 Act's subsections were also extremely controversial, with Democrats (and some begrudgingly supportive, but nonetheless concerned, Republicans) questioning the constitutionality of imposing of criminal penalties for violating the Act's terms, criticizing its broad application to any denial of the right to vote, and bemoaning its interference with state election systems.[227]

Most Republicans tended to resist any characterization of federal power that would make it impossible to confront the day-to-day realities of voter disenfranchisement

223 "Comments of Representative Kerr, 41st Congress, Second Session, May 27, 1870," 42 *Congressional Globe* (Washington, D.C.: Congressional Globe Office, 1870), part 5, p. 3872.

224 "Comments of Representative Potter, 41st Congress, Second Session, May 27, 1870," 42 *Congressional Globe* (Washington, D.C.: Congressional Globe Office, 1870), part 5, p. 3876 ("Many of [the Enforcement Act of 1870's] provisions relate neither to the time, place, nor manner of holding elections, in respect of which Congress is entitled to legislate by the fourth section of the Constitution, nor to the denial or abridgment of suffrage on account of race, color, or previous condition of servitude as to which legislation is authorized by the fifteenth amendment....").

225 "Comments of Representative Bingham, 41st Congress, Second Session, May 27, 1870," 42 *Congressional Globe* (Washington, D.C.: Congressional Globe Office, 1870), part 5, pp. 3871–3872.

226 Franita Tolson, "What Is Abridgment? A Critique of Two Section Twos" (2015) 67 *Alabama Law Review* 433–484, 463 (discussing fraud in northern states).

227 "Comments of Senator Hamilton, 41st Congress, Second Session, May 18, 1870," 42 *Congressional Globe* (Washington, D.C.: Congressional Globe Office, 1870), appendix, p. 355 (disputing that Congress can impose criminal penalties under the Fifteenth Amendment because "the denial of the exercise of a certain power by the Constitution to a State does not thereby confer upon Congress power over the subject-matter of such denial"); "Comments of Senator Casserly, 41th Congress, Second Session, May 20, 1870," 42 *Congressional Globe* (Washington, D.C.: Congressional Globe Office, 1870), appendix, pp. 473–474 (comments of Casserly) (arguing that there was a "difference between legislation by Congress to execute an express power exclusive in itself, and legislation to enforce a limitation of a general power exclusive in the States. In the former case Congress may claim a liberal construction in the aid of its express exclusive power. In the latter case the State has a right to restrict Congress to the very terms of the prohibition. This is especially true when the prohibition affects the power of the State over a subject such as the suffrage.").

and election fraud, both of which necessitated greater federal involvement in both the North and the South. Black voters and Republican officials continued to be assaulted across the South in the fall of 1870 and spring of 1871, providing countless examples of why federal oversight remained necessary.[228] However, the Enforcement Acts as well as the Ku Klux Klan Act, which punished individuals who deprived United States citizens of "any [federal] rights, privileges or immunities,"[229] pushed the boundaries of Congress's authority to reach private individuals under the Reconstruction Amendments. To safeguard its newest stakeholders, Congress would not stop at enacting new statutes and constitutional provisions but also turned to a familiar friend to protect this constituency: its authority under Article I, Section 5 to judge the elections of its members.

6.5 EXPANDED OPPORTUNITY FOR FEDERAL INTERVENTION THROUGH ARTICLE I, SECTION 5

During the chaos of the Civil War, contested elections surged across the South. With the balance of power in Congress (and some might say, the future of the republic) at stake, Republicans leaned into their constitutional authority to judge the elections of their members, using this provision as a tool to secure and solidify their majority in the war-torn and, eventually, restructured southern states.[230]

Starting with the Thirty-Seventh Congress (1861–63), the House considered almost six times as many cases as it had during the antebellum period, where it entertained just under three per Congress, on average. This number would inch upwards during Reconstruction, from nineteen and seventeen in the Thirty-Seventh and Thirty-Eighth Congresses (1863–65), respectively, to as many as thirty-eight cases in the late 1890s, averaging approximately fifteen contested election cases per Congress during this period.[231]

[228] See, e.g., Herbert Shapiro, "Afro-American Responses to Race Violence during Reconstruction" (1972) 36 *Science & Society* 158–170, 163–165; Schaefer, "The Ku Klux Klan," 143–157, 144–145; Herbert Shapiro, "The Ku Klux Klan during Reconstruction: The South Carolina Episode" (1964) 49 *The Journal of Negro History* 34–55, 35–36; Michael Wallace, "The Uses of Violence in American History" (1970–71) 40 *The American Scholar* 81–102, 85–86.

[229] An Act to enforce the Provisions of the Fourteenth Amendment to the Constitution of the United States, and for other Purposes, ch. 22, 17 Stat. 13 (1871) [Ku Klux Klan Act].

[230] Charles H. Rammelkamp, "Contested Congressional Elections" (1905) 20 *Political Science Quarterly* 421–442, 432; Jeffery A. Jenkins, "Partisanship and Contested Election Cases in the House of Representatives, 1789–2002" (2004) 18 *Studies in American Political Development* 112–135, 113.

[231] Jenkins, "Partisanship and Contested Election Cases," 115. According to Professor Jenkins:

> In the Antebellum period, relatively few contested election cases were dealt with in the House – only 107 over the first thirty-six Congresses, or an average of just under three per Congress. However, a significant jump occurred with the Civil War, as nineteen and seventeen cases were considered in the 37th and 38th Congresses (1861–1865). The number of cases remained relatively high for the next thirty-five years, alternating between five cases in the 49th Congress (1885–1887) and thirty-eight cases, the high-water mark for contested election cases, in the 54th

The outcomes of these cases tended to favor the majority party. As Henry L. Dawes, who chaired the House Committee on Elections from the 1860s to 1875, noted, "each case [was] becoming a partisan struggle…There is no tyranny like that of majorities."[232] In general, only half of the decisions from 1789 to 2002 favored the majority party, but importantly, as Professor Jeffrey Jenkins found in a study of over 600 contested election cases, majority party candidates were more likely to bring frivolous challenges (72 percent of all cases), believing that they would be awarded the seat by virtue of their affiliation.

Delving more deeply into the statistics revealed that this assumption was warranted – an assessment of split Committee decisions, where the Committee disagreed about the underlying merits of a nonfrivolous claim, revealed that the majority party candidate won nearly 70 percent of the time.[233] In addition, where the seat flipped from one party to the other as a result of a challenge, 85.8 percent of cases favored the majority party.[234] Very rarely in the history of available cases did the majority party give the seat of an incumbent to a minority party challenger.[235]

The sharp uptick in cases illustrated how election challenges under Article I, Section 5 could produce reasonably reliable partisan outcomes, an advantage that Republicans maximized in the years between the Civil War and the dawn of the twentieth century. One telling example came in 1866, when a heated dispute broke out over a U.S. Senate seat from New Jersey. The Democratic-controlled state legislature had awarded the seat to John P. Stockton, a Democrat, but his arrival in Washington was met with swift resistance.

Leading the charge were Republican senators Charles Sumner and William Pitt Fessenden, who were not just questioning Stockton's credentials. At the heart of their opposition was a strategic calculation: Republicans needed every possible vote in the Senate to override President Andrew Johnson's veto of the Freedmen's Bureau bill, a cornerstone of their Reconstruction agenda.[236] Hanging their hats on procedural objections to Stockton's appointment, they argued that Stockton's selection was invalid because he only received a plurality, not a majority, of the votes in the joint session that elected him. The joint session voted to change the majority requirement to a plurality requirement, but that vote itself only received

Congress (1895–1897). In all, the period between the Civil War and the turn-of-the century, the 37th through 55th Congresses (1861–1899), witnessed 262 contested election cases, or an average of nearly fifteen per Congress.

232 Vincent M. Barnett, Jr., "Contested Congressional Elections in Recent Years" (1939) 54 *Political Science Quarterly* 187–215, 190.

233 Jenkins, "Partisanship and Contested Election Cases," 121.

234 Ibid.

235 See ibid. ("Only fifteen times in a total of 106 cases has a sitting majority party member been unseated in favor of a minority party contestant.")

236 United States Senate, "The Election Case of John P. Stockton of New Jersey (1866)," www.senate.gov/about/origins-foundations/electing-appointing-senators/contested-senate-elections/047John_Stockton.htm.

a plurality.[237] Though the challenge against Stockton came immediately after his election, the Senate allowed him to take his seat, and the case was referred to the Judiciary Committee. The Judiciary Committee recommended that Stockton keep his seat because all state legislatures elected their senators in different ways, but the full Senate voted to deny Stockton the seat, 23–20.[238] The unseating of Stockton gave the Republicans the requisite two-thirds vote needed to override President Johnson's veto of not only that bill in April 1866, but also the second Freedman's Bureau bill in July 1866.

This particular case had reverberations beyond its specific facts, becoming a vivid example of how contested elections could serve purposes far greater than resolving procedural ambiguities. In the hands of determined legislators, they became powerful instruments, not just for upholding constitutional order, but for steering the direction of national policy. By blocking Stockton's appointment, Republicans cleared the path to advance the broader aims of Reconstruction.

The Stockton dispute also led to changes in Senate appointments, more broadly. In response to the wildly inconsistent ways in which states selected senators (and a number of other abuses by states), Congress passed a law to standardize how senators were selected by state legislatures.[239] Enacted in July 1866, the law, enacted pursuant to the Elections Clause, required each house of the state legislature to vote separately for senator and meet in a subsequent joint session. The candidate who was the choice of both houses would automatically be selected; if the vote was divided, the legislature would vote until there was a winner.[240]

During this period, Congress also changed its rules regarding when results would be disregarded if the election was punctuated by intimidation and violence. Prior to 1869, Congress would only throw out election results where the contestant had shown that intimidation and violence on Election Day changed the outcome of the election. In 1870, this rule changed.[241]

In *Hunt v. Sheldon*, for example, the House Committee on Elections, reviewing an election contest from Louisiana's second congressional district, found that there

[237] Ibid.

[238] "John P. Stockton of New Jersey: Thirty-Ninth Congress, First Session," Richard D. Hupman (comp.), *Senate Election, Expulsion and Censure Cases from 1789–1960: Senate Document 71, 87th Congress, Second Session* (Washington, D.C.: United States Government Printing Office, 1962), p. 38.

[239] 39 Cong. Ch. 245, 14 Stat. 243 (July 25, 1866).

[240] See Anne M. Butler et al., *United States Senate Election, Expulsion, and Censure Cases*, 1793–1990 (Washington, D.C.: Gov. Printing Office, 1995), p.129 (noting that, prior to this law, one house of the state legislature could block a senate election by refusing to meet or send members to the joint assembly but, under the 1866 law, the joint assembly has automatic jurisdiction if one house of the state legislature fails to meet).

[241] Chester H. Rowell, *A Historical and Legal Digest of all the Contested Election Cases in the House of Representatives of the United States from the First to the Fifty-Sixth Congress, 1789–1901* (Washington, D.C.: Government Printing Office, 1901; reprinted edition: Westport, CT: Greenwood Press, 1976), pp. 674–675.

was an organized and longstanding campaign of violence and intimidation in some Louisiana parishes to prevent Republicans and Black people from voting.[242] At the beginning of Reconstruction, Republican candidates got a majority of the votes in the district encompassing Orleans and Jefferson parishes; however, in the 1869 elections, the Republican vote fell to less than one-tenth of the tally.[243] In other parishes, practically no Republican votes were cast at all.[244]

Much of the decline was due to efforts by a secret paramilitary organization known as the Knights of the White Camelia, who first used social and business boycotts to punish Republican voters, but quickly turned to violence and murder.[245] The contested election case of *Hunt v. Sheldon* took place under these circumstances. The Committee determined that the intimidation and violence that caused skewed results in some parishes should be thrown out, and that only the election results of peaceful parishes would be counted toward the outcome.[246] This new rule made a difference in a number of contests,[247] although challengers were still required to show that they would have received a sufficient number of votes in peaceful parishes to win their seats.[248]

This violence was not limited to Louisiana, and losing candidates across the former Confederacy were able to challenge their contests with varying results.[249] In *Wallace v. Simpson*, an 1869 South Carolina contested election case, a former colonel in the Confederate army – Simpson – won a congressional election after members of the Ku Klux Klan intimidated voters in six out of nine counties in the district, ultimately disenfranchising 5,700 individuals through violence that took place before and on Election Day.[250] Black and White voters aligned with the Republican Party were lynched, had property stolen, and endured pre-election cannon fire designed to frighten and discourage them from voting.[251] The Committee found that the contestant, Wallace, was entitled to the seat over Simpson because of these disenfranchising efforts.[252]

242 "Hunt v. Sheldon (case on merits), House Committee on Elections, 41st Congress (1869–1871)," in Rowell, *Contested Election Cases*, p. 241.

243 Ibid., pp. 241–242.

244 Ibid., p. 242.

245 Ibid.

246 Ibid.

247 See ibid., p. 675 (citing *Morey v. McCranie*, *Newsham v. Ryan*, and *Darrall v. Bailey*, which were all Louisiana cases with claims of voter intimidation).

248 See "'Sypher vs. St. Martin,' House Committee on Elections, 41st Congress (1869–1871)," in Rowell, *Contested Election Cases*, p. 241 (declaring a seat vacant where one-fifth of the votes were cast in a peaceful parish and the contestant received a small portion of that vote).

249 For detailed descriptions of election-related violence at the hands of the Ku Klux Klan across the south, against both Black and White Republicans, see Elaine F. Parsons, *Ku-Klux: The Birth of the Klan during Reconstruction* (Chapel Hill: University of North Carolina Press, 2015).

250 "Wallace vs. Simpson (case on merits), House Committee on Elections, 41st Congress (1869–1871)," in Rowell, *Contested Election Cases*, pp. 244–245.

251 Ibid., p. 245.

252 Ibid.

In a similar fashion, the 1870 Kentucky election contest of *Barnes v. Adams* involved an allegation by the contestant, Barnes, that former Confederate soldiers had voted in the election.[253] Unlike the *Wallace* dispute, however, there was Klan intimidation before the election, but none on the day of, which made it difficult for the contestant to show that violence and intimidation affected the outcome.[254] The Committee, finding that the numbers returned in the election were similar to prior cycles, let the results stand, and Adams kept his seat.[255] Presumably, the absence of violence on Election Day was not dispositive, as it would have been under the old congressional rules; the fact that turnout remained consistent based on census numbers justified the outcome in *Barnes*.

Throughout the late 1860s and early 1870s, the Ku Klux Klan was a dominant force across the South, intimidating voters in numerous election contests in the former Confederacy and border states.[256] As the cases of *Barnes v. Adams* and *Wallace v. Simpson* illustrate, whether there was recourse for voters in response to this violence was heavily fact dependent. In the 1871 case of *Sheafe v. Tillman*,[257] for example, the challenger, Democrat C. A. Sheafe, received a majority of 1,156 votes based on the original returns, but the governor of Tennessee rejected the votes of Lincoln County due to Klan intimidation and violence before the election.[258] The Committee on Elections seated Lewis Tillman, a Republican, ratifying the governor's rejection of Lincoln County votes that had left Tillman with a majority of 296 votes.[259]

Like the House, the Senate was not immune from its fair share of contested elections, a somewhat surprising fact given that Senators were appointed by state legislatures and not selected by the electorate. Controversies like the one surrounding John Stockton's appointment were not isolated events, and disputes over Senate elections occurred with some regularity.

Notably, there were arguments in several contests that, because of voter intimidation and violence in state legislative elections, the legislature was illegitimate and therefore lacked authority to appoint U.S. Senators. For example, Republican state legislators in Alabama challenged the 1870 appointment of George Goldwaithe on these grounds, arguing that the illegal election of some of the legislators rendered the appointment invalid.[260] Some legislators had been fraudulently elected in

[253] "Barnes vs. Adams, House Committee on Elections, 41st Congress (1869–1871)," in Rowell, *Contested Election Cases*, pp. 244–249.

[254] Ibid., p. 249.

[255] Ibid., p. 248.

[256] See Parsons, *Ku-Klux*.

[257] "Sheafe v. Tillman, House Committee on Elections, 41st Congress (1869–1871)," in Rowell, *Contested Election Cases*, pp. 257–259.

[258] Ibid., p. 258.

[259] Ibid.

[260] United States Senate, "The Election Case of George Goldthwaite of Alabama (1872)," www.senate.gov/about/origins-foundations/electing-appointing-senators/contested-senate-elections/056George_Goldthwaite.htm.

contests marred by violence and intimidation; others had no certificate of election; and some were ineligible to serve under Section 3 of the Fourteenth Amendment being that they were former officials in the Confederacy. While some Republican Senators expressed concerns about voter suppression in Alabama skewing the membership of the Alabama Legislature, the Senate ultimately seated Goldwaithe.[261]

The Committee took a different position with respect to the appointment of North Carolina Senator Zebulon B. Vance. Like Alabama, the North Carolina state legislature was skewed toward Democrats because of voter suppression and a very active Ku Klux Klan presence.[262] Vance's selection was challenged by Joseph C. Abbott, a Republican who moved to North Carolina after the Civil War, was appointed to the U.S. Senate in 1868, and had wide political support among the state's Black voters.[263] By 1870, the Black vote had been sufficiently suppressed such that the North Carolina legislature, controlled by Democrats and former Confederate officials, chose Vance over Abbott.[264] Abbott alleged that Vance was ineligible because he had served in the Confederate army and was the governor of North Carolina during the war, rendering him ineligible under Section 3 of the Fourteenth Amendment. The Senate agreed, declaring the selection void and calling for a new appointment. Instead of selecting Abbott, however, the North Carolina legislature appointed another candidate to the seat.[265]

As these disputes illustrate, the manner in which Congress deployed its power under Article I, Section 5 during Reconstruction varied, but partisan politics played an outsized role in many of the outcomes. Nothing exemplified this more than the series of election contests involving Josiah T. Walls, the same trailblazer who had distinguished himself as a member of Florida's biracial constitutional convention discussed earlier in this chapter.[266]

In 1870, Walls, a Republican, won Florida's at-large congressional seat and endured the first of his many election challenges from Silas Niblack, a White Democrat.[267] On paper, Niblack appeared to have the edge because the county returns gave him a slim majority of 192 votes more than Walls on Election Day. But the reality on the ground told a different story. In three counties within the district, Black voters had faced violent intimidation at the polls. Armed men had shown up to suppress Republican votes, and the state canvassing board responded

261 Ibid. For more on how rival legislatures and illegitimate legislatures raise core questions about the nature of republican government, see Chapter 7.

262 United States Senate, "The Election Case of Joseph C. Abbott v. Zebulon B. Vance and Matt W. Ransom of North Carolina (1872)," www.senate.gov/about/origins-foundations/electing-appointing-senators/contested-senate-elections/059Abbott_Vance_Ransom.htm.

263 Ibid.

264 Ibid.

265 Ibid.

266 See Chapter 6.1 (discussion of Josiah T. Walls).

267 "Niblack v. Walls, House Committee on Elections, 42nd Congress (1871–1873)," in Rowell, *Contested Election Cases*, pp. 282–283.

by discarding the returns from those counties, reasoning that the elections there had been neither free nor fair.[268]

The House Committee on Elections compared the reported turnout in the disputed counties to the 1870 census data, looking to see if the numbers lined up. In their view, turnout had not significantly deviated from expectations.[269] As a result, Walls lost his seat to Niblack, a seemingly straightforward result in light of *Barnes v. Adams*, which also looked at census data in rejecting an election challenge.

But what made the decision striking was its political valence. The Republican-led Committee had ruled in favor of a Democrat, which was unusual during a time when partisan advantage often drove the outcome of contested elections. That is, until one looks at the timing. The Committee deemed Niblack the winner of the seat on January 29, 1873,[270] when there was a little over a month left in the Forty-Second Congress (which ended on March 4th). At the time of his loss, Walls had already won an 1872 election for the newly redrawn second district and would be seated in the Forty-Third Congress, which began on March 4, 1873. In practical terms, Niblack was given a hollow victory, winning a seat that he would hold for little more than a month. Walls, undeterred, was headed back to Washington.

When Walls won re-election in the second district in 1874, he found himself subject to another election challenge, this time by Democrat Jesse Finley, a former Confederate colonel.[271] Although Walls won the election, Democrats took control of the House of Representatives in the 1874 elections and declared Finley the winner of the seat after he contested the results.[272]

Notably, Walls had a majority based on all the returns, but the Committee stated that fraudulent behavior by a Dr. Johnson, who allegedly brought in voters from different counties to pad the voter counts in Columbia County, explained Walls' vote margin.[273] The Committee discarded the votes in Columbia County and seated Finley based on dubious factual allegations.[274]

Despite his accomplishments – Walls would leave Congress after a distinguished political career in state and national politics to go on to become a professor at State Normal and Industrial College for Colored Students (now known as Florida A&M University) – he died in relative obscurity and was buried in an unmarked grave, an event that was not recorded or memorialized by any of the major Florida newspapers at the time.[275]

268 Ibid., p. 283.
269 Ibid.
270 Ibid.
271 "Finley v. Walls, House Committee on Elections, 44th Congress (1871–1873)," in Rowell, *Contested Election Cases*, pp. 305–308.
272 Ibid., p. 308.
273 Ibid., pp. 306–307.
274 Ibid., p. 305.
275 Fry, "A Forgotten Obituary."

Unsurprisingly, Democrat Finley was party to another election contest in 1881, this time facing a White Republican who had prevailed despite extensive voter fraud, intimidation, and violence against Black voters. In *Bisbee v. Finley*,[276] the Committee rejected returns in Hamilton County because Finley's supporters forced Black voters to drink alcohol and vote while intoxicated.[277] Without the votes in Hamilton County, the Republican, Bisbee, had a majority of 645 votes and was awarded the seat.[278] But the most important difference between Finley's 1874 successful contestation and his 1881 failed bid was Republican control of the House of Representatives. In 1880, Republicans edged out the Democratic majority, winning nineteen seats and gaining control of the House of Representatives.[279]

As the tumultuous 1860s and 1870s show, Section 2 of the Fourteenth Amendment was not an articulable, coherent theory of the Constitution if viewed standing alone. Instead, it was a predicate for a nationwide effort to expand the federal presence in state political systems through myriad constitutional and statutory provisions that not only altered the federalism landscape but also pushed the Constitution toward the Democratic theory that Justice Alito thought Section 2 lacked.

These provisions – from the Military Reconstruction Act to the Reconstruction Acts to the Enforcement Acts to constitutional provisions, both old and new – were not only enforcement mechanisms designed to ensure nondiscriminatory access to the ballot, but they also provided vehicles for Congress to reach state and private actors who might undermine suffrage or any right, privilege, or immunity protected by federal law. Unfortunately, this conglomerate of federal constitutional provisions and legislation – powerful when used in the aggregate – would never reach its full potential.

276 "Bisbee v. Finley, House Committee on Elections, 47th Congress (1871–1873)," in Rowell, *Contested Election Cases*, pp. 368–371.

277 Ibid., p. 370.

278 Ibid.

279 History, Art & Archives, U.S. House of Representatives, *Majority Changes in the House of Representatives, 1856 to Present* (Washington, D.C.: U.S. House of Representatives, n.d.), https://history.house.gov/Institution/Majority-Changes/Majority-Changes/.

PART IV

The Politics of Exclusion?

The Triumph of Partisan Politics over Broad Enfranchisement

Nevada Bloomer was a dedicated wife and mother who, if given a choice, would likely have been content to remain unknown to history. She did not protest in the streets, go on hunger strikes, or lobby the government for women's equality. But she was nonetheless involved in one of the most important voting rights cases in Washington territory, a case in which she asked the courts to sanction the right to vote that the legislature had recently extended to women.

Nevada's sudden interest in the women's suffrage movement must have certainly raised some eyebrows. How does someone previously not interested in these matters become the face of women's suffrage in the territory? The answer, in short, was that she was not, and did not want to become, a trailblazer. Instead, she was, in fact, an agent of chaos, drafted into a fight not of her choosing.

Rather than suffragette, she was a co-conspirator in a scheme to undermine women's suffrage in Washington on the eve of statehood. In fact, she believed that politics was the domain of men and was quite content to live her life as the wife of a local business owner.[1] Yet Spokane saloon owners, including Nevada's husband Edward Bloomer, were increasingly concerned about the prospect of prohibition and, more pointedly, the likelihood that women, if enfranchised, would vote in favor of a liquor ban. In the 1880s, the women's suffrage and temperance movements were linked, with prominent suffragists aligning themselves with the Women's Christian Temperance Movement.[2]

1 John Fahey, "The Nevada Bloomer Case: An Obedient Wife Played a Key Role in Delaying Women's Suffrage in Washington" (Summer 1998) 2 *Columbia: The Magazine of Northwest History* 42–45, www.washingtonhistory.org/wp-content/uploads/2020/04/02-2_Fahey-1.pdf.

2 Ibid.

Despite the protests of Bloomer and fellow saloon owners in Spokane, Washington Territory was surprisingly progressive on the issue of women's suffrage for its time. Like most territories striving for statehood, Washington initially limited voting rights to White men. But from its inception, the legal framework allowed room for change.

On March 2, 1853, Congress passed "An Act to Establish the Territorial Government of Washington," which carved out a portion of the Oregon territory to create what would later become Washington state.[3] The Act set up the territorial legislature, consisting of a Council and House of Representatives, as well as the governor's office. These offices were subject to periodic elections, in which those meeting the criteria set out in Section 5 of the Act could vote. Section 5 provided that "every white male inhabitant above the age of twenty-one years, who shall have been a resident of said Territory at the time of the passage of this act and shall possess the qualifications hereinafter prescribed, shall be entitled to vote at the first election...."[4]

However, the Act also built in flexibility for the future, providing that "the qualifications of voters and of holding office at all subsequent elections shall be such as shall be prescribed by the Legislative Assembly," subject to the caveat that "[t]hat the right of suffrage and of holding office shall be exercised only by citizens of the United States above the age of twenty-one years, and those above that age who shall have declared on oath their intention to become such, and shall have taken an oath to support the Constitution of the United States and the provisions of this act."[5]

In short, while Washington began with restrictive voting laws, its founding documents gave the territorial legislature room to expand suffrage. While there was a gender restriction for the first set of territorial elections, it was clear that the Act imposed no further obligation on Washington's legislature to limit suffrage to male inhabitants; Section 5 provided only that electors had to be American citizens (or one who intended to become a citizen) age twenty-one years or older. Notably, the legislature tried to enfranchise women within one year of the passage of the 1853 Act, but the measure failed by one vote.[6] The legislature was finally successful in 1883, and women voted in the territory for four years before the law was invalidated in 1887 on a legal technicality.[7]

One year later, during the last session before statehood, the legislature passed a new law enfranchising women.[8] This latest iteration provided that, subject to a

3 An Act to establish the Territorial Government of Washington, ch. 90, 10 Stat. 172 (1853).

4 Ibid., 10 Stat. 174, s. 5.

5 Ibid.

6 Rebecca J. Mead, *How the Vote Was Won: Woman Suffrage in the Western United States, 1868–1914* (New York: New York University Press, 2004), p. 45.

7 Ibid., pp. 48–49.

8 An Act Prescribing the Qualifications of Electors in the Territory of Washington, Approved January 18, 1888, in Washington Legislative Assembly, *Laws of Washington Territory Enacted by the Legislative Assembly, at Its Eleventh Biennial Session, 1887–8* (Olympia: Thos. H. Cavanaugh, Public Printer, 1888), Ch. LI, pp. 93–94.

residency requirement of six months, "all citizens of the United States, male and female, above the age of twenty-one years … shall be entitled to vote at any election in this territory…"[9] With the passage of this law, prominent Spokane businessmen, including salon owner Edward Bloomer, hatched a plan to challenge the law in court. Under her husband's direction, Nevada Bloomer tried to vote in elections in Spokane Falls, Washington in April 1888, but was turned away by complicit election judge, John Todd. Bloomer sued, alleging that Todd's actions violated the 1888 law that enfranchised women in the territory.

The Washington Territorial Supreme Court ruled against Nevada Bloomer, and in the process, gave Edward Bloomer and John Todd the exact result that they were seeking. Finding that the 1888 law conflicted with the 1853 federal act establishing the territory, the court held that the phrase "white male citizen" as used in the 1853 act was a limit on the legislative power of the territorial legislature that could not be expanded upon.[10] Had Congress meant just "citizens," a phrase that applied to men and women, they would not have added the qualifier that citizens be male to have the right to vote.[11] It was not the legislative intent of Congress, according to the court, that women be electors or serve in elected office. Although the 1853 act empowered the legislature to set voter qualifications for all elections beyond the first set of territorial elections, the court determined that gender was not a qualification that could be expanded upon under the act.[12]

Statehood did little to alter the view that women were not entitled to vote. In *Isaacs v. McNeil*, for example, the Washington circuit court of appeals, citing *Bloomer*, dismissed a case in which a woman sued after being turned away at the polls.[13] Because the election in which the plaintiff was disenfranchised happened after the *Bloomer* decision, the court held that the defendant election judges could not be held liable for treating *Bloomer* as governing law and refusing to receive the plaintiff's vote.[14] The saloon cabal had succeeded.

The circuitous path of voting rights in Washington territory showed how, even in the relatively progressive American west where many states proactively extended

9 Ibid., s. 1, p. 94.

10 *Bloomer v. Todd*, 19 P. 135, 141–142 (Wash. 1888).

11 Ibid., 141 ("…if it had been intended by congress to use the word 'citizen,' in the broad sense claimed for it, then there would have been no occasion for specifying, as congress did, in the first phrase, 'white male inhabitant,' if, in the use of the word 'citizen' in its place in the proviso it was intended to include females as well as males…[t]he power granted by congress in this section not being intended … to extend the first grant made to the 'white male inhabitants,' but to limit it to a smaller class of people in this territory").

12 Ibid., 143 ("In 1852, when this act was passed, the word 'citizen' was used as a qualification for voting and holding office, and, in our judgment, the word then meant and still signifies male citizenship, and must be so construed.").

13 *Isaacs v. McNeil*, 44 F. 32 (C.C.D. Wash. 1890).

14 Ibid.

suffrage rights to women,[15] this group still struggled to stake out their position in the political community of "We the Voters." They had never been able to gain a foothold in the Republican Party on this issue, even as they enjoyed mixed results at the state level. And women were not the only ones left behind. Other minority groups, notably Chinese immigrants and their descendants, found that they also had no place in the community of "We the Voters."[16] So, too, would the initial beneficiaries of the Republican Party – Black men – learn that the party's favor was fleeting.

By the mid-1870s, Republican majorities in Congress had mostly disappeared, and political volatility would come to define the era just as much as economic turmoil. But the shift away from a full commitment to the Reconstruction project started much earlier. The wavering commitment to equal civil and political rights for Black men occurred parallel to the evolution of Republicans from the party of Lincoln to the party of business.

By 1868, each party – Republican and Democrat – crystallized their positions on monetary policy, with the former illustrating a preference for the gold standard and the latter more amenable to paper currency.[17] These policy debates eventually eclipsed the Republican Party's focus on individual rights like suffrage and elevated other aspects of its pre–Civil War ideology, namely the commercialism that accompanied the valorization of free labor.[18] As northern banks became open to the gold standard, due to their investment in federal bonds during the war,[19] this created a new link between the Republican Party and northern capitalism. The previously impenetrable support for the Democratic Party in these corners began to shift.

Ulysses S. Grant hoped that the currency debate would distract from the racial strife that had dominated the country for much of the 1860s and early 1870s.[20] But disagreements about Reconstruction policy made it difficult for the Republican Party to move past the race issue, even if economics would emerge as a competing concern. In 1872, the Republican Party split as reform-minded members, disillusioned with the corruption in Grant's Administration and the continued military

15 "The first victory for [woman] suffrage on the American continent came by action of the Wyoming territorial legislature in 1869. The Utah territorial legislature enacted woman suffrage the following year. Woman suffrage was provided in the constitutions of both of these states when they were admitted to the union, Wyoming in 1890 and Utah in 1896." David R. Berman, "Male Support of Woman Suffrage: An Analysis of Voting Patterns in the Mountain West" (1987) 11 *Social Science History* 281–94, 292 fn 1.

16 See Gabriel Chin, "A Nation of White Immigrants: State and Federal Racial Preferences for White Noncitizens" (2020) 100 *Boston University Law Review* 1271–1314, 1290.

17 Bruce G. Carruthers and Sarah Babb, "The Color of Money and the Nature of Value: Greenbacks and Gold in Postbellum America" (1996) 101 *American Journal of Sociology* 1556–1591, 1564–1565.

18 Samuel DeCanio, *Democracy and the Origins of the American Regulatory State* (New Haven: Yale University Press, 2015), p. 80; Eric Foner, *Free Soil, Free Labor, Free Men: The Ideology of the Republican Party before the Civil War* (New York: Oxford University Press, 1970) (free labor ideology morphed from the idea that one owns his or her labor to the notion of laboring for wages).

19 See Carruthers and Babb, "Color of Money," 1576–1579.

20 DeCanio, *Democracy*, p. 81.

presence in the South, broke away to form the Liberal Republican Party. This splinter group advocated for civil service reform, an end to Reconstruction, and "universal amnesty" for former Confederates. They also embraced the gold standard, making the same appeal to big business as the mainstream Republican Party, but advocated for lower tariffs, which would promote international commerce.[21]

While the Liberal Republicans ultimately failed to win the presidency, the adoption of the Amnesty Act of 1872 – which opened the door for former Confederates to again hold public office – reflected the gains that they had made on changing the party's Reconstruction policy.[22] These changes happened notwithstanding the realities on the ground. For example, in Yazoo City, Mississippi – a majority-Black town that, according to historian Nicholas Lemann, in 1873 held "the only Mississippi election in the century following emancipation in which there was truly free Negro voting" – a violent confrontation erupted between White Democrats and Black Republicans ahead of the 1875 election cycle. The federal government did little to stop this wave of violence, which ultimately led to the collapse of Reconstruction in Mississippi.[23]

As federal enforcement receded, the South entered into a period of economic reorganization that set the stage for new forms of labor exploitation and the continuation of political violence. The demise of the slave-based plantation system and the volatility of the cotton market all but ensured the creation of new industries and the commission of new atrocities. In some places, sharecropping reigned; in others, opportunists turned their attention to the untapped natural resources beneath the soil.

Like many places in central Louisiana, Grant Parish became a haven for oil and gas prospecting in the late 1890s.[24] Once speculators discovered the rich reserves, they hoped that a new industry could displace the plantation economy that had proven lucrative for only a few farmers in the pre–Civil War era. In 1899, prospectors dug an eleven-hundred-foot shaft, finding not oil but the bones of African Americans murdered twenty-six years earlier during the Colfax Massacre. These individuals lost their lives to White Democrats who sought to seize control of the Grant Parish government from Republican officeholders.[25]

The Yazoo City and Colfax Massacres were but two mass casualty events of many that marked the reemergence of the southern White political class, who were not

21 Robert W. Burg, "Amnesty, Civil Rights, and the Meaning of Liberal Republicanism, 1862–1872" (2003) 4 *American Nineteenth Century History* 29–60; Andrew L. Slap, *The Doom of Reconstruction: The Liberal Republicans in the Civil War Era* (New York: Fordham University Press, 2010).

22 Slap, *The Doom of Reconstruction*, p. 184.

23 Nicholas Lemann, *Redemption: The Last Battle of the Civil War* (New York: Farrar, Staus and Giroux, 2006), pp. 100–134.

24 Franita Tolson, "Parchment Rights" (2022) 526 *Harvard Law Review Forum* 525–536.

25 LeeAnna Keith, *The Colfax Massacre; The Untold Story of Black Power, White Terror, and the Death of Reconstruction* (New York: Oxford University Press, 2008), p. xii.

only committed to governments ruled by White men in service to White people but also represented serious challenges to the Republican Party's commitment to universal male suffrage.

The 1890s saw a wave of state constitutional conventions that engaged in the "legal" disenfranchisement of African Americans and poor White people, yet many in Congress still believed they had the constitutional authority to enact legislation to counter these efforts. Congress first tried to police the offending state laws through legislation known as the Federal Elections Bill of 1890,[26] which would have built on the 1870 and 1871 Enforcement Acts and subjected congressional elections to further federal oversight. This legislation ultimately failed, and Congress later sought to invoke the penalty of Section 2 of the Fourteenth Amendment to counter voting discrimination, an effort that was also unsuccessful.[27] Finally, Congress used its power under Article I, Section 5 to refuse to seat representatives elected in races that were marked with racial discrimination and fraud, an uneven but sometimes successful response to southern discrimination.[28]

In sum, the party of Lincoln evolved from an institution that was largely committed to Black male (but not women's) suffrage, to a party in retreat in less than a decade. By the 1890s, Republicans sought to reclaim the mantle of Reconstruction while balancing the economic issues that dominated the latter half of the nineteenth century. During this period, the party advanced, retreated, and then advanced again on the issues of civil and political rights, using its authority in myriad ways to respond to the challenges presented by a Supreme Court that was largely unsympathetic to both African American suffrage and broad congressional power over elections.

But the conservative posture toward federal power that had once made Congress reluctant to use its authority over elections prior to the Civil War – where federalism arguments were used to counter meaningful federal action – would again stymie federal action for almost a century. In the end, both Congress and the Supreme Court abandoned Black voters to southern disenfranchisers, relegating the promise of American democracy to the trash bin.

26 A Bill to amend and supplement the election laws of the United States and to provide for the more efficient enforcement of such laws, and for other purposes, H.R. 10958, 51st Congress, 1st Session (June 14, 1890).

27 See James W. Fox, Jr., "Black Progressivism and the Progressive Court" (2020) 130 *Yale Law Journal Forum* 398–420, p. 410, n. 60.

28 See Chapters 4 and 5.

7

Voting as Deservedness

Policing the Political Community of "We the Voters"

There is a race so different from our own that we do not permit those belonging to it to become citizens of the United States. Persons belonging to it are, with few exceptions, absolutely excluded from our country. I allude to the Chinese race. But by the statute in question, a Chinaman can ride in the same passenger coach with white citizens of the United States, while citizens of the black race in Louisiana, many of whom, perhaps, risked their lives for the preservation of the Union, who are entitled, by law, to participate in the political control of the State and nation, who are not excluded, by law or by reason of their race, from public stations of any kind, and who have all the legal rights that belong to white citizens, are yet declared to be criminals, liable to imprisonment, if they ride in a public coach occupied by citizens of the white race.

—*Plessy v. Ferguson*, 163 U.S. 537, 561 (1896) (Harlan, J., dissenting)

With the Fourteenth and Fifteenth Amendments, Republicans committed to universal male suffrage well beyond what Lincoln outlined in his fateful April 1865 speech, but one should not assume that they were monolithic on this issue. If you have made this assumption, then I have failed in the last six chapters. Nor should you assume that Republicans had, en masse, completely disregarded Lincoln's initial sentiment that the right to vote, even for African Americans, should be earned. Many aspects of the antebellum framework survived the Republican Party's attempt to remake the face of the American political system – yes, the complexion of the electorate changed, but the system still preserved much of the pre–Civil War ethno-cultural-gendered framework of political identity.

Prior to the Civil War, the act of voting was not simply about casting a ballot. Election Day was often a day of revelry, with polling places located in saloons and other male-only spaces that reinforced themes of manhood and community standing as an aspect of electoral politics.[1] Sometimes the reinforcement of traditional male identity, and the bargaining that occurred between political elites, employers,

[1] Richard Franklin Bensel, *The American Ballot Box in the Mid-Nineteenth Century* (Cambridge: Cambridge University Press, 2004), p. x.

and landlords for votes,[2] trumped any concerns about the policy consequences of elections.

In addition, most communities were aware of the "others" in their midst. Physical appearance and cultural background not only determined who would be turned away from the polls in any given precinct, but voting requirements were also used as proxies to further this exclusion.[3] For example, by the mid-nineteenth century, Rhode Island retained a property qualification for the purpose of making it difficult for noncitizens to vote, and New York retained its requirement to limit the ability of Black voters to participate. Almost all other states had abolished these qualifications.[4]

Much of this commitment to the antebellum framework stemmed from the fact that, prior to the war, money and patronage had been the currency of politics.[5] Now, with the emancipation of African Americans from slavery, there would be a much larger group seeking a piece of the political pie. Former Confederates, by betraying the Union, no longer deserved that place at the patronage, spoils, and policy table, whereas the formerly enslaved, many of whom fought bravely for the Union, had earned their spot.[6] Less a shrinking pot, then, and more of replacing the undeserving with the deserving. In essence, Black men had proven that they were part of the same ethno-cultural gendered identity frame such that their enfranchisement should not be disruptive, at least theoretically.

2 Ibid., p. 77 ("A landowner or factory owner could use his power over employers or tenants to influence their voting decisions. This was most commonly and notoriously the case with freedmen in the South following the Civil War. But northern employers could also intimidate their men by threatening to discharge them from their employment.").

3 Ibid., p. xii ("In rural areas, violence and intimidation extended far beyond the immediate vicinity of the polling place … Because rural voters were quickly embedded in their communities, they inevitably carried their social and political histories to the polls with them. Their neighbors, serving as party observers or election judges, knew their names and political leanings and were thus able to dispense with stereotyped physical appearance and ethnic accents that, in the larger cities, served as proxies for partisan affiliation.").

4 Ibid., p. 43. North Carolina was the other outlier. See Stanley L. Engerman and Kenneth L. Sokoloff, *The Evolution of Suffrage Institutions in the New World* (Cambridge, MA: National Bureau of Economic Research, 2001).

5 Between 1830 and 1850,

> men similar in their dissimilarity to their constituencies held office and exercised behind-the-scenes influence. In contrast to the small farmers, indigents, laborers, artisans, clerks, and shopkeepers – the men of little or no property who constituted the great majority of the antebellum population – the men who held office and controlled the affairs of the major parties were everywhere lawyers, merchants, businessmen, and relatively large property owners. In the South they were inordinately men who owned slaves and owned them in unusually large numbers.

Edward Pessen, "How Different from Each Other Were the Antebellum North and South?" (1980) 85 *The American Historical Review* 1119–1149, 1138. Professor Pessen further notes, "most Southern and Northern political activists were similarly ambitious for worldly success, opportunistic, materialistic, and disinclined to disturb their societies' social arrangements." Ibid., 1139.

6 See Richard M. Re and Christopher M. Re, "Voting and Vice: Criminal Disenfranchisement and the Reconstruction Amendments" (2012) *Yale Law Journal* 1584–1670, 1592–1593.

The problem was that this framing of voting as based on deservedness, rather than by right, did not sufficiently disturb the antebellum assumptions that suffrage should be limited to certain groups.[7] The effect of this holdover was disastrous, for it meant that some groups could be excluded based on the belief that: (1) they had not earned the privilege of voting, either through military service or otherwise; or (2) they lacked the male, ethno-cultural identity that pre–Civil War election dynamics operated around.[8] Two groups – women and those of Chinese descent – are examples of how this dynamic played out.[9] In addition, Congress's desire to preserve its own ability to exclude undesirables jeopardized the place of African American men in the political community of "We the Voters" once their deservedness was called into question.[10]

7.1 A NEW PREDICATE FOR DISENFRANCHISEMENT? FEDERAL EFFORTS TO EXCLUDE CHINESE PEOPLE FROM THE POLITICAL COMMUNITY OF "WE THE VOTERS"

As the fierce debates surrounding the Fourteenth and Fifteenth Amendments demonstrated, the promise of equal protection under the law was never intended to be universally applied; women, noncitizens, and felons were clearly on the outskirts

7 Eric Foner, *Reconstruction: America's Unfinished Revolution, 1863–1877* (New York: Harper & Row, 1988), p. 446; Alexander Keyssar, *The Right to Vote: The Contested History of Democracy in the United States* (New York: Basic Books, 2000), p. 81.

8 Laura Free, *Suffrage Reconstructed: Gender, Race, and Voting Rights in the Civil War Era* (Ithaca: Cornell University Press, 2015), p. 34 ("The advocates of free African Americans' political rights initially asserted in conventions and petitions that American democratic ideals and black men's actions, particularly their military service, entitled them to membership in the American political community.").

9 The Irish was another group of immigrants who also challenged pre-conceived notions of who deserved the privilege of voting. As Professor Travis Crum noted in his pathbreaking article on the Fifteenth Amendment, Irish Americans who had gained citizenship through naturalization remained subject to discriminatory state laws (despite being racially White) and their status split the Republican caucus during debates over the Amendment. Some States continued to impose differential voting qualifications even after naturalization. Most infamously, Rhode Island required only naturalized citizens to satisfy a property requirement. Rhode Island's policy – which was designed to disenfranchise a large Democratic voting bloc of Irish Americans – would feature prominently in the debates over the Fifteenth Amendment. See Travis Crum, "The Unabridged Fifteenth Amendment," (2024) 133 *Yale Law Journal* 1039–1161, 1039, 1068, 1077.

10 The fact that some Republicans in Congress were willing to make tradeoffs that directly undermined African American suffrage for both partisan gain and a commitment to avoid punishing "loyal" states further reinforced the tenuousness of the position of African Americans in the community of "We the Voters." See, e.g., Mark A. Graber, *Punish Treason, Reward Loyalty: The Forgotten Goals of Constitutional Reform after the Civil War* (Topeka: University of Kansas Press, 2024), pp. 318, 326–327, 339–340 (detailing how many Republicans supported the admission of Colorado as a state in early 1866 because "Republicans were likely to retain control of Colorado for the foreseeable future" and this support persisted despite the fact that "Colorado was … committed to white supremacy, and the proposed state constitution limited voting to white persons"). Charles Sumner and other Radicals argued that Colorado could not be admitted because this prohibition rendered its government unrepublican in form, in violation of the Guarantee Clause. Ibid., p. 325. Ultimately, Colorado was admitted in 1876 subsequent to the ratification of the Fifteenth Amendment, which barred racial discrimination in voting.

of "We the Voters," but there were others who, like Chinese people, faced barriers to entry such as immigrants from Japan, Korea, and India;[11] Mexican immigrants, despite being granted citizenship by the Treaty of Guadalupe Hidalgo (1848); Native Americans, who were not granted citizenship until 1924; and some European immigrants, most notably the Irish.

In fact, history reveals a recurring pattern that Republicans could not seem to evade as they sought to remake the American electorate: that every major expansion of American democracy has often been accompanied by a corresponding wave of exclusion. The same constitutional amendments that extended rights to millions also revealed deep anxieties about who truly belonged in the American political community.

From this perspective, Charles Sumner's attack on Section 2 of the Fourteenth Amendment, in which he argued that this provision implicitly countenanced racial discrimination, might have been a boon in the short term. As originally reported out of Committee, its text provided that "whenever the elective franchise shall be denied or abridged in any state on account of race or color," then "all persons therein of such race or color" should be removed from the denominator. Sumner's arguments led to the removal of the "race or color" language and expanded Section 2's reach to race-neutral modes of discrimination.[12] But the removal of this language was also tied to the desire of some congressional representatives to permit states to disenfranchise some groups while including them in the basis of population.

The "race or color" language removed from draft Section 2 arguably would have required states to enfranchise their native-born Chinese populations or suffer the penalty of reduced representation.[13] Representative Thaddeus Stevens said as much, noting that, "if they [Chinese people] are excluded by the laws of California

[11] See *Ozawa v. United States*, 260 U.S.178 (1922) (holding that a native of Japan who had resided in the United States for twenty years was not eligible for citizenship); *United States v. Thind*, 261 U.S. 204 (1923) (holding that an immigrant from Punjab, India, was not "a free white person" and could be excluded from admission into the United States),

[12] See Chapter 5.

[13] See "Exchange between Senators Stewart and Johnson, 39th Congress, First Session, February 9, 1866," 36 *Congressional Globe* (Washington, D.C.: Congressional Globe Office, 1866), part 1, p. 766.

Mr. STEWART. Allow me to suggest that under this amendment I do not think Chinamen be counted.

Mr. JOHNSON. Certainly they will be counted in the whole number.

Mr. STEWART. But not in the basis of representation under this amendment. I think the same rule would operate on Chinese as on negroes, for they are "colored." The provision of the amendment is in reference to exclusions on account of race or color.

Mr. JOHNSON. You are very much mistaken. Your State will be the first to say, "We are entitled to just as many Representatives after this amendment passes as before." If you think your people will be satisfied with losing any part of their representation, I submit it to you, perhaps you had better reconsider before you give this vote, because you may lose, and will lose.

Mr. STEWART. I think the Pacific coast would lose representation under this amendment.

because they are Chinese, this amendment operates upon them because they are excluded on account of race." "[T]he word 'race'," he observed, "was inserted for that purpose."[14] Stevens also rejected comparisons between Chinese people and Native Americans, the latter of which had been expressly excluded from representation and taxation in the Three-Fifths Clause of Article I, Section 2 and would continue to be excluded after the ratification of the Fourteenth Amendment.[15] The denial of both representation and suffrage, according to Stevens, lay in the fact that Native Americans, unlike Chinese people, did not pay taxes and "[b]ecause they are a tribal race, [they] have their own separate governments, and, as a general rule, are not citizens."[16] By 1866, it was well established that Native Americans, who had their own form of sovereignty, were distinct from Chinese people, whose native-born offspring automatically became citizens with the adoption of the 1866 Civil Rights Act. They, too, counted as "persons" entitled to be included in the basis of representation and were, therefore, part of the political community of "We the People."[17]

But the fear that Section 2 of Fourteenth Amendment would require the enfranchisement of Chinese people raised significant questions about the construction of racial categories.[18] For those western representatives opposed to the "race or color" language, the idea of losing representation because of their Chinese populations

[14] "Comments of Representative Stevens, 39th Congress, First Session, January 23, 1866," 36 *Congressional Globe* (Washington, D.C.: Congressional Globe Office, 1866), part 1, p. 376. See also "Comments of Senator Buckalew, 39th Congress, First Session, February 21, 1866," 36 *Congressional Globe* (Washington, D.C.: Congressional Globe Office, 1866), part 2, p. 961.

[15] "Comments of Representative Stevens, 39th Congress, First Session, January 23, 1866," 36 *Congressional Globe* (Washington, D.C.: Congressional Globe Office, 1866), part 1, p. 376.

[16] Ibid.

[17] For more on the juxtaposition between citizenship as a legal status versus citizens as holders of rights, particularly as this frame applies to Asian Americans, see Leti Volpp, "'Obnoxious to their Very Nature': Asian Americans and Constitutional Citizenship" (2001) 5 *Citizenship Studies* 57–71.

[18] "Comments of Representative Rogers, 39th Congress, First Session, January 25, 1866," 36 *Congressional Globe* (Washington, D.C.: Congressional Globe Office, 1866), part 1, p. 433:

> There is still another objection, and one not yet alluded to by any gentleman on this floor. It is this: the resolution provides that whenever the elective franchise shall be denied or abridged in any State on account of race or color, all persons of such race or color shall be excluded from the basis of representation Now, here is a great deal of indefiniteness in both those terms, race and "color." What is a race of men? Writers upon the subject of races differ very materially on this point. Some of them would make four or five races; others fifteen; and one whom I might name seems inclined not to limit the number short of a thousand. … the term "color" is nowhere defined in the Constitution or the law. We apply the term to persons who are of African descent whether their color is whiter or darker than ours. Every one who is familiar with the ethnological condition of things here in the United States, and who sees the general mixing up of colors, particularly in the Democratic portion of the country-I allude to that portion south of Mason and Dixon's line must say it with me that the word "color" has no very distinct meaning when applied to the different peoples of the United States of America.

See also Ian H. Lopez, *White by Law: The Legal Construction of Race* (New York: New York University Press, 1996).

signaled northern ignorance about the boundaries of these categories; there could not be a blanket "nonwhite" designation (i.e., prohibiting abridgments based on "race or color") if it meant imparting upon Chinese people the same rights as Black people. "The pagan Asiatic, speaking an unknown tongue" and not "generally a believer in the Christian religion" was, according to Representative Stewart of Nevada, unfit for both citizenship and suffrage; in other words, differences in language and religion distinguished this group from the formerly enslaved.[19] Representative William Higby of California also referred to the Chinese population as a "pagan race,"[20] incapable of citizenship or naturalization. He denied that Chinese people were entitled to exercise the right to vote since they refused to assimilate, unlike "the negro" whom he viewed "as much a native of this country as…myself."[21]

These views were not outside the mainstream. Prior to the Civil War, many states limited suffrage to White men such as Oregon's 1857 Constitution, which provided that "No negro, Chinaman, or mulatto shall have the right of suffrage."[22] There were also a number of state laws that prohibited Asian immigrants from owning property, which was a common requirement to be an elector in some places until the mid-nineteenth century.[23] And the fact that the North would emerge unscathed by Section 2, free to disenfranchise its relatively small population of nonwhite people while the equally loyal western states had to enfranchise their substantially larger Chinese populations to avoid the penalty, was yet another mark against the proposed Fourteenth Amendment.[24] When the "race or color" language was brought up for a vote in the Senate on March 9, 1866, there was widespread resistance. While California's senators voted in favor of the language, it split the delegations of Oregon and Nevada.[25]

19 "Comments of Senator Stewart, 39th Congress, First Session, March 1, 1866," 36 *Congressional Globe* (Washington, D.C.: Congressional Globe Office, 1866), part 2, p. 1104. To be clear, some representatives had similar concerns about the fitness of African Americans for both citizenship and suffrage. See "Comments of Representative Hubbard, 39th Congress, First Session, January 18, 1866," 36 *Congressional Globe* (Washington, D.C.: Congressional Globe Office, 1866), part 1, p. 406.

20 "Comments of Representative Higby, 39th Congress, First Session, February 27, 1866," 36 *Congressional Globe* (Washington, D.C.: Congressional Globe Office, 1866), part 2, p. 1056.

21 Ibid.

22 Constitution of Oregon, s. 6 (1857).

23 Volpp, "Asian Americans and Constitutional Citizenship," 73.

24 "Comments of Senator Stewart, 39th Congress, First Session, March 1, 1866," 36 *Congressional Globe* (Washington, D.C.: Congressional Globe Office, 1866), part 2, p. 1104 ("The non-voting population of the North consists of aliens, women, and minors. The non-voting population of the South consists of negroes, women, and minors. The North will exclude on account of alienage, sex, and age, and avoid the operation of the proviso; while the South and the Pacific coast must either confer universal suffrage on negroes and Chinamen, or lose their just representation. This will ever be a source of discontent, and it will be hard to explain to fair-minded men why an alien, and even an alien enemy, should be represented in the North and a free negro unrepresented in the South.").

25 "Vote on the Joint Resolution, 39th Congress, First Session, March 9, 1866," 36 *Congressional Globe* (Washington, D.C.: Congressional Globe Office, 1866), part 2, p. 1289.

The removal of the "race or color" language ensured that the western states could disenfranchise Chinese people without explicitly invoking the penalty, although the limitation was still implicit in the text since either race or color can be grounds for abridging the right of otherwise eligible men to vote. But an important part of this narrative was that xenophobia and racism, and not just a desire to bring northern states within the scope of Section 2, triggered the removal of this language.

Questions surrounding the political identity of those of Chinese ancestry had become pressing as their numbers steadily grew during the second half of the nineteenth century. It had begun years earlier, when the lure of gold in the hills of California drew hopeful prospectors from across the globe, with most of these individuals settling on the West Coast.[26] In 1858, China, the United States, and several other countries entered into the Treaty of Tianjin (also known as the Treaty of Tien-Tsin),[27] which opened up China to trade and immigration from foreign merchants and citizens. The treaty was mostly one-sided, guaranteeing rights to American citizens traveling in China but saying nothing of the rights entitled to Chinese citizens traveling in America.

Not surprisingly, Chinese people who immigrated to America were subject to racism, discrimination, and violence because they competed against White people for jobs.[28] To curb race-related violence, the federal government entered into several additional treaties with China throughout the 1880s that addressed some of these issues. These agreements sought, at least nominally, to ease international relations and curb domestic unrest. But rather than protecting the rights of Chinese immigrants, federal policy increasingly turned against them. For the rest of the nineteenth century, Congress targeted Chinese immigrants, seeking to deny them citizenship upon arrival and curb their in-migration; very little attention was paid to the rights of their offspring born on American soil.[29]

26 "The earliest American contingent (of immigrants from China) of any size were the 13,000 or so who came to California in 1854, following the discovery of gold there in 1848[.]" Isabella Black, "American Labour and Chinese Immigration" (July 1963) 25 *Past and Present* 59–76, 76.

27 "Treaty of Peace, Amity, and Commerce between the United States of America and the Ta Tsing Empire (China) of 18 June 1858," in William M. Malloy (comp.), *Treaties, Conventions, International Acts, Protocols & Agreements between the United States of America and Other Powers 1776–1909*, Senate Doc. No. 357, 61st Congress, 2d Session, 2 vols. (Washington, D.C.: Government Printing Office, 1910), vol. 1, pp. 211–221.

28 See Black, "American Labour," 64–65; see also Erika Lee, "The Chinese Exclusion Example: Race, Immigration, and American Gatekeeping, 1882–1924" (2002) 21 *Journal of American Ethnic History* 36–62, 37–39, 42. See also Michael Luo, "When an American Town Massacred Its Chinese Immigrants," *The New Yorker*, March 2025 (detailing the 1885 massacre of dozens of Asian immigrants in Rock Springs, Wyoming by White residents).

29 See Beth Lew-Williams, *The Chinese Must Go: Violence, Exclusion, and the Making of the Alien in America* (Cambridge: Harvard University Press, 2021), p. 5. In the 1860s, part of the criticism of Chinese immigrants is that they refused to procreate in the United States which is likely why the rights of native-born Chinese people were not a hot button issue at that point. See "Comments of Representative Higby, 39th Congress, First Session, February 27, 1866," 36 *Congressional Globe* (Washington, D.C.: Congressional Globe Office, 1866), part 2, p. 1056 (noting that Chinese people

The legal silence on this issue persisted until the landmark Supreme Court case *United States v. Wong Kim Ark* in 1898. The plaintiff, a United States citizen of Chinese ancestry, was barred from reentry after he left the country to temporarily visit China.[30] The Court held that, as a U.S. citizen, the plaintiff could not be excluded from the U.S., and in the process, vindicated certain basic rights of citizens.[31] However, this holding was not necessarily in tension with the widespread view among political elites that Chinese noncitizens should not be naturalized.[32]

The exclusion of Chinese immigrants from the communities of "We the People" and "We the Voters" was not a foregone conclusion, despite the grant of citizenship to those born in the United States. As late as the 1860s, foreign-born Chinese people were a part of a larger immigrant population that had been traditionally encouraged to pursue naturalization upon arriving at America's shores, at least initially. While xenophobia was on the rise, there had not yet been any systematic efforts in federal law to exclude Chinese people from the groups of people eligible for naturalization.

For example, in rejecting a proposal by Ohio Republican Robert Schenck that representatives be apportioned "according to the number of male citizens over twenty-one years of age having the qualifications requisite for electors of the most numerous branch of the State legislature,"[33] Representative John Bingham observed that Schenck's proposal would fundamentally change the Constitution's inclusion of immigrants in the basis of representation. "By substituting the amendment…you strike from the basis of representation the entire immigrant population not naturalized, and therefore not yet capable of becoming voters, citizens

"do not propagate in our country. A generation is not growing up in the State [California], except an insignificant few in comparison with the great number among us."). This refusal to procreate probably stemmed from a shortage of Chinese women, who did not emigrate in the same numbers as the men. See Lew-Williams, *The Chinese Must Go*, p. 22.

30 *United States v. Wong Kim Ark*, 169 U.S. 649 (1898) (holding that Chinese people born in America are entitled to the Fourteenth Amendment's guarantee of birthright citizenship).

31 Ibid.

32 See *Civil Rights Cases*, 109 U.S. 3 (1883) (Harlan, J., dissenting). See also *In re Ah Yup*, 1 F. Cas. 223 (C.C.D. Cal. 1878).

33 "Comments of Representative Bingham on the Proposed Substitute by Representative Schenck, 39th Congress, First Session, January 25, 1866," 36 *Congressional Globe* (Washington, D.C.: Congressional Globe Office, 1866), part 1, p. 432 (arguing that Article I, Section 2's inclusion of immigrants in the basis of population was to "encourage immigration"). According to Bingham,

> It will be admitted, doubtless, that the framers of the Constitution inserted this provision to encourage immigration. They did so, not only by this provision of the organic law, which declared that the whole immigrant population should be numbered with the people and counted as part of them, but by the further provision that Congress should have power to pass a uniform naturalization law, and thereby provide that the alien population, by complying with the terms of the statute, should be clothed with the dignity of citizens of the United States and invested with the rights and powers of citizens. There is no provision of the Constitution that is more essential to the future of the Republic than this.

Ibid.

of the United States over twenty-one years of age. I ask the House to consider whether that is wise."[34]

Bingham's expectation that immigrants would be set on a path to citizenship was not a view that applied universally.[35] But many believed this principle applied to Chinese people in 1866, even if the average White American, particularly those who lived on the West Coast, was not favorably inclined toward Chinese immigration.[36] In 1868, America entered into the Burlingame Treaty with China, which encouraged migration between the two countries.[37] Thus, it is not surprising that draft Section 2, prior to the deletion of the "race or color" language, would have significantly limited the states' ability to draw distinctions between immigrant groups in extending the franchise, especially since the federal government would not explicitly come out against immigration from China until the 1880s.

In its final form, however, it was clear from its text that Section 2 was not intended to embrace universal suffrage in its purest sense, implicitly leaving some groups outside of "We the Voters" by virtue of how this provision defined the relevant community based on citizenship and gender.

The Fifteenth Amendment did little to alter this reality, despite its broad prohibition on discrimination in voting on the basis of race, color, or previous condition of servitude (but, notably, not nativity[38]). Even broader versions of the bill like that introduced by Representative Samuel Shellabarger, which would have "prohibited states from denying or abridging the voting rights of any adult male of 'sound mind'" with an exception only for those who engaged in rebellion or similar crimes, failed because, as Professor Alexander Keyssar has noted, "it implicitly would have ended not only racial discrimination but also property, tax, nativity, and literacy

34 Ibid.

35 See Crum, "The Unabridged Fifteenth Amendment," 1076–1077 ("West Coast Republicans feared that naturalization laws might be changed – something that Senator Sumner was, characteristically, proposing to do. In response, West Coast Republicans suggested modifying the Fifteenth Amendment to expressly bar Chinese immigrants and Native Americans from naturalizing.").

36 Throughout the second half of the nineteenth century,

> the massive migration of laborers from China directly to the United States overlapped with domestic fears about American race, class, and gender relations and helped fan the fires of organized anti-Chinese sentiment, especially in the American West. Chinese workers were blamed for competing unfairly with white workers. Chinese as a race were charged with being inassimilable, inferior, and immoral.

Erika Lee, "The 'Yellow Peril' and Asian Exclusion in the Americas" (2007) 76 *Pacific Historical Review* 537–562, 546–547

37 See Lew-Williams, *The Chinese Must Go*, p. 27–28 ("Despite American misgivings about China's 'uncivilized' status, in 1868 the United States agreed to Seward's treaty, which recognized China as 'a most favored nation' and agreed to 'free migration and emigration' between the two countries.").

38 See Crum, "The Unabridged Fifteenth Amendment," 1116 (noting that "Senator Stewart, a primary author and floor manager [of the Fifteenth Amendment]… sent a telegram to a local federal judge – which was soon published – stating that the 'word 'nativity' was stricken from the original draft of the Constitutional Amendment so as to allow the exclusion of Chinese from its benefits.").

requirements" and, in the process, would have taken "a giant step towards a nationally mandated and nationally uniform suffrage."[39]

Indeed, some of the proposals offered during debates over the Fifteenth Amendment – such as Senator George Williams' proposal that empowered Congress to "abolish or modify any restrictions upon the right to vote or hold office prescribed by the constitution or laws of any state" was not offered, according to Professor Travis Crum, in the spirit of protecting or expanding African American suffrage; rather, Williams "feared that the antidiscrimination models [with language broadly forbidding racial discrimination in voting] would enfranchise Chinese American men" should they ever be eligible for naturalization.[40]

Debates during the Fourteenth and Fifteenth Amendments foreshadowed that the implicit exclusion of some immigrant groups from federal protection would become explicit in short order, as history has shown that almost every expansion of the American polity tended to be accompanied by mass exclusion. As Part II of this book shows, for example, the rise of mass politics in the 1830s worked primarily to the benefit of White men, as state courts became more aggressive in excluding free Black men from the electorate.

This trend continued during Reconstruction, but this time against immigrant populations. In 1869 – after Congress passed the Fifteenth Amendment but before ratification – Democrats in Congress tried to force a procedurally unusual vote on a motion declaring that the Amendment was not intended to enfranchise the "Chinese or Mongolians."[41] While this effort to "affirm" the meaning of the Fifteenth Amendment mid-ratification was unsuccessful,[42] in 1870, Congress successfully amended the federal naturalization law to extend citizenship to "aliens of African nativity or African descent" but not to other immigrant populations.[43]

While citizenship and voting were treated distinctly – yet another holdover from the *Dred Scott* era – the Naturalization Act was very much an election-related law in the mold of the Enforcement Acts. It created a path for citizenship for those of

39 Keyssar, *The Right to Vote*, p. 95 (noting that some of the Republican supporters of the Fifteenth Amendment were former Know-Nothings and nativists whose views might have changed with respect to African American suffrage but not necessarily with respect to some immigrant populations nor were they willing to disavow literacy or educational tests as prerequisites to voting as a general matter).

40 Crum, "The Unabridged Fifteenth Amendment," 1095–1096.

41 Ibid., 1120.

42 This motion would have prevented the Fifteenth Amendment from being interpreted to enfranchise Chinese people should the law ever change to allow them to become naturalized citizens. At the time of ratification, however, it was beyond dispute – given that naturalization was limited to White people and there were few native-born Chinese Americans – that "[t]he original intent and original expected application of the Fifteenth Amendment was to keep Chinese immigrants disenfranchised." Ibid., p. 1135, n. 589.

43 An Act to amend the Naturalization Laws and to punish Crimes against the same, and for other Purposes, s. 7 ch. 254, 16 Stat. 256 (1870) See also Volpp, "Asian Americans and Constitutional Citizenship," 73; Xi Wang, *The Trial of Democracy: Black Suffrage and Northern Republicans, 1860–1910* (Athena: University of Georgia Press, 1997), p. 68.

African descent, while also providing for federal oversight of elections in which naturalization certificates were used to establish citizenship.[44] This law was an important part of incorporating African Americans and African people into the community of "We the People," but not to be overlooked is that the law was also about expressly excluding other nonwhite populations, including Chinese immigrants, from the communities of both "We the People" and "We the Voters."

In the decades that followed, the courts followed Congress's lead, routinely denying that Chinese immigrants could be naturalized, a necessary predicate to exercising the right to vote in most states in the Union.[45] And for those of Chinese descent born in the United States, the continued disaggregation of voting and citizenship ensured that this status did not necessarily confer upon them a right of suffrage.[46] The women in the suffrage movement also learned this lesson the hard way.

7.2 WOMEN, THE RIGHT TO VOTE, AND THE PRIVILEGES OF CITIZENSHIP

Unlike Chinese immigrants, disenfranchising the women who were, by all rights, citizens should have been conceptually harder to defend given the majoritarian

44 An Act to amend the Naturalization Laws and to punish Crimes against the same, and for other Purposes, s. 2, ch. 254, 16 Stat. 254 (1870) ("if any person shall in any manner use for the purpose of registering as a voter, or as evidence of a right to vote, or otherwise, unlawfully, any order, certificate of citizenship … unlawfully issued or made … shall be sentenced to be imprisoned"); Ibid., s. 5, 16 Stat. 255–56 (empowering circuit courts to appoint partisan poll watchers in cities of 20,000 or more to oversee registration, voting and vote counting); Ibid., s. 6, 16 Stat. 256 (empowering the marshal of the United States to appoint deputies to preserve order at the polls).

45 See, e.g., *Chapman v. Toy Long*, 5 F. Cas. 497 (C.C.D. Or. 1876) (stating that "all aliens, including the Congo negro, except the Mongolian, are permitted to become naturalized, and therefore qualified to locate and occupy mining lands under them"); *In re Ah Yup*, 1 F. Cas. 223 (C.C.D. Cal. 1878) (regarding the 1870 Naturalization Act, "whatever latitudinarian construction might otherwise have been given to the term 'white person,' it is entirely clear that congress intended by this legislation to exclude Mongolians from the right of naturalization. I am, therefore, of the opinion that a native of China, of the Mongolian race, is not a white person within the meaning of the act of congress."); *In re Kanaka Nian*, 21 P. 993, 993–94 (Utah 1889) ("Some courts had admitted Chinese to citizenship, and [the federal law at issue] was evidently made to prevent such naturalizations and to remove all doubt. We are of opinion that the law authorizes the naturalization of aliens of the Caucasian or white races and of the African races only, and all other races, among which are the Hawaiians, are excluded."); *In re Hong*, 24 P. 156 (Cal. 1890) (invalidating a naturalization certificate that had been issued by a New York court for someone who had been born in China, ruling that such certificates were invalid under federal law); *In re Gee*, 71 F. 274 (N.D. Cal. 1895) (stating that, while "courts of record of a state, having common-law jurisdiction and a clerk and seal, have the power to naturalize, this, obviously, must be done in conformity with the uniform laws promulgated by the congress of the United States. That congress has never contemplated or intended to confer the right of naturalization upon Mongolians, or natives of China, is palpable by a mere reference to the laws upon the subject of naturalization.").

46 See, e.g., *Green v. Shumway*, 39 NY 418 (1868) (noting that a citizen can forfeit his right to vote for failing to meet the qualifications set by law, including a loyalty oath); *Blair v. Ridgely*, 41 Mo. 63 (1867) (same).

impulses that had come to dominate the post–Civil War era. However, the male-centric strands that were interwoven into the boundaries of the political community of "We the Voters" remained intact if for no reason other than Congress's refusal to completely abandon antebellum conceptions of federalism sometimes required endorsing the state's exclusionary impulses in the postbellum period.[47]

When it came to the community of "We the Voters," the longstanding exclusion of women made it easy to ostracize them during Reconstruction. This was true despite the fact that the Lockean notions of political community, upon which the concepts of "We the People" and "We the Voters" were based, did not necessarily dictate the exclusion of women from the community of voters. Locke, arguing that "[t]he Mother too hath her title," refuted that husbands were like monarchs, with absolute control over their wives.[48] Jeremy Waldron has argued that many of Locke's references to the rights of man in his work were not consistent and that, in some places, Locke invoked "man" as a gender-neutral term in arguing that a natural right of liberty and equality accompanied the notion of motherhood.[49] Unfortunately, Section 2's explicit refusal to penalize states for disenfranchising women illustrated that "We the Voters" would not reach its full Lockean potential.

The exclusion of women persisted in part because, prior to the Civil War, Black men painted their desire for the franchise in gendered terms rooted in deservedness, a framing that experienced a renaissance during the 1866 debates over Section 2.[50] For example, between 1837 and 1846, Black leaders in New York worked with White organizations and abolitionists to remove the property requirement for Black voters in the state constitution. Among the arguments lodged by opponents of the property qualification was that it deprived Black New Yorkers "of the rights of citizenship, ignored their service to the state as soldiers, and 'unwarrantably [withheld] rights

47 See Crum, "The Unabridged Fifteenth Amendment," 1076–1077 (noting that "during debates over the Fifteenth Amendment, no proposal that would have mandated women's suffrage ever came to a vote in the House or Senate").

48 John Locke, *Two Treatises on Government* (London: Butler, Reid, Sharpe, and Bumpus, 1821), book 1, ch. VI, § 65, p. 73.

49 In discussing a passage in Locke's *Two Treatises on Government* that deals with the use of pronouns (male, female, and plural), Waldron makes the following observation:

> There's just no way of reading this meditation on words and pronouns and concluding that Locke intended a narrow exclusive male reading of 'men.' You can't even conclude that he was careless on the matter; he approached it more thoughtfully and at greater length than others have done, including others of our generation. It's a fabulously important passage. It is the one place in the *Two Treatises* where Locke associates humankind in general with the Judeo-Christian idea of imago dei, the image of God, in a way that makes absolutely clear that that characterization applies to Eve (the only other member of the species around) as well as to Adam, to women as well as men, and applies to her as it applies to him in virtue of her intellectual nature.

Jeremy Waldron, *'The Mother Too Hath Her Title' – John Locke on Motherhood and Equality*, Radcliffe Institute Lecture, April 27, 2009, https://papers.ssrn.com/sol3/papers.cfm?abstract_id=1687776 (quote located on page 7 of lecture transcript).

50 Free, *Suffrage Reconstructed*, p. 34.

inherent to us as men.'"[51] A statewide political convention of Black men convening about the suffrage issue in 1840 explicitly staked "their claim [to the ballot] upon the possession of those common and yet exalted faculties of manhood." Black men required the ballot, they declared, because "WE ARE MEN."[52]

Coupled with distinguished military service and the formal eradication of slavery, Black men felt they were entitled to a presumption of virtue that could not be easily rebutted and was sufficient to establish their worthiness to be electors. Because they, like their White counterparts, centered maleness as a prerequisite for being a voter, the Civil War and Reconstruction did not change the gendered appeals that undermined universal suffrage. In June of 1869, the Colored Men's Convention of the State of New York convened at Binghamton, still agitating almost three decades later for the removal of all race-based voting restrictions.[53] Although the convention featured both men and women as speakers, the resolutions offered by the Convention were nonetheless premised on the argument that Black men had earned the right to vote and should be the beneficiaries of these efforts. As the Convention noted,

> Resolved, That we refer with just pride to the fact that, those States wherein the colored men have exercised the right of suffrage, there is not an instance on record of their abuse of it; but they have exhibited intelligent discrimination and judgment in the use of the ballot, as they have attested brave and loyal devotion to liberty, justice, and the Union in the use of the bullet.[54]

For their part, women never gave up their efforts to establish their own entitlement to the vote. While their observations about the undeserving nature of some male voters and their appeals to Democratic rhetoric often fell on deaf ears among both White and Black men,[55] women continued to aggressively challenge their exclusion from the political community of "We the Voters" after the Civil War. The inclusion

51 Ibid., p. 33.

52 Ibid.

53 "Colored Men's Convention of the State of New-York," *New-York Tribune*, June 4, 1869, p. 2.

54 Ibid.

55 See "Resolutions Adopted at the Women's Convention held in Salem, Ohio April 19 and 20, 1850: Resolution 11," in Florence E. Allen and Mary Welles (eds.), *The Ohio Woman Suffrage Movement: "A Certain Unalienable Right": What Ohio Women Did to Secure It* (Columbus: Committee for the Preservation of Ohio Woman Suffrage Records, 1952), p. 13 ("Resolved, That the political history of women demonstrates that tyranny the most degrading, cruel and unrelenting, can be exercised and produced, the same in effect under a mild and republican form of government as by an hereditary despotism."). See also "Report on the Enfranchisement of Woman," *The Revolution* (New York), January 15, 1868 ("It is claimed by some that the right to vote is not a natural right, but that it is a privilege which some have acquired, and which may be granted to others at the option of the fortunate holders. But they fail to inform us how the possessor first acquired the privilege, and especially how they acquired the rightful power to withhold that privilege from others, according to the caprice or notions of expediency. We hold this doctrine to be pernicious in tendency, and hostile to the spirit of a republican government…").

of the word "male" in Section 2 of the Fourteenth Amendment, as well as the proposed language of the Fifteenth Amendment, forced the issue of women's suffrage to the forefront of debate.

Notably, prominent suffragettes Elizabeth Cady Stanton and Susan B. Anthony both opposed the new amendments, famously observing that, "in the enfranchisement of black men by the Fourteenth and Fifteenth Amendments to the Federal Constitution, the Congress of the United States has now virtually established on this continent an aristocracy of sex…"[56] Passionately advocating for women's suffrage in their weekly newspaper, *The Revolution*, their appeals showed both a political opportunism in resorting to racist rhetoric designed to call into question whether "ignorant negroes" were more deserving of the ballot than women,[57] but also a political nihilism in demonstrating their willingness to work with anyone, including former Confederates, to advance women's suffrage.[58]

After the ratification of the Fourteenth Amendment, women's suffrage continued to face considerable headwinds. During debates over the Fifteenth Amendment, for example, Ohio's congressional delegation wanted the proposed Amendment's language to explicitly allow discrimination in voting based on sex.[59] And the Enforcement Acts, which provided a federal criminal penalty for violations of state law that governed federal elections,[60] also raised questions about the rights to which women were entitled. Notably, seven of South Carolina's eight Black Congressmen supported women's suffrage and asserted that the 1870 Act actually enfranchised women. In Columbia, South Carolina, at least five Black women – encouraged by African American election officials – registered and voted in October 1870. Unfortunately, these election officials were arrested for allowing these women to vote because their ballots were deemed "fraudulent."[61]

56 "Anniversary of the American Equal Rights Association," *The Revolution* (New York), April 29, 1869.

57 "Women's Suffrage in California," *The Revolution* (New York), April 30, 1868 ("Now, why should not the millions of intelligent women of the country exercise the right to vote ? Was there not at least as much reason for this proposition as the Republican party constantly urged on behalf of ignorant negroes voting? Let women vote and let them represent their constituents on the floor of Congress.").

58 "Who Are Our Friends?," *The Revolution* (New York), January 15, 1868 ("Why wonder that the workers in our cause turned from their theoretical friends to the Democrats in Kansas, who gave us their votes. The party out of power is always in a position to carry principles to their logical conclusions, while the party in power, thinks only of what it can afford to do; hence, you can reason with minorities, while majorities are moved only by votes. We are indebted to the Democratic party for all the agitation we have had on this question for the last four years.")

59 Mathews, *Legislative and Judicial History of the Fifteenth Amendment*, p. 23.

60 See An Act to enforce the Rights of Citizens of the United States to vote in the several States of the Union, and for other Purposes, ch. 114, 16 Stat. 140 (1870) [Enforcement Act of 1870]; An Act to amend an Act approved May 31, 1870, entitled "An Act to enforce the Rights of Citizens of the United States to vote in the several States of this Union, and for other Purposes," ch. 99, 16 Stat. 433 (1871) [Enforcement Act of 1871].

61 Nancy A. Hewitt, "From Seneca Falls to Suffrage?: Reimagining a 'Master' Narrative in U.S. Women's History," in Nancy A. Hewitt (ed.), *No Permanent Waves: Recasting Histories of U.S. Feminism* (New Brunswick: Rutgers University Press, 2010), p. 27.

Even as Congress refused to enfranchise women and they faced challenges locally, some political communities were willing to carve out meaningful spaces for women in the Democratic process. For example, women applied to become or were nominated for positions as voter registrars, with some successfully serving in these positions.[62] They hoped that their service would establish that they, too, were deserving of the vote. These local efforts gave women political visibility and agency, suggesting that the lack of national recognition did not erase their political identity altogether.

In this sense, the decentralized nature of American federalism actually helped the cause of women's suffrage. Women could vote in states like Wyoming, New Jersey, Idaho, and Utah well before the Nineteenth Amendment was ratified. In fact, women gained the right to vote in Wyoming in 1869, only one year after the ratification of the Fourteenth Amendment. But the lack of federal protection meant that they were always subject to being disenfranchised at any moment. Women in New Jersey learned this lesson the hard way after they were disenfranchised in 1807 because elected officials did not like how they exercised their right to vote.[63]

In 1874, the Supreme Court finally confronted the question of whether the Fourteenth Amendment permitted the disenfranchisement of women. In *Minor v. Happersett*, the Court held that the right to vote was not a privilege or immunity of citizenship protected by the Fourteenth Amendment such that women were entitled to be enfranchised under its terms.[64] Along with the *Slaughter-House Cases*,[65] *Minor* was one of the first decisions to resist the notion that the Reconstruction Amendments so fundamentally altered our system of federalism that they changed both the nature of rights and the branch of government responsible for their enforcement.[66] As the Washington Supreme Court would later recognize in *Bloomer*, women were citizens and had always enjoyed this status; however, citizenship and

62 Edmund L. Drago, "Georgia's First Black Voter Registrars During Reconstruction" (1994) 78 *The Georgia Historical Quarterly* 760–93, 765 ("A variety of individuals applied or were nominated for registrar positions, including ex-Confederates, former Union officers, ex-slaves, and at least one woman.").

63 See Robert J. Dinkin, *Voting in America: A Study of Elections in the Original Thirteen States, 1776–1789* (Westport: Greenwood Press, 1982), p. 42 ("The provision in [New Jersey's] constitution that 'all inhabitants … of full age … worth fifty Pounds' could vote was interpreted to include unmarried women otherwise qualified. Although not too many took advantage of this opportunity, some New Jersey women did exercise their franchise rights until the year 1807 when, after several allegations of fraud, an amendment was passed which took away the privilege."). The stated purpose of New Jersey's 1807 law, which was enacted by the state legislature after the results of an Essex County referendum had to be invalidated due to corruption, was to "disenfranchise women, Black people, and immigrants" and limit the franchise to "free, white, taxpaying male citizens" only. Campbell Curry-Ledbetter, "Women's Suffrage in New Jersey 1776–1807: A Political Weapon" (2020) *Georgetown Journal of Gender and the Law* 705–724, 718–719.

64 *Minor v. Happersett*, 88 U.S. 162 (1874).

65 Ibid., 174–178.

66 *Slaughter-House Cases*, 83 U.S. 36 (1872).

suffrage were not co-extensive.[67] Like African Americans enfranchised at the time of *Dred Scott*, the principle that voting rights did not necessarily signal citizenship, and vice versa, remained undisturbed even if a legislature embraced some version of universal suffrage.

In rejecting the argument that voting was a privilege of citizenship protected by the Fourteenth Amendment, *Minor* was also a clear refutation of the premise of George Boutwell's 1869 bill (H.R. 1667) – which proposed both a constitutional amendment and a statute to prohibit racial discrimination in voting – that the Privileges and Immunities Clause of the Fourteenth Amendment protected a right to vote.[68] This view was contested because of the distinction made between civil and political rights during both the passage of the Fourteenth Amendment and the 1866 Civil Rights Act, in which privileges and immunities (but not voting) were thought to fall within the category of civil rights.[69]

In *Minor*, the Court laid to rest the argument that voting was a civil right and/or a privilege of citizenship that Congress could protect under its enforcement authority under Section 5 of the Fourteenth Amendment.[70] Importantly, *Minor* and *Bloomer* indicated that the disenfranchisement of women, absent a federal constitutional amendment, could never render state governments unrepublican in form, even if they were once enfranchised by state law.[71]

The lack of judicial and congressional support was not the only barrier to women's suffrage; marital expatriation also deprived many women of the right to vote. In *Mackenzie v. Hare*, for example, the California Supreme Court held that a woman could not vote in state and federal elections because, upon her marriage to a British

67 *Bloomer v. Todd*, 19 P. 135 (Wash. 1888).

68 See Chapter 6.3.

69 "Comments of Representative Boutwell, 40th Congress, Third Session, January 23, 1869," 40 *Congressional Globe* (Washington, D.C.: Congressional Globe Office, 1869), part 1, p. 558 (citing an opinion from the Kentucky Supreme Court for the proposition that voting is a privilege of citizenship). Opponents accused Boutwell of taking an inconsistent position during debates over the Fourteenth Amendment, claiming that Boutwell denied that the proposed Amendment would confer political rights, and endorsed the distinction between civil and political rights. See, e.g., "Comments of Representative Nicholson, 40th Congress, Third Session, January 23, 1869," 40 *Congressional Globe* (Washington, D.C.: Congressional Globe Office, 1869), part 1, p. 559.

70 The *Minor* Court expressly stated that it was "unanimously of the opinion that the Constitution of the United States does not confer the right of suffrage upon anyone[.]" *Minor v. Happersett*, 88 U.S. 162, 173 (1874). See also *Civil Rights Cases*, 109 U.S.3, 49 (1883) (stating that "the right of suffrage is not a necessary attribute of national citizenship… The right to vote in the States comes from the States… [and] has not been granted or secured by the Constitution of the United States…"); *McPherson v. Blacker*, 146 U.S. 1, 39 (1892) (holding that the Reconstruction Amendments did not alter the balance of power between the states and the federal government such that states who allowed their citizens to vote for electors at the time of the ratification of these Amendments had surrendered their power under Article II to appoint electors permanently).

71 See, e.g, "Exchange between Representatives Niblack and Boutwell, 40th Congress, Third Session, January 23, 1869," 40 *Congressional Globe* (Washington, D.C.: Congressional Globe Office, 1869), part 1, p. 558.

citizen, she assumed her husband's citizenship and was no longer an American citizen (a prerequisite to being an elector in that state).[72] Although the California constitution had been amended in 1911 specifically for the purpose of extending suffrage to women,[73] the court determined that her marriage not only disenfranchised her but robbed her of her political identity.

For decades, resistance to what would ultimately become the Nineteenth Amendment had been centered in traditional ideas of marriage and coverture, with its opponents arguing that women did not need the vote because they were politically represented by the male heads of households.[74] These stereotypes and assumptions hit Chinese women particularly hard. Thanks to immigration patterns, there was a large number of unmarried Chinese men and a smaller number of Chinese women, many of whom turned to prostitution upon arriving to America.[75] This disparity contributed to the view that Chinese culture was sexually deviant.[76] For this reason, being American-born did not necessarily save Chinese women from

72 *MacKenzie v. Hare*, 134 P. 713 (Cal. 1913).

73 California's Equal Suffrage Amendment referendum passed by a vote of 125,037 to 121,450 in October 1911, and, with this victory, "the number of women with full suffrage in the U.S. doubled[.]" Robert P.J. Cooney, Jr., "California Women's Suffrage Centennial: A Brief Summary of the 1911 Campaign," California Secretary of State's Office, www.sos.ca.gov/elections/celebrating-womens-suffrage/california-women-suffrage-centennial. After the enfranchisement of women in California, "[w]omen throughout the country were exultant and gained new hope that [women's suffrage rights] efforts in their own states might yet be successful. With each additional victory, suffragists built up the political power they needed to win passage and ratification of the 19th Amendment to the Constitution, which guaranteed women the right to vote in all the states." Ibid.

74 See, e.g., Kristy Maddox, "When Patriots Protest: The Anti-Suffrage Discursive Transformation of 1917" (2004) 7 *Rhetoric and Public Affairs* 283–310, 290 ("Anti-suffragists claimed that one of their primary disagreements with suffragists was over whether the family or the individual was the basic unit of society. Antis argued that the family was the basic unit of society, and that one person (the man/husband/father) could vote on behalf of the family. A system of women suffrage would suggest, the antis argued, that the individual was the basic unit of society. Some antis went so far as to predict the dissolution of the traditional family unit as a result of women voting; mothers would be too busy to take care of their children and divorces would result from married couples disagreeing on political issues."). There is also evidence of racially based opposition to the Nineteenth Amendment, mainly from southern white men who did not want to give the federal government yet another opportunity to interfere with how the states ran their elections. See Kenneth R. Johnson, "White Racial Attitudes as a Factor in Arguments against the Nineteenth Amendment" (1970) 31 *Phylon* 31–37, 32–33 ("The proposed Nineteenth Amendment would also authorize the federal government to protect the right of women to vote. Southern Democrats had been able to disfranchise Negro men without provoking federal intervention. There was no assurance that the same could be done with Negro women. It was inconceivable that Negro women would be permitted to vote while men were denied that right.").

75 See Stanford M. Lyman, "Marriage and Family among Chinese Immigrants to America, 1850–1960" (1968) 29 *Phylon* 321–330.

76 Leti Volpp, "Divesting Citizenship: On Asian American History and the Loss of Citizenship through Marriage" (2005) 53 *UCLA Law Review* 405–484, 459–460 ("The Chinese immigrant was generally kept from reproducing a heterosexual family, due in part to restrictions on immigration. This fact produced the perception of Chinese men as aberrant and alien, given the notion of the family as the foundation of civil society. Moreover, a large percentage of Chinese women who immigrated to the United States in the early period in fact worked as prostitutes.").

being denied basic rights that were extended to other women; unlike White women, Chinese women still had to fight to be a part of the political community of "We the People," a necessary prerequisite, in most cases, to possessing political rights.[77]

Mackenzie illustrated the extent to which these ideas of deservedness and exclusion continued to live on during Reconstruction, persisting in a political system in which women were ostensibly enfranchised in some places. The decision was no different from early antebellum-era voting rights cases in which citizenship was used as a foil to question the ability of Black men to be competent electors, even in the context of statutes that extended suffrage to that community. *Hobbs v. Foggs*,[78] discussed in Chapter 3, is illustrative of this point. By excluding a free Black man from voting on the grounds that one can be free of bondage and still lack a political identity, the case illustrated an aggressive policing of the community of voters. Even for those who met the legal requirements to be electors, one could still be excluded from the vote because of incompetencies that were viewed as inherent to one's skin color (or, in the case of *Mackenzie*, one's gender).

The continued exclusion of women and Chinese people from "We the Voters" illustrates that Congress did not fully reject antebellum theories of deservedness, nor the view that political space should remain predominantly male, in crafting new political communities in the wake of the Civil War. In doing so, Congress continued to emphasize those aspects of Lockean theory based primarily on the community's right to exclude. Indeed, the period from 1868 to 1872 saw an extension and contraction of Black voting rights in Washington, D.C., that further established that the narrow conception of "We the Voters" that existed prior to the war had only been temporarily reconfigured, rather than completely scrapped. Black men – the initial impetus for reimagining the political community in the post-war period – would prove to be temporary visitors rather than permanent members of "We the Voters."

7.3 RETAINING ONE'S SPACE IN THE POLITICAL COMMUNITY OF "WE THE VOTERS": WASHINGTON, D.C., AS A CASE STUDY IN AFRICAN AMERICAN DISENFRANCHISEMENT

The decisions that Congress made with respect to Black enfranchisement in Washington, D.C., were ultimately the beginning of the end for much of the Reconstruction project, despite the fact that the federal government exercised unparalleled authority over this small microcosm of American society. Importantly,

77 See, e.g., *Ex parte (Ng) Fung Sing*, 6 F.2d 670 (W.D. Wash. 1925) (finding that petitioner, although American born, could not re-enter the United States because, according to the court, "[b]eing of an excluded race, and a citizen of such excluded racial country, she is not eligible to citizenship, and under the law may not be admitted.").

78 *Hobbs v. Fogg*, 6 Watts 553 (Pa. 1837).

Congress faced much of the same opposition in D.C. as it did across most of the North when it came to universal male suffrage. In 1865, residents of Washington, D.C., voted 6,556 to 35 against Black enfranchisement. Voters residing in the Georgetown area also rejected it, 712 to 1.[79] The level of public opposition to Black suffrage in Washington, D.C., remained high in 1866 and would remain so through the 1868 congressional elections, long after Black people in the District were enfranchised.[80] Many opponents questioned why D.C. residents should be punished with "Negro suffrage" despite the fact that they had been loyal to the war effort.[81]

On Wednesday, January 10, 1866, the House debated a bill providing that,

> [F]rom all laws and parts of laws prescribing the qualifications of electors for any office in the District of Columbia the word 'white' be, and the same is hereby, stricken out, and that from and after the passage of this act no person shall be disqualified from voting at any election held in the said District on account of color; and that all acts of Congress and all laws of the State of Maryland in force in said District, and all ordinances of the cities of Washington and Georgetown inconsistent with the provisions of this act, are hereby repealed and annulled.[82]

Representatives hoped that imposing broad enfranchisement in D.C. would sell the country on the idea of Black political rights and, eventually, create an appetite for imposing the penalty of Section 2 of the Fourteenth Amendment, draft language of which had been introduced a few weeks earlier, on those jurisdictions that failed to institute universal manhood suffrage.[83]

As was the case in the debates over Section 2 of the Fourteenth Amendment and the Fifteenth Amendment, criticism of this proposal centered not only on the

79 "Comments of Representative Boyer, 39th Congress, First Session, January 10, 1866," 36 *Congressional Globe* (Washington, D.C.: Congressional Globe Office, 1866), part 1, p. 175 ("I do not dispute the power of Congress to regulate the elective franchise within the limits of the District of Columbia. But I do deny the moral right of Congress to pass this bill, opposed as it is to the will of the people, and therefore in violation of the fundamental principle of popular government.").

80 LaWanda Cox and John H. Cox, "Negro Suffrage and Republican Politics: The Problem of Motivation in Reconstruction Historiography," (1967) *Journal of Southern History* 303–330, 306–307 (detailing the opposition to Black suffrage following the elections of 1868).

81 "Comments of Representative Boyer, 39th Congress, First Session, January 10, 1866," 36 *Congressional Globe* (Washington, D.C.: Congressional Globe Office, 1866), part 1, p. 176. See also "Negro Suffrage in the District," *The Cincinnati Daily Enquirer*, April 8, 1868 (noting that "Michigan has repudiated negro suffrage, but the Senate voted today to fasten it on the helpless people of this District; and not only that, but negroes are not to be excluded from office.").

82 "Consideration of a bill extending the right of suffrage in the District of Columbia, 39th Congress, First Session, January 10, 1866," 36 *Congressional Globe* (Washington, D.C.: Congressional Globe Office, 1866), part 1, p. 173.

83 "Comments of Representative Scoffield, 39th Congress, First Session, January 10, 1866," 36 *Congressional Globe* (Washington, D.C.: Congressional Globe Office, 1866), part 1, p. 179 ("Bestow the elective franchise upon the colored population of this District, and you awaken the hope and ambition of the whole race throughout the country … . If colored suffrage is still considered an experiment, this District is a good place in which to try it.").

presumed unsuitability of African Americans to be electors but also over the exercise of federal power over elections.[84] These efforts toward universal manhood suffrage were hampered by an unlikely alliance of Democrats (who opposed the law for the usual reasons)[85] and Republicans, some of whom were uncomfortable – even in a jurisdiction in which federal power was plenary – with Congress setting voter qualifications.[86]

Adding complexity to this debate were those who advocated for a more limited suffrage because of the persistent belief – a holdover from the antebellum period – that the onus was on the voter to prove that he was worthy of the franchise. For example, Representative Robert S. Hale of New York, a moderate Republican who voiced concerns over whether some African Americans in the District were fit to be electors, offered a motion to limit the right to vote to all D.C. residents who met any one of three qualifications: (1) literacy; (2) taxpaying; or (3) military service.[87] Notably, Hale conceded that his proposal would disenfranchise some White men already entitled to vote in the District but thought this disenfranchisement necessary to "arrive at a fair and just system" that did not make distinctions on the basis of race.[88]

Other representatives were far more comfortable with the notion of educational qualifications (which were far less common in the pre–Civil War era), but balked at the idea of imposing property restrictions (which had been widespread from the founding to the mid-nineteenth century and had led to the disenfranchisement of many a White man).[89] Yet, with Black people emerging from slavery, educational

[84] "Comments of Representative Boyer, 39th Congress, First Session, January 10, 1866," 36 *Congressional Globe* (Washington, D.C.: Congressional Globe Office, 1866), part 1, p. 182.

[85] Ibid., p. 177 (arguing that "the color of the negro is [not] the main obstacle to his admission to political equality ... [rather] the negroes are not the equals of white Americans, and are not entitled by any right, natural or acquired, to participate in the Government of this country."); Ibid., p. 182 (arguing that Congress had legal authority but no "moral right" to pass the D.C. bill "in the face of the almost unanimous expression of the people of this District against it").

[86] Kate Masur, *An Example for the All the Land: Emancipation and the Struggle Over Equality in Washington, D.C.* (Chapel Hill: The University of North Carolina Press, 2010), p. 139 (noting that some Republicans preferred to address the issue of African American suffrage in the District by removing all references to race from local ordinances rather than setting voter qualifications).

[87] "Comments of Representative Hale, 39th Congress, First Session, January 10, 1866," 36 *Congressional Globe* (Washington, D.C.: Congressional Globe Office, 1866), part 1, pp. 178. See also "Comments of Representative Boyer, 39th Congress, First Session, January 10, 1866," 36 *Congressional Globe* (Washington, D.C.: Congressional Globe Office, 1866), part 1, p. 178 (arguing that the reward for military service was emancipation, not suffrage).

[88] "Comments of Representative Hale, 39th Congress, First Session, January 17, 1866," 36 *Congressional Globe* (Washington, D.C.: Congressional Globe Office, 1866), part 1, pp. 281.

[89] See, e.g., "Comments of Representative Rogers, 39th Congress, First Session, January 11, 1866," 36 *Congressional Globe* (Washington, D.C.: Congressional Globe Office, 1866), part 1, p. 201 (arguing that Madison meant to condemn property qualifications and did not intend for citizenship and voting to extend to any but the White man). See also "Comments of Representative Darling, 39th Congress, First Session, January 17, 1866," 36 *Congressional Globe* (Washington, D.C.: Congressional Globe Office, 1866), part 1, pp. 278–279("Sir, whenever the question of negro suffrage has been submitted

restrictions – together with literacy-related prohibitions – could subvert this electorate just as effectively as property qualifications.[90]

Supporters of the D.C. suffrage bill pointed to the relative affluence of the Black community in Washington, D.C., and Georgetown to push back against the argument that their voting rights should be qualified.[91] Representative James Wilson of Iowa noted, for example, that Black men in D.C. "are not all ignorant. Some of them are highly educated, while many of them are possessed of greater educational qualifications than have yet been suggested as a limitation upon the right of suffrage, and very many more come quite up to the proposed standard."[92] Similarly, Representative William Kelley of Pennsylvania argued that "educated, industrious, taxpaying, school-sustaining, church-building people of the District … are shut out of our Democratic Republic," contrary to the vision of James Madison, who would have "denounced such treachery."[93] This bit of hyperbole notwithstanding, it was clear that Black suffrage in the District became a flashpoint for testing the

to the people of my State, I have voted always and steadily for that amendment, unqualifiedly and unhesitatingly. And yet, under the existing circumstances which surround this question in this District, I am not in favor of giving the colored man here the right of suffrage without imposing an educational qualification. The property qualification I consider odious, and disregard it entirely.") See also "Comments of Representative Jenckes, 39th Congress, First Session, January 23, 1866," 36 *Congressional Globe* (Washington, D.C.: Congressional Globe Office, 1866), part 1, p. 387 ("Some of the southern States, up to the breaking out of the war, had constitutions which prescribed a property qualification. Suppose this amendment were adopted and the State of South Carolina chose to annul the constitution recently proclaimed and to go back to that of 1790, and that the word 'white' should be stricken out of it, I desire to ask how many freedmen, how many persons of African descent can be found who own in fee fifty acres of land or a town lot, or who have paid a tax of three shillings sterling. As far as I can ascertain from the statistics there would not be, if that constitution were restored and the word 'white' omitted, over five hundred additional qualified voters in that State. …The same persons who carried that State into the rebellion, and urged secession on her sister States, would still select the Representatives by continuing to hold control in their elections. They would establish more firmly than ever the aristocracy of landholders. There would be an oligarchy which it would be impossible for us to overthrow.").

90 "Comments of Representative Hale, 39th Congress, First Session, January 10, 1866," 36 *Congressional Globe* (Washington, D.C.: Congressional Globe Office, 1866), part 1, p. 180 ("We are again told that the average ability [of African Americans] is below that of the white race. How do you know that? The colored man has never exhibited equal ability, to be sure, but he has never had equal opportunities. The forbidding statutes of the South attest the capacity of the negro. If they really believed his mind was so feeble, why bind it with such heavy chains? If he was incapable of learning, why prohibit it with the penitentiary?").

91 "Comments of Representative Wilson, 39th Congress, First Session, January 10, 1866," 36 *Congressional Globe* (Washington, D.C.: Congressional Globe Office, 1866), part 1, p. 175 ("The value of real and personal property now owned by them is over one million two hundred and fifty thousand dollars. The value of church property held by them is about one hundred and twenty-five thousand dollars, consisting of twenty-one churches, which are supported at a cost of over twenty thousand dollars per annum.")

92 "Comments of Representative Wilson, 39th Congress, First Session, January 10, 1866," 36 *Congressional Globe* (Washington, D.C.: Congressional Globe Office, 1866), part 1, p. 174.

93 "Comments of Representative Kelley, 39th Congress, First Session, January 10, 1866," 36 *Congressional Globe* (Washington, D C.: Congressional Globe Office, 1866), part 1, p. 183.

antebellum framework that voting was a privilege that was earned and relatedly, that Congress should be reluctant to set voter qualification standards, even in domains in which its authority was paramount.

In December 1866, Congress passed an "Act to Regulate the Elective Franchise,"[94] granting Black men in Washington, D.C., the right to vote. Andrew Johnson vetoed the bill on January 5, 1867.[95] Congress overrode his veto,[96] allowing Washington, D.C., to become a high-profile test case for African American suffrage in the post–Civil War era. With the District, Congress was able define the political community without the restrictions of federalism, setting a baseline for what African American suffrage could look like for the rest of the country.[97] The Military Reconstruction Act of 1867, passed two months after the bill enfranchising the residents of Washington, D.C., subjected the former Confederate states to federal oversight just like the District, so the stakes were high.[98]

On one hand, Congress would be able to analogize from its experience with elections in the District as it sought to remake the South, and in the process, try to get as close as possible to this ideal of universal manhood suffrage within a framework in which congressional power, at least temporarily, was just as far reaching. But, on the other hand, many of difficulties that Congress faced in regulating suffrage in the District could not be generalized to congressional efforts to regulate state political systems over the long term – where local violence; the need to rebuild the economic, political, and physical infrastructure; the geographical distance from Washington, D.C.; and the constraints of constitutional text, new and old – complicated the task of remaking and sustaining new political communities in the South.

For this reason, one might view the states and D.C. as studies in contrast, but the D.C. voting bill nonetheless taught congressional Republicans important lessons about what it meant for Black men, as citizens, to be full members of a political community where they might disagree with and challenge White people.[99] For once, federalism was not political foil that Republicans could hide behind in deciding who to disenfranchise, as they experienced first-hand how African Americans defined their political freedom in the post-war era.

94 An Act to Regulate the elective Franchise in the District of Columbia, ch. 6, 14 Stat. 375 (1867).

95 Masur, *Example for the All the Land*, p. 135.

96 Ibid.

97 Ibid. (noting the difficulties faced by Congress because prior to the war, Congress's "antebellum consensus had been to uphold slavery and the black codes in the nation's capital. Now, however, the issue was not simply congressional power per se, but also the fact that Congress threatened to subject white residents to the humiliation of sharing political power with African Americans or, at the extreme, the dreaded possibility of a government controlled by freedmen.").

98 An Act to Provide for the More Efficient Government of the Rebel States, ch. 153, 14 Stat. 428 (1867) [Military Reconstruction Act I]. For more on the Military Reconstruction Act of 1867, see Chapter 6.

99 "Comments of Representative Rogers, 39th Congress, First Session, January 11, 1866," 36 *Congressional Globe* (Washington, D.C.: Congressional Globe Office, 1866), part 1, p. 200.

To sell African American suffrage on the North, Republicans wanted to point to the District as a success story,[100] and there was much to suggest that Black residents who lived there were becoming political force in their own right. Voter registration opened in Washington, D.C., on March 18, 1867, and by its close, African American voter registration came perilously close to outnumbering that of White people – 7,271–8,240.[101] In 1868, the first African American candidates were elected to city office, and Republicans secured the mayor's office after a bitterly fought campaign that same year.[102]

Over the course of these elections, it was clear that the Black community held a conception of political participation that extended beyond voting to encompass full equality across civil, political, and social domains. During the initial debates in the House, the focus on qualified suffrage predominated because of concerns that once Black men achieved political equality, then social equality was inevitable (which, if we are being honest, was much less desirable to White representatives of all political stripes). As historian Kate Masur has noted of White sentiment in the district, "Black men's access to the vote … would lead inevitably down a slippery slope toward office holding, jury service, and ever-more-intimate spaces, to the point where African American men would 'have and hold' whites in the most private of places."[103]

Congress resisted the call for suffrage, qualified by educational or property restrictions, during debates over the Fourteenth and Fifteenth Amendments and over voting in the District. But its later actions in Washington, D.C. – its first real retreat from universal male suffrage – reveals an unfortunate trade-off between the long-term commitment required to achieve full political equality for Black men and the short-term politics that ultimately rendered this commitment politically toxic.

Between 1868 and 1871, African Americans did not simply fall in line behind Republican orthodoxy. Instead, they sought to exercise their political power independently, even if that sometimes meant bucking the party line. While they initially voted as a bloc, this was not always true, particularly as Black men battled with White politicians over the future of Black schools and public employment in the District.[104] The prospect that Black people might care about policy rather than

[100] Masur, *Example for the All the Land*, p. 138 (noting that by the time that the bill was debated in the Senate in December 1866, "moderate Republicans had come to the conclusion that black men's enfranchisement was crucial for meaningful Reconstruction policy.").

[101] Melvin R. Williams, "A Blueprint for Change: The Black Community in Washington, D.C., 1860–1870" (1971/72) 71/72 *Records of the Columbia Historical Society* 359–393, 382.

[102] Ibid., 383.

[103] Masur, *Example for the All the Land*, pp. 127–128 ("Time and again, when African Americans argued that equality before the law must extend beyond the simple absence of discriminatory statutes and encompass public accommodations or public schools, their opponents insisted that they were demanding much-maligned social equality. In the debate about black men's enfranchisement, concerns were rampant that voting rights for black men would lead to racial equality in a range of other semipublic or private spaces.").

[104] Ibid., p. 145.

politics proved especially disconcerting when they began to dominate the election machinery in the District, which, for some elites, confirmed earlier concerns that White people would be shut out of the electoral process.[105]

During this period, Washington, D.C., was governed by a mayor (elected every two years), a Board of Aldermen (fourteen members, two from each district, elected in staggered two-year terms), and a Board of Common Council (a twenty-one-member board elected annually).[106] Black voters enthusiastically participated in the municipal elections of 1867, their first election post-enfranchisement. During these elections, Black people were barred by the city charter from holding office, although many were appointed to prominent positions by the new Board of Common Council.[107] Black voters fought this restriction in the 1868 election, and Carter Steward, a prominent Black merchant, won a seat on the Board of Common Council.[108] Republicans swept the 1869 municipal elections, and it also proved to be a banner year for Black politicians elected to office: not only did Black candidates win Board of Common Council seats from each of the seven districts, but they were also able to secure other elected positions in D.C.[109]

African American support not only proved decisive in the 1867, 1868, and 1869 elections, but these elections also showcased the political diversity within the Black community. Mayor Sayles J. Bowen, a strong supporter of Black equality who came to power in 1868, faced difficulty implementing his agenda because Democrats on the city council were hostile to much of his agenda.[110] In addition, some of his policies generated an opposition movement within the Black community, particularly when he voiced support for congressional legislation that would remove the District's schools from the oversight of the Secretary of the Interior. The legislation, ultimately vetoed by President Johnson, would have placed schools under the control of a single board, thereby depriving the Black community of the influence that

[105] Ibid., p. 131 ("Since the advent of emancipation, black Washingtonians had been arguing that freedom must entail not just the absence of slavery, but also respect for their association and institutional and racial equality in public life. Now, African Americans could use their power as voters to demand concrete changes in municipal policy. With white voters divided between the two major parties, African Americans could wield considerable power if they voted together.")

[106] Williams, "Blueprint for Change," 382.

[107] See Masur, *Example for the All the Land*, p. 148 ("In Washington's first biracial election, the Republican coalition of African Americans and whites, many of whom were Northerners by birth, succeeded in electing the city collector, registrar, and surveyor, as well as four of seven aldermen and thirteen of twenty-one councilmen.").

[108] Ibid., p. 153.

[109] "The election [of 1869], however, resulted in an almost clean sweep for the Republicans. Only three Democrats remained on the Board of Alderman and none on the council. Blacks won more races in that election than at any other time between 1868 and 1871, the year municipal elections ended. A black man won a seat on the council from each of the seven wards. Steward won in a race for the board of aldermen, and Cook became city registrar with a winning margin of more than 5,000 votes over his white Democratic rival." Williams, "Blueprint for Change," 383.

[110] See Masur, *Example for the All the Land*, p. 153.

they had exercised in this space since the antebellum era.[111] Not surprisingly, Mayor Bowen's position alienated prominent Black leaders and also fueled racial tension about school integration in the District between Black and White Republicans.[112]

This dissension had dire consequences in the 1870 municipal elections, as Black councilmen began to take the lion's share of the blame for the fiscal difficulties that the city faced, and fear spread that Black people were ill-equipped to govern. The city faced a considerable budgetary crisis, with Democrats and Republicans alike blaming Mayor Bowen and the Black councilmen for the fiscal mess. In the end, Bowen's nomination for another term as mayor split the Republican Party and, in the 1870 election, he lost by almost 4,000 votes to Matthew G. Emery, a former alderman who also had biracial support.[113] With Emery's election in 1870, four Black politicians aligned with his campaign also won seats on the Board of Common Council.[114] Bowen enjoyed support from only two prominent Black politicians, signaling that African Americans would not sheepishly fall in law behind White Republicans and had become power brokers within the party in their own right.

Within two years, the experiment by congressional Republicans to test suffrage in the District was viewed as both a failure of local governance and a rebuke of Congress's broader policy on Reconstruction.[115] In reality, the condemnation of Black suffrage as a failed experiment emerged because Black people sought to exercise political power in ways that best benefited their community, even if it meant bucking the White Republican politicians who had anointed themselves with the task of dictating how the newly enfranchised should vote and pursue policy.

Washington D.C.'s Black community – consisting of Black laborers willing to strike for better working conditions; Black parents willing to lobby for integrated schools; and Black political factions willing to make alliances to elect a responsive municipal government – did not mirror Congress's ideal of a Black electorate

111 Ibid., p. 156 ("The black public schools were the literal and figurative descendants of the private schools African Americans had struggled to maintain in the antebellum decades. Since the outset of the public school system, African American parents and educators had sought to maintain a voice in the schools' operations and had cultivated relationships with successive interior secretaries to do that.").

112 Williams, "Blueprint for Change," 383; Masur, *Example for the All the Land*, pp. 154–158 (noting that there were arguments in the black community that a mixed school board was acceptable only if the schools were integrated).

113 Williams, "Blueprint for Change," 387.

114 Ibid., 384. See also Masur, *Example for the All the Land*, p. 156 (stating that "Bowen's administration was not entirely satisfying to its African American constituents, however, particularly when it came to the management of Washington's black public schools").

115 Williams, "Blueprint for Change," 392 ("Washington had undergone some basic social and political changes during the eight preceding years and many whites not only felt that the city's 'social revolution' had gone too far, too fast, but that it should not have been initiated in the first place. The *Intelligencer*, reflecting the sentiments of a number of whites, had bitterly attacked three measures passed by Congress: the act emancipating slaves in the city, the law establishing public education for blacks, and the legislation providing black suffrage. Congress, then, was the real initiator of the 'social revolution.'").

that would vote lock step for candidates anointed by Republican elites and blindly endorse Republican policies in gratitude for having the vote.[116] Because of their willingness to exercise their independence, congressional Republicans viewed Black people in the District as no longer deserving of the vote, and many Republicans in Congress pointed to the poor fiscal situation of Washington, D.C., as proof that this trust had been misplaced.[117]

Congress sought to remedy the alleged chaos and embarrassment – indeed, the democracy – that had come out of the 1870 municipal elections by giving itself the power to determine the officials of city government by consolidating D.C.'s government and removing much of the choice from the electorate.[118] This legislation, the District of Columbia Organic Act of 1871, organized the District government into an upper house, governor, and board of public works appointed by the president.[119] The only elective offices were for the House of Delegates and a nonvoting member of the U.S. House, a move that significantly reduced the political power of the Black community in the District after only four years of enfranchisement.[120] The Organic Act, as it turned out, foreshadowed the decline of Reconstruction policy on other fronts as well.

7.4 A FULL RETREAT? SECTION 2 OF THE FOURTEENTH AMENDMENT, THE NINTH CENSUS, AND CONGRESS'S WAVERING COMMITMENT TO UNIVERSAL MALE SUFFRAGE

Congress's retreat in the District came in the midst of discussions about implementing the reduction clause of Section 2 of the Fourteenth Amendment. The D.C. controversy undoubtedly made Congress gun-shy about enforcing Section 2, once it became clear that the provision's mandate of nondiscriminatory access to the ballot would result in the enfranchisement of Black voters who might not blindly follow the party orthodoxy.

As Republicans grappled with the complexities of reapportioning the country in the wake of emancipation, war, and a complete reimagining of "We the People," they once again turned to principles of federalism – just as politicians had in debates

116 See generally Masur, *Example for the All the Land*.

117 Ibid., pp. 197–198 ("The novelty of black men's enfranchisement was fading and the congressional commitment weakening, but among Republicans the dedication to formal racial equality remained. Thus the consolidators professed not to care about black enfranchisement as such but argued … that 'taxpayers' and 'intelligent citizens' favored consolidating the District's government. Claims of special prerogatives for citizens and taxpayers helped consolidators argue for reducing the political power of the capital's poor black residents without offending Republicans in Congress, who rejected outright racism but were not immune to suggestions that freedmen were not ready to vote.").

118 Ibid., p. 194 (noting that "[t]alk of instituting a commission government for the District of Columbia began in the fall of 1865 as a direct response to the debate over black men's enfranchisement").

119 An Act to Provide a Government for the District of Columbia, ch. 62, 16 Stat. 419 (1871).

120 Masur, *Example for the All the Land*, p. 206.

over the Apportionment Act of 1842 – to navigate delicate political terrain. In the mid-nineteenth century, controversy had centered on single-member districts; two decades later, the stakes had shifted to the intertwined challenges of Reconstruction and economic uncertainty. In one of the great historical ironies, the federalism that was discarded for political reasons in the prior controversy would become a refuge to evade constitutional mandates in the latter. But the one consistent theme across decades was that the politics leading to these decisions were fraught; federalism – the way out.

The decay in the political situation was not uni-causal. The nation's policy toward the South often competed with pressing issues of monetary policy, and northern Democrats were able to leverage these issues into electoral victories. For example, Democrats in Ohio were able to successfully make monetary policy an issue in the 1867 elections, building a winning coalition around a plan that would pay off wartime bonds with paper money rather than gold or silver.[121] Because former New York governor Horatio Seymour favored hard money, Democrats threw their support behind him in the 1868 presidential election, a choice that had little chance of success against war hero Ulysses S. Grant, but nonetheless illustrated the importance of the money question.[122]

The money issue did not completely detract from the omnipresent controversy over African American suffrage and, with the ratification of the Fourteenth Amendment on July 9, 1868, the question of how Section 2 of that provision would be implemented. On December 19, 1868, Senator James Harlan introduced the following resolution in the Senate: "Resolved, That the Committee on the Judiciary be instructed to report a bill for the apportionment of representatives in compliance with the provision of section two of the fourteenth amendment to the Constitution of the United States."[123]

This bill stalled, again because of fundamental disagreements about the money question. Reapportionment of the existing districts would have resulted in a larger contingent of representatives from the Midwest who could strong-arm northeastern states on this issue.[124] Section 2 would have to wait.

Delayed implementation, notwithstanding, it was notable that Congress sought to enforce Section 2 after the Fifteenth Amendment had been voted out of Congress and was awaiting ratification by the requisite number of states, illustrating that Section 2 had not become obsolete as critics claimed.[125] But the sheer breadth of

[121] Nicolas Barreyre, "The Politics of Economic Crises: The Panic of 1873, the End of Reconstruction, and the Realignment of American Politics" (2011) 10 *The Journal of the Gilded Age and the Progressive Era* 403–423, 412.

[122] Ibid. See also Mary K. Hammond, "War and Reconstruction" (October 1952) 23/134 *Presidential Elections* 207–214, 213–214.

[123] "Introduction of Resolution by Senator Harlan, 40th Congress, Third Session, December 19, 1858," 40 *Congressional Globe* (Washington, D.C.: Congressional Globe Office, 1869), part 1, p. 158.

[124] Barreyre, "Politics of Economic Crises," 414.

[125] Ibid.

Section 2, now that enforcement was imminent, raised red flags among even its staunchest supporters in Congress.

In December 1869, Representative (and future President) James Garfield, who had viewed Section 2 as a necessary first step toward African American suffrage and representation,[126] now referred to this provision as "radical." As Chairman of the House Select Committee on the Census charged with establishing the population base for purposes of apportionment, Garfield argued that Section 2 was broader than anyone realized at ratification:

> The fourteenth amendment, so far as it related to suffrage, was generally understood as referring exclusively to the denial of the right to vote on account of race or color. But the language of the Constitution is much broader. It is in substance that, wherever the right to vote is denied or abridged in any State, not merely, on account of race or color, but for any other reason than rebellion or crime, in that State the basis of representation shall be reduced proportionately.[127]

Given the mandate of Section 2, the Committee on the Census had to look into every race-based and race-neutral state law that potentially abridged or denied the right to vote, as well as decisions issued by state courts that had implications for voting rights.[128]

That said, the Committee was very deferential to the states, reaching out to governors to confirm that the Committee had properly characterized their laws.[129] The Committee then produced a list of approximatively eighty laws that excluded men from voting. Using these laws as a basis, the penalty could be imposed by taking the ratio of the entire population of male citizens twenty-one years of age to disenfranchised males in that category and using that as the ratio by which to reduce the basis of apportionment. In other words, if a state had 250 men who were 21 years or older and 100 of them were impermissibly disenfranchised, then the number of voting eligible men who counted for purposes of reapportionment would have to be reduced by 40 percent (the ratio is 100:250) to 150 people.[130]

126 "Comments of Representative Garfield, 41st Congress, Second Session, December 8, 1869," 42 *Congressional Globe* (Washington, D.C.: Congressional Globe Office, 1870), part 1, p. 38.

127 Ibid.

128 Ibid., p. 39.

129 Ibid.

130 Ibid. ("[A]fter a very careful study of the whole matter the committee saw no better way of meeting this part of the case than by putting into the schedule two columns, which the gentlemen who have the bill in their hands will see by turning to schedule one, columns fourteen and fifteen. The heading of one of the columns reads thus: 'Male citizens of the United States twenty-one years of age.' There is to be a mark put in that column for every male citizen of the United States-above twenty-one years of age. In the second, column there is to be an entry of all persons described as follows - and here we adopt the language of the Constitution, abridging it - 'Male citizens of the United States twenty-one years of age whose right to vote is denied or abridged on other grounds than rebellion or other crime.' Those two columns being filled, the ratio of the second to the first is the ratio by which we must reduce the total population of any State in order to find its representative population.").

Even for some Congressmen who had not served in the Thirty-Ninth Congress when Section 2 was enacted, they agreed with Garfield that the breadth of its text likely brought a panoply of state laws within its ambit. As one-term Republican Representative Richard Haldeman observed, the penalty can be imposed for

> for abridging the right to vote on account of race or color, ... account of property qualifications, on account of the want of literary qualifications, on account of service in the Army or Navy, on account of poverty, idiocy, or insanity, on account of not taking certain oaths, and ... on account of not being of good character or good behavior.[131]

He further cautioned that, "you are warned in each State to be careful how far you abridge or deny the right of suffrage to its inhabitants on account of the greater or less duration of their residence under penalty of representative diminution."[132] The fact that many laws that had not historically been objectionable came within the scope of Section 2 – the oath requirement was of particular note – gave many representatives significant pause.

In its report,[133] the Committee complied the following chart of the number of states that abridged or denied the right to vote on various grounds:

1. On account of race or color...16 states
2. On account of residence on lands of the United States.......... 2 states
   On account of residence less than required time in the United States...2 states
   On account of residence in State less than required time, (six different specifications)...36 states
   On account of residence in county, city, town, district, &c., (eighteen different specifications)............................37 states
3. Wanting property qualifications or non-payment of taxes, (eight specifications) ....8 states

See also Michael Hurta, "Counting the Right to Vote in the Next Census: Reviving Section Two of the Fourteenth Amendment" (2015) 94 *Texas Law Review* 146, 148 ("Put simply, states that deny or abridge the right to vote of any voting-age citizens – for any reason other than the citizens' rebellion or crimes – shall have their bases for apportionment reduced according to the percentage of such citizens whose right to vote has not been burdened."); "Comments of Representative Crumpacker, Fifty-Sixth Congress, Second Session, January 7, 1901," 34 *Congressional Record* (Washington, D.C.: Government Printing Office, 1901), Appendix, p. 68 ("If a State with a population of 1,500,000 should disfranchise 40 per cent of its male citizens 21 years of age, except for crime, its basis of representation would be reduced in the same proportion, and it would be accorded representation upon a basis of 900,000 instead of 1,500,000.").

131 "Comments of Representative Haldeman, 41st Congress, Second Session, December 8, 1869," 42 *Congressional Globe* (Washington, D.C.: Congressional Globe Office, 1870), part 1, p. 40.

132 Ibid.

133 *The Garfield Report to Congress from the Committee on the Ninth Census*, House of Representatives Report No. 3, 41st Congress, Second Session (Washington, D.C.: Government Printing Office, 1870).

4. Wanting literary qualifications, (two specifications).................2 states
5. On account of character or behavior, (two specifications).... 2 states
6. On account of services in army or navy.................................. 2 states
7. On account of pauperism, idiocy, and insanity, (seven specifications) ....24 states
8. Requiring certain oaths as preliminary to voting, (two specifications)...... ....5 states
9. Other causes of exclusion, (two specifications).......................2 states

Ultimately, the Committee was unable to produce a conclusive number of individuals whose votes had been abridged or denied. Because state governors had to certify the Committee's findings, this was the equivalent of asking a wrong-doer to confirm whether he had broken the law; thus, it was no surprise that the Committee was unable to collect information sufficient to reduce the representation of any state. The Committee also asked citizens to self-report to the census takers whether their voting rights had been violated, even though Congress was still reasoning through what counted as an abridgment or denial of the right to vote for Section 2 purposes.[134]

To be clear, Section 2 faced distinct challenges long before the Committee undertook the work of deciding what constituted an abridgment or denial within the context of the amendment. When reapportionment was debated in 1869–70, the argument persisted that the soon-to-be-ratified Fifteenth Amendment – which explicitly prohibited racial discrimination in voting – would render Section 2 obsolete, although members of the Committee sharply refuted this contention.[135] As Representative Halderman observed, somewhat presciently:

> the States may still deny the right of suffrage to any of the classes that I have enumerated; and in so far as they deny the right of suffrage for idiocy, or poverty, or insanity, or want of property qualification, or want of education, or for wanting a period of residence sufficiently long to satisfy the State legislature, just in that measure shall the penalty be annexed and attached.[136]

Indeed, one of the reasons for the alarm could be buyers' remorse, or more pointedly, the fact that Section 2, as it was designed to do, extended far beyond race discrimination in voting and even beyond the states in the former Confederacy to places that were geographically varied and racially homogenous. For example, the state of Rhode Island, because of voter qualification standards that included

[134] Ibid., p. 53.

[135] George D. Zuckerman, "A Consideration of the History and Present Status of Section 2 of the Fourteenth Amendment" (1961) 30 *Fordham Law Review* 93–136, 112–114.

[136] "Comments of Representative Haldeman, 41st Congress, Second Session, December 8, 1869," 42 *Congressional Globe* (Washington, D.C.: Congressional Globe Office, 1870), part 1, p. 40.

durational residency and property ownership requirements, was at risk of losing one representative because of the penalty.[137]

Despite the mandate that Congress "shall" enforce Section 2, the reapportionment debates in the 1870s showcased a Congress that consistently sought to evade its responsibilities, at times showing undue solicitude to the states. There were repeated attempts to divorce apportionment from the implementation of the penalty which, according to the language of Section 2, must occur during decennial reapportionment.[138] After all, Congress can only "apportion[ ] [Representatives] among the several States according to their respective numbers" by determining how much "the basis of representation therein" should be proportionately reduced because states have abridged or denied the right to vote.[139]

On December 14, 1869, Representative William Loughridge – another congressman who had not been present for Section 2's enactment – proposed an amendment to the census bill providing, "That for the Forty-Second Congress no State shall be reduced in its representation," to separate the increasingly controversial penalty from the census, which had its own share of problems.[140] At the time, some states were facing the prospect of reduced representation because of population loss;[141] the amendment would have prevented reduction for any reason, including decreased population or voting rights violations.

By converting a once-a-decade mandate into a mere suggestion that could be disregarded on a whim, Loughridge's proposed amendment, as well as the refusal to require the census and reapportionment to be undertaken together, cast doubt on whether the Fourteenth Amendment truly transformed our system of federalism from state-centered to Congress centered, at least as it relates to protecting the new community of "We the Voters." And it is not clear that the circumstances justified this abdication.

137 Gerard N. Magliocca, "Our Unconstitutional Reapportionment Process" (2018) 86 *George Washington Law Review* 774, 788–789 (noting that Rhode Island and Arkansas would have lost representation if the penalty was enforced).

138 Hurta, "Counting the Right to Vote in the Next Census: Reviving Section Two of the Fourteenth Amendment," 157 (noting that, during the effort to enforce Section 2 in 1870, implementation was stymied by the fact that "the superintendent of the census was not statistically confident about his reported number of disenfranchisements."). See also "Comments of Representative Garfield, 41st Congress, Second Session, December 13, 1869," 42 *Congressional Globe* (Washington, D.C.: Congressional Globe Office, 1870), part 1, p. 104 (rejecting an amendment that would have required the census and reapportionment to happen by August 15, 1870).

139 United States Constitution Amend. 14, s. 2. See also *The Garfield Report to Congress from the Committee on the Ninth Census*, House of Representatives Report No. 3, 41st Congress, Second Session (Washington, D.C.: Government Printing Office, 1870) (noting that "[t]he census is our only constitutional means of determining the political representative population."

140 "Comments of Representative Loughridge, 41st Congress, Second Session, December 14, 1869," 42 *Congressional Globe* (Washington, D.C.: Congressional Globe Office, 1870), part 1, p. 122. Loughbridge claimed that the amendment would resolve the most serious objections to the census bill, which was that states lacked an opportunity to call a special session of the legislature to draw new districts.

141 Ibid.

Some of the problems related to the scope of Section 2 and its impact on the census were not unique, at least not in and of themselves. Censuses taken in 1850 and 1860 also had to deal with issues of growth and loss of representation, not to mention the unique problems posed by the Three-Fifths Clause.[142] Indeed, one of the immediate issues facing the House was whether Congress could constitutionally conduct an apportionment twice in the same decade, an issue on which there was a sharp divide within the chamber. The last apportionment took effect in March 1863, and some representatives argued that, while Congress "may provide for an enumeration now," it "had no constitutional power to make an apportionment to take effect before the 4th of March, 1873."[143]

In addition, the issues with the census itself – to be distinguished from the debate over Section 2's penalty – highlighted a growing controversy that had lain dormant for much of the 1860s; namely, how to deal with the states in the West, and in particular, the increases in their congressional representation. Since 1870, western representatives had repeatedly spoken out against attempts to conduct the census without reapportioning representatives, warning that those segments of the country entitled to increased representation would unfairly have to wait until as late as 1873 before receiving their due representation in Congress.[144]

The debates over the census and western representation further compounded the practical problems with implementing Section 2, but again these problems were not new. Recall earlier controversies over whether states could disenfranchise the Chinese population, heavily concentrated in the West, despite the removal of the "race or color" language from Section 2.[145] In debates over the Enforcement Act of

[142] For example, regarding the apportionment changes necessitated by the results of the 1860 census, "[t]he Apportionment Act of 1862 set the membership of the House of Representatives at 241 seats. Fifty-seven seats had been allocated to the eleven seceded states, and of these seats fifteen were assigned according to the three-fifths formula for their slave population. Since these states were not represented in the 39th Congress, actual House membership was reduced to 184." George P. Smith, "Republican Reconstruction and Section Two of the Fourteenth Amendment" (1970) 23 *The Western Political Quarterly* 829–853, 830–831.

[143] "Comments of Representative Woodward, 41st Congress, Second Session, December 13, 1869," 42 *Congressional Globe* (Washington, D.C.: Congressional Globe Office, 1870), part 1, p. 105.

[144] "Comments of Representative Judd, 41st Congress, Second Session, December 13, 1869," 42 *Congressional Globe* (Washington, D.C.: Congressional Globe Office, 1870), part 1, p. 104; see also "Comments of Representative Coburn, 41st Congress, Second Session, December 13, 1869," 42 *Congressional Globe* (Washington, D.C.: Congressional Globe Office, 1870), part 1, p. 106 ("The States in the South, where there has been a large increase of representation by reason of the emancipation of the negroes and the conferring of the right of suffrage upon them, and the States in the West which have been growing rapidly within the last eight years – all these States are entitled justly to their fair representation on this floor. Six millions or more of the people of the United States will be disenfranchised for two years…").

[145] See "Comments of Representative Fitch, 41st Congress, Second Session, May 27, 1870," 42 *Congressional Globe* (Washington, D.C.: Congressional Globe Office, 1870), appendix, p. 411 ("I chanced to be present in Washington, although not then a member of this House, and represented to Mr. Boutwell that with the words 'nativity and religious belief' in we could not exclude the Chinese from the ballot if we should so desire, and Nevada would not in my opinion ratify the fifteenth

1870, some representatives argued that states could disenfranchise their Chinese populations on the grounds of nativity and religious belief, which had been removed from the language of the Fifteenth Amendment for expressly this purpose.[146] But the removal of this language from the Fifteenth Amendment did not answer the question of whether disenfranchisement on the basis of nativity and religious belief would trigger the penalty of Section 2. Arguably, it does. While some representatives argued that religion and nativity were exempt, the broad "abridgment" language of Section 2 of the Fourteenth Amendment and Section 1 of the Fifteenth Amendment did not perfectly overlap and could lead to reduced representation for disenfranchisement on these grounds.

But, more importantly, who decides? As the questions surrounding nativity and religious belief abounded, it was unclear who would determine whether states had abridged the right to vote – the Select Committee on the Census; the House of Representatives; or the Secretary of the Interior. For some representatives, delegating this authority to the Secretary raised serious Article I issues,[147] but many of the concerns surrounding the delegation to the Secretary to handle both the census and apportionment turned on the uncertainty surrounding the application of the penalty.[148] Frankly put, the stakes were too high. Representative Hoar offered the following hypothetical:

amendment if it should be so framed as to prohibit the exclusion of the Chinese from the right of suffrage."). See also "Comments of Representative Johnson, 41st Congress, Second Session, May 27, 1870," 42 *Congressional Globe* (Washington, D.C.: Congressional Globe Office, 1870), part 5, p. 3877 (California representative who referred to the Enforcement Act as "an act to foster paganism in the States and Territories of the United States; to foster child murder, to strike down Christianity, and to deprive the people of their liberties" and noting that it was an act "in favor of the Chinaman").

146 See "Comments of Representative Fitch, 41st Congress, Second Session, May 27, 1870," 42 *Congressional Globe* (Washington, D.C.: Congressional Globe Office, 1870), appendix, p. 411(noting that "[t]he language of the fifteenth amendment was subsequently modified and the words 'nativity and religious belief' were striken out…").

147 "Comments of Representative Hoar, 41st Congress, Second Session, December 13, 1869," 42 *Congressional Globe* (Washington, D.C.: Congressional Globe Office, 1870), part 1, p. 107; "Comments of Representative Dickey, 41st Congress, Second Session, December 13, 1869," 42 *Congressional Globe* (Washington, D.C.: Congressional Globe Office, 1870), part 1, p. 106.

148 See "Comments of Representative Allison, 41st Congress, Second Session, December 13, 1869," 42 *Congressional Globe* (Washington, D.C.: Congressional Globe Office, 1870), part 1, p. 109 ("This bill provides the rule of apportionment, and gives proper directions to the Secretary of the Interior; or if it does not now do so sufficiently it ought to be amended so that it shall do so. Under this rule of apportionment those who are excluded and those who are included ought to be defined so clearly that the Secretary of the Interior cannot err, for he is obliged to give at the outset his instructions to the enumerators, and they are to show in their enumeration the number of persons who are excluded from the right of voting, and the number of persons, male citizens over twenty-one years of age, who are entitled to vote in the several States. In this respect there can be no objection at all to this proposition. Is it possible that we are going to leave so grave a question open for the decision of the Secretary of the Interior or for the decision of the House of Representatives in 1873 or at any future time? It is a question that must be decided in the very beginning in order that the enumerators and the district superintendents and the Superintendent of the Census may know what persons to return, and whether they are within the prohibitions of the fourteenth constitutional amendment.").

> Suppose the Secretary of the Interior disqualifies a certain number of persons in Massachusetts by his interpretation of the fourteenth amendment thereupon, when the members of Congress come here this House determines that the Secretary of the Interior was wrong in his decision and rejects or admits the member from Massachusetts elected under the Secretary's statement; will not that change the ratio of representation of every State of this Union by an act of this House?[149]

These enforcement difficulties notwithstanding, there wasn't a clear consensus among members of the House that Section 2 should be ignored. As John Bingham observed,

> It is our duty, manifestly our duty by the express provision of the fourteenth article of amendments to the Constitution. Having had some part in preparing that amendment, having had something to do with its recommendation to the people of the United States and in common with them in bringing it to effect in the Constitution of the country, I propose to abide by it no matter what political party may be affected by carrying it into effect by legislation, in order that the whole people may be represented, and to let them be represented in the Forty-Second Congress, in accordance with the letter as well as with the spirit of the Constitution.[150]

Conducting the census in accordance with Section 2 was, for representatives like Bingham – who had been present in the Thirty-Ninth Congress and played a key role in the Fourteenth Amendment's adoption – an official recognition that the days of slavery were over and Black men were now a part of the community of "We the Voters." All other issues were tangential to the symbolism of according to African American men full political representation. To proceed otherwise would subvert one of the core purposes of Reconstruction and undermine the provision that was supposed to be the crown jewel of the Fourteenth Amendment.[151] For these individuals, the practical difficulties were not – indeed, could not be – insurmountable.[152]

[149] "Comments of Representative Hoar, 41st Congress, Second Session, December 13, 1869," 42 *Congressional Globe* (Washington, D.C.: Congressional Globe Office, 1870), part 1, p. 109. But see "Comments of Representative Coburn, 41st Congress, Second Session, December 13, 1869," 42 *Congressional Globe* (Washington, D.C.: Congressional Globe Office, 1870), part 1, p. 109 (refusing to consider the possibility because "it is to be presumed that the Secretary of the Interior is a man of common sense").

[150] "Comments of Representative Bingham, 41st Congress, Second Session, December 13, 1869," 42 *Congressional Globe* (Washington, D.C.: Congressional Globe Office, 1870), part 1, p. 105.

[151] "Comments of Representative Maynard, 41st Congress, Second Session, December 13, 1869," 42 *Congressional Globe* (Washington, D.C.: Congressional Globe Office, 1870), part 1, p. 107. See also "Comments of Representative Dickey, 41st Congress, Second Session, December 13, 1869," 42 *Congressional Globe* (Washington, D.C.: Congressional Globe Office, 1870), part 1, p. 106 ("The simple enumeration by the enumerators under the census does not furnish the basis of representation. You must then examine the constitutions and laws of the several States, to see whether there is any limitation upon the right of any portion of the people to vote. If there is then their representation in Congress is to be reduced, and the apportionment of the State that limits the right of any portion of its people to vote must be made to conform to that fact.").

[152] "Comments of Representative Maynard, 41st Congress, Second Session, December 13, 1869," 42 *Congressional Globe* (Washington, D.C.: Congressional Globe Office, 1870), part 1, p. 107 ("Let me remind gentlemen that until within comparatively a few years nearly one half of the States of this

In the end, the Committee, and ultimately the entire Congress, declined to impose Section 2 on states that violated the right to vote of otherwise qualified citizens. Instead, Section 6 of the 1872 Apportionment Act mostly restated the text of Section 2, providing:

> That should any State, after the passage of this act, deny or abridge the right of any male inhabitants of such State, being twenty-one years of age, and citizens of the United States, to vote at any election named in the amendments to the Constitution, article fourteen, section two, except for participation in the rebellion or other crime, the number of Representatives apportioned in this act to such State shall be reduced in the proportion which the number of such male citizens have to the whole number of male citizens twenty-one years of age in such State.[153]

So why did Congress fail to enforce Section 2? In some ways, the failure to commit to universal male suffrage for African Americans, first in Washington, D.C., and later with Section 2 of the Fourteenth Amendment, was in the direct lineage of the disenfranchisement of other groups – notably Chinese immigrants and women. Once Congress actively sought to retain the power to exclude groups from the political community of "We the Voters," based on notions of deservedness that stem from an antebellum framework that it had once tried to escape, this meant that the initial beneficiaries could become casualties of the war once they, too, were perceived as undeserving. An economic crisis in 1873, followed by a political one in 1874, would push Congress further away from an already incomplete vision of universal male suffrage.

Congress's actions during this period – ostensibly a second founding, a new beginning – seemed irrational if events are viewed in isolation: the extension of suffrage in Washington, D.C., then the withdrawal of political rights for Black people in the District; the passage of the Fourteenth Amendment, then punting on the enforcement of its most central provision; a commitment to voting rights for some groups but explicitly not others, and so on. Yet the passage of the Fifteenth Amendment and the subsequent implementation of the Enforcement Acts counter this narrative of a complete retreat. Indeed, the enduring unpopularity of African American suffrage in 1871–72 meant that some branch, besides Congress, also had to step in to protect the new residents in the community of "We the Voters."

As the next chapter shows, the Enforcement Acts forced the courts to take on a starring role in the Reconstruction project, and Congress resorted to other tools at its disposal – namely Article I, Section 5 and the Elections Clause – to address

Union did not elect their Representatives until after the termination of the preceding Congress… Now, if you should by law postpone the election of members of the Forty-Second Congress until May, 1871, we can during the next session of this Congress so arrange matters that the election for members of the Forty-Second Congress can be held in accordance with the returns of the ninth census.").

153 An Act for the Apportionment of Representatives to Congress among the several States according to the ninth Census, ch. 11, s. 6, 17 Stat. 29 (1872).

remaining inequities after the courts proved to be more foe than friend. But, as illustrated by the failure of the Federal Elections Bill of 1890, even these efforts would be stilted, uneven, and ultimately, unsuccessful, as shifting political winds, continuing economic turmoil, and a lack of true commitment to full equality resulted in a piecemeal approach to voting rights enforcement over the remainder of the century.

8

Congressional Power at Its Nadir

Federalism, Judicial Supremacy, and the Long Kiss Goodnight

Decades before Black Tuesday, when stock markets spiraled out of control in October 1929, Jay Cooke and Company filed for bankruptcy, setting off an economic depression from which the country would not be able to emerge for the remainder of the nineteenth century. The 1929 crash is far more famous, but the financial crash leading to the Panic of 1873 also had appreciable and catastrophic economic consequences. Even more pointedly, the 1873 crash occurred at a transformational political time, changes that cannot be divorced from their fiscal implications. The dawn of a financial crisis meant that the Democrats, or the party of secession, could successfully run for office based on the very issues – monetary policy, the economy – that stagnated enforcement of Section 2 the year before and use their new majority to kill Reconstruction in its entirety.

In other words, when Jay Cooke went bankrupt in September 1873, squandering his fortune on railroads that never neared completion, his actions burst both the credit bubble and the Reconstruction bubble.[1] The Black men who had proven their mettle by fighting for the Union – and had shown that Black people were worthy of the vote through their service – were now in competition for jobs that were few and far in between.[2] White people, some of whom were once allies, viewed the right to vote as an unjustified subsidy to Black men who might exercise their political power in deleterious ways, by supporting policies that would aid Black people, at the expense of White people, at a time when all were suffering.

On the heels of the Panic of 1873, Democrats retook the House of Representatives in the 1874 elections for the first time since the Civil War. In some ways, the

[1] Nicolas Barreyre, "The Politics of Economic Crises: The Panic of 1873, the End of Reconstruction, and the Realignment of American Politics," (2011) 10 *The Journal of the Gilded Age and the Progressive Era* 403–423.

[2] Ibid., 408–409 ("Social consequences were particularly severe in the 1870s: Workers real wages collapsed, bottoming in 1880 at their 1860 level. Many others lost their jobs. Thousands were laid off in the coal and iron areas of Ohio, Pennsylvania, and Illinois. Approximately a fourth of the labor force in New York City was unemployed during the first winter after the panic. Farmers also suffered, as priced dropped (especially wheat) and mortgages became unavailable for several months and remained too expensive afterwards.").

economic situation was a welcome distraction for many parts of the country experiencing Reconstruction fatigue and who were tired, frankly, of hearing about the atrocities in a region that did not even seem to be a part of the United States. Instead of focusing on the misfortune that Black people continued to experience across the South as they and their Republican allies fought to maintain control of state houses in the former Confederacy, attention turned to the money question and whether the country's primary legal tender should be gold, or the greenbacks that the Union had used to finance the war.[3]

Democrats had been able to successfully run on this issue in some state races in the 1860s. The Panic of 1873 provided another opportunity for the money question to take front and center over Reconstruction policy.[4] And like Reconstruction, the money question was sectional, but this time the division was Midwesterners against Northeasterners. These sectional differences meant that Reconstruction policy became a chip to be bartered and bargained as soft-money Midwesterners, who outnumbered members from any other section in the Forty-Third Congress as of December 1873,[5] hoped to gain an advantage over hard-money Northeasterners. When President Grant vetoed a moderate fiscal measure that would have added a limited number of banknotes in circulation as a means of addressing the Panic,[6] it set the Republican Party up for an electoral shellacking.

The 1874 elections represented a historic loss for Republicans. As historian Nicholas Barreyre has noted, they went "from a 70 percent majority to a 37 percent minority" in the House.[7] "They kept a majority of seats only in 12 of the 37 states, saving New England but losing key midwestern states such as Illinois, Indiana, and Ohio and losing all but South Carolina in the South." According to this account, the reckoning was not limited to federal elections. Gubernatorial elections were just as discouraging, as Democrats won California, Missouri, New Jersey, New York, and even Massachusetts.[8] While an economic crisis turned the party of secession into the majority party in the House, the national story should not obscure that the Democratic Party remained just as split as the Republicans, particularly at the state level.

Nowhere was this split more evident than Louisiana. The push by Republicans during the 1867 constitutional convention to adopt universal male suffrage had created a majority-Black electorate in the state. General Philip H. Sheridan, responsible for overseeing the military district containing Texas and Louisiana established

3 Ibid., 410.

4 Ibid., 413 ("Hard-money men explained that the panic had been brought on by the speculation encouraged by the gap in value between specie and greenbacks. … On the other hand, soft-money men analyzed the panic as the result of a severe stringency of money: For them, the crisis would not have happened had the volume of currency not been kept excessively small.").

5 Ibid., 414.

6 Ibid., 415.

7 Ibid., 416.

8 Ibid.

by the Military Reconstruction Act, refused to register White voters who did not swear loyalty to the Union.[9] Only half of the eligible White voters were registered in those two states, resulting in 83,000 registered Black voters as compared to 55,000 White voters. Of the delegates elected to the fall 1867 Louisiana constitutional convention, over half of them were Black.[10] In the April 1868 elections, this diverse electorate approved the new constitution and elected Republicans of all stripes – Black, White, and mulatto – to the governorship and the state legislature, where they held a 56–45 majority in the state house and a 20–16 majority in the state senate.[11] Henry Warmoth, an Illinois native who migrated to Louisiana after the war, assumed the governorship, but most symbolic of this new chapter in Louisiana politics was the fact that the lieutenant governor, Oscar J. Dunn, was formerly enslaved.[12]

But New Orleans, Shreveport, and other big cities where such coalitions were possible with federal oversight were far different places than rural Louisiana, where a little over 1400 White people voted for the 1868 Constitution.[13] The racial egalitarianism of the new state government did not translate to the local level, where the Ku Klux Klan and the Knights of the White Camelia – counting among their ranks an estimated half of all White men in southern Louisiana – terrorized the formerly enslaved and actively worked to keep them away from the polls.[14] By the fall 1868 elections, African American turnout in some parishes diminished to almost zero.[15]

Republicans in some local areas found creative ways to insulate Black political power from insurgent White supremacists. Calhoun's Landing, home to Willie Calhoun (a former slaveowner turned Republican state legislator), became one such safe haven for African Americans and their Republicans allies in rural Louisiana. Calhoun was the only White planter in central Louisiana to make land available to the formerly enslaved in the post–Reconstruction period.[16]

In 1869, Calhoun enlisted his colleagues in the state legislature to create an entirely new political subdivision out of his family home: Grant Parish, namesake of President Ulysses S. Grant, with its county seat in Colfax, so named after Vice President Schuyler Colfax.[17] One of eight new parishes created between 1868 and 1873, Grant Parish was, importantly, a parish with a majority-Black electorate – slightly edging

9 Charles Lane, *The Day Freedom Died: The Colfax Massacre, the Supreme Court, and the Betrayal of Reconstruction* (New York: Henry Holt & Co., 2009), pp. 38–39.

10 Ibid., pp. 37–38.

11 Ibid., p. 38.

12 See A.E. Perkins, "Oscar James Dunn" (1943) 4/2 *Phylon* 102–121.

13 Lane, *The Day Freedom Died*, p. 38.

14 Ibid., pp. 38–39.

15 Ibid., p. 40 (noting that the federal government failed to deploy forces to protect black voters; as a result, "[t]he Republican vote practically vanished").

16 Thomas Howell, "Finding the Line: The Origin of Grant Parish and the Recent Dispute over Its Boundary" (2010) 51 *Journal of the Louisiana Historical Association* 215–230, 219–220.

17 Joel M. Sipress, "From the Barrel of a Gun: The Politics of Murder in Grant Parish" (2001) 42 *Louisiana History: The Journal of the Louisiana Historical Association* 303–321, 305.

out White people 2,414 to 2,101 – and notably, a place where Black people served in government roles such as justice of the peace and constable.[18]

This progress was short-lived, however. In 1870, Governor Warmoth replaced the parish's judge, William B. Phillips, and its sheriff, Delos White, with more conservative Republicans who tended to sympathize with ex-Confederates.[19] Within one year, Warmoth had undermined one of the central justifications for the new parish – to protect Republicans from threats of White violence. The dissension in the parish came to a boiling point in September 1871, when a mob of White vigilantes set fire to the homes of both Phillips and White, murdering White as he fled the burning building. Although neither man was African American, their strong support of Black political and civil rights meant that their lives were forfeit. Indeed, the fact that the new sheriff, Alfred Shelby, and his deputy, Christopher Columbus Nash, were unindicted participants in White's murder, illustrated the extent to which the government in Grant Parish had become irrevocably broken.[20]

Governor Warmoth proved to be more foe than friend to Republicans in Grant Parish, impeding the federal investigation into White's death and preventing the state militia from rounding up White supremacists who continued to commit outrages against Black and White Republicans.[21] The Governor also continued to tinker with the Grant Parish government, appointing to important posts White supremacists like William Cruikshank, namesake of the famous Supreme Court case.[22]

The upheaval in Grant Parish, contrary to its initial promise, was a microcosm of a larger political struggle between Governor Warmoth, who represented a more conservative faction of the Republican Party, and the so-called Custom House faction of the party, or radical Republican officials from the North whose control of the New Orleans Custom House gave them substantial power over revenue and patronage.

To oppose Warmoth, Custom House Republicans partnered with Democrats to elect an anti-Warmoth Republican as Speaker of the Louisiana House of Representatives in January 1872.[23] Governor Warmoth attempted to bribe legislators to change their votes, leading four state legislators aligned with the Custom House to swear out a criminal complaint against the Governor and a number of his legislative allies for violating state and federal election laws.[24] As Governor Warmoth made bail, so too would Delos White's killers, free to return to Grant Parish to further terrorize Black people in the area.

18 Lane, *The Day Freedom Died*, p. 45. See also Howell, "Finding the Line," 216, 220, 223.

19 Lane, *The Day Freedom Died*, pp. 49–50.

20 Robert M. Goldman, *Reconstruction & Black Suffrage: Losing the Vote in Reese and Cruikshank* (Lawrence: University Press of Kansas, 2001), p. 45.

21 Lane, *The Day Freedom Died*, pp. 56–59.

22 Ibid.

23 Ibid., pp. 53–65.

24 Ibid., pp. 60–61.

The division within the Louisiana Republican Party, culminating in the arrest of the Governor, reflected the split in the party nationwide. In 1872, the liberal Republican national convention in Cincinnati nominated Horace Greeley for president,[25] an effort comprised mostly of anti-Grant Republicans and Democrats who opposed the corruption of the Administration and the continuation of Reconstruction policies.

At the state level, Warmoth mirrored this effort to displace pro-Grant Republicans, aligning himself with Louisiana Democrats to support the gubernatorial campaign of John McEnery, a planter with a reputation for virulent anti-Black sentiment. The Custom House threw their support behind pro-Grant candidate, William Pitt Kellogg, leading to a hotly contested election that would result in both sides claiming victory and armed militia entering New Orleans to install McEnery as the governor.[26]

Grant Parish also produced a fusion ticket, made up of Democrats alarmed at what they perceived to be "Negro rule" and conservative Republicans. As a part of this ticket, Christopher Columbus Nash – one of Delos Whites' accused murderers – ran for sheriff. The 1872 election in the parish, much like parishes across the state, was punctuated by voter fraud, violence, and the massive disenfranchisement of Black voters. Fusionist candidates for governor, sheriff, and judge claimed victory, despite the fact that registered Black and mulatto voters in the parish outnumbered White people 776 to 630.[27]

With help from the ballot tampering that took place in parishes across the state, McEnery had more votes than Kellogg in the governor's race and, like candidates in Grant Parish, also claimed victory.[28] Warmoth, as Governor, controlled the election machinery and backed McEnery's claims of victory.[29] The Warmoth-controlled State Returning Board, tasked with certifying all elections, declared McEnery the winner (among the many actions of the canvassing board that would be subject to a congressional investigation, detailed below).[30]

25 James M. McPherson, "Grant or Greeley? The Abolitionist Dilemma in the Election of 1872" (1965) 71 *The American Historical Review* 43–61, 50–51.

26 Lane, *The Day Freedom Died*, p. 62.

27 Ibid., p. 65.

28 Oliver P. Morton, "History of the Troubles in the Pelican State – Terrible Massacres by Ku-Klux and White Leaguers" [Transcript of Speech at Indianapolis of September 18, 1874], *New York Times*, September 23, 1874, p. 2 ("The Democratic Party went into that election in 1872 relying wholly and entirely on fraud for their success .... Gov. Warmoth ... succeeded in bringing in returns, many of them forged and altered in New Orleans, showing that John D. McEnery, the Democratic candidate for Governor, was elected over Kellogg."); S.M. Booth, "Letter to the Editor," *Chicago Daily Tribune*, December 16, 1872, p. 3 ("No one disputes that the Greeley Electoral and the McEnery State tickets had the most votes. But the plea is, that, if those who were not allowed to register had been registered, and had voted, as it is claimed they would, for the Administration ticket, it would have been elected.").

29 See Althea D. Pitre, "The Collapse of the Warmoth Regime, 1870–72" (1965) 6/2 *Louisiana History: The Journal of the Louisiana Historical Association* 161–187, 177 n. 70 (discussing an 1870 election bill that gave Warmoth, as Governor, the "authority to appoint the state and parish registrars" and create "a returning board before which the governor was required to lay all of the election returns").

30 Ibid., 181.

Despite these declarations, both McEnery and Kellogg proceeded as if they each were the lawful executive of the state, creating competing election boards to verify their respective elections and filling state and local vacancies with their supporters.[31] Kellogg named Republicans to various offices statewide, including to the government in Grant Parish, and McEnery installed his people in these same slots.

In December 1872, Custom House Republicans impeached Governor Warmoth for his role in the voting irregularities and fraud that dominated the election.[32] The governor's term ended in January 1873, before his impeachment trial could take place,[33] and McEnery, with the support of an armed militia, was installed as Governor.[34]

In response, President Grant backed Kellogg's government with military force,[35] despite doubts by Republicans in Congress that there was a legitimate government in Louisiana given the widespread fraud in the 1872 election. President Grant sent troops to New Orleans, who defeated McEnery's militia at the Battle of Canal Street and secured the governorship for Kellogg.[36] Kellogg's Administration was on shaky ground for its entire duration, culminating in an angry mob storming the statehouse in 1874 and briefly controlling state government until President Grant sent troops to regain order.[37]

Prior to President Grant's military intervention, Kellogg tried to cut a deal with the Fusionist slate in Grant Parish to bolster his political position. He pledged to install their candidates – for tax collector, clerk, recorder, and police jury – in exchange for their support, not realizing that many of these individuals had been involved in the fire that burned the homes of Phillips and White; were complicit in White's subsequent murder; and had tried to steal the 1872 election through fraud.

31 Ibid., 181–85.

32 Charles L. Dufour, "The Age of Warmoth" (1965) 6/4 *Louisiana History: The Journal of the Louisiana Historical Association* 335–364, 362. See also Morton, "Troubles in the Pelican State" ("It is a matter of proof taken before the committee at Washington, and is proven on the record by numerous witnesses, that the Democratic politicians of Louisiana made a coalition with Warmoth upon the express understanding and estimate that the control of the machinery of the election was equal to 20,000 votes. They believed that through him they could carry the State; without him they knew they could not do it."). For thirty-five days prior to Kellogg assuming office, Warmoth's Lieutenant Governor – P.B.S. Pinchback – was recognized by the Grant Administration as Louisiana's Governor, and as such, the first Black governor in the country. See, e.g., "Pinchback Recognized by the President as the Legal Executive," *Daily Post*, December 13, 1872; see also Pitre, "Collapse of the Warmouth Regime," 185.

33 Dufour, "Age of Warmouth," 363.

34 Lane, *The Day Freedom Died*, p. 13.

35 Ibid., p. 185.

36 Ulysses S. Grant, "Message to the Senate of the United States of January 13, 1875, Regarding the Affairs in Louisiana," *Congressional Record*, 43rd Congress, 2nd Session (Washington, D.C.: Government Printing Office, 1875), v. 3, pp. 414–415.

37 See Lane, *The Day Freedom Died*, pp. 217–240 (discussing in detail the rise, and eventual control, of the Louisiana government by the White League until displaced by federal troops).

Once Kellogg realized his error, he refused to appoint Nash as sheriff but was willing to compromise on other offices, an offer that the Fusionists soundly rejected amid promises that Grant Parish would erupt in bloodshed.[38] Once his offer of compromise was rebuked, Kellogg formally appointed two Republicans – a Black man, R.C. Register, as parish sheriff and Daniel Shaw, a White man, as judge.

And erupt in bloodshed it did. On March 25th, Sheriff-elect Register and Judge-elect Shaw sought to vindicate their claim as the parish's only legitimate government by taking control of the Grant Parish courthouse, which was the center of government for the parish. The next day, they swore in Republicans for the offices of sheriff, recorder, and police jurors.

On March 27th, the Fusionists, emboldened by an erroneous newspaper article that listed Christopher Columbus Nash as the incoming sheriff, decided to retake the courthouse. Even though Fusionists knew that the news report was incorrect (and despite the fact that they had clearly rejected the Governor's offer of compromise), they used the article to bolster their claims that they were the legitimate governing faction of Grant Parish.

On April 1st, about a dozen Fusionists rode into Grant Parish, leading to a number of skirmishes with Republicans. Over the next ten days, the Fusionists grew to more than 150 White men. With Fusionists patrolling the woods surrounding Colfax, Black people crowded into the Colfax courthouse to avoid being caught, or at worst, killed.[39] Many of the White Republican leaders went to New Orleans to plead for military assistance, leaving the courthouse guarded by a predominantly Black (and poorly armed) militia with very little military experience.

On Easter Sunday, April 13, 1873, the Fusionists attacked the courthouse, opening fire on the occupants. Because of its limited arsenal, the Black militia was forced to surrender after two hours. As the militia members came out of the courthouse amid promises that they would not be harmed if they laid down their guns, the courthouse's Black defenders were met with gunfire. The White mob systematically chased down and murdered dozens of Black men, chasing those who fled into the woods and shooting them.[40] The mob then set the courthouse on fire, and shot the remaining men who emerged, unarmed, from the building after another baseless reassurance of safe passage. For the few Black men taken as prisoners of war, they, too, found themselves on the other end of a shotgun.[41] In all, the band of Fusionists, Democrats, and White supremacists murdered somewhere between 50 and 150 Black men at the Colfax courthouse that day.[42]

38 Ibid., pp. 64–94 (detailing the development of Kellogg and Nash's relationship and subsequent conflict).

39 Sipress, "Barrel of a Gun," 318.

40 Lane, *The Day Freedom Died*, pp. 100–102.

41 Ibid., pp. 104–07; Sipress, "Barrel of a Gun," 304.

42 The number of dead is disputed. Compare Eric Foner, *Reconstruction: America's Unfinished Revolution, 1863–1877* (New York: Harper & Row, 1988), p. 589 (estimating 50 deaths) with Danny Lewis, "The

The Department of Justice indicted ninety-eight White men under the Enforcement Act of 1870, arguing that they had, among other things, conspired to deprive the murder victims of their right to vote, petition the government, and bear arms.[43] These indictments were brought in a political environment in which almost all White people in Grant Parish refused to testify despite being well aware of the carnage on April 13th; in fact, the defendants were able to pay dozens of White people to travel to New Orleans and testify on their behalf.[44] Three defendants were convicted,[45] but the Supreme Court, in *United States v. Cruikshank*, quashed the indictments, finding that the defendants had not violated the victims' constitutional rights.[46]

The *Cruikshank* Court conceded that, with respect to the right to petition the government, "[t]he very idea of a government, republican in form, implies a right on the part of its citizens to meet peaceably for consultation in respect to public affairs and to petition for a redress of grievances[,]" but "the conspiracy was to prevent a meeting for any lawful purpose whatever."[47] In other words, the right to petition the government for the redress of grievances is federally protected by the Privileges and Immunities Clause of the Fourteenth Amendment, but the indictment did not allege that the defendants had conspired to prevent a meeting that had been assembled for this purpose. Inartful drafting provided the Court with the excuse that it needed to ignore the rights violation.

Second, the Court found that neither the right to bear arms nor the right to vote were rights granted by the Constitution; instead, the Second Amendment declared only that "it shall not be infringed by Congress"[48] and there was no constitutional provision that "confer[red] the right of suffrage upon any one."[49] To the claim that the disenfranchisement was racially motivated, triggering the protections of the Fifteenth Amendment, the Court rejected the argument that the denial of voting rights in Grant Parish was race–based, noting that "we may suspect that race was the cause of the hostility [but] it [was] not so averred."[50]

Only rarely had lower courts convicted individuals for denying the rights of African Americans based on an implicit assumption that the Fourteenth Amendment had

1873 Colfax Massacre Crippled the Reconstruction Era," *Smithsonian Magazine*, April 13, 2016, www.smithsonianmag.com/smart-news/1873-colfax-massacre-crippled-reconstruction-180958746 (estimating 60 to 150 dead).

43 Lane, *The Day Freedom Died*, pp. 12, 123–125.

44 LeeAnna Keith, *The Colfax Massacre; The Untold Story of Black Power, White Terror, and the Death of Reconstruction* (New York: Oxford University Press, 2008).

45 "Louisiana Affairs: The Conviction of the Grant Parish Prisoners," *New York Times*, June 19, 1874, p. 5. Notably, much of the press coverage painted the black defenders of the Colfax Courthouse as the aggressors and instigators of the massacre. Ibid.

46 *United States v. Cruikshank*, 92 U.S. 542, 559 (1875).

47 Ibid., 552–553.

48 Ibid., 553.

49 Ibid., 554.

50 Ibid.; see also *United States v. Reese*, 92 U.S. 214 (1876).

nationalized the Bill of Rights, the restrictions in which now applied to both the states and the federal government.[51] In the *Slaughter-House Cases*, the Supreme Court called this assumption into question; *Cruikshank* rejected it outright.

In the *Slaughter-House Cases*, the Supreme Court interpreted the Privileges and Immunities Clause to protect only those rights incidental to national citizenship, rather than the more expansive collection of rights advanced by the plaintiff butchers seeking to overturn a state-granted monopoly that undermined their ability to engage in their profession.

The rights protected under the Clause, according to the Court, included the "right to peaceably assemble and petition for redress of grievances, the privilege of the writ of habeas corpus … [t]he right to use the navigable waters…"; in other words, the Court held that all rights that citizens had prior to the ratification of the Fourteenth Amendment were the rights that they possessed post-ratification.[52] The antebellum status quo, decimated by the Reconstruction project, had found a savior in the Court. By the same reasoning, the charges in the *Cruikshank* indictment alleging that the defendants had conspired to commit murder were also dismissed because there was no federally protected right involved.

Third, the *Cruikshank* Court affirmed the principle that the Fourteenth Amendment only applied to state action, and not the actions of private individuals; thus, a private individual's deprivation of a fellow citizen's life, liberty, or property without due process of law did not violate the Fourteenth Amendment.[53] Given this holding, it was no surprise that, post-*Cruikshank*, Christopher Columbus Nash – the unindicted participant in the murder of Delos White; the unwavering election denier who sought to undermine the 1872 election results; and the unrepentant ringleader of the Colfax Massacre – formed a unit of the White League to continue his work of terrorizing, intimidating, and lynching Black voters.[54] The Supreme Court had effectively endorsed the outsourcing of violence and discrimination, limiting the ability of federal officials to address violence (even from those, like Nash who, as a former deputy sheriff, had straddled the worlds of public and private).

Despite *Cruikshank* and other decisions that significantly curtailed the ability of Congress to respond to voter disenfranchisement through federal legislation, Congress continued to use its authority under Article I, Section 5 to police

[51] See, e.g., *United States v. Hall*, 26 F. Cas. 79 (C.C.S.D. Ala. 1871) (Congress can punish private individuals under Section 5 of the Fourteenth Amendment who conspire to deny the civil rights of African Americans, including under the First Amendment). See also *United States v. Crosby*, 25 F. Cas. 701 (C.C.D.S.C. 1871) (Congress can criminalize conspiracies by private individuals to deny voting rights under the Fifteenth Amendment).

[52] *Slaughter-House Cases*, 83 U.S. 36 (1872).

[53] *United States v. Cruikshank*, 92 U.S. 542, 554–555 (1875).

[54] Sipress, "Barrel of a Gun," 314; James K. Hogue, "The Battle of Colfax: Paramilitarism and Counterrevolution in Louisiana," June 27, 2006 (unpublished article) (available at www.racialviolenceus.org/Articles/hogue-colfax.pdf).

congressional elections. From 1872 until the end of the decade, it was clear that partisan control of Congress, as well as a pragmatic assessment of the facts on the ground, tended to dictate the success of these challenges.

8.1 THE POLITICAL BACKLASH OF THE 1870S: PROTECTING "WE THE VOTERS" AND THE CONSTITUTION OF POLITICAL RIGHTS

The upheaval in the South following the 1872 elections – and again in 1874 and 1876 – put to the test the Constitution of Political Rights constructed by Republicans in the wake of the Civil War. With the ratification of the Fifteenth Amendment just ahead of the 1872 election cycle, the landscape of American suffrage shifted. No longer solely a matter for the states, the right to vote was now understood as a federally protected political entitlement, one meant to be exercised under the shield of national authority.[55] The vision was bold: to replace the uncertain legacy of the "alter or abolish" right with a stable, federally anchored political community – "We the Voters" – capable of generating Democratic outcomes free from intimidation and violence.

But that vision was immediately put to the test. Republican losses in the elections of 1872 and 1874 not only tested the fate of this community but also whether the reconstructed governments created to protect it would endure. Will the tools of the Constitution of Political Structure, potent from 1866 until 1872, prove resilient in an era of divided government? Put differently, could the new political community of "We the Voters" survive when its existence was no longer backed by a unified federal resolve?

In answering these questions, Louisiana once again became a case study, where the fallout from post-election violence extended well beyond the horrors of the Colfax Massacre and the betrayal of the Supreme Court's *Cruikshank* decision. With the dispute over who – Kellogg or McEnery – was rightfully elected governor, the state was thrust into a constitutional crisis that blurred the line between legal authority and political force. From 1873 to 1880, the upheaval in Louisiana politics led to no less than eight different men being appointed to represent the state in the Senate, appointments that took place in contexts punctuated by massive disenfranchisement.[56]

In February 1873 (42nd Congress), the Senate refused to seat John Ray and William L. McMillen on the grounds that their elections were fraudulent. Ray was appointed to the U.S. Senate by the Republican-controlled legislature, which

[55] See Anne M. Butler et al., *United States Senate Election, Expulsion, and Censure Cases, 1793–1990* (Washington, D.C.: Gov. Printing Office, 1995), pp. 182–187.

[56] "The Louisiana Cases (1873–80)" in Butler et al., *Senate Election, Expulsion, and Censure Cases*, pp. 61–62.

was aligned with Governor Kellogg. McMillen was appointed by the Democratic-controlled legislature, loyal to Governor McEnery.[57] Both of their respective certificates were also signed by competing secretaries of state. The battle between Kellogg and McEnery had left the state with two competing governments, and by extension, two legislatures, each asserting its right to appoint a U.S. Senator.

At the heart of the dispute was more than just a contested Senate seat – it was a question of who truly governed Louisiana, forcing the U.S. Senate to confront a fundamental constitutional question about legitimate republican government.[58] In the course of determining the lawful government of Louisiana, the Senate Committee on Privileges and Elections found that the 1872 elections were conducted in violation of the Fifteenth Amendment and the Enforcement Acts of 1870 and 1871 because Governor Warmoth and the canvassing board had disregarded the votes of African Americans in violation of state law.[59]

More than ten thousand Black men were disenfranchised across the state, with Ray's team presenting four thousand affidavits to support this allegation. Governor Warmoth, through his partnership with the state's Democratic Party, appointed Democratic parish registrars who manipulated voter rolls to favor White voters and disenfranchise Black voters.

These registrars changed registration sites without notifying Black residents and imposed requirements that disproportionately affected Black people, such as demanding proof of age when many former slaves lacked birth certificates. Additionally, in Grant Parish – site of the Colfax Massacre – a plantation owner threatened to evict Black tenants if they voted Republican.[60] Warmoth then had the returns submitted to him, rather than the secretary of state, as the state constitution required.[61] A week after the election, Warmoth was elected chairman of the canvassing board (the "Warmoth" Board), an obvious conflict of interest resulting from Warmoth's belief that, according to the Senate Committee, "the board, as constituted, would not do his bidding or execute his schemes."[62]

Conversely, the Committee also determined a federal district court had illegally restrained the board from canvassing the results to prevent McEnery from being declared the winner of the gubernatorial election.[63] Judge Edward Durell had intervened in the dispute by issuing orders that effectively sidelined the

57 Sen. Report No. 457, 42nd Cong., 3d Sess. (February 20, 1873).

58 Ibid., p. 1 ("The extraordinary fact that two men are claiming to be the governor of said State, and that two men are certified, under the great seal of the State, to have been elected to one and the same seat in the Senate, and the resolution of the Senate requiring your committee to inquire and report whether there is any existing State government in Louisiana. and how and by whom it is constituted, have compelled your committee to inquire fully into the condition of things in that State … .").

59 Ibid., XI–XII.

60 Lane, *The Day Freedom Died*.

61 Sen. Report No. 457, 42nd Cong., 3d Sess. (February 20, 1873), p. VI.

62 Ibid.

63 Ibid., p. XIII.

state's official canvassing board (the "De Feriet" Board) – which was appointed by Warmoth a few weeks after his failed attempt to capture the election apparatus had led to two competing canvassing boards (the "Warmoth" Board and the "Lynch" Board, respectively), each claiming the authority to act.[64] Judge Durell authorized the Lynch Board to canvass the results and issued an order seizing the Louisiana State House to prevent "unlawful assemblage" by Governor McEnery and those aligned with his Administration who had previously been certified as winners by the De Feriet Board.[65]

The Lynch Board declared Kellogg the winner, despite the absence of official election returns and without conducting an independent canvass. This action was widely criticized as an overreach of federal authority into state election matters, as federal courts had no jurisdiction – in the eyes of the Senate Committee – to determine which canvassing board was the lawful one given that these were appointed state officers and the court's jurisdiction derived solely from allegations that there had been violations of the Fifteenth Amendment.[66] The House Majority later deemed Judge Durell's intervention illegal, with the Senate Report on the incident describing the actions by Durrell as "the saddest chapter in this melancholy business."[67] In 1874, a House Committee recommended Durell's impeachment for his role in the election dispute, but he resigned to avoid the proceedings.

In the end, Congress rejected both Ray and McMillen, using the controversy surrounding the 1872 elections as an opportunity to assert its power to determine, first, that there was no legislature in Louisiana that had clear authority to appoint a U.S. Senator and second, to call for new elections. After a month-long investigation, the Senate Committee determined that neither the Republican nor the Democratic legislature had clear legal authority to appoint Senators due to the illegitimacy of the Warmoth and Lynch canvassing boards (which, in turn, meant that neither board had authority to certify legislative elections). While the Committee's majority report criticized the Republican legislature for usurping power and denounced the federal court's intervention, it also argued that recognizing the McEnery (Democratic) government, elected only through the disenfranchisement of Black voters, would mean endorsing a government "based upon fraud, in defiance of the wishes and intention of the voters of that State."

These disputes struck at the heart of a fundamental constitutional question: what did it mean for Congress to guarantee a "republican form of government" under the Guarantee Clause? One obvious answer, from *Ray v. McMillen*, was that

64 Ibid., p. VII–VIII, IX.

65 Ibid., p. XVI–XVII.

66 Ibid., p. XIII ("What jurisdiction had the Federal court to determine the right between these contending boards? They were State officers, and it is not alleged in the bill that any colored man was deprived of any right which had resulted in the election of Hatch and Da Ponte. Besides, the question of right to this office was entirely collateral in the proceedings.").

67 Ibid., p. IX.

republicanism required Congress to reject the result of elections marred by racial discrimination in voting. Yet Congress, rather than approaching this as a matter of consistent constitutional principle, often seemed to toggle between engagement and avoidance, its posture shaped less by theory than by partisan expediency. The fact that *Ray v. McMillen* was resolved a few weeks before a new Senate, still dominated by the Republican Party, took their oath lessened the stakes some.

But there was another lesson here as well: federalism. Federalism constrained Congress, not only the enforcement of the Reconstruction Amendments, but also with respect to enforcing the republican guarantee and utilizing its authority under Article I, Section 5. In *Ray v. McMillen*, Congress was unwilling to empower courts to completely displace state authority over elections in furtherance of African American voting rights while also acknowledging its authority to dismiss election results tainted by racial discrimination. But Congress quickly learned that its decision to reject both candidates altogether, as it did in the case of *Ray v. McMillen*, or not take any action at all, as it would in the example that follows, can have the same impact on the partisan composition of the Senate as choosing a legislature directly.

Like Louisiana, Alabama was another state in which two governments claimed dominion, creating similar issues over the meaning of republican government and who had been duly elected to state government. By the time of the 1872 election, the state found itself in the grip of a full-blown political standoff – two competing legislatures (the "court house" legislature and the "state house legislature," respectively), each claiming legitimacy, each determined to send its own man to the United States Senate.[68]

At the state capitol, the Democrats, newly empowered and eager to reassert control over Alabama's government, convened the "state house" legislature and chose Francis W. Sykes as their Senator. A number of individuals in the state house legislature had certificates of election but, according to the Senate Committee on Privileges and Elections, "are conceded not to have been elected."[69] Meanwhile, just a few blocks away, the Republicans – still clinging to the remnants of their Reconstruction authority – held their own session in the Montgomery County courthouse as the "court house" legislature, re-electing George E. Spencer, a Union officer turned politician, to the same Senate seat. Both men packed their bags and traveled to Washington, each carrying documents certifying their election – each convinced he was the rightful representative of Alabama.

Spencer's credentials were issued by the Republican-controlled legislature and certified by the governor, while Sykes's were issued by the Democratic-controlled legislature. Given that both Spencer and Sykes had credentials from rival legislatures – each claiming to be the lawful body – the Senate recognized this as an exceptional case that could not be resolved by the general rule that a claimant with

68 "Sykes v. Spencer," in Butler et al., *Senate Election, Expulsion, and Censure Cases*, pp. 178–181.
69 Ibid. See also Sen. Report No. 457, 42nd Cong., 3d Sess. (February 20, 1873), p. 60.

"regular" credentials – on their face not raising a question about their legality – to take his seat provisionally while any challenge was ongoing. Both sets of credentials were referred to the Committee on Privileges and Elections, but by tradition and procedure, Spencer was allowed to take his seat temporarily.

Senators debated whether the governor's certificate (favoring Spencer) should outweigh the record of the legislature that elected Sykes. Some argued that in cases of dual legislatures, the Senate was not bound by the governor's certificate and must thoroughly examine the legitimacy of each claim. Sykes, represented before the Senate Committee on Privileges and Elections by former Confederate general John Tyler Morgan, argued that the Democratic-controlled legislature – the one meeting at the capitol – was the legitimate government of Alabama. Therefore, it followed, so was their choice for Senator. Morgan himself would be at the center of an election contest four years later in which Spencer, then the incumbent, would allege, unsuccessfully, that the 1876 elections were punctuating by fraud and racial disenfranchisement such that Morgan's appointment was illegitimate.[70]

In 1872 (42nd Congress), Spencer was more successful in keeping his appointment to the Senate than he would be four years later, even if inadvertently. Despite the arguments laid out by Sykes and Morgan, the Senate Committee never made a definitive ruling, finding that "it would not be competent for the Senate to inquire into the rights to hold seats of the eight or nine members whose rights to seats were disputed, in order to determine which of the two bodies was the legal legislature"; it was enough that "the persons claiming to be the legislature who voted for Mr. Spencer constituted a quorum of the members actually elected."[71] By punting, the Committee failed to answer the core constitutional question: Which of Alabama's two legislatures, and by extension which senator, was the legitimate expression of a republican form of government? Instead, the issue was quietly left to wither, and politics, not principle, carried the day. Spencer was a Republican, and so, in a Republican-controlled Senate, he kept his seat – not by legal triumph, but by partisan inertia.

As these examples illustrate, Congress rarely chose between rival legislatures, which would directly threaten the principles of federalism that had ostensibly survived the adoption of the Reconstruction Amendments.

But sometimes politics dictated a different course of action, leading Congress to cast off its self-imposed federalism constraints just as it had decades earlier with the Apportionment Act of 1842 and all of the subsequent upheaval over the course of that decade surrounding the slavery issue in the territories.[72]

70 Ibid.

71 Ibid.

72 Congress declined to choose between competing governments in Louisiana, but it sided with the Democratic legislature in South Carolina following the election of 1876. See "Corbin v. Butler," in Butler et al., *Senate Election, Expulsion, and Censure Cases*, p. 198 (recognizing the legitimacy of the

The election of 1876, and the compromise of 1877 – leading to the removal of many of the remaining federal troops from the South and the official federal recognition of Democratic state governments elected through force, fraud, and violence – presented such circumstances.[73] For example, Congress ratified the 1876 appointment of L.Q.C. Lamar to the Senate, despite the fact that he was appointed by a Mississippi legislature whose legitimacy, like that of the rival Louisiana legislatures, was in doubt due to the fact that the elections of many of its members were tainted by racial discrimination. Lamar, and some of his colleagues in the legislature, had also served in the Confederacy, a disqualification for office that had not been removed by Congress as required by Section 3 of the Fourteenth Amendment.[74] Yet Congress seated Lamar anyway, and in the process, endorsed the Democratic legislature in Mississippi as the legitimate state government. Just as President Rutherford B. Hayes, to secure the office of the presidency, had recognized the so-called Redeemer governments that restored White Democratic control to much of the South, Congress, in short order, would also show its Reconstruction fatigue by supporting the federal retreat from the South in its own way.[75]

In the wake of the 1876 election, Republicans continued to lose ground in the Senate, and so too would Article I, Section 5 lose its stature as a go-to weapon to fight fraudulent elections and, in the process, further define the meaning of the republican guarantee. Notably, Republican control of Congress would go from 51 to 20 Republican/Democrat in the 43rd Congress (1873–75) to 44–28 in the 44th Congress (1875–77) to 39–35 in the 45th Congress (1877–79). With the 1878 elections, Democrats gained control of the Senate for the first time since the Civil War, controlling 42 seats in the 46th Congress to Republicans' 31 seats.

It was not that history stopped or the text of Article I, Section 5 disappeared. When Republicans finally lost the Senate in 1878, just as they had lost the House four years earlier, the focus of contested elections shifted north, west, and to the midwest. Indeed, the cases coming out of other parts of the country illustrate how attention had moved away from the South,[76] which was clearly a lost cause (not to be confused, of course, with "The Lost Cause").

For example, in 1879, Congress allowed former Confederate Wilkinson Call – once denied his seat in 1865 – to represent Florida in the Senate, which effectively

Democratic controlled South Carolina legislature, and its authority to appoint senators, over the rival Republican legislature as a part of the broader federal retreat from the South in 1877).

73 Foner, *Reconstruction*, pp. 580–582 (noting that, in exchange for Democratic support of his presidency, Rutherford B. Hayes removed federal troops and allowed the redeemer governments in Louisiana and South Carolina to come to power).

74 "LQC Lamar (MS)" in Butler et al., *Senate Election, Expulsion, and Censure Cases*, pp. 203–204.

75 Edward L. Ayers, *The Promise of the New South: Life after Reconstruction* (New York: Oxford University Press, 1992), p. 8.

76 See, e.g., "John J. Ingalls (KS)" in Butler et al., *Senate Election, Expulsion, and Censure Cases*, p. 219; "La Fayette Grover (OR)," in Butler et al., *Senate Election, Expulsion, and Censure Cases*, p. 211; "Charles H. Bell (NH)," in Butler et al., *Senate Election, Expulsion, and Censure Cases*, p. 216.

sounded the death knell for Article I, Section 5's ability to protect "We the Voters" or to stand as an instantiation of broad congressional power under the Constitution of Political Structure.[77] Republicans lost interest in Reconstruction. America lost interest in Reconstruction. Chaos reigned in the South.

It was not until a Republican resurgence following the 1888 election that southern states like Louisiana would make a meaningful return to the annals of contested election cases that came before Congress.[78] And even then, partisan control of that body was outcome determinative for these contests. During this period, there might have been enough Republicans to fight – both in Congress and candidates willing to bring the challenges – but this was not always enough to win.[79]

8.2 THE SUPREME COURT'S WAR WITH CONGRESS: RECONSTRUCTION AT THE BRINK

In some ways, the increased polarization and contentious political landscape were only the tip of the iceberg following devastating Republican electoral losses in the 1870s and the withdrawal of federal troops from the South after the 1876 election. Republicans also had to contend with a judicial environment that was significantly more hostile than when they first embarked on the work of Reconstruction in the 1860s.

The rank formalism of the *Cruikshank* decision was a blow to the Enforcement Act of 1870 and, by implication, broad congressional enforcement authority. The Court adhered to this path of obstruction in *United States v. Reese*, which held that Congress exceeded the scope of its authority under the Fifteenth Amendment in enacting Sections 3 and 4 of the Enforcement Act of 1870 to prohibit all abridgments of the right to vote, rather than just race-based abridgments.[80] While *Cruikshank* was narrower than *Reese* because it did not invalidate those provisions of the Enforcement Act upon which the indictments were based,[81] *Cruikshank*

77 "Davidson v. Call," in Butler et al., *Senate Election, Expulsion, and Censure Cases*, p. 239 (discussing Call's first Senate appointment).

78 See, e.g., "Coleman v. Buck (1895–1897)," in Asher C. Hinds, *Hinds' Precedents of the House of Representatives of the United States*, 5 vols. (Washington, D.C.: United States Government Printing Office, 1907), v. 2, p. 617; United States House of Representatives, "Committee on Elections Report on the Contested Election Case of *Alexis Benoit v. Charles J. Boatner*," 54th Congress, 1st Session, Report No. 867 (Washington, D.C., Government Printing Office, 1896).

79 See, e.g., "Beattie v. Price, House Committee on Elections, 54th Congress (1897)," in Chester H. Rowell, *A Historical and Legal Digest of all the Contested Election Cases in the House of Representatives of the United States from the First to the Fifty-Sixth Congress, 1789–1901* (Washington, D.C.: Government Printing Office, 1901), pp. 527–528 (declining to vacate an election where Black supporters were murdered and White Democrats formed a new republican organization to exclude Black voters because these injustices were insufficient to void the contestee's win).

80 *United States v. Reese*, 92 U.S. 214 (1876). See also Introduction.

81 Goldman, *Reconstruction and Black Suffrage*, pp. 105–106.

nonetheless reinforced the cramped view of congressional power endorsed in earlier decisions like *The Civil Rights Cases* and the *Slaughter-House Cases*.

In the *Slaughter-House Cases*[82] and the *Civil Rights Cases*,[83] the Court found that the recently ratified Fourteenth Amendment did not alter our system of federalism by shifting the responsibility of protecting civil rights from the states to the federal government.[84] As mentioned prior, the *Slaughter-House Cases* interpreted the scope of the Privileges and Immunities Clause of the Fourteenth Amendment, while the *Civil Rights Cases* resolved the constitutionality of the Civil Rights Act of 1875, which, among other things, prohibited discrimination in places of public accommodation. In the latter case, the Court held that Congress's power under Section 5 of the Fourteenth Amendment was not broad enough to reach private discrimination. While these cases did not deal with elections, *Reese* and *Cruikshank* made it clear that the judicial threat to broad congressional power extended to voting rights enforcement efforts.[85]

The consensus view in Congress had been that the enforcement clauses of the Fourteenth and Fifteenth Amendments operated in a manner similar to the Necessary and Proper Clause of Article I.[86] Even John Bingham, the primary drafter of Section 1 of the Fourteenth Amendment, sanctioned this idea, arguing that "adding an amendment to the Constitution to operate on all the States of this Union alike [will give] Congress the power to pass all laws necessary and proper to secure to all persons … their equal personal rights."[87] But the Court was of a different mind, challenging Bingham's conception of federal power under the Reconstruction Amendments throughout the 1870s and 1880s.

In resisting most arguments that the Amendments changed the balance of power between the states and the federal government, the Court could have easily used a similar approach to the Elections Clause.[88] Prior to Reconstruction, there was

82 *Slaughter-House Cases*, 83 U.S. 36 (1872).

83 *Civil Rights Cases*, 109 U.S. 3 (1883).

84 Ibid., 24 ("[H]is redress is to be sought under the laws of the State; or, if those laws are adverse to his rights and do not protect him, his remedy will be found in the corrective legislation which Congress has adopted, or may adopt, for counteracting the effect of State laws, or State action, prohibited by the Fourteenth Amendment."); *Slaughter-House Cases*, 83 U.S. 36, 77 (1872) (declaring it was not "purpose of the fourteenth amendment, by the simple declaration that no State should make or enforce any law which shall abridge the privileges and immunities of citizens of the United States, to transfer the security and protection of all the civil rights which we have mentioned, from the States to the Federal government").

85 See *Civil Rights Cases*, 109 U.S. 3, 24 (1883); *Slaughter-House Cases*, 83 U.S. at 77.

86 See, e.g., "Comments of Senator Thurman, 41st Congress, 1st Session, May 20, 1870," 42 *Congressional Globe* (Washington, D.C.: Globe Office, 1870), pt. 4, p. 3663. ("[T]hat provision about appropriate legislation is nothing more than the old provision in the Constitution which gives Congress power to pass all necessary and proper laws for carrying the provisions of the Constitution into effect, and is to be interpreted in the same light.").

87 "Comments of Representative Bingham, 39th Congress, 1st Session, January 9, 1866," 36 *Congressional Globe* (Washington, D.C.: Globe Office, 1866), pt. 1, p. 158.

88 Compare *United States v. Reese*, 92 U.S. 214 (1876) (making no mention of the Elections Clause in its analysis).

not much mention of the Elections Clause in the Supreme Court's jurisprudence, much less any thorough analysis of the meaning of its terms.[89] The absence of substantial precedent meant that there was a risk that the Court would interpret the Clause's provisions narrowly, especially since Congress itself had declined to read the Clause broadly until right before the Civil War.[90]

But there were some bright spots that demonstrate that the end of Reconstruction was not linear, with an ending that was foretold. Despite unfavorable jurisprudence, a reality in which the Elections Clause was narrowly interpreted never materialized. Since the Elections Clause was a part of the original Constitution and explicitly delegated to Congress substantial authority over federal elections, cases litigated under the Clause provide a nice counterpoint to those decided under the Reconstruction Amendments, which did not contain such explicit language and consequently were not viewed as liberally.[91] Contrary to *Reese*, *Cruikshank*, and other cases interpreting the scope of the Reconstruction Amendments, the Court's jurisprudence interpreting the scope of federal power under the Elections Clause was surprisingly generous.

Two cases, involving a range of election-related offenses, are especially instructive here. In *Ex parte Clarke*,[92] an election judge violated state law by opening a previously sealed poll book before turning it over to the county clerk.[93] *Ex parte Siebold* involved an election judge prosecuted under state law for stuffing the ballot box.[94] Other defendants were also indicted and had committed a range of violations from ballot box stuffing to turning away lawful voters at the polls.[95] The issue before the Court in both cases was whether Congress had the authority to make the violation of a state election statute a federal offense under the 1870 Enforcement Act since the violations occurred in the context of a federal election.[96]

89 See, e.g., *Dred Scott v. Sandford*, 60 U.S. (19 How.) 393 (1856) (Curtis, J., dissenting) (referencing the Elections Clause in a brief discussion of the meaning of the word "regulate"); *Prigg v. Pennsylvania*, 41 U.S. 539, 586 (1842) (making passing reference to the Elections Clause).

90 See Chapter 4.

91 The Elections Clause complicates the overly simplistic view of the Reconstruction-era Court as state friendly, or alternatively, overtly hostile to congressional power. See Pamela Brandwein, *Rethinking the Judicial Settlement of Reconstruction* (New York: Cambridge University Press, 2011), p. 53 (noting the failure of most of the legal literature to recognize the Reconstruction-era Court's willingness to hold states accountable); John B. Gates, "Partisan Realignment, Unconstitutional State Policies, and the U.S. Supreme Court, 1837–1964," (1987) 31 *American Journal of Political Science* 259–280, 264 ("From 1837 to 1860 the Court struck down 17 state policies, or less than one statute a year. On the other hand, between 1860 and 1878 the Court declared 58 state policies unconstitutional, or more than three each year."). While the Court actively resisted a broad reading of the Reconstruction Amendments, it was much more solicitous in interpreting the Elections Clause.

92 100 U.S. 399 (1879).

93 Ibid., 401–402.

94 *Ex parte Siebold*, 100 U.S. 371, 379 (1879).

95 Ibid., 377–379 (enumerating charges against other defendants).

96 Ibid., 382.

Section 5515 of the United States Revised Statutes, originally Section 22 of the Enforcement Act of 1870, did not define the substantive offenses that violated its terms, instead incorporating state law and other federal laws by reference.[97] In defending this regime of concurrent state and federal regulation over congressional elections, the *Siebold* Court noted that Congress could act pursuant to the Elections Clause, which empowered that body to "make or alter" state regulations, free of the usual concerns about state sovereignty present in other contexts.[98] Congress can make its own regulations pursuant to the Clause, and where its regulations conflict with state law, the Court recognized that federal law "necessarily supersedes" state law because "the power of Congress over the subject is paramount."[99]

Congress did not have to defer to state sovereignty under the Elections Clause because, as the *Siebold* Court noted, "[n]o clashing [of jurisdictions and conflict of rules] can possibly arise. There is not the slightest difficulty in a harmonious combination into one system of the regulations made by the two sovereignties, any more than there is in the case of prior and subsequent enactments of the same legislature."[100] While avoiding this clash might require a certain level of cooperation on the part of the two governments, the Court was clear that this cooperation occurred at the prerogative of Congress.[101] In other words, federal law was always paramount.

The Court's disregard of state sovereignty, unusual given the controversy over the Reconstruction Amendments, was tied to the explicit language of the Elections Clause ("make or alter") that contemplated a concurrent regime of election regulation in contrast to the Fourteenth and Fifteenth Amendments where Congress's authority to enact "appropriate" legislation was significantly more ambiguous. Under the Clause, Congress could act at any time in supplementing or displacing state law, could incorporate state law by reference, and had both civil and criminal authority.[102]

97 "An Act to enforce the Rights of Citizens of the United States to vote in the several States of the Union, and for other Purposes," ch. 114, s. 22 16 Stat. 145 (1870) [Enforcement Act of 1870], codified at U.S. Rev. Stat. s. 5515 (2nd ed. 1878) (punishing election officers who violate "neglect or refuse to perform any duty in regard to such election required of him by any law of the United States, or of any State or Territory thereof").

98 *Ex parte Siebold*, 100 U.S. 371, 392 (1879) ("[W]e think it clear that the clause of the Constitution relating to the regulation of such elections contemplates such cooperation whenever Congress deems it expedient to interfere merely to alter or add to existing regulations of the State.").

99 Ibid., 384.

100 Ibid.

101 Ibid., 386 ("The State may make regulations on the subject; Congress may make regulations on the same subject, or may alter or add to those already made. The paramount character of those made by Congress has the effect to supersede those made by the State, so far as the two are inconsistent, and no farther. There is no such conflict between them as to prevent their forming a harmonious system perfectly capable of being administered and carried out as such.").

102 See Richard M. Valelly, "Partisan Entrepreneurship and Policy Windows," in Stephen Skowronek and Matthew Glassman (eds.), *Formative Acts: American Politics in the Making* (Philadelphia: University of Pennsylvania Press., 2007), p. 131 (calling the Court's decisions in *Clarke* and *Siebold* "stunning" by finding the "regulatory jailing of state and local elections officials .. perfectly constitutional," which the Court accomplished by relying on "a centralizing and muscular reading of Article I, Section 4").

In contrast, the dissenters in *Ex parte Siebold* and *Ex parte Clarke* applied the same federalism restrictions to the Elections Clause that had stymied congressional enforcement of the Fourteenth and Fifteenth Amendments. In his dissent in *Ex parte Clarke*, Justice Field denied that there could be federal incorporation of state law offenses because such incorporation would extend both the power of Congress and the jurisdiction of the courts, intruding on the sovereignty of the states.[103] This critique mischaracterized Congress's authority to "make or alter" state regulations, which arguably included the power to enact a criminal code for federal elections, even if such regulations derive solely from state law. In essence, Justice Field's criticism of Congress was for that body's lack of originality (i.e., its borrowing of state law offenses) rather than a critique based on substance (i.e., concern about the actions being criminalized).

Indeed, the "no incorporation by reference" argument proved too much. As the Court recognized in *Minor v. Happersett* in famously denying that women had a right to vote,[104] federal law does not create voters; instead, the right to vote itself is a creature of state law, incorporated by reference into the Constitution.[105] Requiring Congress to articulate with specificity each crime that came within the purview of Section 5515, instead of allowing that body to incorporate state law by reference, was arguably Justice Field's attempt to impose procedural hurdles – the nineteenth-century equivalent of a presumption against preemption or a clear statement rule – to limit the scope of federal law.[106]

103 *Ex parte Clarke*, 100 U.S. 399, 408 (1879) (Field, J., dissenting). As Justice Field argued,

> There is no doubt that Congress may adopt a law of a State, but in that case the adopted law must be enforced as a law of the United States. … The judicial power thus defined may be applied to new cases as they arise under the Constitution and laws of the United States, but it cannot be enlarged by Congress so as to embrace cases not enumerated in the Constitution …. To authorize a criminal prosecution in the Federal courts for an offence against a law of a State is to extend the judicial power of the United States to a case not arising under the Constitution or laws of the United States.

Ibid. Notably, Justice Field's arguments echoed those made by his older brother, David Dudley Field, a lawyer who also argued that the Enforcement Acts were unconstitutionally broad. See David Dudley Field, "Centralization in the Federal Government" (1881) 132 *The North American Review* 407–426, 412–413 (arguing that Enforcement Acts "are in themselves a displacement of State power far beyond anything written in the early days of the Constitution … [and] the theory on which they rest would, if carried out to its logical results, lead to the practical absorption in the central government of all the chief functions of sovereignty").

104 *Minor v. Happersett*, 88 U.S. 162 (1874).

105 Ibid., 171 ("The United States has no voters in the States of its own creation. The elective officers of the United States are all elected directly or indirectly by State voters.").

106 Compare *Arizona State Legislature v. Arizona. Independent Redistricting Commission*, 576 U.S. 787 (2015) ("The Arizona Legislature urges that the first part of the Elections Clause, vesting power to regulate congressional elections in State 'Legislature[s],' precludes Congress from allowing a State to redistrict without the involvement of its representative body, even if Congress independently could enact the same redistricting plan under its plenary authority to 'make or alter' the State's plan.").

In suggesting that Section 5515 impermissibly commandeered state law and state officials, Justice Field analyzed whether the Elections Clause, as predicate authority for this provision, was similarly constrained by federalism concerns as the Reconstruction Amendments.[107] He questioned the impact of Section 5515 on *state* elections because of that provision's influence on the validity and scope of state regulations.[108] This concern was valid only if the Elections Clause preserved a decisive role for state authority that would constitutionally require Congress to consider the impact of any federal regulations on state elections, and there was no reason to believe that the Clause contained any such requirement.[109] To read the Clause in this manner would not only deny Congress the sovereignty to which it was rightly entitled, given the Clause's delegation to Congress of the authority to "make" its own laws or "alter" existing state laws, this reading would also prioritize state sovereignty over federal power.[110]

In re Coy, decided in 1888 on the eve of Reconstruction's last act, was a decision in which the Court recognized that, contrary to Justice Field's arguments in *Ex parte Siebold* and *Ex parte Clarke*, Congress's authority under the Elections Clause was not diminished simply because a federal regulation may affect state and local elections.[111] In that case, the relevant federal law made it a crime for any election official to "violate or refuse to comply with his duty" at "any election for representative or delegate in Congress," but defendant election inspectors argued that they could not

107 *Ex parte Clarke*, 100 U.S. 399, 409 (1879) (Field, J., dissenting) ("The act of Congress asserts a power inconsistent with, and destructive of, the independence of the States. The right to control their own officers, to prescribe the duties they shall perform, without the supervision or interference of any other authority, and the penalties to which they shall be subjected for a violation of duty is essential to that independence. If the Federal government can punish a violation of the laws of the State, it may punish obedience to them, and graduate the punishment according to its own judgment of their propriety and wisdom. It may thus exercise a control over the legislation of the States subversive of all their reserved rights.").

108 *Ex parte Clarke*, 100 U.S. 399, 412–413 (1879) (Field, J., dissenting) ("So far as the election of State officers and the registration of voters for their election are concerned, the Federal government has confessedly no authority to interfere. And yet the supervision of and interference with the State regulations, sanctioned by the act of Congress, when representatives to Congress are voted for, amount practically to a supervision of and an interference with the election of State officers, and constitute a plain encroachment upon the rights of the States, which is well calculated to create irritation towards the Federal government, and disturb the harmony that all good and patriotic men should desire to exist between it and the State governments.").

109 This is true even though courts have been conditioned to worry about state sovereignty, even when unnecessary. See Justin Weinstein-Tull, "Election Law Federalism," (2016) 114 *Michigan Law Review* 747–801, 765 (discussing a Ninth Circuit decision that upheld the NVRA as a proper exercise of congressional power under the Elections Clause but expressed that the burden on California's sovereignty was of "constitutional concern").

110 See *Ex parte Siebold*, 100 U.S. 371, 391–392 (1879) ("The more general reason assigned, to wit, that the nature of sovereignty is such as to preclude the joint cooperation of two sovereigns, even in a matter in which they are mutually concerned, is not, in our judgment, of sufficient force to prevent concurrent and harmonious action on the part of the national and State governments in the election of representatives. It is at most an argument ab inconveniente. There is nothing in the Constitution to forbid such cooperation in this case.").

111 *In re Coy*, 127 U.S. 731 (1888).

be indicted under federal law because they were tampering with the returns of state and local elections, not the U.S. House election.[112] The Court found this argument "manifestly contrary to common sense" because the "purpose of both systems of legislation is to remove the ballot-box as well as the certifications of the votes cast from all possible opportunity of falsification, forgery, or destruction."[113]

The Elections Clause cases of the 1870s and 1880s may seem like a bit of a shocker given the Court's unyielding determination to read the Reconstruction Amendments narrowly. These cases, when contrasted with *Cruikshank* and *Reese*, engage views of congressional power that seem diametrically opposed. The latter cases dealt with Amendments that sought to maintain some sort of federalism balance with respect to voter qualifications – preferring state to federal regulation in this domain, while the former centered on a provision, the Elections Clause, that eschewed state sovereignty altogether in the context of federal election administration.[114]

There is some explanation for the obvious tension between the two lines of jurisprudence. The text of the Elections Clause empowered Congress to determine (through its ability to "alter" state regulations or "make" its own) the circumstances under which voting takes place for certain federal elections ("time, place, and manner"). This language, centering on federal power, was not a textually friendly home for the Court's desire to preserve much of the pre–Civil War system of federalism.

The Reconstruction Amendments, in contrast, directly touched on the question of who should vote. Given these substantive distinctions, the Court had no choice but to read the Elections Clause more liberally than the Amendments in the context of federal elections. Congress's power over federal election administration is plenary, and as such, undeniably broader than its authority to regulate voter qualifications that don't implicate certain categories (i.e., race and, later, gender and age). That power lies with the state.

While each level of government is ostensibly committed to a particular regulatory domain by the constitutional text, this did not resolve the issues that had arisen when the line between election administration and voter qualifications became

112 Ibid., 749–751, 753.

113 Ibid., 755. See also Vallely, "Partisan Entrepreneurship," pp. 135–136 (arguing that the Court rejected the claim because "during the elections the state and local elections officials had, for all intents and purposes, become officers of the United States and were subject to the jurisdiction of the United States").

114 As the *Cruikshank* Court observed, "[T]he right of suffrage is not a necessary attribute of national citizenship; but that exemption from discrimination in the exercise of that right on account of race, &c., is. The right to vote in the States comes from the States; but the right of exemption from the prohibited discrimination comes from the United States. The first has not been granted or secured by the Constitution of the United States; but the last has been." *United States v. Cruikshank*, 92 U.S. 542, 555–556 (1875). Compare *United States v. Harris*, 106 U.S. 629, 639 (1883) (emphasizing federalism principles inherent in the Fourteenth Amendment and stating that "when … the laws of the State, as enacted by its legislative, and construed by its judicial, and administered by its executive departments, recognize and protect the rights of all persons, the amendment imposes no duty and confers no power upon Congress").

blurry. As early as 1875, the Court resisted the urge to read the Elections Clause as an express limit on Congress's ability to regulate voter qualifications.

In *Minor v. Happersett*,[115] the majority observed that, "It is not necessary to inquire whether this power of supervision thus given to Congress [under the Elections Clause] is sufficient to authorize any interference with the State laws prescribing the qualifications of voters, for no such interference has ever been attempted. The power of the State in this particular is certainly supreme until Congress acts."[116] "[U]ntil Congress acts" suggests that the *Minor* Court was reserving judgment on this issue, but by 1884, the Court definitively resolved whether Congress could protect the right to vote through its authority under the Elections Clause. And the answer was yes – a qualified yes – but yes, nonetheless.

In *Ex parte Yarbrough*,[117] for example, the Court rejected a writ of habeas corpus from defendants seeking to invalidate their convictions under Sections 5508 and 5520 of the Enforcement Act for assaulting a Black man exercising his right to vote. The Court sustained the indictments. While the Fifteenth Amendment did not shift the responsibility for protecting all voters from the states to the federal government, this responsibility did shift as it pertains to the right to vote free of racial discrimination.[118] Congress was even more empowered to provide this protection in the context of federal elections. Notably, the Court held that the Fifteenth Amendment "gives no affirmative right to the colored man to vote," but ultimately concluded that "it is easy to see that under some circumstances it may operate as the immediate source of the right to vote."[119] Those circumstances were present where Congress was exercising its authority under the Elections Clause, as it was in *Yarbrough*, to regulate national elections.[120]

115 For more on *Minor v. Happerset*, see Chapter 7.

116 *Minor v. Happersett*, 88 U.S. 162, 171 (1874).

117 *Ex parte Yarbrough*, 110 U.S. 651 (1884).

118 Ibid., 664 ("The Fifteenth Amendment of the Constitution, by its limitation on the power of the States in the exercise of their right to prescribe the qualifications of voters in their own elections, and by its limitation of the power of the United States over that subject, clearly shows that the right of suffrage was considered to be of supreme importance to the national government, and was not intended to be left within the exclusive control of the States.").

119 Ibid., 665.

120 See Ibid., 662:

> It is said that the parties assaulted in these cases are not officers of the United States, and their protection in exercising the right to vote by Congress does not stand on the same ground. But the distinction is not well taken. The power in either case arises out of the circumstance that the function in which the party is engaged or the right which he is about to exercise is dependent on the laws of the United States. In both cases it is the duty of that government to see that he may exercise this right freely, and to protect him from violence while so doing, or on account of so doing. This duty does not arise solely from the interest of the party concerned, but from the necessity of the government itself, that its service shall be free from the adverse influence of force and fraud practised on its agents, and that the votes by which its members of Congress and its President are elected shall be the free votes of the electors, and the officers thus chosen the free and uncorrupted choice of those who have the right to take part in that choice.

In *Yarbrough*, the negative inference in the Fifteenth Amendment that the right to vote could not be abridged on the basis of race was converted into an affirmative power that Congress could invoke broadly to protect suffrage from race-based abridgments in the context of federal elections, *even from private individuals*, thanks to the Elections Clause.[121] However, when Congress sought to protect the right to vote in the absence of alleged racial discrimination, as was the case in *Reese*, or where there was "nothing to show that the elections voted at were any other than State elections,"[122] as in *Cruikshank*, then federalism once again became a decisive factor that cut against the exercise of federal authority. In other words, strict formalism prevailed over functional solutions.

In the end, *Ex parte Clarke* and *Ex parte Siebold* proved to be small victories that did not do much to offset the damage that the Court inflicted in *Reese* and *Cruikshank*. A few years later, the 1891 case of *United States v. Brewer*[123] quashed indictments under Section 5515, the same statute that the Court had held to be constitutional in *Ex parte Clarke* and *Ex parte Siebold*. The indictment alleged that defendants – election judges and an election officer – failed to perform duties required by state law; namely, they did not open the ballot box at the close of the election, in the place where the election was held, and read the names of the ballots in the presence of voters.[124] The Supreme Court sided with the defendants, finding that Tennessee law did not explicitly impose any such duty on them.

The relevant state laws provided:

> Sec. 1067. The officer or person and judges appointed to hold an election shall not proceed to or commence counting out the votes given in the election until the polls shall have been closed.
>
> Sec. 1068. When the election is finished, the returning officer and judges shall, in the presence of such of the electors as may choose to attend, open the box and read aloud the names of the persons which shall appear in each ballot; and the clerks, at the same time, shall number the ballots, each clerk separately.[125]

Ibid. See also Vallely, "Partisan Entrepreneurship," p. 135 ("a unanimous Court ruled that in order to protect the electoral processes that made it a national representative assembly, Congress could protect the right to vote of any citizen, Black or white.").

121 *Ex parte Yarbrough*, 110 U.S. 651, 666 (1884) ("[W]hile it may be true that acts which are mere invasions of private rights, which acts have no sanction in the statutes of a State, or which are not committed by any one exercising its authority, are not within the scope of that amendment, it is quite a different matter when Congress undertakes to protect the citizen in the exercise of rights conferred by the Constitution of the United States essential to the healthy organization of the government itself."). This distinction – between Congress exercising its Fifteenth Amendment authority and Congress acting pursuant to both the Elections Clause and the Fifteenth Amendment – became more and more significant as the Court increasingly diminished the scope of the Fifteenth Amendment in the ensuing decades. See, e.g., *James v. Bowman*, 190 U.S. 127 (1903) (finding that the Fifteenth Amendment cannot be violated by private individuals, just the state).

122 *United States v. Cruikshank*, 92 U.S. 542, 556 (1875).

123 *United States v. Brewer*, 139 U.S. 278 (1891).

124 Ibid., 282.

125 Ibid., 286–287.

The Court determined that the statute did not require "distinctly and specifically, and in words required in a criminal statute" that the box shall be opened and the votes counted at the place where the election was held.[126] Instead, the relevant provisions of state law should have imposed the duty in clear language, given that violation of its terms would constitute a crime.

Brewer bookended a chapter in the Court's history where strictly construing the law to dismiss indictments was one of the most common tactics used to undermine federal voting rights efforts.[127] During this period, the Court often prioritized formalism over substance, making it exceptionally difficult for the federal government to enforce the Fifteenth Amendment. *Ex parte Yarbrough*, *In re Coy*, *Ex parte Siebold*, and *Ex parte Clarke* were, at best, rare exceptions to the Court's overly formalistic and constrained approach.[128] Yet it was precisely these exceptions, and their broad reading of the Elections Clause, that gave Republicans the confidence to act boldly and push new federal legislation, the proposed Federal Elections Bill of 1890, when they regained control of Congress in 1888.

8.3 ELEVATING THE STRUCTURAL CONSTITUTION: LESSONS FROM THE ELECTIONS CLAUSE AND THE FEDERAL ELECTIONS BILL OF 1890

There was a need for new federal legislation after a decade plus of judicial obstruction, particularly given the limits of some of the tools that derived from the Constitutional of Political Structure. Congress continued to use its authority under Article I, Section 5 to displace elections in which legal voters were disenfranchised, power that was exercised well beyond the context of racial discrimination in voting and free of judicial interference.[129] But this authority could only be used on

126 Ibid., 287.

127 See, e.g., *Blitz v. United States*, 153 U.S. 308 (1894) (partially dismissing an indictment alleging that the defendant double voted in a congressional election because the indictment did not establish whether the defendant cast his vote for federal officials, state officers, or both). See also *Connors v. United States*, 158 U.S. 408 (1895) (sustaining an indictment that described, with particularity, how the defendant prevented election judges from counting the votes after an election).

128 See Chapter 9.

129 See, e.g., "House Committee on Elections, *Cook v. Cutts*, Sixth Congressional District of Iowa," in James H. Ellsworth (ed.), *Digest of Election Cases: Cases of Contested Elections in the House of Representatives, Forty-Seventh Congress* (Washington, D.C.: Government Printing Office, 1883), p. 243 (resolving disputes over state laws pertaining to voter registration); "House Committee on Elections, *Bisbee v. Finley*, Second Congressional District of Florida," in Ellsworth (ed.), *Digest of Election Cases*, pp. 172–173 (verifying whether individuals had been erroneously disenfranchised because of a belief that they were convicted felons); "House Committee on Elections, *Lowe v. Wheeler*, Eighth Congressional District of Alabama," in Ellsworth (ed.), *Digest of Election Cases*, p. 64 (determining whether votes were lawfully cast under the applicable Alabama state law which prohibited embellishments on the ballot). In resolving these cases, the House operated in a judicial role, but free of any actual judicial oversight: it heard sworn testimony from voters, elected officials, and poll workers from various precincts within the congressional district; reviewed the governing statutes under state law; used evidentiary rules to weigh testimony; and applied the relevant state law to the facts of the

a case-by-case basis to challenge the results in individual congressional elections rather than to protect voters in the act of exercising their right to vote. Congress primarily relied on the Enforcement Acts[130] and the Ku Klux Klan Act for this purpose.[131]

Before the Supreme Court sharply limited the scope of the 1870 Enforcement Act in *United States v. Reese*,[132] attorneys from the Department of Justice brought thousands of cases across the South between 1871 and 1875 against White supremacists and former Confederates who committed outrages against African Americans. Logistics made a high success rate for these prosecutions impossible, as most cases involved overworked prosecutors and law enforcement officers who had to gather evidence of crimes committed in the dead of night; cajole terrified witnesses afraid to testify; search for suspects who had the support of a sympathetic community; and provide sometimes false assurances that there would not be retribution toward those who cooperated with the criminal investigation.[133] Federal law enforcement officers and prosecutors also investigated these crimes not without risk to themselves. Arresting a suspect with force, for example, could result in federal officers being arrested by local authorities.[134]

While the clearance rate for Enforcement Act cases was about 17 percent in 1870 as compared to 41 percent for other criminal cases, the conviction rate was much higher – 74 percent as compared to a rate of 53 percent for other federal criminal cases.[135] Enforcement Act cases were brought in both the North and the South, but the majority of these were in the former Confederate states. In 1871, approximately 70 percent of cases were in Tennessee with almost all cases concentrated in this state and four others: Alabama, Mississippi, North Carolina, and South Carolina. By 1872, the conviction rate in the South was 90 percent.[136]

dispute to resolve these election contests. See De Alva Stanwood Alexander, *History and Procedure of the House of Representatives* (Boston, New York: Houghton Mifflin Co., Riverside Press, 1916), p. 313 (noting that the House's Article 1, Section 5 power has "neither appeal nor review. Although precedents be ignored, statutes neglected, and the rules of evidence disregarded, there is no redress."). For its part, the Supreme Court has treated issues surrounding the procedures used to resolve election contests as nonjusticiable political questions. *See Barry v. United States ex rel. Cunningham*, 279 U.S. 597 (1929) (holding that the Senate's decision to hold a witness in contempt during proceedings to resolve an election dispute was nonjusticiable).

130 An Act to enforce the Rights of Citizens of the United States to vote in the several States of the Union, and for other Purposes, ch. 114, 16 Stat. 140 (1870) [Enforcement Act of 1870]; An Act to amend an Act approved May 31, 1870, entitled "An Act to enforce the Rights of Citizens of the United States to vote in the several States of this Union, and for other Purposes," ch. 99, 16 Stat. 433 (1871) [Enforcement Act of 1871].

131 An Act to enforce the Provisions of the Fourteenth Amendment to the Constitution of the United States, and for other Purposes, ch. 22, 17 Stat. 13 (1871).

132 *United States v. Reese*, 92 U.S. 214 (1876).

133 Robert J. Kaczorowski, *The Politics of Judicial Interpretation: The Federal Courts, Department of Justice and Civil Rights, 1866–1876* (New York: Fordham University Press, 2005), pp. 48–49.

134 Ibid., pp. 47–48.

135 Ibid., p. 65.

136 Ibid., p. 71.

Congress, while not indifferent to the difficulties of prosecuting these cases, was likely encouraged by the successes (although it might also have been waiting to see what the Supreme Court's reception to the Enforcement Acts would be). The Court, for its part, did not seem anxious to engage the situation. In *United States v. Avery*,[137] an Enforcement Act case decided in 1872, the Court avoided entering the fray and dismissed the case for jurisdictional reasons.

The results in the lower courts were somewhat mixed. Some judges had proven to be quite hostile to the Enforcement Acts, resisting the idea that voting rights protection had shifted from the states to the federal government. For example, the assault of a Black man in his home to prevent him from exercising his right to vote did not, according to a South Carolina federal district court the 1871 decision of *United States v. Crosby*, implicate any right protected by the U.S. Constitution.[138]

In contrast, future Supreme Court justice William B. Woods determined, in the federal district court case of *United States v. Hall*, that Ku Klux Klan members who had committed violent acts against Black people attending a Republican political meeting, culminating in the murder of two people, had violated the attendees' First Amendment rights of speech and assembly.[139] *Hall*, decided in 1871, stood in stark contrast to *Cruikshank*, in which the Supreme Court found that the victims' rights to bear arms, assemble, and vote had not been violated in remarkably similar circumstances.

When the Supreme Court finally issued a substantive decision and invalidated Sections 3 and 4 of the Enforcement Act of 1870 in *United States v. Reese*, Congress reauthorized Section 4 relying, not on the Fifteenth Amendment, but on its authority under the Elections Clause to enact what would now be known as Section 5506 of the Revised Statutes. Like its predecessor, Section 5506 punished those "who, by any unlawful means, hinders, delays, prevents, or obstructs, or combines and confederates with others to hinder, delay, prevent, or obstruct, any citizen from voting at any election in any state, territory, county, city, or parish."[140]

Lower courts rejected arguments challenging Section 5506 as unconstitutional that were based on the Court's decision in *United States v. Reese*. In the 1891 case of *United States v. Belvin*, for example, a district court in the eastern district of Virginia rejected the argument that Section 5506 exceeded the scope of Congress's authority.[141] The district court distinguished *Reese* by noting that the defendant in that case had been charged with violating an individual's right to vote, with no allegation that the violation was based on race, under a version of Section 5506 enacted pursuant to the

137 *United States v. Avery*, 80 U.S. 251 (1872) (finding that it lacked jurisdiction under the Judiciary Act of 1802 to hear criminal cases brought under the Ku Klux Klan Act).

138 Richard Claude, "Constitutional Voting Rights and Early U.S. Supreme Court Doctrine," (1966) 51/2 *The Journal of Negro History* 114–124, 116.

139 *United States v. Hall*, 26 F. Cas. 79 (C.C. S.D. Ala. 1871).

140 An Act to enforce the Rights of Citizens of the United States to vote in the several States of the Union, and for other Purposes, ch. 114, s. 4, 16 Stat. 141 (1870), codified at U.S. Rev. Stat. s. 5506 (2nd ed. 1878).

141 *United States v. Belvin*, 46 F. 381, 382–383 (E.D. Va. 1891).

Fifteenth Amendment. The *Belvin* defendants were charged with hindering voting in the context of a congressional election, which was well within Congress's purview.

An earlier eastern district of Virginia case, also from 1891 and relied on by the *Belvin* court, had rejected a constitutional challenge to Section 5506 on similar grounds.[142] In *United States v. Munford*, the district court read the Elections Clause as broad authority for this provision, noting that "If congress can provide for the manner of election, it can certainly provide that it shall be an honest manner; that there shall be no repression of voters and an honest count of the ballots. There is little regarding an election that is not included in the terms, time, place, and manner of holding it."[143]

While the remedial measure at issue was inappropriate under the Fifteenth Amendment, Section 5506 was a valid exercise of federal power under the Elections Clause.

In addition to reauthorizing legislation struck down by the Court, Congress attempted to enact new legislation under the Elections Clause. In 1890, Henry Cabot Lodge introduced the Federal Elections Bill to "secure entire publicity in regard to every act connected with the election of members of Congress."[144] Following a wave of support for election reform, Lodge proposed this legislation after the Republicans gained majorities in both houses of Congress in 1888 – the first time since 1874 – and sought to overcome the political stalemate that had hampered enforcement of the federal election laws then on the books.[145] The bill was the only piece of election legislation to gain significant traction and almost become law since Reconstruction.

This legislation, proposed under the Elections Clause rather than the Reconstruction Amendments, sought to extend the reach of the 1870 and 1871 Enforcement Acts by instituting federal supervision of congressional elections if 100 people within any given congressional district request federal intervention.[146]

142 *United States v. Munford*, 46 F. 381 (E.D. Va. 1891).

143 Ibid.

144 Henry C. Lodge and Terence V. Powderly, "The Federal Election Bill," (1890) 151 *The North American Review* 257–273, 257; see also A Bill to amend and supplement the election laws of the United States and to provide for the more efficient enforcement of such laws, and for other purposes, H.R. 10958, 51st Congress, 1st Session (June 14, 1890).

145 Richard E. Welch, Jr., "The Federal Elections Bill of 1890: Postscripts and Prelude" (1965) 52 *The Journal of American History* 511–526, 512 ("[I]n the election of 1888 the Republicans won control of Congress as well as the presidency, and the latter office would be held by Benjamin Harrison. Harrison stood with such old-time Republican senators as [George Frisbie] Hoar [floor manager of the Bill in the Senate] and [William E.] Chandler in refusing to admit that the aims and ideals of Radical Reconstruction had been disproved or that the Republican party had outgrown its concern for the southern Negro. The motives of these 'old-fashioned Republicans' offered a strange blend of political opportunism and political idealism. They were determined to spite Grover Cleveland and revive the ideals of Charles Sumner.").

146 Lodge and Powderly, "Federal Election Bill," 266; see also A Bill to amend and supplement the election laws of the United States and to provide for the more efficient enforcement of such laws, and for other purposes, H.R. 10958, 51st Congress, 1st Session (June 14, 1890); J. Morgan Kousser, *The Shaping of Southern Politics: Suffrage Restriction and the Establishment of the One-Party South, 1880-1910* (New Haven: Yale University Press, 1974), pp. 29–30.

The 1890 bill exemplified the under-utilized potential of federal authority in the aggregate; if enacted, it would have been a time, place, and manner statute that strengthened the 1870s Enforcement Acts – enacted pursuant to the Fourteenth and Fifteenth Amendment and the Elections Clause – to protect voters in both the North and the South. Referred to as the "Lodge Force Act," the bill was so controversial, according to *The New York Times*, that major issues were being neglected to focus on its potential passage.[147]

The Federal Elections Bill raised interesting questions about whether Congress had constitutional authority under the Elections Clause to assume control of federal elections, which, in the view of critics, was a far different power than regulating their "manner," as the text permitted.[148] The bill would have appointed election officers from the two major political parties to oversee congressional elections, from voter registration to the certification of the winners.[149] While these officers could not directly override the state law that governed federal elections, they had investigative power that allowed them not only to secure evidence of voter disenfranchisement for later prosecutions against state officials, but also to publicize their wrongdoing.[150]

Because state law remained the framework for federal elections, this suggested that the bill wasn't as far reaching as its critics contended;[151] nonetheless, the proposal did represent a significant change in the basic structure of the system. The bill, if enacted, would have installed a chief election supervisor in each judicial circuit in the country to take applications from citizens requesting federal assistance.[152] Under this new regime, federal election supervisors would no longer oversee only registration and voting. Their duties would have also included:"[I]nspecting the registration

147 "Gorman on the Stump: He Tells Truths about the Tariff and Force Bills," *New York Times*, October 4, 1891, p. 20.

148 "Comments of Representative Holman, Fifty-First Congress, First Session, July 1, 1890," 21 *Congressional Record* (Washington, D.C., Government Printing Office, 1890), part 7, p. 6843 (pointing to federal laws that require single-member districts and ballots as "manner" regulations under the Elections Clause, and noting that the Federal Elections Bill presented a "new and startling question" of whether Congress can "not only prescribe rules as to the procedure in these elections of Senators and Representatives, but through its own agents take charge of these elections and decide and declare the result").

149 Lodge and Powderly, "Federal Election Bill," 257–258.

150 Ibid., 258.

151 The misnomer, "Force Act," was more of a reflection of the controversy surrounding the proposal as opposed to its scope. See Xi Wang, *The Trial of Democracy: Black Suffrage and Northern Republicans, 1860–1910* (Athens: University of Georgia Press, 1997), pp. 233–237 (noting that Republicans considered separating state and federal elections, or alternatively, taking the power of conducting congressional elections away from the states before settling on a regime of federal oversight). Democrats referred to the Lodge Bill as a "Force Act" as a nod to an earlier voting rights bill that had failed in 1875. J. Morgan Kousser, *Colorblind Injustice: Minority Voting Rights and the Undoing of the Second Reconstruction* (Chapel Hill: University of North Carolina Press, 1999), p. 18.

152 Wang, *Trial of Democracy*, p. 266; A Bill to amend and supplement the election laws of the United States and to provide for the more efficient enforcement of such laws, and for other purposes, H.R. 10958 51st Congress, 1st Session (June 14, 1890), s. 2.

lists; verifying a doubtful voter's name, identity, and residential information; placing an oath before a voter when his qualifications were challenged; making a list of all voters; making and certifying statements of the votes cast in his election district; and assisting the court in preventing illegal immigrants from voting."[153]

Most importantly, the bill allowed the United States Board of Canvassers to determine the winner of a congressional election, even if the state certified a different candidate than the Board.[154] The losing candidate could appeal the Board's decision, but only in federal court.[155]

Much like debates over the Apportionment Act of 1842, federalism would once again make an appearance in debates over the Lodge Force Act as critics framed the bill, not only as undemocratic, but as a usurpation of and unconstitutional interference with state power.[156] The ability to override a state-certified winner in a congressional election, leaving the outcome of federal elections almost entirely in the hands of federal judges and election supervisors, led one representative to argue that the bill represented "an absolute and complete change in our system of government."[157]

[153] Wang, *Trial of Democracy*, p. 237; A Bill to amend and supplement the election laws of the United States and to provide for the more efficient enforcement of such laws, and for other purposes, H.R. 10958, 51st Congress, 1st Session (June 14, 1890), s. 8.

[154] Lodge and Powderly, "Federal Election Bill," 266 ("Where an entire Congressional district is placed under the law, a United States Board of Canvassers appointed for the district receives the supervisors' returns, and on those returns issues a certificate to the candidate who appears to be elected. If that certificate agrees with the certificate of the State officers, the name of the candidate who holds them both is, of course, placed upon the roll of members of the House. If the two certificates disagree, then the certificate of the United States board is prima-facie evidence and places the name of the holder upon the roll of Representatives ...."); A Bill to amend and supplement the election laws of the United States and to provide for the more efficient enforcement of such laws, and for other purposes, H.R. 10958, 51st Congress, 1st Session (June 14, 1890), ss. 15–16.

[155] Lodge and Powderly, "Federal Election Bill," 258 (noting that the "Circuit Court of the United States ... has power to set aside the certificate of the canvassers and virtually decide whose name shall be placed on the roll of the House"); see also Welch, "Federal Elections Bill of 1890," 514 (noting that "the judges of the federal circuit courts in 1890 were mostly Republican appointees"); Lodge and Powderly, "Federal Election Bill," 258 (conceding that this was the only point in the legislation where "the United States take what may be called control of any essential step in the election of Representatives.").

[156] See "Comments of Representative Breckinridge, Fifty-First Congress, First Session, July 1, 1890," 21 *Congressional Record* (Washington, D.C.: Government Printing Office, 1890), part 7, pp. 6853, 6856. See also "Comments of Representative Mills, Fifty-First Congress, First Session, July 1, 1890," 21 *Congressional Record* (Washington, D.C.: Government Printing Office, 1890), part 7, p. 6858 (arguing that the bill was undemocratic because it would have permitted the House to "disregard the certificates given by the chosen officers of the people who have voted for the Representatives"). Contrary to these assertions, Lodge argued that the legislation would not disturb state election laws. See Lodge and Powderly, "Federal Election Bill," 258 ("The State systems, whether they provide for the secret and official ballot or otherwise, are all carefully protected under this law against any interference from United States officers."); see also Wang, *Trial of Democracy*, p. 234 (arguing that Lodge believed "the best way to eliminate southern suppression of black votes was to carry out comprehensive ballot reform").

[157] "Comments of Representative Holman, Fifty-First Congress, First Session, July 1, 1890," 21 *Congressional Record* (Washington, D.C.: Government Printing Office, 1890), part 7, pp. 6844–6845 (referring to the bill as "[a] mean, petty system of espionage on the citizens of our country").

Democrats warned that the bill would cause widespread violence and disruption, prompting a minority of representatives from the House Committee on Elections to propose an amendment that would have left control of congressional elections in the hands of state officials.[158]

Supporters of the bill pointed to the lack of checks within state systems to prevent fraud from occurring. Some states, including North and South Carolina, made county canvassing boards judicial officers and removed any oversight of election returns from state courts. As one congressman observed, this structure resulted in the wrong man being elected to a congressional seat in South Carolina because the unchecked county canvassing board, appointed by the Governor, had thrown out votes for his opponent.[159]

Instead of denying the existence of fraud, some Democrats focused on its inevitability, arguing that the various election frauds would cancel themselves out, so federal oversight was unwarranted.[160] Others tried to deflect attention away from the improprieties committed by state and local officials by pointing out that the bill was a partisan measure, designed to bolster electoral support for the Republican Party just as the Apportionment Act of 1842 and single-member districts had secured the electoral position of the Whigs just as they, for the only time in history, controlled all three branches of government.[161]

158 See "Comments of Representative Buckalew, Fifty-First Congress, First Session, July 1, 1890," 21 *Congressional Record* (Washington, D.C.: Government Printing Office, 1890), part 7, p. 6851. ("[T]his amendment now proposed by the minority of the committee, when properly understood by the House, is simply this: That the existing system for State elections for Representatives in Congress, including all the proceedings of returns, shall be left unimpaired. The election will be held by the proper State officers. In the first place, the election returns will be carried in such States as mine to a court a day or two after the election, all the returning judges appearing there, the court being empowered to correct errors or any apparent frauds. Then they pass to the district returning boards, which is merely a mere matter of form now in those, and then to the proper high State officers, the secretary of the Commonwealth, … and then the returns come here [to Congress] and are prima facie evidence of what the people have done.") (emphasis omitted)). See also Kousser, *Colorblind Injustice*, p. 39.

159 "Comments of Representative Rowell, Fifty-First Congress, First Session, July 1, 1890," 21 *Congressional Record* (Washington, D.C.: Government Printing Office, 1890), part 7, p. 6852.

160 "Comments of Representative Breckinridge, Fifty-First Congress, First Session, July 1, 1890," 21 *Congressional Record* (Washington, D.C.: Government Printing Office, 1890), part 7, p. 6854 ("Any Federal election law, in my judgment, is unwise … . With the States controlling their elections there can be only local frauds and only temporary mischief. In the give and play of counteracting forces these frauds will generally offset each other. The average result in a series of years will about be equal on either side …").

161 See "Comments of Representative Caruth, Fifty-First Congress, First Session, July 1, 1890," 21 *Congressional Record* (Washington, D.C.: Government Printing Office, 1890), part 7, p. 6858 ("This is an effort here, Mr. Speaker, to perpetuate you Republicans in power. For the first time in quite a number of years the Republican party finds itself in possession of the executive office and of both bodies constituting the legislative department of the Government. The methods by which it secured this supremacy were, to say the least, questionable. The party fought with a desperation which seemed born of despair.").

Criticism of the bill was not limited to southern Democrats. Some representatives were troubled because it would apply nationwide, a concern that ignored the fact that election fraud was rampant across the country.[162] Yet nationwide application was a further indication that supporters were concerned less about focusing on specific practices enacted with discriminatory intent, which would have limited the scope of the bill mostly to the South, and more on fraudulent or discriminatory practices that had the effect of undermining the integrity of elections more generally.[163] While the purpose of the original federal election laws was to protect African American voters, enforcement efforts had shifted to securing Republican majorities in northern states.[164] During the congressional debates, fraud in elections held in Chicago and New York was as much a topic of discussion as the discriminatory practices in the South.[165]

But few could deny that the South was the bill's primary target.[166] First, most of the fraud identified by its supporters had occurred in southern states.[167] Second, the

[162] See "Comments of Representative Hill, Fifty-First Congress, First Session, July 1, 1890," 21 *Congressional Record* (Washington, D.C.: Government Printing Office, 1890), part 7, p. 6847 ("After days and days of talking against this bill in every conceivable form … we find them advocating its application, if enacted into law, not merely to a few Congressional districts, not merely to a few cities and localities where it is needed in this country, but to every Congressional district. The constitutional argument is forgotten, the great expense to the people of the United States is forgotten, all the arguments that they have used against this bill are forgotten for the time, and they are ready to fall in and adopt the amendment … extending the operations of this bill to every Congressional district, making it not voluntary but compulsory, regardless of expense and regardless of constitutional law."). But see "Comments of Representatives Hemphill and Richardson, Fifty-First Congress, First Session, July 1, 1890," 21 *Congressional Record* (Washington, D.C.: Government Printing Office, 1890), part 7, p. 6848 (arguing that the Bill should apply nationwide otherwise "there will be gentleman upon this floor who will be seated here under the State law, others will be seated under the United States law … [a]nd some without any law"); "Comments of Representative Hemphill, Fifty-First Congress, First Session, July 1, 1890," 21 *Congressional Record* (Washington, D.C.: Government Printing Office, 1890), part 7, p. 6848 (noting that the law only goes into operation if 100 people in a district request oversight).

[163] As previously noted, Lodge explicitly stated that the Bill would leave in place state election laws, most of which were adopted with discriminatory purpose. See Lodge and Powderly, "Federal Election Bill," 258; Wang, *Trial of Democracy*, p. 234.

[164] See Scott C. James and Brian L. Lawson, "The Political Economy of Voting Rights Enforcement in America's Gilded Age: Electoral College Competition, Partisan Commitment, and the Federal Election Law" (1999) 93 *The American Political Science Review* 115–131, 115 (noting that "the Republican promise of black voting rights was gradually crowded out by a preoccupation to contain Democratic registration and voter fraud in the competitive swing states in presidential elections").

[165] See "Discussion between Various Congressmen, Fifty-First Congress, First Session, July 1, 1890," 21 *Congressional Record* (Washington, D.C.: Government Printing Office, 1890), part 7, pp. 6846–6847, 6849; Lodge and Powderly, "Federal Election Bill," 258. See also Wang, *Trial of Democracy*, p. 225 (noting that the Republican Party's 1888 platform emphasized "equal suffrage instead of black suffrage … although black suffrage was intended to be the object of attention").

[166] Wang, *Trial of Democracy*, pp. 234–235, 238.

[167] See "Comments of Representative Oates, Fifty-First Congress, First Session, July 1, 1890," 21 *Congressional Record* (Washington, D.C.: Government Printing Office, 1890), part 7, p. 6862 (noting:

legislation would have strengthened the system of federal oversight already in place in the southern states as a result of federal elections laws enacted between 1870 and 1872.[168] The 1890 bill, despite its geographic breadth, would have inevitably brought national attention back to the fraudulent and discriminatory practices in the South.

Southerners were right to be concerned about the effect of the Federal Elections Bill on their decades-long campaign to disenfranchise African Americans. The bill arguably would have had its biggest impact on preventing states from applying their election laws in a disparate manner, and much of the former Confederacy relied on unequal application to maximize the disenfranchisement of minorities and those White people who did not support the Democratic Party.

For example, the system of periodic voter registration that many southern states used during the 1870s and 1880s depended, for broadest impact, on the significant discretion that state law delegated to registrars.[169] As J. Morgan Kousser noted in his seminal study of these practices:

> According to the North Carolina law of 1889, for instance, registrars, appointed indirectly by the Democratic legislature, could require that a voter prove "as near as may be" his "age, occupation, place of birth and place of residency … by such testimony, under oath, as may be satisfactory to the registrar." Black men born into slavery were often ignorant of their exact ages; streets in Negro areas often had no names, houses no numbers…. Registration officials in Florida merely erased Republican names and then refused to meet with the voters so that they could re-register.[170]

Like North Carolina and Florida, the registration requirements in an 1896 Louisiana law were very effective in disenfranchising African Americans and their White allies. Louisiana's voter rolls were inflated, as reflected by the fact that 103.2 percent of White people and 95.6 percent of African Americans were registered to vote in 1897, but it was still instructive that, just one year later, mandatory re-registration had reduced these figures to 46.6 percent and 9.5 percent, respectively.[171] While

"It is said by the advocates of this bill that they have found that frauds have been committed in one district out of the eight in Alabama, in two districts of Arkansas, one in South Carolina, one in Virginia, and one in Mississippi" but arguing that "such a law as that proposed will … set us [the South] back to the days of violence which were prevalent there twenty years ago."). This does not mean that fraud was not prevalent in the North. See Wang, *Trial of Democracy*, p. 225 ("The election frauds in northern cities, where large numbers of foreign immigrants lived and voted, presented a problem no less urgent than black disenfranchisement in the South and probably even more threatening as it spread nationwide.").

168 See Chapter 6.

169 Kousser, *Southern Politics*, p. 48 ("The key disfranchising features of the Southern registration laws were the amount of discretion granted to the registrars, the specificity of the information required of the registrant, the times and places set for registration, and the requirement that a voter bring his registration certificate to the polling place."). Voter registration systems remain legal today. See *Kramer v. Union Free School District No.* 15, 395 U.S. 621 (1969).

170 Ibid. (first alteration in original).

171 Ibid., p. 49 ("The law as administered reduced white registration by nearly 60 percent and Negro by 90 percent.").

the constitutional requirements for voter registration did not change, discriminatory administration all but ensured a reduction in the size of the electorate.

The Federal Elections Bill, with its proposed regime of federal oversight, would have eliminated the ability of registrars handpicked by Democratic officials to engage in widespread disenfranchisement. It was clear from the structure of the law that Congress did not actually believe that voter registration systems were presumptively unlawful or unconstitutional, but Congress recognized that voter registration, along with other laws adopted throughout the 1870s and 1880s, had operated to deprive large segments of the population of the right to vote.

The same argument could be made with respect to literacy tests, which also depended on the discriminatory actions of registrars to narrow the electorate. In fact, as late as 1959, the Supreme Court upheld the facial constitutionality of these devices as "one fair way of determining whether a person is literate, not a calculated scheme to lay springes for the citizen" so long as they were "applicable to members of all races."[172] Yet the discretion delegated to election administrators guaranteed that literate African Americans would not be able to register to vote, and illiterate White people would still be able to cast a ballot. Although literacy tests were legal, the Federal Elections Bill would have limited the discretion given to registrars to use these devices as a means of furthering racial and partisan discrimination.[173]

With the Federal Elections Bill, Congress sought to build on the earlier Enforcement Acts and favorable Supreme Court precedents that had explicitly recognized that Congress had broad authority under the Elections Clause to protect federal elections.[174] Nonetheless, the perception that Congress was legislating toward the outer limits of its constitutional power carried political risk that ultimately manifested at the ballot box.

Republicans enacted five Enforcement Acts in the early 1870s, which contributed to the electoral defeat that cost them control of Congress in 1874 for the first time since the Civil War.[175] Republican support for the Federal Elections Bill would similarly cost them in the 1890 elections, with fissures in the Republican caucus ultimately leading to the bill's defeat in 1891, followed by huge Republican losses in the 1892 elections.[176]

172 *Lassiter v. Northampton County Board of Elections*, 360 U.S. 45, 53–54 (1959).

173 To be fair, it is not clear whether federal administration of a literacy requirement would have had less of an impact on the electorate than administration by the state because many individuals, both African American and White, were deterred from even trying to register because they did not want to publicly expose their illiteracy. See Kousser, *Southern Politics*, p. 59.

174 Franita Tolson, "The Elections Clause and the Underenforcement of Federal Law" (2019) 129 *Yale Law Journal Forum* 171–184.

175 Wang, *Trial of Democracy*, pp. 110–113.

176 Vallely, "Partisan Entrepreneurship," p. 127 (noting that the bill "died on January 26, 1891" and "[d]espite the passage of eighteen months time, Democrats actually ran against the Federal Elections Bill in 1892"); "Wanted, a Trust Moses Who Can Save the Perplexed Bay State Republicans," *New York Times*, June 3, 1891, p. 3 ("There was no popular demand for the Force bill so persistently

The Democrats (with the help of some Republicans) ultimately killed the Lodge Force Act in Congress, but the wheels of disenfranchisement, more far reaching than prior efforts, had already been set in motion.[177] The *Chicago Tribune*, in 1892, colorfully referred to the recently deceased bill as "last year's bird's nest" with "no eggs in the nest, and no birds anticipating ... a brood from that nest."[178] But for Southerners, the latent prospect of federal oversight led to the systematic and "legal" disenfranchisement of African Americans and poor White people across the South in an effort to preempt the Republican majorities that might result from increased federal oversight.[179] As the next chapter shows, by 1908, every southern state adopted various limitations on voting – complicated voter registration systems, the Australian secret ballot,[180] poll taxes,[181] more expansive literacy tests,[182] and multiple-box laws,[183] to name a few. All of these laws were extremely effective in circumscribing the electorate.[184]

Discriminatory implementation, while still important, became less central to the restrictive election regimes that were more far reaching than their predecessors and, ostensibly, were "constitutional" under the Fifteenth Amendment. The 1890 Federal Elections Bill, if enacted, would have made it difficult for state officials to exercise the discretion that they retained under state law to ensure the virtual elimination of African Americans from the electorate. Accordingly, the response of many

championed by Messrs. Hoar and Lodge. The voters of Massachusetts gave the measure only scant favor, and yet it was known that the Speaker secured the unanimous support of the Republican delegation for the tariff and other pet schemes in which he was interested by designating Mr. Lodge as their promoter and recognized sponsor on the floor of the House. The interests of the State as a manufacturing and purchasing community were therefore bartered and pledged in favor of a bill that evoked no enthusiasm among the thoughtful, but rather excited positive hostility.").

177 Welch, "Federal Elections Bill of 1890," 515 (noting that some Republicans wanted to table the Elections Bill in order to push through the McKinley tariff).

178 "The Race Question: Halsted Wants the Fifteenth Amendment Knocked Out," *The Chicago Daily Tribune*, August 1, 1892, at 10.

179 Kousser, *Southern Politics*, p. 30 ("Despite the mildness of the Lodge Bill, the Democrats were correct in fearing its possible consequences. Had it been enacted and enforced (and had the Southern states not passed disenfranchising laws), the bill would have increased the number of Southern Republicans and Populists in Congress and focused attention on the malodorous Southern election practices. These exposures and the increased strength in Congress of Southerners opposed to the Democratic party might well have led Congress to pass stronger legislation, which would have added further to the erosion of Democratic power, and so on and on.").

180 See ibid., p. 53 (noting that "there is little question that the secret ballot was adopted in the South primarily to purge the electorate of illiterates"); ibid., pp. 55–56 (looking at Arkansas, Alabama, and Louisiana and noting that, because of the Australian ballot, the "decline in participation varied from 8 percent to 28 percent of the white adult males, and from 15 percent to 45 percent of the Negro adult males").

181 See ibid., pp. 63–82.

182 See ibid., pp. 56–62.

183 See ibid., p. 50 ("Under the eight-box laws, separate ballots for president, congressman, governor, state senator, etc., were supposed to be deposited in the proper boxes; if the ballots were distributed otherwise, they were not counted.").

184 See ibid., pp. 32–33.

southern states after its failure was to limit this discretion to avoid triggering the attention of federal officials.

Elected officials also wanted to eliminate the need for partisans within the Democratic Party to engage in the fraud and violence that had characterized southern elections, which brought with it unwelcome attention from Congress and the Department of Justice.[185] Since the Federal Elections Bill's purpose was to ensure compliance with state and federal law, southern states subverted the bill by adopting facially neutral voter qualification standards that would narrow the electorate without the explicit need for force or fraud.[186]

185 See Lodge and Powderly, "Federal Election Bill," 259 ("There is absolutely nothing in this bill except provisions to secure the greatest amount of publicity in regard to elections and to protect the ballot-box by making sure the punishment of those who commit crimes against the suffrage. It interferes with no man's rights; it changes no local system; it disturbs no local officers; but it gives publicity to every step and detail of the election, and publicity is the best, as it is the greatest, safeguard that we can have in this country for good government and honest voting.").

186 Kousser, *Southern Politics*, p. 32; Michael J. Klarman, "The Puzzling Resistance to Political Process Theory," (1991) 77 *Virginia Law Review* 747–832, 792–793 ("The South was anything but politically 'solid' through the 1880s (except as to presidential contests); Democrats faced close competition from an assortment of independent, Republican, and Populist candidates, often emerging victorious only with the aid of rampant ballot fraud and voter intimidation. For this reason, the Lodge Federal Elections Bill of 1890 … aroused great anxiety in the South, leading to a formalization and extension of disfranchisement techniques that already had proven quite successful by 1890." (footnote omitted)).

9

In Congress We Trust?

A Final Curtain Call for the Reconstruction Project

The final collapse of Reconstruction in the 1890s and early 1900s across the South, culminating in the adoption of new state constitutions that represented the end of the fragile political order that emerged in the aftermath of the Civil War, brings us full circle. In the face of Redemption-era disenfranchisement and violence, Congress and the courts systematically abandoned the full arsenal of federal authority – both the new constitutional tools forged during Reconstruction and the older powers long available under the original Constitution – retreating instead to the cramped confines of Madisonian federalism.

Slavery had once served as the wedge issue that led Congress to tolerate unrepublican governments before the Civil War – where the language of federalism and states' rights validated the counter-majoritarianism of the planter class that had co-opted the federal government – and Jim Crow would assume that role during Redemption and Restoration. This reversion back to the Madisonian mean recentered the states as the ultimate arbiters of civil and political rights, allowing them to construct political communities on exclusionary terms, even when those parameters clashed with the more inclusive vision promised by the Guarantee Clause.

The boundaries of the political communities of "We the People" and "We the Voters," both of which had been radically reconceptualized during Reconstruction, would once again become heavily policed to keep out those who had, briefly, enjoyed membership. Just as the Colfax Massacre had marked the triumph of the "alter or abolish" principle over the promise of voting rights a decade earlier, so too would the Wilmington Insurrection of 1898, discussed in this chapter, reflect the enduring power of violent exclusion as a tool of statecraft. Unchecked violence across the South would remind the former beneficiaries of the Reconstruction project that their time in these communities had come to an end.

The case studies in disenfranchisement that are presented in Chapter 9 – focusing on Mississippi, Virginia, North Carolina, South Carolina, and Alabama – each illustrate the systematic dismantling of the inclusive political communities of "We the Voters" and "We the People" that Congress had built by redefining the Constitutions of Political Structure and Political Rights. When attempts to enforce

Section 2 of the Fourteenth Amendment sputtered and then died at the turn of the century, coupled with Congress's unceremonious retreat from robust oversight of its members' elections under Article I, Section 5, this was the final signal that the Civil War's great constitutional experiment had come to an end.

9.1 SETTING THE STAGE FOR JIM CROW: MISSISSIPPI AS PARADIGM

Mississippi was the first state to call a constitutional convention to revisit its voting laws in response to the proposed Lodge Force Act.[1] Its new 1890 constitution introduced an onerous residency rule, requiring that voters live "in this State two years, and one year in the election district, or in the incorporated city or town, in which he offers to vote."[2] Voters also had to be registered "within four months next before any election at which they may offer to vote."[3]

The constitution imposed a literacy test that required potential voters to read a provision of the state constitution, which would disenfranchise African Americans at the registration stage, rather than having to resort to the widespread fraud at the ballot box that was prevalent prior to the convention.[4] The addition of a so-called understanding clause provided an out for White voters who, despite being illiterate, could register if they understand a provision of the state constitution, read to them by the registrar, and explain that provision to the registrar's satisfaction.[5]

The state's new $2 poll tax disenfranchised African American voters in most of Mississippi's counties.[6] Although the constitution indicated that the tax was for the "aid of the common schools," the text lacked any penalty for failure to pay, an

1 See Michael Perman, *Struggle for Mastery: Disfranchisement in the South, 1888–1908* (Chapel Hill: University of North Carolina Press, 2001), p. 75 (stating that the Federal Elections Bill "presented not only the alarming prospect of an increased federal presence in southern congressional elections but also the likelihood that federal officials would see for themselves how the vote was manipulated in black-majority districts. This kind of scrutiny could be obviated by redefining suffrage rights constitutionally in such a way as to place them outside the scope of a law intended simply to supervise elections.").

2 Constitution of the State of Mississippi art. XII, s. 251 (1890) (amended 1968).

3 Ibid.

4 Ibid., art. XII, s. 244 (repealed 1975).

5 Perman, *Struggle for Mastery*, p. 86 (noting that, in Mississippi, "the white-county representatives realized that, without the elastic 'understanding' clause, thousands of white voters would be confused or deterred by the secret ballot and eliminated by the poll tax"); see also Constitution of the State of Mississippi art. XII, s. 244 (1890) (repealed 1975) ("On and after the first day of January, A. D., 1892, every elector shall, in addition to the foregoing qualifications, be able to read any section of the constitution of the state; or he shall be able to understand the same when read to him, or give a reasonable interpretation thereof.").

6 See Perman, *Struggle for Mastery*, p. 88 ("By July 1891, when thirty-two of Mississippi's sixty-five counties had paid [the poll tax], 44,971 whites but only 17,331 blacks had cleared the pecuniary hurdle."); see also Constitution of the State of Mississippi art. XII, s. 243 (1890) (repealed 1975).

indication that its adoption had little to do with raising revenue.[7] The state's redistricting plan guaranteed that the political strength of majority-African American counties would be significantly diluted, further undermining a group already unable to advocate for themselves at the ballot box.[8]

The criminal justice system was a key element to facilitating the quest to turn Black people into political nonages, outside the boundaries of "We the Voters." Mississippi used its criminal law to not only streamline the Black population into convict leasing and peonage, but also to limit their political participation. The Mississippi Constitution disenfranchised any person "convicted of murder, rape, bribery, theft, arson, obtaining money or goods under false pretense, perjury, forgery, embezzlement, or bigamy."[9] This provision, which remains in effect today, was a cornerstone of the effort to disenfranchise Black voters; as the Fifth Circuit Court of Appeals recognized in the 2022 case of *Harness v. Watson*, "Section 241 was reconfigured in the 1890 Constitution to eliminate voter disenfranchisement for crimes thought to be 'white crimes' and by adding crimes thought to be 'black crimes.'"[10] The court also conceded that, had the law never been amended, it would be a clear violation of the Equal Protection Clause of the Fourteenth Amendment.

The Fifth Circuit's recognition that the 1890 convention was "motivated by a desire to discriminate against blacks"[11] was the only concession that the court made in acknowledging the discriminatory origins of the state's felon disenfranchisement law. Instead, the court found that, because Section 241 had been re-enacted twice since 1890 – once in 1950 and again in 1968 – the deliberative process surrounding amended Section 241 was sufficient to break the inference of discriminatory intent that would otherwise establish a Fourteenth Amendment violation.[12]

Oddly, the deliberative process that the court heralded as a sign of race-neutral decision-making resulted in additional felonies being added to the list of disenfranchising crimes with each subsequent amendment. As it stands, nearly 16 percent of Black voters in Mississippi are disenfranchised because of Section 241.[13] The *Harness* Court's view that discriminatory taint can be cleansed through the amendment process ignores that Section 241 was a part of an ongoing and systematic effort to create, and then maintain, an all-White electorate in the state through *legal* discrimination.

Put differently, the facial neutrality of the language was key to furthering White supremacy one hundred years ago, when there was no judicially actionable concept

7 Constitution of the State of Mississippi art. XII, s. 243 (1890) (repealed 1975) ("No criminal proceedings shall be allowed to enforce the collection of the poll-tax.").

8 Perman, *Struggle for Mastery*, p. 87.

9 Constitution of the State of Mississippi art. 12, s. 241 (1890).

10 *Harness v. Watson*, 47 F.4th 296, 300 (5th Cir. 2022).

11 Ibid.

12 Ibid., 310.

13 The Sentencing Project, *Locked Out 2020: Estimates of People Denied Voting Rights Due to a Felony Conviction* (October 2018), www.sentencingproject.org/app/uploads/2022/08/Locked-Out-2020.pdf.

of discriminatory intent. Allowing the chain of discrimination to be broken through statutory amendment, while ignoring that the law is as wildly effective now in disenfranchising Black voters as it was a century ago, disregards how facially race-neutral laws have once again emerged as the primary vehicle for facilitating racial discrimination.

The judicial head-in-the-sand approach embraced by the *Harness* Court was prevalent in the U.S. Supreme Court in the 1890s. In the 1898 case *Williams v. Mississippi*, the Supreme Court found that the Mississippi Constitution – which, as the Fifth Circuit acknowledged, was adopted in a process "steeped in racism" – did not violate the Federal Constitution.[14] Even though discriminatory implementation of the state's voting laws meant that the defendant in *Williams* was indicted by an all-White, all-male grand jury selected from the state's predominantly White voting rolls, the facially race-neutral language of the state constitution meant that there was no Fourteenth Amendment violation.

By adding a layer of formalistic neutrality between the discriminatory action and its victim – in *Harness*, by reauthorizing a discriminatory law in an ostensibly race-neutral process to cleanse it of discriminatory taint;[15] in *Williams*, by relying on all White voter rolls to comprise the jury rather than directly excluding Black people from the jury pool[16] – this neutered the ability of the courts to effectively police discrimination. Justice McKenna's observation in *Williams* – that as long as "the operation of the constitution and laws…reach weak and vicious White men as well as weak and vicious black men…[i]t cannot be said that the denial of the equal protection of the laws arises primarily from the constitution and laws of Mississippi" – would fit comfortably in the Fifth Circuit's *Harness* opinion, written over a century later.[17] Very little had changed.[18]

Although elected officials felt a sense of urgency because of threats posed by the Lodge Force Act, the reality was that Mississippi's 1890 convention was the culmination of a decades-long effort to disenfranchise the state's Black voters. Indeed, the withdrawal of federal troops from the South after the 1876 presidential election was

14 *Williams v. Mississippi*, 170 U.S. 213 (1898).

15 Compare *Abbott v. Perez*, 585 U.S. 579 (2018) (holding that a prior legislature's discriminatory intent does not carry over to a subsequent legislature, which is presumed to have acted in good faith even when enacts the discriminatory redistricting maps drafted by the prior legislature).

16 Compare *Strauder v. West Virginia*, 100 U.S. 303 (1879) (invalidating a state law that, on its face, explicitly excluded Black people from jury service). See also "No Discrimination: The Election Law of Mississippi Sustained by the Supreme Court," *Baltimore Sun*, July 21, 1898 ("In disposing of the case, Justice McKenna said that it could not be held that either the constitution of the State or the laws enacted under its provisions discriminate directly against the negro race.").

17 *Williams v. Mississippi*, 170 U.S. 213, 222 (1898).

18 As Professor Richard Pildes has noted, *Williams* left open the possibility that discriminatory effects could potentially violate the Constitution, but *Giles v. Harris*, discussed later in this chapter, effectively foreclosed this possibility. Richard H. Pildes, "Democracy, Anti-Democracy, and the Canon" (2000) 17 *Constitutional Commentary* 295, 298 n. 12.

a pivotal moment in all southern states, including Mississippi, as it signaled a new era of racial discrimination in voting. The number of Black legislators had already dropped from 115 in 1867 to 16 in 1876; by 1896, no Black legislators remained.[19]

Many congressional districts that were once guaranteed Republican seats became Democratic districts. For example, the Second Congressional District in Mississippi, which was vacant from 1860 to 1869, had been safely Republican since 1870. In 1876, the district elected its first Democrat since the Civil War, a feat that, as the House Committee on Elections observed, had been achieved by terrorizing Black voters.[20] In *Chalmers v. Morgan* (1889), a contested election in the second congressional district during the Fifty-First Congress (1889–91), the Committee noted how that election had been marked by disenfranchising techniques that became commonplace after the Democrats gained control of the Mississippi district thirteen years earlier. These tactics included:

- Constructing partisan election boards that had no members other than Democrats, or having Republican representatives who, by reason of ignorance and illiteracy, were not "competent and suitable men";
- Removing duly qualified and registered voters from the voter registration lists; and
- Stealing or unlawful removal of ballot boxes (or hiding boxes from the view of the United States supervisors).[21]

Despite the irregularities in the 1888 race, the Republican-led Committee concluded that there was insufficient evidence to show that the contestee, Democrat James B. Morgan, was unlawfully elected. The contestant, Independent James R. Chalmers, had not established that the fraud was widespread enough to call the outcome into doubt.

While some precincts had clearly been marred by fraud and disenfranchisement, there were enough precincts where this was not the case, which meant that the Committee could not conclude that Chalmers had won the election.[22]

19 Alexander Tsesis, *We Shall Overcome: A History of Civil Rights and the Law* (New Haven: Yale University Press, 2008), p. 117.

20 "Chalmers v. Morgan (1889–1891)," in Asher C. Hinds, *Hinds' Precedents of the House of Representatives of the United States*, 5 vols. (Washington, D.C.: United States Government Printing Office, 1907), v. 2, p. 498. The committee noted,

> Not to indulge in further comment on this subject, it will be manifest to any fair-minded man who will read the testimony in this case, that measures were resorted to in many places in the Second Congressional district of Mississippi at the election in question, to terrorize the colored voters and to keep them from the polls, and the record abounds in proof that many of the colored men were prevented by fear from attempting to exercise their right of suffrage. Nor is evidence wanting that this is a favorite method of long standing of "shutting down upon" the Republican voters of this district, which up until 1876, and prior to the inauguration of the "shotgun policy," was a Republican district by a large majority. Ibid.

21 Ibid.

22 Ibid.

The Committee presumed that ballot boxes that did not appear to have been tampered with were valid (even if these boxes were in precincts with other boxes that had been compromised), a contention that a minority of the Committee challenged given the widespread fraud.[23]

Chalmers v. Morgan illustrated that Republican control of Congress did not necessarily guarantee favorable results for Black voters. Another contested election case from this period, *Hill v. Catching*, also failed to overturn election results despite the existence of widespread fraud and racial discrimination in voting.[24] The relevant rule at the time was that the person challenging the election had to prove that the outcome would have been different in the absence of fraud, although Republicans would relax this rule in subsequent Congresses. In determining the outcome in *Hill v. Catching*, Democrats voted cohesively in favor of Catching, a fellow Democrat, but the Republican Party did not uniformly support Hill, the Republican contestant. The split among Republicans led to an outcome in which the fraud was deemed not dispositive to the outcome.

This was certainly an odd result, given that the Committee could not help but note the extent of the disenfranchisement, which seemed more far reaching than what had been at issue in *Chalmers v. Morgan*:

> In a majority of the precincts, about which evidence was taken, we find that the precinct inspectors appointed to represent the Republicans were either Democrats in fact, or were incompetent and untrustworthy. ... In several large Republican precincts no elections were held, and it is manifest that the neglect to hold elections was intentional and for the purpose of depriving contestant of the votes which he otherwise would have received. In one instance the poll books were carried off to prevent the holding of an election. While there is some conflict in the evidence, we are convinced that the whole matter was arranged at a Democratic meeting the night before the election.[25]

The Committee found that these facts went to the weight that the Committee should ascribe to the evidence, rather than used to render the results invalid.

A number of election contests in the Fifty-First Congress came to a similar result: yes, there was fraud, but not enough to make a difference in the outcome.[26] Contestants often had to establish that the entire election machinery had been captured to make headway on their claims. For example, in the Arkansas case of *Featherston v. Cate*, the Committee invalidated an election in pretty dystopian

23 Ibid., p. 499.

24 "Hill v. Catching (1889–1891)," in Hinds, *Hinds' Precedents of the House of Representatives of the United States*, v. 2, p. 509.

25 Ibid., p. 510.

26 "Kernaghan v. Hooker (1889–1891)," in Hinds, *Hinds' Precedents of the House of Representatives of the United States*, v. 2, p. 512; "Atkinson v. Pendleton (1889–1891)," in Hinds, *Hinds' Precedents of the House of Representatives of the United States*, v. 2, p. 451.

circumstances: an armed mob took control of the election machinery in the district; the sheriff failed to deliver ballots as the law required; and the county clerk failed to certify votes for the contestant in various townships where elections were held.[27] The contestant was able to show that, but for these outrages, the outcome would have been different.

Comparatively, the contested elections in Mississippi involved a mix of fraudulent results from some precincts and legitimate results from others, and the Committee was not willing to throw out lawful ballots with those that were fraudulent. One has to admire their ability to separate the wheat from the chaff, or it may have been that the thin margin in which they were operating made Republicans reluctant to be viewed as overtly partisan – in 1888, Republicans only had an eleven-seat majority in the House of Representatives. Altering election outcomes in which the fraud was clear, undisputed, and pivotal to the outcome was arguably a barrier against claims of partisanship.

Because the bar had been set so high, it came as no surprise that Congress's response to Mississippi's 1890 constitution was mostly nonexistent. In 1895, the Republican-controlled House Committee on Elections heard a series of cases in which the contestants explicitly argued that the Mississippi Constitution was void and that elections held under its terms should be set aside. In each of the three cases – *Newman v. Spencer, Ratcliff v. Williams,* and *Brown v. Allen*[28] – the contestants challenged the validity of Section 241 of the Mississippi Constitution. In addition to its strict residency requirements and felon disenfranchisement language, Section 241 also codified the state's poll tax, which required:

> Every male inhabitant of this State, except idiots, insane persons and Indians not taxed, who is a citizen of the United States, twenty-one years old and upwards… and who has paid, on or before the first day of February of the year in which he shall offer to vote, all taxes which may have been legally required of him, and which he has had an opportunity of paying according to law, for the two preceding years, and who shall produce to the officers holding the election satisfactory evidence that he has paid said taxes, is declared to be a qualified elector…[29]

Apparently, the Committee was not troubled by the fact that voters in a mostly agrarian society, whose income came from the fall harvest (August–November), had to pay a poll tax in February for an election the following November. Instead, the Committee concluded that, "a decision that the constitution of the State of Mississippi was invalid would not necessarily deprive the State of representation in

27 "Featherstone v. Cate (1889–1891)," in Hinds, *Hinds' Precedents of the House of Representatives of the United States*, v. 2, pp. 456–458.

28 "Newman v. Spencer; Ratcliff v. Williams; Brown v. Allen (1895–1897)," in Hinds, *Hinds' Precedents of the House of Representatives of the United States*, v. 1, p. 976.

29 Constitution of the State of Mississippi art. XII, s. 241 (1890).

Congress" and dismissed the contests. How one can be duly elected by an electorate determined by a void instrument remains a mystery.

Mississippi's constitution served as a model for other states seeking to emulate its success in disenfranchising African Americans,[30] but the effect of some of the restrictions on White voters did not go unnoticed.[31] While Mississippi viewed these voters as unfortunate casualties of a hard-fought war between the races, other states – like Virginia – experimented with different variations of Mississippi's approach to maximize African American disenfranchisement while limiting the impact on White voters.

9.2 "IF YOU ARE IN LINE, YOU CAN VOTE": NOT IN VIRGINIA

Although Mississippi was the first mover, the pace of Jim Crow and formal disenfranchisement varied across the South. Virginia – the seat of the Confederacy – was a bit behind the ball relative to its sister states. Prior to 1901, there had been piecemeal efforts toward disenfranchising Black people through segregated lines, long wait times, and hyper technicalities but nothing as expansive amending the state constitution to change voter qualification standards.[32]

Formal Jim Crow would come later, when the state's Democrats became a party unified behind White Supremacy, rather than a many-headed beast battling over the public debt and against the biracial, fusion politics of the "Readjusters," who advocated for reducing the debt, improving the public school system, and abolishing the poll tax.[33] Prior to the 1901 constitutional convention, Congress played an important, but inconsistent, role in policing the fraud and discrimination that would have otherwise derailed African American representation in the state.

For example, the 1889 election contest of *Langston v. Venable*, decided during the Fifty-First Congress (1889–91), involved a successful challenge filed by John M. Langston before the Republican-controlled House Committee on Elections. Langston contested the results of the election in Virginia's Fourth Congressional

30 "Comments of Representative Crumpacker, Fifty-Sixth Congress, Second Session, January 7, 1901," 34 *Congressional Record* (Washington, D.C., Government Printing Office, 1901), Appendix, p. 68 (noting that "by operation of the law in the State of Mississippi over 42 percent of the male inhabitants 21 years of age who are citizens of the United State are disfranchised, while in the State of Massachusetts not exceeding 3 per cent are disfranchised.").

31 See Perman, *Struggle for Mastery*, p. 89 ("According to the secretary of state's records, the vote in the 1892 congressional election was a mere 69,905 white votes and 9,036 black out of a total state population of 1.27 million. The fact that the white vote had also fallen considerably caused little concern.").

32 The use of segregated lines had long been a tactic used by White election administrators to disenfranchise African Americans who had been able to successfully navigate the obstacle of voter registration. See, e.g., "Stovell v. Cabell (1882)," in Hinds, *Hinds' Precedents of the House of Representatives of the United States*, v. 1, p. 877 (involving a similar claim). See also Brent Tarter, *The Grandees of Government: The Origins and Persistence of Undemocratic Politics in Virginia* (Charlottesville: University of Virginia Press, 2013), p. 263.

33 Tarter, *The Grandees of Government*, pp. 245–246.

District, which was marked by the same fraud at the ballot box that was commonplace across the South prior to the disenfranchising constitutional conventions.

Langston, like Josiah T. Walls of Florida, was a Renaissance man. He had served as a conductor on the Underground Railroad; was the first Black person admitted to the Ohio bar; had been appointed inspector general of the Freedmen's Bureau; was the founding dean of Howard Law School in Washington, D.C.; and served as President of Virginia State University.[34] Langston was also the Minister of Haiti under President Rutherford Hayes; Minister of the Dominican Republic under President Chester A. Arthur; and, sadly, the first and only Black member of Congress (both chambers!) elected from Virginia for almost a century.

This latter accomplishment had almost been denied to Langston. The reported results of the November 1888 election had Langston's Democratic opponent, E.C. Venable, ahead by 641 votes. The House Committee on Elections, while noting that "mere irregularities in the conduct of the election" were usually not actionable, found that the election in the Fourth Congressional District suffered from fatal errors.[35] For example, election administrators did not count lawful ballots cast for Langston because of mistakes that voters made with respect to other races on the ballot.[36] There were other irregularities in the election as well including: last minute changes to the composition of the election judges (almost all of whom refused to testify about the election); ballots cast in excess of the number of names on the poll lists; and the relocation of the election from its usual site.

Finally, some majority-African American precincts reported results favorable to Venable on Election Day, but Black voters filed affidavits stating that they were prevented from voting. In the sixth ward of Petersburg, Virginia, for example, election administrators had voters stand in lines segregated by race. Because Black voters outnumbered White voters 3-to-1 in that precinct, Black people were disproportionately impacted when the poll closed at sunset, and people still in line were turned away. Fourteen White voters were disenfranchised because of the segregated lines, as compared to the 308 Black voters who were rejected, mostly because of delays by election officials who claimed that they could not find their names in the registration book.[37]

Langston v. Venable also established the lengths to which White Democrats would go to prevent African Americans from testifying about their disenfranchisement,

34 Maxwell Bloomfield, "John Mercer Langston and the Rise of Howard Law School" (1971/1972) 71/72 *Records of the Columbia Historical Society* 421–438.

35 "Langston v. Venable (1889–1891)," in Hinds, *Hinds' Precedents of the House of Representatives of the United States*, v. 2, p. 486.

36 Ibid. ("This vote was regularly returned to the county commissioners, but not counted for the alleged reason that the same returns showed certain votes cast for candidates for President and Vice-President instead of for electors of President and Vice-President. For this mistake of the judges not only the electoral vote of this precinct was thrown out, but the vote for every other candidate upon the ticket was rejected by the county commissioners.").

37 Ibid., p. 491.

even in the context of an official congressional proceeding. Langston and his attorney deposed many of those Black men disenfranchised on Election Day as a part of their filing before the House Committee on Elections. During one such deposition, a witness, F.N. Robinson, was arrested by a deputy United States marshal after his direct examination because the opposing counsel swore out a warrant, falsely accusing Robinson of a crime. Because Robinson was arrested prior to the cross-examination, the counsel objected to Robinson's testimony on the grounds that they had not cross-examined him.[38]

Despite these shenanigans, the Committee found that it was unable to count 124 votes because these individuals had not been deposed as a part of the proceeding. While these votes would have been relevant for determining whether Venable would keep his seat, they could not be added to Mercer's total.[39]

In coming to this conclusion, the Committee referenced the election contest of *Waddill v. Wise* (1889),[40] which had similar facts as *Langston v. Venable*. Like *Langston*, the *Waddill* contest also involved the disenfranchisement of African American voters who waited in segregated lines but were then turned away when the polls closed at sunset, following a series of manufactured delays by election administrators and frivolous challenges by poll watchers.[41] In *Waddill*, the contestant was able to call these individuals as witnesses, whereas Langston was not able to do so (in part because of the mischief of opposing counsel in making witnesses unavailable).[42]

Even without these 124 votes added to his total, however, Langston was able to establish a plurality of 731 votes over Venable, giving him the seat. The circumstances surrounding *Langston v. Venable* were a paradigmatic example of consistent malfeasance by election officials to prevent Black voters from successfully casting their ballots, malfeasance that the House Committee on Elections inconsistently policed in challenges arising during this period.[43]

For example, in *Wise v. Young*, out of the Fifty-Fifth (1897–99) Congress, the House confronted claims that Virginia election officials rejected lawful votes, fraudulently marked the ballots of illiterate voters, and falsified returns to help elect the

[38] Ibid., p. 492.

[39] Ibid. ("The committee is, however, of the opinion that if these 124 votes equaled or exceeded the plurality returned for the contestee, so that the legality of the election depended upon them, it would invalidate his election with no further proof and make a new election necessary...Taking this view of the case, the 124 voters prevented from casting their ballots must be considered for the purpose of unseating the contestee only, but cannot be considered in favor of contestant's right to his seat.").

[40] "Waddil v. Wise (1889–1891)," in Hinds, *Hinds' Precedents of the House of Representatives of the United States*, v. 2, p. 469.

[41] Ibid., p. 470.

[42] The problems in these cases were often evidentiary. See "Stovell v. Cabell (1881–1883)," in Hinds, *Hinds' Precedents of the House of Representatives of the United States*, v. 1, p. 877.

[43] Compare "Chalmers v. Morgan (1889–1891)" in Hinds, *Hinds' Precedents of the House of Representatives of the United States*, v. 1, p. 499; "Hill v. Catching (1889–1891)," ibid., p. 509.

Democrat, Young.[44] In some ways, Virginia law helped to facilitate this fraud even without the formal amendment that would come later. State law required that election administrators have different partisan affiliations but provided no penalty should this provision be violated. In addition, the form and arrangement of Virginia's Australian ballot,[45] which had byzantine requirements instructing voters to mark "through three-fourths of the name" of the candidates whom the voter did not want to select (as opposed to simply circling the name of the voter's preferred candidate), was not provided to the voter prior to Election Day.[46] This meant that illiterate voters had no way to familiarize themselves with the ballot ahead of time and were left to the day-of whims of election judges.

The Committee on Elections tasked with adjudicating *Wise v. Young* found themselves bound by the Virginia Supreme Court's holding that the Australian ballot was constitutional.[47] *Wise v. Young* nonetheless determined that the ballots of voters negatively affected by the law should be counted.[48] As the Committee noted, "nearly one-sixth of the entire vote cast for congressmen were thrown out as defective, and one-fourth of the entire vote cast for Presidential electors."[49] The majority found that there were ten precincts in which voters claimed that they intended to vote for the Republican Wise, but with the "help" of election judges, all of whom were Democrats, their ballots were marked for Democrat Young. In addition, a number of Black voters testified that they were refused registration, but had they been allowed to register, they would have cast their votes for Wise.[50] There was also significant evidence of ballot box stuffing.

The Committee concluded that, because of this fraud, the votes for Democrat Young from these precincts had to be discarded. In forty-four other precincts, Wise produced testimony from almost 5,000 voters who intended to vote for him even though election administrators reported only 3,729 votes in his favor from those precincts. In twenty-nine precincts, voters were obstructed and delayed from casting ballots, much like the voters seeking to vote in the election between Langston and

44 "Wise v. Young (1897–1899)," in Hinds, *Hinds' Precedents of the House of Representatives of the United States*, v. 2, p. 650.

45 The term "Australian secret ballot" is "applied to the particular form which America borrowed from Australia and which the State of Massachusetts led the way in adopting in 1889. But it is also used to designate any secret ballot printed and furnished by the State." Philip L. Allen, "The Multifarious Australian Ballot" (1910) 191/654 *North American Review* 602–611, 602.

46 See "Wise v. Young (1897–1899)," in Hinds, *Hinds' Precedents of the House of Representatives of the United States*, v.2, p. 651 ("The ballot was marked by drawing a line through the names of the candidates whom the elector did not wish to vote for, and no name was to be considered scratched unless the mark extended through three-fourths of the name.").

47 Ibid.

48 Ibid. (the Committee found that it could not count ballots that had failed to mark "through three-fourths of the name" of rejected candidates as the law required, even if the intent of the voter was apparent from the ballot).

49 Ibid., p. 651.

50 Ibid., p. 652.

Venable. Once all of these votes were included in the tally, the number was more than sufficient to establish that Wise was the winner of the seat.

Wise v. Young occurred on the eve of substantial changes to Virginia's election system. Virginia delegates, like their counterparts in Mississippi over a decade earlier, descended upon Richmond in 1901 for the express purpose of crafting a document that would facilitate the "legal" disenfranchisement of Black voters, or in the words of delegate Carter Glass: "Discrimination! Why, that is precisely what we propose; that, exactly, is what this Convention was elected for – to discriminate to the very extremity of permissible action under the limitations of the Federal Constitution, with a view to the elimination of every negro voter who can be gotten rid of, legally…"[51]

Many of the delegates recalled a time, in 1869, in which the state constitution had come perilously close to being amended to disenfranchise White Confederates; the fact that Republicans had not won statewide office since 1882 did not stop Virginia Democrats from pointing to this moment to raise the specter of "Negro rule."[52]

In 1901, delegates to the state constitutional convention, made up entirely of White males, adopted a constitution that, like its sister states, targeted African Americans in intent and effect. Drafted by Carter Glass, its suffrage provisions, which went into effect in 1902, contained a residency requirement for all potential voters – two years in the State, one year in the precinct – but otherwise limited registration to military veterans, their children, property owners, or those who could pass a literacy test or explain any section of the state constitution.[53]

The poll tax, also a prerequisite to registration, required that voters be paid up for three years prior to when they cast a ballot.[54] Notably, military veterans – including those who served in the Confederate army – were exempt from paying the poll tax.[55] While the Supreme Court would sustain the constitutionality of literacy tests over a half century later,[56] Virginia's $1.50 poll tax would be struck down in the watershed 1966 case of *Harper v. Virginia State Board of Elections*, which formally recognized

51 *Report of the Proceedings and Debates of the Constitution Convention of the State of Virginia*, 2 vols. (Richmond: Hermitage Press, 1906), v. 2, p. 3076.

52 Wythe W. Holt, Jr., "The Virginia Constitutional Convention of 1901–1902: A Reform Movement Which Lacked Substance" (1968) 76/1 *Virginia Magazine of History and Biography* 67–102, 70.

53 Constitution of the State of Virginia art. II, s. 19.

54 Art. II, s. 20 of the Virginia Constitution provided that:

> After the first day of January, nineteen hundred and four, every male citizen of the United States, having the qualifications of age and residence required in section Eighteen, shall be entitled to register, provided…That he has personally paid to the proper officer all state poll taxes assessed or assessable against him, under this or the former Constitution, for the three years next preceding that in which he offers to register; or, if he come of age at such time that no poll tax shall have been assessable against him for the year preceding the year in which he offers to register, has paid one dollar and fifty cents, in satisfaction of the first year's poll tax assessable against him…

55 Ibid., art. II, s. 22.

56 *Lassiter v. Northampton County Board of Elections*, 360 U.S. 45 (1959).

a constitutionally protected right to vote in state elections under the Fourteenth Amendment.[57]

The 1902 state constitution also centralized election administration to give state officials greater control over the political community of "We the Voters," a departure from the decentralized process that had been integral in facilitating disenfranchisement through fraud and disparate implementation.[58] This decentralization had led to ballot stuffing, subterfuge, and violence that, as historian Brent Tarter has observed, disgusted many Virginians,[59] and because of Congress's power under Article I, Section 5 to judge elections, did not necessarily ensure a particular outcome for federal races. Limiting the ability of African Americans to become registered voters, as the 1902 constitution did, solved a lot of these problems.

Importantly, its provisions did not entirely eliminate local administrator discretion. The laws subsequently passed to implement the new constitution subjected voters to a labyrinth of annual re-registration requirements that gave local officials significant discretion over whether poor White men and all Black men qualified as voters. Thus, the disenfranchisement of at least some poor White men was inevitable, and Carter Glass's observation, during the convention, that the constitution's provisions "would 'not necessarily deprive a single White man of the ballot but will inevitably cut from the existing electorate four-fifths of the negro voters'" was not entirely correct.[60] But, as to Black men, it was mostly accurate.

Virginia's constitution was as brutally effective as those in its sister states – in 1900, approximately 147,000 Black voters were on the rolls. By 1904, two years after the constitution was ratified, this number had fallen by 85 percent.[61] Notably, the

57 *Harper v. Virginia State Board of Elections*, 383 U.S. 663 (1966).

58 Constitution of the State of Virginia art. II, s. 25.

59 Tarter, *The Grandees of Government*, pp. 263–264. According to one election official, proud of his handiwork:

> A judge of the election would take the Republican ticket in his left hand, from the voter, but put in the box a Democratic ticket, which he had concealed in his right hand. Another common trick was to put a handful of Democratic tickets in the ballot box, when the Republican judge was taking a drink of water or liquor, or had turned his back. Sometimes, when the judge would go to dinner or to the toilet, a duplicate box, filled with Democratic tickets, would be substituted for the original box. Then sometimes the Democrats would have two tickets printed, a large one that most people voted, and which was shown around, and a very small one which the Republicans never saw until the ballot box was opened at night. The old reliables would fold three or four of these small tickets into such a small package that the size was no larger than a regular ticket. When the ballot box was opened, all seemed very much surprised that it contained many more tickets than voters. Of course, this trick was pulled off in the Republican precincts. The officials either had to throw out the whole vote in that precinct or blind-fold a judge and get him to draw out the excessive number of tickets.

Ibid.

60 Ibid., p. 267.

61 Kevin Anderson, "Civil Rights Groups Respond," in Michael A. Smith, *Much Sound and Fury, or the New Jim Crow?: The Twenty-First Century's Restrictive New Voting Laws and their Impact* (New York: State University of New York Press, 2022), p. 147.

Virginia Constitution was not submitted to the voters out of fear that the White men disenfranchised under its provisions would not vote for it.[62] Delegates simply declared that the 1902 constitution replaced its 1870 counterpart, which meant that this anti-democratic and anti-republican document ironically went into effect without popular support.

Long before Virginia's discriminatory constitution would shrink the electorate by double digits, Congress realized that policing select elections through its power under Article I, Section 5 would not be enough to counter sustained efforts to eject African Americans from the political community of "We the Voters," particularly when these efforts were punctuated with extreme violence. Indeed, the process of Black disenfranchisement in North Carolina led to a coup on American soil – namely, the overthrow of a biracial government in Wilmington, North Carolina, in 1898.

9.3 THE RESURGENCE OF ALTER OR ABOLISH: THE DEMISE OF REPUBLICAN GOVERNMENT IN NORTH CAROLINA

Between Reconstruction and Redemption, Wilmington, North Carolina, maintained a hierarchy similar to that which had existed prior to the Civil War: a business class that included the planters who dominated the economic pyramid; White working-class laborers in the middle; and free Black people at the bottom (a class that now included the formerly enslaved). Wilmington, the state's largest city at the time, had a robust Republican Party that maintained a dominant presence even as North Carolina itself was being "redeemed" by Democrats and former Confederates.[63]

The violent events in Wilmington in 1898 occurred at the tail end of almost three decades of political upheaval across the state, and this episode would demonstrate that the most violent form of alter or abolish, presumably displaced by a Civil War and subsequent constitutional amendment, had not only survived but thrived. After the November 1870 impeachment of William Woods Holden, the Republican governor who tried to bring Klansmen to justice for persecuting Black people,[64] Democrats effectively controlled the state government for much of the next two decades. Republican candidates were usually victorious only where federal troops were present to ensure somewhat free elections.

Black officeholders were successful in some of these elections, most notably in the "Black Second" district where voters routinely elected Black officials to state and

62 Tarter, *The Grandees of Government*, p. 270 ("Eleven months after the Constitution of 1902 went into effect, the Supreme Court of Appeals took judicial notice that all of the state officials, including members of the General Assembly and the judges of the court themselves, had taken an oath to support and defend the new constitution and were exercising their duties under it.").

63 LeRae Umfleet, *Report of the 1898 Wilmington Race Riot Commission* (Raleigh: North Carolina Department of Cultural Resources, 2006), https://digital.ncdcr.gov/digital/collection/p249901coll22/id/5842/.

64 Ibid., p. 23.

federal office.[65] But post-1876, the party was subject to many of the same repressive tactics as Republicans elsewhere across the South: gerrymandering;[66] voter suppression; racial propaganda in newspapers; and violence and intimidation. With the re-election of Zebulon Vance, North Carolina's wartime governor (and the subject of an 1868 Senate election challenge discussed in Chapter 6), the end of the Republican Party's presence in statewide politics was assured.[67]

While Black voters remained loyal to the Republican Party during the 1880s, the party's diminishing presence meant that Black support became attractive to any coalition seeking to upset the Democratic Party's control of the election apparatus. Republicans did not become competitive again until the mid-1890s, when they partnered with the Populist Party to challenge Democratic dominance in statewide politics. The Populist Party created a biracial coalition centered around economic issues, offering possible solutions to the financial problems that plagued Black people and poor White people alike throughout the latter half of the nineteenth century.[68] The party also offered a pipeline for less affluent White men to exercise meaningful political power; a split within the Democratic Party (which also included a faction of "Reform" Democrats willing to solicit Black support) also provided an opening for the Populists to successfully compete in the 1894 and 1896 elections.[69] As a result of their partnership, Republicans and Populists gained control of the state legislature and Wilmington's local government.[70]

During this period, the House Committee on Elections used its authority under Article I, Section 5 to police North Carolina elections that had been marred by substantial fraud and disenfranchisement, but with mixed results. In *Williams v. Settle*, a case from the Fifty-Third Congress (1893–95), the Democrat-led House Committee on Elections rejected ballots from voters improperly registered by state officials through no fault of their own because the North Carolina Supreme Court had already determined that those votes were invalid.[71] North Carolina law stated that, "No registration shall be valid unless it specifies, as near as may be, the age,

65 Benjamin R. Justesen, "Black Tip, White Iceberg: Black Postmasters and the Rise of White Supremacy in North Carolina, 1897–1901" (2005) 82 N.C. Hist. Rev. 193–227, 194 ("Three of the five Republicans elected to Congress from the Second District between 1874 and 1890 were African American, serving a total of five terms. Each insisted on his limited patronage right to appoint other black officeholders.").

66 Umfleet, *1898 Wilmington Race Riot Report*, p. 24.

67 Ibid., p. 25.

68 "The political landscape of North Carolina was extremely complex throughout the 1890s. Members of the Populist Party, led by reformers and grass-roots activities, had aligned themselves with Republicans and African Americans to smash the hegemony of the Democratic Party in 1894." James M. Beeby, "Red Shirt Violence, Election Fraud, and the Demise of the Populist Party in North Carolina's Third Congressional District, 1900" (2008) 85/1 *The North Carolina Review* 1–28, 4.

69 Umfleet, *1898 Wilmington Race Riot Report*, pp. 37, 40.

70 Ibid.

71 "William v. Settle (1893–1895)," in Hinds, *Hinds' Precedents of the House of Representatives of the United States*, v. 2, p. 536.

occupation, place of birth, and place of residence of the elector, as well as the township or county from whence the elector has removed, in the event of removal, and the full name by which the voter is known."[72]

While the minority also endorsed the proposition that the Committee should follow state court interpretations of state law, they accused the majority of citing to the dissent rather than the majority opinion, which noted that these votes should not be disregarded if there was a "failure [by the registrar] to enter upon the registration books such facts connected with [the voter's] history as the statute requires."[73] Thus, the proposition that the House Committee on Elections was bound by a state court determination of state law seemed to be a nonpartisan proposition, but there was often partisan disagreement about what the state court actually held and which portions of state court opinions should be controlling.

Nevertheless, the Committee, particularly at times in which its composition was majority Republican, was unequivocal in rejecting election results where there was uncontradicted evidence that election officials purposely disenfranchised voters. In *Martin v. Lockhart* (Fifty-Fourth Congress) (1895–97), the Committee heard evidence that election officials had rejected voters by claiming nonexistent irregularities with their registrations or after frivolous challenges.[74] Noting the discriminatory implementation of the North Carolina's voter registration law, the Committee observed that:

> The Constitution of the State provided that there should be a registration of voters, and that "no person shall be allowed to vote without registration." And the law required the registration to specify certain things in order to be valid. It was admitted by one of the election officers in this precinct, a partisan of sitting Member, that during the registration he allowed ignorant voters to give defective particulars, not such as the law required, and wrote those particulars as given, when he knew that by registering them in such a way he was giving an excuse for the rejection of their votes when challenged. Thus, an ignorant voter, when asked his residence, would give the name of the plantation where he was employed instead of the township. The registrar knowingly recorded this defective description. In this precinct 307 White men and 414 colored men were registered, and of these, the votes of 1 White man and 167 colored men were rejected, some on grounds absolutely frivolous.[75]

North Carolina election officials also tried to generate confusion by marking the ballot boxes with "indistinct letters" rather than using the plain lettering required by law. As a result of these improprieties, the full House voted to seat the contestant, Populist Charles H. Martin, rather than the sitting Democrat, James Lockhart,

[72] Ibid.

[73] Ibid., p. 537.

[74] "Martin v. Lockhart (1895–1897)," in Hinds, *Hinds' Precedents of the House of Representatives of the United States*, v. 2, p. 627.

[75] Ibid., pp. 627–628.

by counting the lawful ballots that had been rejected and discarding questionable returns from precincts in which the poll list showed discrepancies.

Similarly, in *Pearson v. Crawford* (Fifty-Sixth Congress) (1899–1901), the Republican-led House Committee on Elections overturned an election marked by bribery and numerous improprieties, including actions by officials who improperly registered voters in places other than those mandated by state law.[76] The Committee also rejected votes from a precinct in which the election judges stuffed ballot boxes.[77]

Despite using its power under Article I, Section 5 to aggressively police congressional elections across the South, this authority would be insufficient to stop the tide of violence from a motivated population of White supremacists. Such was the case in Wilmington, North Carolina, on November 10, 1898.

The fusion politics in the state led to the election of a biracial government in Wilmington in 1897. This government generated hostility from prominent White men, who were concerned about increasing Black prosperity, which they perceived as inversely related to a decline in White prominence. White elites in the city formed secret groups in 1897–98, most notably the White Government Union and the Red Shirts, with the end goal of securing the success of the Democrat Party and disenfranchising African Americans in the 1898 elections.[78]

Throughout the mid-1890s, the Democratic Party increased its efforts to suppress the Black vote in Wilmington, winning big in the 1898 elections by using fraud and violence to deter Black voters. Nevertheless, the fusion government that controlled the city did not come up for re-election in 1898 and became an attractive target of the Red Shirts following the November elections.

On November 9th, a group of White men gathered in the local courthouse to write "The White Declaration of Independence," which demanded that "Negro rule" be brought to an end because "the Negro has demonstrated by antagonizing our interests in every way, and especially by his ballot."[79] What followed was post–Election Day violence by a White mob that concluded with the murder of dozens of Black men; the destruction of Wilmington's Black newspaper, *The Record*; and a successful coup d'état that displaced the mayor, the Board of Aldermen, and the chief of police.[80]

Not surprisingly, the horrific violence in Wilmington; the reemergence of robust electoral competition; and the prospect of an active House of Representatives that could displace problematic elections generated an interest

76 "Pearson v. Crawford (1899–1901)," in Hinds, *Hinds' Precedents of the House of Representatives of the United States*, v. 2, pp. 681–682.

77 Ibid., pp. 683–684.

78 Umfleet, *1898 Wilmington Race Riot Report*, p. 55.

79 Ibid., p. 115.

80 Ibid., pp. 121, 154. See also David Zucchino, *Wilmington's Lie: The Murderous Coup of 1898 and the Rise of White Supremacy* (New York: Atlantic Monthly Press, 2020).

in "legal" discrimination in North Carolina, just as it had in other southern states. But instead of blindly following its sister states, North Carolina legislators viewed Louisiana as the paradigm.

With its 1898 Constitution, Louisiana adopted a residency requirement that reduced the size of the electorate.[81] Poll tax and literacy qualifications also mirrored those present in other state constitutions, requiring that a voter "read and write, and … demonstrate his ability to do so when he applies for registration, by making … written application therefore."[82] Over time, Louisiana's literacy requirement gained a reputation as one of the most stringent in the country, requiring not only that voters read and write but also the "ability … to make arithmetical calculations … in the presence of the registration officer."[83]

But for these purposes, it was Louisiana's grandfather clause, designed to insulate White people from being disenfranchised, that captured the imagination of North Carolina disenfranchisers.[84] Grandfather clauses had been around since the mid-nineteenth century. This device served as a temporary measure to protect illiterate and poor White men from disenfranchisement by allowing them to rely on their lineage to register to vote.[85] Unlike the literacy test or "understanding" clauses, the grandfather clause did not require the assistance of election administrators to reach its full disenfranchising potential.[86] It was, unfortunately for Black voters, fully self-executing.

Between 1899 and 1901, North Carolina amended its constitution to adopt a grandfather clause like that in Louisiana. Instead of a safe-harbor provision that gave significant discretion to election supervisors to register illiterate White people, the grandfather clause prevented anyone entitled to vote prior to January 1, 1867 (or before the ratification of the Fourteenth and Fifteenth Amendments) from being "denied the right to register and vote at any election in this state by reason of his failure to possess the educational qualification prescribed in section four of this article," that is, the literacy requirement under which every voter had to be able to "read and write any section of the constitution in the English language."[87]

81 See Constitution of the State of Louisiana art. 197, s. 1 (1898) ("He shall have been an actual bona-fide resident of this State for two years, of the parish one year and of the precinct in hich [sic] he offers to vote six months next preceding the election … .").

82 Ibid.

83 See "Comments of Representative Crumpacker, Fifty-Sixth Congress, Second Session, January 7, 1901," 34 *Congressional Record* (Washington, D.C.: Government Printing Office, 1901), Appendix, p. 70.

84 See Constitution of the State of Louisiana art. 197, s. 5. See also R. Volney Riser, "Disenfranchisement, the U.S. Constitution, and the Federal Courts: Alabama's 1901 Constitutional Convention Debates the Grandfather Clause" (2006) 48 *American Journal of Legal History* 251–253 (noting that "North Carolina's disenfranchisers had recast Louisiana's grandfather clause as a tried and true landmark of American constitutional development" because the Louisiana law had never been judicially invalidated).

85 Riser, "Disenfranchisement, the U.S. Constitution, and the Federal Courts," 237–279, 247–248.

86 Ibid., 251.

87 Constitution of the State of North Carolina art. VI, §§ 4–5 (1901).

North Carolina also borrowed piecemeal from other states in constructing its disenfranchising regime. Like Mississippi, for example, North Carolina also imposed a poll tax[88] and more stringent residency requirement.[89]

In the end, the 1901 North Carolina Constitution eliminated Black political influence in the state. The grandfather clause provided no avenue for registration for Black people, who were disenfranchised in the state prior to 1867. The literacy requirements were discriminately applied to Black voters, further undermining their political rights. In many counties, Black electoral participation was wiped out completely in no small part due to the state's poll tax. In 1896, roughly 126,000 Black North Carolinians were registered to vote.[90] By 1902, only about 4.2 percent of African American voters (or about 6,000 people) remained on the rolls, a drop of almost 95 percent.[91] By 1910, few Black voters existed and no Black legislators had served in the General Assembly in a decade.[92]

While there had been a decline in Black voting and Black officeholding over the preceding three decades – with a brief spike in Black participation in the mid-1890s thanks to fusion politics that generated some electoral wins – the state constitution ensured that "We the Voters" would remain an all-White space for the next two generations. And key to this success was not only a willingness to, but also a lack of consequences for, violently overthrowing any duly elected, diverse governments that could challenge the construct of "We the Voters" as a racially homogenous political community.

9.4 "GOOD LUCK WITH THE EIGHT BOXES": VOTER DISENFRANCHISEMENT IN SOUTH CAROLINA (WITH A SPECIAL NOD TO THE SEVENTH CONGRESSIONAL DISTRICT)

South Carolina Democrats had engaged in a two-decade quest to disenfranchise its Black majority, the state's largest demographic from 1820 to 1930.[93] In 1882, the Republican Party, which, by this time, was made up almost entirely of Black voters,

88 Ibid., art. VI, § 4 (1901) (amended 1920) ("[A]nd before he shall be entitled to vote he shall have paid on or before the first day of March of the year in which he proposes to vote his poll tax as prescribed by law for the previous year."). After disenfranchisement, North Carolina collected the poll tax from African Americans to fund African American schools.

89 Ibid., art. VI, § 2 (1901) (amended 1920) ("He shall have resided in the state of North Carolina for two years, in the county six months and in the precinct, ward or other election district in which he offers to vote four months next preceding the election … .").

90 Zucchino, *Wilmington's Lie*, p. 379.

91 Ibid.; Glenda E. Gilmore, *Gender and Jim Crow: Women and the Politics of White Supremacy in North Carolina, 1896–1920* (Chapel Hill: University of North Carolina Press, 1996), p. 125.

92 Justeen, "Black Tip, White Iceberg," 226; J. Morgan Kousser, *The Shaping of Southern Politics: Suffrage Restriction and the Establishment of the One-Party South, 1880–1910* (New Haven: Yale University Press, 1974), p. 241.

93 George B. Tindall, *South Carolina Negroes, 1877–1900*, reprinted ed. (Columbia: University of South Carolina Press, 2003), p. 1.

aligned themselves with White Democrats who had become disillusioned with their party over economic matters, resulting in both factions throwing their support behind the 1882 slate of the Greenback Party.[94]

Prominent Black Republicans routinely endorsed Greenback candidates, a coalition that caused significant alarm in a Democratic Party mired in internal disputes that had split its coalition. In the November 1882 elections, South Carolina's Greenback candidate for governor lost to the Democratic nominee but garnered a not inconsequential number of votes – 17,719 votes, compared to the winning candidate's 67,158 votes. Not surprisingly, this increase in fusion politics coincided with increased violence and new voting restrictions.[95]

Prior to the fall 1882 elections, the South Carolina state legislature adopted one of the most extensive disenfranchising regimes in the South. Notably, the laws were facially race-neutral – extending the right of suffrage "without distinction of race or color or former condition" so long as one is a "male citizen of the United States, of the age of twenty-one years and upwards, not laboring under the disabilities named in the Constitution … who shall have been a resident of the State for one year, and in the County in which he offers to vote for sixty days next preceding any general election."[96]

But the devil was in the details or, in this case, in the voter registration rules. The law enacted a one-time voter registration requirement for 1882 designed to substantially reduce the state's electorate. Section 93 of the General Statutes required the Supervisor of Registration to make a list of all qualified voters, but the supervisor only had to provide three weeks' notice of the time and place where prospective voters could register. Voters were given between one and three days to register.[97]

To avoid disenfranchising those White voters unable to register within this truncated window, the law permitted these individuals to appear before the Supervisor, who could "open his books at the County seat, to correct errors in registration, and to register such electors as failed to register at their respective precincts."[98] The Supervisor could also unilaterally add voters to the rolls who had not requested to be registered:

> At the conclusion of the registration hereinbefore provided for, the Supervisor of Registration shall revise the list; and in case it be made to appear to his satisfaction that there is a qualified voter in a precinct who has failed to register, he may, upon such evidence as he may think necessary, in his discretion, permit the name of such voter to be placed on said list, and issue a certificate therefore.[99]

94 Ibid., pp. 49–50.

95 Ibid., pp. 50–51.

96 *General Statues and Code of Civil Procedure of the State of South Carolina* (Columbia: James Woodrow, State Printer, 1882), tit. 2, ch. VII, s. 89, pp. 35–36.

97 Ibid., s. 93, p. 37 ("The time for registration shall not be less than one nor more than three days at each registration precinct").

98 Ibid.

99 Ibid. See also Kousser, *The Shaping of Southern Politics*, p. 89.

Unless the Supervisor of Registration added a voter who had missed the window at the close of registration, the one-to-three-day window was the only opportunity that voters had to register until *after* the next general election for State officers.[100] At that point, the law established a permanent registration scheme moving forward. Starting at the end of the 1884 election cycle, prospective voters could register "on the first Monday in each month, to and until the first Monday of July, preceding the following general election," after which registration would be closed until after the next election cycle, or fall 1886 (and so on).[101]

Election registrars also had broad authority to determine the eligibility of prospective voters, empowered by law to "administer to each person offering to vote an oath that he is qualified to vote at this election," according to the state constitution, with few restrictions on how this authority could be exercised.[102]

In lieu of the traditional literacy test, the law required voters to cast ballots in eight separate boxes that corresponded to each contested office – governor, lieutenant governor, other state officers, circuit solicitor, state senator, members of the state house, county officers, and congressional representatives.[103] Votes placed in the wrong box were discarded.[104] To prevent this regime from disenfranchising illiterate White people, the law empowered election officials to read the labels on the box upon a voter's request.[105]

The success of the state's restrictive voter registration and multiple-box laws was best indicated by the precipitous drop in the Republican Party's share of the vote in presidential elections during that decade, which fell from 58,071 in 1880 to 13,740 in 1888.[106] Despite the disenfranchisement, African Americans continued to be elected to office well into the 1890s. Like the Fourth Congressional District in Alabama,[107] Democrats gerrymandered a majority-Black district during the 1882 redistricting process to limit Republican influence – here, the Seventh Congressional District.

[100] *General Statues and Code of Civil Procedure of the State of South Carolina*, tit. 2, ch. VII, s. 94, p. 37.

[101] Ibid. ("When the said registration shall have been completed, the books shall be closed, and not reopened for registration, except for the purposes and as hereinafter mentioned, until after the next general election for State officers. After the said next general election the said books shall be reopened, for registration of such persons as shall thereafter become entitled to register, on the first Monday in each month, to and until the first Monday of July, inclusive, preceding the following general election, upon which last named day the same shall be closed and not reopened for registration, until after the said general election; and ever after the said book shall be opened for registration of such electors, on the days above mentioned, until the first day of July, preceding a general election, when the same shall be closed as aforesaid, until the said general election shall have taken place."). See also ibid., ch. VII, s. 107, p. 41 ("The general elections in this State shall be held on the first Tuesday following the first Monday in November in every second year ...").

[102] Ibid., s. 111, p. 42.

[103] Ibid., s. 116, p. 43.

[104] Ibid., s. 115, p. 43.

[105] Ibid., s. 117, pp. 43–44. See also Kousser, *The Shaping of Southern Politics*, p. 89.

[106] Tindall, *South Carolina Negroes*, p. 94.

[107] See Chapter 9.5. See also Introduction.

This district elected three Black men to office: Robert Smalls, Thomas Ezekiel Miller, and George Washington Murray.

Smalls – widely known as the "Gullah Statesman" – was a colorful character, rising to prominence during the Civil War when he stole a Confederate ship, the *Planter*, from Charleston harbor, delivered it to the Union navy, and later captained the *Planter* in a number of skirmishes with the Confederate navy.[108] Like his counterpart Josiah T. Walls in Florida, Smalls was a delegate to his respective state constitutional convention, served as a member of its state legislature, and, in 1874, was finally elected to the House of Representatives.

Prior to representing the Seventh Congressional District, Smalls faced a series of election contests in 1876 and 1878 against Democrat George Tillman in the Fifth Congressional District. In 1878, the Democratic-controlled House Committee on Elections found that Republican election administrators, without the knowledge or consent of the one Democratic administrator, illegally moved a polling place to allegedly enable Black Republicans to double vote.[109] After discarding half of the district's votes, the Committee declared the seat vacant.

Smalls, who had won the election, retained his seat in the 46th Congress because the full House never took up the case. Smalls won re-election in 1880, but was defeated in 1882 by a White Republican, E.W.M. Mackey. Smalls regained the seat, now in the Seventh Congressional District, after Mackey's death and was elected to a full term in 1884. In 1886, he lost his seat to Democrat William Elliott.[110]

Despite the fact that the Seventh Congressional District was a majority-African American district and would presumably be reliably Republican, Congress heard a series of election challenges from that district over the next two decades. This district was nearly always contested because Democrats continued to compete for the seat using force and fraud, and Republicans had almost no control over the election machinery after 1878, leaving room for malfeasance by Democratic election officials.

In 1888, Congress confronted the legality of South Carolina's 1882 voter registration law in deciding an election contest from the Seventh Congressional District between Thomas Miller and his Democratic opponent, William Elliott (*Miller v. Elliott I*).[111] Elliott was certified as the winner, but Miller alleged that fraud and irregularities led to Elliott's victory. In resolving the case, a majority of the House Committee on Elections determined that South Carolina's 1882 voter registration law was unconstitutional because of discriminatory application with respect to African American voters. According to the Committee:

108 "Robert Smalls Elected to Congress," *Chicago Daily Tribune*, March 19, 1884. See also Tindall, *South Carolina Negroes*, p. 55.

109 "Small v. Tillman (1875–1880)," in Hinds, *Hinds' Precedents of the House of Representatives of the United States*, v. 2, pp. 183–184.

110 Tindall, *South Carolina Negroes*, p. 55.

111 "Miller v. Elliott (1889–1891)," in Hinds, *Hinds' Precedents of the House of Representatives of the United States*, v. 2, p. 493.

> [T]housands of Republicans of the Seventh district were deprived of such certificates of registration as the managers would recognize. Hundreds of them went to the polls and presented their old certificates, only to find their names stricken from the books. Many of them were voters who had not changed their residence, even within the precinct of their residence. Some who, after much trouble, had secured transfer certificates, went to the polls and found that the description copied into the precinct registry did not agree with the description in their certificates, and so were unable to vote.[112]

The Committee also found that South Carolina's multiple-box law, which (if you recall) required voters to place their votes in the ballot boxes that corresponded to each office, was a violation of the state constitution. The Committee recognized that requiring voters to put their ballots in the proper box, otherwise it be discarded, was nothing more than "an educational test."[113]

Election administrators, who shifted the boxes and caused Miller to lose a thousand votes (according to federal election supervisors overseeing the election), further exacerbated the disenfranchisement that voters faced in the district. In one precinct in particular, the votes of Black Republicans never reached the county board.[114] The actions of the election administrators, according to the Committee, constituted a "crime at common law … [which makes it unlawful] to enter into a conspiracy to commit any offense against the purity and fairness of a public election."[115] While adding numbers to Miller's column, the Committee rejected ballots cast for Elliott, noting that there was substantial fraud and ballot box stuffing that gave Elliott the edge over the Republican Miller. In the end, the Committee awarded the seat to Miller,[116] based in part on their independent determination that the 1882 voter registration law was unconstitutional.

In 1890, Miller successfully defended his seat in the Seventh Congressional District in a contest, once again, against Democrat William Elliott (*Miller v. Elliott II*).[117] The election contest came down to alleged malfeasance by election officials. These officials rejected ballots that had been cast for Miller in four counties, on the grounds that the ballots were one-sixteenth of an inch too short and not printed on white paper as required by law. Once these votes were discarded, Elliott appeared to be the winner of the seat by 478 votes, a decision affirmed by the South Carolina Supreme Court in November of that year.[118]

112 Ibid., p. 494.
113 Ibid., p. 495.
114 Ibid., p. 496.
115 Ibid.
116 Ibid., p. 497.
117 "Miller v. Elliott (1892–1894)," in Hinds, *Hinds' Precedents of the House of Representatives of the United States*, v. 2, p. 527.
118 Ibid., p. 528.

Miller contested the election results. In *Miller v. Elliott II*, a majority of the House Committee on Elections, now controlled by Democrats, sided with Elliott, noting that Miller's ballots not only destroyed the secrecy of the ballot because they were easily identifiable, the fact that the ballots were printed on "dirty white paper" rather than "plain white paper" with his name dropped lower down on the ticket and visible from the back "enable[ed] the name to be easier seen."[119] The majority found that the South Carolina law requiring that the ballot be of "plain white paper of two and a half inches wide by five inches long, clear and even cut, without ornament, designation, mutilation, symbol, or mark of any kind whatsoever…" was mandatory and not optional, such that Miller's deviations from the law required that nonconforming ballots be discarded.[120] By this point, it would have been symbolic to displace Elliot since the Committee issued its report on February 23, 1893 – about two weeks before the end of the Fifty-Second Congress (1891–93). Miller was therefore able to retain his seat.

In 1892, George Washington Murray defeated Miller in the Republican primary for South Carolina's seventh district and went on to win the general election to serve as the district's representative in the Fifty-Third Congress (1893–95). Although successfully elected, Murray found himself in a vastly different political environment than Miller had been in just a few years earlier.

Murray, along with other prominent African Americans, served as delegates to the 1894 state constitutional convention, which adopted a more onerous voter registration regime than that which existed under the 1882 statute. Murray, for his part, raised money to fund litigation to challenge the earlier registration law and prevent the restrictions adopted during the 1894 constitutional convention from going into effect.[121] These new voting restrictions furthered the central aim of the constitutional convention, which was to eliminate any possibility that rival factions within the Democratic Party could rely on African American voters to swing an election.[122]

While South Carolina did not adopt the Australian secret ballot, which could have had a negative impact on illiterate White residents,[123] its 1895 constitution finished the job started by its 1882 voter registration law, which had disenfranchised 75 percent of the African Americans in the state by minimizing the political influence

[119] Ibid., p. 529.

[120] Ibid., p. 528.

[121] W. Lewis Burke, "Killing, Cheating, Legislating, and Lying: A History of Voting Rights in South Carolina after the Civil War" (2006) 57 *South Carolina Law Review* 859–888, 871.

[122] Perman, *Struggle for Mastery*, p. 96.

[123] Kousser, *The Shaping of Southern Politics*, p. 53 ("About one of every four white males of voting age in the United States in 1900 had been born abroad, two-thirds of these in non-English-speaking countries…. It seems probable, therefore, that many immigrants did not have a sufficient command of English to complete their ballots unassisted."). A good point of comparison is Louisiana. The secret ballot had a devastating impact on its electorate in the 1896 elections, where the vote shrank from 206,354 in the April state elections to 101,179 in the November general election. Perman, *Struggle for Mastery*, p. 136.

of the small Republican and Black voters remaining in the electorate.[124] The 1895 amendment required:

(a) Residence in the State for two years, in the County one year, in the polling precinct in which the elector offers to vote four months, and the payment six months before any election of any poll tax then due and payable ....
(b) Registration, which shall provide for the enrollment of every elector once in ten years ....
(c) Up to January 1st, 1898, all male persons of voting age applying for registration who can read any Section in this Constitution submitted to them by the registration officer, or understand and explain it when read to them by the registration officer, shall be entitled to register and become electors ....
(d) Any person who shall apply for registration after January 1st, 1898, if otherwise qualified, shall be registered: *Provided,* That he can both read and write any Section of this Constitution submitted to him by the registration officer or can show that he owns, and has paid all taxes collectible during the previous year on property in this State assessed at three hundred dollars ($300) or more.[125]

The state constitutional provision in subsection (b) was more restrictive in some ways than the 1882 law because it required re-registration every ten years, whereas the 1882 law established a one-time registration requirement.[126] The three-year safe harbor in subsection (d) gave illiterate White people a three-year window to register without hindrance, subject to the discretion of the registration officer.

The law was stunningly effective. African Americans in the lower house of the state legislature, for example, amounted to nine representatives after the 1882 elections, but that number dropped to one representative by 1896.[127] Some free Black men, who voted Democratic prior to war, continued to serve in public offices in some counties, but with these exceptions, the decline in Black political power was almost absolute.[128]

South Carolina's 1882 law, which faced opposition from conservative Democrats, White Republicans, and African Americans because it impeded the type of fusion politics that had, on occasion, allowed Black voters to be the swing bloc, was upheld

124 Burke, "Killing, Cheating, Legislating, and Lying," 871 ("The 1882 registration law only allowed new voters to register only on the first Monday of each month and only through the month of July in order to vote in that year's fall election. The limitation was vigorously enforced with respect to blacks and white Republican.").

125 Constitution of the State of South Carolina art. II, s. 4 (1895) (amended 1971).

126 See Kousser, *The Shaping of Southern Politics*, p. 92.

127 Tindall, *South Carolina Negroes*, p. 59.

128 Ibid., p. 66. See also ibid., p. 67 ("In the Tillmanite state convention of 1890 a rule was adopted providing that in the Democratic primaries 'only white Democrats shall be allowed to vote, except that negroes who voted for Gen. Hampton in 1876, and who have voted the Democratic ticket continuously since, may be permitted to vote.' This rule, with the passage of years, rapidly eliminated the Negro members of the party.").

by the South Carolina Supreme Court in the 1894 case of *Ex parte Lumsden*.[129] However, this did not deter new litigants from challenging the 1895 voter registration scheme put in place by the new state constitution.

Lawrence Mills, a Black tailor, brought a lawsuit claiming that the new voting restrictions were unconstitutional. Amazingly, he had been successful in the lower court, with a federal district court judge declaring the state's registration laws to be unreasonable.[130] Much of the district court's analysis had to do with a comparison between the 1895 law and the state's 1868 law, which coincided with Congress's readmission of South Carolina back in the Union.

Upon readmission, Congress determined that South Carolina had established a republican government due to its adoption of universal male suffrage: one only had to be a twenty-one-year-old male citizen who had resided in the state for a year and registered as least two months prior to the election.[131] The district court, citing the Reconstruction Act that readmitted South Carolina back in the Union, noted that the Act limited the power of the state to change suffrage requirements after admission. Moreover, despite its facial neutrality, the district court concluded that the 1895 statute violated the Fourteenth and Fifteenth Amendments since the defendants admitted that the law was enacted with discriminatory intent.[132]

The district court was reversed on appeal by both the Fourth Circuit Court of Appeals and the U.S. Supreme Court.[133] The Supreme Court relied on the mootness doctrine to dismiss the case, noting that the election in which Mills sought to vote had already happened. Thus, the Court could not grant relief. This formalistic approach allowed the Court to evade a number of then pressing questions: (1) whether it had any obligation to police voting rights given that the then-Democratically controlled Congress would be unlikely to do so, and (2) whether the Reconstruction Acts, which readmitted the Confederate states with the understanding that they not change their constitutions to disenfranchise legal voters, were judicially enforceable. By dismissing *Mills v. Green* as moot, the Court, for all intents and purposes, answered these questions in the negative.

129 *Ex parte Lumsden*, 19 S.E. 553 (S.C. 1894).

130 *Mills v. Green*, 67 F. 818 (D.S.C. 1895).

131 Ibid., 829 ("While, as a rule, the rights of a citizen of a state are such as all citizens of the United States enjoy, yet this plaintiff has also certain rights under the constitution of South Carolina by virtue of the act of congress of June 25, 1868, which was accepted and acted upon by that state; in which it is provided that the constitution of said state shall never be so changed as to deprive any citizen or class of citizens of the United States of the right to vote in said state who are entitled to vote by the constitution of the same, recognized in said act, except as a punishment for crime.").

132 Ibid., 832 ("If we may judge of what the intention of the legislature was by the inevitable result of its enactment – as we are assured we can – then the one object that controlled the minds of those who formulated the enactment I have been considering was how to successfully destroy the greatest number of the ballots of the citizens of African descent, while at the same time to interfere with as few as possible of those of the white race. The fact is that, with a candor that was as frank as it was amazing, this was virtually admitted during the argument of this case.").

133 *Green v. Mills*, 69 F. 852, 862 (4th Cir. 1895).

Between 1895 and 1901, the majority-Republican Congress got the chance to weigh in on both of these questions. Redistricted into South Carolina's first congressional district in 1894, Republican George Washington Murray defeated William Elliott after contesting the election results before the House Committee on Elections, now dominated by Republicans, and was seated in the Fifty-Fourth Congress (1895–97).[134] The Committee found that, on election day, election administrators did not open the polls in areas where Murray enjoyed considerable support. Because "voters can not be deprived of their ballots by the neglect or failure of regularly appointed managers to qualify and act," the Committee added 217 voters to Murray's column.[135]

In addition, the House Committee on Elections had previously determined that South Carolina's voter registration law was unconstitutional as applied in *Miller v. Elliott I*, a decision ratified by the full House, so the Committee also added 156 votes for Murray from qualified individuals unable to obtain a registration certificate (or who were given erroneous registration certificates) and not allowed to vote. The Committee found that these efforts to disenfranchise Black voters, through discriminatory application of the 1882 voter registration law, was part of a far-reaching conspiracy to elect Elliott. For example, the city of Charleston, which had 8000 prospective Black voters and 6000 prospective White voters, had Election Day turnout that instead was 10:1 White to Black voters because, according to the Committee:

> [T]he board of supervisors fraudulently impeded and prevented the registration of colored voters, and committed intentional errors in the execution of registration certificates for illiterate voters... A common excuse for rejection of ballots was that certificates held by the voter failed to give the number of the precinct, or the correct number of the ward in which the voter lived, or the proper number of his residence. The fact that these errors appeared always with certificates held by colored voters is significant. That the voters holding such certificates were illiterate was sufficient excuse for their ignorance of the condition of the certificates...[136]

Challengers from the Democratic Party were also present at every precinct and worked in conjunction with the election administrators to determine who should vote. As the Committee observed, "The familiarity of the challengers with the registration books and the kinds of certificates held by the voters evidenced their preparation for their part in the plan, which was to point out the defects in the certificates of registration...."[137]

[134] *Mills v. Green*, 159 U.S. 651, 658 (1895).
[135] "Murray v. Elliott (1895–1897)," in Hinds, *Hinds' Precedents of the House of Representatives of the United States*, v. 2, p. 598.
[136] Ibid.
[137] Ibid., p. 599.

Finally, the existence of dead and absent voters on the registration lists reinforced the Committee's conclusion that the election was tainted. The Committee concluded, based on all of the evidence before it, that Republican Murray won the seat by 434 votes once the ballots of disenfranchised African Americans were included in the total.

The House reaffirmed its views regarding the unconstitutionality of South Carolina's voter registration regime in the contested election case of *Wilson v. McLaurin*. Also resolved during the Fifty-Fourth Congress (1895–97), this election contest, like *Murray v. Elliott*, involved claims that thousands of Black voters had been illegally prevented from registering to vote.[138] While *Murray v. Elliott* dealt with discriminatory application of the state's voter registration regime, *Wilson v. McLaurin* tackled a conflict between the state voter registration statute and the state constitution.

In *Wilson*, the Committee held that the 1882 registration law violated the state constitution on its face because the statute, "by its specific terms, extended the period of residence required by the constitution of South Carolina."[139] Notably, the Committee felt empowered to resolve the facial constitutionality of the law because there was no South Carolina Supreme Court precedent on point.[140]

Five years after *Wilson v. McLaurin*, in *Johnston v. Stokes*,[141] the Republican-controlled House again confronted the impact of the state's restrictive voter registration regime on an election in the Seventh Congressional District for a seat in the Fifty-Seventh Congress (1901–03). The contestant, Johnston, claimed that the state's 1882 voter registration law was unconstitutional under both state and federal law. Not only did the voter registration system significantly reduce the opportunities to register, but it was also discriminately applied. According to Representative McCall, the only member of the House Committee on Elections to find that the seat should be declared vacant:

138 "Wilson v. McLaurin (1895–1897)," in Hinds, *Hinds' Precedents of the House of Representatives of the United States*, v. 2, p. 601.

139 Ibid., p. 602.

140 Ibid. ("A majority of this committee has reached the conclusion that the voters of the district now in consideration who were qualified under the constitution of South Carolina and who were rejected under color of the enforcement of the registration law are entitled to be heard in this contest. In this conclusion no violence is done to the doctrine that 'where the proper authorities of a State have given a construction to their own statutes that construction will be followed by the Federal authorities.' While the supreme court of South Carolina has not passed decisively upon the statute in question the people themselves, the highest authority in that State, have decreed its disappearance from the statute book."). To be clear, the presence of controlling state supreme court precedent would not always be a barrier to a determination that the governing law facilitated fraud. See "Wise v. Young (1898–1901)," in Hinds, *Hinds' Precedents of the House of Representatives of the United States*, v. 2, p. 651.

141 "*Johnston v. Stokes*, House Committee on Elections, 56th Congress (1901)," in Chester H. Rowell, *A Historical and Legal Digest of all the Contested Election Cases in the House of Representatives of the United States from the First to the Fifty-Sixth Congress, 1789–1901* (Washington, D.C.: Government Printing Office, 1901; reprinted edition: Westport: Greenwood Press, 1976), p. 531.

> The law only provides one registration place in each county, and only one day for registration each month from December to June, inclusive. Although the constitution provides that a male person otherwise qualified shall have the right to vote who has resided in the precinct six days before the election, the registration law, in fact, denied him registration, and, consequently, the right to vote unless he had resided in the precinct on the 1st day of July preceding the election. This provision is clearly repugnant to the constitution of South Carolina, which, under the pretense of regulating suffrage, imposes a new qualification upon it and is, therefore, unconstitutional.[142]

In addition, those who were able to comply with these requirements were routinely denied the opportunity to register, even after traveling over great distances:

> The testimony shows that many voters, some of them coming 30 or 40 miles, appeared regularly at the places of registration from month to month, and were denied registration by means of a systematic obstruction. It shows further that many thousand men who had the constitutional qualification, but were not registered, and who therefore had the right to vote if the registration laws were unconstitutional, expressed their desire to vote by going to the polls.[143]

The minority report, which also found the law unconstitutional, declared that the contestant was entitled to the seat despite the general rule, adhered to by both Representative McCall and the majority, that "lawful votes tendered but not received can not be made available to either party."[144]

Relying on the contested election case of *Miller v. Elliott I* and the district court's opinion in *Mills v. Green*, both of which found the 1882 law unconstitutional, three members in the minority noted that the declarations of disenfranchised voters were sufficient to establish that the contestant would have garnered additional votes but for the registration laws.[145] The full House ultimately agreed with Representative McCall and declared the seat vacant – contrary to cases such as *Wilson v. McLaurin* in which the Committee stated that this remedy was generally disfavored[146] – and, notably, reaffirmed that South Carolina's voter registration law was unconstitutional as it had previously declared in *Miller v. Elliott I*.

Despite Republicans' aggressive use of its Article I, Section 5 power, George Washington Murray would be the last African American elected from South Carolina until James Clyburn's successful 1992 campaign to the U.S. House of

[142] Ibid., p. 531.

[143] Ibid.

[144] Ibid., p. 532.

[145] "*Johnston v. Stokes*, House Committee on Elections, 56th Congress (1901)," in Rowell, *A Historical and Legal Digest of all the Contested Election Cases*, p. 533.

[146] "Wilson v. McLaurin (1895–1897)," in Hinds, *Hinds' Precedents of the House of Representatives of the United States*, v. 2, p. 602 ("The election is only to be set aside when it is impossible from any evidence within reach to ascertain the true result – when neither from the returns, nor from other proof, nor from all together can the truth be determined. Nothing short of the impossibility of ascertaining for whom the majority of the voters were given ought to vacate an election.").

Representatives. To go from being a majority of the lower house of the state legislature at the height of Reconstruction to having no representation at the state or federal level three decades later made it clear that the campaign of voter suppression in the state had succeeded.[147]

9.5 THE FIGHT AGAINST "LEGAL" DISENFRANCHISEMENT: THE FOURTH CONGRESSIONAL DISTRICT OF ALABAMA AND THE GHOST OF CHARLES MILLER SHELLEY

Despite existing trends favoring disenfranchisement through legal channels, Charles Miller Shelley – yes, *that* Charles Miller Shelley, the Confederate brigadier general and congressman that you met in the introduction[148] – was adamantly opposed to amending the Alabama Constitution to disenfranchise African Americans in the state. One would think that Shelley would take the opposite position, given that he lost an 1878 election challenge in Congress because of the widespread fraud and disenfranchisement undertaken on his behalf. As it turned out, stuffing the ballot box and intimidating Black voters did not guarantee Democratic success and could lead to troublesome congressional proceedings. Yet Shelley, state chairman of the Anti-Ratification Democratic Campaign Committee, worried that a new constitution, with colorblind language restricting suffrage, would disadvantage White men in the state and threaten the one goal that had to trump all others: establishing and preserving White supremacy.[149]

The widespread agreement about this end goal notwithstanding, the best means for securing White supremacy in Alabama had long been in question. Prior to the state constitutional convention, state legislators – in coordination with the state's congressional delegation – had actively worked to repeal the Fifteenth Amendment with no success.[150] Absent direct repeal, amending the state constitution – like sister

[147] Pildes, "Democracy, Anti-Democracy, and the Canon," 303.

[148] See Introduction.

[149] "Movement against the New Constitution: Democrats of Alabama Who Oppose Its Ratification Prepare for the Campaign," *Louisville Courier Journal*, September 15, 1901; "Active Fight: Against New Constitution in Alabama," *Louisville Courier Journal*, September 22, 1901.

[150] The following resolution was offered:

> To the senators and representatives from Alabama in the congress of the United States, requesting their support of the bill pending seeking to repeal the fifteenth amendment to the constitution of the United States:
>
> Whereas, the Honorable Oscar W. Underwood, representative from the ninth congressional district of Alabama in the congress of the United States has introduced into said congress a bill, seeking the repeal of the fifteenth amendment to the constitution of the United States, and whereas, we favor the passage of such measure, therefore, Be it resolved by the house, the senate concurring, that the senators and representatives from the State of Alabama are hereby requested to use their best efforts for the passage of such bill, and that the secretary of State is hereby requested to furnish a copy of this resolution to each of said senators and representatives.

states Mississippi, Virginia, North Carolina, and South Carolina had done to their governing documents in the 1890s and early 1900s – offered a workaround that could achieve similar results.[151]

In 1901, delegates descended on Montgomery to memorialize African American disenfranchisement (and, contrary to earlier reassurances, the disenfranchisement of poor White men) in the state constitution.[152] What resulted was a two-tiered approach to suffrage: a temporary plan that would permit White men (from the desired socioeconomic background) to register without hindrance until January 2, 1903, and a permanent plan that would make it difficult for anyone to join the voting rolls absent assistance from discerning election administrators. Anyone who registered before January 1, 1903 under the temporary plan would be registered permanently; anyone who registered after that date had to re-register yearly.[153]

The two-tiered approach addressed concerns raised by Shelley and also by the various constituencies who did not object to disenfranchisement, per se, but worried about the means for achieving it. Go too far and there was a risk of disenfranchising too many White men. Go too far and there was a risk of raising the ire of the federal government. Fail to go far enough and African Americans could still wield enough influence to affect state politics.[154] Where these delegates landed was a complete oxymoron: disenfranchisement within the constraints of the Federal Constitution.

The Alabama Constitution, as amended, enfranchised every male citizen, twenty-one years and older, as well as noncitizens over twenty-one intending to apply for citizenship.[155] After setting age, gender, and citizenship qualifications that were standard in most state constitutions at the time, the convention engaged in a number of disenfranchising mechanisms to create, and subsequently maintain, an all-White electorate. The first was the restrictive residency requirement in Section 178, requiring lawful voters to "have resided in the state at least two years, in the county one year, and in the precinct or ward three months," and to "have paid on or before the first day of February next preceding the date of the election at which he offers to vote, all poll taxes due from him for the year nineteen hundred and one, and for each subsequent year."[156] While Alabama's poll tax was not cumulative like that in

Journal of the House of Representatives of the State of Alabama, Regular Session, 1901, p. 183. See also "Comments of Congressman Bowie," reprinted in "The 14th and 15th Amendments," *Nashville Tennessean*, August 15, 1904 ("That this amendment [the Fifteenth], if adopted at all, was done by methods grossly fraudulent, history leaves no reason whatever to dispute.").

151 Kousser, *The Shaping of Southern Politics*, p. 166.

152 Ibid., p. 169.

153 R. Volney Riser, *Defying Disfranchisement: Black Voting Rights Activism in the Jim Crow South, 1890–1908* (Baton Rouge: Louisiana State University Press, 2010), p. 121.

154 Riser, "Disenfranchisement, the U.S. Constitution, and the Federal Courts," 237–279, 241, 243 (2006).

155 Constitution of the State of Alabama art. VIII, s. 177 (1901).

156 Ibid., art. VIII, s. 177

Georgia, the $1.50 tax, owed by those aged 21 to 45 years old, was more than most people could pay.[157]

The evil genius of the Alabama Constitution was, like North Carolina and Louisiana, its grandfather clause in Section 180, which removed longstanding Black voters from the rolls. Under Section 180, those who met the requirements in Sections 177 and 178 were entitled to register prior to December 20, 1902, if they served in any American War of the nineteenth century (or were the descendants of those who served in these wars) including, notably, as land or naval forces of "the Confederate States, or of the State of Alabama in the war between the states."[158] This language meant that the formerly enslaved who had served as Union soldiers could not register pursuant to the grandfather clause.[159] This provision also generated the most opposition among the delegates, who were concerned that the obviously disingenuous tactic, widely reviled when adopted in Louisiana and North Carolina several years prior, would invite attention from the federal courts.[160]

Alternatively, if a person was one "of good character and who understand[ ] the duties and obligations of citizenship under a republican form of government," he was also permitted to register.[161] The character requirement and understanding provision, implemented at the local level, ensured that African Americans would not be permitted to vote even if they otherwise meet the constitutional requirements.

After January 1, 1903, the requirements to vote in Alabama became more stringent, with the state instituting both a literacy test and a property qualification to register. Applicants had to "read and write any article of the Constitution," and own forty acres of land or personal property worth three hundred dollars or more, with all property taxes being paid and current.[162] Again, discriminatory implementation at the local level ensured that African Americans, even if they could meet these requirements, would be prevented from registering.[163]

Finally, Section 182 of Alabama's constitution guaranteed that many Black people would never again qualify as electors. This provision disenfranchised "[a]ll idiots and insane persons" as well as those convicted of a laundry list of crimes that well exceeded the restrictions in the Reconstruction Act readmitting Alabama back into the Union and limiting disenfranchisement to those who committed common

157 Ibid., art. VIII, s. 194. The constitution explicitly prohibited any attempts to collect a delinquent poll tax. Ibid.

158 Ibid., art. VIII, s. 180.

159 Riser, *Defying Disfranchisement*, p. 183 (discussing a few black union veterans who threatened lawsuits and were added to the voter rolls under the temporary plan). Many veterans sought to use the impractical judicial appeals process built into the new constitution, but these efforts were met with little success. Ibid., p. 184.

160 Riser, "Disenfranchisement, the U.S. Constitution, and the Federal Courts," 246.

161 Constitution of the State of Alabama art. VIII, s. 180 (1901).

162 Ibid, s. 181. See also Kousser, *The Shaping of Southern Politics*, p. 169.

163 Constitution of the State of Alabama art. VIII, s. 186 (1901) (delegating voter registration duties to county boards).

law felonies.[164] As of 1890, the state had leased more than 800 of its convicts to the Tennessee Coal and Iron Company, generating 6 percent of its yearly revenue.[165] The ability to disenfranchise Black people convicted of crimes while feeding them into the newly burgeoning industry of convict leasing would prove to be a boon for the state.

Black people in Alabama did not stand by idly as the law was debased and corrupted into a tool of White supremacy. Not only did they turn out in large numbers to vote against the proposed constitution,[166] they had also been active in fighting these discriminatory tactics well before the state constitution was amended in 1901. During the 1880s and 1890s, they turned to Congress, with both candidates and voters challenging fraudulent elections in Alabama in which there had been massive disenfranchisement.

The Fourth Congressional District in Alabama, originally gerrymandered in the early 1880s as a safe Republican seat, exemplified this practice. Known as "the black fourth" for its majority-Black population, Democrats were elected from the district for many years through force and fraud.[167] The fourth district was at the heart of

164 Section 182 provides:

> The following persons shall be disqualified both from registering, and from voting, namely: All idiots and insane persons; those who shall by reason of conviction of crime be disqualified from voting at the time of the ratification of this Constitution; those who shall be convicted of treason, murder, arson, embezzlement, malfeasance in office, larceny, receiving stolen property, obtaining property or money under false pretenses, perjury, subornation of perjury, robbery, assault with intent to rob, burglary, forgery, bribery, assault and battery on the wife, bigamy, living in adultery, sodomy, incest, rape, miscegenation, crime against nature, or any crime punishable by imprisonment in the penitentiary, or of any infamous crime or crime involving moral turpitude; also, any person who shall be convicted as a vagrant or tramp, or of selling or offering to sell his vote or the vote of another, or of buying or offering to buy the vote of another, or of making or offering to make a false return in any election by the people or in any primary election to procure the nomination or election of any person to any office, or of suborning any witness or registrar to secure the registration of any person as an elector.

Ibid., s. 182. The Supreme Court invalidated this provision in its 1985 decision in *Hunter v. Underwood*, 471 U.S. 222, 233 (1985).

165 Paul M. Pruitt, "Convict Lease System and Peonage," in Thomas C. Holt et al. (eds.), *The New Encyclopedia of Southern Culture*, 24 vols. (Chapel Hill: University of North Carolina Press, 2013), v. 24, p. 50. The Supreme Court would invalidate Alabama's system of convict leasing in a number of high-profile cases. See *Bailey v. Alabama*, 219 U.S. 219 (1911); *United States v. Reynolds*, 245 U.S. 133 (1914). Initially, the Court declined to intervene and prevent Alabama's peonage system. See *Clyatt v. United States*, 197 U.S. 207 (1905); see also Daniel A. Novak, *The Wheel of Servitude: Black Forced Labor after Slavery* (Lexington: University Press of Kentucky, 1978), pp. 49–50.

166 "Blacks Shut Out: Alabama's New Constitution Is Ratified by a Large Majority," *Louisville Courier-Journal*, November 12, 1901.

167 "How the Democrats of the IVth Alabama Congress District Rolled up a Majority of 13,150 Votes for Mr. Turpin – Fraud in Bewildering Variety," *New York Tribune*, March 9, 1890 (noting that, with a fair election in the district, "the Republican majority would exceed 16,000"). See also "Victim of the Majority: Another Sacrifice to Republican Injustice," *New York Times*, June 3, 1890 (noting that in the census of 1880 the population of the district was 32,820 White people, 6,500 of whom were voters, and 135,893 Black people, 27,000 of whom were voters).

the election contest in which the Republican-controlled Forty-Seventh Congress (1881–83) declared that the Republican candidate, James Q. Smith, rather than Charles Miller Shelley, was entitled to the seat.[168] After the seat was declared vacant because Smith died,[169] Shelley was re-elected to fill the vacancy for the rest of the Forty-Seventh Congress, and was then elected for a full term in the Forty-Eighth Congress (1883–85).

Notably, Shelley's opponent during that second election contested the results, and the contest was (somewhat) successful. The Democratic-controlled Congress seated Republican George Henry Craig on January 9, 1885. According to the *Chicago Tribune*, which reported on the longstanding fraud in the district, "[I]t was so clear that Shelby [sic] had received the certificate in consequence of fraud that even a Democratic committee was obliged to report against him."

Shelley, however, had the last laugh – as the *Tribune* observed, the matter was allowed to drag along and Craig was not seated until two weeks before the final adjournment.[170] This same delay tactic had been used by a Republican-led Congress, which seated Republican Josiah Walls' Democratic opponent after a successful election contest a little over a month before the end of the Forty-Second Congress.[171]

Despite successful contests against him in the Forty-Seventh and Forty-Eighth Congresses, even if hollow victories at best, Shelley was publicly regarded as "[t]he only Democrat who ever successfully defied the efforts of his republican opponent to unseat him."[172] This moniker reflected that the prevailing political winds, guided by the invisible hands of fraud and electoral violence, were difficult to redirect even with federal intervention. For the rest of the 1880s – indeed, the remainder of the century – the Fourth Congressional District oscillated between Democratic and Republican officeholders, despite an 1891 gerrymander designed to make it into a safe Democratic district.[173]

In *McDuffie v. Davidson* (Fiftieth Congress) (1887–89), the Democratic-controlled House found, unsurprisingly, that Republican John Van Patter McDuffie was not entitled to the seat in the Fourth Congressional District, despite substantial witness evidence that the vote had been tampered with by election officials.[174] In 1888,

[168] "How the Democrats Win: The Gross Frauds Practiced in the Fourth Alabama District," *Chicago Daily Tribune*, April 18, 1890 (noting that "Gen. Shelby [sic], Democrat, was certified as elected, having obtained a majority by the simple process of rejecting all the returns from colored precincts").

[169] "James Q. Smith Obituary," *Philadelphia Inquirer*, May 13, 1882. Smith died a little over a month before the Committee declared him the winner of the seat.

[170] "How the Democrats Win: The Gross Frauds Practiced in the Fourth Alabama District," *Chicago Daily Tribune*, April 18, 1890.

[171] See Chapter 6.

[172] "The Redistricting of Alabama: The Fourth District Is Now Made Safely Democratic," *The Atlanta Constitution*, February 13, 1891.

[173] Ibid.

[174] "McDuffie v. Davidson (1887–1889)," in Hinds, *Hinds' Precedents of the House of Representatives of the United States*, v. 2, pp. 421–422. This evidence is also discussed in *McDuffie v. Turpin I*.

Republicans gained control of Congress, using the malfeasance that took place in the Fourth Congressional District as a part of their campaign appeal.[175] Democrats had not only deprived the Illinois-born McDuffie of his seat, lamented the *Chicago Tribune* in February 1888, but the Republicans (then in the minority) had also been able to show "a record of fraud … that would put the Chicago election crooks to shame…."[176]

At least initially, the new generation of Republican Congressmen who assumed power after the 1888 elections were well-positioned to pick up the mantle of Reconstruction and offer hope to African Americans seeking to vote. In *McDuffie*, they had staked out strong positions while in the minority, calling out the fraud and violence in the Fourth Congressional District that undermined the promise of Reconstruction years after its supposed end. Throughout the 1880s and 1890s, however, Republicans would gain, lose, and then gain control of Congress – and this yo-yo, coupled with their reluctance to appear overtly partisan, made efforts to protect Black voting rights as uneven in Alabama as it had been in Mississippi, Virginia, and the Carolinas.

For example, *McDuffie v. Turpin I* (Fifty-First Congress) (1889–91) ended very differently from *McDuffie v. Davidson*, even though this contest was resolved during the same Congress in which the Committee had upheld the results in the fraudulent contests out of Mississippi.[177] The Republican-led House Committee on Elections found that the history of contested elections in the district created a presumption against the legitimacy of the returns.[178] Election officials reported 13,000 votes in favor of Democrat Turpin, even though Black voters had a 20,000 vote majority in the district.[179] In Lowndes County, the ratio of Black to White voters was 5:1; in Percy County, this number was 3:1.[180]

Unsurprisingly, the House found that the reported numbers could not possibly be credible, given that the majority of Black voters were Republicans who maintained an active presence in the district.[181] "If the certified returns in this case are true," the Committee noted, "it follows … that all the White voters and at least 11,800 colored men voted for the [Democratic] contestee, while only 5,625 voted for contestant and

[175] "A Disgraceful Record: Something about Crooked Elections in Alabama," *The Chicago Tribune*, February 22, 1888.

[176] Ibid.

[177] "McDuffie v. Davidson (1887–1889)," in Hinds, *Hinds' Precedents of the House of Representatives of the United States*, v. 2, pp. 421–422.

[178] "McDuffie v. Turpin (1889–1891)," in Hinds, *Hinds' Precedents of the House of Representatives of the United States*, v. 2, p. 479. See also "Threet v. Clarke (1889–1891)," in Hinds, *Hinds' Precedents of the House of Representatives of the United States*, v. 2, p. 467.

[179] "How the Democrats Win: The Gross Frauds Practiced in the Fourth Alabama District," *Chicago Daily Tribune*, April 18, 1890.

[180] "How the Democrats of the IVth Alabama Congress District Rolled up a Majority of 13,150 Votes for Mr. Turpin – Fraud in Bewildering Variety," *New York Tribune*, March 9, 1890.

[181] Ibid. ("The evidence shows that 97 percent of the votes polled in the district were cast for the Republican ticket… .").

more than 11,500 did not vote at all."[182] The Committee went on to note the various efforts to perpetuate the fraud including the appointment of disloyal and illiterate Republican inspectors[183]; a refusal by the sheriff to accept Republican returns[184]; and a failure to open polling places in majority-Republican areas.[185]

There was also a violent assault on Republicans by a deputy sheriff seeking to prevent an accurate accounting of the vote.[186] The sheriff killed one Republican poll watcher and wounded two others who were assembling evidence for an election contest on behalf of McDuffie.[187] This evidence would have shown the variance between the number of votes actually cast and the number of votes recorded. As the Committee noted with respect to one precinct in the district:

> Here we have 170 voters declaring at the polls their intention to vote the Republican ticket, taking the ticket from one chosen by them to issue tickets by prearrangement, holding their tickets in such a way that they could be seen until voted, and then having their names registered so as to be able to prove how they voted. These acts are a part of the res gestae of the election – the deliberate declaration of the voters while engaged in the act of voting, not only of how they voted but of their utter want of confidence in the election board, upon which they had no representation.[188]

There would be a repeat of this election in the next Congress, resulting in *McDuffie v. Turpin II* (Fifty-Second Congress) (1891–93).[189] After Republican McDuffie lost the general election to Turpin, he again contested the results before the House Committee. Like the election two years earlier, officials reported that Democrat Turpin defeated McDuffie by a large margin that McDuffie claimed was a result of a conspiracy among election officials to disenfranchise Black voters. And like the prior election contest, there was widespread evidence that the vote was illegitimate because election officials had refused to open polls, falsified returns, and prevented Black voters from casting ballots, consistent with the history of the district.[190]

Yet the House Committee on Elections, now controlled by Democrats after the historic Republican defeat following the failure of the Lodge Force Bill,[191] found

[182] "McDuffie v. Turpin (1889–1891)," in Hinds, *Hinds' Precedents of the House of Representatives of the United States*, v. 2, p. 479.

[183] Ibid., p, 481.

[184] Ibid., p. 484.

[185] Ibid., p. 485.

[186] Ibid., p. 481 (citing *McDuffie v. Davidson*).

[187] "How the Democrats of the IVth Alabama Congress District Rolled up a Majority of 13,150 Votes for Mr. Turpin – Fraud in Bewildering Variety," *New York Tribune*, March 9, 1890.

[188] "McDuffie v. Turpin (1889–1891)," in Hinds, *Hinds' Precedents of the House of Representatives of the United States*, v. 2, p. 482.

[189] "McDuffie v. Turpin (1891–1893)," in Hinds, *Hinds' Precedents of the House of Representatives of the United States*, v. 2, p. 520.

[190] Ibid., p. 522.

[191] A Bill to amend and supplement the election laws of the United States and to provide for the more efficient enforcement of such laws, and for other purposes, H.R. 10958, 51st Congress, 1st Session (June 14, 1890).

this evidence to be insufficient to establish that there was fraud. The Committee rejected the witnesses who reported the fraud at the polls, finding them "ignorant" or too far away from the ballot boxes to be credible; notably, this evidence had been key in the challenge two years earlier. Whereas the lists used to keep an accurate account of the vote had been dispositive before the Republican House, their Democratic counterparts found that it would set a "dangerous precedent" should "the actual returns, as made by the inspectors and sworn officers of the election … be disregarded and impeached by returns made out by irresponsible partisan workers at the polls."[192] And finally, to add insult to injury, the Committee not only denied that African Americans were reliable Republican voters,[193] but asserted that the history of the district was irrelevant in determining the existence of fraud.[194]

The Democratic-leaning *N.Y. Times* had suggested as much in reporting on *McDuffie v. Turpin I* years before; it was entirely plausible, the *Times* noted, that McDuffie was unpopular among Black voters, who changed their ballots at the last minute in support of Turpin and made sure to do so out of the purview of disapproving Black leaders.[195] Unsurprisingly, Democrats adopted a similar line of reasoning in *McDuffie v. Turpin II*.

Despite being the subject of three election contests, McDuffie would serve as a congressman for less than one year, from June 1890 to March 1891. The disastrous November 1890 elections had essentially foreclosed one of the few avenues that Black voters had left to protect their voting rights, at least temporarily. As hope dimmed for congressional intervention, Black voters in Alabama continued to fight for their rights, turning to the courts as a last resort to resolve the decades-long battle that culminated in the disenfranchising 1901 state constitution.

9.6 THE ROAD TO *GILES V. HARRIS* AND THE COMPLETE ABDICATION OF THE FEDERAL COURTS

At the turn of the twentieth century, Booker T. Washington was not only the most famous Alabamian, but one of the most famous Americans. Advisor to several presidents, Washington was also founded Tuskegee University in 1881. Publicly, he advocated that Black people should focus on their labor rather than tackling racial discrimination and Jim Crow head on, placing him at odds with other Black

192 "McDuffie v. Turpin (1891–1893)," in Hinds, *Hinds' Precedents of the House of Representatives of the United States*, v. 2, p. 522.

193 See, however, "How the Democrats of the IVth Alabama Congress District Rolled up a Majority of 13,150 Votes for Mr. Turpin – Fraud in Bewildering Variety," *New York Tribune*, March 9, 1890 (stating that "any colored Democrats whatever in the district does not affect a dozen precincts, or more than 200 voters in all.").

194 "McDuffie v. Turpin (1891–1893)," in Hinds, *Hinds' Precedents of the House of Representatives of the United States*, v. 2, p. 522.

195 "Victim of the Majority: Another Sacrifice to Republican Injustice," *New York Times*, June 3, 1890, p. 1.

leaders of the time period, most notably W.E.B. DuBois. While these philosophical differences between Washington and DuBois are very much a part of Washington's legacy, less well known is that Booker T. Washington had the unique distinction of being one of the few Black men registered to vote under Alabama's restrictive voting regime adopted in 1901 – indeed, one of the only 3,000 Black voters who were able to register[196] – while also bankrolling the litigation that challenged its constitutionality.[197]

Washington's presence on the voting rolls was supposed to signal that Black voters could register under the new restrictions; his prominence and accommodationist message made him an obvious candidate for inclusion, meant to illustrate that respectable Black property owners could be voters. But a token he was.

John Knox, president of the 1901 Alabama constitutional convention, famously opened the proceedings with the same overarching goal as Virginia delegate Carter Glass – "to establish white supremacy in this state" – with the same qualification – "within the limits imposed by the Federal Constitution."[198] While the Supreme Court, almost nine decades later, would view these comments as evidence of intentional racial discrimination in violation of the Fifteenth Amendment with respect to Alabama's felon disenfranchisement law,[199] in 1901 Alabama sought to join the ranks of Mississippi and other southern jurisdictions in endorsing a vision of the Fifteenth Amendment that permitted states to enact laws that were facially race-neutral, but had a disparate racial impact or could be discriminately enforced.

During this period, the federal judiciary heard cases dealing with southern racial discrimination and disenfranchisement, involving racist tactics that were later outsourced to the north. For example, in 1887, the Texas legislature sent a proposed constitutional amendment to voters that authorized voter registration for cities of 10,000 or more people, after rejecting a proposal in 1876 that would have mandated voter registration statewide.[200] In practice, this meant new restrictions were concentrated in places like Dallas, Galveston, Houston, Austin, and a number of other cities in which the Republican Party no longer had a significant presence, but where poor White people (aligned with the Populist Party) and African Americans were still numerous enough to make the difference in close elections.[201]

Voters finally approved this law following an 1891 mayoral election in Dallas in which the incumbent mayor, supported by a majority of Black and working-class

[196] Pildes, "Democracy, Anti-Democracy, and the Canon," 303.

[197] Riser, *Defying Disfranchisement*, pp. 10, 99–100.

[198] Ibid., p. 184.

[199] *Hunter v. Underwood*, 471 U.S. 222 (1985).

[200] The 1869 Constitution required voter registration, and the system was subject to so much abuse that delegates to the 1875 constitutional convention rejected a similar measure. In 1887, voters rejected a proposal that would have implemented a statewide system of voter registration. This law was finally approved in 1891. See www.sll.texas.gov/assets/pdf/braden/26-article-vi.pdf.

[201] Patrick G. Williams, "Suffrage Restrictions in Post-Reconstruction Texas" (2011) 68 *Journal of Southern History* 31–64, 33.

White precincts, defeated the candidate endorsed by local Democratic leaders.[202] Local leaders urged the legislature to resubmit the proposal to the voters, especially since voter registration requirements had proven wildly effective in suppressing the vote in other southern states.[203] The durational residency requirement imposed by the state constitution,[204] coupled with local registration and re-registration requirements, ultimately disenfranchised many minorities residing in urban areas.

Mason v. State of Missouri was the northern counterpart to the Texas voter registration litigation, involving a challenge to a state law that required voter registration for cities with more than 100,000 residents.[205] At the time, St. Louis was the only city that met this population requirement. The plaintiff, a St. Louis election official tasked with implementing the registration requirement, argued that the law violated the Federal Constitution because St. Louis residents were subject to a registration requirement that did not apply to residents of other cities.[206]

Deferring to the state supreme court, the U.S. Supreme Court rejected this challenge on the grounds that the state constitution did not expressly limit the legislature's authority to treat cities differently. Because the right to vote derives from state law – and the state supreme court determined that state law had not been violated by the registration requirement – the Court found there was no violation of the Equal Protection Clause of the Fourteenth Amendment.[207]

The notion that a potential federal constitutional violation can be negated by a state court interpretation of state law may seem like an unorthodox position to endorse, especially for an institution that once deemed itself solely responsible for determining what the U.S. Constitution means.[208] Yet *Mason* and other voting cases decided at the turn of the century provide important context for understanding how massive disenfranchisement can occur "within the limits imposed by the Federal Constitution."

One such way was through aggressive use of jurisdictional doctrines. In *Luther v. Borden*,[209] the Supreme Court laid the foundation for its abdication from certain political disputes, which it liberally took advantage of during Redemption and

202 Kousser, *The Shaping of Southern Politics*, p. 203.

203 Franita Tolson, "What Is Abridgment?: A Critique of Two Section Twos" (2015) 67 *Alabama Law Review* 433–483.

204 Article VI of the Texas Constitution provided that: "Every male person…who shall have attained the age of twenty-one years, and who shall be a citizen of the United States, and who shall have resided in this State one year next preceding an election, and the last six months within the district or county in which he offers to vote, shall be deemed a qualified elector…"

But see *Dunn v. Blumstein*, 405 U.S. 330 (1972) (invalidating unreasonable durational residency requirements as a prerequisite for voter registration).

205 *Mason v. State of Missouri*, 179 U.S. 328 (1900).

206 This would be an obvious violation of the Equal Protection Clause today. See, e.g., *Bush v. Gore*, 531 U.S. 98 (2000).

207 *Mason v. State of Missouri*, 179 U.S. 328, 335 (1900).

208 *Marbury v. Madison*, 5 U.S. 137 (1803).

209 See Chapter 4.

Restoration. For example, the facts of *Taylor v. Beckham*, decided by the Court in 1900, arose from a dispute in Kentucky's 1900 gubernatorial election that demonstrated how the selective use of these doctrines could facilitate a discriminatory status quo.

In *Taylor*, the Democratic candidates for governor and lieutenant governor contested an election in which the Kentucky State Board of Election Commissioners initially certified their Republican opponents as the winners. The Board, after a recount, ultimately determined that the Democratic candidates received the highest number of legal votes. Both houses of the Kentucky General Assembly ratified the decision by the Board to award the offices to the Democratic candidates, but the Republicans refused to surrender their offices after the Democratic candidate for governor was assassinated weeks after the election. The Republican candidates alleged that contest proceedings were not valid and that the Board and the General Assembly had engaged in a conspiracy to deny them the offices that they had legitimately won on Election Day.[210] The Democratic candidates sued in response to the Republicans' actions, arguing that their failure to vacate these offices rendered Kentucky's government unrepublican in form, in violation of the Guarantee Clause.

Citing *Luther v. Borden*, the Supreme Court declined to resolve which slate of candidates had been lawfully elected to the offices of Governor and Lieutenant Governor. Finding that this was purely a state matter that warranted no federal intervention, the Court noted that "the legislative, executive and judicial departments of the State are peacefully operating by the orderly and settled methods prescribed by its fundamental law … and any remedy beside that is to be found in the august tribunal of the people…."[211]

The Court's holding that a lack of violence in the state counsels against federal intervention was striking, as this was similar to the determination made by President Tyler in the context of the Rhode Island dispute almost sixty years earlier. By 1900, the federal courts were on board with the idea that the federal government should only enforce the republican guarantee when legitimate state government is threatened by violent overthrow.[212] Yet there was no such intervention when White supremacists overthrew the duly elected government in Wilmington, North Carolina a year earlier.

The revival of the political question doctrine was also indicative of a broader trend in the Court's case law involving the use of jurisdictional doctrines to convert voter disenfranchisement and election issues into state, rather than federal, issues. In *Mason v. State of Missouri*, discussed above, the Court also questioned whether the plaintiff, a St. Louis election official, had standing to challenge the state voter

210 *Taylor v. Beckham*, 178 U.S. 548 (1900). See also Edward Foley, *Ballot Battles: The History of Disputed Elections in the United States* (New York: Oxford University Press, 2016).

211 Ibid., 580.

212 See, e.g., *Pacific States Tel. & Tel. Co. v. Oregon*, 223 U.S. 118 (1912); *Taylor v. Beckham*, 178 U.S. 548 (1900).

registration law on behalf of St. Louis voters.[213] His standing was at issue because he was not alleging that it was his right to vote that was being violated.[214]

While rejecting his claims on the merits, the Court distinguished an earlier case, *Wiley v. Sinkler*,[215] in which it determined that it had subject matter jurisdiction over a case in which the plaintiff had been disenfranchised in the context of a federal election. The defendant election administrators in *Wiley* argued that the Court lacked jurisdiction because voter qualification standards are determined by the states, not the federal government. The Court rejected this argument, noting that the offices that were the focus of the election – here, for the House of Representatives – were created by the U.S. Constitution, which also sets out how these seats should be filled.[216] The Court also distinguished *Minor v. Happersett*'s premise that the Constitution "does not confer the right of suffrage upon anyone[,]" and clarified that, while the *Minor* Court was correct that "the right is not definitely conferred on any person or class of persons by the Constitution alone…the court did not intend to say that, when the class or the person is thus ascertained, his right to vote for a member of Congress was not fundamentally based upon the Constitution, which created the office…."[217]

Despite presenting a stronger claim than the *Mason* plaintiff, at least as it pertains to standing, the *Wiley* plaintiff lost his case, which brings us to the second way in which the Court lent its imprimatur to disenfranchisement efforts: through unduly strict formalism. Despite finding the existence of subject matter jurisdiction, the Court dismissed the *Wiley* plaintiff's case, noting that, while the plaintiff established that he had the requisite qualifications to be an elector in South Carolina, his complaint failed to allege that he had actually registered to vote in the state.[218] Consequently, the plaintiff had not alleged facts sufficient to establish a federal cause of action.

The Court's effort to limit federal oversight of voting and elections did not just stop with its own jurisprudence. The Court actively undermined Congress's authority to protect voting rights. First, as the relevant case law has shown us, the Court had been very aggressive about limiting Congress's exercise of its Fifteenth Amendment authority to address race-based disenfranchisement and to prevent Congress from exercising a plenary and broad authority to protect voters from disenfranchisement, more generally.

Two of these cases were discussed extensively in Chapter 8. In *United States v. Reese*, the Court quashed an indictment against election inspectors who refused

[213] *Mason v. State of Missouri*, 179 U.S. 328 (1900).

[214] Ibid., 333 ("The assertions referred to, it must be borne in mind, are made by a public official who is seeking to avoid the performance of duties enjoined upon him by the law in question, and who does not allege that any particular rights possessed by him as an individuals have been expressly invaded.").

[215] *Wiley v. Sinkler*, 179 U.S. 58 (1900).

[216] Ibid., 63.

[217] Ibid.

[218] Ibid., 66.

to count the ballots of Black voters, finding that Congress could only prohibit race-based disenfranchisement and not disenfranchisement more broadly when enacting legislation pursuant to its Fifteenth Amendment enforcement authority.[219] Similarly, *United States v. Cruikshank* quashed an indictment under Section 6 of the Enforcement Act of 1870 involving the murder of dozens of Black men at the Colfax County courthouse in Louisiana in the wake of the 1872 election, finding that there was no allegation that the denial of voting rights was racially motivated.[220]

The Court would follow a similar path in the 1903 case of *James v. Bowman*. In *James*, the defendant, a private citizen, was indicted for bribing and intimidating African Americans from voting in a Kentucky congressional election, in violation of the Enforcement Act of 1870 (codified as Section 5507). This statute criminalizes retaliation against those exercising the right to vote protected by the Fifteenth Amendment.[221] Section 5507 prevents the use of bribery or threats to "depriv[e] such person of employment or occupation, or of ejecting such person from a rented house, lands, or other property, … refus[e] to renew leases or contracts for labor, or by threats of violence to himself or family." Additionally, like Section 4 of the Act (at issue in *Reese*), this provision lacked a limitation to race-based bribery, threats, deprivations, or denials (even though it specifically references the right to vote as protected by the Fifteenth Amendment).

The *James* Court quashed the indictment, finding that the defendant could not be prosecuted under Section 5507 because there was no allegation that the bribery and intimidation were because of race. According to the Court, "an indictment which charges no discrimination on account of race, color or previous condition of servitude is likewise destitute of support by [the Fifteenth] amendment."[222] While the victims were African American and the rights infringed protected by the Fifteenth Amendment, the Court held that this was merely descriptive and did not show that these voters were "bribed because they were colored men."[223]

Second, robust enforcement of a very formalized version of the state action doctrine – that is, the idea that "No State shall" language in the Fourteenth Amendment means what it says – had long been a way for the Court to limit Congress's ability to address private discrimination.[224] *James v. Bowman* expanded this practice to the Fifteenth Amendment, hobbling federal civil rights enforcement efforts well into the 1940s.[225] The defendant indicted in *James* was a private

219 *United States v. Reese*, 92 U.S. 214 (1876). See also Chapter 8.
220 *United States v. Cruikshank*, 92 U.S. 542 (1875). See also Chapter 8.
221 See An Act to enforce the Rights of Citizens of the United States to vote in the several States of the Union, and for other Purposes, ch. 114, 16 Stat. 140 (1870). See also Chapter 5.
222 *James v. Bowman*, 190 U.S. 127, 139 (1903).
223 Ibid.
224 *Civil Rights Cases*, 109 U.S. 3 (1883).
225 *Grovey v. Townsend*, 295 U.S. 45 (1935); *Nixon v. Condon*, 286 U.S. 73 (1932); *Nixon v. Herndon*, 273 U.S. 536 (1927) (collectively referred to as the "White Primary Cases").

individual; the indictment did not allege any wrongdoing by the state of Kentucky. In the Court's view, because the Fifteenth Amendment stated that the right to vote "shall not be denied or abridged by the United States or by any state" on account of race, Congress lacked authority, pursuant to Section 2 of the Amendment, to criminalize discriminatory actions by private individuals.

Notably, the Court acknowledged that Congress has authority, under the Elections Clause, to broadly regulate federal elections beyond prohibiting race-based discrimination but denied that Section 5507 was enacted pursuant to this provision. The Court noted that Section 5507 applied to "all elections, state or federal, and it does not purport to punish bribery by any voter. On its face, it is clearly an attempt to exercise power supposed to be conferred by the Fifteenth Amendment in respect to all elections."[226]

In so holding, the Court completely ignored that the Senate version of the Enforcement Act of 1870, which was the version that ultimately became law, sought to enforce not only the Fifteenth Amendment, but also the Fourteenth Amendment and the Elections Clause.[227] Instead, a rigid formalism, applied with the intent to minimize the federal footprint in state political systems, won the day. *James v. Bowman* was not a surprise to anyone who had been paying attention; indeed, the U.S. Supreme Court had signaled the demise of the Reconstruction project – on life support for decades – a year before *James* in a case called *Giles v. Harris*.

Jackson Giles, a forty-four-year-old political activist, was born in slavery and had held many jobs (in agriculture, as a grocer, a newspaper publisher, janitor) but his most important occupation was his decades-long dedication to dismantling White supremacy and Jim Crow.[228] Giles, head of the Colored Man's Suffrage Association, challenged Alabama's new suffrage restrictions that, under its 1901 Constitution, had disenfranchised him and other Black men in the state. Notably, Giles attempted to register under the temporary plan but, as the Supreme Court conceded, was not allowed to register despite being "subject to none of the disqualifications set forth in the constitution of Alabama."[229]

Given the posture of the case – a motion to dismiss in which the Court had to assume the truth of all allegations – the Court deferred to Giles' arguments that White men registered with ease; that election registrars assumed their positions solely for the purpose of ensuring that Black men could not do the same; and that

[226] *James v. Bowman*, 190 U.S. 127, 140 (1903).
[227] See Chapter 6. See also *United States v. Cruikshank*, 92 U.S. 542 (1875) (finding that the Fourteenth Amendment does not reach actions by private individuals in the context of Section 6 of the Enforcement Act of 1870).
[228] See Brian Lyman, "The Journey of Jackson Giles," *Montgomery Advertiser*, January 27, 2022, www.montgomeryadvertiser.com/in-depth/news/2022/01/27/jim-crow-alabama-jackson-giles-supreme-court/7995760002/.
[229] *Giles v. Harris*, 189 U.S. 475 (1903).

the entire registration scheme itself constituted a wholesale fraud.[230] It was also evident that Giles and others similarly situated had suffered a clear harm based on the facts alleged – the registration scheme prevented them from voting in the November 1902 election, yet the Court, resolving the case in 1903, found that since "[t]his election has gone by … it is impossible to give specific relief with regard to that."[231]

Like *Taylor v. Beckham*, resolution of the case turned solely on jurisdictional issues rather than the strict formalism that had doomed the plaintiffs in *Mason* and *Wiley*. The first was whether Giles met the amount in controversy requirement, which was then set at $2,000. The Court declined to dismiss the complaint for failing to meet this amount, noting that this issue "was not raised in the Circuit Court" and "could have been remedied by amendment."[232]

Instead, the Court focused on Giles' request for equitable relief, which would require the Court to declare Alabama's registration scheme unconstitutional or, alternatively, add Giles and others similarly situated to the voter rolls. In rejecting Giles' claims, the Court created a diabolical catch-22: if Alabama's registration scheme was a fraud, as Giles claims, then how could the Court add him to the rolls? To do so would "make the court a party to the unlawful scheme by accepting it and adding another voter to its fraudulent lists."[233] And if the registration scheme was motivated by discriminatory intent, as Giles claimed, "it would be a new doctrine in constitution law that the original invalidity could be cured by an administration which defeated their intent."[234]

The Court's creative (not a compliment) approach to resolving Giles' claims should not obscure the core holding, which was that the Supreme Court could not and would not enforce political rights. Or, as Justice Holmes succinctly put it, "equity cannot undertake now, any more than it has in the past, to enforce political rights."[235]

Giles did not go quietly. Instead of accepting at face value the Court's dubious claims about its jurisdiction over political matters, he refiled his case, asking instead for money damages rather than the equitable remedy that he had initially requested. Unfortunately, this effort also met with little success. In *Giles v. Teasley*, decided in 1904, the Court simply deferred to the Alabama Supreme Court's finding that if the Alabama registration scheme was unconstitutional, then "the defendants were wholly without authority to register the plaintiff as a voter, and their refusal to do so cannot be made the predicate for a recovery of damages against them."[236] And even

[230] Ibid., 482–483.
[231] Ibid., 484.
[232] Ibid.
[233] Ibid., 486.
[234] Ibid., 487.
[235] Ibid.
[236] *Giles v. Teasley*, 193 U.S. 146, 160 (1904).

if such a predicate existed, the defendants, as election registrars, were acting in a judicial capacity and were therefore entitled to immunity.[237]

Giles v. Teasley not only rejected any judicial oversight of southern political systems, the decision also insulated those perpetuating the discrimination from any legal liability. Unlike the prior challenge in *Giles v. Harris*, the *Teasley* case took place after Alabama's temporary plan protecting voters registered before 1902 had expired, which meant that any hope of legal recourse had also expired.

Legal battles notwithstanding, those advocating for African American voting rights were also losing the public relations campaign, as the view that disenfranchisement was a political wrong, rather than a legal one, gained steam in the North. A regent for the New York state university system, C.A. Gardner, reflected on this shift in a 1903 convocation speech to a crowd of educators in Albany. In his widely reported remarks, Gardner observed, "that under the new constitutions the South is disenfranchising the negro and excluding him from office. If under the same constitution whites can vote and negroes equally cannot, that, I admit, is a political wrong, and for it there is no justification."[238]

Yet, while conceding the wrongfulness of the act, he cautioned northerners against quick judgment of Southern officials, embracing wholeheartedly the Supreme Court's approval of these regimes: "Does it lie with the Empire State, so often bowed down with shame for the corruption of its great cities, to cast the first stone?…And by whose authority do you say they are illegal? So far, every decision of the Supreme Court has sustained them! By whose warrant do you declare that the South is disenfranchising the negro?"

Thus, the message to Giles and other Black men similarly situated was loud and clear: the federal courts are closed, and you have lost the messaging battle. The Republican-led Congress would soon finish what the Democrats started in the Alabama contested election case of *McDuffie v. Turpin II* – using political opportunism and scapegoating of African Americans to align their approach with that of an unsympathetic Court that had washed its hands of the project of Reconstruction.

9.7 A COURT AND A CONGRESS ON THE SAME DISENFRANCHISING PAGE: THE END OF AN ERA

Republicans took back the House and the Senate during the Fifty-Fourth Congress (1895–97), control that they retained until the Sixty-Second Congress (1911–13). Most of this period was one of unified government and presented a window of opportunity not seen since the days of Reconstruction, but it was an open question as to whether this new generation of Republicans would continue the legacy of Sumter, Bingham,

237 Ibid.

238 "Educators in Albany: In Annual Convocation Regent C. A. Gardiner Says Education Is the Key to Negro Problem," *New York Tribune*, June 30, 1903.

Boutwell, and others.[239] When Alabama amended its constitution in 1901, Congress was well-positioned to meet this new challenge and had intervened, albeit sporadically, in the years since Republicans regained control of government.[240]

But the establishment of an enduring congressional majority would not generate the consistent federal protections for which African Americans had hoped and labored toward for decades. This was true for a number of reasons that have been well canvassed in the literature. To list some of the commonly accepted wisdom on this topic: Republicans had become the party of business by the 1890s;[241] American imperialism made it difficult to address racial discrimination in voting on the national stage;[242] and northern states continued to discriminate at the ballot box, making it difficult for Republicans to take the moral high ground with respect to discrimination in the South.[243] These efforts were also significantly hampered by the fact that, post-1894, not only did Congress have to police the South with fewer tools than they had in the 1870s, but they also had to do so in a political environment in which most people, if the disastrous election of 1890 was any indication, did not want to relitigate Reconstruction.

The fact that the Supreme Court that was not amenable to a broad reading of the Reconstruction Amendments was an added complication, stymieing the federal response regardless of which institutional actor was tasked with enforcing these provisions. Its decision in *McPherson v. Blacker* – decided in 1892, a few years before *Mills* and *Giles* opened the door for the mass disenfranchisement of African Americans across the South – rejected the argument that Section 2 of the Fourteenth Amendment created an affirmative right to vote, noting that there "is no color for the contention that under the amendments every male inhabitant of the State being a citizen of the United States has from the time of his majority a right to vote for presidential electors."[244]

239 See Chapter 6.

240 See, e.g., "Aldrich v. Plowman, House Committee on Elections, 55th Congress (1898)," in Rowell, *A Historical and Legal Digest of all the Contested Election Cases*, p. 555 ("The result of our investigation is the conclusion that every precinct in Dallas County in which a contest is made is fatally tainted with fraud that the returns therefrom must be entirely disregarded[.]").

241 After the 1896 election, "[t]he victorious Republicans … sought to preserve U.S. industrial development by thwarting radical democratic ideas[.] … [T]he general pattern was for party strength on currency, expansionism, business, and taxation to rise" during the period to follow. David Brady and Joseph Stewart, Jr., "Congressional Party Realignment and Transformation of Public Policy in Three Realignment Eras" (1982) 26 *American Journal of Political Science* 333–360, 351.

242 See Sam Erman, *Almost Citizens: Puerto Rico, the U.S. Constitution, and Empire* (New York: Cambridge University Press, 2018).

243 Alexander Keyssar, *The Right to Vote; The Contested History of Democracy in the United States* (New York: Basic Books, 2000), Chapter 4 (discussing concerns about northern hypocrisy with respect to issues of discrimination and disenfranchisement that surrounded the adoption of the Fifteenth Amendment).

244 *McPherson v. Blacker*, 146 U.S. 1, 39 (1892) (also reaffirming *Minor v. Happersett*, 88 U.S. 162 (1875), which permitted the disenfranchisement of women on the grounds that the right to vote is not a privilege or immunity of citizenship within the context of the Fourteenth Amendment).

But there were some Republicans willing to continue the fight, as the violence across the South and the spate of constitutional conventions designed to memorialize African American oppression illustrated the need for stronger measures to police southern disenfranchisement efforts. In 1899, Edgar D. Crumpacker, a Republican member of the House of Representatives from Indiana, introduced a proposal to implement Section 2 of the Fourteenth Amendment and reduce the congressional representation of Mississippi, South Carolina, Louisiana, and North Carolina as a penalty for disenfranchising large segments of their electorates.

On March 3, 1899, the last day of the Fifty-Fifth Congress (1897–99), the House Committee on the Census voted a bill out of committee, H.R. 11982, which would require the director of the census to furnish Congress with statistical information regarding the number of men of voting age in each state (broken down by race).[245] Representative Crumpacker, chairman of the Committee, used this information to determine how many voters in southern states had been unconstitutionally disenfranchised so as to trigger the penalty of Section 2.[246]

Though H.R. 11982 would not come up for a vote, the issue of reduction would become a subject of intense debate in early 1901, culminating in a motion by Crumpacker on January 8, 1901, to re-commit an apportionment bill, H.R. 12740, to the House Census Committee, presumably so his own bill, which would have reduced representation but kept the number of representatives in the House at 365, could be substituted.[247]

Noting the mandatory nature of the penalty – "the provision is plain, clear, and mandatory" – Crumpacker criticized many of the bills then pending for failing to comply with the constitutional requirements of Section 2. Outside of the Fifteenth Amendment, reduction was the "only repressive force under the control of Congress to prevent abuses of the vast power of the respective States" who "may fix an age limit so high that it would disfranchise 60 per cent of its male citizens, or impose a property qualification that would operate in the same manner, or establish a literary standard for suffrage that would disfranchise all who are unable to read and to read and translate the Greek language, without violating any federal law."[248]

245 "Comments of Representative Crumpacker, Fifty-Fifth Congress, Third Session, March 3, 1899," 32 *Congressional Record* (Washington, D.C., Government Printing Office, 1899), part 3, p. 2936.

246 United States House of Representatives, "Black Americans in Congress: The Fifteenth Amendment in Flesh and Blood, 1870–1901: The Demise of Reconstruction," https://history.house.gov/Exhibitions-and-Publications/BAIC/Historical-Essays/Temporary-Farewell/Legislative-Interests/.

247 "Comments of Representative Crumpacker, Fifty-Sixth Congress, Second Session, January 8, 1901," 34 *Congressional Record* (Washington, D.C.: Government Printing Office, 1901), part 1, p. 748. See also Perman, *Struggle for Mastery*, pp. 224–225. Crumpacker appeared to be picking and choosing his battles. He preferred a larger House but likely assumed that a bill that both enlarged the House and imposed the penalty of reduction would not pass. See "Comments of Representative Crumpacker, Fifty-Sixth Congress, Second Session, January 7, 1901," 34 *Congressional Record* (Washington, D.C.: Government Printing Office, 1901), Appendix, p. 67.

248 See "Comments of Representative Crumpacker, Fifty-Sixth Congress, Second Session, January 7, 1901," 34 *Congressional Record* (Washington, D.C.: Government Printing Office, 1901), Appendix, p. 68.

He spoke passionately in favor of reducing southern representation, detailing the specific provisions that had been drafted and implemented to make it difficult or impossible for thousands of people to vote, and then using voting statistics to demonstrate that the laws had the desired effect.[249] Unlike Republicans who sought to enforce Section 2 in 1872, Crumpacker had significantly more confidence that Congress could distinguish between an unconstitutional abridgment and denial of the right to vote and the state's "interest of fair and orderly elections."[250]

Crumpacker took a very broad view of what was permitted in the name of fair and orderly elections – "[t]he Australian system of voting, the official ballot, registration laws, whether a fee be charged the voter for registration or not, primary laws and requirements of the same general character which affect the mode of exercising the right of suffrage rather than the right itself are mere regulations for the orderly administration of elections and to protect their purity...."[251] He further concluded that "laws denying the right of suffrage to idiots, insane persons, and persons under guardianship" as well as "residence requirement[s]" which "exists in every State in the country" would not necessarily trigger the penalty of Section 2.[252]

Ironically, it was by subverting many regulations that might nominally "abridge and occasionally deny a voter the right of suffrage" – most of which did not, in Crumpacker's view, trigger the penalty – that the southern regimes of the 1880s and 1890s were at their most effective. If you will recall, the 1889 North Carolina registration law asked for specific information, such as street names and demographic information, that formerly enslaved Black voters were known to lack. Similarly, South Carolina's 1882 law, which provided limited notice to voters about registration and gave them between one and three days to register, was later struck down by a federal court. Registration regimes could be pedestrian or pernicious, depending on how they were structured.

To his credit, Crumpacker acknowledged that there were circumstances in which a commonly accepted practice could become an abridgment, where "regulations may be carried to such a degree as to seriously impair the right to vote; and when they are, they become qualifications." Thus, the Australian ballot used in many southern states could become an educational qualification if designed to operate as a bar to voting; for example, where a state that used the Australian ballot prohibits assistances to those who are illiterate with the end result that the voter could not choose his candidate of choice (a regulation that Crumpacker refers to as the

249 "Comments of Representative Crumpacker, Fifty-Sixth Congress, Second Session, January 7, 1901," 34 *Congressional Record* (Washington, D.C.: Government Printing Office, 1901), Appendix, pp. 69, 70–72 (noting "there is no difficulty in ascertaining with reasonable certainty the number of disenfranchisements occasioned by educational and property laws").

250 "Comments of Representative Crumpacker, Fifty-Sixth Congress, Second Session, January 7, 1901," 34 *Congressional Record* (Washington, D.C.: Government Printing Office, 1901), Appendix, p. 68.

251 Ibid., p. 69.

252 Ibid.

"Dortch" law), this could trigger the penalty of Section 2. While the Dortch law had been upheld in state court, the fact that its legality was not universal was relevant in determining whether the law constituted an abridgment.[253]

Importantly, Crumpacker seemed most trouble by the literacy tests and grandfather clause provisions that had become staples of the disenfranchising southern constitutions, which he thought impossible to defend as ballot integrity measures given their disparate impact.[254] For example, he described Louisiana's voter registration regime as "an unblushing attempt to evade the Federal Constitution," given that

> [t]he applicant for registration must not only be able to read and write, but he is required to fill out a blank application, without the aid of memorandum or suggestion by any other person, giving his name, the day, the month, and the year of his birth, his exact age in years, months, and days, the place of his birth, the place and duration of his residence, and the number of the precinct or ward in which he is a voter. In addition to all this, he must have paid a poll tax of $1 a year, on or before the 31st day of December, for two years prior to his registration.[255]

Referring to these requirements as "extraordinary," Crumpacker pointed to the state's grandfather clause as proof that it was "by indirection applied applicable to the colored citizen only" since Black people were not subject to being grandfathered in, having not voted prior to January 1867.[256] The effect of these restrictions was clear: before the adoption of the 1896 constitution, the average vote per congressional district was 16,020 voters; two years later, this average had fallen to 5,546.[257]

Crumpacker described the Mississippi Constitution in similar terms, framing the record before the Supreme Court in *Williams v. Mississippi* – which had upheld that constitution as consistent with the Fifteenth Amendment – as lacking evidence that showed the constitution "was not fairly administered" and concluding that "if such disclosures had been made its decision would likely have been different."[258] This was an assertion that was likely untrue, given the well-known and widely publicized statements made by delegates to virtually every southern convention that the purpose was to disenfranchise Black voters as well as the fact that each regime was structured to inflict race-neutral harms in a targeted manner. Indeed, Crumpacker noted as much in his discussion of the constitutions of North Carolina and South Carolina, both of which had laws that, in his view, operated as

253 Ibid.

254 Ibid., p. 73. Crumpacker seemed to think the grandfather clause problematic in any circumstances but noted that "[j]ust educational and property qualifications may be enacted."

255 "Comments of Representative Crumpacker, Fifty-Sixth Congress, Second Session, January 7, 1901," 34 *Congressional Record* (Washington, D.C.: Government Printing Office, 1901), Appendix, p. 70.

256 Ibid.

257 Ibid.

258 Ibid., p. 71.

educational requirements that – although facially race-neutral – could be disproportionately applied against Black voters.[259]

Like Crumpacker, several other representatives were quite vocal in their support for reduced representation in the southern states, and all of them relied on the effects of the discriminatory provisions on the electorate in arguing for the imposition of Section 2. On January 5, 1901, Representative William Shattuc emphasized that the plain text of Section 2 *required* Congress to reduce congressional representation in states that made it difficult, if not impossible, for those qualified to exercise the right to vote:

> In four of these States in the past ten years they have placed amendments in their constitutions and have placed laws upon their statute books that disfranchised from 40 to 50 per cent of the voters of their States.
>
> The defense employed in the seventies, that the abridgment of the electorate was the act of individuals and not of the State, no longer holds good.
>
> In four of the Southern States the denial of the right to vote to 40 or 50 per cent of the male members, 21 years of age or over, and citizens of the United States, is no longer the act of individuals but of the States.
>
> ....
>
> [Laws in the south intended to limit participation in elections] developed in various forms, as will be shown later, but nowhere to the extent of wholesale disfranchisement as in four of the States—Mississippi, Louisiana, South Carolina, and North Carolina.
>
> Even in the South these four States occupy a position of their own in this matter ....[260]

Shattuc then outlined the state statutes and constitutional provisions intended to limit African American voting rights including the literacy and "understanding" requirements in the constitutions of Mississippi and South Carolina as well as the grandfather clause in North Carolina.[261] He also proposed a separate resolution that would have established a special Committee to investigate disenfranchisement for purposes of apportionment, a proposal that never came to a vote.[262] Notably, Shattuc did not limit his attacks to the states' desire to exclude African Americans; instead, he observed how the laws were exclusionary across the board, disenfranchising almost half of the male population (including White men) in the offending states.

Representative Marlin Olmsted of Pennsylvania proposed an unsuccessful resolution in January of 1901, requiring the House Census Committee to investigate

[259] Ibid., pp. 71–72 (describing South Carolina's eight box law and North Carolina's "educational and poll-tax standard of suffrage").

[260] "Comments of Representative Shattuc, Fifty-Sixth Congress, Second Session, January 5, 1901," 34 *Congressional Record* (Washington, D.C.: Government Printing Office, 1901), part 1, pp. 601–602.

[261] Ibid., p. 602.

[262] Ibid., pp. 599–603.

reduction, either as a Committee or through an appointed sub-committee.[263] Among the evidence that Olmsted relied on was the significant decline in African American turnout in congressional elections.[264] Most importantly, Olmstead presented evidence of the discriminatory effect of those laws that had been adopted by constitutional conventions in the former Confederate states which, as mentioned earlier, had eliminated half of eligible voters and had reduced African American voter registration by an even larger margin. The disparity was quite stark when compared to the voting regulations in the North, which never impacted more than 8 percent of potential voters.[265] As this chapter shows, all of these laws were race-neutral.

Unsurprisingly, efforts to enforce Section 2 were met with firm opposition from southern representatives, who argued that only a law that is racially discriminatory on its face can trigger the penalty of Section 2. For example, Representative William Kitchin of North Carolina argued that Section 2 could be enforced only if a state denied the right to vote to its citizens under the Fifteenth Amendment, and further, that a state only violated the Fifteenth Amendment if it explicitly barred voting by qualified individuals "on account of race, color, or previous condition of servitude."[266] Otherwise, he argued, states had the power to impose any voter qualifications they wished:

> When the fifteenth amendment says that the States shall not deny or abridge the right to vote on account of race, color, or previous condition of servitude, the mentioning of these three conditions, in my judgment, is an exclusion of all others, and is tacit permission to the States for any other cause than race, color, or previous condition of servitude to abridge or deny the right of suffrage without penalty. I call the attention of the gentleman' from Indiana [Representative Crumpacker] to this proposition, that when the State of Massachusetts has an educational qualification, and the State of Pennsylvania a tax-paying qualification, it is not a denial of the right of suffrage.[267]

As we know from Chapter 6, playing the Fifteenth Amendment against Section 2 of the Fourteenth to prevent the latter's enforcement was not new. Indeed, such arguments cropped up every time Congress's attention turned south. In the wake

263 "Comments of Representative Olmstead, Fifty-Sixth Congress, Second Session, January 3, 1901," 34 *Congressional Record* (Washington, D.C.: Government Printing Office, 1901), part 1, p. 520; "Comments of Representative Olmstead, Fifty-Sixth Congress, Second Session, January 5, 1901," 34 *Congressional Record* (Washington, D.C.: Government Printing Office, 1901), part 1, p. 609.

264 Perman, *Struggle for Mastery*, p. 225. ("Mississippi's seven [congressional] districts polled a mere 27,045 votes in 1898, compared to a turnout of 62,652 in 1890. The vote in South Carolina's seven districts fell from 73,522 in 1890 to 28,831 in 1898. And Louisiana's six districts returned 74,542 votes in 1890 and only 33,161 in 1898. In each state, there was one district with between 160,000 and 200,000 inhabitants that gave its sitting congressman about 2,000 votes.").

265 Ibid., p. 226.

266 "Comments of Representative Kitchin, Fifty-Sixth Congress, Second Session, January 7, 1901," 34 *Congressional Record* (Washington, D.C.: Government Printing Office, 1901), part 1, p. 648.

267 Ibid., pp. 648–649.

of the Lodge Force Bill's failure, an editorial in the *Chicago Daily Tribune* offered a scathing indictment of the Fifteenth Amendment, noting that it had "not established manhood suffrage, but has largely prevented it."[268]

Echoing arguments from the early days of Reconstruction that the Fifteenth Amendment superseded the Fourteenth, the writer asserted:

> The fifteenth says the thing shall be, and the legal presumption is that they shall be of the Constitution must be in fact. Therefore, the provisions of the fourteenth amendment for restricting political capacity in proportion to disenfranchisement are in the air. That are, in fact, unconstitutional. Taking the two amendments together they invite precisely the construction that the nullifiers have placed upon them and playing the one against the other…if the fifteenth amendment were out of the way the fourteenth would gradually but surely enforce itself.[269]

In other words, while the villains might change, the arguments had not.

Opponents of reduction attacked the renewed efforts to enforce Section 2 as a relic of the Reconstruction-era that was too impractical to actually implement, or offered the hopeful fiction that the racial inequities in voting would eventually right themselves.[270] Others denied that African Americans were being disenfranchised at all, an argument that could, after all, be made with a straight face in light of the facial neutrality of the new state regulations that cloaked exclusion in the language of literacy tests, onerous registration requirements, poll taxes, grandfather clauses, and administrative discretion.[271]

In the end, Congress's efforts to operationalize Section 2 ultimately faltered because of basic problems of implementation and concerns about efficacy. It was

268 "The Race Question: Halsted Wants the Fifteenth Amendment Knocked Out," *The Chicago Daily Tribune*, August 1, 1892, p. 10.

269 Ibid. See also Rufus Bullock, Letter to the Editor, "Southern Representation," *New York Tribune*, April 29, 1903 (arguing that "the second section of the Fourteenth Amendment cannot be depended upon to reduce representatives from states that exclude votes because of color." To attempt this would be as the Tribune has said, "a cowardly abandonment of the negro and an acquiescence in the repeal of the Fifteenth Amendment.").

270 See Perman, *Struggle for Mastery*, pp. 225–228. See also "The Voting Privilege," *The Nashville American*, April 22, 1903 ("A suffrage law that would deny the ballot to nobody because of the color of his skin, but which would grant it to nobody not worthy; by fair and reasonable test, to exercise it would be a law to which no wise and good citizen could object. We shall come to that eventually.").

271 "Comments of Representative Holman, Fifty-First Congress, First Session, July 1, 1890," 21 *Congressional Record* (Washington, D.C.: Government Printing Office, 1890), part 7, p. 6845 (Comments of Rep. Holman) ("It is said that this Federal interference in elections is necessary to protect in the right of voting the colored people of the South. [sic] But will this Federal interference be beneficial to the colored people? We meet almost daily in this city with colored people from the South who give us assurance of the prosperity and progress of their race in the Southern States."). See also "The Voting Privilege," *The Nashville American*, April 22, 1903 ("But if the North which must recognize the difficulties with which the South has had to deal will keep hands off, the South, in a few years, will have election laws very much like those they have in other States and which apply alike to black and white.").

not clear that the census contained the information that Congress needed to accurately determine the penalty in any given state, a problem similar to that which Congress faced in enforcing Section 2 over two decades earlier.[272] There were also questions surrounding whether Section 2 would cost the South enough seats to make any difference in the political prospects of African Americans in the region.[273] Indeed, the fact that poor White people had also been turned away from the polls was framed as a positive that undermined the notion that the southern constitutions were designed to disenfranchise Black voters.[274] But most importantly, the fact that Crumpacker's bill targeted four southern states, and not northern and western states who were just as guilty of abridging and denying the right to vote,[275] made it difficult to refute that the bill was intended to do nothing more than stoke sectional animosity and secure political advantage for the Republican Party.[276]

Crumpacker's motion ultimately failed, as would the more limited proposal, H.R. 329. The latter bill targeted the same four southern states and required the census director to gather demographic data to determine how much representation each state would lose.[277] But unlike the Crumpacker bill, H.R. 329 would not have directly reduced the states' representation and would have only reported those states that were eligible for reduction.[278]

[272] "Comments of Representative Crumpacker, Fifty-Sixth Congress, Second Session, January 7, 1901," 34 *Congressional Record* (Washington, D.C.: Government Printing Office, 1901), Appendix, p. 71–72 ("The new apportionment must be made by the Fifty-sixth Congress next winter, and there appears no way to get the sort of information necessary to make a basis of representation on the number of males of voting age until Congress passes a law directing the Census Bureau to extend the scope of the census, so as to find out just what number of adult males are deprived of suffrage. Manifestly, this cannot be done in time for the next apportionment."). See also Chapter 6.

[273] "Negroes: Not So Generally Disenfranchised in the South as Many Suppose," *Louisville Courier Journal*, August 12, 1900 (estimating that states across the South would lose, at most, ten-to-twenty seats in the aggregate if Section 2 is implemented).

[274] "Comments of Representative Fox, Fifty-Sixth Congress, Second Session, January 7, 1901," 34 *Congressional Record* (Washington, D.C.: Government Printing Office, 1901), Appendix, p. 75.

[275] Ibid., pp. 75, 78 (stating that Massachusetts and Wyoming both have literacy requirements for voters in their state constitutions).

[276] Ibid., p. 75 (noting that the representation of Massachusetts should be reduced by two "on account of the denial to certain classes of the right of suffrage" and that the Mississippi Constitution of 1890s suffrage requirements borrowed from that state).

[277] *Congressional Record*, 56th Cong., 2d sess., February 27, 1901, vol. 34, part 4, p. 3182 (H.R. 329).

[278] The resolution's conclusion read:

> *Resolved*, That the Committee on Census shall be, and is, authorized and directed, either by full committee or by such subcommittee or subcommittees as may be appointed by the chairman thereof, to inquire, examine, and report in what States the right to vote at any election for the choice of electors for President and Vice-President of the United States, Representatives in Congress, the executive and judicial officers of a State, or the members of the legislature thereof, is denied to any of the male inhabitants of such States 21 years of age and citizens of the United States, or in any way abridged, except for participation in rebellion or other crimes, and the proportion which the number of such male citizens shall bear to the whole number of male citizens 21 years of age in such State.
>
> Ibid.

Together, these and other unsuccessful legislative efforts represented a brief rise of "reduction" as a political issue at the turn of the twentieth century. Yet the failure to impose the penalty in 1899 and 1901 – when the Republicans had control of both the presidency and Congress – was concrete proof (to the extent that more proof is required) that Republican support for African American suffrage had waned, and the pivotal year of 1866 was well in the rearview.

In 1902, Republicans retained majorities in both houses of Congress, which would – again – seem to leave the party well-positioned to use their authority under Article I, Section 5 to police the administration of congressional elections by southern states that had actively worked to disenfranchise African Americans. Republicans also swept the 1904 elections, providing a sufficient cushion that should have prompted a more significant legislative and/or institutional response to the formal disenfranchisement efforts in the South, particularly in light of the lack of judicial support.

The issue of reduction came up again after the election of 1904, with the same results as the prior efforts: failure. Democrats again framed their opposition in terms of the inequitable treatment of the South relative to, in their view, an equally racist North. John Sharp Williams, House minority leader, threatened that "the South voluntarily would forego representation in Congress rather than acknowledge the rightfulness of political serfdom or the inequality of the states within the Union."[279]

As mentioned prior, memoirs from prominent Republicans released decades after Reconstruction provided the fuel that southern Democrats needed to challenge the validity of the Fourteenth and Fifteenth Amendments. In 1895, former congressman John Sherman, recognizing the salience of politics on the effectiveness (or ineffectiveness) of the Fourteenth and Fifteenth Amendments, wrote about the missteps of the Thirty-Ninth and Fortieth Congresses that were almost certainly informed by the then-present reality of Redemption, Restoration, and the practical invalidation of the Reconstruction Amendments in the South:

> It is a question of grave doubt whether this amendment [the Fifteenth], though right in principle, was wise or expedient. The declared object was to secure impartial suffrage to the negro race. The practical result has been that the wise provisions of the Fourteenth Amendment have been modified by the Fifteenth Amendment. The latter amendment has been practically nullified by the action of most of the states where the great body of this race live and will probably always remain. This is done, not by an express denial to them of the right of suffrage, but by ingenious provisions, which exclude them on the alleged ground

279 "Passive Resistance for South – Williams: Democratic Leader's Plan to Defeat Representation," *New York Times*, December 3, 1904 (noting that "a great many Northern people do not count the negroes or the South as a part of the population of this country, and the cry went up that 'one white man in the South should not have as much power as two or three white men in the North'…").

> of ignorance, while permitting all of the white race, however ignorant, to vote at all elections. No way is pointed out by which Congress can enforce this amendment. If the principle of the Fourteenth Amendment had remained in full force, Congress could have reduced the representation of any state…This simple remedy, easily enforced by Congress, would have secured the right of all persons…[280]

Like C.A. Gardner, the regent to the New York university system, Sherman would conclude that, "I see no remedy for this wrong except the growing intelligence of the negro race, which, in time, I trust, will enable them to demand and receive the right of suffrage."[281]

For Sherman, implementing the "simple" remedy of Section 2, which in 1872 had stumped him and his colleagues, was a lost opportunity that now rendered African Americans helpless in the face of widespread discrimination. Sherman, writing over two decades later, recognized that Democratic control of Congress meant that Section 2 was effectively dead. Yet Republican control of Congress at the turn of the century did not change this state of affairs, and the threat of reduced representation remained just that: a threat.

Indeed, one of the most egregious failures of the Republican-controlled House came, not in the context of reduced representation under Section 2, but in an area where the political considerations posed less of a barrier: Article I, Section 5. In *Dantzler v. Lever*, the House had to resolve an election contest in the Fifty-Eighth Congress (1903–05) involving South Carolina's Seventh Congressional District. This case set the tone for congressional enforcement efforts for the first half of the twentieth century. While the contestant, Alexander Dantzler, clearly lost the election – he received 167 votes to Asbury Lever's 4,220 votes – his contest raised a fundamental question about the continuing validity of the Reconstruction Acts that readmitted the former Confederate states.

Pursuant to the Reconstruction Act of June 25, 1868,[282] South Carolina and several other Confederate states agreed "that the constitution of neither of said States shall ever be so amended or changed as to deprive any citizen or class of cities of the United States of the right to vote in said State who are entitled to vote by the constitution thereof herein recognized… ." It is this provision that, if you will recall, the district court relied on in *Mills v. Green* to invalidate South Carolina's 1882 voter registration law. However, in 1895, South Carolina amended its state constitution to impose educational and property qualifications that were not present in the state constitution accepted by Congress in June 1868 as a condition of readmission. Dantzler argued that this conflict between the Reconstruction Act and the 1895

[280] John Sherman, *Recollections of 40 years in the House, Senate and Cabinet*, 2 vols. (Chicago: The Werner Company, 1895), vol. 1, p. 450–451.

[281] Ibid.

[282] The Reconstruction Acts are discussed in Chapter 6.

constitution rendered the November 1902 election in the Seventh Congressional District null and void.[283]

In rejecting Dantzler's claim, the House Committee on Elections relied on the same creative catch-22 that the Supreme Court had used in the Alabama case of *Giles v. Harris*. If the November 1902 election was not valid because of the 1895 South Carolina Constitution, it would follow that "no election could be held to fill the vacancy until after the South Carolina Constitution of 1895 and the election laws under it had been changed."[284] Like the *Giles* Court, who argued that it had no power to add anyone to a fraudulently constructed voter roll, the House Committee on Elections took this logical fallacy to its most extreme endpoint:

> It follows, therefore, quite logically that if the House should unseat the contestee on the ground that no valid election was held or could be held in his district under the present constitution and election laws of South Carolina, a similar construction would require the House, in the case of contest, to unseat all of the Members from South Carolina and from most of the other Southern States, and that new elections could not be held to fill the vacancies until the respective constitutions of these States had been changed so as to comply with the reconstruction acts.[285]

The Committee – less than one year after the Supreme Court decided *Giles v. Harris* – denied that Congress must provide a remedy in these circumstances: "If any citizen of South Carolina who was entitled to vote under the constitution of that State in 1868 is now deprived by the provisions of the present constitution he has the right to tender himself for registration and for voting, and in case his right is denied, to bring suit in a proper court for the purpose of enforcing his right or recovering damages for its denial."[286] Notably, the House Committee on Elections came to this conclusion less than two years after its decision in *Johnston v. Stokes*,[287] where the Committee was willing to enforce the very rights that it now claimed could only be vindicated through the courts.

The House Committee on Elections reaffirmed this position in a second election challenge between Dantzler and Lever in the Sixtieth Congress (1907–09), a challenge that received a stinging rebuke by a Committee that was tired of revisiting the question of whether the disenfranchising constitutions in the southern states violated the Reconstruction Acts. Instead of directly confronting the legality of these disenfranchising regimes, the Committee adopted the same reasoning underlying its resolution of the 1902 election contest:

283 "Dantzler v. Lever (1902–1906)," in Hinds, *Hinds' Precedents of the House of Representatives of the United States*, v. 2, p. 742.

284 Ibid., p. 743.

285 Ibid.

286 Ibid.

287 "Johnston v. Stokes, House Committee on Elections, 56th Congress (1901)," in Rowell, *A Historical and Legal Digest of all the Contested Election Cases*, p. 531. See also Chapter 9.4.

> Contestant claims that if the citizens of the Seventh Congressional District of South Carolina who could have voted under the terms of the constitution of 1868 had been permitted to vote, he would have been elected, and he asserts that many thousands of colored voters in the Congressional district entitled to vote under the constitution of 1868 were deprived of the right to vote under the educational and property qualifications of the constitution of 1895. … It would seem that if no valid election was held in the Seventh Congressional District of South Carolina…then no election could be held to fill the vacancy until after the South Carolina constitution of 1895 and the election laws under it had been changed. …
>
> However desirable it may be for a legislative body to retain control of the decision as to the election and qualification of its members, it is quite certain that a legislative body is not the ideal body to pass judicially upon the constitutionality of the enactments of other bodies. We have in this country a proper forum for the decision of constitutional and other judicial questions…[288]

In *Dantzler v. Lever I* and *II*, Congress expressly ceded its authority over these election disputes to the courts. Unsurprisingly, after 1910, the number of contested elections challenging voting discrimination in the South dwindled to almost nothing.

Despite clear evidence that Congress was unwilling to protect political rights, the justices doubled down on their refusal to intervene. In *Jones v. Montague*,[289] decided in 1904, the Court dismissed a challenge to the state of Virginia's new voting regulations after the plaintiffs attempted to register to vote but were turned away. Like *Mills v. Green*, the Court held that no relief was available since the election had already occurred, a decision that, coupled with *Dantzler v. Lever I* and *II*, brought a decisive and swift end to the four-decade federal effort to incorporate African Americans into the political community of "We the Voters."

[288] *Dantzler v. Lever*, House Report No. 1817, 60th Cong., 2d Sess. (1990), p. 2.
[289] *Jones v. Montague*, 194 U.S. 147 (1904).

Epilogue

Lessons from a Failed Political Experiment

Enacted in reconstruction times, when it was deemed necessary to carry out those measures, the purpose for which they were framed having happily passed away, we feel that they can not be too quickly erased from the statute books…Let every trace of the reconstruction measures be wiped from the statute books; let the States of this great Union understand that the elections are in their own hands…

—Majority Report, Committee on Privileges and Elections, Repeal of Federal Election Laws, 1893[1]

'[T]he Framers of the Constitution intended the States to keep for themselves, as provided in the Tenth Amendment, the power to regulate elections'… The Voting Rights Act sharply departs from these basic principles…Our country has changed, and…Congress must ensure that the legislation it passes to remedy [racial discrimination] speaks to current conditions…

—*Shelby County v. Holder*, 2013[2]

On December 14, 1893, the U.S. Senate Committee on Privileges and Elections submitted a report recommending the repeal of most Reconstruction-era federal voting rights legislation. Among the targeted statutes were the 1870 and 1871 Enforcement Acts, which had been integral in increasing Black voting in the South despite persistent and unyielding opposition by both the legislatures of the former Confederate states and the United States Supreme Court.

A little over three years after a new generation of Republicans sought to enhance these laws by proposing an omnibus election bill that failed by one vote, Congress – now controlled by the Democratic Party – wanted to decimate voting rights enforcement efforts at the federal level entirely. In 1894, Democrats repealed most of the Reconstruction-era legislation, including most of the Enforcement Acts

1 United States Senate Committee on Privileges and Elections, "Majority Report: Repeal of Federal Election Laws," S. Rep. No. 113 (1893).
2 *Shelby County. v. Holder*, 570 U.S. 529 (2013).

of 1870 and 1871.[3] In addition, the Democratic-led Congress declined to act on proposals to investigate allegations of Black disenfranchisement in a number of contests, all signs that congressional protection for Black voting rights was solely dependent upon the party in power.

The Republicans fought these efforts after regaining control of Congress following the 1894 elections. They tried, at various points, to implement Section 2 of the Fourteenth Amendment and to aggressively police congressional elections pursuant to Congress's authority under Article I, Section 5. Yet Republicans' commitment to Black equality was waning, and by 1910, federal efforts to protect Black voting rights were, for all intents and purposes, dead.

There are innumerable explanations for this abandonment: Reconstruction fatigue, a constitutional system naturally resistant to broad structural change, political expediency, the seemingly unbreakable will of southern White supremacists, a shift to economic issues, etc. Whatever the reason, the nineteenth-century Congress was ill equipped to be the long-term savior of the formerly enslaved and showed themselves unable to shake off their own biases and limitations that would allow them, as a legislative body, to stand in the gap as a change agent.

As early as 1866, Congress had laid the groundwork for the exclusion of certain groups from the political community – women and those of Chinese descent were notable examples – even as it expanded voting rights for Black men. With the acquisition of new territories at the turn of the twentieth century – including the Philippines, Guam, and Puerto Rico – the federal government's justification for why residents of these territories were unfit for citizenship (and the exercise of rights) bore a strong resemblance to arguments offered by southern disenfranchisers in the post–Reconstruction period that Black people suffered from the same disability.[4] Because a rising tide never lifted all boats, at least with respect to federal voting rights protections, Black enfranchisement was abandoned once it became politically expedient to do so.

For the next seven decades, federal civil rights and voting rights legislation died in a Congress dominated by powerful southern representation. Their opposition to civil

[3] An Act to repeal all statutes relating to the supervisors of elections and special deputy marshals, and for other purposes, ch. 25, 28 Stat. 36 (1894). More provisions were repealed in 1909 and 1911. See An Act to Codify, revise, and amend the penal laws of the United States, ch. 321, 35 Stat. 1088 (1909); An Act to codify, revise, and amend the laws relating the judiciary, ch. 231, 36 Stat. 1087 (1911).

[4] See Richard H. Pildes, "Democracy, Anti-Democracy, and the Canon" (2000) 17 *Constitutional Commentary* 295–317, 305 ("National political reaction to Southern disfranchisement was quiet for many reasons, including that the federal government was seeking to restrict suffrage in newly acquired territories, such as the Philippines and Puerto Rico, and territories it effectively controlled, such as Cuba."); R. Volney Riser, "The Burdens of Being White: Empire and Disenfranchisement" (2001) 53 *Alabama Law Review* 243–272, 244 (noting that elected officials in Alabama "viewed American imperialism as something more than a shield for disenfranchisement … Alabama, like Britain, France, and Germany, faced the question of how to seize and maintain control of nonwhite populations, and W.M. Banks [a delegate to the 1901 state constitutional convention] believed the state should offer itself as a model."). See also Sam Erman, *Almost Citizens: Puerto Rico, the U.S. Constitution and Empire* (New York: Cambridge University Press, 2019).

rights also ensured that the Democratic Party operated as separate southern and northern factions, rather than as a truly unified organization. This was a rift that would, inevitably, split the party apart. The late 1950s saw an opening for federal action; although it was limited at first,[5] this intervention represented a sign of changing times.

As support for civil rights grew nationwide and the Supreme Court seemed poised to put its legitimacy on the line for equality,[6] President Lyndon B. Johnson and Congress rose to the occasion in the mid-1960s with the passage of a package of initiatives that included the Civil Rights Act of 1964,[7] the Voting Rights Act of 1965,[8] and the Fair Housing Act of 1968,[9] to name a few landmark pieces of legislation. The cooperation of all three branches, after decades of desuetude, marked a watershed moment in American history.

The moments leading up to the adoption of the Voting Rights Act of 1965, in particular, represented a Second Reconstruction; or, more pointedly, a moment in which the nation was at a precipice where it could rekindle and possibly fulfill the promise of democracy that had existed from 1866 until the early twentieth century. The Act not only represented a radical reimagining of the political community of "We the Voters" – incorporating minority voters who had been excluded from this world for decades – but it also reenergized Congress's role in voting rights enforcement.

To be clear, this was not a moment in which Congress was starting over. Congress's renewed efforts to protect Black people in the twentieth century reflected lessons learned from an earlier time. The 1960s-era federal civil rights legislation was crafted in response to the limits that the Supreme Court had placed on Congress's enforcement authority in the 1870s, 1880s, and 1890s.

For example, is there a state action requirement to reach private discrimination under the Fourteenth and Fifteenth Amendments?[10] No problem: enact the 1964 Civil Rights Act pursuant to the Commerce Clause, which has no state action requirement.[11] Concerned about the federalism issues raised by continuous federal

5 An Act to provide means of further securing and protecting the civil rights of persons within the jurisdiction of the United States, 71 Stat. 634, Pub. L. No. 85–315 (1957).

6 See *Brown v. Board of Education*, 347 U.S. 483 (1954).

7 An Act to enforce the constitutional right to vote, to confer jurisdiction upon the district courts of the United States to provide injunctive relief against discrimination in public accommodations, to authorize the Attorney General to institute suits to protect constitutional rights in public facilities and public education, to extend the Commission on Civil Rights, to prevent discrimination in federally assisted programs, to establish a Commission on Equal Employment Opportunity, and for other purposes, 78 Stat. 241, Pub. L. No. 88–352 (1964).

8 An Act to enforce the fifteenth amendment to the Constitution of the United States, and for other purposes, 79 Stat. 437, Pub. L. No. 89–110 (1965).

9 An Act to prescribe penalties for certain acts of violence and intimidation, and for other purposes – Title VII: Fair Housing, 82 Stat. 73, Pub. L. No. 90–284 (1968).

10 See *Civil Rights Cases*, 109 U.S. 3 (1883); *James v. Bowman*, 190 U.S. 127 (1903).

11 See *Katzenbach v. McClung*, 379 U.S. 294 (1964). See also Reba G. Rasor, "Regulation of Public Accommodations via the Commerce Clause – The Civil Rights Act of 1964" (1965) 19 *Southwestern Law Journal* 329–369.

oversight of state political systems?[12] No worries, include a sunset provision on the law.[13] And so it went as Congress attempted to bypass the judicially imposed limits on its authority from a century earlier. It was, truly, a second (and this time, more enduring) attempt at Reconstruction.[14]

But the civil rights laws of the 1960s were also, importantly, shaped by what had long been considered an acceptable use of Congress's enforcement authority. It used to be the case that a system of federal oversight for federal elections was not problematic, in and of itself. Thus, the Enforcement Act of 1871, which included such a system, provided an important blueprint for these congressional voting rights efforts in the 1960s.[15]

In addition, tailoring the regime of oversight to single out a particular region had also not been an issue, at least within certain parameters. Section 2 of the Fourteenth Amendment, although it has remained unenforced since its conception, was specifically designed to target the former Confederate states, but it has nonetheless provided a foundation for the preclearance regime of the Voting Rights Act that ultimately remade political systems across that region. These earlier precedents laid the foundation for the revolution that was to come.

The Voting Rights Act of 1965, and more pointedly, sections 4(b) and 5 of that provision, built on a Reconstruction framework that produced a more egalitarian political system in ways in which the radicals of days old could only hope. As discussed in the Introduction, these provisions suspended all voting-related changes in certain jurisdictions with a history of voting-related discrimination, located mostly in the South, until those changes were approved by the Attorney General or the United States District Court for the District of Columbia.[16] Sections 4(b) and 5 completely remade the southern electorates, finally bringing minority voters into the fabric of American democracy.[17]

12 See *Civil Rights Cases*, 109 U.S. 3, 25 (1883) ("When a man has emerged from slavery, and, by the aid of beneficent legislation, has shaken off the inseparable concomitants of that state, there must be some stage in the progress of his elevation when he takes the rank of a mere citizen and ceases to be the special favorite of the laws, and when his rights as a citizen or a man are to be protected in the ordinary modes by which other men's rights are protected.").

13 See *South Carolina v. Katzenbach*, 83 U.S. 301 (1966).

14 See Michael J. Klarman, "Brown, Racial Change, and the Civil Rights Movement" (1994) 80 *Virginia Law Review* 7–150, 81–84 (discussing several post-*Brown* events that influenced the particular timing of the civil rights movement of the 1960s).

15 An Act to amend an Act approved May 31, 1870, entitled "An Act to enforce the Rights of Citizens of the United States to vote in the several States of this Union, and for other Purposes," ch. 99, 16 Stat. 433, 434 (1871).

16 An Act to enforce the fifteenth amendment to the Constitution of the United States, and for other purposes, s. 2, 79 Stat. 437, Pub. L. No. 89–110 (1965).

17 The impact of the Voting Rights Act and its enforcement on Black voters in the former confederate states cannot be understated. By 1969, the percentage of registered Negroes in the Deep South ha[d] more than doubled. In the previous seven and a half years this percentage had only increased by only one-seventh. Experience under the Voting Rights Act of 1965 ha[d] also shattered the long cherished myth that federal assumption of traditionally local functions would impair efforts to persuade local

In June 2013, the U.S. Supreme Court invalidated Section 4(b) of the Act in *Shelby County v. Holder*, finding that the coverage formula was an "extraordinary and unprecedented" intrusion on state sovereignty that, when viewed through the Court's twenty-first-century lens, failed to account for the substantial decrease in racial discrimination in voting since the Act was passed in 1965.[18]

While the narrative in these pages stops a full century before *Shelby County*, this book nonetheless provides important context that establishes that this decision was not only misguided but also ahistorical. Congress crafted the preclearance regime of the Voting Rights Act of 1965 to be responsive to the constitutional challenges lodged against federal voting rights legislation enacted in the nineteenth century. Rather than "extraordinary and unprecedented," the Act was built on a blueprint and foundation laid by Congress during its first foray into federal voting rights enforcement.

To be clear, this epilogue is not an attempt to lodge a comprehensive and complete assessment of *Shelby County v. Holder* nor do I engage with the recent decision in *Louisiana v. Callais*, which has been similarly devastating to minority voting rights. The decision is complicated. Also, I well recognize that there is a century of history that bears on the status of modern voting rights efforts that is not covered in this book. Instead, I want to invite readers to contemplate a much more narrow insight, one that can safely be gleaned from the almost two hundred years of history in these pages: that many of the federalism and political process objections lodged against the 1965 Voting Rights Act have their genesis in the opposition to nineteenth-century federal civil rights and voting rights laws that came from the Waite and Fuller Courts.[19] Indeed, Congress took these criticisms into account in crafting the Voting Rights Act, with the preclearance regime reflecting lessons learned from earlier efforts that had failed.

With the Supreme Court's decisions in *Shelby County v. Holder* and *Louisiana v. Callais*, America is at a point where we can either relitigate the now-defunct Second Reconstruction, or instead (and perhaps preferably), rise to the moment and create another path forward in which America can finally, and permanently, become the

officials to fulfill their responsibilities. Federal intervention into voter registration spurred country registrars to do their duty. Unwilling to defer to federal examiners, many previously recalcitrant registrars complied with the new law. Since July 1965, the vast majority of new Negro voters ha[d] been registered by local officials." Allan Lichtman, "The Federal Assault against Voting Discrimination in the Deep South 1957–1967" (1969) 54/4 *Journal of Negro History*, 346–367, 367.

18 *Shelby County. v. Holder*, 570 U.S. 529, 531 (2013). See also *Louisiana v. Callais*, 608 U.S. __ (2026) (narrowing the scope of Section 2 of the VRA as it applies to racial gerrymandering claims); *Petteway v. Galveston County*, 111 F. 4th 596 (5th Cir. 2024) (en banc) (holding that the VRA does not protect coalition districts); *Brnovich v. DNC*, 594 U.S. 647 (2021) (narrowing the scope of Section 2 of the VRA as it applies to vote denial claims); *Arkansas State Conference of the NAACP v. Arkansas Board of Apportionment*, 86 F.4th 1204, 1216 (8th Cir. 2023) (finding no private right of action for suits brought under Section 2 of the VRA).

19 Supreme Court Historical Society, "The Waite Court, 1874–1888," https://supremecourthistory.org/history-of-the-courts/waite-court-1874-1888/; Supreme Court Historical Society, "The Fuller Court, 1888-1910," https://supremecourthistory.org/history-of-the-courts/fuller-court-1888-1910/.

democracy that we hold out to the world. Either *Shelby County* is an invitation to a second phase of Redemption and Restoration, in which the gains of the prior generation will be forever lost to a tide of voter suppression and antidemocratic actions by political elites, or it is a chance for a Third Reconstruction, in which we build a new foundation for the democracy to which we aspire.[20] Importantly, drawing parallels between the enforcement efforts of the late nineteenth century and those of the mid twentieth century illustrates that voting rights advocates must blaze a new path on these issues, rather than recreate the efforts of half a century ago. In enacting the VRA, Congress tried to be responsive to century-old concerns about its power to protect the right to vote, and in the end, the Court invalidated Section 4(b) of the Act anyway.

Another lesson that emerges from connecting our present challenges to our historical failures is that Congress cannot simply replicate its past attempts by reauthorizing a new coverage formula. Maybe the solution is for Congress to tap into its underutilized constitutional authority under either the Elections Clause or Article I, Section 5, or implement the penalty of reduced representation under Section 2 of the Fourteenth Amendment. As history shows, these constitutional provisions represent broad sources of congressional authority that defy the federalism narrative currently championed by the Roberts Court. Or perhaps the answer lies, not with Congress, but with "We the People," a premise that I explore in my next book that picks up around 1910 and carries us into modern day.[21] Maybe the answer is both.

20 Michael Perman, *Struggle for Mastery: Disfranchisement in the South, 1888–1908* (Chapel Hill: University of North Carolina Press, 2001), pp. 10–11 (describing Reconstruction as a period of "voter disenfranchisement"; Redemption as a period of "vote manipulation"; and Restoration as a period of "voter elimination").

21 See Franita Tolson, *In the People We Trust? Expanding Voting Rights from the Progressive Era to the Present* (manuscript in progress and on file with the author).

Index

Printed in the United Kingdom by TJ Clays Ltd.